THE BOMBERS

THE ILLUSTRATED STORY OF OFFENSIVE STRATEGY AND TACTICS IN THE TWENTIETH CENTURY

ROBIN CROSS

Macmillan Publishing Company
New York

The Bombers was conceived, edited and designed by
Grub Street

Copyright © 1987 by Grub Street
Text copyright © 1987 by Robin Cross
Color artwork by Sarson and Bryan
Lineartwork by Mark Stirling and Barrie Ibbotson

Macmillan Publishing Company
866 Third Avenue,
New York, N.Y. 10022
Collier Macmillan Canada, Inc.

Library of Congress Cataloguing-in-Publication Data

Cross, Robin.
   The bombers: the illustrated story of offensive strategy
and tactics in the twentieth century.

   Includes index.
   1. Bombing, Aerial—History.   2. Bombers.   I. Title.
UG700.C76   1987   358.4′2′09   87-11074
ISBN 0-02-528930-6

Macmillan books are available at special discounts for
bulk purchases for sales promotions, premiums, fund-
raising, or educational use. For details, contact:

Special Sales Director
Macmillan Publishing Company
866 Third Avenue
New York, N.Y. 10022

1 0 9 8 7 6 5 4 3 2 1

Printed in Italy

The author would particularly like to thank the
following for their help in the preparation of
this book:
The Air Gunners Association, Bill Wilcox,
H D 'Roger' Coverley, Alec Thorne,
Jack Catford, Boris Breslof, Peter Richard,
John Albers, Kenneth Wakefield, Gerry Goldie,
Graeme Andrew, Brian Williams, the RAF
Museum, Hendon, and the Reference,
Documents and Sound Archives Departments
of the Imperial War Museum.

CONTENTS

SECTION ONE

THE BIRTH OF THE BOMBER

1.1 INTRODUCTION

THE POSSIBILITY OF BOMBARDMENT FROM THE AIR EXERCISED men's minds long before the problems of powered flight were solved. In *The Arabian Nights*, Sinbad the Sailor tells of the destruction of a ship by two Rocs, fabulous birds 'carrying great stones ... in their claws'. But it was not until the dawn of the 20th century that Sinbad's vision stood on the threshold of becoming reality.

The first military airman had been Capitaine Coutelle of the French Revolutionary Army, who in 1794 went aloft in a tethered balloon to 'examine the works of the enemy, his positions and his forces'. However, while balloons remained without power and at the mercy of the elements, they had limited potential as weapons of war. A new phase in the evolution of lighter-than-air machines opened on September 24, 1852 when the French engineer Henri Giffard took off from the Paris race course in a balloon equipped with a 3 hp steam engine driving a propeller and steered by a rudimentary vertical rudder. The crucial breakthrough came in 1885 with the development of the internal combustion engine, designed by both Daimler and Benz. This was a lightweight, high-performance power plant which, when combined with a navigable airship, promised to open up a new range of military applications.

During the American Civil War, Graf (Count) Ferdinand von Zeppelin, a young German officer serving as a military attaché with the Army of the Potomac, made his first ascent in a tethered observation balloon. His subsequent experiences as a balloonist kindled an interest in flying machines which became an obsession. On March 25, 1874 he committed his 'Thoughts About an Airship' to his diary, and in 1887 he wrote to the King of Wurtemburg outlining the military potential of airships for scouting and raiding in warfare. In 1898 von Zeppelin established the Joint Stock Company for the Promotion of Airship Flight. In the same year work began on his first rigid airship, *LZI*. On July 2, 1900 the massive 'Zeppelin', as all the Count's airships were inevitably dubbed, was eased out of its floating hangar on Lake Constance for its maiden flight. *LZI* proved difficult to control and structurally weak and was broken up three months later when the Count ran out of money, an early example of the financial problems which beset all ambitious aviation projects.

The German military remained resolutely unenthusiastic about von Zeppelin's grand designs, and the series of spectacular disasters which overtook his early airships confirmed their scepticism. It was not until March 1909 that the German Army took delivery of *LZ3A*, designated Luftschiffe 1 [*LZ1*]. Thereafter the German airship program lurched forward in fits and starts, its erratic course dictated by the Zeppelins' limited performance, lingering suspicions about their vulnerability, and the military's confusion as to their proper role. Mere lip service was paid to the widely held view that the Zeppelins' primary role was that of long-range reconnaissance aircraft, cruising at high altitude and commanding views of vast war zones through high-powered Zeiss lenses. In reality the Army's Zeppelins were confined on maneuvers to short-range missions which they lacked the flexibility to undertake.

More sinister than the airship's capacity as a scouting craft was its potential as a bombing weapon, an instrument of 'frightfulness' raining death and destruction from the skies. Britain was

Balloons at war. Thaddeus S C Lowe supervises the inflation of the observation balloon Intrepid during the American Civil War battle of Fair Oaks. The smoke and the dust from the front line can be seen rising on the horizon.

particularly vulnerable to air attack since many of her most important civil and military centers were situated in that part of the country nearest to Continental Europe. In October 1908 Britain's Committee of Imperial Defence set up a sub-committee, headed by Lord Esher, to investigate 'the dangers to which we would be exposed on sea or land by any development in aerial navigation reasonably probable in the near future', and to decide in the light of the knowledge thus gained the 'naval and military advantages that we might expect to derive from the use of airships or aeroplanes'.

For those concerned about a new form of warfare in the skies there was precious little comfort to be gained from the provisions of international law. In 1899 the Hague Conference had prohibited for a period of five years the discharge of projectiles and explosives from balloons 'or by any other new methods of a similar nature'. When this article came up for renewal in 1907, the majority of the contracting powers declined to do so, arguing that flying machines engaged on reconnaissance or any other military duties would be legitimate targets of attack and thus should not be deprived of the means of retaliation. It was agreed that the vaguely worded prohibition already placed by the Conference on the bombardment of 'undefended villages, dwellings or buildings' by both land and sea forces should also be applied to flying machines.

Responding to these developments, the Aerial League of the British Empire, formed at the beginning of 1909, was agitating to 'secure and maintain for the Empire the same supremacy in the air as it now enjoys on the sea.' One of its most vociferous spokesmen was Lord Montagu of Beaulieu, who in a speech delivered to the National Defence Association on April 21, 1909 painted a vivid picture of a paralysing air attack on London's 'nerve centers' – the Houses of Parliament, government offices, the General Post Office, and telephone exchanges. At the time Lord Montagu's predictions had a science fiction quality about them, derived perhaps from the work of another member of the Aerial League, H G Wells. In 1908 his book *War in the Air* had portrayed an aerial invasion in which New York's Brooklyn Bridge is 'broken down' by a single airship in its passage overhead, and 'The City Hall and the Court House and the Post Office were a heap of blackened ruins after the first day of the enemy's visit'.

How much was being undertaken in Germany to fulfil these dire prophecies? In the summer of 1912 von Zeppelin's commercial airship company, DELAG, was secretly informed that its air crews were henceforth to join the military reserve and participate in regular exercises with the Army and Navy. After taking a ride in a DELAG ship, the Chief of the General Staff, Helmuth von Moltke, wrote a memorandum urging the purchase of 20 airships of 'the latest model'. The latest model was the Schutte-Lanz *SL1*, whose advanced design features set the standard for all subsequent Zeppelins. The optimism of 1912 infected the previously cautious Navy, which obtained the Kaiser's consent for a five-year airship program. But within a year the Navy's program had been canceled after the loss, in swift succession of its first two airships, *L1* and *L2*. *L1* was destroyed in a squall while flying in the High Seas Fleet maneuvers; *L2* blew up a month later while undergoing its

acceptance trials. By August 1914 the Naval Airship Division had taken delivery of only one more Zeppelin, *L3*.

Overall, the German experience with giant rigid airships between 1908 and 1914 had not been entirely happy. Picture postcards depicting the destruction of British warships by fleets of Zeppelins were eagerly bought by the public, but the reality failed to match these garish propaganda images. In 1913 the General Staff had produced a secret paper entitled *Aircraft in the Service of the Army*. It dwelt at length on the airship's reconnaissance role and on the principles governing the bombing of targets in the enemy's rear areas – troop encampments, railheads, supply depots and so on. But none of this theorizing had been put to the test when war began. After their disappointing performance in the 1910–11 war games, the giant rigids found no military employment with the Army until the maneuvers of 1913, in which two Zeppelins took part. In August 1914 the German Army deployed eight rigid airships: *LZ6*, *LZ7*, *LZ8*, *LZ9* and the *Sachsen* (requisitioned from DELAG) on the Western Front; in the East, *LZ14* at Konigsberg, *SL2* at Liegnitz for cooperation with the Austro-Hungarian Army, and *LZ5* at Posen under the command of Eigth Army. The Navy could call on *L3* and the requisitioned *Hansa* and *Viktoria Luise*. None of these airships was equipped to wage war.

Airships versus Airplanes

While Graf von Zeppelin was struggling to raise money for his airship program, developments of deeper significance were taking place on the other side of the Atlantic. By 1905 the Wright brothers had built Flyer III, the first practical airplane in history, fully controllable and capable of flights of more than 30 minutes duration. On October 5, 1905 they established an endurance record when Flyer III covered 24.25 miles in 38 minutes 3 seconds. Two weeks later they approached the US War Department with a proposal to build a military machine. The offer was unceremoniously refused, a fate which also befell the Wrights' attempts to sell a machine to the British Admiralty and War Office.

Despite the failure of their military initiative, the Wrights' achievements stimulated a spate of activity

SL2, A Schütte-Lanz rigid purchased by the German army in 1914, which incorporated the advanced design features pioneered by SL1, which was completed in 1911. Its hull, constructed of laminated aspen wood to allow greater flexibility, reflected the shipbuilding background of Professor Schütte and his technical staff. More significant was the shape of the hull, carefully streamlined and with simple cruciform fins, rudders and elevators at the stern, replacing the complicated box-like control surfaces of the contemporary Zeppelins. The keel was placed inside the ship's hull, providing an internal gangway, and the crew rode in streamlined gondolas. The propellers were not shaft-driven, as in the Zeppelins, but directly coupled to engines at the rear of the gondolas. With the exception of the wooden framework, all these design elements were adopted in the later Zeppelin program. The 'super-Zeppelins' which appeared in 1915 owed much to the brilliant work of the Schütte-Lanz team.

The first airplane built under military contract. Orville Wright flies over Fort Myer, piloting the tail-first biplane in which he crashed and was severely injured on September 17, 1908. His passenger, Lieutenant Thomas E Selfridge, was killed in the accident.

In the summer of 1910 the German Army began the training of volunteer officer pilots at Doberitz, near Berlin. In October 1912, while it was indulging one of its periodic bouts of disillusion with the rigid airship, the Army decided to expand the Doberitz establishment into a Fliegertruppe attached to the Pioneer Gardekorps. In the autumn of 1913 Idflieg (Inspectorate of Military Aviation) was set up, headed by an Inspecteur der Fliegertruppen, Oberst von Eberhardt, who was responsible for four Flieger Bataillonen, each comprising three companies and based on garrison towns across the Reich (Nr1–Nr4). A Saxon unit formed the 3rd Company of Flieger Bataillone Nr1. In addition the Bavarian Army, jealously guarding its independence, formed a two-company Flieger Kompanie. Mobilization plans involved the formation of a number of Feldflieger Abteilungen from these garrison units to serve with the Army in the field.

In August 1909 the US Army took delivery of a Wright Flyer, designating it Model A. The *Washington Star* rather grandly dubbed it 'Aeroplane No. 1, Heavier-than-Air Division, United States Aerial Fleet'. For some time it remained the only aeroplane in the 'Aerial Fleet'. It was not until March 1911 that Congress allocated the first $25 000 instalment of a $125 000 appropriation for Army flying. A month later the Signal Corps took delivery of a Wright Model B and a Model D pusher designed by Glenn Curtiss.

Second only to the Wrights as a pioneer of American aviation, Glenn Curtiss had scored a considerable triumph at the 1909 Rheims aviation rally, on successive days piloting his Golden Flyer biplane to victory in the Gordon Bennett Trophy and the Prix de la Vitesse. Back in the United States Curtiss began some of the first experiments with the dropping of bombs from aeroplanes. As early as June 30, 1910 he piloted his Golden Flyer over the outline of a battleship (marked with flags), dropping dummy bombs from a height of 50 ft. The first test with live bombs was made in January 1911, during Army exercises near San Francisco, by Lt Myron S Crissy and Philip Parmalee flying a Wright biplane. In spite of this promising start the US military authorities' interest in aviation began to recede. When war broke out in Europe the US Army had only 20 aircraft in service, all of them obsolete, and an establishment of 60 officers and 260 other ranks.

Much of the progress made in the United States before 1914 was the result of individual initiative rather than official encouragement. A notable enthusiast was Lt Riley Scott, whose bombsight of 1911 – a simple affair of wires and nails – was installed in a US Army Wright Model B. The bomb-aimer lay in a prone position, looking down at the target through a mica window, a development which anticipated the bombing methods evolved years later. In a series of passes over a 4 × 5 ft target, Scott released a single 18-pound bomb from a canvas sling under the passenger seat. From an altitude of 400 ft he was able to place each projectile to within 10 ft of the target. The US War Department remained unimpressed, Scott resigned his commission in disgust and took his sight to Europe where in January 1912 he won the Michelin bomb-dropping competition.

September 1909 saw the first big aviation rally in

by European designers and aviators. On July 2 1909 Louis Blériot piloted his Blériot XI monoplane across the English Channel, taking off from Les Baraques, near Calais, at 4.41 am and landing at Northfall Meadow, near Dover, 76 minutes later. Not only did he win the £1000 prize offered by the *Daily Mail* newspaper for the first cross-Channel flight; he also demonstrated that Britain could no longer rely absolutely on her isolation from the Continent as the single most important factor on which her national security rested. The following month saw the opening of the Rheims Aviation Week, the first of the great flying competitions which acted as the forcing beds of European aircraft design in the years leading up to World War I.

The military began to take an interest in heavier-than-air machines. In France airplanes participated in the Grandes Manoeuvres of 1910. By the end of the year there were 39 French military pilots and 29 military aircraft of Blériot, Breguet, Farman, Voisin, and Antoinette design, operating under the umbrella of the newly formed Inspectorate of Military Aeronautics.

Italy, the Air Circuit at Brescia, and the appearance of the first indigenous aircraft designs from Giovanni Caproni. Two years later an Italian officer, Giulio Douhet, published a seminal essay entitled *Rules for the Use of Aircraft in War*. Douhet was one of the few military men who understood that a combination of mass production and modern technology would transform warfare into an unlimited struggle between whole nations. Into this scenario, Douhet inserted a sweeping role for the emerging air corps, which would bomb the defensive positions in the enemy's line, his rear areas and routes of supply, communications networks and most significantly, his sources of production and population centers. To accomplish this, the air corps would necessarily act as an *independent* striking force, freed from a purely tactical subordination to the Army or Navy.

In 1911 there was no air corps capable of projecting such power on to or beyond the battlefield. But in the autumn of that year Douhet's theories were put to a more limited test in North Africa. On September 29, Italy declared war on Turkey after the latter's refusal to agree to the Italian military occupation of Tripolitania and Cirenaica. Attached to the Italian Expeditionary Force was a small aviation battalion, under the command of Captain Carlo Piazza, comprising two Blériot XIs, three Nieuport monoplanes, two Farman biplanes, and two Etrich Taubes.

On November 1 a member of the aviation battalion, Lieutenant Gavotti, took off in an Etrich Taube carrying four 4.5-pound Cipelli bombs in a leather bag. The detonators were stuffed in his pocket. Circling round a Turkish encampment at Ain Zara, he placed one of the bombs on his knees, fitted the detonator and dropped it over the side of his Taube. He then flew on to the oasis at Taguira, where he repeated the exercise with the remaining three bombs. Gavotti touched down after a 56-mile trip, having successfully accomplished history's first bombing raid undertaken by an element of an organized military unit.

In Italy in 1913, Giovanni Caproni completed work on the prototype of the first big three-engined aircraft designed specifically as a bomb carrier, the Ca30. In Russia parallel development was racing ahead under the direction of the brilliant designer Igor Sikorsky, whose giant Ilya Muromets Type A (IM Type A) took off on its maiden flight on December 11, 1913. The IM Type A had a wingspan of 113 ft, was capacious, luxuriously appointed with a fully enclosed cabin, and had a viewing platform on the top of the fuselage – where adventurous passengers could take a bracing turn outside, clinging to the safety rail in the slip-stream. Sikorsky recalled that it was 'just like Jules Verne, only more practical'. The Tsar had closely followed Sikorsky's progress and the Russian General Staff were also impressed with the military potential of Sikorsky's giant aircraft both for strategic reconnaissance and as bomb carriers. An order was placed for ten machines.

In Britain military flying had begun in 1878 with the building of a balloon at the Woolwich Arsenal. The Balloon Section was incorporated into the Royal Engineers in 1890 and saw action in the Boer War, directing the fire of British artillery at Magersfontein and during the Battle of Lombard's Kop. In October 1910 the Balloon Section was provided with funds 'to afford opportunities for aeroplaning'. Six months later the Army acquired some heavier-than-air machines after the expansion of the Royal Engineers' Balloon Section into an Air Battalion. By the summer Britain's first air force had assembled: six Bristol Boxkite biplanes, a battered Henri Farman pusher, a heavily modified Howard Wright biplane, and a Blériot XI monoplane which was the personal property of Lieutenant B A Cammell.

Senior officers were not impressed and General Nicholson, the Chief of the Imperial General Staff, considered that aviation was a useless and

Igor Sikorsky (left) poses proudly aboard the Russki Vityaz (Russian Knight) with his co-pilot and (center) the Grand Duke Nikolai, C-in-C of the Russian armed forces and a keen supporter of air power. Russki Vityaz was powered by four Argus tractor power plants mounted on the leading edge of the lower wing and flew for the first time on July 23, 1913. It had a useful load of 1540 pounds, in addition to its crew of seven. In the Military Trials of 1913 its airframe was written off in an accident, but the undamaged engines were salvaged for use in the Ilya Muromets (IM) Type A, named after a hero in Russian folklore.

A Be2a of No. 2 Squadron, RFC, at Larkhill in 1913. Designed as an inherently stable reconnaissance platform, the BE2a could also carry 100 pounds of bombs. Maximum speed was 70 mph at sea level and endurance three hours. A BE2a piloted by Lieutenant H D Harvey-Kelly was the first RFC aircraft to land in France on the outbreak of war.

expensive fad advocated by a handful of cranks. Nevertheless, at the beginning of 1912 the Committee of Imperial Defence recommended the establishment of a 'Flying Corps' with separate Military and Naval Wings serviced by a Central Flying School. This led to the formation of the Royal Flying Corps on April 13, 1912. However, interservice rivalry kept the Naval and Military Wings apart. Their effective separation was officially recognized in July 1914 when the Military Wing became the Royal Flying Corps (RFC) and the Naval Wing became the Royal Naval Air Service (RNAS). It was the RNAS which was to set the pace.

The Army remained almost exclusively preoccupied with the development at its Royal Aircraft Factory of an inherently stable reconnaissance machine, the BE2. The Army's approach to aviation remained cautious and bureaucratic while that of the RNAS was characterized by innovation and experiment. The RNAS pursued an independent training and procurement policy, encouraging private British manufacturers like Short and Sopwith and acquiring French and German machines for comparison. The Navy had traditionally played a wide-ranging strategic role, with the emphasis on mobility and flexibility of response, and the air enthusiasts in the RNAS grasped the opportunity offered by the airplane as an offensive weapon. The RNAS already envisaged its aircraft flying long distances to bomb enemy warships, dockyards and shore installations. While Army pilots groped their way across the country using the maps in Bradshaw's railway guide, the RNAS was developing specialized air navigation aids and its first primitive hand-held and fuselage-mounted bombsights. Machine-guns were taken aloft and experiments conducted to test the effectiveness of bomb and torpedo-dropping gear. In the summer of 1913 the RNAS took delivery of the first British machine designed specifically as a bomb carrier. This was the Bristol TB8 biplane, a two-seater with the bomb-release and prismatic

bombsight in the front cockpit and the controls in the rear. The offensive load consisted of 12 ten-pound bombs housed in a revolving container beneath the fuselage. As the lowermost bomb left its mounting, the rack turned to place the next bomb in position and automatically set the fuse. The bombs could be dropped both individually and in a batch.

On the Eve of Battle

In the 11 years following the Wrights' pioneering flights, aviation had laid claim to a rapidly growing industry geared to an accelerating rate of technological change and improvement in performance. Airplanes had climbed to over 20 000 ft, flown faster than 120 mph, and remained airborne for over six hours. Nevertheless, by the summer of 1914 neither the airship nor the airplane had staked a convincing claim as a major weapon of war. The Zeppelin, thought to be capable of paralysing the military and communications sinews of a nation in a few devastating hours, had simply not been equipped to wage war. The future of aerial bombardment was to lie with the purpose-built bomber, but only in Italy and Russia had the first steps been taken down this road, with the introduction of the Caproni Ca30 and the conversion of Sikorsky's massive Ilya Muromets long-range transports to military use.

The light, flimsy airplanes of the day, with their ability to take off from any level grass field, moderate fuel consumption and minimal logistical requirements, had won the grudging acceptance of Europe's General Staffs – as reconnaissance machines. However, doubts as to their true value remained deeply ingrained, particularly at the highest level. In July 1914, less than a month before he sailed for France in command of the British Expeditionary Force's 1st Corps, General Sir Douglas Haig told his staff officers: 'I hope none of you gentlemen is so foolish as to think that aeroplanes will be usefully employed for reconnaissance purposes in war'. During the next four years the relentless 'purposes of war' were to shape a formidable air weapon.

1.2 WESTERN FRONT 1914–15

IN THE HIGH SUMMER OF 1914 THE MOMENT arrived for the European powers to put their infant air forces to the test. On July 28, a month after the assassination at Sarajevo of the Archduke Franz Ferdinand by Slav nationalists, Austria-Hungary declared war on Serbia. Two days later the Tsar ordered a general mobilization of Russia's armed forces. German mobilization followed on the afternoon of August 1, four hours after the German ultimatum to St Petersburg had expired. Simultaneously the telegraph flashed mobilization orders through France. On August 3 Germany declared war on France – on the false pretext that French airplanes had bombed Nuremberg – and advanced German units pushed into Luxembourg. Britain was inexorably sucked in to the conflict, declaring war on Germany on August 4. Within two weeks the bulk of the British Expeditionary Force (BEF) had crossed to France.

The great German deployment preliminary to the execution of the Schlieffen Plan – the advance intended to swing through Belgium and capture Paris – was made with seven armies and 1.5 million men. In comparison with the millions of troops on the move, the opposing air forces were tiny. Between August 13 and 15 the RFC flew its 63 front-line aircraft to France. Of the four squadrons available, Nos 2 and 4 were equipped with BE2s, No. 3 with Blériot monoplanes and Farman biplanes, and No. 5 with Farmans, Avro 504 biplanes and Factory-built BE8s.

The first pilot to land in France, on August 13, was Lt H D Harvey-Kelly, flying a BE2a, No. 347. The RFC established its first headquarters at Maubeuge (where Capitaine Coutelle had made his historic balloon reconnaissance flight 120 years before). Reconnaissance was still the order of the day, and at 0930 hrs on August 19, Captain (later Air Chief Marshal Sir) Philip Joubert de la Ferté of No. 3 Squadron in a Blériot, and Lt G W Mapplebeck of No. 4 Squadron in a BE2a took off to make the first observations from the air of the advance and dispositions of the enemy. They both got lost and Joubert did not return until late in the afternoon, having landed twice to ask the way!

There was, perhaps, still an air of comedy about an untried air force which boasted an intriguing mixture of hastily commandeered transport vehicles, one of which – No. 5 Squadron's ammunition and bomb lorry – still bore the scarlet livery of a famous sauce manufacturer and the legend 'The World's Appetizer'.

Little or no thought had been given to the best means of delivering the projectiles the vehicle carried. In the swirling confusion of the opening weeks of the war the four RFC squadrons under the command of Major-General Sir David Henderson strove to interpret the ebb and flow of battle and observe the location and composition of the German field formations and the movement of their reinforcements. The science of 'seeing from the air', still in its infancy, faced its first serious test over a war zone too large to be covered comprehensively either by the aircraft of the Allies or by their German opponents. But during the retreat from Mons the daily reconnaissance sorties took a more aggressive turn, with pilots dropping hand grenades and petrol bombs on the enemy.

This was done without the benefit of either sights or bomb-dropping gear; the pilots went aloft with grenades stuffed into their pockets and larger missiles hanging from their flying gear or slung on cords along the fuselage of their aircraft. These were tossed over the side at low altitude to ensure a degree of accuracy, tactics which exposed valuable aircraft to virtually point-blank machine-gun and rifle fire. These dangers did not deter an RFC pilot on September 1 from dropping two bombs on columns of German cavalry converging on a crossroads at Villers-Cotterets, northeast of Paris, provoking a stampede. Three days earlier, on August 29, while No. 4 Squadron was at Compiègne, a German machine flew over their camp and dropped three bombs. Second-Lieutenant N C Spratt immediately took off in pursuit of the enemy aircraft in a Sopwith Tabloid and, as a squadron officer noted in his diary, 'made 20 rings round it and fairly put the wind up the German, and then came back'. Some reports of the incident describe Spratt bombarding the enemy machine with flechettes – pointed and fluted steel darts about five inches long normally dropped from cannisters in quantities of up to 500. On reaching the ground from 5000 ft, the flechette attained the speed of a rifle bullet. Intended for use against German troop concentrations and horse-lines, the flechette proved a disappointment; even in a combat area, anything but a direct hit was a waste of effort.

Another aggressive RFC pilot was Lieutenant L A Strange of No. 5 Squadron. On August 28 he was aloft in his Farman biplane, No. 341, with Captain Penn Gaskell as his observer: '*I* SPENT the morning … fixing up a new type of petrol bomb to my Henri Farman and in the morning Penn Gaskell and I went to try it out. We dropped two bombs on either side of the road north of St Quentin, where we found a lot of German transport; returning ten minutes later to have another go at the same lot, we found them moving south, so we dropped down to a low height and flew along over the road, where we managed to plant our bombs right on to a lorry which took fire and ran into a ditch. The lorry behind it caught fire as well, and both were well ablaze when we left. It was not a serious loss to the German army, but it sent us home very well pleased with ourselves. That same evening a German machine dropped three bombs in our aerodrome and one fell fairly close to our transport, but luckily it did not burst. We all made a rush to the spot to grab bits of the bombs as souvenirs and found that they were full of shrapnel bullets.*'

The RFC was moving into unknown territory, with all the risks that improvization brought with it. That summer Sergeant Reginald King was a rigger with No. 5 Squadron: '*B*OMBS, WELL, THEY WERE only like grenades. We had one kind of bomb which we hung up in the undercarriage of the Henri Farman, and it contained two gallons of petrol and in the nose there was a very light cartridge. When this* *bomb was dropped the cartridge would explode and set fire to the petrol - and that was a primitive fire bomb.... They also had small grenades which they hung on the nacelle of the aircraft, and the pilot would take them out of the rack and throw them at his target. They had a cap at the top, and when he was ready to throw them down he undid the cap, put the detonator on, took them out of the rack and just threw them down. For some reason or other the tail on these bombs was too short ... it was about a quarter of an inch iron rod some six inches long. They wanted to extend this by 12 inches. So they took these bombs, without their detonators, and gave them to the smith, with his little portable forge, and he actually welded a piece of metal on to the live bomb. He was careful to keep it cool all the while with water, and when that job was on we gave him a very wide berth. He would say, "What are you chaps walking right over there for? What's the matter?" And for the best part of the day he merrily worked on a great pile of these bombs'.*

'Doves' and 'Carrier-Pigeons'

When war came, the German air corps was completely subordinated to the tactical requirements of the army. It possessed some 264 airplanes, the bulk of which were mobilized into 33 Feldflieger Abteilungen, each of six machines. These were assigned to duties with their allotted Army headquarters and individual Army Corps.

The most numerous German type was the elegant bird-winged Etrich Taube. In common with all German military airplanes, it was unarmed and its role was purely reconnaissance, a task which it performed with spectacular success in East Prussia, covering the Russian advance in the campaign which preceded Von Hindenburg's crushing victory at Tannenberg (August 26–29). Like the BE2c, the Taube's principal asset was its inherent stability. In the West, the Taube added bombing to its reconnaissance duties. On August 30 the Sunday calm of Paris was disturbed by four small bombs which fell near the Gare de L'Est, killing one civilian and injuring four others. In a nearby street a message fell to earth, written on a streamer attached to a sandweighted rubber pouch: 'The German army is at the gates of Paris. There is nothing for you to do but surrender. Leutnant von Hiddessen'. That evening the German Army despatches announced that an airplane attached to IX Corps had 'successfully' bombed Paris.

Far from alarming the citizens of Paris, the attention paid to them by this and subsequent Taubes became the source of enormous popular interest. Two more raids followed: on August 31, when one of two bombs dropped failed to explode and there were no casualties; and on September 1, when six bombs killed three and injured 16. When on September 3 three more Taubes droned over the rooftops of Paris, its citizenry were well-prepared for the visit, arming themselves with binoculars and opera glasses and newspaper diagrams of the Taube's distinctive silhouette. The profit-minded did brisk business selling seats in the best vantage points, particularly Montmartre. The German pilots entered into the carnival spirit, flying circuits round the Eiffel Tower while French riflemen blazed away at them from its upper stories.

After September 3 the visits were halted. This coincided with von Kluck's decision to wheel the German 1st Army southward and in front of Paris, exposing his flank to the French counter-stroke on the Marne. Had his pilots' attention remained on the capital, rather than being directed to the southeast, they would have observed the build-up to the French attack on the German right flank.

By the time the Taubes reappeared over Paris on September 8, von Kluck was on the point of ordering a withdrawal to the Noyon-Verdun line. On this occasion the aircraft dropped no bombs, but one of them was brought down by ground fire north of the capital near the Fort de Celles. The pilot crashed near a unit of troops on trench-digging duty; when he pulled out a pistol and attempted to resist capture, he was beaten to death with shovels and picks.

The last attack was made on October 12, when two Taubes dropped incendiary bombs. In a total of ten attacks, 16 planes had dropped approximately 56 bombs, none of them heavier than ten pounds. Eleven people had been killed and 47 injured.

These raids had been little more than a flamboyant diversion from the Taubes' reconnaissance flights, exciting intense curiosity but inflicting very little damage. However, on the northern wing of the German advance, Major Wilhelm Siegert was planning a more ambitious aerial offensive. In the autumn of 1914 he obtained permission from the German High Command (Obersten Heeresleitung, or OHL) to assemble a special unit, recruited from the air corps' most experienced pilots, for cross-Channel raids against Britain. A temporary airfield was established at Ghistelles, near Ostend, for the two 18-aircraft wings of the Fliegerkorps des Obersten Heeresleitung, code-named the 'Carrier-Pigeon Unit of Ostend' (Brieftauben Abteilung Ostend). The aircraft at Siegert's disposal were Type B Aviatik and Albatros two-seater reconnaissance biplanes modified to carry four 20-pound bombs. Defensive armament consisted of Mauser rifles issued to the aircrew. To increase the unit's mobility, Siegert housed the officers in railway carriages.

It was Siegert's aim to launch his bombing offensive from Calais, but the German advance came to a halt well short of this objective, leaving the British mainland out of combat range. Thus between September 1914 and the beginning of January 1915 the Carrier-Pigeon Unit's activities were confined to daylight raids on Dunkirk, Nieuport, Furnes and La Panne. In Siegert's words, 'After that the enemy's aerial defenses so increased in efficiency that it was impossible to undertake further work with any hopes of reasonable success'. Siegert turned to night bombing, and on the night of January 28/29, 14 of his aircraft attacked Dunkirk. Shortly afterwards the unit was transferred to the Eastern Front, where in March 1915 it operated with some success during the Battle of Gorlice-Tarnow.

In October 1914 Siegert's ambitions were pre-empted by another army air unit, Feldflieger Abteilung 9. On October 25, two of its Taubes took off to attack Dover. Poor visibility forced one of them to turn back but the other, piloted by Leutnant Karl Kaspar, claimed to have bombed the port.

Strategic and Tactical Bombing

Although Feldflieger Abteilung 9's raid was an isolated effort, verging on the puny, its operations touch on the important distinction between strategic and tactical bombing - one of the principal themes running through the history of aerial bombardment.

Siegert's aims were essentially *strategic* but, lacking the means to accomplish them, he was obliged to switch the Carrier-Pigeon Unit to purely *tactical* operations. Expressed in the simplest form, tactical operations are those carried out in co-ordination with surface forces which directly assist the land or naval battle. Strategic operations are aimed at the enemy's capacity to make war, hitting vital industries, those civilians employed in them, and the communications networks and energy supplies which sustain them. The US Strategic Bombing Survey expressed the distinction in a metaphor: 'Strategic bombing bears the same relationship to tactical bombing as does the cow to the pail of milk. To deny immediate aid and comfort to the enemy, tactical considerations dictate upsetting the bucket. To ensure eventual starvation, the strategic move is to kill the cow'. Thus to attack the enemy's airfields and aircraft is tactical, while to attack the factories which produce them is strategic.

The key factor is the nature of the target not, as is sometimes supposed, the size of the aircraft involved or the distance flown to the objective. When during World War II, four-engined Lancaster bombers of 5 Group, RAF Bomber Command, flew 1100 miles from Scotland to strike at the German battleship *Tirpitz* in Tromso Fjord, in northern Norway, they were undertaking a tactical mission. And when in the early months of 1945 the US Navy launched strike forces of single-engined aircraft against aircraft factories only 100 miles distant on the Japanese mainland, their mission was strategic.

The very words 'strategic bombing' evoke those chilling images of total devastation, aerial photographs of the blackened shells of Germany's cities in the spring of 1945. In the autumn of 1914 frail biplanes carrying 20-pound bombs represented that terrible power only in an embryonic form. Nevertheless, even at this stage, the strategic concept was eagerly embraced by British naval aviation.

The RNAS and Strategic Bombing

On September 3, 1914 the hard-pressed British War Office had ceded the air defense of the British Isles to the Royal Navy. Admiralty defense policy had long rested on the assumption that, in the event of war, Zeppelins would be despatched across the North Sea to raid Britain's cities. Not content merely to wait passively for their arrival overhead, the Admiralty had concluded the best form of defense was attack, and that the German airships should be destroyed in their hangars. This suited the energetic First Lord of the Admiralty, Winston Churchill, who saw in this policy a golden opportunity to involve the Navy in the great land battle raging across the Channel - albeit only on its coastal fringes.

Already in Belgium was the Eastchurch squadron of the Royal Naval Air Service (RNAS), led by the remarkable Squadron Commander C R Samson, one of the pioneers of British air power. On August 27, Samson had flown to Ostend at the head of a mixed unit comprising three BEs, two Sopwith Tabloids, two Blériot monoplanes, one Henri Farman, one Bristol biplane and a Short seaplane which had had its floats exchanged for wheels. The force was accompanied by the semi-rigid airship *Astra-Torres 3*, which at the time was the only RNAS aircraft armed with a machine-gun. Three days later - with the fate of the BEF hanging in the balance at Mons - the order came to return to England. On September 1 the RNAS aeroplanes flew to Dunkirk, where Lieutenant Lord Edward Grosvenor crashed his Blériot and delayed the party for three days. While they waited Samson received fresh orders from the Admiralty: '*T*HE ADMIRALTY CONSIDERS IT *extremely important '...to deny the use of territory within a hundred miles of Dunkirk to German Zeppelins and to attack by aeroplanes all airships found replenishing there'.*

Reinforced with an improvized squadron of armored cars, Samson threw his tiny command into the confused spasm of fighting - the so-called Race to the Sea - which followed the breakdown of the Schlieffen Plan and preceded the descent into trench warfare. While his armored cars ranged across the Belgian countryside, Samson drew up plans to bomb the Zeppelin sheds at Cologne and Düsseldorf. Since its arrival in France his force had been divided into Nos. 1, 2 and 3 Squadrons. These designations were more optimistic than realistic as there were only 12 aircraft at his disposal, a motley collection of Sopwiths, BEs, Blériots, a Deperdussin monoplane and two Bristol TB8s.

The aircraft in Samson's command were hardly more sophisticated as fighting machines than his collection of primitive armored cars. For bombing the principal available weapon was the pear-shaped, impact-detonating 20-pound Hale bomb. The bomb contained a 4.5-pound bursting charge of Amatol (a mixture of TNT and ammonium nitrate). It was armed by a fusing mechanism activated by a small propeller behind the tail fins which started to revolve when the missile was dropped.

On September 3 three Sopwith Tabloids flew to Ostend to make ready for an attack on German airship sheds to be launched from an airfield being prepared at Antwerp. They were picketed on the leeward side of the sand dunes where on September 12 they were sent cartwheeling to destruction by a gale force wind. It was not until ten days later, on September 22, that the first British raid on Germany was mounted. The aircraft involved were: Be2a No. 50, flown by Major C L Gerrard (flight leader); Sopwith Tractor Biplane No. 906, flown by Flight Lieutenant C H Collet; Sopwith Churchill No. 149, flown by Squadron Commander Spenser D A Grey with Lieutenant Newton Clare; and Sopwith Tabloid No. 168, piloted by Flight Lieutenant R L G Marix. The BE2a and the Tractor Biplane were tasked to attack the Zeppelin shed at Düsseldorf; the Churchill and the Tabloid were to fly to Cologne. When the aircraft took off they flew into a dense mist spreading from the River Roer some miles east of the Rhine. Only Flight Lieutenant Collet succeeded in finding his target, gliding towards the Zeppelin shed from 6000 ft, the last 1500 ft through thick mist. He emerged barely a quarter of a mile from his objective

Avro 504B, No. 1009, of No. 1 Squadron RNAS with its pilot Flight Lieutenant A W Bigsworth, who on May 16/17, 1915 attacked and badly damaged *LZ39* over Ostend, a feat which gained Bigsworth the DSO.

and released three bombs at 400 ft. One exploded short of the shed, and the others failed to detonate. All four aircraft were back in Antwerp by 1300 hrs.

On September 27 reinforcements arrived in the shape of Squadron Commander A M Longmore, in his RE5, and six other aircraft. On September 30 Longmore, accompanied by Flight Lieutenant E Osmond, took off in his RE5 to attack the railway junction at Cambrai. Descending through cloud over the target, Longmore signalled Osmond to drop three improvized bombs (of French manufacture) over the side of the aircraft. On the same day a similar raid was made by Flight Lieutenant E T R Chambers.

At the end of September, with Antwerp menaced by German heavy artillery, Samson launched further air attacks on the Zeppelin sheds alongside the Rhine. The RNAS airfield lay between Antwerp and the tightening German encirclement. Under incessant bombardment two Sopwith Tabloids – neat little wood and fabric biplane scouts evolved from a pre-war racing model – were readied for a sortie.

The evacuation of Antwerp was imminent when, at 1320 hrs on October 8, Squadron Commander Spenser D A Grey took off in No. 167 and set course for Cologne. He was followed ten minutes later by Flight Lieutenant R L G Marix in 168, bound for Düsseldorf. Take-off had been delayed by poor weather conditions and, on arrival over Cologne, Spenser Grey found that the Zeppelin shed was obscured by cloud. He came down to 600 ft and for ten minutes flew through a barrage of fire in a vain attempt to locate his target. Finally giving up, he dropped his two 20-pound bombs on the railway station in the middle of the city. He returned to Antwerp at 1645 hrs, barely an hour before the order was given to evacuate the city.

Arriving over the Zeppelin shed at Düsseldorf, Marix dived to 600 ft before releasing his bombs. Thirty seconds later the roof of the shed collapsed as the fully inflated Army Zeppelin ZIX inside exploded, sending sheets of flame to a height of 500 ft. Marix's Tabloid had been badly damaged by ground fire and, with his fuel exhausted, he force-landed some 20 miles from Antwerp. He borrowed a bicycle from a friendly Belgian peasant and rode most of the way back to base, completing the journey by car.

When Antwerp was evacuated, the RNAS established itself at Dunkirk, which was to become its largest single operational base for most of the war. Its location, strategically placed on the left flank of the Allied line and at the end of one of the vital cross-Channel arteries, encouraged the RNAS to diversify its operations into virtually every aspect of aerial activity, from sea patrolling to strategic bombing. This tendency was encouraged by the relative freedom which the Admiralty allowed its successive commanders and the elasticity of the RNAS' organization compared with the RFC's strict dependence on the requirements of the Army in the field. Moreover the Dunkirk station's rapid evolution was bound up with Churchill's vigorous efforts to find an offensive role for the Navy, of which the RNAS was a small but highly individualistic part, appealing irresistibly to the First Lord's buccaneering instincts.

In spite of worsening weather conditions, Samson strove to maintain the pressure, and early in November a number of attacks were made on Bruges, where the Germans were assembling U-boats from sections transported there by rail. On November 3 a Short Seaplane aimed two 100-pound bombs at Bruges' railway station, one of which exploded in some nearby sidings.

The withdrawal to Dunkirk had placed the Zeppelin sheds alongside the Rhine outside the range of Samson's aircraft. Consideration was quickly given to alternative targets and the spotlight fell on the Zeppelin factory at Friedrichshafen, a strategic target situated on the shores of Lake Constance. Under the overall direction of Noel Pemberton Billing (a celebrated pre-war aviation pioneer by now in the Royal Navy's Volunteer Reserve) detailed plans were drawn up in conditions of the greatest secrecy. To reach the target it was necessary to overfly some 250 miles of hostile territory, wooded and mountainous terrain contiguous with the Black Forest. The airfield at Belfort, on the Franco-Swiss border, was chosen as the base from which to launch the raid, its vast airship hangar providing the RNAS' pilots and aircraft with a secure hiding place from the prying eyes of enemy agents. The machines selected for the operation were Avro 504s, the first of this type to go into service with the RNAS.

Accompanied by 11 mechanics, the crated-up Avro 504s were transported by special train to Belfort, arriving under cover of darkness on November 13. Sixteen hours after their arrival they had been reassembled, loaded with fuel and fitted with improvized under-wing bomb-racks carrying four Hale bombs. Bad weather then closed in and the four pilots selected for the operation (Squadron Commander E F Briggs, Flight Commander J T Babington, Flight Lieutenant S V Sippé and Flight Sub-Lieutenant R P Cannon) were forced to stand by until conditions improved in the small hours of November 21. After a final check at 0930 hrs the four Avro 504s took off at five-minute intervals, led by Squadron Commander Briggs in No. 873. Cannon, in No. 179, broke his tailskid on take-off and abandoned the mission. The others flew on to a point north of Basle and then, at 5000 ft, followed the Rhine to Lake Constance. Flight Lieutenant Sippé's log takes up the story: '**11.30** *AM: ARRIVED at extreme end of lake and came down to within 10 ft of the water. Continued at this height over lake,* *passing Constance at a very low altitude, as considered less likelihood of being seen. Crossed lake and hugged north shore until five miles from objective. Started climb and reached 1200 ft. Observed 12 or 14 shrapnels bursting slightly north of Friedrichshafen. Presumed these were directed against No. 873.*

11.55 am: When half a mile from the sheds put machine into dive, and came down to 700 ft. Observed men lined up to right of shed, number estimated 300–500. Dropped one bomb in enclosure to put gunners off aim, and, when in correct position, two into works and shed. The fourth bomb failed to release. During this time very heavy fire, mitrailleuse and rifle, was being kept up, and shells were being very rapidly fired. Dived and flew north until out of range of guns, then turned back to waterside shed to try to release fourth bomb. Bomb would not release; was fired on by machine-guns (probably mitrailleuse), dived down to surface of lake and made good my escape.

'1.50 pm: Arrived Belfort'.

Of the eleven bombs released over the target, two had fallen on the airship sheds, damaging one of the Zeppelins under construction and blowing up a gasworks in a spectacular explosion. Babington flew back to within 35 miles of Belfort before making a forced landing. Squadron Commander Briggs was less lucky. His fuel tank was holed by machine-gun fire and he came down near the Zeppelin factory. After landing he was attacked and injured by German civilians, but on his arrival at Friedrichshafen's Weingarten hospital he was treated with every respect and courtesy by the local military.

On November 25 it was the turn of one of Samson's TB8s, which successfully bombed the German gun batteries at Middelkerke. Just under a month later Samson achieved a notable 'first', flying his Maurice Farman, loaded with 18 16-pound bombs, on a night attack against the U-boats sheltering in Ostend.

Samson's historic night raid was a prelude to the attack launched on December 25 by RNAS seaplanes on the Imperial Navy's Zeppelin shed at Nordholz, eight miles south of Cuxhaven. In conception the raid was a classic example of the Royal Navy's tradition that the defense of Britain began at the highwatermark of the nearest enemy port; for the first time in the history of naval warfare, shipboard aircraft were to be employed as the sole striking arm of the fleet.

The nine seaplanes selected for the raid – three Short Folders, four Short 74s and two Short 135s (Nos. 135 and 136) – were to be transported to within striking distance of the German coastline aboard the former passenger packets *Engadine*, *Empress* and *Riviera*, each of which had been converted into a seaplane carrier at the beginning of the war. Accommodation for the aircraft consisted of canvas screens erected on the ships' forecastles and afterdecks.

The Short 74 was an improved version of the Navy's first seaplane, the Short S41 of 1912. The Folder was so named because its wings could be swung back from their 67 ft span to no more than 12 ft, facilitating shipboard storage. It was powered by a 160 hp Gnôme rotary which gave it a maximum speed of 78 mph and a fully loaded weight of 3040 pounds. The two 135s had been ordered by the

Navy in September 1913 and were advanced versions of the Folder, with a shorter upper wing span of 54 ft 6 in. No. 135 was delivered before the outbreak of war and was powered by a 135 hp Swiss-designed single-row, water-cooled Salmson radial; No. 136 had a more powerful engine, a two-row 14-cylinder Salmson developing 200 hp.

At 0600 hrs on Christmas Day the three seaplane carriers reached a point 12 miles north of Heligoland, escorted by the light cruisers HMS *Arethusa* and HMS *Undaunted* and a protective screen of eight destroyers of Third Flotilla. Ahead of them was a piquet line of submarines which had sailed from Harwich at 0500 hrs on December 24. At 0700 hrs, in the bone-numbing cold of the North Sea and conditions of considerable confusion, seven of the seaplanes took off; the remaining two failed to 'unstick' and were taken back on board their carriers. In racks underneath the center sections of the seaplanes were slung three 20-pound Hale bombs. The combined weight of the bursting charges in these 21 projectiles was less than the similar charge in just one of the 13.5 in common shells in the magazine of the battleship *Iron Duke*, Admiral Jellicoe's flagship.

The seven seaplanes flew eastward into an ominously thickening haze. By the time they crossed the coast they were enveloped in a dense bank of fog. Had the sun been bouncing off the massive revolving hangar at Nordholz – 597 ft long, 114 ft wide and 98 ft high – the glare would have led them straight to the target. But widely separated and lost in the fog, they jettisoned their bombs on the coastline and countryside. It is just possible that one of the pilots released his bombs close to the target, unaware that the Zeppelin shed lay below, concealed by the fog. Little if any damage was suffered by the military installations on which the pilots later claimed to have dropped their bombs.

The first three seaplanes returned at 1000 hrs, shortly after *Empress*, the slowest of the carriers, had fought a spirited engagement with the Zeppelin *L6*, which had caught up with the British force at about 0930 hrs. *Empress* had taken immediate evasive action, zigzagging through the water while *L6* ponderously tried to match her course, firing a machine-gun from the forward gondola and dropping three 50 kg bombs, all of which fell harmlessly into the sea. When *Arethusa* and *Undaunted* came to *Empress*'s rescue, *L6* broke off its attack. During these last hectic moments of the operation *Empress* was also bombed by two German seaplanes, a Friedrichshafen FF29 and a Friedrichshafen 19, the latter dropping several bombs (probably 4.5 kg Carbonits) from a height of about 1600 ft. This machine was so badly damaged by fire from the British converted six-pounder anti-aircraft guns that it 'completely collapsed' on landing at its base on Heligoland, and had to be written off.

Three more pilots were later picked up by *E11*, one of the British submarines. The remaining pilot was picked up by a Dutch trawler and interned for a while in Holland before returning to his unit.

In January and February 1915 RNAS aircraft, including seaplanes from *Empress*, flew missions all along the Belgian coast, from Zeebrugge to Ostend. On February 12, 21 land planes and six seaplanes took off, 15 of the former and only one of the seaplanes

In his autobiography *Flights and Fights*, Samson vividly recalled the historic raid on Ostend:

'When I got over the harbour I could see no signs of any submarine. I therefore determined to bomb the batteries just to the south of the town, where there would be little risk of killing civilians. The lights of the town were all lit, and the view was splendid. The flash of the guns and the glare of the bursting shells was a wonderful sight all along our line from Dixmude to Ypres. By the time I reached 1000 ft I opened out my engine and turned south, passing along the seafront of Ostend. As soon as the noise of my engine was heard, pandemonium started. Star shells, rockets and searchlights played into the sky, and the lights of the town went out in about two minutes, but they stayed long enough for me to pick out my objective. I let go my 18 bombs in salvoes of threes, and the flash of their explosions was a most satisfying sight. Having unloaded my cargo I set out directly to seaward. By this time the air was alive with shrapnel, but all well away from me; the searchlights were sweeping the sky, but all the beams were well above me. Getting out to about four miles to seaward, I headed for home, turning round every now and then to look at the view. The air behind me was a mass of bursting shells, rockets and star shells, and it was certain that the Hun was badly shaken.'

The Handley Page 0/100, the first true British bomber. The observer lay prone, just behind the pilot, to aim and release bombs, tugging on the latter's left or right boot to alter direction on the bombing run. Sub-Lieutenant Paul Bewsher, who flew 0/100s with 3 Wing, has described the crucial moment of a raid: *'I lifted my seat and crawled to the little room behind, which vibrated fiercely with the mighty revolutions of the engines. I stood on a floor of little strips of wood, in an enclosure whose walls ... were of tightly stretched canvas which chattered and flapped a little with the rush of the wind from the two propellers whirling scarcely a foot outside. Behind was fitted a petrol tank, underneath which hung the 12 yellow bombs. I lay on my chest under the pilot's seat and pushed to the right a little wooden door, which slid away from a rectangular hole in the floor through which came a swift updraught of wind. Over this space was set the bombsight with its ranging slide bars painted with phosphorescent paint. On my right, fixed to the side of the machine, was a wooden handle operating on a metal drum from which ran a cluster of release wires to the bombs further back. It was the bomb dropping lever, by means of which I could drop all my bombs at once, or one by one, as I wished'.*

locating their targets. In the course of this busy day Flight Lieutenant Marix bombed the railway station at Ostend harbour, scoring a direct hit and starting a large fire: in all 61 bombs were dropped, a total weight of 1820 pounds. Two days later Samson wrote, 'An aeroplane with a determined pilot has all the chances on its side'. This was an accurate enough observation before the introduction of the Fokker Eindecker, with its forward-firing, synchronized machine-gun, and at a time when the German anti-aircraft defenses were still relatively ineffective (although on February 16 they accounted for four out of 25 RNAS machines). Nevertheless, the damage which Samson's machines could inflict, however gallantly they were flown, was akin to a swarm of gnats stinging a rhinoceros. Samson admitted as much in a memorandum he submitted to the Admiralty on February 6:' *PRACTICAL EXPERIENCE ... HAS shown me that bomb dropping is only successful at the present moment when carried out by aeroplanes carrying a number of bombs. 100 pound bombs are wanted against submarines. I am quite confident of being able to use 200 hp Short seaplanes adapted as aeroplanes for this work. They should carry four 100 pound bombs, and would be used at night'.*

Before Samson could fully develop this theory he was recalled to Britain, and in March 1915 sent to the Dardanelles at the head of No. 3 (Aeroplane) Squadron, RNAS. It was not long before he was coaxing a Farman into the air armed with a 500-pound bomb. On September 7, 1915 he flew the same aircraft, this time carrying two 112-pound bombs, on a mission against the railway bridge over the River Maritza, scoring a direct hit and halting traffic for two days.

The Handley Page 0/100

The vigorous bombing campaign mounted by the RNAS in the opening months of the war played an important part in the development of the first series of large British bombing aircraft, the 'bloody paralyzer' advocated by the Director of the

Admiralty Air Department, Commodore Murray F Sueter. On December 28, 1914 a specification was issued calling for a land-based twin-engined patrol bomber capable of attaining a minimum speed of 72 mph, climbing to a height of 3000 ft in ten minutes and carrying an offensive load of six 112-pound bombs. Handley Page responded with a design for a bomber, designated Type 0/100, with a wingspan of 114 ft, two 150 hp Sunbeam engines, a fuel load of 200 gallons of petrol and 30 gallons of oil, a bombsight, a Rouzet wireless telegraphy transmitter-receiver and a crew of two protected from small arms fire by armor plate.

The first prototype, No. 1455, was flown a year later on December 18, 1915. It was powered by two water-cooled 12-cylinder Vee-type Rolls Royce Eagle engines installed as tractors in armored nacelles, each of which contained an armored fuel tank. The Eagles could develop 300 hp at 2000 rpm but to ensure reliable running they were derated to 250 hp at 1600 rpm. The crew of three sat in a cockpit enclosure glazed with bullet-proof glass and reinforced with armor plate; in the production models, however, the enclosure and much of the armor plating was removed. The cross-braced box-girder fuselage was made in sections, as were the 100 ft wings, which could be folded to enable the aircraft to be stowed in the standard Bessoneau canvas field hangars of the time. The undercarriage was built almost entirely of faired steel tube, and each of the four wheels was fitted with a large shock absorber. The release gears for the standard bombload of 16 112-pound bombs were mounted on four crossbeams in the fuselage above the bomb-cell floor, which was a 'honeycomb' grid with 16 spring-loaded flaps separately pushed open by each bomb as it fell. The first four prototypes were not fitted with any armament, but those ordered for the RNAS were modified to incorporate a Scarff ring mounting in the nose for either one or two double-yoked Lewis machine-guns; the upper rear cockpit housed either one Lewis gun on a rocking post mounting, or more usually two Lewis guns, each on an individual bracket at either side of the cockpit. A further Lewis gun was mounted to fire backwards and downwards through a trapdoor in the floor of the fuselage abaft the mainplanes. Delivery of the 0/100 to the RNAS began in September 1916.

The French Take the Lead

The Handley Page 0/100 was designed to carry and deliver bombs in level flight against a specific target at medium or long range. It was a true bomber, as opposed to the general-purpose types which had been pressed into service at the beginning of the war. Perhaps the most efficient airplane in this latter category was the French Voisin 3, a sturdy pusher biplane of steel-tube structure powered by a 120 hp Canton-Unné nine-cylinder liquid-cooled engine. On October 5, 1914 a Voisin 3 of Escadrille VB24, with an 8 mm Hotchkiss machine-gun mounted in the nose of its nacelle, demonstrated its all-round capability by shooting down an Aviatik two-seater near Rheims in the first aerial fire fight of the war.

The first French bombing raid of the war was made on August 14, 1914 when a single machine, piloted by Lieutenant Césari with Caporal Prudhommeaux as observer, attacked a Zeppelin shed near Metz. The first step in the evolution of a French bombing strategy was taken five weeks later with the appointment of Commandant Barès as the Director of Aeronautics at the French General Headquarters. In the early weeks of the war Barès had secured permission for the use of bombing aircraft to complement counter-battery observation operations. On October 8 a memorandum issued by the General Headquarters specified the objectives for aerial bombardment, such as troop concentrations and communications. By November four escadrilles had been assigned to bombing operations, and at the end of the month Barès formed the first Groupe de Bombardment (Bombardment Group) composed of VB1, VB2 and VB3, a total of 18 Voisins led by Commandant Göys, another vigorous proponent of air power. Groupe de Bombardement 1 was under the overall control of General Joffre, the French Commander-in-Chief, at General Headquarters – an indication of its fundamentally strategic character.

From the outset Barès demonstrated his determination to use his bombers not merely as an adjunct to the artillery in the battle zone but as a force capable of striking at the communications systems and war industries deep in the heart of the German homeland. Operations began on December 4, with a raid on the railway station at Freiburg, to all intents and purposes an 'undefended town' situated well behind the German lines. Meanwhile Barès was hard at work drawing up a plan of bombardment which identified targets according to their importance and vulnerability. The program was approved by Joffre in January 1915, and out of a proposed new 75 escadrilles, 21 were earmarked for bombing operations. A new Bombardment Group, GB2, was formed at the beginning of January 1915, under Commandant Laborde, followed in March by GB3 under Capitaine Fauré. To gain experience, GB3 was stationed in Alsace, a relatively quiet sector, from which it launched a series of raids on Altkirch, Mülheim and Freiburg. May saw the formation of GB4 and its immediate employment in a tactical role in the fighting in the Artois sector.

At this stage in the war the pusher types, like the Voisin 3 and the Farman F.40 encountered little or no resistance in the air. The fact that the pusher layout rendered them completely blind from the rear presented no problem until the appearance in August 1915 of the Fokker Eindecker armed with a synchronized, forward-firing machine-gun. In the first year of the war, the pusher's machine-gun, mounted in the nose of its tub-like nacelle, had a much less restricted field of fire than those installed in the German tractor types.

On April 22, 1915 a sinister green cloud swirled across No-Man's-Land towards the French lines at Ypres. In an attempt to break the deadlock, the Germans had opened over 500 cylinders containing 168 tons of pressurized chlorine gas, which was carried by the wind towards the French positions along a four-mile front, causing 15 000 casualties, one-third of them fatal.

The French quickly discovered that the gas was being manufactured by the Badische Anilin und Soda Fabrik (BASF) at Ludwigshafen near Mannheim. This target was assigned to GB1, operating from an airfield at Malzéville near Nancy.

The raid was planned with immense attention to detail. The BASF factory was located at the extreme limit of the Voisin's range – its combat endurance being approximately five hours – and, under the supervision of Gabriel Voisin, the Groupe's aircraft were fitted with larger fuel tanks. Arrangements were made to obtain accurate meteorological reports prior to the launching of the mission, as a miscalculated headwind could spell disaster for the entire raiding force. The crew of each aircraft was provided with an enlarged photograph of the works at Ludwigshafen and Oppau, with the precise objectives clearly marked and numbered.

Commandant Göys ordered the attack on Ludwigshafen to go ahead in the small hours of May 26. The 18 aircraft made their rendezvous over Baccarat and then flew eastwards to the objective in rough formation based on escadrilles. With the smoke of Ludwigshafen's factories rising on the horizon, Göys' Voisin was forced down with engine failure. He was taken prisoner but later escaped and found his way back to France. The remaining 17 airplanes flew on, commencing their attack at 0600 hrs. In half an hour of bombing, the French machines dropped 87 bombs from a height of approximately 5000 ft. All 17 aircraft returned to Malzéville without any further trouble other than two pilots slightly wounded by anti-aircraft fire. This success prompted General Headquarters briefly to consider increasing the strategic bombing force from 21 escadrilles (126 machines) to 60 escadrilles, each comprising ten aircraft. Two months later, as the French offensive reached a peak of activity, a report was prepared proposing the creation of a bombing force of 750 aircraft to be thrown into an all-out campaign against the industrial center of Essen.

By July GB2, GB3 and GB4 were also concentrated at Malzéville. At the end of the month 45 aircraft of GB1 and GB2 took off to bomb industrial plants at Pechelbronn while GB3 made a diversionary raid on the military barracks at Saverne, an early example of one of the ploys which was to become standard British practice in World War II. Only 15 aircraft succeeded in finding the industrial target, and the attack was rendered ineffective by the failure of most of the bombs to explode.

In August, under the driving leadership of a new commander Commandant Roisin, the four Groupes embarked on a fresh offensive. Saarbrucken was attacked by GB1 and GB2 on August 9, 21 of the 28 aircraft involved arriving over the target. On August 14, GB1 was switched to the tactical bombing of military installations near St Mihiel, but this was the prelude to a big attack on August 25 in which 62 machines of GB1, GB2 and GB3 flew to raid the blast furnaces and steel works at Dillingen. Fifty machines reached the target, and only one failed to return. By now the French had formulated well-thought-out tactics, most of which were soon to be adopted by the RFC. At the start of a raid the Group Commander was the first to take off, leading the formation throughout the mission. His aircraft was distinguished by a tricolor rosette on the sides of the fuselage and front of the nacelle and metal pennants mounted on the rear center struts. As soon as all the aircraft had made their rendezvous over a given point well behind the lines and out of the immediate sight of the enemy, the Group Commander fired a series of flares and then led off towards the objective with his engine well throttled down, the rest of the force maintaining as close a formation as was practicable. Over the target the aircraft would come in at varying heights, making the task of the anti-aircraft gunners more difficult. The French preferred to make their bombing run down-wind, which minimized the effect of any errors made in calculating the direction of the wind. It also reduced the time during which a pilot making a straight and level run was exposed to anti-aircraft fire, but had the disadvantage that any slight error in releasing the bombs was greatly magnified by the increased speed of the aircraft. At the beginning of September GB3 was despatched to the Artois sector on tactical duties. GB1 and GB2 attacked Saarbrucken on the 6th, 25 out of 40 machines reaching the target. There was a considerable tactical success a week later, on the 13th, when 19 aircraft bombed the railway junction at Trier, halting all traffic for three days. However, the tide was going out for the first French bombing offensive. The General Headquarters had lost faith in the value of strategic bombing and reacted by breaking the Malzéville force up, converting many of its aircraft into gun-buses (avions-canons) armed with 37mm Hotchkiss guns for strafing trains and troop columns. Only two escadrilles were retained at Belfort to bomb industrial targets.

Tactical Bombing

By the end of March 1915 the RFC's strength in France had risen to seven squadrons and one wireless unit flight, a grand total of 85 aircraft in the line with 80 in reserve. The front-line figure had doubled to 161 by September, but as yet there was little attempt to assign aircraft to specific operations. Throughout the first year of the war each squadron had muddled through with a multiplicity of types pressed at various times into every aspect of aerial warfare. It was not until July 25, 1915 that No. 11 Squadron arrived in France equipped exclusively with the Vickers FB5 two-seat pusher assigned specifically to 'fighting duties'.

During the opening months of the War the RFC had focused its attention almost entirely on reconnaissance. But the arrival of trench warfare forced a reappraisal of the value of bombing operations. By its very nature, this new form of warfare resulted in the more or less static concentration of large numbers of troops and quantities of equipment in or immediately behind the front line. The increasingly familiar features of the trench system – troops moving up to the Front or back to the rear areas, ammunition dumps, billets, and headquarters buildings – presented a range of inviting targets to bomb-carrying aircraft. Of greater significance than these harrassing operations was the role earmarked for the RFC in the big offensives planned for the spring of 1915. When the first big push was made against the German line, the RFC would be called upon to prevent or delay the arrival of enemy reinforcements, with particular attention being paid to the rail systems which brought them up to the front line.

It is significant, however, that a directive on bombing issued by RFC HQ on February 15, 1915 gave no systematic technical guidance on the appropriate tactics to adopt when attacking any of the long and varied list of targets it contained. The directive confined itself to the pious hope that, "Accuracy to within 50 yards is essential. If it cannot be obtained from a height of 5000 to 6000 feet, the target must be attacked at low altitude – 500 feet".

In the absence of any but the crudest bombsights and bomb release gear, the 'option' of 500 feet became an operational necessity. Major Gordon Burge who in 1915 was flying BE2cs, put it quite simply: 'The technique was to glide down on your target, take a sight on the target – purely by eyesight – and release your bomb when you were low enough'.

The RFC's first attempt to co-ordinate tactical bombing operations with a major offensive came on March 10, 1915 when 2 and 3 Wings* supported the attack made by Haig's First Army at Neuve Chapelle. On the first day of the Neuve Chapelle offensive Captain L A Strange of No. 6 Squadron was flying a BE2c loaded with three 25-pound bombs. His target was the railway station at Courtrai. When he took off the weather was breaking up, with clouds at 2000 ft and poor visibility. Strange crossed the lines between the clouds, but a shell bursting nearby sent him up into them, navigating his way through cloud until he emerged north of Courtrai. Diving through a low bank of cloud east of the town, he came down to within 200 ft of the railway, following the track towards the station. A sentry on the platform opened fire on him as he approached, but Strange silenced him with a grenade thrown over the side of the BE2c. His aircraft flashed over the station roof and Strange dropped his bombs on a train standing on the other side.

The BE2c aeroplane was singularly ill-fitted for the offensive role into which it had been thrust. Altogether a total of 1117 BE2cs were delivered to the RFC but the loss rate suffered by the type was extremely severe. Its inherent stability, which was its principal asset as a reconnaissance aircraft, so reduced its maneuverability that in combat it came close to being a flying coffin. Moreover, the observer in the front cockpit was so surrounded by struts and wires that his machine-gun was virtually useless. To enable the BE2c to operate as a bomber it was flown as a single-seater. It normally carried its bombload in racks beneath the fuselage and inboard under the lower wings. An exception was the BE2c supplied to the RNAS and fitted with a RAF 1a engine; these machines were frequently fitted with a rack, capable of taking three bombs, below the engine's sump. A number of the RNAS machines also flew with the front cockpit faired over.

The RFC's first ventures into tactical bombing provide a catalogue of exceptional gallantry and heavy loss. On April 26, during fighting in the Ypres salient, Lieutenant W B Rhodes-Moorhouse of No. 2 Squadron, flying a BE2b loaded with a 100-pound bomb, attacked Courtrai railway station. Met with heavy rifle and machine gun fire, he went down to 300 ft before releasing his bomb. Mortally wounded, he flew 35 miles back to his aerodrome and on his return insisted on delivering his report before receiving any attention. He died on the following day

*The formation of Wings – each attached to an Army – had been approved in December 1914.

and a month later received the posthumous award of the Victoria Cross, the first VC given for work in the air.

On May 9 the fighting at Aubers Ridge had been opened by a number of bombing raids which preceded the usual artillery bombardment. The bombing, planned to interrupt rail communications and harrass rear areas and army HQs, achieved little success. None of the bombs dropped was observed to hit their targets. At this time both the RNAS and the French Groupes de Bombardement were achieving better results and in an attempt to solve this pressing technical problem a conference, attended by representatives from the French air service the RFC the RNAS, was held on August 7, 1915. One of the gloomier documents under review at the conference was an RFC memorandum prepared in July, which contained a detailed analysis of the results of bombing operations undertaken by the three services on the Western Front between April 1 and June 18. In 483 operations a total of 4062 bombs had been dropped with little apparent material result. Attempts to hinder enemy movements by bombing rail junctions and stations had been made on 141 occasions during which 991 bombs had been dropped; of these "it appears that only three attempts were at all successful ". This depressing summary overlooked the genuine achievements of the RNAS, although the figures indicating percentage successes demonstrate that of the attacks against Zeppelins in their sheds – principally naval targets – 25 per cent were successful.

The RFC's immediate reaction to these figures was to scale down tactical bombing operations. Army commanders were instructed to limit bombing attacks by aircraft under their command to a number of specified targets within the close reconnaissance area of the army. Sustained attacks on the enemy's railway system would be carried out under the authority of GHQ as part of the overall Allied plan. The RFC's most committed advocate of bombing, Colonel F H Sykes – Sir David Henderson's Chief of Staff – had been transferred to the Dardanelles in May 1915, having been rejected by Kitchener as Henderson's successor in France on the grounds of inexperience. On August 19, 1915 Henderson returned to the War Office as Director of Military Aviation and was succeeded as GOC in France by Major-General H M Trenchard.

Gruff to the point of inarticulacy and startlingly blunt about the sacrifices he expected his aircrew to make, 'Boom' Trenchard was nevertheless an inspiring leader and an implacable advocate of maintaining the offensive in the air. He was an indifferent pilot himself, having qualified in 1912 in spite of being blind in one eye. In later years, when he had been virtually canonized as "the Father of the RAF" he was always quick to point out that his predecessor as GOC in France, Henderson 'had twice the insight and understanding'. Nevertheless, it was Trenchard who was to exert a crucial influence on British air policy during World War I and in the post-war years virtually single-handedly securing the survival of the RAF as an independent service. As we shall see, however, his powerful advocacy of strategic bombing in the interwar years has tended to obscure the more conservative approach he adopted to this form of warfare from 1916 to 1918.

Bombsights

One of the most pressing problems which Trenchard faced on assuming command of the RFC was the lack of efficient bombsights. In the spring of 1915 there were only two makeshift sights available, the nail sight and the lever sight, both of which had been developed by the RNAS. The former was a practical application of a primitive sight developed by the RNAS in 1913 – a hand-held piece of board with a spirit level attached and two nails positioned to indicate the dropping angle. The bombs were released when the two pins came into line. This sight was only useful for dropping bombs from a fixed height and at a fixed speed, and the lever sight incorporated modifications which allowed for the dropping of bombs from varying heights and varying speeds. The two pins – the foresight and the backsight – pivoted on a lever, enabling the line of sight to be set at a dropping angle established by consulting tables for height and groundspeed.

It was not until mid-summer 1915 that the first standard bombsight went into service. It was developed by an RFC officer, Lieutenant R B Bourdillon, who in December 1914 had joined the newly established experimental flight at the Central Flying School. Serving as an intelligence officer with III Corps, Bourdillon had collaborated with Lieutenant Strange on a simple 'wires and nails' sight little different from that developed several years earlier by the American, Lieutenant Riley Scott.

Early versions of the CFS sight were received by the RFC in time to be used in the Battle of Loos, the third and last attempt by the British Commander-in-

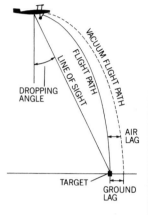

FLIGHT PATH
VACUUM FLIGHT PATH
LINE OF SIGHT
DROPPING ANGLE
AIR LAG
TARGET
GROUND LAG

CFS 4B BOMBSIGHT

The novel feature of this sight was a timing scale which enabled a pilot in the air, with the aid of a stopwatch, to measure his groundspeed by two sights taken on one object. To give the correct angle for bomb dropping, the moveable foresight was then set on a timing scale to correspond with the time interval, recorded in seconds on the stopwatch between the two sightings. Using the CFS sight, it was still necessary to bomb directly up or down wind. Calibration of the CFS sight was achieved in a series of experiments which used an electrically operated camera obscura to measure the difference between the trajectory of a bomb falling through the air and that of a bomb falling through a vacuum. the latter being ascertained by simple calculation. The photographs taken by the camera obscura established the height,

track and groundspeed of an overflying aircraft, whose release mechanism triggered a wireless signal the moment the bomb was dropped. The invariable point of impact of the 'vacuum' bomb could then be calculated and the distance measured between that and the impact of the real bomb as the aircraft passed over the camera. This gave the 'ground lag'. Further

calculations were made to determine the 'air lag' – the horizontal distance at any height between the flight path of the 'vacuum bomb' and that of the real bomb; and the 'time lag' – the difference between the time it took for the real bomb to fall from a known height and that of the 'vacuum bomb' falling through the same distance.

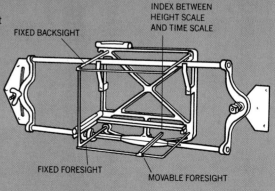

INDEX BETWEEN HEIGHT SCALE AND TIME SCALE

FIXED BACKSIGHT

FIXED FORESIGHT

MOVABLE FORESIGHT

A Voisin Type L pusher, trim in comparison with some of the later 'chicken coop' types. Its small 130-pound bombload was housed on the cockpit floor until it was time for the observer to toss them over the side.

Chief Sir John French to break the trench deadlock with a frontal assault. The artillery bombardment preceding the attack began on September 21, 1915 and two days later the RFC's 2 and 3 Wings and No. 12 (HQ) Squadron, which had arrived in France on September 6, began a series of strikes at rail communications in the battle zone. The target area – agreed at a conference attended by representatives of the British and French air services – was the important Lille-Douai-Valenciennes railway triangle.

On September 23, 3 Wing struck at the Douai-Valenciennes line while 2 Wing and No. 12 Squadron concentrated their efforts on the Lille-Valenciennes axis. The deepest penetrations extended as far as 36 miles behind the German lines. Bad weather halted operations on the 24th but bombing was resumed on the following day. In the five days between September 23–28, the RFC aircraft had dropped 82 100-pound bombs, 163 20-pound bombs and 26 small incendiary bombs – a total of nearly five and a half tons. Casualties during this period were two aircraft and two pilots, who returned wounded. In this and subsequent attacks ending on October 13 the railway lines were damaged in 16 places, five trains were partially wrecked, a signal box was destroyed and sheds at Valenciennes set ablaze. According to the German records the bombing at Valenciennes on September 26 blew up armored trains and halted traffic for several days. However, although these attacks undoubtedly hindered transportation of troops to the front line, it would seem that no German units were late in taking up their positions.

New Tactics

In the autumn of 1915 the RFC began a reappraisal of its bombing tactics. Although it still favored the employment of aircraft against moving trains in single or small numbers, it began to emphasize the concentration of all available aircraft to bomb a single objective together. In turn this raised the issue of formation flying, a tactic not formally adopted until January 1916 but one which was beginning to take shape at Wing level. One of the RFC's long-stated objections to formation flying was that a group of aircraft offered an exaggerated target to German anti-aircraft gunners. At this stage the adoption of formation flying was largely an informal

business, with each Wing evolving tactics which suited its own purposes and achieved a practicable degree of compactness. Urgency had been added to these deliberations by the appearance in the summer of 1915 of the Fokker M5K single-seater monoplane – the Eindecker – fitted with a machine-gun synchronized to fire directly through the propeller arc. It was the first true fighter, and a formidable opponent. The first Eindecker victory came on July 1 when Leutnant Kurt Wintgens of Feldflieger Abteilung 6b shot down a French Morane two-seater. In the hands of brilliant pilots like Otto Parschau, Max Immelmann and Oswald Boelcke it established such an ascendancy over Allied aircraft that the mauling the French and British air services received between August 1915 and January 1916 became known as the 'Fokker Scourge'. On January 14, 1916, RFC HQ ordered that reconnaissance aircraft were always to be escorted by at least three combat machines flying in close formation, and that a mission was to be abandoned if one of the escort became detached.

The RFC also experimented with a number of counter-measures to protect bombing aircraft. It was thought that if the target was no more than 30 miles from the lines, the bombers would be adequately protected by 'fighting aircraft' flying offensive patrols between the bombers and the enemy aerodromes. A misplaced faith in this tactic led to the conclusion that bombing aircraft could dispense with the observer and close escort, an illusion shattered in the skies over the Somme battlefield in July 1916. For more distant objectives, two out of every ten bombing planes would substitute an observer armed with an extra Lewis gun for its bombload.

The RFC was also turning its attention to operating at night, and at the beginning of February 1916 it obtained permission for the night bombing of points up to six miles over the lines, the number of aircraft initially being limited to two from an Army in any one night. The first RFC night raid was made by the light of the full moon on February 19 when Captains E D Horsfall and J E Tennant of No. 4 Squadron, both flying BE2cs without an observer, raided the aerodrome at Cambrai. Tennant, carrying seven 20-pound Hale bombs and four incendiaries, flew over the aerodrome's line of sheds at a height of 30 ft, splinters from his exploding bombs shredding his aircraft's wings. After his first run he banked to the left and opened up the throttle to make another pass over the sheds with his incendiaries. At first his engine failed to pick up, but after an anxious interlude at 10 ft he came in for another attack, placing three of his incendiaries into a shed. Horsfall's two 112-pound bombs stubbornly refused to leave their racks over the aerodrome, but he managed to drop them on the return journey.

This was to be the only RFC night raid for some time, but in March and April a considerable amount of night-flying practice was undertaken behind the British lines. On the Western Front, strategic bombing remained little more than a dream for the RNAS's Dunkirk contingent. But, through the night skies over England, the Zeppelins of the German Navy's Airship Division were turning H G Wells's pre-war fantasies of aerial warfare into a semblance of reality.

1.3 THE ZEPPELIN OFFENSIVE

IN *THE WORLD CRISIS* (1922), CHURCHILL wrote that from the opening days of the war there was a widespread fear in Britain that 'at any moment half a dozen Zeppelins might arrive to bomb London, or what was more serious, Chatham, Woolwich or Portsmouth'.

When they came, the Zeppelins' first blows were delivered against European rather than British targets. Instead, the Zeppelins themselves suffered a series of crippling reverses. Before August was out *LZ6*, *LZ7* and *LZ8* – flying low and slow over the Western Front – were brought down by gunfire. On August 28, *LZ5* suffered a similar fate on the Eastern Front.

Amid this succession of crushing failures, the newly commissioned *LZ9* achieved a minor success when bombing Liége, although half of its improvized bombs (converted artillery shells with a blanket wrapping to provide stability) failed to explode. By the end of the month the Zeppelins were more prudently flying at night and on August 26, in company with the former DELAG ship *Sachsen*, *LZ9* began a week-long bombardment of Antwerp, using for the first time newly developed shrapnel and incendiary bombs.

The initial deployment of the Army's Zeppelins bordered on the suicidal. The predictably disastrous results badly dented OHL's faith in the airship. Although a small number of Army ships were later used on bombing raids over Britain, it was the German Naval air service which exploited the Zeppelin to its fullest extent, not only in strategic raids over Britain but also in reconnaissance and fleet co-operation over the North Sea, its principal task throughout the war. In four years the Naval Airship Division made 971 scouting flights over the North Sea and 220 over the Baltic.

At the end of August 1914, Konteradmiral Paul Behncke, Deputy Chief of Naval Staff, wrote to his superior Admiral Hugo von Pohl urging him to launch airship raids on the London docks. But the build-up of the Airship Division remained relatively slow: by Christmas it had only six Zeppelins on its strength and the construction of new airship bases was still in progress. In London, however, the airship menace continued to hover menacingly over the War Council's deliberations, and on January 1 Winston Churchill warned the Council about a planned night attack by up to 20 airships, which he considered the Navy would be powerless to prevent. The First Sea Lord, Admiral Fisher, was so alarmed that he predicted a horrible massacre and suggested that the only counter would be to announce that, if bombs were to fall on Britain's capital, German prisoners of war would be shot in reprisal.

In Germany Admiral von Pohl had ignored his deputy's advice. He was attached to the Imperial Headquarters in Luxembourg and was well aware of the Kaiser's reluctance to approve a policy of bombing operations against England. Nevertheless, by the turn of the year he had yielded sufficiently to petition the Kaiser to launch a series of cross-Channel raids. The Kaiser agreed to sanction airship attacks on England but initially insisted on their limitation to docks, shipyards and other military facilities on the Lower Thames and the East coast. He expressly forbade the bombing of private property and historic buildings; nor was there to be any bombing of London itself. On January 10, 1915 the High Seas Fleet was informed of the Kaiser's decision.

In command of the Naval Airship Division was Korvettenkapitan Peter Strasser, one of the air service's outstanding leaders. Appointed at the end of 1913 when the Division was at a particularly low ebb, he was an officer of immense drive and ability, who from first to last led his men from the front. His first attempt to raid England had been made three days after receiving the Kaiser's authorization but had been frustrated by bad weather. He tried again on January 19: *L3* and *L4* took off from their base at Fuhlsbüttel, bound for the River Humber area; *L6*, with Strasser on board, flew from Nordholz, setting a course for the River Thames estuary. Engine failure forced *L6* back when it was still 90 miles from the English coast. *L3*, commanded by Kapitanleutnant Hans Fritz, was blown south of its intended landfall and at 2020 hrs arrived over Great Yarmouth. Fritz released a parachute flare and five minutes later began his attack from a height of 5000 ft, dropping six 110-pound HE bombs and seven 6.5-pound incendiaries. *L4* crossed the coast only a few miles away, but quickly became lost in the dark and squally conditions. Later its commander, Kapitanleutnant Magnus von Platen-Hallermund, claimed to have attacked military installations between the rivers Tyne and Humber, attracting heavy artillery fire from 'a big city'. In fact the bulk of his bombload had fallen on or around the small town of King's Lynn in Norfolk. At one point he had unwittingly passed directly over the royal palace of Sandringham.

Flying the Zeppelin

The arrival of the Zeppelins threw Britain's primitive air defenses into confusion, and only two Vickers FB4 Gunbus aircraft got airborne. Their attempts to shoot down the enemy ended in near-farce. Both force-landed and one was fired on by an RNAS armoured car patrol. Five civilians had been killed and 16 injured in the first Zeppelin raid; the damage caused was estimated at £7740. There was public outrage in Britain and public rejoicing in Germany.

The airships which flew on the raid of January 19 were 'm' class Zeppelins; 518 ft long, they were powered by 210 hp Maybach engines giving a top speed of 52 mph; with a bomb-load of between 1100 and 1430 pounds, they had a combat ceiling of about 5000 ft. Flying these colossal aerial machines was something akin to an art, combining the sciences of aerostatics, aerodynamics, structural and mechanical engineering and navigation. An even more important part of a commander's equipment was the instinctive ability to interpret the moods of the sky and to anticipate what might go wrong before it happened. Good airship commanders were born rather than made, and they have justly been compared with the great clipper ship captains in the heyday of sail. Like his maritime equivalent, the airship commander steered a craft which despite its massive size was constantly at the mercy of the unpredictable forces of Nature. Within a month both *L3* and *L4* became victims of bad weather, wrecked in forced landings on the Danish coast.

Crucial factors in airship performance were temperature and barometric pressure, both of which had a direct bearing on height and lift. The static-lift generated by the hydrogen-filled gas cells was higher in cool air and in periods of high pressure, owing to the greater weight of air displaced. Therefore the colder months of the year presented the best conditions for successful Zeppelin operations. Landing was a particularly tricky procedure, and in low cloud and fog could prove a nerve-racking ordeal. Each airship base was equipped with a kite balloon capable of carrying a man above the clouds to signal directions from the ground to the airship commander. In conditions of deep cloud, the airship commander could only feel his way from one landmark to another, groping his way down to base. If the base was completely invisible, he might stop his engines to listen for the throaty roar of the 300 men in the handling crew shouting in unison.

The men who flew in these colossal machines worked in a strange world of throbbing engines, faintly glowing dials and gauges, whispered orders, and the ceaseless squeaking of wires and struts under strain. Oberleutnant Ernst Lehmann commanded *LZ12*, one of the Army airships based in Belgium. On March 17, he set out on what proved to be an abortive mission against England: '*U*NDER *us, on the shimmering sea, cruised enemy patrol boats. I prudently ordered the lights out. In the control car the only light was on the dial of the machine telegraph.... On the narrow catwalk between the rigging and the tanks, we balanced ourselves as skillfully as if we were walking in the broad day light down a wide street. I was wearing fur-lined shoes; and this thick footwear was not solely a protection against the cold. The hobnailed army boot might have damaged the ship's metal frame [or struck fatal sparks], and shoes with rubber or straw soles were therefore regulation.*

In the pale glimmer coming through the hatchway, I saw the bombs hanging in the release mechanism like rows of pears. Besides explosive bombs weighing from 125 to 650 pounds, there were phosphorus bombs for igniting fires in the bombarded objectives. The safety catches were not yet off but my Bombing Officer was already lying on his stomach staring impatiently through the open trap door ... While von Gemmingen [Leutnant Max von Gemmingen, a nephew of Count Zeppelin] discussed with the Bombing Officer the co-operation between him and the control car, I continued the inspection and descended to the aft engine car, which swayed under the ship like a celestial satellite. The car was enclosed and so crowded by the two 210 hp Maybach motors that the two mechanics could scarcely turn around. The noise of the motors drowned out every word, and the Chief Machinist simply raised his hand which meant that everything was OK. The air in this nutshell was so saturated with gasoline fumes and exhaust gases I almost choked, until I opened the outlet and let the icy stream in. ...'

It was on this raid that Lehmann made the first operational experiments with an observation capsule lowered up to 2500ft from the Zeppelin and connected by telephone to the control gondola. This device enabled an observer with a good head for heights to guide the airship while it remained concealed above the clouds.

German naval communications had been compromised early in the war when the High Sea Fleet's secret code and signal books and cypher keys had fallen into the hands of British intelligence. By mid-April 1915 British intelligence had made another breakthrough. Among the signals transmitted by Zeppelins on leaving base – and intercepted by coastal wireless direction finding stations – was the cryptic phrase 'only HVB on board'. HVB was an abbreviation for Handelsschiffs-verkehrsbuch, the German Navy's code book for signalling merchant shipping, which it already knew was not secure and therefore was of no great significance. On missions over England airship crews were forbidden to carry the more highly classified naval codes and publications. Therefore if 'only HVB was on board', it was a clear indication that the Zeppelin was bound for England.

Prior warning of a Zeppelin raid was of little use if the haphazard collection of aircraft based in Britain for home defense continued to experience the utmost difficulty in intercepting the enemy raiders and were equipped with few convincing weapons to destroy them. Pilots had little or no experience of night flying and at this stage in the war their chances of making a safe landing on their own airfields were about as slim as their hopes of seeing a Zeppelin. War Office returns for June 1915 show that there were only 20 aircraft available for the defence of London, most of them Martinsyde S.1 scouts and BE2cs: The sluggish Martinsyde took over 21 minutes to reach a height of 6000 ft carrying a standard load of six tube-launched incendiary bombs, three powder bombs and carriers, 12 Hale grenades and 150 incendiary darts; the BE2c took at least an hour to reach 13 000 ft. One of the more optimistic weapons fitted to some aircraft was the 'Fiery Grapnel', a grappling iron on a cable which was meant to engage the outer envelope of a Zeppelin and detonate an explosive charge.

LZ38's Raids

The first successful raid on England by an Army airship was made on April 29/30 by *LZ38*, a four-engined Zeppelin of one million cubic feet capacity commanded by the energetic and efficient Hauptmann Erich Linnarz. Crossing the coast north of Felixstowe in the small hours of the morning, *LZ38* bombed Ipswich and Bury St Edmunds before flying back over the coast at Aldeburgh at 0200 hrs. On the night of May 9/10 *LZ38* returned to bomb Southend. London had been Linnarz's original target, but there was still some confusion about the restrictions the Kaiser had placed on bombing the capital. Initially the Army favoured a liberal interpretation of 'the London docks', assuming that this could be stretched to embrace the entire city area east of the center. In March, however, the Kaiser made it clear that this went beyond 'his wishes and desires'. Early in May the order was amended to permit attacks on all military targets east of the Tower of London, but the Kaiser's authorization was delayed until end-May.

On May 16/17, British aircraft engaged Zeppelins for the first time. The Admiralty had notified the RNAS in France of a raid by *LZ38*. Nine aircraft of No. 1 Squadron from Dunkirk and Furnes took off to intercept *LZ38* on its return journey. Instead, several of the pilots intercepted *LZ39*, which was returning from a raid on Calais. Squadron Commander Spenser D A Grey and Flight Sub-Lieutenant R A J Warneford, both flying Nieuports, attacked the Zeppelin at 0355 hrs, Grey with a Lewis gun and Warneford with a .45 in rifle firing 'flaming bullets' and handled by his observer. Ten minutes later Flight Lieutenant A W Bigsworth, flying an Avro 504B, climbed above the Zeppelin over Ostend and at about 10 000 ft dropped four 20-pound bombs on the colossal target below. Five gas cells were ruptured, the rear starboard propeller badly damaged and one member of the crew killed. *LZ39* limped home billowing smoke.

The Kaiser had vacillated for three weeks before giving his permission for the bombing of targets in east London. The first raid on the capital was made on the night of May 31/June 1 by *LZ38*, which scattered 30 small HE bombs and 90 incendiaries in

Above: *L13*, commissioned on July 25, 1915 and dismantled on December 11, 1917. It made a total of 159 flights, and participated in 17 raids and 45 scouting flights. Note the upper gun platform on the top of the hull above the control gondola.
Left: The Zeppelin's secondary upper gun position, aft of the rear rudder. Gunners were not allowed to fire their machine-guns when the ship was climbing and valving gas. Perhaps the Zeppelin's single most important defensive weapon was its ability to climb at a speed which easily outstripped that of obsolescent home defense types like the BE2c.

an arc from Stoke Newington to Leytonstone. Rioting broke out in London's East End as the population vented its fury on premises owned by people of German descent. A week later *LZ38's* short and vigorous operational career was brought to an end. On the night of 6/7 June it had set out in company with *L9*, *LZ37* and *LZ39* to bomb London. All three of the Army airships were forced to abandon their missions: *LZ38* developed engine trouble and returned to its base at Évère, near Brussels; navigational problems forced *LZ37* and *LZ39* to turn back. *L9*, commanded by Kapitan-leutnant H Mathy, switched its attack to Hull, dropping ten HE bombs and 50 incendiaries. Twenty-four civilians were killed and 40 injured.

In France, No. 1 Squadron RNAS was already involved in a raid on the Belgian airship sheds when it received news of the Zeppelin sorties. *LZ38* had just completed docking when the Henri Farmans of Flight Lieutenant J P Wilson and Flight Sub-Lieutenant Mills attacked the airfield scoring direct hits on the hangar and destroying the airship. Time was also running out for *LZ37*. Flight Sub-Lieutenant R A J Warneford, (the attacker of *LZ39*) was on his way from Dunkirk to raid the Zeppelin sheds at Berchem St Agathe with six 20-pound bombs hanging from his Morane Saulnier Type L monoplane. He spotted *LZ37* over Ostend and after a patient hour-long pursuit, during which he came under heavy defensive fire from the Zeppelin, he succeeded in pushing his Morane to 11 000 ft, about 4000 ft above *LZ37*. Over Ghent he put the Morane into a steep glide, leveling out 150 ft above *LZ37* and releasing his six bombs in quick succession. While the last bomb was still in the air *LZ37* exploded in a mass of flame, tossing the flimsy Morane around the sky in the blast.

Zeppelins in the Ascendant

It was not until September 8/9 that the Naval Airship Division mounted its first effective raid on London. At 2240 hrs *L13*, captained by Heinrich Mathy, dropped a sighting stick of bombs on Golders Green in north London and the bulk of its load (including a 660-pound bomb) in a line running from Euston to Liverpool Street. Twenty-six people were killed, 94 injured and the damage caused estimated at £554,287.

The last and most serious raid of 1915 came on October 13/14, when the Naval Zeppelins *L11*, *L13*, *L14*, *L15* and *L16* took off to attack London. Anti-aircraft fire forced *L11's* commander to jettison his bombs in open country around Coltishall; *L13* became lost and bombed Woolwich and Guildford; *L14* followed a meandering course which took it south of the River Thames estuary to Shorncliffe camp, where its bombs killed 15 soldiers, and then back to Tunbridge Wells and Croydon before it passed across southern London on its return journey. *L15*, powered by new 240 hp HSLu engines, was the only Zeppelin to penetrate to central London, dropping 30 bombs between the Strand and Limehouse. *L16's* commander mistook the River Lea for the Thames and bombed the small town of Hertford.

The inadequacy of the British home defenses had been exposed, and the balance sheet for 1915 made depressing reading. In 19 raids, 37 tons of bombs had been dropped, causing over £800 000 worth of damage – most of it by *L13* on September 8/9 – and killing 209 people. No airships had been downed and only two interceptions had been made during the course of the raids.

The crisis was exacerbated by the divided control the RFC and the RNAS continued to exercise over air defense* and their constant bickering over the most suitable tactics to counter the Zeppelins. At the heart of the dispute was a fundamental disagreement over the usefulness of the airplane as a weapon against the Zeppelin. The RNAS was quick to endorse the view, expressed in a report issued by the Board of Invention and Research in September 1915, that night flying against the airships was 'ineffective, costly and dangerous'. Instead the RNAS urged the adoption of the system employed in Paris, which concentrated on observers, searchlights and anti-aircraft batteries. By contrast the RFC took a more positive line, recommending that the effectiveness of night-flying aircraft should be increased. RFC planning for home defense was based on the assumption that airship counter-measures required the co-ordination of search-lights, anti-aircraft batteries, ground observer cordons, directional wireless equipment and night-flying aircraft. But in the autumn of 1915 aircraft were still flying standing patrols at heights of up to 10 000 ft, often with each airfield only sending up one machine at a time, keeping within visual distance of its base.

However, technical improvements were beginning to work their way into service. They included an illuminated instrument panel, landing lights, and a simple ground-to-air signalling system.

The overriding problem remained the destruction of the Zeppelin once it had been intercepted and engaged by a fighter. One answer was the Ranken dart, an iron-pointed tube weighing about one pound and containing black powder and an explosive charge. Vanes in its tail sprang open to engage the airship's envelope after it had been penetrated by the cast-iron point, simultaneously activating a detonator rod. Sparks from the black powder were intended to accelerate the ignition of the escaping hydrogen by the dart's HE charge. Up to 24 Ranken darts could be carried in a canister for launching from heights between 150 and 700 ft above the target. The Ranken went into service early in 1916 at a time when the only serious alternative anti-Zeppelin weapons were the 20-pound bomb of the type successfully used by Lieutenant Warneford, or the 10-pound and 14½-pound (Mk II) carcass bombs, incendiary devices dropped through a tube in the aircraft's fuselage.

The machine-gun was regarded as a secondary weapon whose bullets were unlikely to prove fatal but might cause sufficient gas loss to cripple an airship on its return journey. Moreover, it was

The destruction of *LZ37* on June 7, 1915 by Flight Sub-Lieutenant R A J Warneford of No. 1 Squadron, RNAS, flying a Morane Saulnier L3253. *LZ37* was an 'm' type Zeppelin with a capacity of 794 500 cu ft, 518 ft long and powered by three 630 hp Maybach engines. Both of its gondolas were of the open type, with the propellers mounted on outriggers. The keel was externally mounted and widened at the center to accommodate a small cabin housing wireless and bomb racks. Remarkably one of *LZ37's* crew survived the fiery descent. Helmsman Alfred Mühler was trapped in the forward gondola, which fell one and a half miles before crashing through the roof of a convent and depositing him on a bed. Warneford was awarded the Victoria Cross for his achievement, but only ten days after his duel with *LZ37* he was killed in a flying accident.

* A formal agreement was reached in February 1916: 'a) The Navy to undertake to deal with all hostile aircraft attempting to reach this country, whilst the Army undertake to deal with all such aircraft which reach these shores. b) All defense arrangements on land to be undertaken by the Army, which will also provide the aeroplanes required to work with the home defense troops and protect garrisons and vulnerable areas and the flying stations required to enable their aircraft to undertake these duties'. On February 16 Field Marshal Lord French, C-in-C Home Forces, assumed responsibility for the home defense of London.

wrongly believed that the exhaust gases from the Zeppelin's motors were turned into the airship's ring space, making it extremely difficult to ignite any hydrogen escaping from punctured gas cells. Work was under way on the development of specialized anti-airship incendiary ammunition, but it was not until February 1916 that the Admiralty placed an order for 500 000 rounds of the Brock explosive bullet; the RFC followed suit in April, with an order for the Buckingham incendiary bullet and in August placed an experimental order for 500 000 rounds of the Pomeroy incendiary bullet. Probably the first pilot to fire the Brock bullets on an anti-Zeppelin sortie was Captain A T Harris of No. 39 Squadron, flying a BE2c, who on April 25/26 fought a brief, inconclusive engagement with LZ97 before his Lewis gun jammed. Harris was to go on to greater things, as C-in-C, Bomber Command, 1942–1945.

On January 18, 1916 Vizeadmiral Reinhold Scheer, the new commander of the High Seas Fleet, approved plans drawn up by Strasser (now a Fregatten-kapitan) for a fresh airship offensive against England. Three attack zones were specified: England North, from the Tyne to Edinburgh; England Middle, from the Humber to the Tyne; and England South, in which London was the principal target.

On the night of January 31/February 1 the Naval Airship Division launched its biggest attack to date, sending L11, L13, L14, L15, L16, L17, L19, L20 and L21 to raid Liverpool. They failed to find the target, dropping 205 HE and 174 incendiaries on towns as widely scattered as Loughborough, Ilkeston, Scunthorpe, Derby and Burton-on-Trent. Problems with the new Mayback 240 hp HSLu engines probably accounted for the loss of L19, which came down in the North Sea. The trawler King Stephen was in the area but her skipper left the survivors to drown, on the grounds that had he rescued them they might have overpowered his small crew.

It had been a disappointing night for Strasser, but in Britain the results of the night's activity produced serious shockwaves. In the Midlands, factory workers were reluctant to continue night shifts for at least a week after the raid, and munitions production fell away alarmingly as a result. In the House of Commons there were demands for reprisals. Rear-Admiral C L Vaughan-Lee, Director of Air Services, submitted a memorandum in which he argued that the best response was 'an organized and systematic attack on the Germans at home'. He proposed that 'a definite policy of retaliation be laid down and carried into effect without delay', and that 'French bases for long-range operations be obtained with the co-operation of that government'. Echoing the RNAS' continuing scepticism about the value of the airplane in a *defensive* role against the Zeppelin, Vaughan-Lee concluded by suggesting that, if necessary, pilots for this long-range force should be taken from the RNAS' chain of coastal stations in Britain. Arguments about strategic bombing were fast acquiring a political dimension.

When Hull, which had no anti-aircraft defenses, was raided on March 5/6, indignation spilled over into civil disturbances. However, on the night of March 31 the anti-aircraft guns achieved their first success when at 2145 hrs the battery at Purfleet scored a direct hit on L15, one of ten Zeppelins flying that night. Within minutes two gas cells were empty

and others badly damaged. At the moment L15 was hit, it was being stalked by Lieutenant Alfred de Bathe Brandon, No. 19 Squadron RAS (Reserve Aeroplane Squadron), flying a BE2c. Ten minutes later he found the Zeppelin again, dived to within 400 ft and dropped three Ranken darts. These were followed by two more batches of darts and an incendiary bomb. All of them missed their target, probably because the crippled L15 was flying extremely slowly and in an abnormal attitude. It was becoming increasingly nose-heavy, and in a desperate attempt to stay airborne the crew jettisoned everything movable, including the machine-guns and all but enough fuel to reach Belgium. But just over two hours later, with its back broken, the Zeppelin came down in the sea 15 miles north of Margate.

There was a lull in airship activity in the early summer which coincided with a reorganization of the British air defenses. A 'barrage line' of airplanes and searchlights was set up on the east and south-east coasts to intercept raiders as they arrived over Britain and flew out. Guns and searchlights were integrated into the RFC's communications network. England and Scotland were divided into Warning Control Areas approximately 30 miles square; it took a Zeppelin about 30 minutes to cross one of these areas, and so it became possible to implement a series of alerts, a factor which greatly reduced the time previously lost in munitions factories and other industries vital to the war effort.

Meanwhile the German Naval Airship Division was readying itself for a renewed effort, buoyed up by the introduction of the new 'r' type Zeppelins, the first of which was L30.

L33–Super-Zeppelin

L33 was the fourth of the 'r' Types, the so-called 'super-Zeppelins', and was commissioned on September 2, 1916. Its massive streamlined (644 ft 9 in) hull contained 19 gas cells which were separated by the main transverse rings (the largest spanning 78 ft 6 in) firmly braced and installed at 10-m intervals. The light weight and gas tightness of the cells was achieved by lining them with goldbeater's skin, the delicate outer membrane covering the cecum (blind gut) of cattle. Each animal yielded only one skin measuring not more than 39 by 6 inches and each of L33's gas cells required 50 000 of them. The preparation of the goldbeater's skin was an extremely delicate and costly business, and the bill for L33 probably equaled the cost of the construction of 15 of the British Short bombers which were soon to come into service.

Ballast in L33 was provided by 30 800 pounds of water mixed with glycerin as an antifreeze and contained in 14 bags of rubberized cloth. The ballast was discharged from aluminum tubes which were streamlined where they projected through the Zeppelin's outer covering. To lighten the ship at short notice, in the event of an emergency on take-off or landing, additional water ballast was carried in smaller bags of 550-pounds capacity, known as 'breeches', stored fore and aft. Frequent soakings from these quickly discharged 'breeches' was an occupational hazard borne stoically by the Zeppelin handling crews.

L33's bomb capacity was almost five tons, but the

standard load was four 660-pound bombs, 40 128-pound and 60 25-pound incendiaries. The bombs were suspended vertically from racks amidships. The heaviest bombload carried over England was by *L31* on September 23/24, 1916 comprising four 660-pound bombs, 40 128-pound and 60 incendiaries, a total weight of 9250 pounds. The bombsight, made by Carl Zeiss of Jena, was located in the control gondola to the right of the rudder man. In combat, the executive officer was the bomb-aimer, first setting the ship's altitude (from the altimeter) on the sight and then measuring the speed over the ground by timing with a stopwatch the passage of an object between two cross-hairs supposedly measuring an interval of 300 m on the ground. Compensating curves allowed for the adjusting of the sight for the differing ballistic properties of the various bombs carried by the ship. The Zeiss sight was a precision instrument, which could also be used to take drift readings, but airship officers seem to have received little training in its proper use.

On the icy, windswept reaches of *L33*'s upper hull were two gun platforms. The main platform was located at the bow, some 60 ft above the control gondola, and housed three 8-mm Maxim-Nordenfelt machine-guns firing a mixture of armor-piercing and explosive shell. When not in use the guns were swathed in cloth jackets to prevent the cooling water freezing solid. Communications with the control gondola were maintained by a speaking tube. Perched dizzily aft of the rear rudder was a secondary upper gun position for a machine-gun with a wide arc of fire mounted on the central girder just beyond the edge of the platform. The four upper machine-guns were used with the utmost caution. In combat, if the ship's cells were punctured or if it was rising fast with hydrogen hissing out of the valves, machine-gun fire directed at attacking aircraft was highly inadvisable. Two more machine-guns were installed at the rear of the control gondola, firing out of side windows in a manner which anticipated the waist positions in the B-17 Flying Fortress of World War II. Two machine-guns were fitted in similar fashion in the rear engine gondola, and there were also machine-gun positions in the two wing gondolas slung amidships, although these were rarely used. All in all, the machine-guns provided a debatable degree of protection. In an emergency they were usually the first items to be thrown overboard.

The nerve center of the ship was the cramped control gondola, located below the centerline 72 ft from the tip of the Zeppelin's nose.

On the starboard side of the control gondola was the rudderman, one of whose duties was to watch the ship's small magnetic compass – the much more accurate gyro-compass was ruled out because of its weight. Navigation in a Zeppelin remained a relatively hit and miss affair to the end of the war and was one of the principal factors limiting its effectiveness as bomber. The magnetic compass frequently froze up at altitude, despite its 40 per cent alcohol content; after a long flight at over 13 000 ft *L45*'s compass was covered by ice one millimetre thick. Dead reckoning, in a ship flying above the clouds and at the mercy of strong high-altitude winds, could be little more than guesswork. Some commanders took star sightings at sunset from the upper gun position, using a standard maritime sextant, but this required a clear sky and a

well-defined sea or cloud horizon. From the spring of 1915 Zeppelin commanders relied heavily on radio bearings and even attempted to use them as a blind bombing aid when there was dense cloud cover. But their ignorance of such distorting phenomena as 'night effect' and 'aeroplane effect' could lead them miles astray. Even the ablest commanders could, on occasion, become hopelessly lost: on the night of August 2/3 1916 the best of them all, Kapitan-leutnant Heinrich Mathy, dropped his bombs into the sea off Dover while under the impression that he was attacking London. It was not until the winter of 1917–18 that the German radio direction-finding system was drastically overhauled. Two new sending stations were established at Tondern and Cleve, 250 miles to the southwest in the Rhineland. These transmitted directional signals at regular intervals, 15 minutes before and 15 minutes after the hour. Using these signals an airship commander could determine his position merely by using a stopwatch and grand circle charts. The system also eliminated the frequent overloading of the airships' special wavelengths with constant requests for bearings.

Immediately behind the control gondola was the forward engine car, with its Maybach six-cylinder HSLu motor driving a 17 ft-diameter propeller. The rear engine gondola housed three Maybachs, two of them installed side by side. The wing gondolas contained just enough space for a single Maybach and the mechanics. Each of the engine gondolas was surmounted by large air-cooled radiators, which produced considerable drag. At altitude icing-up was a serious problem, and it was not unusual for layers of ice weighing 5000 pounds or more to build up on the Zeppelin's outer cover.

Zeppelin crews learnt to live with the intense cold. The temperature in the control gondola rarely rose above freezing point, and layers of fur-lined clothing were often supplemented by wads of newspaper stuffed inside crewmen's coveralls. Food provided some comfort: '*W*E GOT SAUSAGES, GOOD butter, thermos flasks containing an extra brew of coffee, plenty of bread, chocolate and 50 grams of rum or brandy per man ... We had several peculiar and very practical kinds of tinned food, which might be described as chemical and gastronomical miracles. There were tins containing hashes and stew which were heated up by a certain chemical process as soon as you opened them. We were not allowed to cook anything on account of the danger from inflammable gas*'.

End of a Dream

Impressive though they were, the super-Zeppelins did not add greatly to the problems already faced by the British home defense as neither their speed (63 mph) nor their ceiling (11 500 to 13 000 ft) represented a significant advance on earlier types.

At the end of July and in early August 1916 a series of raids probed the region between the Thames and the Wash. Then, on the night of August 8/9, the focus shifted to the northeast before moving back to London on August 24/25, when Heinrich Mathy's *L31* became the first Zeppelin to bomb the capital since October 1915, killing nine people, injuring 40 and causing over £100 000 worth of damage. A week later, on September 2/3, the German Army and the Navy combined – for the first and last time – to mount the biggest airship raid on London.

Sixteen airships flew that night, but atrocious weather scattered them and only one, the Army Schutte Lanz ship *SL11* commanded by Hauptmann Schramm, penetrated to within seven miles of the center of London. At 0205 hrs it was intercepted over the suburbs of north London by Lieutenant William Leefe Robinson of No. 39 Squadron, flying a BE2c armed with a Lewis gun firing Brock and Pomeroy bullets. Robinson recalled: *I SACRIFICED HEIGHT (I was still at 12 900 ft) for speed and made nose down in the direction of the Zeppelin. I saw shells bursting and night tracer shells flying around it. When I drew closer I noticed that the anti-aircraft aim was too high or too low; also a good many some 800 ft behind. A few tracers went right over. I could hear the bursts when about 3000 ft from the Zeppelin. I flew along about 800 ft below it from bow to stern and distributed one drum along it (alternate New Brock and Pomeroy). It seemed to have no effect; I therefore moved to one side and gave it another drum distributed along its side – without apparent effect. I then got up behind it (by this time I was very close – 500 ft or less below) and concentrated one drum on one point (underneath rear). I was then at a height of 11 500 ft when attacking the Zeppelin. I had hardly finished the drum before I saw the point fired at glow. When the third drum was fired there were no searchlights on the Zeppelin and no anti-aircraft was firing. I quickly got out of the way of the falling, blazing Zeppelin and being very excited fired off a few red Very lights and dropped a parachute flare'.*

The Zeppelins' Response

Strasser's reply was a large-scale operation on September 23/24: *L13, L14, L16, L17, L21, L22, L23* and *L24* attacked the Midlands; the super-Zeppelins *L30, L31, L32* and *L33* steered courses for London. It was *L33*'s first raid. Commanded by Kapitan-leutnant der Reserve Alois Bocker, a veteran merchant marine officer, it had been only three weeks in service. Bocker steered his airship in from the east, making landfall at Foulness at 2240 hrs, flying up the Lower Thames and arriving over east London shortly after midnight. Meeting heavy anti-aircraft fire, he twice dropped magnesium parachute flares in an attempt to dazzle the gunners with the blazing light suspended in the sky beneath his ship. Dropping ballast, he pushed *L33* up to 13 000 ft before releasing two 660-pound bombs, eight 220-pound, 32 128-pound, and 20 incendiaries.

Suddenly *L33* was trapped in the probing beam of a searchlight and the control gondola illuminated so brightly that one could have read a newspaper in the glare. Leaning out of a ventilation hatch in the gangway amidships was Chief Machinist's Mate Adolf Schultz, who was counting the searchlight beams sweeping the sky. As he reached 30, he was thrown about by a tremendous detonation overhead. An anti-aircraft shell had burst inside one of the forward gas cells, expelling hydrogen in great gusts. Losing height and jettisoning all movable objects, including the machine-guns, Bocker turned the

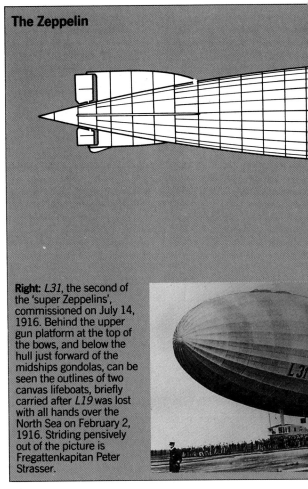
crippled Zeppelin for home, only to be intercepted over Chelmsford by Lieutenant A de Bathe Brandon of No. 39 Squadron flying a BE2c whose Lewis gun fired a combination of Brock, Pomeroy and Sparklet ammunition. As he closed on the Zeppelin, Brandon's automatic fuel pump failed, forcing him to pump fuel by hand. Coming up behind *L33*, he pulled his Lewis gun down to load it, whereupon it tumbled into his lap. Having overshot the Zeppelin, he reasserted control over his unruly weapon and attacked *L33*'s rear port side, emptying a drum of Brock ammunition and watching the bullets burst along the hull without any discernible effect. Inside *L33*'s hull, fuel from burst tanks was sluicing down the gangway, but still it failed to catch fire.

The gunners on the top platform watched helplessly as the little biplane flitted in and out of the searchlight beams, a minnow tormenting a stricken whale. On his second pass Brandon's machine-gun jammed, and it seems likely that he attempted to climb above *L33* to drop a batch of Ranken darts. At this point he lost contact, but by now the Zeppelin was doomed. As damage reports flooded into the control gondola, *L33* suddenly fell 3000 ft in four minutes, forcing Bocker to fly at such a steep nose-high angle that every crew member had to cling to the nearest fixed object to avoid sliding aft. Across the Essex fields below, *L33*'s progress could be traced by a trail of jettisoned clothing, ammunition boxes and

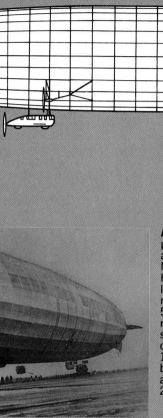

Above: *L32*, built principally of duralumin and powered by six 240 hp Maybach six-cylinder HSLu engines. Its overall length was 649 ft 5 in and maximum diameter 78 ft 5 in. *L32* had a cruising range of 2300 miles, top speed of 62.6 mph and operational ceiling of 17 000 ft. Average bombload was 4-5 tons and the crew numbered 22.

Left: The elevator man's post on the port side of the control car of *L59*, with control wheel, inclinometer, altimeter and, above, pulls for gas valves and water ballast controls.

Middle: The control gondola of *L54*, which along with *L60* was destroyed in its shed at Tondern on July 19, 1918 by a strike from the British carrier *Furious*.

tool cases. At 0030 hrs, with fuel left for only one hour's flight and the sailmaker still gallantly scrambling from girder to girder at the top of the hull in a vain attempt to staunch the flow of escaping gas, Bocker sent a last radio message *en clair*: 'Need help, mouth of Thames, *L33*'. Down to 500 ft, *L33* was caught in a sudden down-current and at 0120 hrs crashed into a field at Little Wigborough near the Blackwater estuary. It was dragged along the ground for another 100 yards before coming to rest, miraculously without bursting into flames.

The 22 crewmen leapt to safety, one of them landing heavily and breaking his ribs. In the control gondola Bocker made a pile of the crew's papers and the ship's classified documents and then ignited it with a signal flare. The papers and *L33*'s outer fabric covering went up in flames, but there had been so much gas lost that the ship's framework remained virtually intact, providing British intelligence with a priceless insight into Zeppelin construction.

The End of L.31 and L.32
L31 and *L32* had kept company until 2245 hrs when they crossed the English coast at Dungeness. While Kapitanleutnant Mathy pushed on towards London, *L32*'s commander, Oberleutnant Peterson, was forced by engine failure to circle for an hour over Dungeness Point. Getting under way again, *L32* crossed the River Thames about 12 miles east of

London, attracting fierce anti-aircraft fire. With searchlight beams striking its hull, the Zeppelin was intercepted by No. 39 Squadron's Lieutenant F Sowrey in a BE2c. After a 25-minute pursuit Sowrey closed to attack at a height of 13 000 ft, flying so close underneath *L32*'s hull that he could see the great wooden propellers churning the air. Throttling down, he emptied a drum into the Zeppelin's belly, the only effect being to make it 'wriggle' and alter course. Under heavy fire from the airship's gondola guns, Sowrey pressed home two more attacks spraying his fire the length of *L32*'s envelope. Having exhausted a third drum he saw flames leap from several points in the hull and seconds later *L32* was plunging earthward in a ball of fire. Near the wreckage, embedded up to the waist in the ground, was found the body of the ship's executive officer, Leutnant zur See Karl Brodrück, who had jumped rather than burn to death. The charred remains of the other 21 members of the crew were found trapped in the shattered gondolas and crushed under the Zeppelin's twisted girders. RFC personnel, sifting through the wreckage, also found the crew's breakfast - black bread, bacon and potatoes, which had been cooked in *L32*'s fiery descent.

The tide had turned and henceforth Strasser permitted only the newer airship types to attack London, while the Army never again raided the capital. Morale was at a low ebb in the Airship

Division, but another raid was ordered for October 1. While five naval airships went on a 'mystery tour' of the English Midlands, the resourceful Mathy in *L31* struck straight for London. As he entered the searchlight zone he steered to the northwest and, hoping to elude the anti-aircraft defenses, cut his engines and drifted for a while southeastward with the wind. At about 2340 hrs *L31* was coned by searchlights and shot down by Second Lieutenant Wulstan Tempest of No. 39 Squadron in a BE2c.

The last raid of 1916 brought further disasters for the German Airship Division. On November 27/28 nine naval airships attacked Tyneside and the Midlands. On this occasion the defenses outside London proved effective. Forty fighter sorties were flown: RNAS BE2cs from Burgh Castle and Bacton shot down *L21* off Yarmouth; *L34* was destroyed off the mouth of the Tees by Second Lieutenant I V Pyott of No. 36 Squadron flying a BE2c.

The Height-Climbers

As ever, Strasser reacted vigorously to these setbacks and attempted to wrest back the initiative with the introduction of the so-called 'height climbers'. Convinced that drastically improved performance was the best answer to the British defences, he placed his faith in a new breed of Zeppelin designed to operate well beyond the range of both fighters and anti-aircraft guns. Weight had to be sacrificed to gain height, and this was achieved by a series of economies so progressively severe that some of the later types could not be maneuvered at high speeds and low altitudes lest the aerodynamic forces in the dense air broke their backs. Bomb and fuel loads were reduced, and Strasser even toyed with the idea of discarding the upper gun platform, although he finally rejected this economy. A more streamlined control gondola was developed and the clumsy rear gondola housing three engines, each driving its own propeller, was aerodynamically cleaned up and redesigned to hold two engines geared to a single propeller. The modifications were achieved in stages, beginning in January and February 1917 when *L35*, *L36*, *L39*, *L40* and *L41* each had a rear engine removed, which raised their ceiling to 17 000 ft. The 't' class *L44* was built with an improved and streamlined rear gondola, and by the time the 'v' class *L64* was commissioned in March 1918 the economies had been taken to their limit. The space between *L64*'s mainframes had been increased from 34 ft to 50 ft; there were five fewer large braced rings and the number of gas bags was reduced to 14. Resonance phenomena, caused by the wide spacing of the rings, led to unexpected vibration problems. Power was provided by five over-dimensioned and super-compressed Maybach 'altitude motors', each delivering a continuous 245 hp at up to 5900 ft and 142 hp at 19 700 ft. With a bombload of 6500 pounds, *L64*'s operational ceiling was 21 000 ft.

Crew comfort (never the Zeppelin's strong point) was one luxury which the height climbers could not afford. To freezing temperatures was added the agony of altitude sickness which was only partially alleviated by the provision of bottles of compressed oxygen and later 'bombs' of liquid air stored in the gondolas. Without the liquid air, crewmen could develop a disabling fatigue reducing them to a state of apathy, and with the slightest physical exertion ran the risk of crippling headaches and nausea. At heights of 16 000 ft and over an excursion to the aluminum flush-toilet installed in the hull (a round-trip of about 100 yds) would leave a man so exhausted that he was quite useless for the rest of the raid.

At these altitudes machinery suffered as badly as men. Engine failure was likely to be followed immediately by the freezing of the radiators and the cooling systems. In *L44* different coefficients of expansion of duralumin and steel caused the engine telegraph wires and rudder and elevator control cables to slacken off markedly at extreme height, although they 'took up' again at lower altitudes. Similarly, the control gondola's celluloid windows, 'set up' taut at the factory, could split above 16 000 ft.

The Zeppelin offensive was fast approaching a point at which it could no longer effectively be sustained. In 1916 there had been 22 airship raids; during the whole of 1917 there were only seven. In the summer of 1917 the Army decided to abandon airship operations, and the Kaiser himself began to query their usefulness. Other more immediate pressures were bearing down on Strasser. At the same time as the Army withdrew from airship operations it had been decided to boost airplane construction to counter the (unrealized) aerial threat from the United States, which had entered the war on April 6. The so-called 'Amerika Progamm' could only be pursued at the expense of the Airship Division, and on July 27 General Erich Ludendorff, the First Quatermaster-General, proposed that the Navy's Zeppelin building program be halted immediately to conserve dwindling supplies of aluminum and rubber. After much bitter wrangling with the Naval Staff, Ludendorff conceded that airship raids could be continued on central and northern England, which was beyond the range of the two-engined Gotha GIV bombers now operating against the British mainland, but insisted that airship replacements should be held down to half a ship per month. He was supported by the Kaiser, who in an Imperial Order dated August 17 directed that Germany's rubber and aluminum should be conserved to build up the Army's airplane strength. Henceforward the Navy was to be limited to 25 airships whose primary role was to be reconnaissance.

Midsummer Madness

At this point Strasser's determination to regain the initiative betrayed him into launching a major raid at a time of year when his airships would only have a few hours of midsummer darkness while they were over England. On June 16/17 six airships were detailed for a raid on London. High winds prevented two of them from leaving their sheds and two more turned back with engine failure, leaving *L42* and *L48* to press home the attack. Designed to operate at a height of 20 000 ft, *L48* crossed the English coast near Orfordness at 18 000 ft. The time was 0145 hrs. An hour later, after making an ineffectual attack on Harwich, the Zeppelin radioed its base for a wireless bearing and was informed that tailwinds for the homeward flight could be expected at 11 000 ft. Kapitanleutnant Eichler brought *L48* down to 13 000 ft and steered northeast, a faulty course dictated by a frozen compass. Engine trouble

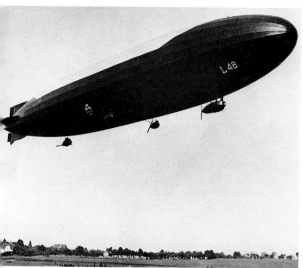

reduced speed to 33 mph and at 0330 hrs, over Aldeburgh, L48 was shot down by the combined efforts of three aircraft: an FE2b flown by Second Lieutenant F D Holder; a BE12 flown by Captain L P Watkins; and a DH2 flown by Captain R H M S (later Air Marshal Sir Robert) Saundby.

Rocked by an explosion following the hits of the British bullets, and in flames, L48 slid down stern-first at an angle of 60 degrees, crashing into a field near Theberton, Suffolk. Miraculously three crewmen survived, though one died from his injuries 18 months later.

Seventy miles away, in the control gondola of L42, Kapitanleutnant Martin Dietrich watched the end of L48: '*AT 3.35 TWO POINTS ABAFT THE PORT beam, a red ball of fire suddenly appeared, which quickly grew bigger and in falling showed the shape of a Zeppelin airship. The burning ship was at the same altitude as L42, therefore between 4000 and 5000 m. Some 500 m higher a plane was clearly visible, which twice fired a bright light*'.

While they flew at 18 000-20 000 ft, the height-climbers remained immune from fighter attack. But at these extreme altitudes they were almost pathetically vulnerable to adverse weather conditions, as was demonstrated in the so-called 'Silent Raid' of October 19/20, 1917. Eleven airships were despatched to raid industrial targets in the north of England, rising to altitudes of 16 000-20 000 ft as they approached the English coast. Here their difficulties began, as the light winds which had been forecast were replaced by gales blowing from the northeast and heralding the onset of a deep depression. Freezing temperatures, engine failure, height sickness and navigational confusion - and above all the failure quickly to appreciate the sudden onset of extremely hazardous conditions - combined to turn the operation into a fiasco. L41 succeeded in bombing the Austin vehicle factory at Longbridge, on the outskirts of Birmingham, while its commander Hauptmann K Manger was under the impression that he was attacking Manchester further to the north. L45 was blown south across the Midlands, dropping bombs on Northampton, in the belief that it was Oxford, and then careering onwards until, in the

words of the rudderman Heinrich Bahn: '*AT about 11.30 we began to see lights below and as the lights continued so it suddenly dawned upon us that it could only be the city of London that we were crossing in the air. Even Kölle (the commander) looked amazed ...*'

Kölle released the remainder of his bombs and turned east. Over the Medway L45 was intercepted by a BE2c of No. 39 Squadron flown by Second Lieutenant T B Pritchard, who opened fire from about 2000 ft below the Zeppelin. L45 immediately altered course to the south, gained height and outran the BE2c but, according to Bahn, '*IT WAS THEN that our misfortunes began. Hahndorff reported to Kölle that the engine on the port wing car was scarcely working - he thought owing to the sooting of the plugs. The plugs were cleaned by the engineers but, alas, their hands were so cold and they themselves so clumsy with lassitude and fatigue owing to the height that, by the time the plugs were cleaned and replaced, the engine ceased to function*'.

L45 was driven over France, a second engine failing at dawn and a third shortly after it passed over Lyons. With its fuel almost exhausted, the Zeppelin finally came to rest on an island in the River Beuche.

At 0400 hrs L55 came under fire through a gap in the clouds. Its commander, Kapitanleutnant Flemming, believed that he was over Dover; in fact his Zeppelin was racing through the sky above the Western front between St Quentin and Rheims. Nearly four hours later L55 reached the greatest height attained by an airship - 24 000 ft - before force-landing in a forest clearing in Thuringia, 200 miles south of its base.

L44, crippled by engine failure, drifted over the French trenches, where it was shot down by 75 mm artillery fire. L49 and L50 both witnessed its destruction, but this left their commanders none the wiser as to where they were. Shortly afterwards L49 was forced down near Bourbonne-les-Bains by French fighter aircraft of Escadrille N. 152 ('Les Crocodiles') and the exhausted crew taken prisoner by an aged huntsman. The Zeppelin was captured intact and its design copied and distributed to the Allied powers; the first US rigid airship, Shenandoah, owed much to the design of L49.

L50 also came under attack from 'Les Crocodiles', and its commander, realising that with one engine out of action he had no hope of making sufficient headway against the wind, deliberately crashed the Zeppelin. Before all of its crew could jump clear the wind caught L50 and whirled it away again, with four men still trapped on board. It was blown across France and, poignantly, was spotted flying at a great height by the crew of L45 as they were being taken prisoner. It was last seen over Fréjus, heading out into the Mediterranean Sea with a number of French seaplanes in vain pursuit.

Four Zeppelins were lost in the 'Silent Raid', so-called because of the unusual atmospheric conditions over England which muffled the sound of the airship's motors. Five more Zeppelins, L46, L47, L51, L58 and SL20, were lost at the end of the year, on December 27, when fire swept through the sheds at

L48, the first of the 'u' type Zeppelins to carry a streamlined control gondola. Note the under-side of the hull and gondolas, doped black to counter British search-lights. L48 was shot down over England on June 16/17, 1917. There were three survivors, one of them the ship's executive officer Otto Mieth, who was in the control gondola when disaster struck: '*I had just returned to my station after despatching a radiogram reporting the success of the raid ... when a bright light flooded our gondola, as if another searchlight had picked us up. Assuming that we were over the sea, I imagined for a moment that it must come from an enemy war vessel, but when I glanced up from my position, six or eight feet below the body of the ship, I saw that she was on fire. Almost instantly our 600 ft of hydrogen was ablaze. The quickest death would be the best; to be burned alive would be horrible. So I sprang to one of the side windows of the gondola to jump out. Just at that moment a frightful shudder shot through the burning skeleton and the ship gave a convulsion like the bound of a horse when shot. The gondola struts broke with a snap, and the skeleton collapsed with a series of crashes like the smashing of a huge window. The gondola was now grinding against the skeleton, which had assumed a vertical position and was falling like a projectile ... I wrapped my arms about my head to protect it from the scorching flames ... That was the last thing I remember ... There was a tremendous concussion when we hit the earth. It must have shocked me back to consciousness for a moment, for I remember a thrill of horror as I opened my eyes and saw myself surrounded by a sea of flames.*'

Shortly afterwards Mieth was dragged from the wreckage, his legs broken, by civilians and police who had arrived on the scene.

L53 being walked into the building shed at Friedrichshafen in 1917, with the naval ensign hanging from its tail post. The 'v' class *L53* made its maiden flight on August 18, 1917. It was the last Zeppelin to be destroyed by British forces when on August 11, 1918 it was shot down by Lieutenant S D Culley. Perhaps even more spectacular than the giant airships were some of the sheds which housed them. The famous revolving 'Nobel' shed at Nordholz weighed 4000 tons and was 653 ft long. Its electrically driven turning mechanism could be stopped within a millimeter of the required position.

Ahlhorn in circumstances which have never been satisfactorily explained. On July 19, 1918 *L54* and *L60* were destroyed in their shed at Tondern by seven Sopwith Camels launched from the converted cruiser HMS *Furious* in the first successful operation flown by shipborne aircraft against a land target.

Assailed by this succession of disasters, Strasser retained an unquenchable optimism which was boosted by the arrival, at the beginning of July, of *L70*, the first of a new class and the last word in height-climbers. Just under 694 ft long, with a gas capacity of 2 195 800 ft and powered by seven Maybach MBIVa 'altitude motors', this sleek black-skinned monster easily attained 19 700 ft statically and 23 000 ft dynamically on its trials. The fastest airship of the day, with a top speed of 81 mph, *L70* could carry a bombload of 8000 pounds.

On August 5, 1918, with Strasser on board and in company with *L53*, *L56*, *L63* and *L65*, it flew from Nordholz on the last big raid of the war. Once again Strasser had made the reckless decision to launch a raid in the most unfavorable conditions; indeed, never had a Zeppelin attack been attempted when the barometric pressure was so low. The predicted westerly winds fell away and at 1830 hrs *L70*, *L65* and *L63* found themselves flying some 60 miles off the English coast in broad daylight. At 2100 hrs Strasser broke radio silence to give his final attack directions to the Zeppelin commanders. Sadly, even these were in error, as they were based on misleading radio bearings which placed Strasser at least 50 miles west of his actual position. At 2200 hrs *L70*, *L65* and *L63* were flying in a broad V-formation about 18 miles off the coast, with Strasser's flagship occupying the southernmost position. Minutes later *L70* was engaged by a DH4 of No. 4 Group, RAF, flown by Major Egbert Cadbury with Captain Robert Leckie as observer. Even at *L70*'s altitude of

18 000 ft the fast rugged DH4 – the outstanding day bomber of the war – was more than a match for the Zeppelin. Cadbury came in head-on and slightly to port in order to 'avoid any hanging obstructions'. In the rear cockpit Leckie swung his single Lewis gun to bear. It was not fitted with sights and the first rounds missed the enormous target, flaming away for several hundred feet beyond *L70*'s hull. Leckie made a small correction and *L70*'s fate was sealed. The Pomeroy bullets blew a gaping hole in the Zeppelin's outer fabric, starting a fire which rapidly spread from stem to stern. For a moment *L70*'s bow reared up, as if in a last struggle to escape, and then it plunged seawards, a blazing mass which broke in two as it disappeared into a thick layer of cloud at 11 000 ft.

After making an abortive attack on *L65*, which had swung north after watching the destruction of *L70*, Cadbury turned for home, landing at the aerodrome at Sedgeford. The raid ended with the remaining Zeppelins, now in the grip of terminal navigational confusion, dropping their bombs into the sea at distances of up to 70 miles from the coast.

It was the end of the airship dream and the final shattering blow to the morale of the Airship Division. Five days later *L53* was shot down at a height of 18 500 ft in the Heligoland Bight by a Sopwith Camel piloted by Lieutenant S D Culley and launched from a large floating platform towed by the destroyer HMS *Redoubt*. There were no survivors.

Conclusion

During the course of World War I Germany built 88 airships, 73 of them for the Naval Airship Division. Over 60 were lost. Accidents and forced landings caused by bad weather accounted for 34, and the remainder were shot down by Allied aircraft and groundfire. In 51 raids on Britain the Zeppelins delivered 5806 bombs (196½ tons), killing 557 people, injuring 1358 and causing some £1.5 million worth of damage. In the final analysis, the damage inflicted by the Zeppelins was insignificant, but as Strasser pointed out at the end of 1917, 'It is not upon the direct material damage that the value of the airship depends but rather on the general result of the German onslaught upon England's insularity, otherwise undisturbed by war'. Circumstances had forced even the indomitable Strasser to lower his sights, but to a great extent he had succeeded in the later aim of tying down in England large numbers of men and substantial amounts of equipment which might otherwise have found employment on the Western Front. The British Official History recorded of the airships: '*THE THREAT OF THEIR RAID-ing potentialities compelled us to set up at home a formidable organization which diverted men, guns and aeroplanes from more important theatres of war. By the end of 1916 there were specially retained in Great Britain for home anti-aircraft defense, 17 341 officers and men. There were 12 RFC squadrons, comprising approximately 200 officers, 2000 men and 110 aeroplanes. The anti-aircraft guns and searchlights were served by 12 000 officers and men who would have found a ready place, with continuous work, in France or in other war theatres*'.

This was Strasser's true monument.

1.4 THE SOMME AND THE BATTLE FOR AIR SUPREMACY

A T THE BATTLE OF LOOS (1915) THE BEF's ammunition requirement was 35 000 rounds for heavy artillery and about 500 000 for the field batteries. In June 1916, as General Rawlinson's Fourth Army prepared for the big push on the Somme, over three million rounds of ammunition were accumulated behind the lines. The artillery concentration of 1537 guns (467 of them heavy), one gun to every 20 yards of front, was a record at the time but one which was to be far surpassed later in the war. Machines had taken over from men on a scale which outstripped the generals' ability to control them.

As the BEF expanded to meet the colossal new demands of war, so the RFC also increased in size. In January 1916 it was reorganized into brigades, one to each army, a process completed on April 1, 1916 when IV Brigade was formed to support Fourth Army. Each brigade comprised a headquarters, a balloon wing, an aircraft park, an army wing of two to four squadrons and a corps wing of three to five squadrons (one squadron for each corps). At the RFC's Headquarters there was an additional wing to provide reconnaissance for GHQ and, later, to undertake additional fighting and bombing duties.

The French and German air services were also in the process of rapid tactical and organizational change. Out of the battle for air superiority fought by the French escadrilles de chasse and the German Kampfeinsitzerkommandos over the shell-churned landscape of Verdun evolved the prototypes of specialist fighter aircraft units. On the urging of Oswald Boelcke, one of the outstanding aces of the early part of the war, the Germans then embarked on the creation of 37 special fighter squadrons (Jagdstaffeln or Jastas), each with 14 aircraft. On August 27 Boelcke, recently recalled from the Eastern front, established the headquarters of Jasta 2 at Bertincourt, south of Bapaume on the front of the German Second Army.

The Bombing Plan

On June 23 the final German thrust at Verdun spent itself at Belleville Height. The next day the rumble of guns was heard to the north as the week-long British bombardment on the Somme began. For the long-prepared offensive the RFC had concentrated 167 aircraft in the battle area, facing a German strength of 129 machines. An important feature of the RFC's plans for the opening phase of the battle was a bombing offensive designed to strike at German communications and headquarters. The more distant targets were assigned to the RE7s of 9 (Headquarters) Wing's 21 Squadron. The RE7 was an ungainly two-seater biplane, with a maximum speed of 85 mph, specifically designed to accommodate the Royal Aircraft Factory's 336-pound bomb and its dropping mechanism (alternatively it could carry two 112 pound bombs supplemented by a number of 20-pounders). In spite of the growing realization of the importance of defensive armament, the RE7's observer and Lewis gun were located in the front cockpit, with its hopelessly restricted field of fire; a small number of RE7s were later modified to carry the observer in a third cockpit to the rear of the pilot and fitted with a Nieuport ring-mount for a single Lewis gun.

The tactical bombing of the German rail system was entrusted to the BE2cs from Nos. 2 and 10 Squadrons of I Brigade, 7 and 16 Squadrons of II Brigade and 12 and 13 Squadrons of III Brigade. Each of the BE2cs was to fly from the airfields in Fourth Army's rear area and then return to its base at the end of the day's operations.

On July 1, the first day of the Somme offensive, railway bombing was undertaken by 12 BE2cs of II Brigade and 16 from I and III Brigades. The aircraft flew without an observer and unescorted, carrying two 112-pound bombs. In the morning the detachments from I and II Brigades arrived at Fienvillers and Vert Galand respectively, and soon after midday began flying out at intervals. By the evening of July 3 eight of the BE2cs were missing, one pilot had returned badly wounded, and nearly all the remaining aircraft had been damaged to a greater or lesser extent. The offensive patrols flown by Nos 27 and 60 Squadrons were wholly inadequate to protect the BE2cs and Trenchard stopped further bombing attacks on trains by the BE2cs and returned to bombing in heavily escorted formations.

Although they found themselves initially at a numerical disadvantage, the Germans were able to mount a vigorous response to the RFC's bombing sorties, particularly those in which formation had been lost. Lieutenant J A Brophy, flying an RE7 with No. 21 Squadron described one such raid, on July 11, in his diary. After an initial general observation on the 'poor formation, leaving us in danger of being separated and "done in" by Huns', he continues:

' T HE COLONEL [LIEUTENANT-COLONEL H C Dowding*] decided he'd lead us to show us how. He was to lead and Captain Carr and I were next and four others in pairs behind, and nine scouts. At 6000 ft we met thick clouds and when I came through I couldn't see anyone anywhere, so I just flew around and finally sighted three machines. I went over and found Carr and the Colonel and two scouts, so I got into place and the Colonel went over the lines and kept circling to get higher, for half an hour, right over the lines. I thought this was a very foolish stunt, as I knew the Huns could see us and would be waiting for us. I was very surprised that they didn't shell us, but there was a battle on, and they were probably too busy.... When we did cross over with only two scouts, we hadn't been over for more than a couple of minutes before I saw three Fokkers coming towards us, and a couple of LVGs climbing up to us. Another Fokker was up above me, and behind, between our two scouts. I knew he was going to dive at one of us, but expected the scout to see him and attack him, so I

---

* The CO 9 Wing; later C-in-C Fighter Command during the Battle of Britain, 1940

Captain H Wilkins of No. 27 Squadron, RFC, (standing with bandaged head and back to the camera) gazes on the wreckage of his Martinsyde G. 102, A3986, in which he was forced down on July 28 by a two-seater of Fliegerabteilung 45. Serving with No. 27 Squadron at the same time was Lieutenant L S Campbell:

'The Martinsyde was a delightful machine for leisurely pleasure flying but totally unsuited for daylight bombing or indeed for any kind of war mission. In the ordinary way it was very slow but when loaded with bombs it became heavy, sluggish and cumbersome and took ages to answer the controls ... When a formation of Martinsydes was attacked there was only one thing it could do and that was to put its nose down into a steep dive and with added speed to zig-zag its way back home ... though far from safety-proof it did make it more difficult for the enemy scouts to register a hit'.

didn't bother about him, but began to get the stopwatch-time of my bombsight to set it for dropping. While I was doing this I suddenly heard the pop-pop-pops of machine-guns, and knew that the Huns had arrived. I looked and saw them diving in amongst us and firing. There were seven LVGs and three Fokkers as far as I could make out, but they were so fast that I could hardly watch them. Our scouts went for them, and I saw the Colonel turn about. My gun being behind me I couldn't get in a shot, and turned around after Carr and the Colonel.... The Colonel was hit and so the show was over. He had about a dozen bullets in his machine and was hit in the hand. His gun was shot through and his observer hit in the face. He probably won't try to lead us out again'.

From mid-July to early August Trenchard mounted a series of attacks on the Douai-Oppy-Corons 'railway triangle'. On July 18, 20 and 28 Corons was subjected to night raids by the BE2cs of No. 13 Squadron. The main bombing south of the Ancre fell to the RE7s of No. 21 Squadron, the BE12s of No. 19 Squadron and the Martinsyde G102s of No. 27 Squadron, which had been only the second unit flying single-seaters to go to France specifically for air fighting duties. In its G100 form the Martinsyde had been developed as a long-range, single-seater escort fighter, but it was too large and too hard to handle in combat with agile German scouts, and the broad-chord wings restricted the pilot's field of vision. Reassigned to ground-attack and bombing duties the G102, nick-named 'The Elephant', was powered by a Beardmore 160 hp six-cylinder liquid-cooled in-line engine, giving it a maximum speed of 95 mph at 6500 ft and a combat endurance of about five hours with an offensive load of two 112-pound bombs or one 230-pounder. Standard armament was two Lewis guns.

During the Somme offensive No. 27 Squadron was involved in a curious incident, related by Oswald Boelcke in his memoirs. The great ace, flying his Fokker DIII and leading a formation of five Albatros DIs and Halberstadt DIIs of Jasta 2, attacked a formation of six Martinsydes near Bapaume. After a brief dogfight Boelcke's first victim 'fell like a sack'. Then he fastened on behind another Martinsyde, pouring fire in at close range. To his amazement the bomber continued to fly in tight circles. 'I said to

myself', wrote Boelcke, 'the fellow is long since dead and the machine is flying so because its steering apparatus is fixed in the correct position. I therefore flew quite close and saw the occupant leaning over to the right, dead in his cockpit. So that I should know which of the machines I had shot down (surely it must go down) I noted the number – 7495 – left him and took on the next'. The stricken Martinsyde was flown by the dead hand of Second Lieutenant H A Taylor.

Boelcke had blooded Jasta 2 over the Somme. On September 17 he selected four pilots, including Leutnant Manfred von Richthofen, to accompany him on the Jasta's first offensive patrol. Flying Albatros DIIs, they intercepted a formation of eight BE2cs of 12 Squadron escorted by six FE2bs of No. 11 Squadron, just after the BE2cs had bombed Marcoing. In the subsequent dogfight von Richthofen, flying Albatros DII No. 491/16, scored the first of his 80 victories. Four of the FE2bs were shot down and two BE2cs before the remainder were extricated by a fighting patrol of No. 60 Squadron.

From mid-July German airfields were added to the RFC's list of targets. The big airfield at Douai was attacked four times between July 19 and September 7, and other targets included the fields at Quéant, Bertincourt, Beaucamp and Valenciennes. The last was bombed on September 7 by aircraft of No. 12 Squadron led by Captain E J Tyson, who navigated by compass through and over dense cloud for over 70 minutes before bringing his formation down directly over the objective. The planning and co-ordination of bombing operations, and the tactics employed, were now becoming more sophisticated. On September 25 a carefully planned attack was launched on railway communications in the Douai area. First, diversion-ary raids were launched on enemy airfields at Provin, Tourmignies and Phalempin. Between 1320 and 1400 hrs each field was bombed by two FE2bs of 25 Squadron escorted by an FE8 of 40 Squadron. The FE2bs dropped phosphorus bombs, which kept the landing grounds shrouded in smoke, mixed with the odd 20-pound bomb to remind the temporarily blinded enemy of the continued RFC presence overhead. At the same time a similar formation of three aircraft made the first attack on trains running along the line near Libercourt. Captain R Chadwick, flying an FE2b, hit a troop train on the main line with a 20-pound bomb and strafed the soldiers who emerged from the wrecked train. The main line was now blocked, and as a second train came to a halt it was attacked by the FE2b flown by Second Lieutenant Woollven. The main raiding force – seven BE2cs of No. 16 Squadron and 6 FE2bs of No. 23 Squadron escorted by FE8s of 40 Squadron – was now approaching Libercourt station, on which its bombs – 14 112-pound and 34 20-pound – began to fall at 1350 hrs. Only one German pilot appeared over the target and he quickly made off when he was attacked.

In spite of these successes the RFC's hard-won, and temporary, air superiority over the Somme had been bought at a very high price. By November 17, as the battle stuttered to a halt, overall RFC statistics showed a total of 35 Squadrons, but also listed 409 pilots or observers killed, wounded or missing, with a further 268 pilots struck off the strength from other causes. Moreover, in the previous month the German air service had undergone a wholesale reorganization in which Generalleutnant Ernst Wilhelm von Hoeppner had emerged as Kommandierender General der Luftstreitkrafte (Kogenluft), in overall command of German aviation with the sole exception of the Bavarian units. The war in the air was gathering pace.

The RNAS and Air Policy

January 1916 – March 1917

In the winter of 1915–16 the Zeppelin campaign had prompted demands for reprisal raids to be made on targets in Germany. The initiative still lay with the RNAS. The impulse for the RNAS's enthusiasm for strategic bombing lay in the experience it had gained during the first 12 months of the war. Both at Dunkirk and later in the Dardanelles bombing had become one of the principal tasks undertaken by RNAS units. In the background, but a pointer to the future, was the development of the Handley Page 0/100, the 'bloody paralyzer' specified by Murray Sueter, which had flown for the first time in December 1915. In addition, the RNAS had, quite simply, more men and equipment than it could employ on purely naval duties.

By the end of 1915 the RNAS was forming the nucleus of a bombing squadron, based at Detling in Kent, for operations against the German industrial towns of Essen and Düsseldorf. In February 1916 it began to take delivery of the Sopwith 1½ Strutter, an aircraft which derived its distinctive name from its use of pairs of long and short center-section struts. The 1½ Strutter was a large biplane with a wingspan of 33 ft 6 in and length of 25 ft 3 in. Developed in its Admiralty Type 9700 form, it was a two-seater escort fighter initially powered by a 110 hp Clerget 9Z rotary engine, giving it a maximum speed of 106 mph at sea level and 87 mph at its service ceiling of 15 000 ft. Novel structural features included air brakes on the trailing edge of the lower wing's center-section and a tailplane whose incidence could be adjusted in flight. In its two-seater form the 1½ Strutter could carry a bombload of up to 160 pounds on racks under the fuselage or lower mainplane. Defensive armament reflected the new demands of aerial fighting: a Lewis gun mounted on a Scarff pillar (later Nieuport or Scarff No. 2 rings) in the observer's cockpit and a Vickers machine-gun firing through the propeller arc using the Scarff-Dibovski synchronizing gear. The bombing version of the 1½ Strutter, Admiralty Type 9400, was flown as a single-seater with its maximum bombload of 260 pounds housed in the space formerly occupied by the observer and released through spring-loaded trap doors in the fuselage underside. Some of the bombers had a single Lewis gun mounted in the upper center-section in addition to the synchronized Vickers. The pilot's field of vision was restricted and on some aircraft transparent panels were fitted in the mainplanes near the center-section.

3 Wing Operations

Detling was far from being the ideal base from which to mount bombing operations against Germany, as the direct route to the nearest targets lay over neutral Holland. An alternative was soon provided by the French air service, with whom the Admiralty had forged close links in the winter of 1915. On May 1, 1916 Captain W L Elder travelled to Paris to discuss plans for a joint strategic bombing campaign to be flown from bases in France. Significantly, neither the British War Office nor the British War Cabinet was informed about these moves! Nevertheless, on 5 May the personnel and aircraft of the new bombing force moved from Detling to Manston, becoming 3 (Naval) Wing. Two weeks later an advance party travelled to Luxeuil-les-Bains, 25 miles northwest of Belfort in the Vosges, to prepare the necessary facilities for the main force's arrival.

It was not until October 3 that 3 Wing was able to begin independent operations. The air battle over the Somme placed such a strain on the RFC's resources that Trenchard obtained priority for the delivery of 60 1½ Strutter fighters as soon as they became available. At the end of August, 3 Wing had only 13

Sopwith 1½ Strutters of 5 Wing preparing to set out on a mission from Coudekerque airfield in February 1917.

operational Strutter bombers at Luxeuil, while its French counterpart, Groupe de Bombardement 4, was committed to assembling a force of 50 aircraft by early September. In order to raise the strength of 3 Wing to two squadrons the Admiralty purchased a number of French Breguet V pusher bombers.

The French air service's determination to press ahead was underlined in October when Colonel Barès, a leading advocate of strategic bombing, visited London for discussions with the Admiralty aimed at the extension of Anglo-French co-operation. After the talks with Barès, the Admiralty sent a memorandum to the Air Board (which had succeeded the Joint War Air Committee) urging that, '...it should be definitely laid down that the Navy should keep an effective force of at least 200 bombers in France (to include Dunkirk) and if this policy commends itself, it is considered that orders for 1000 Hispanos and 1000 Clergets engines would not be excessive for the RNAS alone'.

This forced an immediate reply from Henderson, arguing that bombing was 'an unimportant duty compared with fighting or reconnaissance, nor does it seem to fall in any way within the sphere of Naval Duties'. Henderson had a powerful ally in Trenchard, and it is the latter's hand which can be detected in a letter which General Haig, the British C-in-C in France, wrote to the War Office on November 1. After lambasting the judgement of Colonel Barès, particularly over 'the bombing of open towns merely for the sake of terrorizing the civil population', Haig insisted that the only way to bring the war to a successful conclusion was by 'a decisive victory over the enemy's forces in the field'. Long-range bombing was entirely secondary to the tactical requirements of the land forces.

It was against this acrimonious background that 3 Wing made a modest start to its operations on July 3, when two 1½ Strutters flew with aircraft of Groupe de Bombardement 4 to attack petrol storage facilities at Müllheim. Overall planning remained in the hands of the French and was based on a program which concentrated its efforts on the war industries in the Saar-Lorraine-Luxembourg regions, whose blast furnaces produced half of Germany's steel requirements and lay within 70 miles of the French airfield at Nancy.

At the beginning of October, 3 Wing was preparing for its first big daylight raid, an operation stemming from an order issued on September 3 by Barès to Capitaine Happe, commander of the French bomber squadrons at Luxeuil, to attack the Mauser rifle factories at Oberndorff. The flight to and from the target was particularly challenging to the pilots, involving some 220 miles of cross-country flying over the inhospitable terrain of the Vosges and the Black Forest. For the raid 3 Wing was divided into Red and Blue Squadrons, the former comprising two flights of 1½ Strutters and the latter one flight of 1½ Strutters and one of Breguet Vs. Each flight was made up of five or six aircraft. The combination of Breguets and 1½ Strutters greatly increased the problems of co-ordination as the French bomber's performance was markedly inferior to that of the British aircraft. It took twice as long to reach 10 000 ft as the 1½ Strutter (49 minutes as opposed to 25) was unstable fore and aft, sluggish in the turn, and all but impossible to fly on instruments.

On October 12 the weather cleared sufficiently for the raid to go ahead. Starting at 1315 hrs the flights took off at ten-minute intervals. The Sopwiths flew in an upwardly staggered V-formation, with a single escort fighter keeping station 750 ft above the leader in the opening of the V behind the formation. The Breguets, escorted by two fighters above and behind, formed a triangle with the machines staggered downwards to provide maximum mutual protective fire. Altogether 34 French and 21 British aircraft took off to attack Oberndorff. The two flights of Red Squadron, one of which was escorted by the top naval ace of the war, Sub-Lieutenant Raymond Collishaw, made their rendezvous without incident and bombed their target according to plan, forming into line over the objective, bombing in succession and then re-assuming formation for the return flight. On their way back they were attacked by a Fokker DII, which forced the machine flown by Flight Lieutenant Butterworth down on a German airfield. Collishaw might have saved Butterworth but his engine cut out just as he moved in to attack.

By the time Blue Squadron's 1½ Strutters took off, the weather had closed in and the aircraft failed to make a rendezvous. One crashed 25 minutes after take-off and the others returned independently to the airfield. Flying above the dense cloud cover, Wing Commander R B Davies and his escort flight of three aircraft anxiously awaited the arrival of the Breguets. Then Davies saw 'a disturbance in the white layer below and the top-plane of a Breguet appeared. The machines came out one by one, looking like a string of hippos emerging from a pool'. The Breguets failed to find their target, bombing Donaueschingen which they mistook for Oberndorff, and lost two machines over Alsace to German fighters. With the formation drifting towards Switzerland, and internment, one of the escorting fighter pilots, Flight Sub-Lieutenant Redpath, took the initiative, dived in front of the Breguets, made a sharp turn and led them to safety.

About 20 British and French aircraft bombed the target, nine failing to return. For the French, however, the results were discouraging: two of their Farmans and four of their Breguets had been shot down, as well as a Breguet V borrowed from the RNAS. Fighter escort had been provided by the famous Escadrille Lafayette, but the limited range of their Nieuport 17s prevented them from staying with the bombers for very long. Norman Prince, one of the original seven members of the Escadrille Lafayette, crashed on landing and later died of his injuries.

The raid had exposed the vulnerability of the French pushers on daylight missions and henceforward they were restricted to operating at night. Bad weather continued to frustrate flying from Luxeuil and the focus shifted to the advanced French base at Nancy, the springboard for a campaign against the Saar-Lorraine-Luxembourg industrial complex.

3 Wing was soon on the move again, this time to the airfield at Ochey, 12 miles southwest of Nancy, from which on November 11, 15 bombers with an escort of seven fighters flew against the steelworks at Völklingen in the Saar basin, some 70 miles distant. However, a number of factors combined to limit operations to only four more raids by the end of the year: wear and tear on the 1½ Strutters' 130 hp

French armorers maneuver a bomb into position·in a Farman HF 27. Powered by a 160 hp Canton Unné engine, the HF 27 could carry about 550 pounds of bombs with an endurance of four hours.

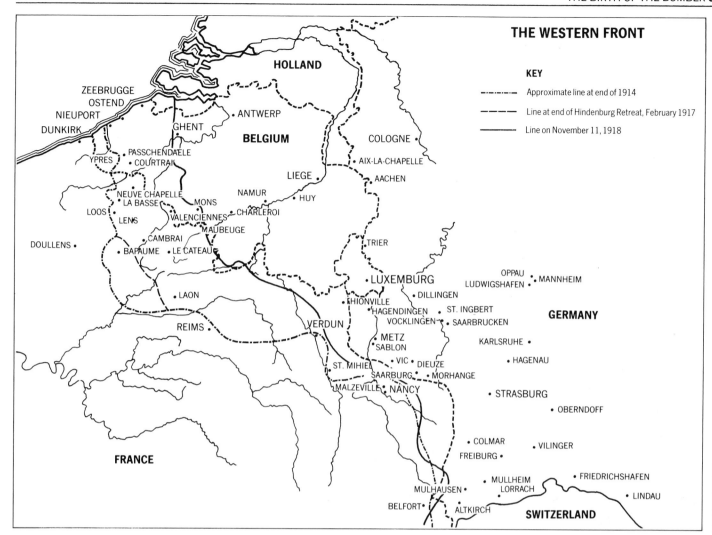

THE WESTERN FRONT

KEY

–·–·–·– Approximate line at end of 1914

– – – – – Line at end of Hindenburg Retreat, February 1917

———— Line on November 11, 1918

Clerget engines; increasingly bad weather and poor visibility over the targets; and the lake of mud masquerading as an airfield at Ochey, which prompted Elder to report, 'It is almost impossible for machines to get off owing to the depth of the mud; accidents to propellers are frequent'.

Nevertheless, both morale and operational efficiency had reached a new peak by the end of the year. According to Wing Commander Davies,

WHEN WE WENT TO ATTACK WE USUALLY met with the same half-hearted interference from German aircraft and the self-confidence of our young pilots rose rapidly. My idea was to keep the flights in close-locked formation, with fighters supporting the bombers on the outward and return journeys. However the bomber pilots had discovered that once their bomb loads were gone they had the legs of the fighters. So as soon as their bombs had been released, they took to opening the throttle and going off on their own in search of Germans. I gave up trying to stop this as it was resulting in quite a number of Germans shot down'.

In the winter of 1916–17 German air defense was still largely ineffective and unable to provide adequate cover for the long, narrow 200-mile-long band of territory which contained the principal industrial targets in the Saar-Lorraine-Luxembourg complex. Balloon barrages were now being flown over 3 Wing's main objectives and a number of single-seater units had been established in the industrial regions of western Germany from Cologne to Freiburg. Their activities were limited to picking off stragglers, and they rarely engaged a tightly held formation.

However, it was clear that the superiority enjoyed by single-seater bombers escorted by two-seater fighters would last only as long as the Germans failed to throw their full weight behind air defense. Wing Commander Davies had doubts about the long-term future of the single-seater bomber, particularly if the enemy was to introduce large numbers of two-seater aircraft to attack the fighter escorts and force the bombers to break formation: '*IT WILL BE OF great importance for the bombers to defend themselves without breaking formation. The type most suitable for this will be a two-seater bomber, but it will not be an advantage if speed, climb or maneuvering power have to be sacrificed to obtain the extra lift required. In my opinion it will be well worth experimenting with a type of machine similar*

'The Bloody Paralyser': Handley Page 0/100 1459, one of the first two machines to go into operational service in the winter of 1916.

to the present Sopwith, but carrying a passenger and gun and greatly reduced weight of bombs. With such machines there will be no need of escorting fighters, and all machines in the flight will then not be very greatly reduced, while it is probable that very greatly increased accuracy of dropping will be obtained by carrying a passenger to work the sighting arrangements'.

Atrocious weather conditions restricted 3 Wing to only one raid in January, when 24 aircraft flew to attack the blast furnaces at Saarbrücken-Burbach. In the freezing weather 16 machines reached the target and five cases of severe frostbite were reported after the raid. On the ground aircraft engines froze up in the unheated hangars. Early in February it became impossible to start the engines, and it was not until February 25 that the weather cleared sufficiently to permit another raid on Saarbrucken-Burbach. The temperature rose at the beginning of March, but at the same time thick fog rolled over 3 Wing's principal targets. Developments in the United Kingdom were also conspiring to frustrate the Wing's ambitions. Aircraft production was failing to keep pace with the RFC's requirements and the RNAS was called upon to place fully equipped and manned fighter squadrons at the disposal of RFC HQ. From the end of January a number of 3 Wing's pilots were transferred to Dunkirk to fly tactical missions on the Western Front.

Shortly afterwards, on April 14, 3 Wing flew its last missions. Two attacks were made on Freiburg, ostensibly in direct retaliation for a long string of German 'atrocities' culminating in the torpedoing of the hospital ship Asturias on March 20. Pilots were given clear instructions to aim at the center of the town. Twenty-five British and 15 French aircraft were involved and 3 Wing lost four machines – three 1½ Strutter escorts (which were now rapidly being outclassed by German fighters) and one bomber.

The disbandment of 3 Wing marked the end of the first sustained British strategic bombing offensive. Most of the Wing's Sopwith bombers were turned over to the French and their aircrew posted to RNAS squadrons on loan to the RFC. Bad weather and its own limited resources had confined 3 Wing's operations to a mere 18 raids, and it is interesting to note that during the same period 4 and 5 Wings at Dunkirk had flown 52 missions, principally of a tactical nature, over the same ranges. Nevertheless, 3 Wing had gone some way towards wresting the strategic initiative from the Germans whose Zeppelins, while causing little material damage, had disrupted British war production and lowered civilian morale. In the process the Wing's brief operational career raised the hopes of its supporters that strategic bombing might yet provide the key to unlock the bloody deadlock of trench warfare.

The Handley Page 0/100

In November 1916 3 Wing took delivery of the first two service 0/100s, Nos. 1459 and 1460, the latter flown into Luxeuil by Squadron Commander John Babington. The third Luxeuil-bound 0/100, No. 1463 piloted by Lieutenant Vereker, took off on New Year's Day. Vereker lost his way in unbroken cloud over the Channel and, with fuel running low came down to 500 ft before making a landing in the first suitable field. Unfortunately, Vereker had put his machine down behind enemy lines, near Laon, a fact he rapidly discovered when a German patrol arrived on the scene. Vereker attempted to scramble back into his cockpit, from which he had ventured in order to discover his whereabouts, only to be ignominiously hauled down by the seat of his pants. The 0/100 was dismantled and transported to Johannisthal, where it was rebuilt and closely examined. Legend has it that on one test flight No. 1463 was taken up to a height of 10 000 ft under the eyes of the Kaiser by no less a person than

Freiherr Manfred von Richthofen, but it crashed before a full assessment of its capabilities could be made.

At 3 Wing the 0/100's capabilities were not immediately appreciated by Captain Elder, who reported magneto trouble and distorted propellers, 'through either inefficient design or bad material, as far as one can judge, from the former'. The 0/100 was flown operationally for the first time on the night of March 16/17, 1917, when No. 1460 raided the railway yards at Moulins-les-Metz. The bomb doors proved troublesome; the technical expert, Lieutenant Commander E W Stedman having to push the bombs out by hand. On later raids, brown paper was used to cover the grid opening. The bombs fell through the paper when released. This improvization subjected the 0/100's crew to ferocious blasts of cold air on the return journey.

On the night of April 5 both of 3 Wing's 0/100s took off to raid the railway junction at Arnaville, and on April 14 a single machine attacked the furnaces at Hagendingen while the other bombed the depot and airfield at Chambley. This was a modest beginning but already the striking power and cost-effectiveness of the big bomber were becoming clear. The magnificent Rolls Royce Eagles gave the aircraft an endurance of 9½ hours with an all-up weight of 5½ tons, including 380 gallons of fuel and ten 112-pound bombs. Operating at shorter range with 250 gallons of fuel in tanks in the rear of the engine nacelles and 70 gallons in the fuselage, the 0/100 could carry 14 112-pound bombs. With the removal of the fuel in the fuselage, the offensive load could be increased to 16 112-pound bombs. In the four operational flights made between March 16 and April 14, 3 Wing's 0/100s had dropped almost as much explosive (4800 pounds) as the combined total (4940 pounds) delivered by 21 1½ Strutters, accompanied by ten escort fighters, in the raids of February 25 and March 16.

When 3 Wing was disbanded its two 0/100s were sent to join 5 Wing at Coudekerque, initially flying daylight missions against the U-boat bases at Zeebrugge and Ostend. Later targets included the long-range heavy shore batteries sited by the Germans along the dunes from Middelkerke to the Dutch frontier at Sluys.

On April 23 three 0/100s of 5 Wing, each carrying 14 65-pound bombs, located five German destroyers off Ostend, and badly damaged one of them. Three days later, in a similar engagement, 0/100 No. 3115 was shot down and ditched in the sea, three of its crew being taken prisoner. This marked the end of daylight sorties for the 0/100 and subsequently night attacks were concentrated on the docks at Bruges and Zeebrugge, where U-boats were refueled and resupplied. Only the 0/100 and the landplane version of the Short 184 seaplane, the Short bomber, were capable of carrying the 520-pound 'light case' and 550-pound 'heavy case' bombs developed to deal with submarine pens and shore batteries, both of which were heavily protected with concrete. The Short was a stop-gap bomber which had gone into service with No. 7 Squadron at the end of 1916. A big two-seater three-bay biplane with an 85 ft wingspan and a generously proportioned curved fin, it was powered by a 250 hp Eagle engine, giving it a maximum speed of 77 mph at 6500 ft and a range of over 400 miles. It could carry up to 920 pounds of bombs (standard loads were four 230-pound or eight 112-pound) and defensive armament was provided by a single Lewis gun mounted in the rear (observer's) cockpit. The Short bomber first saw action on November 15, 1916 when four machines, each armed with eight 65-pound bombs, raided submarine pens at Zeebrugge. In all 83 were built.

The Short's slow speed quickly relegated it to night-flying operations alongside the 0/100s, of which there were 20 in Nos. 7 and 7A (subsequently 14) Squadrons by September. Initially flying was restricted to bright, moonlit nights but by the late summer of 1917 night flying training had improved to such an extent that only the worst weather kept the bombers grounded.

Only one 0/100 was used outside Europe. Early in 1917 Commodore Murray F Sueter, who had been transferred to the Mediterranean, called for a heavy bomber to attack the enemy cruisers *Goeben* and *Breslau* anchored at Constantinople. Sueter had originally requested a floatplane conversion of the 0/100, a suggestion which was politely declined by Handley Page, who eventually delivered No. 3124, fresh from the production line at Cricklewood. On May 23, piloted by Squadron Commander Kenneth Savory, it left Hendon on the first stage of a 2000-mile flight to Mudros, on the Aegean island of Lemnos, via Villacoublay, Lyons, Fréjus, Pisa, Rome, Naples, Otranto and Salonika. Mudros was reached on June 8 after 55 hours in the air.

Savory's first two attempts to bomb Constantinople, on July 3 and 8, were foiled by strong headwinds. On July 9 he succeeded at the third attempt, reaching Constantinople at midnight after a flight of 3 hours and 15 minutes. Savory circled the city for half an hour at 1000 ft, dropping eight 112-pound bombs on the *Goeben* in Stenia Bay, two more on the steamer *General* (then being used as the German HQ) and the last two on the Turkish War Office.

The Ilya Muromets Type B, predecessor of the Type V.

On September 30, after three months of short-range bombing and anti-submarine patrols, the 0/100 took off once more for Constantinople with Lieutenant J Alcock at the controls. Engine failure forced the aircraft down in the Gulf of Xeros, near Suvla Bay, and the crew were taken prisoner.

Russia, Italy and the first 'Heavies'

The 0/100 was not the first of the heavy bombers. While work was proceeding on the prototype at the Handley Page factory at Cricklewood, the Russian Ilya Muromets (IM) four-engined bombers were flying operationally on the Eastern Front.

The Russian military were no different from their western European counterparts and at first greeted the arrival of the IM Type Vs with a great deal of scepticism, a point of which seemed to have been confirmed by the poor performance of the first two IMs on the Northwest Front in the early months of the war. However, with the active support of the Grand Duke Nikolai Nikolayevich, Commander-in-Chief of the armed forces, Igor Sikorsky had obtained a second chance for his giant aircraft and installed himself at Yablonna, near Warsaw, as test pilot, flight instructor and on-the-spot designer.

Before the arrival of the Type Vs early in 1915, the Eskadra Vozdushnikh Korbablei (EVK) or Flying Ship Squadron, formed in December 1914, had operated Type Bs. Captain Gorshkov, in *Kievsky* flew the unit's first mission on February 15 and on March 6 dropped ten 35-pound bombs on Willenburg during a flight which lasted four hours.

The IMs proved themselves to be extremely rugged aircraft, capable of absorbing considerable punishment and remaining airborne, not least because of their specially designed fireproof fuel tanks and the installation of armor protection under the pilot's cabin. The heavy defensive armament

they carried – some IMs bristled with seven or more machine-guns – made them a daunting prospect for German fighters on the Eastern Front. It was not until September 12, 1916 that one of the IMs was shot down in combat, and only after it had disposed of three of its attackers and badly damaged a fourth. Another example of the aircraft's durability was provided on June 6, 1915 when an IM was caught 40 miles inside enemy territory by a swarm of German fighters which quickly put two of its engines out of action and mortally wounded the commander. Harried all the way, the IM still managed to regain the safety of its own lines. It is a measure of the aircraft's psychological effect that in the spring of 1916 the great German ace Oswald Boelcke was despatched to the Eastern Front to raise morale.

By the summer of 1915 the value of the IM bomber was no longer questioned by the military, and as soon as the EVK was operating ten aircraft it began flying sorties in which several bombers combined against a single target. At the end of the year the EVK had made over 100 sorties, delivering 22 tons of bombs and incurring no losses as a result of enemy action. By then the Type G had gone into production. In most respects similar to the Type V, the Type Gs were powered by a mixture of 170hp Sunbeam Cossacks and 220hp Renaults, supplemented by RBVZ engines in the outboard positions. Combat experience resulted in a considerable strengthening of the defensive armament, to five machine-guns. Later, on Sikorsky's urging, a tail gun position was added to the G2 and G3 variants which could be reached from the cabin by a man lying prone on a small trolley which ran the length of the fuselage. The G2 also incorporated a nose gun and the G3 added two beam machine-guns.

The largest of the Muromets series was the IMYeA, with a wingspan of 113ft 2in and a gross weight of 15432 pounds. This colossus never went into production, but a few of the slightly smaller IMYe1s were built, armed with seven machine-guns and powered by four 220 hp Renaults. The IMYe2, the last of the line, carried no fewer than eight machine-guns and, in an experimental version, was fitted with a 50-mm quick-firing cannon.

Eighty IMs had been built when the Russian Revolution of October 1917 brought an end to production. In three years they had flown 450 missions and dropped 65 tons of bombs with a loss of only three aircraft. After the Russo-German armistice of December 15 several of the IMs fell into German hands, some 30 were destroyed by EVK personnel and the remainder appropriated by the Bolsheviks and the counter-revolutionary White Army. IMs saw service in the Northern Group of the 'Red Air Fleet of the Workers and Peasants Army' and in 1921–22 a few undertook less warlike duties, plying as experimental passenger and freight liners. In 1924 the last surviving IM was pressed into service as a training aircraft at the Serpukhov School of Bombing.

Technically ahead of their time, heavily armed and equipped with an accurate bombsight designed by Captains Ivanov and Zhuvavchenko, the IM bombers might have exerted a considerable influence on the Eastern Front had it not been for persistent maintenance problems and the inescapable difficulties of obtaining engines and spare parts. They remain among the 'might-have-beens' of the early history of aerial warfare.

Italy was the next country to introduce heavy bombers into service, following its declaration of war against Austria–Hungary on May 24, 1915. These were aircraft of the three-engined Caproni series, developed before the war and modified considerably during the course of the conflict.

The first to fly operationally, in the late summer of 1915, was the Ca32 (military designation Ca.3), powered by three 100 hp Fiat liquid-cooled engines. The Ca32's range of 340 miles gave it a strategic capability but when operations began it was restricted to tactical objectives – railroads, supply depots, troop concentrations and airfields – to the rear of the Austrian armies.

The Ca32, of which 164 were built, was followed into service at the end of 1916 by the Ca33. Similar in layout to its predecessor, its distinctive structure incorporated large wings of 73 ft span, two booms supporting the tailplane, elevators and three polygonal rudders. Powered by three Isotta-Fraschini V4B engines, each developing 150 hp, the Ca33 had a maximum speed of 85 mph at sea level, a service ceiling of 13 450 ft, endurance of three hrs 30 minutes and could carry a bombload of 1000 pounds. The crew consisted of two pilots, an observer, whose cockpit was located in the nose and fitted with a ring-mounted machine-gun, and a rear gunner. Muffled against the howling slipstream, the rear gunner stood in a kind of cage mounted at the level of the trailing edge of the upper wing and over the pusher engine at the rear of the central fuselage.

The cockpit instrumentation on the Capronis was fairly primitive, as Lieutenant E J Furlong discovered when, in 1917, he travelled to Italy with an RFC/RNAS contingent for a conversion course on the big biplane: 'NONE OF US WERE MULTI-engine pilots at the time, so we had to learn how to fly multi-engined aeroplanes.... The air speed indicator was a rough and ready affair consisting of what we called a "penny on a string", a little round disc on a spring on one of the struts outside the cockpit. When the wind was blowing on it, it was blown backwards and when the wind wasn't so strong, it came forward. Behind it was a plate on which were the two words "Minima" and "Maxima". If you let it get below "Minima" you stalled, and if you got above "Maxima" presumably the wings fell off. But that was the only indicator. There was no actual "miles per hour" sort of indication at all. You simply knew you had to fly within these limits.... There was practically nothing that I recall in the way of instruments, except perhaps an oil gauge for each engine and a rev counter.... I don't even recall an altimeter. The aircraft was very noisy and when in the air it was very unbalanced – very tail heavy – and there was no adjustment on the tail or bias on the rudder, so all the correction had to be done by the pilot, and this was quite hard work. If you were flying solo, you had literally to jam your elbow into your stomach and hold the stick forward with one hand while you operated the ailerons with the other. There was a sort of wheel on the top of the stick. So that was pretty heavy work. If you'd been flying like that for the best part of an hour you knew all about it'.

The aircraft in the Ca3 series were all biplanes, but the Ca4 series introduced a colossal triplane, the Ca40. The most effective machine in this series was the Ca42. Twenty-three Ca42s were built, of which six were supplied to the British RNAS. E J Furlong gained some experience of the Ca42, which in some respects he found easier to fly than the Ca33: 'The Triplane was more manageable, although it was still fairly heavy on the tail. It felt a bit faster although we had no means of knowing by how much because of the lack of instruments'.

Throughout the war tactical operations remained the principal preoccupation of the Italian air service, but a number of strategic raids were executed, principally at the instigation of the flamboyant soldier-poet Gabriele D'Annunzio. Vienna, some 250 miles from the Capronis' main base at Pordenone, was well out of range, but there was a string of tempting targets only 100 miles away along the Adriatic coast, among them the city and seaport of Trieste and the naval bases at Pola, Kotor and Sebenico. Kotor was one of the first bases to be hit, by a special unit of Capronis known as Distaccamento AR (Detachment AR), so-called because of the name of its commander Captain Armani. Pola also suffered the attentions of the Capronis, particularly in a big raid on October 2, 1917. However, at the end of the month, following the defeat at Caporetto, the Pordenone base fell into German hands, curtailing any further strategic operations. Subsequently one Ca33 unit, 18 Gruppo commanded by Captain de Riso, was based in France at Ochey, flying its three squadrons against targets on the Marne in the spring of 1918 and against supply centers north of Rheims, Thionville, Sablon, St Quentin and Metz.

The Italian air service contrived at least one final spectacular fling with an operation which had originally been planned in the summer of 1917 for two Ca33s of 4a Squadriglia. The target was to be Vienna and the load carried not bombs but

Ca42

The aircraft in the Ca3 series were all biplanes, but the Ca4 series introduced a spectacular triplane, the Ca40. The most effective machine in this series was the Ca42, with a wingspan of 98 ft and powered by three Isotta Fraschini six-cylinder liquid-cooled in-line engines, each of which developed 270 mph. The bombload, housed in the streamlined coffin-like canister between the wheels of the landing gear, was a formidable 3197 pounds. However, this was offset by a relatively poor performance: a maximum speed of 78 mph at sea level and a service ceiling of only 9840 ft. The rear gunner's cage was eliminated and replaced with a gun, or pair of guns, mounted in the tail booms. The extra armament was sorely needed as the 'built-in headwind' of the massive aircraft made it easy meat for enemy scouts on daylight missions.

The Caproni Ca42 triplane, of which 23 were built by the Italians and six supplied to the RNAS.

propaganda leaflets. To prepare the aircraft for the mission massive auxiliary fuel tanks were fitted to the Capronis, at the expense of all armament, giving them a range of about 550 miles and no margin for error. The mission was delayed for a year, and when it was finally launched on August 9, 1918 it was flown by an aircraft markedly different to the huge Caproni. With a wingspan of just under 30 ft, the Ansaldo SVA5 light bomber was a midget compared with the Ca33, but it was one of the outstanding aircraft of the war. A trim single-seater originally designed as a fighter and powered by a 220 hp SPA six-cylinder liquid-cooled in-line engine, the SVA5 had a maximum speed of 143 mph and a ceiling of 22 000 ft. In service from the beginning of 1918, it equipped six squadrons and proved outstanding in reconnaissance and bombing roles, with a range of

600 miles (double that of the Capronis) carrying an offensive load of 200 pounds. For the propaganda raid on Vienna eight SVA5s of 87 Squadriglia ('Serenissima') were fitted with an extra 66-gallon fuel tank, and one of them was specially modified from a single- to a two-seater to accommodate D'Annunzio and the pilot Captain Natale Palli. After a flight of three hours 30 minutes the SVA5s appeared over Vienna at 0920 hrs and, flying in close formation, swept across the city scattering leaflets and taking photographs. Turning for home, the machine piloted by Lieutenant Giuseppe Sarti developed engine trouble which forced him down near Wiener Neustadt. The remainder returned to their San Pelagio base at 1240 hrs, at the end of a round trip of 620 miles, almost 500 miles flown over enemy territory.

1.5 THE FIRST BATTLE OF BRITAIN 1917–18

THE NIGHT OF NOVEMBER 27/28, 1916 HAD been a particularly bad one for the German Naval Airship Division, witnessing the destruction of *L34* and *L21* by British home defense fighters. Barely six hours after the wreckage of *L21* slid beneath an ugly oil slick in the North Sea, a series of small explosions punctuated the bustle of central London between the Brompton Road and Victoria Station. They were caused by six 22-pound bombs dropped by a single-engined LVG CII biplane of Marine Landflieger Abteilung 1 piloted by Deck Offizier Paul Brandt with Leutnant Walther Ilges as observer.

In broad daylight and undetected, the LVG had approached London from the south to deliver its bombs from a height of 13 000 ft, optimistically aiming them at the Admiralty building but, literally, missing by a mile. This audacious sortie was Leutnant Ilges' fourth flight over the British mainland, and his last. Over the English Channel the LVG developed engine trouble, forcing Ilges and Brandt down near Boulogne, where they were captured by a French patrol who discovered a large-scale map of London still in their possession.

Since Leutnant Caspar's abortive raid on Dover at the end of October 1914, there had been a sporadic series of German hit and run raids against southern seaports and coastal shipping flown by the float-planes of See Flieger Abteilung 1 (SFA 1), which had become operational at Zeebrugge in December 1914. The most ambitious floatplane raid was mounted on March 19, 1916, when four Friedrichshafen FF3-bfs, one Hansa-Brandenburg NW and one Gotha-Ursinus WD attacked Dover, Deal and Ramsgate, killing 14 and injuring 26.

The authorities' growing confidence in the home defense organization remained unruffled by the pinpricks of the floatplane raids or the apparently receding menace of the Zeppelin. Convinced that the airships' days were numbered, consideration was now given to the reallocation of home defense resources to other more hard-pressed areas.

The German air service did not remain idle. Korvettenkapitan Peter Strasser sought to rein-vigorate the flagging Zeppelin offensive with the introduction of the 'height-climbers', previously described. On April 19, 1917 four torpedo-carrying Gotha WD11s of SFA1, accompanied by one fighter escort and a W/T communications aircraft, launched a daring but unsuccessful attack on coastal shipping. Just over two weeks later, on May 6/7, London ex-perienced its first night attack by an airplane. The raid was an apparently 'freelance' effort flown by an Albatros CVII of Feldflieger Abteilung 19, based near Ostend.

The Albatros's lone sortie was the prelude to a long-planned strategic bombing campaign against the British mainland. In the winter of 1916 the Kogenluft, Generalleutnant von Hoeppner, had advised OHL that 'since airship raids over London had become impossible', immediate consideration should be given to the launching of airplane attacks.

He went on to propose the creation of a new squadron equipped with 30 of the Gotha GIV twin-engined bombers, then still under development and due to enter service in February 1917. The projected bombing offensive was given the codename *Turkenkreuz* ('Turk's Cross').

The origins of the plan lay in Major Wilhelm Siegert's 'Carrier-Pigeon Unit' formed in the autumn of 1914. Siegert was now Inspector-General of the Kommandieren General der Luftsstreitkrafte and his old unit had expanded into Kampfgeschwader der Obersten Heeresleitung 1 (Battle Squadron No. 1 of the Army High Command, and in abbreviated form Kagohl 1). Kagohl 1 was called upon to provide three of its six Staffeln (flights) as a nucleus for the new strategic unit, designated Kagohl 3 and soon dubbed the Englandgeschwader, with an initial strength of four flights. This was to be the élite of the Kaiser's bombing squadrons and the first to be given a purely strategic role, attached to the German Fourth Army but operating quite independently and reporting directly to OHL. Its first commanding officer was Hauptmann Ernst Brandenburg and his orders were to 'disrupt the British war industry, disorganize the communications between coastal ports and hinder the transport of war materials across the Channel'.

The twin-engined bomber which equipped Kagohl 3 was the first major production variant of the G class of aircraft produced by the Gothaer Waggonfabrik AG. The first of these *Grosskampf-flugzeugen* ('battle airplanes'), the GI designed by Oskar Ursinus, appeared in January 1915. It was followed by the GII, designed by Hans Burkhard; a three-bay biplane powered by two 220 hp Benz engines driving pusher propellers. By the end of 1915 there were fewer than 20 GIs and GIIs at the front, and the GIII – which entered service in the autumn of 1916 – proved another transitional model. Powered by two six-cylinder 260 hp Mercedes DIVa liquid-cooled in-line engines, the GIII incorporated a novel feature which was to reappear in the GIV and GV – a hatch in the rear fuselage which gave the after gunner a downward field of fire covering the blind spot below the aircraft. In the GIV this was refined into a more sophisticated 'tunnel' arrangement which increased the gunner's field of fire.

The Englandgeschwader Attacks

In April 1917 the Englandgeschwader left its tem-porary home at Ghistelles in Belgium to occupy permanent bases at St Denis-Westrem (13, 14 Staffeln), Gontrode (15, 16 Staffeln) and, shortly afterwards, Mariakerke (two new flights, 17 and 18 Staffeln). Commanded by a Staffelnführer, each flight was equipped with six GIVs. British intelligence about Kagohl 3's aircraft remained limited, as is demonstrated by an official letter to all units which advised that the best way to attack a Gotha '...is from below and behind, that is, under their tails. An attacker in this position is safe, and he is completely outside the enemy's field of fire'. German intelligence was equally sketchily informed about the British home defense, but a considerable measure of protection was afforded the Gotha by its attack altitude of 16 000 ft. Once unburdened of its bombs, the aircraft could climb even higher to evade the British fighters on the return journey.

On Friday, May 25, the Englandgeschwader mounted its first raid on the British mainland. Twenty-three Gothas took off, and almost immediately engine failure forced down one of them near Thielt. The remainder landed at Nieuwmunster to refuel. Over the Channel, the machine commanded by Leutnant Walther Aschoff began to lose power in the starboard engine. After firing several red flares to indicate that he was turning back, Aschoff swung over the Belgian coast. The 21 remaining Gothas flew on, forming into two tight clusters as they crossed the Essex coastline between the Blackwater and Crouch estuaries at 1700 hrs, and then droning on towards towering banks of cloud which were forming over Gravesend. The cloud forced them to turn south, bombing Lympne airfield on the way before arriving over Folkestone, about two miles from Shorncliff army camp.

Most of the Gothas' bombs, dropped from 16 000 ft and aimed at Shorncliff camp, fell on Folkestone, killing 95 civilians, injuring 195 and causing nearly £20 000 worth of damage. The only home-based aircraft to make contact with the raiders were flown by two ferry pilots. More than 70 home defense sorties were hampered by cloud, confusion, and the low performance of their aircraft.

As they neared the Belgian coast at a height of 18 000 ft the Gothas came under attack from nine Sopwith Pups of Nos. 4 and 9 (RNAS) Squadrons from Dunkirk. The RNAS pilots subsequently claimed two Gothas, one shot down into the sea and the other forced down out of control. However, the German reports list only one loss, a Gotha which crashed near Bruges, killing its crew.

On June 5 the Gothas returned, 22 aircraft

attacking the Admiralty docks at Sheerness and the proving grounds at Shoeburyness, losing one straggling machine (possibly to anti-aircraft fire) on the return flight. Brandenburg was now under intense pressure to bomb London, and the moment arrived eight days later on June 13, when a force of 14 Gothas dropped a total of 72 bombs in the area of Liverpool Street Station.

Brandenburg became a hero overnight and was awarded the Pour le Mérite by the Kaiser at the Supreme Headquarters at Kreuznach. After spending the weekend there, Brandenburg took off for Ghent in an Albatros two-seater piloted by Oberleutnant Freiherr von Trotha. The Albatros crashed, killing von Trotha and seriously injuring Brandenburg, who was replaced as commander of the Englandgeschwader by Hauptmann Rudolf Kleine, a much-decorated veteran of Kagohl 1 and a fully qualified pilot (a distinction among Kagohl commanders who were customarily observers).

In Britain the June 13 raid precipitated a furious debate on the state of home defense. Unlike the Zeppelins, frequently blundering blindly over great tracts of central England, the Gothas had struck bold and hard and in broad daylight at the very center of the biggest city in the world. The psychological effect was tremendous. On the Western Front at least 2500 men were dying every day. In London 162 people were killed in the first Gotha raid – and an immediate furore erupted.

Reluctantly Haig agreed to the release of No. 56 Squadron (SE5as), to be posted to Bekesbourne in Kent; and the diversion of No. 66 Squadron (Sopwith Pups) to Calais to fly high-altitude formation patrols over the Channel, a task for which the Pup, with its ceiling of 18 000 ft, was well qualified. Haig added the rider that both squadrons were to return to their normal duties in France by July 5.

The day before the two squadrons resumed their duties in France, Kleine launched the first raid under

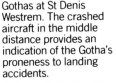

Gothas at St Denis Westrem. The crashed aircraft in the middle distance provides an indication of the Gotha's proneness to landing accidents.

his command. Twenty-four Gothas took off to bomb naval installations at Harwich and Felixstowe, 18 of them reaching their targets but dropping most of their bombs into the sea. Over 100 home defense aircraft took off to intercept the raiders but the Gothas encountered only one machine, a DH4 which was being given an endurance test over the Channel by Lieutenant John Palethorpe, accompanied by Air Mechanic James Jessop. The DH4 attacked. Jessop got in a burst before himself being killed by fire from the Gothas. Thirty miles north of Ostend the Gothas were intercepted by four Sopwith Camels of No. 4 Squadron (RNAS), fending off a series of attacks without loss.

On July 6 Sir John French, now C-in-C United Kingdom, wrote to Robertson, painting a gloomy picture of the forces at his disposal. There were available only 21 home defense fighters whose performance gave them a chance of successfully engaging the Gothas – 12 Sopwith Pups, six DH4s and three SE5s. French concluded, '...if London is again subjected to attack, the results may be disastrous'.

Kleine made sure that French's prophecy came true by launching a raid on the following day. At 1000 hrs 21 Gothas appeared over London, dropping their bombs in a rough triangle bounded by Kentish Town, Hackney and Tower Hill, killing 57 people, injuring 193 and causing £205 622 worth of damage.

In spite of the outcry provoked by the second raid on the capital, the home defense could derive some encouragement from its performance. In all, 108 sorties were flown and a number of pilots intercepted and engaged the Gothas before they reached central London. At least 20 pilots made interceptions on the Gothas' outward flight, one bomber was shot down and several others badly damaged. The Gotha commanded by Leutnant S R Schulte force-landed on the beach at Ostend with 88 bullet holes in the fuselage. Three more Gothas were written off in landing accidents. Two RFC aircraft were lost and

their crews killed, while a third returned with the pilot wounded.

Within hours of the second German raid on London the War Cabinet had directed Haig to release from the Western Front 'two good squadrons'. Haig feared their loss would prejudice 'the fight for air supremacy preparatory to forthcoming operations ... Withdrawal of these two squadrons will certainly delay favourable decision in the air and render air victory more difficult'. A compromise was reached which resulted in the arrival of No. 46 Squadron at Sutton's Farm airfield on July 10.

The increasing sophistication of long-range bombing operations was underlined by the importance at Kagohl 3's Gontrode headquarters of the meteorological expert Leutnant Walther Georgii. However on August 18, the commander of Kagohl 3, who carried the aggressive spirit up to and beyond the borders of recklessness, chose to ignore Georgii's warning against flying that day. Twenty-eight Gothas took off, 13 from Gontrode and 15 from St Denis Westrem, flying straight into a strong southwest headwind which forced Kleine to turn back when barely over the English coastline. At the mercy of a ferocious tailwind, four Gothas crashed into the sea, while the remainder drifted across neutral Holland, south of the Scheldte, where Dutch gunners accounted for another bomber, bringing it down on the Belgian side of the border. Two more Gothas made forced landings in Holland, where their crews were interned. Striving to maintain a semblance of formation, Kleine took the Gothas down to 1000 ft to avoid the risk of mid-air collisions in the clouds blowing in from the sea. Four more bombers ran out of fuel before they reached Ghent, force-landing where they could. Five hours after take-off the remaining Gothas struggled down at Ghent in a series of 'controlled crashes'. It had been Kagohl 3's own version of the disastrous 'Silent Raid' flown by the Naval Airship Division on October 19/20, 1917.

Gothas Raid London, June 13, 1917

At 1000 hrs 20 GIVs took off from Gontrode airfield, south of Ghent. By the time the Belgian coast was crossed at Zeebrugge, two of the bombers had fallen out with engine trouble. With the coastline of the Thames estuary looming ahead, another Gotha left the formation and bombed Margate before returning to Gontrode. Over Foulness Island three aircraft fired flares to indicate that they were turning back. At least one of them raided Shoeburyness and another attacked the Victoria Royal Docks before returning for home. The remaining 14 tightened up into a diamond formation and, flying at 16 500 ft, approached London north of their principal aiming areas, turning over Tottenham to fly back over the City. Over Regent's Park, Hauptmann Brandenburg – leading the formation in his distinctive red-tailed Gotha – fired a single white flare. The formation swung round to begin bombing at 1135 hrs. Conditions were perfect as each Gotha broke formation to select a target almost at leisure. One bomb hit a school in Poplar, killing 16 young children. Home defense fighters failed to make a single interception on the Gothas' inward journey, and only a handful struggled to within combat range as the bombers droned homewards. The observer in a Bristol Fighter of No.35 (Training Squadron), piloted by Captain C W E Cole-Hamilton, was killed in a sharp combat with three of the Gothas over Southend. All the Gothas returned safely.

The aircraft in the foreground, with the distinctive 'serpent' motif, is the machine piloted by Leutnant Kolberg and commanded by Leutnant Aschoff. The GIV was powered by a Mercedes DIVa engine and, with its all-plywood fuselage and ailerons on both top and bottom wings, was stronger and easier to fly than its predecessors. It combined an ungainly appearance with high performance, possessing a ceiling of 20 000 ft and cruising speed of 80 mph. The maximum bombload of 1100 pounds could be carried either externally or internally. Smaller bombs were hung on racks located within the fuselage between the pilot and the rear gunner. Projectiles of 110 pounds and over were shackled under the wings and the twin-wheeled landing gear, the standard cross-Channel load being six 110-pound bombs. The aircraft's principal weakness was a proneness to landing accidents, control becoming more difficult as the center of gravity shifted with the release of the bombs and the consumption of most of the fuel. Initially the Gotha's range was insufficient for a non-stop flight to London, necessitating a refueling halt on the Belgian coast on the outward journey. Later the addition of a reserve fuel tank made the stop redundant.

The Gotha's bomb release

Right: Muffled against the elements, a Gotha gunner demonstrates the oxygen equipment for operating at altitude. The bombers carried two cylinders of oxygen, the flow of which was regulated by a valve and inhaled through a mouthpiece. Aircrew were reluctant to use the oxygen, not only because of its unpleasant side effects but also because it was thought to be 'unmanly'. Bravado was the norm in a unit which contained such colorful characters as

Oberleutnant Fritz Lorenz, who as the result of a flying accident sported a prosthetic gelatine nose which he reshaped every morning. Lorenz commanded a Gotha with Lo-Ri2 emblazoned on the front of the fuselage – 'Lo' for Lorenz and 'Ri' for Oberleutnant Richter, who had been killed while test-flying 'Lo-Ri 1'. On the top of the Gotha's wings Lorenz had painted his motto, 'Eisern und Irre' – Iron and Madness.

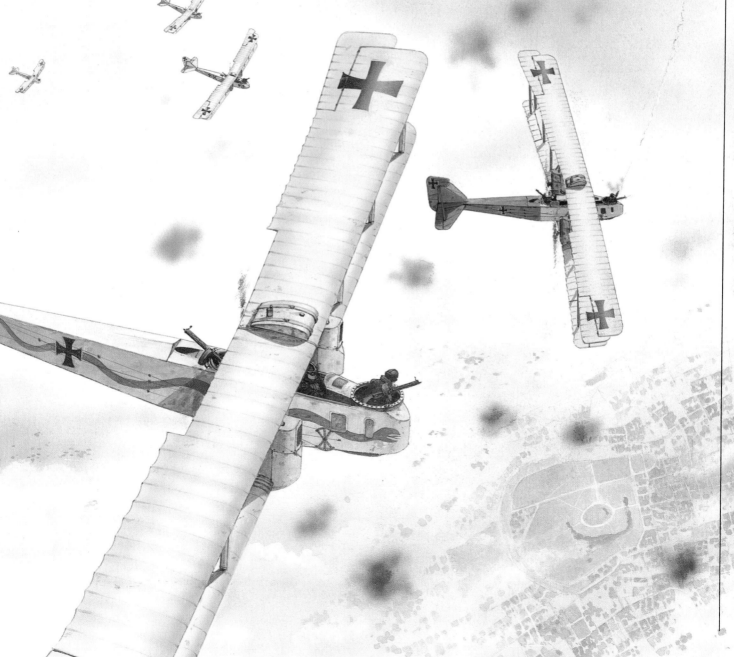

Gotha GIVs parked outside the Zeppelin shed at Gontrode. The Gotha was flown by a crew of three, commanded by the observer, who was also the navigator and bombardier, occupying the 'pulpit' position in the Gotha's bulbous box-like nose. The observer's cockpit was crammed with equipment: a 7.92mm ring-mounted Parabellum machine-gun; the Gorz bombsight, the principal component of which was a vertically mounted telescope over three feet long; and one of the two cylinders of compressed oxygen carried by the Gotha for operating at altitude.

Only four days later Kleine mounted another raid with his depleted forces. But his plan to push home a two-pronged attack on Dover and, depending on the circumstances, Sheerness, Southend or Chatham, proved another fiasco. Of the 15 Gothas which took off only ten reached the English coast, the others turning back with engine trouble, among them the machine commanded by Kleine. The formation was spotted at 1006 hrs by the Kentish Knock lightship, and its slow progress over the last 20 miles to the English coast allowed the home defense fighters ample time to gain height. The Gothas could manage only hurried and indiscriminate bombing of Margate and Dover, two of them falling to anti-aircraft fire and a third to the combined efforts of three RNAS pilots, Flight Lieutenant A F Brandon (flying a Sopwith Camel from Manston), Flight Commander G E Hervey (flying a Sopwith Pup from Dover) and Flight Lieutenant H S Kerby (flying a Sopwith Pup from Walmer). The Gothas never returned to bomb England by day.

The Smuts Report
While the Gothas prepared to switch to night bombing, British air policy was undergoing a fundamental change which was to have far-reaching consequences. Reacting to the Gotha raids, the British Prime Minister, David Lloyd George, appointed a member of the War Cabinet, General Jan Smuts, to head a committee of inquiry examining the state of 'air organization and home defense against air raids'. Smuts' report was divided into two halves: recommendations for air defense and proposals outlining a new structure for the nation's air forces to be used an an 'independent means of war operations'.

In the first half of this report, which was produced in just over a week, Smuts noted that London occupied 'a peculiar position in the Empire of which it is the nerve center'. Exceptional measures had to be taken for its defense, since it was possible that the capital 'would through aerial warfare become part of the battle front'. His first recommendation was for the appointment of an air defense chief, responsible to French and 'specially charged with the duty of working out all plans for the defense of the capital'. The London Air Defense Area (LADA), as it became known, was to include all the territory within the range of the Gothas and its first commander was Major-General E B 'Splash' Ashmore, an artillery officer and qualified pilot. Smuts also secured three extra home defense squadrons, Nos. 44, 112 and 61, and in August work began on an eastern 'gun barrier' around London. The battle against the U-boats – which was now entering a critical phase – was still the top priority and initially only 34 anti-aircraft guns were available for the barrier. Behind the barrier, Ashmore deployed his fighters to patrol the courses flown by the Gothas into London. The two defense zones were divided by a 'green line', the guns being given priority in the outer zone while the fighters took over in the inner.

The second part of Smuts' report was completed on August 17, and in its sweeping conclusions are to be found the seeds of the British strategic air offensive of World War II. In the relatively short time it had taken him to prepare the report, Smuts had been captivated by a vision of air power: '*As far as can at present be foreseen there is absolutely no limit to the scale of its future independent war use. And the day may not be far off when aerial operations with their devastation of enemy lands and destruction of industrial and populous centres on a vast scale may become the principal operations of war, to which the older forms of military and naval operations may become secondary and subordinate.*

The magnitude and significance of the transformation now in progress are not easily recognized. It requires some imagination to realise that next summer, while our Western Front may still be moving forward at a snail's pace in Belgium and France, the air battle front will be far behind on the Rhine, and that its continuous and intense pressure against the chief industrial centers of the enemy as well as on his lines of communications may form an important factor in bringing about peace'.

Alongside this vision of a new form of warfare to replace the old which had failed so spectacularly and bloodily in the mud of Flanders, Smuts presented the immediate means of reorganizing the British air service. First was the establishment of an Air Ministry 'to control and administer all matters in connection with aerial warfare of all kinds whatsoever'. Second, the creation of a single, separate air service by the merging of the RNAS and the RFC.

Smuts was not alone in his advocacy of a bombing campaign to be launched against Germany in 1918 but his arguments, and those of his supporters, were based on a crucially false premise. Sir William Weir, Director-General of Aircraft Production, had assured the Cabinet that increased production for 1918 would leave a 'surplus' of 3000 aircraft available for a bombing offensive. Neither Trenchard nor Haig had any faith in Weir's optimistic forecasts. Both of them were keenly aware that the original RFC expansion target of 1916 was still far from being met and both of them knew, as the Cabinet seemingly did not, that there was an inevitable lag between increased production levels and the appearance of trained crews ready for operations.

The Gothas by Night

The Germans had considered the possibility of night bombing as early as February 1917 when in a study entitled *Air Attacks on England*, Oberleutnant Weese proposed the introduction of 'rolling day and night raids'. Weather permitting, a campaign would be waged in which morning and afternoon attacks, each made by a Geschwader of 45 aircraft, were to be followed by a night raid flown by a Geschwader 30 strong. The aim was to 'break the will' of the British people. In his paper Weese had urged the formation of a bombing force of at least 120 aircraft, forecasting that 'the possibility of attacking London by day can be calculated to last two months, three at most, by which time the effectiveness of the defenses will force a change to attack by night'.

Weese had been remarkably prescient. The daylight offensive had lasted just three days under three months. Steadily increasing losses had obliged Kleine to turn to night attacks, a temporary expedient which became permanent when the new Gotha V, delivered in August, failed to achieve a performance significantly superior to that of the GIV. Nevertheless aircrew valued the GV because its fuel tanks were located in the fuselage, instead of under the engines, which greatly reduced the risk of fire in crashes and forced landings.

Operating by night conferred a number of advantages. The difficulties of navigation were offset by the fact that Kagohl 3 no longer needed to maintain the pretence that it was bombing targets of 'military importance'. London itself had become the target, which simplified matters considerably. Moreover, the British air defenses, having mastered the Zeppelin and the daylight Gothas, were forced to return to square one. Although many pilots had gained considerable night flying experience against Strasser's airships, they were now presented with a more elusive quarry: harpooning the Naval Airship Division's 'whales' had turned into swatting at Kagohl 3's 'mosquitos'.

Kagohl 4 opened the night offensive when one of its single-engined aircraft made a probing low-level attack on Dover on the night of September 2/3. On the following night Kleine led five Gothas of Kagohl 3 in a raid on Chatham. Four aircraft bombed the town, and two of their 110-pound bombs caused direct hits on a drill hall which was being used as a temporary dormitory, killing 130 naval recruits and injuring 88. Home defense units made no interceptions but the night's most significant events were the sorties flown by three Sopwith Camels of No. 44 Squadron, commanded by the 22-year-old Captain Gilbert Ware Murlis-Green, a veteran of the Macedonian front, where he had flown against Gotha GIIs and GIIIs. These sorties demonstrated that the Camels – which were notoriously difficult to handle – could be flown safely at night, hammering the first nail in the coffin of the firmly held belief that night-fighter operations could best be flown by low-performance, inherently stable types like the BE2c.

On September 4/5, Kleine turned his attentions to London. Starting at 2030 hrs, 11 Gothas took off at five-minute intervals. Signal flares were fired from behind the German lines to guide the bombers across Belgium. Two Gothas turned back with engine trouble and the remainder, now widely scattered, crossed the English coast at varying points on the southeast coast from Orfordness to Dover between 2220 hrs and 0010 hrs. Five Gothas penetrated to London and the first bombs fell at 2320 hrs, one of them exploding near Cleopatra's Needle on the Thames Embankment, rupturing a gas main and fatally injuring two passengers in a passing tram. One Gotha was shot down by anti-aircraft fire, crashing into the sea off Eastchurch.

Following the raid Major-General Ashmore was bombarded with all kinds of advice on the best way to deal with the raiders. One of the more grandiose schemes involved the floodlighting of most of southeast England with nearly 2000 searchlights. As Ashmore dryly observed, 'It would have been cheaper to move London'. A more practical measure, already well in hand, was the erection of a balloon barrage on the northern and eastern outskirts of London in a series of 'aprons', comprising three Caquot-type balloons flying at 500-yard intervals and linked with cables from which 1000 ft-long steel wires hung vertically every 25 yards. The balloons' operating height was 7500 ft, later increased to 9500 ft. The first of the 20 planned aprons became operational in October, but only ten were in place by the summer of 1918. While the aprons went up, Ashmore began work on an elaborate system of anti-aircraft fire to bring down the raiders. The London Metropolitan Area was divided into numbered squares. The unseen raiders were plotted by sound and 'curtains' of fire were aimed in their path as they crossed from square to square. The curtains were given charming names – 'Woodpecker', 'Ace of Spades', 'Cosy Corner' – belying their purpose. By the end of October, London's defenses consisted of some 90 such curtains.

On September 24 Kleine pushed the night raids into a higher gear. What later became known as the 'Harvest Moon Offensive' opened with a two-pronged attack in which 16 Gothas flew against London and 11 Zeppelins took off to raid the Midlands and the northeast. Thereafter there were five more raids on London, the last being flown on the night of October 1/2, when 12 out of 18 aircraft succeeded in dropping their bombs somewhere on the British mainland. At the end of the week-long bombardment British casualties numbered 114 killed – several of them by shrapnel from anti-aircraft guns – and 334 wounded. On the night of September 30 over 14 000 shells were fired in the barrage over London without scoring any hits. Equally disturbing was a report submitted by the Royal Arsenal, Woolwich, stating that on September 25, after the first raid, only one third of the night shift in the filling factory turned up for work, causing an 80 per cent drop in output. When the Gothas arrived over London on the night of September 30 nearly 300 000 people took refuge in the underground railway system, throwing it into complete chaos. Thousands more trekked out into the surrounding countryside, a pattern repeated in World War II.

Three days after the last of the 'Harvest Moon' raids the Kaiser awarded Kleine the Iron Cross. The decoration had been acquired at a heavy price. Between September 24 and October 1, 92 Gothas had been despatched, of which 55 had crossed the English coast. Fewer than 20 had reached London to deliver their bombs. Thirteen aircraft had been lost, the equivalent of two Staffeln, or one-third of Kleine's squadron.

The R-Types

On the night of September 28/29, the 25 Gothas which took off to bomb London were accompanied by two of the giant multi-engined R-types. These were among the most remarkable military aircraft ever to fly operationally.

Directly influenced by Igor Sikorsky's development of the IM series in 1913–14, Count Ferdinand von Zeppelin had embarked on a similar programme to produce a long-range bomber or *Riesenflugzeug* ('giant airplane' – the R-type classification was not officially authorized until November 1915). Designed in the winter of 1914 by B G Klein and H Hirth at the Versuschbau GmbH Gotha-Ost (Experimental Works, Gotha-East), the three-engined prototype, VG01, made its first flight on April 11, 1915. The Siemens Schuckert Werke AG was also pursuing a similar line with its RI. The SSW RI was powered by three 150 hp Benz BIII engines and had a wingspan of 92 ft.

From the outset these aircraft were designed to fulfil a requirement which placed them in a class of their own, and which in turn determined their size and configuration. The crucial specification was that the engines had to be fully accessible, serviceable and – like those of the Zeppelin – capable of being repaired in flight. It was beyond the capacity of contemporary aircraft engines to carry the huge bombloads and quantities of fuel over the range envisaged for the R-types without constant servicing and maintenance. Therefore large engine rooms or nacelles were designed into the R-type concept, spacious enough to house the air mechanics who would tend the giant aircraft's engines.

The development of the R-types remained in a constant state of flux throughout the war, and even in 1918 there was no agreement on the ultimate configuration. From the beginning the principal differences of opinion were over the rival claims of centralized and decentralized engines. Decentrally powered R-types were distinguished by engines mounted in port and starboard nacelles, with in some cases an additional one or two engines installed in the nose. In the centrally powered R-types the

engines were located in the fuselage, coupled to one or more common gear boxes and driving from one to four propellers through a system of clutches, transmission shafts and gears.

In the early days of the R-type the decentralized configuration raised doubts about the aircraft's ability to withstand the problems of assymetric flight in the event of the failure of one or more of the engines. In practice the failure of all the engines in one nacelle did not endanger the aircraft. By careful control setting and throttling back of the opposing engines, an experienced pilot could maintain straight and level flight. Moreover, in the decentralized R-type the aircraft could be maneuvered by throttling back the port or starboard engines, a procedure considered to be extremely useful in gusty weather. With a more favorable distribution of engines, fuel and bombload, lighter, simpler and more robust engine bearings, and increased useful load, the decentralized aircraft became the mainstays of the R-type squadrons on the Western front. Nevertheless, internally engined R-types continued to be built right up to the end of the war. Still uncompleted in November 1918 was the SSW RVIII 23/16, the largest aircraft built by any nation during World War I. Powered by six 300 hp Basse und Selve BuSIVa engines it had a wingspan of 157 ft 6 in – 55 ft greater than that of the World War II Lancaster.

The Eastern Front

In October 1915, SSW RI was attached to Feldfliegerabteilung 31 at Slonim on the Eastern front. Plagued by technical problems, it never flew any bombing missions and by the spring of 1916 had been dismantled for shipment back to Berlin. Feldfliegerabteilung 31 had originally provided a Sonderkommando (special unit) to take delivery of SSW RI in Berlin and, under the command of Oberleutnant Krupp, this eventually became Rfa (Reisenflugabteilung) 501. Also serving on the Eastern front was Rfa 500, which had taken delivery of VGOII and III, the last powered by six 160 hp Mercedes in-line engines, four of which were installed in tandem in two nacelles, each driving a propeller, and the remaining two in the nose of the fuselage. In company with RMLI (the rebuilt VGOI), the German Navy's land-based R-type, VGOIII undertook the unit's first

The Staaken RVI formed the backbone of the German R-plane force in the West. This is *R.29*, powered by four 245 hp Maybach MbIVa engines mounted in the front and rear of the two nacelles and each independently driving a single propeller through a reduction gear box and short transmission shaft. A small cockpit for the engineer was situated between the engines. The RVI had provision for nose, dorsal, ventral and upper wing machine-gun positions. The bombload was carried internally in the central section of the fuselage underneath the fuel tanks. Bomb racks for 18 220-pound bombs in three rows of six each were provided, but the 660-pound and 2200-pound bombs had to be carried semi-externally. Over short ranges a bombload of 4500 pounds could be lifted; endurance could be stretched to ten hours by the installation of extra fuel tanks. On May 9, 1918 *R.29* was wrecked while landing in fog at Scheldewindeke.

successful raid, bombing a rail junction in Estonia on August 13, 1916.

Both squadrons experienced teething troubles, particularly with the Maybach Hs engines. When Krupp visited the Maybach works at Friedrich-shafen to supervise testing, he was treated to a demonstration of the power plants purring along serenely at cruising speed on their stands, much as they would on an airship. When he asked the engineers to raise the Maybachs to full throttle, to simulate the R-type's take-off, they burned out within a few minutes.

At the front, the Maybachs required a considerable degree of pampering. The R-types were drawn out of their hangars on special tracks, or by teams of oxen, to save the engines from being used for taxying. In the air considerable physical demands were made of the pilots. Two complete turns of the steering wheel were needed to operate VGOII's ailerons. In summer pilots frequently discarded their flying coats and helmets, sitting at the controls in jackets and open-neck shirts and, according to Rfa 500's technical officer Richard Lühr, 'sweating like bulls'.

Although the early R-types were barely able to cope with the demands of combat service, the experience gained on the Eastern Front later proved invaluable in the West. Crews were able to come to grips with the problems of night flying, navigation and target location, and in the process instrumentation and wireless equipment were developed and adapted to the long-range bombing role.

In July 1917 Rfa 501, commanded by Hauptmann Richard Bentivegni, was transferred to Berlin to train on the new Staaken RVI bombers. The RVI formed the backbone of the R-type squadron in the West, and 18 of these machines were built, the longest production run. Approximately twice the size of the Gotha GV, the RVI's loaded weight was 25 269 pounds, almost the same as that of a fully loaded Heinkel He111H of World War II. Wingspan was 138 ft 5 in, nearly twice that of the Heinkel. The RVI's engines, mounted in the front and rear of each nacelle and independently driving a single propeller, were either four 260 hp DIVa Mercedes or four 245 hp 'overcompressed' MbIVa power plants from Maybach. The flight mechanic sat in a small cockpit between the engines. Maximum range with 700 gallons of fuel and a bombload of 1653 pounds was 900 km. Up to 18 220-pound bombs could be carried internally in the centre section of the fuselage, but the RVI's 660-pound and 2200-pound bombs had to be carried semi-externally. The standard bombload was approximately 2600 pounds, and twice this weight could be lifted over short distances. There was provision for nose, dorsal, ventral and – on at least two of the RVIs – upper-wing machine-gun positions; three guns were usually carried on operations. Each RVI flew with a crew of seven: a commander/navigator and two pilots, a wireless operator, two flight mechanics and fuel attendant. The commander directed the bomb run from the observation post in the nose. In common with the Gothas, the R-types were prone to landing accidents, particularly in conditions of reduced visibility. However, their low landing speed lessened impact and generally allowed the crew to escape the almost inevitable fire.

In August 1917 Rfa 501 was transferred from Berlin to Belgium. On September 25 an RFC reconnaissance aircraft photographed one of the R-types parked on the airfield at St Denis Westrem. Curiously, British intelligence made nothing of this, and as a result the appearance of the R-types caused considerable confusion in the air defense. At a distance of 20 miles, listening posts frequently took the throbbing engines of a single R-type to be a formation of Gothas droning overhead. Their wireless signals were mistaken for those of Zeppelins seeking radio bearings. Night fighter pilots, who were by now developing special skills for intercepting Gothas, repeatedly failed correctly to estimate the distance between their aircraft and the R-types, as the British Neame sights were calibrated to accommodate the smaller wingspan of the Gothas. An R-type filled the sights at twice the distance, encouraging the pilots to fire at too great a range to inflict any damage. It was not until December 18, after the eighth R-type sortie, that the home defense forces were informed that giant aircraft were flying against London.

The Incendiaries

In 1915 nearly 70 per cent of the bombs dropped by the Zeppelins in four separate raids were incendiaries. Serious fires had resulted from only one attack, on September 8, but in the autumn of 1917 a new 10-pound incendiary bomb was developed with the aim of delivering hundreds of these projectiles from the comparatively few Gothas at Kagohl 3's disposal. It was anticipated that on a night of strong wind the fires started by the bombs would merge and spread unchecked through the older, more vulnerable parts of the City of London.

At the beginning of the war Grand Admiral Tirpitz had addressed himself succinctly to the morality of such a bombardment: 'I am not in favor of "frightfulness" ... Single bombs from flying machines are wrong: they are odious when they hit and kill an old woman ... If one could set fire to London in 30 places, then what is odious would retire before something fine and powerful. All that flies and creeps should be concentrated on that city'.

On the night of October 31/November 1, 22 Gothas took off for London carrying a total bombload of over six tons, of which half comprised the new incendiary bombs. Only ten Gothas reached London, bombing its eastern perimeter, but most of the incendiaries refused to ignite. All the Gothas left London unscathed but five crashed on landing. In London the authorities were still experimenting with all manner of air raid warning systems, and on this occasion the 'All Clear' was given by several hundred Boy Scouts on bicycles.

At Kagohl 3's headquarters the inconclusive results of the raid prompted a searching analysis of training and operational procedure. Closer attention was now paid to weather forecasts, and at the beginning of December Kagohl 3 initiated a meteorological flight of single-engined Rumpler CIVs, equipped with R/T, which observed and reported on weather conditions off the English coast before a decision was made to launch a raid. At about this time Kagohl 3 also acquired a new name, Bombengeschwader OHL3 (Bogohl 3).

On December 5 Leutnant Georgii informed Kleine

Classification of the R-types, many of which were one-offs, is somewhat confusing. The functional letter classification was preceded by the manufacturer's name and followed by a Roman numeral to indicate the model (or design) number of the aircraft – ie Staaken RIV. In addition the Army aircraft were assigned a military serial number followed by two digits representing the year in which the aircraft was ordered – eg AEG R1 21/16. Because relatively few R-types were built during the war, it was customary to refer to individual machines by their functional letter and serial number – ie R21, R55. The serial numbers ran consecutively from R1/15 to R86/18.

that conditions were perfect for a second incendiary raid. In clear moonlit skies the first probing attacks were made by an R-type and two Gothas, which dropped about 3000 pounds of bombs (two-thirds of them incendiaries) on Sheerness. Two hours later RVI R.39 and three Gothas flew in over the north coast of Kent to bomb the Whitstable-Margate-Dover area. The main attack developed between 0430 and 0540 hrs when six Gothas dropped over 5000 pounds of incendiaries on London, starting a number of blazes which were rapidly brought under control by the fire-fighting services. Only eight civilians died in this raid, but the material damage was estimated at £93 000.

There were to be no more attempts to mount large-scale incendiary raids. In the summer of 1918 the Germans developed the Elektron bomb, consisting almost entirely of pure magnesium, which burnt at a heat of between 2000 and 3000 degrees Fahrenheit. Thousands of these bombs were readied for a series of devastating fire raids, but they were never used. On August 8 over 400 British tanks broke the German front on the Somme, and with that OHL realised that the war was lost. Fire raids on London would not only have invited severe reprisals but would also have compromised the armistice negotiations which were now seen as inevitable. Permission to use the new bombs over London was refused. At the Ghent airfield the message canceling the first Elektron raid was received less than an hour before Bogohl 3's Gothas were due to take off.

The End of the Gothas

On December 12, 1917 Hauptmann Kleine was shot down and killed by Captain Wendel L W Rogers of No. 1 Squadron, RFC, while flying on a tactical mission near Ypres. Rogers had become the first Allied pilot to shoot down a Gotha in France.

Kleine was succeeded temporarily by the senior flight commander, Oberleutnant Richard Walter, an experienced and more cautious airman whose first raid was launched on the dark night of December 18. Thirteen of the 15 Gothas despatched reached the English coast, six of them penetrating to London and bombing between 1910 and 2035 hrs. They were followed by the six-engined R.12, which dropped two 660-pound bombs and a small quantity of incendiaries. A total of 11 300 pounds of bombs were dropped, causing the worst damage to property since the Zeppelin raid of September 8/9, 1915. The biggest fires could be seen over 50 miles away.

Captain Murlis Green, flying a Sopwith Camel armed with two upward-angled Lewis guns mounted on the top wing, was patrolling at a height of 11 000 ft when at 1915 hrs he spotted the exhaust flames of a Gotha piloted by Leutnant Friedrich Ketelsen. The fighter pilot made four attacks, despite a frozen gun, and the distraction of gun flash and searchlights. Murlis Green hit the Gotha's starboard engine and Ketelsen ditched in the sea off Folkestone. Two crewmen were rescued, but the unfortunate Ketelsen drowned. Murlis Green was the first pilot to destroy a Gotha at night over England.

Fog prevented any major operations until an abortive raid, on January 25, by three R-types, all of which were forced to turn back. Three days later 13 Gothas and two R-types tried again. The first

aircraft took off in perfect conditions, but a sudden build-up of fog grounded several of the later machines and forced another six to return to base. Of the two R-types, R. 35 was forced back with engine trouble after jettisoning its bombs in the sea off Ostend. Its companion, R. 12, fared better, forcing down a Bristol Fighter of No. 39 Squadron on its inward journey across Essex and dropping over 2000 pounds of bombs over central London before returning safely to base. One 660-pound bomb fell on the Odhams Print Works in Long Acre, killing 38 and injuring 85 in the worst single bombing incident in the war. Only three Gothas reached the capital, the remainder attacking Ramsgate, Margate, Sheerness and the area around Sandwich. One Gotha, GV/938/16, was shot down in flames on its return journey by two Sopwith Camels of No. 44 Squadron, flown by Captain G H Hackwill and Second Lieutenant C C Banks, whose aircraft was armed with two forward-firing Vickers machine-guns and, unconventionally, an upward-firing Lewis gun armed with RTS explosive bullets. When the gallant Brandenburg returned to reassume command in February, he found a depleted and demoralized unit.

On January 29 four R-types of Rfa 501 launched the squadron's first independent raid on London. R. 12 turned back over the Channel with engine trouble, bombing fortifications around Gravelines on its return journey. R.26 penetrated no further inland than Rayleigh in Essex, where failing power in two of its engines forced its commander to release his bombs and head back to Belgium. R. 39 had a more eventful trip. On its inward journey it came under attack from a BE12b of No. 37 Squadron and then, having scattered its bombs between Acton and Richmond, it was intercepted by a Sopwith Camel flown by Second Lieutenant R N Hall of No. 44 Squadron. Diving away to escape Hall's attentions, and mistakenly identified by the anti-aircraft batteries below as a formation of Gothas, R. 39 successively encountered Captain F C Luxmore of No. 78 Squadron, flying a Camel, and Captain Hackwill of No. 44 Squadron before clearing the coast at Hythe on its outward journey.

R. 25, which had crossed the coast near Foulness at 2250 hrs, had an equally stimulating and potentially more hazardous series of encounters with British aircraft. Between 2315 hrs and midnight the R-type came under attack from five fighters, the last of them flown by the redoutable Murlis Green. Pressing home the attacks at close range and firing about 800 rounds at the giant bomber, the home defense pilots succeeded in putting one of R. 25's port engines out of action. Lumbering on at reduced height and speed R. 25 finally dropped its bombs on open ground at Wanstead from a height of 6000 ft. When it landed it was found to have been hit 88 times. The R-type's survival was a tribute to the coolness of its crew and the robustness of its design. However, the German report on the raid advised that, in future, raids on the British capital should be restricted to nights when there was little or no moon.

The R-type's durability was again demonstrated on the night of February 16/17 when R. 12 blundered into the balloon apron at Woolwich. It was an indifferent climber and, crossing the coast at 8200 ft, had managed to gain only another 1300 ft on the approach to London. This was insufficient to clear the apron, which *R. 12* struck with its starboard wing at 2215 hrs. In his report *R. 12's* commander, Oberleutnant Hans-Joachim von Seydlitz-Gerstenberg wrote: '*T*HE AIRCRAFT WAS FIRST *pulled to starboard, then port and finally slipped out of control to the port side. The first pilot, Leutnant Gotte, immediately throttled down all engines, then opened up the throttles on only one side, whereby the aircraft regained equilibrium once again, after having fallen 300 m. The impact of the balloon apron was so severe that the starboard mechanic fell against the glowing exhaust stacks, which severely burnt his hands, and the port aileron control cables sprang from their roller guides. The aircraft itself remained intact with the exception of minor damage to the leading edge of the starboard wing, propeller and mid-fuselage section*'.

Having survived this mid-air collision with minimal damage, *R. 12* flew on to bomb the Beckenham area southeast of London before returning to base. On the same raid *R. 39* dropped the first 1000 kg (2204-pound) bomb on England, aiming east of the City and hitting the Royal Hospital Chelsea. Meanwhile, *R. 33* limped back from the south coast with its port engines stopped by interrupted oil circulation and the rear starboard power plant reduced to half power. A machine-gun and sundry items of loose equipment were thrown overboard in an attempt to maintain altitude, but *R. 33* drifted down to 6500 ft before a mechanic restored power to the rear port power plant by holing a tank with a pocket knife and using his cupped hands to transfer oil to the engine.

On March 7 Rfa 501 transferred from the airfield at Gontrode to Scheldewindeke, which had been provided with a specially constructed concrete apron for the giant aircraft, the first of its kind. That night the R-types put in their biggest effort against London, despatching six aircraft. Only three bombed the capital, and on its return journey *R. 27* came down in No-Man's-Land. It crashed sufficiently near the German lines for its engines and instruments to be salvaged by infantry units before it was destroyed by British artillery fire.

On March 21, under cover of heavy fog, General Ludendorff launched the last great German offensive of the war on the Somme. Throughout April the Englandgeschwader flew tactical missions on the Western Front, supporting the drive to capture the Channel ports. On May 9 four of Rfa 501's R-types took off to bomb Dover before heavy weather closed in, grounding the Gothas which were to follow them. First, they were radioed to change course and bomb alternative targets on the French coast. Then, with the weather deteriorating fast, they were recalled. *R. 32* was the first to attempt to land at the fog-bound field at Scheldewindeke, guided in by searchlights. After a number of abortive passes over the field, it overshot, plunged straight into the ground and blew up in a sheet of flame as its unreleased bombs exploded. *R. 39* touched down safely, but *R. 26* and *R. 29* chose to ignore frantic orders to put down at Ghistelles – where conditions were improving – and attempted blind landings. *R. 26* flew straight into the ground, killing all its crew with the exception of a mechanic; *R. 29* crashed into the treetops on the edge of the airfield. The fuel tanks burst but the aircraft

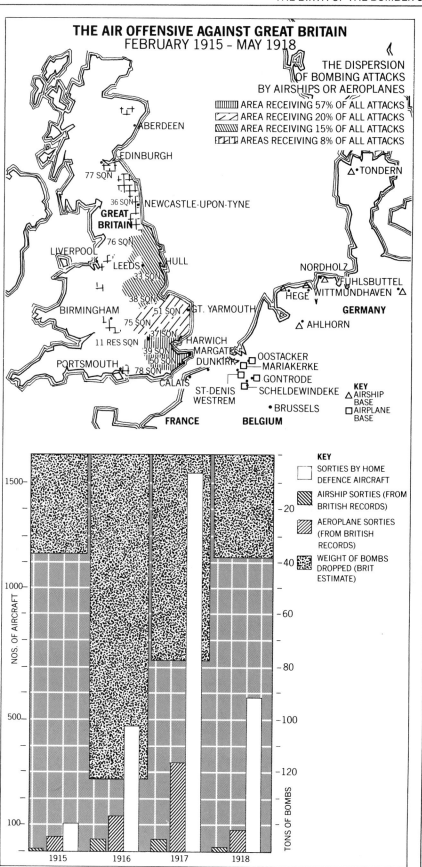

did not catch fire, thanks to the quick-witted pilot who immediately shut off the engine ignition and motor-dynamo.

Ten days later, on the night of May 19/20, Brandenburg assembled a force of 38 Gothas and two single-engined weather reconnaissance aircraft for Bogohl 3's last maximum effort against London. After the disaster of May 9 Rfa could only muster three R-types, R. 13, R. 12 and R. 39, the last carrying a 2200-pound bomb. Eighteen Gothas and one R-type reached London, the attack continuing from 2330 to 0030 hrs. Three Gothas were shot down and a fourth crash-landed.

Brandenburg planned more raids on London, but his strategic offensive had run its course. When on May 27 the Germans threw in a big attack on the Aisne, Bogohl 3, Rfa 501 and Rfa 500 (which had been transferred to France in February 1918) were committed to tactical operations on the Western Front. It was a task for which the R-types had never been designed. The enormous amount of work necessary to prepare one of these giant aircraft for flight (each one required a minimum groundcrew of 40) meant that only one sortie could be flown in a night. Significantly, only once had the all six of Rfa 501's R-types gone into action together in the campaign against London. In eight months only 11 raids had been flown by a total of 30 machines. But 28 of them had dropped their bombs on the British mainland and Rfa 501 had suffered no personnel or aircraft losses to enemy action. On these operations the R-types had proved themselves reliable machines and steady gun platforms with which the British night fighters had found it extremely difficult to come to grips. Flying at short range over the maelstrom of the Western Front they were far more vulnerable.

On the night of June 1/2 R. 37 was brought down by anti-aircraft fire near Betz after a raid on Paris, the first of the R-types to be lost in action. On August 10/11 R. 43, a five-engined RXIV prototype delivered in April 1918, took off to attack Doullens, a target only 40 miles behind the front line. R. 43's armament of six machine-guns – one on each of the upper wings and two each in dorsal and ventral positions – reflected the greater intensity of night fighter activity on the Western Front, but they were no defense against the Sopwith Camel of Captain A B Yuille of No. 151 Squadron. Yuille closed to within 25 yards, settling well below and behind the bomber's tail. His first three bursts put one of R. 43's engines out of action. Two more and the fuselage was ablaze around the rear gunner's cockpit. R. 43 slipped sideways and then fell in flames.

On the following night the new R. 52 crashed near Villers le Tour, killing Hauptmann Schilling, commander of Rfa 500, and four members of the crew. This was the only instance when an R-type crashed because of uncontrollable flight maneuvers. Battle damage probably caused the loss of R. 31 and R. 34 before the Armistice.

In October the Englandgeschwader fell back to Evre, near Brussels, dumping their unused Elektron incendiaries in the River Scheld. Within 48 hours of the signing of the Armistice on November 11, the remaining Gothas were handed over to a commission of British officers. 'Outwardly they looked perfect', Leutnant Aschoff recalled, 'but our mechanics would never have allowed us to fly those machines'. Of the remaining R-types, R. 30 was hired by an American showman and, with the legend 'Fletcher's World' painted on its fuselage, flew passengers on joy-rides from an airstrip near Berlin. R. 37, R. 69 and R. 70 found employment in the postwar Russo-Polish conflict, ferrying huge quantities of currency printed in Berlin to the Ukrainian government. R. 70 made the first flight in June 1919, landing at a specially prepared strip at Kamenets-Podolsky. Shortly afterwards it was confiscated by the Romanians after making a forced landing in Bessarabia. R. 69 also suffered the indignity of confiscation when, after completing a successful delivery, it landed outside Vienna. It was carrying 22 passengers, including 15 members of a Ukranian delegation, two repatriated prisoners of war and a couple of Russian honeymooners. R. 39, veteran of 20 missions, was shot down by Polish border troops near Ratibor on August 4, 1919.

Conclusion

In all, 60 Gothas were lost during operations flown against the British mainland. Twenty-four were shot down or disappeared over the sea. The remaining 36 were written off in landing or approach crashes. Bogohl 3 lost 137 aircrew dead and 88 reported missing*. No R-types were lost to enemy action over England and their crews achieved an impressive 93 per cent of missions completed. With a maximum speed of around 80 mph, the R-types were much slower than the Gothas, but their extra engines made them far more reliable and more difficult to shoot down. As Captain Yuille demonstrated, it was necessary to close to almost point-blank range to be sure of a kill. On occasion the R-types' dawdling pace was a positive advantage; its slow progress and the noise it generated confusing spotters and listening posts below. As a result they were able to exercise a quite disproportionate strategic effect on the British home defenses. On the night of February 17/18, 1918 a single machine, R. 25, reached London, hitting St Pancras railway station with a stick of eight 110-pound bombs. This lone aircraft caused 69 defense sorties to be flown and several thousand rounds of anti-aircraft ammunition to be vainly expended. In some areas panicky gunners up to 20 miles from R. 25's flight path were firing blindly into the sky.

If obsolescent types are disregarded, there were 145 Sopwith Camels and 55 Bristol Fighters flying on home defense duties over England by the end of the war, a sizeable force but arguably not large enough seriously to weaken British air strength on the Western Front. Nevertheless, the psychological effects of the German raids were to linger long after 1918. In *Europe in Arms* (1937) Basil Liddell Hart wrote: 'To anyone who analyses the comparatively slight material results of the air raids in 1914–18, it is remarkable to find what a profound psychological impression they made, and have left ... The effects have not disappeared with the cessation of the cause; they are traceable in the general tendency among the public, whenever they think of war, for the thought to be associated immediately with the idea of being bombed from the air. And from this apprehension springs a natural exaggeration'.

*Including losses on the Western Front.

1.6 AN INDEPENDENT FORCE

KAGOHL 3's ATTACKS ON LONDON IN THE summer of 1917 finally propelled the British War Cabinet into the arms of the strategic bombing enthusiasts. Among the most vociferous was C G Grey, who in an open letter to the Air Board argued, 'Behind Germany's army lies the sources from which it is fed. The iron mines, the steel works, the armament factories ... Instead of bowing to popular clamor for reprisals – mere retaliatory raids in revenge after every enemy attack – let us take the invasion of Germany from the air as a serious problem of war.'

The Air Board was already in the grip of advanced bomber mania and by early September 1917 orders, had been placed for over 2700 DH4 day bombers and 300 Handley Page night bombers. At the end of the month the Air Board noted that it could use 'every bombing machine we could get', predicting a monthly production rate of 300 of the new DH9s by the end of January 1918 and 200 Handley Page 0/400s by the following June. Touring bomb-damaged streets in London, Lloyd George promised the far from friendly crowds who gathered round him that, 'We shall bomb Germany with compound interest'.

On September 5 the War Cabinet agreed that 'we must carry the aerial war into Germany, not merely on the ground of reprisal'. Having received assurances from Sir William Weir, Director-General of Aircraft Production, that the necessary aircraft and personnel would be available for the task, it summoned Trenchard to England on October 1. Trenchard flew in the following day, suffering the mild indignity of being fired on by anti-aircraft batteries, which mistook his two-seater for a German raider.

Trenchard returned to France with orders for Haig, directing the C-in-C to detach a day and night bombing squadron from 9 (HQ) Wing and as soon as possible, 'to undertake a continuous offensive by air, against such suitable objectives in Germany as can be reached by our aeroplanes'. Amid these rapid developments a note of caution was sounded by one of the earliest advocates of strategic bombing, Minister of Munitions Winston Churchill. Warning that by itself an air offensive could not bring victory, he noted: 'nothing that we have learned of the capacity of the German population to endure suffering justifies us in assuming that they could be cowed into submission by such methods or, indeed, that they would not be rendered more desperately resolved by them'.

At the meeting of October 2, Trenchard had told the War Cabinet that the airfield at Ochey, earmarked for the bombing offensive, would be operational within six days. Later that day he was somewhat more frank with a journalist friend, confiding that 'the long-range bombing squadrons are not ready yet and will not be till winter'. He had a point. In the newly formed 41 Wing, under the command of Lieutenant-Colonel C L N Newall, there were three squadrons – No. 55 (DH4s) for day bombing; and No. 100 (FE2bs) and No. 16 Naval Squadron (originally designated 'Naval A' and flying Handley Pages) for night bombing. The principal theme which runs through the history of the subsequent bombing offensive is the gulf between the aims of the Air Staff in London – nursing dreams of victory through air power – and the limitations of the force which was deployed in France to seek this end. At the turn of the year planning was proceeding on the assumption that the number of available bomber squadrons would rise to 25 by the end of May 1918 and to 40 by the following July. In June 1918, when Major-General Trenchard took command of the newly formed Independent Force, he had only five squadrons at his disposal, a figure which would rise to nine by the end of the war.

The DH4 Response

On October 17, 41st Wing launched its first raid, on the large steelworks at Saarbrucken-Burbach. Eleven DH4s of No. 55 Squadron took off, eight of them bombing the target and, according to German records, causing 17 500 marks worth of damage, killing four people and injuring nine. Four days later No. 55 Squadron despatched 12 DH4s to raid the factories and railyards at Bous, lying on the Moselle north of Hagendingen about 60 miles from Ochey. Only one aircraft turned back with engine trouble, and the remainder pressed on to bomb the target. Flying away from the railyards, the DH4s were bounced by a formation of ten German Albatros DIs. In the ensuing meleé the squadron claimed four DIs shot down for the loss of one DH4, piloted by Captain Daniel Owen, who although badly wounded in the left eye, managed to fly his aircraft down to land behind the German lines.

The raid of October 21 provides an early example of the rugged qualities of the DH4, an outstanding two-seater day bomber and a classic military aircraft. Defensive armament was provided by a Constantinesco-synchronized .303 Vickers machine-gun mounted on the decking to the port of the pilot; and by one or two Lewis guns mounted on a Scarff ring in the observer's cockpit. Combat experience demonstrated that the twin Lewis arrangement had a considerable psychological effect on enemy pilots, who seldom pressed home an attack if they saw two guns in the observer's cockpit.

The DH4's pilot sat several feet ahead of the observer, rather unsatisfactory communication being by means of a pair of string 'reins' and, in some cases, a voice tube. Set in the floor immediately behind the rudder bar was the Negative Lens Sight, consisting of a square plane-concave glass plate through which four sighting wires were visible. The sight was usually calibrated for use at 15 000 ft at 70 mph, 10 000 ft at 80 mph and 6000 ft at 90 mph and could be employed for both up and down wind attacks. However, it was not a precision instrument, as Lieutenant Farrington of No. 55 Squadron recalled: 'I personally used the lens of the bombsight fitted in the floor of the machine merely as a glass to look through to ensure that I was flying perpendicularly over the target. There is a tendency when looking over the side of the machine to tilt it unconsciously, thus appearing vertically over the target when one is not'.

Flying the DH4 in winter and at altitude imposed great physical demands on both pilot and observer.

To combat the cold aircrew cocooned themselves in layers of silk, wool and leather, so that they resembled large brown grubs squeezed into their cockpits. Some of them resorted to the 'winter warmer', a tobacco tin stuffed with smouldering rags, frequently suffering blistered thighs in the process. Some aircrew experimented with electrical flying kit in which a wire-strung vest was connected, through the gloves, to a power-plant. When their DH4 went into a dive, the system overheated and burnt fingers were a common complaint. Lengthy spells at heights over 15 000 ft frequently led to nose and ear infections, while exposure to fuel and exhaust fumes affected the chest and stomach. Oxygen could be gulped up a tube and inhaled through a fur-trimmed mask, but the flow was erratic and the mask irritating to faces chapped raw by the howling slipstream.

Formation Flying

DH4 missions were invariably unescorted, relying on close formation flying and mutual supporting fire for effective defense. No. 55 Squadron was a crack DH4 unit and it is worth examining its methods in some detail. The squadron specialized in long-distance raids, carrying fuel for five hours which, with a wind of not more than 15 mph, placed targets 120 miles from the British trenches within range. Normally a mission was flown by 12 machines, divided into two formations of six. After warming up their engines, a flight could be airborne in about 30 seconds, the flight leader of No. 1 Flight climbing on full power to 700 ft, then throttling back to allow the others to formate. His observer checked that all the aircraft were in position and fired the first Very light, which gave the signal to 'leave rendezvous'*.

On a long-distance raid one hour's flight time was allowed behind the British lines to gain a height of 15 000 ft. With the course set, the leader adjusted the pace of the formation so that the slowest machine was not quite flying at full throttle, giving his pilots a feeling of confidence that they would not straggle as they had a few revs in hand. Each pilot would then begin the neck-chafing routine of scanning the sky for enemy aircraft, splitting it into sections: port tip to center section, straight ahead; center section to starboard tip, straight ahead; starboard tip, above and curving round to port tip. From time to time the pilot would also go into a gentle weave to give the observer a chance to cover the blind spot astern and below.

Formation flying required a degree of skill and concentration which was frequently beyond the ability of the inexperienced pilots who invariably occupied positions 4 and 6 (see diagram). Their training had not prepared them for the constant adjustment of throttling and trim required to keep station, or for the fatigue induced by flying at altitude with full fuel and bombloads. It was the inexperienced pilots who were most likely to straggle and fall victim to predatory German fighters.

When two formations were flying, No. 2 was subordinate to the first, with the leader of No. 1 Flight assuming the responsibility for the route taken, height flown and approach made to the target. The second formation would fly either to the half right or half left of the lead flight, this being determined by the position of the sun, the quarter from which enemy aircraft almost invariably chose to launch their attacks.

Over the target, No. 2 Flight would fall in behind the first, dropping its bombs in turn and then re-assuming its position as soon as possible. A mile or so from the target No. 1 Flight's leader fired a white Very light and thereafter the pilots would watch for the release of his bombs, usually from a height of 15 000 ft, dropping theirs immediately afterwards. This was often the point of maximum danger and there was scant time for pilots to place their bombs individually while watching for the leader's signals, holding formation, co-operating with their observers and shooting at any enemy aircraft coming at them head-on or flashing across their noses. No. 55 Squadron preferred the upwind approach, which made the ground speed over the target as slow as possible.

After releasing his bombs, the leader executed a deliberate turn, enabling his flight to regain formation. If the sun was on either flank of the formation he would also take care to turn into it, so that enemy aircraft could not attack out of its concealing glare and on to his DH4s' tails. On the return flight the two formations would climb all the way, crossing the lines at 17 000 ft.

The DH4's rival as a day bomber was the superb Breguet Br.14B2. As well as equipping the revived French bombardment units, the B2 was flown by the first day bomber squadron of the American Expeditionary Force, 96th Aero. On July 10, 1918 this

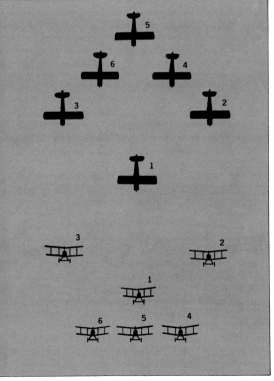

A DH4 formation
The flight leader, carrying a streamer on each wing tip and one on his tail, flew at the head with aircraft Nos. 2 and 3 some 50 ft above him to his half left and right. Aircraft Nos. 4, 5 and 6 flew below the leader, Nos. 4 and 6 to the half right and left of Nos. 2 and 3. No. 5, the deputy leader, flew at the rear of the formation. Nos. 4, 5 and 6 flew as close to 2 and 3 as possible and some 50 ft below the formation leader. This gave the formation the maximum compactness and the observers the maximum concentration of fire in a vertical as opposed to horizontal plane. The leader, with machines above and below him, was afforded considerable protection from enemy fighters.

*Other Very signals were: White (leader) – east or west of the lines this meant 'washout' and the mission was abandoned: east of the lines it could also mean 'hold formation'. Red (any other member of the formation) – 'Attacked, need help'. Red (leader) – 'Rally on me!' Green (any member of the formation) 'Forced to return'.

squadron, led by its commanding officer Harry M Brown, took off to raid Conflans in heavy rain. Under a low cloud ceiling, Brown lost his bearings, came down through the cloud and landed the formation at Coblenz, 90 miles northeast of his objective. Shortly afterwards a Rumpler-borne message was delivered addressed to General W Mitchell, commander of the Air Service of the American First Army: 'We thank you for the fine airplanes and equipment which you have sent us, but what shall we do with the Major?'

41 Wing Operations

On October 24, 1917 it was the turn of 41 Wing's night bombers to make their debut. On a foggy, squally night, nine Handley Pages of 'A' Naval took off to attack the Burbach works, and 16 FE2bs of No. 100 Squadron were despatched against the railyards between Falkenburg and Saarbrucken. 'A' Naval could not find the target and two machines failed to return, but No. 100 Squadron reported several direct hits on the railyards [and one, by a 230-pound bomb, on a train caught in the raid].

Originally designed as a fighter, the FE2b pusher had entered service in 1915. On June 18, 1916, near Annay, Lieutenant McCubbin and Corporal Waller, flying an FE2b of No. 25 Squadron, shot down the great German ace Max Immelmann in his Eindecker. However, by 1917 the FE2b had become obsolescent as a fighter and achieved a new lease of life as a stopgap night bomber, arriving at the front in this new role in March 1917 with No. 100 Squadron whose machines were specially modified with a sim-

plified undercarriage for flying at night. Powered by a Beardmore 160 hp engine, the FE2b could carry a single 230-pound bomb or, more usually, two 112-pound and a number of 25-pound bombs housed in racks under the wings and fuselage. The observer's cockpit contained a single pillar-mounted Lewis gun and, as a more or less standard fitting, a second Lewis gun was located on a telescopic pillar mounting between the cockpits. To man this gun the observer stood on the cupboard which contained spare parts and other miscellaneous equipment, firing back over the upper wing.

The FE2b's pusher layout provided excellent forward visibility but during the winter of 1917–18 conditions for the aircrew, in their exposed cockpits, were particularly severe. Frequently they struggled to find their targets blinded by rain and sleet, or groping through fog banks on instruments, the pilots keeping the aircraft level with a combination of air sense and 'feel'. During its first month of operations 41 Wing dropped over 11 tons of bombs in eight raids. But with the onset of bad weather in November only five more raids were possible before the turn of the year. The Germans made life more difficult by bombing Ochey twice in November and twice in December, damaging 16 of the Wing's aircraft in the attack of December 4/5. Nevertheless, the area around 41 Wing remained a hive of activity. In February it was placed under a new headquarters, VIII Brigade, and Newall promoted to Brigadier-General. At the same time work was proceeding on three new night-bomber and three day-bomber airfields.

The DH4, the first British airplane to be designed specifically for day bombing, was the finest aircraft of its type used by any World War I air force.

DH4

The classic day bomber of World War I. Originally powered by the 250 hp Rolls Royce Eagle VI, later models of the DH4 had the 275 Eagle VII and finally the 375 hp Eagle VIII, the last giving it a top speed of 133 mph at 10 000 ft and a ceiling of 22 000 ft. The basic offensive load, accommodated in racks beneath the lower wings, consisted of two 230-pound bombs or four 112-pound bombs.

Breguet Br14B2

Superb French day bomber, which entered service in 1917. Largely built of the light alloy duralumin and powered by a 300 hp Renault engine, the Br14 could climb to 16 500 ft in 40 minutes, achieve 110 mph at 6500 ft and carry up to 660 pounds of bombs, the standard offensive load being 32 18-pound bombs. Using an experimental 320 hp Renault with a multistage centrifugal blower allowing maximum power up to 18 000 ft, one Br14 attained a speed of 112 mph at 22 000 ft.

Most of the raids undertaken between November and January were flown over short ranges, but on February 18/19 No. 100 Squadron made an effective raid on Trier, a round trip of 200 miles which strained the FE2bs' endurance to the limit. On this raid one of the squadron's aircraft flew so low over the town that the German anti-aircraft guns ceased firing, having been depressed so far that they ran the risk of shooting up Trier rather than shooting down the impudent British raider.

During this period the day bombers were also active, and the raid of February 20 provides an example of the difficulties under which they were flying. Captain J B Fox led ten DH4s of No. 55 Squadron against Mannheim, with Kaiserslautern as an alternative target. Shortly after take-off at 0846 hrs one bomber spun from 5000 to 1000 ft and the shaken crew decided to return to base. In heavy cloud another aircraft lost touch with the formation,

and it too returned. Leading the formation over No-Man's-Land at 14 000 ft, Fox encountered a buffeting headwind which soon placed both of the original targets out of range. Eventually he decided to bomb the cloud-covered town of Pirmasens, whose workshops produced German army boots by the tens of thousands. In his report Fox noted that it had been a 'very quiet journey' with 'no trouble being experienced with either anti-aircraft fire or enemy aircraft'.

The relative quiet was soon shattered when VIII Brigade was thrown into the battle to stem the Ludendorff offensive. Between March 23 and May 16 the Brigade flew more than 200 bombing sorties, the majority of them in tactical support of the ground forces. Railway communications rather than German heavy industry were the principal targets, temporarily reversing the priorities established in October 1917. Another prime target of a purely military nature was the German headquarters at Spa, which No. 55 Squadron attacked unsuccessfully on three occasions.

During the hectic days of the Ludendorff offensive No. 100 Squadron flew one of its most spectacular raids. On March 24/25, 14 FE2bs were despatched against the Metz-Sablon railway triangle. The squadron dropped 69 bombs on or near the objective and, according to the German report, 'Several bombs fell on the main No. 6 Track in the station. Fifteen trucks caught fire and seven munitions wagons amongst them exploded. Tracks Nos. 6 and 16 were very extensively damaged and others also suffered (20 in all). The whole train exploded, blew up and burnt itself out ... the force of the explosion was so great that the building south of the gasometer had its roof blown off and exploding shells damaged the machinery'. All the FE2bs returned safely.

By the end of May the impetus of the Ludendorff offensive was ebbing away, and No. 55 Squadron found itself reassigned to attacking industrial targets. Night raids were still meeting only token resistance, but there was a disturbing acceleration of enemy activity during daylight operations. On May 16, 12 DH4s set out for Saarbrucken, where a series

of dogfights boiled up over the target. One DH4 was shot down in flames, and on their return three more machines were discovered to be so badly damaged that they had to be written off.

The Arrival of the DH9

On May 3, 1918 VIII Brigade was joined by No. 99 Squadron, equipped with the new DH9 day bomber. Superficially similar to the DH4, the DH9 had a slim streamlined nose surmounted by the exposed cylinders of its Beardmore-Halford-Pullinger (BHP) engine. It was the failure of this engine, designed to yield 300 hp but in practice capable of only 230 hp, which lay behind that aircraft's disappointing performance. With a full bombload the DH9 could only struggle up to 15 000 ft – 7000 ft lower than the ceiling of the DH4. Its endurance was only marginally better, but this was offset by its excessive proneness to engine failure, and above 10 000 ft frequent carburation problems pushed fuel consumption up to a prohibitive 15 gallons an hour. Of 848 attempted DH9 sorties by individual aircraft between June and November 1918, no fewer than 123 were forced to turn back with engine failure.

In the DH9 the pilot's and observer's cockpits were

A pilot and observer watch an air mechanic arming a bomb under an FE2b of No. 142 Squadron at an airfield near St Omer, July 1918.

placed close together, answering one of the principal criticisms of the DH4, but in turn this gave the aircrew the same, rather than different, blindspots. It also made them more vulnerable to an accurate burst of fire. In addition the design requirement which placed the DH9's radiator under the fuselage, just ahead of the undercarriage, increased the size of the target vulnerable to attack from below by at least 30 per cent. All in all, the DH9 could not fly high enough, fast enough or far enough to evade the German fighters, which were able to dictate the terms on which the British bomber's daylight missions were flown. The DH9's frailty was quickly exposed. On May 29, 12 machines set out for the Metz-Sablon railway triangle, only for six of them to return with engine trouble. A week earlier a new DH9 squadron, No. 104, had joined VIII Brigade. Its operational life was blighted by heavy casualties, which began almost immediately when arriving in darkness over the airfield at Azelot, two of the squadron's aircraft crashed on landing.

By the time No. 104 Squadron flew its first mission, on June 8, VIII Brigade had become the Independent Force, under the command of Major-General H M Trenchard, who had previously spent a brief and stormy period in London as the first Chief of Air Staff. When Trenchard assumed his new command in France, the air services had undergone the major organizational change outlined in the Smuts report. On April 1 the RFC and the RNAS were merged into the world's first fully independent air force, the Royal Air Force (RAF). From that date all the old RNAS squadrons were re-numbered – No. 1 (Naval) Squadron became No. 201 Squadron Royal Air Force, No. 2 (Naval) Squadron became No. 202, and so on.

The new Chief of Air Staff, Major-General Sykes, had been given a sweeping brief for the Independent Force: 'the demobilization of the German Armies-in-the-Field by attacking the root industries which supply them with ammunitions'. Trenchard was directed to concentrate on this aim to the exclusion of strategic reconnaissance or attacks upon the enemy's airfields, railway centers or transport. The primary objective was the 'obliteration' of the German chemical industry, which supplied the materials for explosives, propellants and poison gas.

Sykes had a more realistic grasp of the possible, warning the War Cabinet that decisive results could not be expected for at least a year. At the end of April 1918 Sykes produced a paper which outlined an offensive aimed at key German industries. However, even this appraisal of strategic bombing was wildly optimistic, suggesting that as much as 95 per cent of the German magneto industry could be destroyed in as few as three raids. In similar fashion it was anticipated that up to 80 per cent of the German chemical industry could be wrecked in 12 raids, the destruction of each of the principal works being accomplished by a total of 1000 DH4 sorties in a single raid. In this context it is salutary to note that during its lifetime the Independent Force's DH4s flew approximately 2500 sorties. A single raid of 1000 sorties remained in the realms of fantasy – in June 1918 the Force never managed more than 45 sorties in a single 24-hour period.

While the Air Staff and the politicians in London proposed, at the front Trenchard disposed. His initial plan was to use a force of nine squadrons to attack 'the big industrial centers on the Rhine' when weather permitted. When long-distance raiding was impossible, his aircraft would fly against the steel-making areas closer at hand. He also suggested using the two Handley Page squadrons based in Dunkirk to attack the submarine facilities at Ostend and Zeebrugge and the employment of army bombing squadrons in raids on the Gotha bases in Belgium. This was a modest program more in keeping with the five squadrons at Trenchard's disposal – Nos. 55, 94 and 104 for day bombing; and 100 and 216 (formerly 'A' Naval) for night operations. It was of this force that the Deputy Chief of the French General Staff, General Duval, remarked sarcastically, 'Independent of what? Of God?'

Independent Force Operations

In spite of this unpromising start Trenchard had two factors working for him: the close support of the French General Castelnau, in whose sector the Independent Force was based; and the relatively free hand he was given by Sykes to run his own show. From the beginning Trenchard used this freedom to ignore Sykes' brief.

In June 1918 only 14 per cent of the Independent Force's 77 raids were directed against the German chemical industry and 13 per cent against the iron and steel industry. By contrast over 50 per cent of the missions flown were against the rail networks, the majority of the targets lying within 75 miles of the base at Nancy. Additionally some 13 per cent were flown against German airfields, ensuring that almost 75 per cent of the 66 tons dropped fell on non-strategic targets.

In July bad weather limited the tonnage dropped to 88 in 116 raids, but the pattern remained essentially the same, with only 18.5 per cent of the Force's raids directed against the chemical and steel industries. Attacks on enemy airfields had risen to 28 per cent of the total, with the FE2bs of No. 100 Squadron conducting what was almost a private war against the German bomber base at Bourlay, on which they dropped almost 20 tons of HE by the end of August. The German home defenses were also improving and daylight raiding was becoming increasingly costly.

A system of Observation and Alert Posts had been established at intervals between the front line and the interior, situated at the highest points in their respective zones and connected to command positions by telephone. Their sole duty was to report the whereabouts and probable direction of hostile machines to the important industrial centers and anti-aircraft headquarters. Both searchlight and anti-aircraft batteries were becoming more efficient. The much-raided BASF factory near Mannheim was protected by 20 10.5 cm guns and a number of captured Russian pieces. The 10.5 cm anti-aircraft gun could fire a shell to 20 000 ft and each battery was crewed by officers and men drawn from the Landwehr (a form of Home Guard). They were housed in quarters 50 yards from the emplacements, which were revetted and provided with deep ammunition pits.

British aircrew new to the front quickly learned to read the anti-aircraft danger signals. Noiseless white puffs by day, or red pinpricks of light by night, meant that the shells were bursting at a safe distance. A dull 'whoof', accompanied by a blink of red light was countered by a height or course adjustment. A brilliant flash and a sharp tearing noise followed by a shower of splinters was a warning that shells were bursting uncomfortably close. Even closer, and the aircrew would smell the rank odor of cordite, instinctively duck as shrapnel splattered through spars, and then listen for the ominous drumming of rent fabric. Balloon barrages dangling steel cables were now in place at heights between 5000 ft and 7500 ft around the principal industrial targets; at Saarbrucken there were no fewer than 249 balloons, with aprons, arrayed in two layers several hundred feet apart.

The balloons claimed one British victim, an FE2b piloted by Lieutenant L G Taylor. The FE2b was returning from Treves with its rudder-controls damaged by anti-aircraft fire. After surviving a hair-raising descent, Taylor discovered that the cable of the balloon had sawed halfway through his machine.

Fighter defenses had been stepped up, and in the spring of 1918 there were ten home defense squadrons – Kampfeinsitzerstaffeln, or 'Kests' – each comprising 13 aircraft and stationed along the Rhine and in Alsace-Lorraine. They were equipped with a mixture of types including Albatros DVs, Pfalz DIIIs and Fokker Dr1s, flown mainly by novice pilots and veterans resting from front-line duties. Their tactics were to maneuver in groups of six to eight above the day-bomber formations while two or three machines concentrated on a single British aircraft from below and at very close range.

The Handley Page 0/400

In July, 16 of the Independent Force's machines were lost to enemy action, as well as 41 from other causes. The bulk of them were DH9s. On July 31 12 DH9s of No. 99 Squadron took off to raid Mainz, with Saarbrucken as a secondary objective. Three returned with engine trouble and one was shot down by enemy scouts on the flight to the objective. Shortly afterwards the remainder were attacked by a large number of German fighters, estimated by some observers to be as many as 40, and three more were shot down. Their leader decided to divert to Saarbrucken with the remaining five DH9s, but soon found his formation under attack again, losing three more of his machines in a running dogfight. The remaining two DH9s returned home safely, but this one disastrous raid put No. 99 Squadron out of action for a month while replacement pilots were learning how to fly in formation.

In August more powerful reinforcements arrived in the shape of Nos. 97, 115 and 215 Squadrons, all of which were equipped with the Handley Page 0/400. The 0/400 was an improved version of the 0/100, of which a total of 46 had been built. As a result of operational experience the 0/400 incorporated a completely redesigned fuel system in which the fuel tanks were removed from the engine nacelles and positioned above the bomb bay, with two small gravity tanks installed in the upper wing. The standard power plants were two two 360 hp Rolls Royce Eagles, but a number of 0/400s were fitted with 250 hp Sunbeam Maori and 260 hp Fiat A-12bis engines. Maximum speed was 95 mph and the 0/400's operational ceiling was 8500 ft. Defensive armament was provided by one or two Lewis guns mounted in both the nose and rear cockpits; in the latter position one gun was fired sideways or backwards from a raised platform while the second could be fired downwards and backwards through a trapdoor in the floor of the fuselage. The 0/400's load was 2000 pounds maximum, only slightly less than that carried by a flight of DH4s. The bomb release mechanism was by means of Bowden cables operated by the observer/front gunner from the cockpit in the 0/400's nose, reached by a small opening in the bulkhead which separated it from the pilot's cockpit. Initially the bombsight used was Lieutenant-Commander Wimperis's High Altitude Drift Sight Mk1a (mounted on the 0/400's nose) which took account of the aircraft's height above the target, its airspeed, the wind velocity and the amount of drift when flying across the wind. The end of the war also saw the appearance of the Course-Setting Bombsight (also designed by Wimperis), which incorporated a compass to enable bombing to be carried out in any direction relative to the wind. The Course-Setting Bombsight remained standard RAF equipment for another 20 years, and a modified version was still in service at the beginning of World War II.

The arrival of the 0/400s shifted the balance of the Independent Force's operations towards night bombing. However, disaster still haunted the DH9 squadrons. On August 22, 13 DH9s of No. 104 Squadron took off in two formations, of six and seven aircraft, to bomb the BASF factory at Mannheim. At 0740 hrs, just before the two flights crossed the lines, the single reserve machine turned for home. Immediately afterwards the DH9s encountered heavy anti-aircraft fire which brought down one machine. As the guns ceased firing, eight enemy scouts were spotted and a few bursts were exchanged at long range while the German fighters hovered on the flanks of the DH9 formations, waiting for stragglers to lose station. At this point Lieutenant J Valentine fired a flare to indicate that his engine was failing, and began to lose height. Harassed all the way by the German fighters, Valentine nevertheless managed to land his machine behind enemy lines. The other DH9s flew on, for the moment unmolested. Over the Vosges mountains Captain McKay, leader of the second flight, developed engine trouble, force-landed and was taken prisoner. Approaching Mannheim at 11 500 ft, the DH9s arrived at the city's outskirts at 0800 hrs, encountering 15 Fokker and Pfalz scouts and Halberstadt two-seaters. During the bombing run there was a fierce battle, which broke up the formation and forced the DH9s down to 6000 ft, where they were at the mercy of the German fighters. The leader of No. 1 flight, Captain J B Home-Hay, was shot down, quickly followed by another aircraft in the flight. The vicious dogfight continued for about ten minutes before Lieutenant Bottrill, tying a handkerchief to his Scarff ring, attempted to rally the scattered formation. The five surviving aircraft fought their way back to base, landing at 0930 hrs. In a little over four hours No. 104 Squadron had lost seven out of 12 machines and most of its best aircrew.

Night Raiding

The organization of most night raids left a great deal of initiative in the hands of the aircrews. Geoffrey Linnell, a Handley Page pilot with the Independent Force, recalled: 'We are told in the afternoon that we must prepare to bomb a certain railroad station or a certain town. It was up to us to plan out our own compass course. We were told the rough idea of the direction, the strength of the wind, but it was up to us entirely to plot our own course. We had to find our own way to the target and back again'.

The sensation of flying in a Handley Page at night has been vividly described by W E D Wardrop, an observer with No.7 squadron, RNAS, at Coudekerque: 'On an ordinary dark clear night, with no moon, the roads would appear a darkish color and the forests and woods very black, and rivers a dark gray. And on a moonlit night the roads would appear almost bluish – wonderful – and even railway lines would shine up more or less silvery. And forests and woods become very clearly defined. We always welcomed a moonlit night'.

Maps and the countryside below were the principal navigational aids to familiar targets: 'We didn't bother much with watching the compass... because I could tell from the landmarks. In fact I got so used to it that I could almost go to sleep and wake up and tell you where I was in a few seconds, provided the visibility was right'.

On the return journey navigation was aided by 'lighthouses' – beacons which flashed identity messages in morse code. Once a 'lighthouse' was identified, a fix could be obtained as the distance of each beacon from the aircraft's home station was known. Use was also made of a system originated by the German air service, in which batteries in a known location fired color-coded flares when they heard an aircraft overhead. Conditions in the big bombers were rudimentary: 'We had no oxygen, of course, but the heating was running from the engine. The exhaust at the back was all right, but we had sheepskin boots and leather clothing, and fur-lined gloves and helmets. I personally used to wear a silk stocking over my head before I put my helmet on. I also used to have silk gloves underneath my fur-lined gloves. They were most effective... We were also supposed to have whale oil. We never saw any... I used to put Vaseline on my face'.

Frostbite was always a danger: 'Unfortunately I was frostbitten on one occasion because one or two bombs got jammed, and I couldn't release them with my gloves on. So I took my gloves off and made certain that the bombs went, and I couldn't get my glove on again. For three days I was going crazy with the pain'.

The Badische Works Raid by No. 215 Squadron, August 25, 1918

In sharp contrast to the heavy daylight losses suffered by the Independent Force's DH9s was the carefully planned night attack by two 0/400s on one of the most stubborn targets in Germany. The movements of the two aircraft were co-ordinated in advance. The 0/400 piloted by Captain W B Lawson was to approach Mannheim at 5000 ft, drawing enemy fire. When he was joined by the 0/400 flown by Lieutenant M C Purvis, Lawson was to 'veer off four miles, shut off our engines, turn and glide silently towards the target'. The four-mile glide was calculated to bring him over the target at 1000 ft, an altitude at which the 0/400 would be safe from blast.

The two bombers made a successful rendezvous over Mannheim, but Lawson began his glide too soon. Lieutenant H B Monaghan (a pilot who had volunteered to fly with Lawson as gunner) recalled, 'The silence was startling with only the whistle of the flying wires and the soft sound of the wind to break the quiet … I stood on a wooden lattice support with my arms resting on the fuselage, gazing at the countryside below'. Lawson's mistimed glide brought him over the Badische factory at 200 ft, the 0/400 bucking wildly as its bombs exploded. A searchlight swayed towards the bomber, obligingly illuminating a church steeple directly in its path while Monaghan tossed 20-pound Cooper bombs over the side, 'looking down a long street and seeing, with astonishment, a house topple into the road-way'.

Lawson remained over the target for seven minutes, strafing the works and its searchlights with machine-gun fire. As he flew away Purvis glided in to bomb from 400 ft and sweep the town with 1100 rounds of machine-gun fire. A division of the works was put out of action for two weeks, but the damage was limited by the failure of many of the bombs to explode.

The disasters of August 22, and the successful 0/400 mission of August 25 against the Badische Anilin factory equally underlined the appalling cost of daylight bombing without the protection of long-range escorts. It was thus somewhat ironic that Trenchard's final reinforcements were the new DH9as of No. 110 Squadron, which had been donated by the Nizam of Hyderabad. Although it was powered by the 12-cylinder Liberty engine, whose 400 hp made it the most powerful in operational use, the eagerly awaited replacement for the DH9 proved to be almost as big a disappointment in service. It ceiling was 3000 ft lower than the DH4 and a speed of 120 mph at 10 000 ft could not match the DH4's 133 mph at the same altitude. Its endurance was an hour less, and its loss rate with No. 110 Squadron – 17 aircraft shot down and another 28 written off in two months of service – exceeded that of the DH9.

In September the Independent Force was re-organized into three Wings: 41 Wing, equipped with day bombers (excluding No. 110 Squadron); 83 Wing, equipped with the Handley Page squadrons; and 88 Wing, which comprised No. 110 Squadron and No. 45 Squadron, the latter flying Sopwith Camels in an abortive attempt to solve the escort problem (which failed because the Camel lacked the range for the task). During the month the Independent Force reached a peak of activity, dropping over 178 tons of bombs, most of them in a tactical role in support of the American First Army's offensive at St Mihiel. In the effort to pinch off the German salient, 1481 Allied aircraft were committed – the biggest concentration of air power in one operation in the whole of the war.

At the end of the month the Independent Force was, at the request of Marshal Foch, employed in the big offensive in the Verdun sector aimed at cutting off large numbers of retreating German troops. Once again No. 99 Squadron suffered heavily, losing five out of seven DH9s in a raid on Metz on September 26 and a sixth in a landing accident. The momentum of long-distance night bombing was also maintained, but also at some cost. On the night of September 16/17 all the night squadrons were in action against targets in Cologne, Frankfurt, Coblenz and Trier. It was a bad night for the Handley Pages, seven of which were lost to enemy action and three more in forced landings behind the Allied lines. No. 215 Squadron despatched five machines: three left to bomb Cologne, one turning back with engine trouble and two failing to return; another machine failed to return from Frescaty, and the aircrew who flew to bomb Mannheim were posted missing. No. 97 Squadron despatched five machines to Frankfurt, but only one reached the target, causing considerable damage with nine 112-pound bombs and four cases of incendiaries. The success of this sortie prompted Sir William Weir to suggest to Trenchard that, 'I would like it very much if you could start a really big fire in one of the German towns.... If I were you, I would not be too exacting as regards accuracy in bombing railway stations in the middle of towns. The German is susceptible to bloodiness, and I would not mind a few accidents due to inaccuracy'.

These remarks reflect the ebb and flow of argument between those who still believed in the Independent Force's capacity to inflict widespread damage on German war industry and those who were by now convinced that the *psychological* impact of bombing the German civilian population was more important. Three months earlier Sykes had also pondered the 'dislocation of municipal and industrial organization ... the aim of such attacks would be to sow alarm ... set up nervous tension, check output and generally tend to bring military, financial and industrial interests into opposition.... The wholesale bombing of densely populated industrial centers would go far towards destroying the morale of the operatives'.

However, the pace of the Independent Force's activities was gradually slackening. In October bad weather reduced the tonnage dropped to 97, and on 19 days and 22 nights of that month even short-distance raids were ruled out by fog and low cloud. Most of the Force's operations continued to be in support of the Franco-American offensive in the Rheims-Verdun sector, with over 70 tons of bombs dropped on railroads and German airfields. Nevertheless, there were some notable operations of a strategic nature, among them the raid of October 21/22 in which a 1650-pound bomb dropped by an 0/400 of No. 97 Squadron completely demolished a munitions plant at Kaiserslautern. The 20 ft-long bomb was too large to be stowed internally, and was shackled under the 0/400's fuselage.

The Handley Page V/1500

As the war drew to a close, frantic efforts were made to bomb Berlin. Early in November consideration was given to a plan to raid the German capital with

0/400s flying from an airfield north of Prague. This hasty improvization was still-born, as there was already a bomber designed specifically for the task, the Handley Page V/1500.

Designed and built in conditions of great secrecy, the prototype V/1500 had flown for the first time in May 1918. In spite of its great size, it was a more robust and better-engineered aircraft than the German R-types. The V/1500 had a 126 ft wingspan and was powered by four 375 hp Rolls Royce Eagle VIIIs mounted in tandem pairs midway between the wings. The tractor engine on each side drove a two-bladed airscrew and the pushers powered a four-blader of similar diameter. The aircraft's two most striking features were a tail gun position, with catwalk access, and its very heavy bombload, rising to a maximum of 30 250-pound bombs on short-range missions. A 3300 pound bomb was designed specifically for the V/1500, and two of these bombs could be accommodated under the fuselage. Its combat range of 1100 miles placed Berlin within reach of V/1500s flying from the east coast of Britain with a reduced bombload of 1000 pounds.

While the prototype was nearing completion, 27 Group, a special unit to fly the V/1500, was assembled under the command of a vastly experienced airman, Colonel R H Mulock. At the end of August 27 Group, consisting of 86 and 87 Wings, was formally established at Bircham Newton, near King's Lynn, in eastern England.

Production estimates (optimistic as ever) forecast that eight V/1500s would be ready to enter service in October, 13 by early November and 42 by the end of the year. In June the program suffered a serious setback when the single prototype, which had already been troubled by problems with the control surfaces, crashed on a test flight, killing all its crew. The first production model was not test flown until August 28, but continuing problems with the rudder and ailerons, engine placement and radiators led to extensive modifications.

While the V/1500's teething problems were being overcome, the Air Staff continued to weave fantasies of the mass destruction the new giant bombers would visit on the cities of Germany. As late as September 30 a Staff paper outlined the advantages of the combined use of incendiaries and HE on population concentrations. It estimated that the V/1500 could deliver 16 000 'Baby Incendiaries', laying down a belt of fire 60 yards wide and 2500 yards long: 'If the target is large, the operation may be described as simply a plastering of the locality with a predetermined density of fire nuclei'. However, before the paper was circulated, the War Cabinet had decided that the destruction of German towns with incendiaries in what were to all intents and purposes 'terror' raids, was to be undertaken only as 'a defensive act of retaliation'. The painful progress of the V/1500 towards operational readiness inevitably limited the Air Staff's expansive horizons, and more realistic planners turned their attentions to attacks on Hamburg and Berlin with the essentially politico-strategic aim of producing 'results of a disintegrating character, ie they would

Above: The Handley Page V/1500. It never flew in anger in World War I but a single machine was used in air control operations on the North-West Frontier immediately after the war.
Left: Pilot and observer of a Handley Page heavy bomber, photographed at an airfield near Cressy, France, in September 1918. The observer's Lewis gun is mounted on a Scarff ring.
Far Left: Two Handley Page 0/400 bombers at Coudekerque airfield on April 20, 1918.

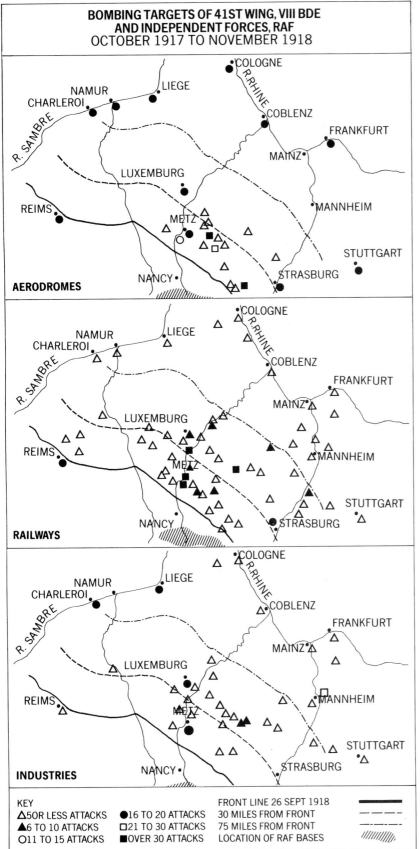

BOMBING TARGETS OF 41ST WING, VIII BDE AND INDEPENDENT FORCES, RAF OCTOBER 1917 TO NOVEMBER 1918

AERODROMES

RAILWAYS

INDUSTRIES

KEY
△ 5 OR LESS ATTACKS ● 16 TO 20 ATTACKS FRONT LINE 26 SEPT 1918
▲ 6 TO 10 ATTACKS □ 21 TO 30 ATTACKS 30 MILES FROM FRONT
○ 11 TO 15 ATTACKS ■ OVER 30 ATTACKS 75 MILES FROM FRONT
LOCATION OF RAF BASES

tend to set the capitalists and masses against the military'. Bombing, it was hoped, would finally bring Germany to the point of collapse.

By the beginning of October modification and flight testing of the two completed V/1500s were progressing and Mulock felt sufficiently confident to inform Trenchard that they would soon be ready to fly to Berlin under suitable weather conditions. Mulock selected two crews and directed his Meteorological Section to make weather forecasts for 'the whole area concerned, Norfolk, "X", and Nancy' – the 'X' clearly referring to Berlin. A map in Mulock's papers shows the route chosen for the raid: 240 miles from Bircham Newton to Borkum and then a 300-mile leg to Berlin; after bombing, the V/1500s would set a course for one of the Independent Force's airfields at Nancy. It was left to Mulock to decide when to launch the operation but, as he recalled, during the closing days of the war the Air Staff became alarmed that 'we might push off and take a chance' on bombing Berlin. He was 'withdrawn from my unit and kept in London the last ten days of the war', returning to Bircham Newton on the afternoon of November 10 – 'They thought it was too big a temptation to leave in the hands of anybody'. Early on November 11 Mulock received a signal from Trenchard: 'Hostilities cease today at 11.00. You will not carry out operations without orders from this HQ'. The bomber on which the Air Staff's hopes were pinned stayed on the ground.

The Independent Force: Assessment
Perhaps the single most important feature of the Independent Force's operational career was that, under Trenchard's command, it was *not* used primarily as a strategic bombing weapon. From the beginning of June to the end of September 1918 only 16 per cent of the Force's raids were aimed at German chemical and steel plants. In October Trenchard was no longer able to choose his targets as the bulk of his aircraft were heavily committed to the tactical support of the final Allied offensives.

Trenchard believed that, with the relatively small numbers of aircraft at his disposal and the constant difficulties imposed on long-range bombing by the weather, significant destruction of the German war industries could only have been achieved if the conflict 'had lasted at least another four or five years'. This makes good sense when one considers that at its peak the Independent Force could muster only 120 aircraft. In April Lord Tiverton, who had flown with No. 3 Wing in 1916 and was one of the most vigorous advocates of strategic bombing, had estimated that a force of over 700 aircraft would be needed to exert a decisive influence on the course of the war. Weight was added to this argument in the following June when a sample target analysis of bombing results indicated that only 23·5 per cent of bombs dropped could be expected to be effective in the selected target area.

Postwar confirmation of Trenchard's caution came with the findings of a British Air Ministry commission sent to Germany to assess the effects of British bombing raids. The report observed that, 'It is very noteworthy how surprisingly little damage has been throughout four years of war, and on no occasion has a works been forced to close down for more than a week as the direct result of bombing'.

Both the 230-pound and 112-pound bombs were found to have been disappointing in their effects on blast furnaces and factories. At plants like the BASF works at Mannheim the buildings and machinery were 'so massive and solidly built that in some cases 230-pound bombs … have been telescoped and not exploded. At Hagendingen a 230-pound bomb pierced the roof of the Central Power Station, striking one of the alternator armatures. The whole bomb telescoped, the fuse being shot right into the bomb'. The report also noted the frequency with which bombs failed to explode, estimating that up to 25 per cent of the bombs dropped on Saarbrucken were 'blinds' or duds.

Some loss of production was caused by the practice of sounding air raid warnings over the whole area in which the British bombers were operating. For example, the Roechligsche E and S Werke of Völklingen lost 15 563 tons of steel production in the last year of the war, but this represented only 4·6 per cent of the factory's 1913 production of over 340 000 tons. Lost man-hours and shaken civilian morale were contained within tolerable limits (as they were to be in Germany during World War II, until late 1944, when the Anglo-American bomber forces were delivering approximately 90 000 tons of bombs a month to the German heartland).

Even when assessing the tactical bombing of the Metz-Sablon railway triangle, barely 12 miles behind the German lines, the results were disappointing. In spite of the occasional British success, the lines were never completely closed to traffic and the efficient deployment of Eisenbahn Truppen (special units responsible for clearing wreckage and restoring flow) underlined the difficulty of severely disrupting a railway network. On July 16, 1918 No. 99 Squadron recorded one of its major successes, dropping 20 bombs on the sidings at Thionville and blowing up a big munitions train and ten locomotives. The flames could be seen 20 miles away, but within 48 hours the line had been cleared and traffic was rolling again.

In a memorandum of August 13, 1918 Major-General F H Sykes, Chief of Air Staff, wrote: '*Ex-perience has shown that a bridge offers so small a target that even from low altitude it is exceedingly difficult to hit: even direct hits will not as a rule cause any very prolonged interruption of traffic. To destroy a bridge an air attack in considerable strength and carried out from low height is necessary. Such an operation must inevitably be costly as all important bridges are very strongly defended against aircraft attack'.*

The truth of Sykes' words was being simultaneously demonstrated on the Western Front in the series of furious air battles which developed as the Allies attempted to seal off the battlefield at Amiens by the destruction of the bridges in the immediate area and to the east of the fighting. Between August 8 and 14, over 700 day and night sorties were flown against these bridges and over 57 tons of bombs dropped without any of them being seriously damaged. An indication of the ferocity of the fighting in this sector is provided by a raid on the railway station at Peronne on August 10 in which 12 DH9s of Nos. 27

and 49 Squadrons were escorted to the target by 40 SE5as and Bristol Fighters from Nos. 32 and 62 Squadrons. The bridges survived but the German air corps did not, chewed up in the relentless attrition over the battlefield. This was a classic air superiority encounter, and a hint of the lessons which were to be bitterly learnt by the US 8th Air Force in the skies over Germany in 1943–45. Rather than being the means of winning air superiority through bombing, the bomber could be made the means by which an air superiority battle could be provoked and won.

As with the German Zeppelins and Gothas, the most tangible achievement of the Independent Force was to divert enemy equipment and personnel from front-line service. During the night of September 16/17, when seven 0/400s were lost, it was estimated that over 16 000 anti-aircraft shells had been expended and 173 searchlights brought into action in the area under attack. In contrast there were only six home defense squadrons stationed in the areas attacked by the Independent Force, far fewer than the postwar Air Ministry estimate of 330 fighters.

But British losses were heavy, reaching a peak in September when 37 machines were shot down over enemy territory and 54 crashed on the Allied side of the lines. Thus in a single month the Force had lost 75 per cent of its establishment of 122 aircraft. During the same period No. 5 Group, flying long-distance raids from Dunkirk, lost only one of its 58 DH9s and a single 0/400. The severe Independent Force losses can, in part, be attributed to Trenchard's unyielding belief in attrition. Privately he expressed the view that the RNAS units lacked 'ginger', but his unceasing pursuit of battle prompted the Official Historian to observe: 'It has been said that the air offensive was responsible for severe casualties, which led to the sending of reinforcements to France before they were adequately trained, with the result that they were offered as somewhat easy targets, so that the circle of heavy casualties and ill-trained reinforcements became a vicious one'.

At the same time tactical bombing had achieved a degree of sophistication undreamt of in the autumn of 1914, when L E Strange was lobbing grenades from the cockpit of his Avro 504. In the closing months of the war effective procedures were developed to use the tactical day bombing squadrons of the Army Wings under the direction of the Counter Battery Office. Important targets (bodies of troops, artillery on the move or motor transport convoys) which were beyond the effective range of the artillery or which, because of their importance, required very intensive bombardment, were pinpointed and attacked from the air with a high degree of success.

Tactical operations at night also took their toll. For example, on August 21/22, FE2bs of No. 102 Squadron flew a total of 38 sorties against troops, trees and transport. The machine flown by Lieutenant J Farley dropped six 25-pound bombs on a column of horse transport on the Albert-Bapaume road, scoring at least one direct hit and scattering the rest. It would have taken hours to reorganize the column, calming panicking horses, righting overturned wagons and reforming demoralized drivers in the dark and glutinous mud which for the troops on the ground was the enduring feature of war on the Western Front.

SECTION TWO
THE INTER-WAR YEARS

2.1 1920s: THE COMMAND OF THE AIR

I T IS ARGUABLE THAT THE COURSE OF WORLD WAR I MIGHT HAVE been the same had the aeroplane never been invented. But if the aeroplane had failed to exercise a decisive influence on the war, the war had exercised a decisive influence on the aeroplane. Only four years separated the fragile Avro 504, with its 80-pound bombload, from the Handley Page V/1500, designed to carry 90 times that weight of bombs to attack continental targets from bases in Britain. The relentless dynamic of war had not only accelerated the work of aircraft designers and engineers but had also established patterns for the use of air power, by different types of military aircraft designed to fulfil specific roles, that are still recognizable today.

With peace came the rapid dismantling of the air fleets amassed during four years of war. The RAF's inventory for October 1918 reveals that it had 22 171 airplanes in service and in store, with 37 702 engines. There were 291 175 RAF personnel and nearly 350 000 men and women in the aircraft industry, which as the war drew to an end was churning out 2668 machines a month. By January 3 1920, 26 087 officers, 21 259 cadets, and 227 229 non-commissioned ranks had left the RAF, whose strength had dwindled from a wartime peak of 188 operational squadrons to 33 in March 1920, with eight of these still in the process of formation.

Britain's Postwar Bombers
The hard core of Britain's postwar bomber squadrons were equipped with the DH9a and two aircraft which had arrived too late to see operational service on the Western Front. In the summer of 1918 contracts had been placed for no fewer than 1275 of the twin-engined De Havilland DH10 bomber, powered by the 400 hp American Liberty engine. Owing to the slow supply of the Liberty, only eight DH10s had been delivered to the RAF by October 31, 1918. Following the Armistice, production contracts were slashed, and the DH10 eventually saw service with No.120 Squadron in the United Kingdom, with No.216 in Egypt and with No.60 in India, where it was used to quell tribal uprisings during the years 1920–23, after which it was withdrawn from service. The DH10 was also used to pioneer long-distance mail services, an early example of the interaction between the military and civilian sides of aviation which was to be an important feature of the interwar years.

The twin-engined Vickers Vimy was another casualty of peace. It had been designed in 1917 as a heavy bomber, capable of carrying an offensive load of 2500 pounds a distance of 985 miles. However, only one Vimy reached the Independent Force before the Armistice and the type never flew operationally against Germany. Its fame rests on Alcock and

Brown's Atlantic crossing in June 1919, when their Vimy flew 1890 miles in 16 hours 12 minutes.

The close linkage between postwar civil aviation and bomber development can be seen in the origins of the Handley Page Hyderabad, which was evolved from the company's W8b commercial airliner. The prototype, which flew for the first time in October 1923 and was developed to meet the Air Ministry Specification 31/22, was substantially similar to the airliner which three years earlier had won the Ministry's heavy commercial aircraft competition. The Hyderabad was a conservative biplane successor to the 0/400, constructed principally of wood, with fabric-covered wings, fuselage and tail unit. It was powered by two 450 hp Napier Lion engines. The first RAF squadron to take delivery of the Hyderabad was No.99 based at Bircham Newton. A total of 45 Hyderabads were ordered by the RAF, but not all of them were completed as such, for the Hyderabad was withdrawn from front-line service in 1930 to be replaced by the Handley Page Hinaidi, the prototype of which had been converted from an early production Hyderabad in the spring of 1927.

A more successful but equally conservative type was the twin-engined wood and fabric-covered Vickers Virginia, originally designed as a long-range successor to the Vimy and the RAF's principal heavy night bomber between 1924 and 1937. In all a total of 126 Virginias went into service with nine UK-based bomber squadrons.

The outstanding British light day bomber of the late 1920s was Sydney Camm's Hawker Hart, which had first flown in June 1928, powered by a supercharged Rolls Royce FX1 engine. Among the indelible images of British aviation technology of the interwar years are photographs of the Hendon Air Display with RAF Harts executing immaculate Squadron Wing Drill over the upturned faces of immense crowds, the gunner's hand signalling the change of maneuvers. A supremely elegant all-metal two-seater biplane, whose 37 ft 3 in upper wings were slightly swept back to improve the pilot's view,

the production Hart was powered by a 525 hp 1B Kestrel (developed from the FX1), giving it a speed of 184 mph at 5000 ft – in the late 1920s a full 10 mph faster than the RAF's standard day fighter, the Bristol Bulldog. The Hart could climb to 10 000 ft in eight minutes, with a ceiling of 21 350 ft. Its offensive load was 520 pounds, carried in racks beneath the lower wings, and defensive armament was provided by a forward-firing Vickers gun and a ring-mounted Lewis gun in the observer's cockpit. With 83 gallons of fuel the Hart had a range of approximately 450 miles.

The first squadron to receive Harts was No. 33 at Eastchurch, the type subsequently equipping six UK-based squadrons and seven overseas. The Hart was an early version of a familiar modern type, the MRCA or multi-role combat aircraft. A cost-effective, high-performance general-purpose machine, it proved itself in the 'air control' operations which enabled the RAF to demonstrate a practical role for an independent air force in the interwar years.

Trenchard and Air Control

In the immediate years following the end of World War I, the principal achievement of the British Chief of Air Staff, Sir Hugh Trenchard, was to ensure the survival of the RAF as an independent service. Both the Army and the Royal Navy pressed for its disbandment and the reinstatement of their own 'private' air forces, and it was not until December 1919 that the formal plan for the permanent peacetime establishment of the RAF was placed before Parliament. The financing of the service was limited by the Cabinet decision to restrict the air estimate to £15 million for the next five years.

Moreover, overall policy was to be determined on the assumption that Britain would not be involved in another major war for at least ten years – the so-called 'Ten Year Rule'.

While Trenchard had little room for maneuver in the United Kingdom, greater possibilities existed for the RAF overseas. Thus in 1920, 19 of the 25 available squadrons were stationed abroad: eight in India, three in Mesopotamia, seven in Egypt and one for general co-operation with the various naval bases. Their job was to police the Empire and those territories which had fallen under British control by League of Nations mandate. In the straitened economic circumstances of the postwar years the policy of air control exercised in these far-flung and frequently inhospitable parts of the world would become virtually the *raison d'être* of the RAF's existence.

The use of air power as an arm of Imperial policy had been foreseen before World War I. As early as 1909 Arthur Lee, Member of Parliament for Fareham, had suggested the employment of airships as an economic method of mounting punitive expeditions in the colonies. Between 1915 and 1917 BE2cs of No.31 Squadron had been used with some success

Above: Designed in 1922 to replace the Vimy, the Vickers Virginia remained in service with the RAF from 1924 to 1937. In spite of its engagingly obsolete appearance and maximum speed of 108 mph, it equipped front-line bomber squadrons for several years after the RAF had raised the world speed record to more than 400 mph with the streamlined Supermarine S.6B monoplane racing seaplane.
Left: The modified Vickers Vimy MkIV bomber in which Captain J Alcock and Lieutenant A Whitten-Brown flew from New-foundland to Ireland on June 14/15, 1919.

against large bodies of dissident tribesmen on the North-West Frontier, acting as artillery spotters and ground-attack aircraft.

By the end of 1928 there were eight squadrons in India, with Nos. 11 and 39 introducing the Westland Wapiti IIa, designed as a replacement for the DH9a, which had proved a rugged and adaptable instrument of air control in the 1920s.

By 1933 the squadrons in India were re-equipping with Harts. The Hart was also to play an important part in air control in the Middle East, where the end of the war had seen the dismemberment of the old Ottoman Empire. A huge area had been carved up into separate states, three of which – Mesopotamia (Iraq), Transjordan and Palestine – were assigned by a League of Nations mandate to British control. In Mesopotamia there was a British garrison of equivalent strength to two divisions and five squadrons of obsolescent aircraft, but these proved quite inadequate to police the long and turbulent borders, across whose northeastern corner Kurdish rebels, supported by infiltrating Turkish troops, passed virtually at will. At the Cairo Conference in March 1922 Trenchard secured agreement to a proposal that the bulk of the ground forces should be withdrawn, to be replaced by eight RAF squadrons and a mixed brigade of British and Indian infantry, some native levies and four squadrons of RAF-manned Rolls Royce armored cars. Based at Hinaidi, near Baghdad, were Nos. 45 and 70 Squadrons, equipped with twin-engined Vickers Vernon transports (modified Vimys incorporating the latter's wings and tail with a roomy fuselage), Nos. 8 and 30 with DH9as, and No. 1 flying Sopwith Snipe single-seat fighters. Two more DH9a squadrons, Nos. 84 and 55, were stationed respectively at Shaibah, near Basra, and Mosul. In the northeast, at Kirkuk in the foothills of the Zagros mountains on the Persian-Kurdish border, was No. 6 Squadron, flying Bristol Fighters.

The DH9a, sturdy workhorse of air control operations in the 1920s. The demands of 'colonial' duties meant that the 'Nine-Ack' invariably took off festooned with water bottles, emergency rations, medical kits and spare parts. With a 450-pound bombload and fore and aft machine-guns, this reduced the DH9a's top speed to 114 mph.

Learning the Part

The quality of the small air contingent in Mesopotamia was extremely high, and in one unit brought together three men who were later to play crucial roles in the bombing offensive against Germany in World War II. No. 45 Squadron was commanded by Squadron Leader Arthur Harris, who in 1942 was appointed C-in-C Bomber Command. One of his flight commanders was Flight Lieutenant R H M S Saundby, who was to become Harris's wartime deputy; the other was Flight Lieutenant R A B Cochrane, the future Air Officer Commanding (AOC) No. 5 (Bomber) Group. It was not long before the energetic Harris had calculated that a single Vernon was capable of carrying a bombload equivalent to an entire squadron of DH9as and had instructed his riggers and armorers to fit the lumbering transports with bomb racks and sights. Harris had holes cut in the nose of the Vernons, enabling the bomb aimer to lie prone and look down, forward and below, to the approaching target. According to Harris' biographer: 'A CRUDE BUT effective bombsight was developed and installed in this nose position, together with an improvized automatic bomb release gear, consisting of a long piece of rubber shock absorber cord combined with a trigger to operate the bomb release cables, which ran back to the bomb racks under the wings, singly or in salvo. Thus the bomb aimer could watch the target coming up into his sights and trip the trigger mechanism at the appropriate moment'.

Acting as his own bombardier, Harris threw the squadron into rigorous training, using 20-pound Cooper bombs. Eventually the modified transports achieved an accuracy of 10 to 15 yards from 2000 ft, which was not particularly difficult when the Vernon was crawling upwind with a groundspeed of only 40 mph but good enough to wipe the floor with

the rival DH9as and Bristol Fighters in a bombing competition organized by Harris. Before he left Mesopotamia in 1924, Harris had further refined his methods, raising the squadron to a high degree of efficiency in night flying and developing a marker bomb to be dropped by the most experienced crew, a crude demonstration of the later Pathfinding technique. Harris recalled: '*WE MADE OUR marker bombs by the simple process of screwing two pieces of bent tin on the back of a 20 pound practice bomb, into which we clamped a white Very light. Between the clamp and the Very light we inserted a striker so that when the bomb hit the ground the Very light was detonated and shot up into the air, illuminating the surroundings for a few moments and leaving a trail of smoke from the point where it had hit. Of course, the nights were very clear out there and visibility was excellent – and we flew at only one or two thousand feet, never more than three thousands ... So you can see, target-finding was not too difficult. And our crude marker bombs were very effective under those conditions*'.

Air control had its critics, even among those involved in the operations. Nevertheless, it was a cost-effective way of enabling the RAF to maintain a high profile while at the same time providing operational experience for its aircrew. In his book *Air Bombardment*, Air Chief Marshal Saundby wrote. 'The opponents of air control had predicted that the use of bombs would leave a legacy of hatred and ill-will. In fact nothing of the kind happened, and airmen were held in great respect. No airman who fell into tribal hands during air control operations was killed or even ill-treated'. Significantly, however, Saundy continues, 'No great efficiency was demanded for the small types of bomb that were adequate for air control purposes. The crews were trained to bomb into the wind, taking a long straight run at the target, and they became used to tactical methods that would be quite out of the question in a major war'.

Douhet, Mitchell and Air Power

In the 1920s the prospect of another major conflict was all but unthinkable to the politicians and populations of the Western democracies. But in the immediate aftermath of war two airmen, Douhet and Mitchell, were already 'thinking the unthinkable', and in the process elevating the bomber to the status of a revolutionary instrument of warfare.

General Giulio Douhet had joined the Italian Army as an artillery officer. Before World War I he had commanded Italy's embryonic air corps, but in 1916 he was court-martialed for criticising his superiors. In February 1918 he was recalled to head the Central Aeronautical Bureau; two years later his sentence was expunged and he was promoted to the rank of General. After the Fascist take-over in 1922, Douhet withdrew from public life to concentrate on writing about air power.

In 1921 he published *Command of the Air*, which was revised in 1927. Among many other writings Douhet also produced a fictional account of a future war between France and Germany, entitled *La Guerra del' 19..*, which was published in 1930, the year of his death. In common with many a seminal thinker, Douhet's theories were to be debated and dissected by disciples who had not read a word he had actually written. It was only after his death that widespread translations of his work became freely available outside Italy.

The principal thrust of Douhet's argument was that in any future war victory would be secured by the nation which could dominate the skies and bring the enemy to its knees by bombarding its industries and cities. In this new form of warfare ground forces would be deployed purely defensively, holding a front while the issue was decided in the air above them. Speed and utter ruthlessness were of the essence. In *La Guerra del' 19...* Douhet pictures France with its cities transformed into 'flaming masses' by an hour's bombing from a fleet of 1500 German 'battle planes' and suing for peace within 36 hours of the opening of hostilities. Douhet took a slide rule to these prophecies of mass destruction: he calculated that 20 tons of bombs would level everything within a circle 500 m in diameter. Thus a fleet of 1000 bombing aircraft could destroy 50 of these 500 m areas during the course of a single day. Civilian morale, subjected to the consequences of such a massively concentrated attack on virtually undefended cities, would crack within hours: '*WHAT COULD HAPPEN TO A SINGLE CITY in a day could also happen to 10, 20, 50 cities. And, since news travels fast, even without telegraph, telephone or radio, what I ask you would be the effect on civilians of other cities, not yet stricken but equally subject to bombing attacks? What civil or military authority could keep order, public services functioning and production going under such a threat?... Normal life would be impossible in this constant nightmare of imminent death and destruction. And if on the second day another 10, 20 or 50 cities were bombed, who could keep all those panic-striken people fleeing to the open countryside to escape this terror from the air?*'

Hindsight enables us to see that the bomber is only one element in the military equation. Douhet was convinced that it was the single dominant factor in warfare, which had rendered all others obsolete. He discounted the fighter altogether, assuming that the interception by fighters of self-defending bomber fleets flying zigzag courses would be virtually impossible. This was perhaps a pardonable error in the late 1920s, when emerging bomber types such as the Hawker Hart flew faster than most fighters and radar still remained in the realm of science fiction. But having wished fighters out of existence and replaced them with all-purpose 'battle planes', Douhet then argued that no emphasis need to be placed on speed, asserting that 'it is of so little importance that technical advances may soon produce bombing and combat planes which, while retaining other basic characteristics unaltered, will have a speed of 10 to 20 mph'. It is easy now to scoff at such wildly inaccurate predictions, but in many important areas Douhet correctly foresaw the future, notably in his preference for the industrial over the military objective and the use of the incendiary

Air Control

Hawker Harts K2109, K2102 and K2119 of No. 11 Squadron, based at Rawalpindi, bomb a village of the Madda Khel tribe on India's North-West Frontier in May 1938. Air control was a cost-effective method of maintaining law and order in a turbulent part of the world where fighting has always been a way of life. The traditional method of dealing with the tribesmen's sporadic forays was the despatch by the Army of a punitive expedition. This force was invariably ambushed by the tribesmen, providing them with an enjoyable fight and, if they were lucky, substantial quantities of captured weapons and ammunition. Next, a bigger column would set off to engage the tribesmen in a pitched battle, which it usually won. Then money was poured into the region, roads built, and allowances paid to the local chiefs to keep the peace. This would continue until the inevitable arrival of economies, whereupon the cycle would begin again.

Air control was seen as an effective alternative to the military stages in this sequence. The method employed was simple. First a message was delivered or air dropped to a lawless tribal leader instructing him to submit himself to a court of law. If he refused, leaflets were dropped over his village informing the inhabitants that it would be bombed on a certain date. This gave them time to evacuate their homes and then, if it was still considered necessary, the village was bombed. The stated aim was not to kill people, or even to cause extensive damage. Rather the intention was to disrupt the tribespeople's daily lives, depriving them of shelter and comfort and access to their pastures. Frequently the bombing produced a capitulation without any troop movements, but occasionally sterner measures were taken. Geoffrey Tuttle, a flight commander in No. 5 (Army Co-operation) Squadron, based at Rawalpindi, recalled: 'if they went on being troublesome, we would warn them that we would bomb an assembly of people. An assembly was normally defined as ten people. This isn't a good idea in a modern society but I think it important to emphasise that we were all trained as professional assassins and we wanted to see if we could kill people. We didn't know them and weren't fighting a crusade; we were merely exercising our professional skill. Indeed in my case I can remember actually finding nine people and saying "That's within ten per cent and that's good enough", so I blew them up'. The tribesmen were not noted for their friendliness towards captured servicemen, and aircrew always carried a 'blood chit', a piece of paper stating that if their captors handed them in they would receive a reward.

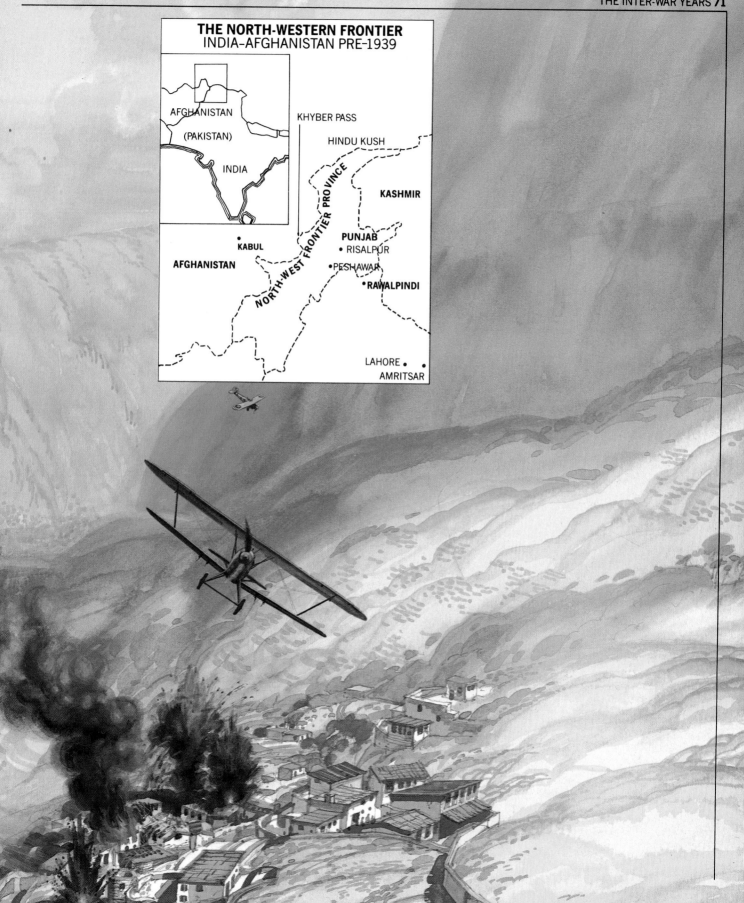

THE NORTH-WESTERN FRONTIER
INDIA–AFGHANISTAN PRE-1939

AFGHANISTAN

(PAKISTAN)

INDIA

KHYBER PASS

HINDU KUSH

KASHMIR

NORTH-WEST FRONTIER PROVINCE

PUNJAB

KABUL

RISALPUR

AFGHANISTAN

PESHAWAR

RAWALPINDI

LAHORE

AMRITSAR

bomb. None of these ideas was new, but Douhet's achievement lay in placing these arguments at the heart of a complete body of military doctrine developed and disseminated over a number of years.

Douhet was the reformed rebel turned theoretician. Brigadier-General William Mitchell's crusade to demonstrate the practical applications of air power also led him into conflict with authority and eventual court-martial. The leading American advocate of air power, Mitchell had commanded the flying units with the United States First Army in France. Of the 45 combat squadrons operational at the time of the Armistice, seven were assigned to bombing duties, equipped with the French Breguet Br14B2 and the British DH4, and flying principally in a tactical role supporting ground forces. Towards the end of the war Mitchell secured approval to form and train a US element to join the Independent Force, but peace arrived before any of the American aircrew had flown operationally.

Mitchell shared with Douhet the fervent belief that an air force must be a separate service, not merely an adjunct to the Army and the Navy. However, in the postwar United States the American General Staff were reluctant to countenance a separate air arm. They believed that the airplane, like the tank, was simply a new weapon to be employed in support of troops on the ground. Moreover, the United States was retreating into isolationism, strategically protected by the vastness of the Atlantic and the Pacific Oceans, the latter policed by its powerful Navy based in Hawaii and the Philippines. In 1919 a thorough-going demobilization began in which the air service was quickly reduced from nearly 200 000 personnel to a mere 10 000, leaving 27 first-line squadrons based in the various Army Corps areas. Only one formation, 2nd Bombardment Group, was specifically assigned to bombing duties.

In 1919 Mitchell was appointed Director of Military Aeronautics under the Director of the Air Service. Like Trenchard in Britain, his principal problem was the inadequate provision of funds for development of an air service in an environment glutted with war surplus aircraft and equipment. Most of Mitchell's aircraft were built from European-derived designs, an exception being the Glenn-Martin twin-engined bomber, which made its maiden flight on August 17, 1918. Clearly showing the influence of the Handley Page 0/400, which had been built under licence in the United States, the MB-1 was powered by two 400 hp Liberty engines, carried a crew of four, defensive armament of five machine-guns and a maximum bombload of 1040 pounds. Like the 0/400, the wing panels outboard of the engine nacelles could be folded back alongside the fuselage. After the Army Requisition Act of 1920 the Air Service was provided with increased research and procurement funds, enabling it to order an advanced version, the MB-2, powered by 420 hp Liberty 12s and capable of carrying a bombload of 1800 pounds. The MB-2 received the Army designation NBS-1 (Night Bomber Short Range).

Mitchell's enthusiasm for a long-range bomber then led to the development of one of the inter-war years' most engaging follies, the XNBL-1 (Experimental Night Bomber Long Range) designed by Walter Barling. A giant triplane of 120 ft span with two tailplanes and four fins, the Barling bomber was powered by four Liberty engines – equal to the task of getting the Barling into the air with a full load but scarcely able to propel the monster through it. In 1925, after the expenditure of $325 000, the project was abandoned.

The Barling episode was characteristic of the Mitchell style. Unlike the systematic, dispassionate Douhet, the American was a fierce controversialist who could never restrain himself from denouncing his opponents as reactionary bigots blinded by ignorance and self-interest. Ultimately this made Mitchell extremely vulnerable to counter-attack, as the violence of his polemics gained him many powerful enemies and also alienated potential supporters.

Mitchell shared Douhet's belief in the fragility of civilian morale under air attack, arguing that a relatively modest amount of bombing could paralyse industrial activity. In *Skyways, A Book on Modern Aeronautics* (1930) he envisaged a possible enemy attack on American cities:' IT IS UNNECESSARY *that these cities be destroyed, in the sense that every house be leveled to the ground. It will be sufficient to have the civilian population driven out so that they cannot carry on their usual vocations. A few gas bombs will do that...'*

And in *Winged Warfare* (1930) he observed, ' IN *future the mere threat of bombing a town by an air force will cause it to be evacuated, and all work in the factories to be stopped. To gain a lasting victory in war, the hostile nation's power to make war must be destroyed – this means the factories, the means of communication, the food producers, even the farms, the fuel and oil supplies, and the places where people live and carry on their daily lives. Aircraft operating in the heart of an enemy country will accomplish this object in an incredibly short space of time'.*

In other respects Mitchell took a different view from Douhet. The Italian was writing from a European perspective about conflict between neighbors whose principal cities and industrial complexes could be quickly reached by air and, in the case of Italy, about a nation protected by the Alps from the rapid development of a surface attack. With some candour he observed, 'In all probability if I were considering a conflict between Japan and the United States, I would not arrive at the same conclusions'. Such a conflict fitted neatly into Mitchell's viewpoint, which was geared towards a global application. In particular Mitchell was a tireless advocate of the opening up of the Arctic air routes between the continents and the importance of Alaska as the strategic key to the Pacific. While Mitchell was assistant chief of the Air Corps, an Army squadron of three aircraft flew around the world, crossing both the Pacific and the Atlantic by the island routes.

Above all, Mitchell declined to ignore the enemy's land and surface forces. In doing so he developed what amounted to an obsession with the airplane's ability to destroy every kind of surface vessel. Mitchell sought to establish an independent role for the air corps by proving that his bombers, rather than the Navy's warships, could act as 'the first line of national defense'. His persistence led to Congressional approval of a series of tests involving the bombing of capitulated German warships. Between July 13 and 21, 1921 Mitchell's Martin MB-2s flew against a succession of warships anchored off the Virginia Capes, some 97 miles from the bombers' base at Langley Field. The cruiser *Frankfurt* was sunk with 600-pound bombs; the destroyer *G-102* was 'dive-bombed' by an SE5a carrying 25-pound anti-personnel bombs and then finished off with 300-pound bombs; finally the heavily compartmented battleship *Ostfriesland* was sent to the bottom by a combination of 1000- and 2000-pound bombs. In September the obsolete US battleship *Alabama* suffered a similar fate, sinking like a stone after a direct hit from a 2000-pound bomb. These heavy missiles had been produced specifically for the task, and work was under way on a 4000-pound bomb, which was dropped from an 0/400 on the Aberdeen Proving Grounds on September 28. Further bombing tests were carried out in 1923 on the battleships *Virginia* and *New Jersey*, but they did little to alter the course of the debate which had begun after the initial 1921 series.

The Navy had accused Mitchell of conducting a purely artificial exercise. Things might have been different had the warships been under way and capable of defending themselves. Ironically, while conceding little publicly, the service's tacticians had taken careful note of the bombing trials, and as a result aviation was to play an increasingly

important part in the Navy's planning. But it was Mitchell who lost the argument. When in September 1925 the Navy airship *Shenandoah* broke up with the loss of 14 lives, Mitchell issued a statement charging the US War and Navy Departments with incompetence, criminal negligence and what amounted to 'treasonable administration of the national defense'. This intemperate outburst led to Mitchell's court-martial and suspension from duty for five years. He resigned in February 1926 to devote the last ten years of his life to demonstrating that 'the airplane is the arbiter of our nation's destiny'.

In Britain the theories of Douhet and Mitchell found a supporter in the Chief of Air Staff, Sir Hugh Trenchard, who believed that no system of air defense could be effective and that the only way to stem an air attack was by launching a crushing counter-offensive. In Trenchard's words, 'The nation that could stand being bombed the longest would win in the end'.

On the morality of bombing civilians, Trenchard conceded that a policy of deliberate terror might be contrary to the accepted rules of war, while adding the rider, '... it is an entirely different matter to terrorize munitions workers (men and women) into absenting themselves from work or stevedores into abandoning the loading of a ship with munitions through fear of air attack upon the factory or dock concerned'. Trenchard's belief in the strategic role of the bomber, both as a means of defending Britain and inflicting a speedy defeat on her enemies, became the principal justification for an independent RAF.

A 100-pound phosphorus bomb explodes over the disused American battleship *Alabama* during bombing trials organized by Brigadier-General Mitchell in September 1921. The aircraft responsible for this spectacular display is an MB-2-NBS-1; the object of the exercise was to demonstrate how chemical missiles could 'make the decks and below decks of any war vessel a floating hell'. *Alabama* was bombarded with phosphorus, tear gas and incendiaries before being sunk by a 2000-pound bomb.

2.2 1930s: THE BOMBER WILL ALWAYS GET THROUGH

THE EARLY 1930s SAW A RADICAL SHIFT IN the shape, construction and capabilities of military aircraft. The world's first all-metal design, the Junkers 1 monoplane, had appeared at the end of 1915. However, the wooden fabric-covered biplane held sway until the late 1920s, when the widespread use of metal endowed large aircraft with sufficient strength to adopt the monoplane form.

In France the metal chosen by most designers was the light alloy duralumin, used in the construction of the Lioré et Olivier Le0 12, a two-seat twin-engined biplane which appeared in 1924 and equipped an experimental night bomber squadron. A civil version of this design, the Le0 121, led to the development of a slightly larger bomber, the Le0 20, of which 320 were eventually built for the French air service.

The Le0 20 remained in service until 1933, but a more successful French all-metal biplane was the Breguet 19 two-seat light bomber designed to replace the celebrated Br14. The Br19 was a robust aircraft with clean lines and a single-strut sesquiplane lay-out which made for easy building and maintenance, an asset underlined by the large number of different power plants it accommodated during its 15-year life. From 1925 about 1000 Br19s were produced in France, serving in a reconnaissance role (Br19A.2), as a day/night bomber (BR19B.2) and as a long-range reconnaissance type (Br19GR).

The heavy bomber tradition had been established in Russia before World War I, with Igor Sikorsky's Ilya Muromets. In 1926 the Soviet Central Aero and Hydrodynamic Institute (Ts AGI) and the Special Technical Bureau began work on a significant new heavy bomber, designated ANT-6 and evolved from the TB-1, a twin-engined cantilever low-wing monoplane constructed of Kolchug aluminum sheeting. The new bomber emerged in December 1930 as the TB-3. During the 1930s the aircraft underwent a series of modifications, including the adoption of a smooth skin surface and the reduction of defensive armament from ten DA-2 machine-guns installed in open positions to three ShKAS guns in manually operated nose and dorsal turrets. By the summer of 1934 over 250 TB-3s had entered service, assigned to bombing, cargo and paratroop transportation duties and exploration work with Soviet Arctic expeditions. A small number were also used in 'parasite' fighter experiments.

In 1926 the German designer Dr Adolph Rohrbach perfected the stressed-skin monoplane, requiring no bracing. This technical advance was incorporated in the British Beardmore Inflexible of 1928. This 16.5-ton giant was a monoplane, of 175ft 6in wingspan, constructed almost entirely of duralumin. It was powered by three 650hp Condor II engines, one of which was installed in the nose. Though the Beardmore prototype was on the grand scale, it was so heavy that it proved unable to carry any useful load and it was eventually scrapped.

The first all-metal heavy bomber to enter British service was of more modest dimensions and backward-looking design. The Handley Page

Hinaidi II, first flown in November 1931, would have been reassuringly familiar to World War I veterans of the Independent Force. The Hinaidi was an ungainly biplane, with a fixed four-wheel main undercarriage, whose all-metal airframe was hidden by a fabric covering. Its two 440hp Bristol Jupiter VIII radials gave it a cruising speed of 75mph at 5000ft with a bombload of 1500 pounds and a modest operating radius of 100 miles. The aircraft took nearly an hour to climb to 13000ft. The crew sat in open positions, muffled against the slipstream, and defensive armament was provided by three hand-held machine-guns in nose, dorsal and ventral positions. The bombsight was the Course Setting Mark VII, into which the bombardier set the aircraft's speed and altitude, the bombs' ballistic data, and the estimated wind speed and direction. The sight was not gyroscopically stabilized, which meant that to align his aircraft on the target during a bombing run the pilot could only make unbanked turns. These could be achieved much more easily in a biplane than in a monoplane. In 'peacetime' conditions trained crews could use the Mark VII to achieve accuracies of within 50yds from 10000ft, flying at 85mph.

Cautious Modernizing

Late in 1933 the Hinaidi began to be replaced by the Handley Page Heyford, designed by G R Volkert. One of the most distinctive of all British military aircraft, it was the last of the RAF's heavy biplane bombers. Appropriately the first squadron to take delivery of the new bomber was No.99, based at Upper Heyford in Oxford. In a sense the Heyford was a big biplane inside which there was a monoplane struggling to get out. The upper wing, bearing two 525hp Rolls Royce Kestrel III engines, was shoulder mounted on the upper fuselage. Some distance below the slender fuselage, and supported by heavy interplane struts, was the lower mainplane, in whose thick center section a maximum bombload of 3500 pounds could be stored. The large main landing wheels were protected by fairings attached to the wing's leading edge. The crew of five – pilot, co-pilot and three gunners – sat in open cockpits. Defensive armament consisted of single hand-trained Lewis guns in nose, dorsal and ventral 'dustbin' positions. In spite of its curious appearance, the Heyford's lay-out conferred a number of significant advantages; its height above the ground of 20ft 6in gave fitters and groundcrew head-high clearance under the fuselage to carry out speedy servicing and reloading of the bomb bay. In addition each member of the crew had an exceptionally good field of vision and fire, although landing the Heyford was a tricky business. Production came to an end with the Heyford III, powered by the 640hp Kestrel VI. In all, the Heyford served until 1937 with 11 first-line UK-based bomber squadrons.

The RAF's first cautious experiment with an all-metal cantilever monoplane came in November 1936 when No.38 Squadron, based at Mildenhall, took

delivery of the Fairey Hendon. Like the ill-fated Fairey Fox, the Hendon was a one-squadron aircraft and only 14 were built. The Hendon had a distinctive profile, with a fuselage which possessed almost constant depth from nose to tail, immensely thick wings and a 'trousered' undercarriage. Powered by two closely cowled Kestrel VI engines, driving three-bladed Fairey-Reed metal propellers, the production MkII had a maximum speed at 15 000 ft of 155 mph and could cruise at 133 mph. The pilot's cockpit was canopied and, because of the aircraft's speed, the front gunner/bombardier was protected against the slipstream by a rotating domed cupola. Access to the tail gunner's position was by a corrugated duralumin sheet catwalk. The lay-out of the Hendon's flying and control surfaces in relation to the nose, dorsal and tail gun positions ensured that a blind spot did not exist more than 22 ft from the aircraft. Maximum bombload was 1660 pounds with a range of 1360 miles.

The Fairey Hendon never flew operationally but it gently pushed the RAF into the era of the modern monoplane bomber. As late as July 6, 1935, when King George VI reviewed RAF squadrons at Mildenhall and Duxford, there was not a single monoplane to be seen.

The United States

In the early 1930s a revolution was taking shape in the United States, which would make Britain's bomber force appear positively antique. It was in North America, with its burgeoning airline industry, that successive technological innovations were swiftly absorbed into new military types which were to set the standards for almost all the bombers which flew in World War II.

An early example of this process can be seen in the Boeing YB-9 of 1931. An all-metal cantilever low-wing monoplane carrying its 2260-pound bombload entirely enclosed within its semi-monocoque fuselage, the YB-9 also featured a retractable undercarriage. At the cost of only a little extra weight this eliminated the severe drag penalty imposed by the fixed undercarriage – as much as 15 per cent of the total profile drag on an aircraft like the Handley Page Hinaidi. Only seven YB-9s were built, but its advanced features were consolidated a year later in the Martin Model 123 bomber, which entered service with the US Army Air Corps in 1935 as the B-10. The most advanced bomber of its day, the B-10 was an all-metal monoplane with fully enclosed bombload and positions for its five-man crew,

The standard Soviet heavy bomber up to 1941, the TB-3, was an ideal choice for carrying and dropping paratroops. The Russians were pioneers of this technique but did little in the war to exploit the technical expertise they had gained in the 1930s. The TB-3 had 133 ft span wings of exceptional thickness and strength, braced with five spars and built in three sections. Powered by geared and supercharged 920 hp M-34RN engines, it had a range of 1350 miles with a bombload of 4409 pounds. A maximum load of 12 800 pounds, stowed internally and externally, could be carried over short distances.

Right: Handley Page Heyfords of Nos. 10 and 99 Squadrons at RAF Mildenhall for the Royal Review of July 6, 1935.
Below: The Handley Page Harrow prototype K6933, which first flew on October 10, 1936. Sixty-two MkII Harrows were produced, powered by 925 hp Pegasus XX engines and equipped with power-operated turrets.
Below Right: Boulton Paul Overstrands of the RAF's No. 101 Squadron, the first British bombers equipped with power-operated turrets.

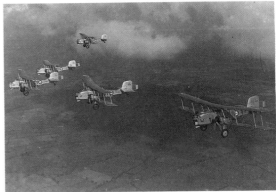

retractable undercarriage with braked main wheels, flaps and a variable-pitch airscrew. This last innovation eliminated the inefficiencies of converting engine power into thrust at the high and low speed ends of the aircraft's performance envelope. This was a crucial advantage for bomber aircraft, ensuring that less engine power was wasted on take-off or during the cruising phase of flight, which in turn significantly increased the aircraft's range.

In 1934 five B-10s flew non-stop from Alaska to Seattle, a demonstration of the bomber's range which revived the controversy, originally started ten years earlier by Mitchell, over the competing claims of land-based long-range aircraft and the US Navy's warships for the principal role in national defense. The Army Air Corps was sufficiently encouraged by the performance of the B-10 to issue a specification (under the designation 'Project A') for an offensive anti-shipping bomber capable of making a direct flight from the United States to Alaska, Panama or Hawaii. To a 5000-mile range were added requirements for a speed of 200 mph and a payload of 2000 pounds.

In June 1934 the Boeing Aircraft Company, designer of the revolutionary 247 transport, was awarded the preliminary contract, under the terms of 'Project A', to build a single aircraft designated XBLR-1 (Experimental Bomber Long Range 1), later simply XB-15. Boeing's own designation was Model 294, but hardly had work begun on the giant four-engined bomber envisaged by its designers when the Army solicited tenders for an aircraft to replace the B-10, capable of carrying a ton of bombs over a

distance of 2000 miles at over 200 mph. The prototype of such an aircraft was to be ready to fly within 12 months.

Boeing immediately switched its priorities, combining the work already devoted to the Model 294* with the proven success of the 247 to produce the four-engined Model 299 (prototype X13372), which flew for the first time on July 28, 1935. The gleaming new aircraft made a spectacular debut. Massive by the standards of the day but with a streamlined profile tapering to a large tail, the Model 299 weighed 21 600 pounds empty and was provided with five (unarmed) gun emplacements which instantly earned it the nickname 'Flying Fortress'. The power plants were four Pratt and Whitney radials, which gave X13372 a performance which effortlessly outstripped the Army Air Corps' original specifications. Tests demonstrated that the Fortress had a maximum speed of 236 mph at 10 000 ft and a service ceiling of 24 600 ft. Normal operating range with a bombload of 4000 pounds (four times that of the B-10) was 2400 miles. There was a price to be paid for this level of performance – $260 000 per aircraft, three times as expensive as the submissions placed by Douglas for the X13372's competitor, the twin-engined B-18, a military derivative of the DC2 commercial airliner.

Three weeks after its maiden flight, X13372 made an impressive 2100-mile non-stop flight from Seattle to the AAC evaluation center at Wright Field,

*The XBLR-1 first flew on October 18, 1937 and saw service as the XC-105 in a cargo and personnel transport role.

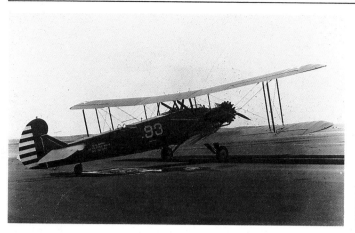

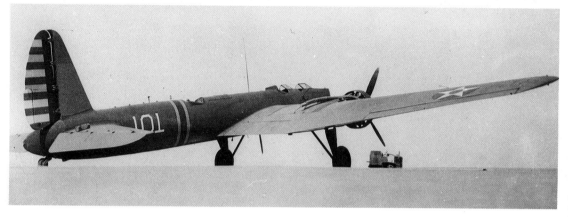

Above left: A Keystone Y1B-4, one of a complicated series of twin-engined bombers produced in the United States in the 1920s by the Keystone Aircraft Corporation.
Above right: The Martin B-10, which appeared in prototype form in the early months of 1932 and was to revolutionize multi-engine bomber design.
Left: The Boeing YB-9, an interim bomber design, of all-metal construction and with retractable undercarriage, which first flew in April 1931. Although not built in quantity and used only on a trial basis by the US Army Air Corps, the YB-9 offered a considerable improvement over its Keystone predecessors. However, its top speed of 188 mph and bombload of 2260 pounds was soon to be overshadowed by the B-10.

Dayton, Ohio – covering the distance at an average speed of 232 mph. However, the aircraft's triumphal progress was temporarily halted on October 20 when it was destroyed in a take-off accident. The field was left open for the more mundane Douglas B-18. Nevertheless, X13372 had demonstrated such potential that the AAC placed an order for 13 pre-production models (designated Y1B-17) and a 14th airframe for evaluation trials. Nearly a ton heavier and seven feet longer than X13372, the Y1B-17 was powered by four 930 hp Wright Cyclone Gr-1820-39 (G2) engines, which pushed the top speed up to 265 mph at 14 000 ft, and the ceiling to 30 000 ft. An extra crew member could be accommodated, and the flight deck was redesigned to place the pilot and co-pilot alongside each other.

In trials undertaken by 2nd Bombardment Group, the Y1B-17s registered nearly 10 000 flying hours and almost two million miles in all-weather conditions without a single accident.

A further dramatic improvement to the bomber stemmed directly from a remarkable incident in the spring of 1938 when a YB-17, crammed with instruments collecting performance data, stalled in a storm over Langley Field and survived no fewer than nine spins before being brought down to land by Lieutenant William Bentley. Theoretically the aircraft's wings should have sheared off under such stress, but they only suffered minor damage and a few popped rivets. The AAC's reaction was to fit as an aircraft the airframe which had been ordered for ground tests on stress levels. Redesignated Y1B-17A (No. 373369), it was powered by four 1000 hp

Cyclone radials, each fitted with a Moss-General Electric supercharger. The combination of new engines and a supercharger pushed the Y1B-17A through the 300 mph barrier, although its effective maximum speed was 295 mph at 25 000 ft. Service ceiling soared to 38 000 ft and range leapt to 3600 miles. Standard operational payload was estimated at 2500 pounds over a range of 1500 miles. Here, it seemed, was a strategic bomber in a class of its own. But in spite of its impressive profile not everyone was impressed. A critical note was struck by Air Commodore Harris, who had inspected a Y1B-17 when visiting the United States as a member of the British Purchasing Commission. In his report he wrote: 'Far from being a "Fortress", this aircraft is practically indefensible against any modern fighter'.

The first Fortress production contract, for the modest total of 39 aircraft, was placed in the same year. The resulting B-17Bs incorporated a number of modifications, including a cleaned-up nose, altered settings for the turbo superchargers, a new hydraulic braking system, and enlarged rudder and flaps. By the time the last of the B-17Bs was delivered in March 1940 the war storm had broken in Europe.

The USAAF also possessed a sophisticated tachometric bombsight, the Norden, which it claimed would enable a bombardier to drop a bomb 'in a pickle barrel from 25 000 ft'. The principal component of the Norden's sighting head was a gyro-stabilized, motor-driven telescope, through which the bombardier viewed the target during the bombing run. Having set into the sight the appropriate windspeed and altitude calculations, and the bombs' ballistic data, the bombardier held the telescope's sighting graticule over the target. Precise information on the aircraft's movement over the ground was fed into the Norden's sighting computer, generating course corrections which enabled the bombardier to control lateral movements of the aircraft through the Automatic Flight Control Equipment (AFCE). The act of keeping the sight pointed at the target commanded the aircraft to steer for an accurate bombing run, making correctly banked turns. The bombs were dropped automatically at the release angle calculated by the sight's computer. The bombardier would then cut out the sight and restore control of the aircraft to the pilot. The Norden was a fancy instrument, and in the ideal, clear conditions of American training grounds, bombardiers used it to achieve impressive results. However, as will be seen, such conditions were rarely present in the skies over Europe during World War II.

Germany Rearms

After World War I Germany was disarmed under the terms of the Treaty of Versailles. Its Air Corps was disbanded and from April 1922 only light civilian aircraft with a maximum speed of 110 mph and an endurance of two and a half hours could be built in Germany. An International Military Control Commission was given the task of making sure that these rules were observed.

Covert methods were employed to maintain a German foothold in military aviation. Help came from an unlikely source. The terms of the Treaty of Rapallo provided for the resumption of diplomatic relations and the expansion of trade between Germany and the Soviet Union. It was also the cover for secret negotiations which resulted in a Soviet agreement to furnish German aircrew with training facilities at an airfield hidden away at Litepsk, 250 miles south of Moscow on the road between Ord and Tambov.

By the early 1930s a new breed of German bombers began to emerge, among them the Junkers Ju52/3m, the most celebrated trimotor type ever built. Pioneers of all-metal aircraft, with their distinctive corrugated skin, the Junkers Flugzeug und Motorenwerke of Dessau had received a number of secret military orders in the 1920s. One of them resulted in the Ju52 transport, powered by a single 800 hp Junkers L-88 engine, which flew for the first time on October 13, 1930. Eighteen months later, after a comprehensive re-design, a three-engine development appeared powered by a trio of 575 hp BMW-built Pratt and Whitney Hornet radials. Designated Ju52/3m, the trimotor entered production as a commercial transport with Deutsche Lufthansa and a number of foreign airlines.

In January 1933 Adolf Hitler maneuvered himself into power as Chancellor in a Nazi-Nationalist coalition. The rearmament of Germany quickly moved into a higher gear. The Reichskommissariat für die Luftfahrt (Government Aviation Inspectorate), headed by the World War I ace Hermann Goering, and the covert Luftschutzamt (Department of Air Raid Protection) were merged into a single ministry, the Reichsluftfahrtministerium (RLM), under the control of Goering and tasked with the development of a new German air service, the Luftwaffe. At the same time aero clubs throughout Germany were absorbed into the nation-wide Deutscher Luftsportsverband (DLV), which was run along para-military lines by another World War I fighter ace, Bruno Loerzer.

Under the direction of the RLM the Ju52 was adapted as a Behelfskampfflugzeug (auxiliary bomber) to fill a gap created by the disappointing performance of the Dornier Do11c. By the time the existence of the Luftwaffe was officially announced in February 1935, 450 Ju52/3mg3e four-seater bombers had been delivered, comprising two-thirds of the total Geman bomber force. With a top speed of 180 mph at sea level and an operational ceiling of 20 700 ft, the Ju52/3mg3e had a range of 795 miles with a maximum bombload of 2205 pounds. Defensive armament was provided by two hand-trained 7.9 mm MG-15 machine-guns, one in a dorsal position and the other installed in a ventral 'dustbin'. The aircraft first flew operationally in the late summer of 1936, when 20 were despatched to Spain after the outbreak of the Spanish Civil War.

In 1934, as the Ju52 went went into full-scale production, the designers at the gleaming new Heinkel factory at Rostok-Marienehe were working on a twin-engined machine which could equally well be used as a high-speed civil or military aircraft. On February 24, 1935 the He111a (later designated He111V1) took off on its maiden flight. Conceived by the brothers Siegfried and Walter Günter, the all-metal He111a boasted exceptionally clean aerodynamic lines, with distinctive elliptical wings, fully retractable undercarriage and variable-pitch airscrews driven by 660 hp BMW VI water-cooled engines. As a medium bomber it could be armed with three defensive 7.9 mm machine-guns – in nose, dorsal and ventral 'dustbin' positions – and an internal bombload of 2205 pounds. The fourth prototype, the ten-seat transport version designated He111V4D-AHAO, was publicly unveiled at Berlin-Tempelhof on January 10, 1936, while the He111V3 provided the prototype for the first military pre-production version the He111A-0. At the Rechlin proving ground, Luftwaffe test pilots complained that the He111A-0 required excessive stick pressures and was an unforgiving aircraft to fly. The ten He111A-0s which had been produced were successfully off-loaded on to the Chinese government and a single machine – fitted with new 1000 hp Daimler Benz DB600A power plants and designated He111V5D-APYS – was delivered to Rechlin in the spring of 1936. Following the tests an order was placed for ten He111B-s, four of which later saw service at the beginning of the Spanish Civil War in an experimental bomber Staffel, VB88.

A bulk order quickly followed for 300 He111B-1s, with a cruising speed of 214 mph, operational ceiling of almost 23 000 ft and range – with full armament and 3307-pound bombload – of 559 miles. The only comparable contemporary European medium bomber was the Italian Savoia Marchetti S.79, another civil transport derivative, which possessed a cruising speed of 233 mph, service ceiling of 21 200 ft and a range of 1181 miles with a bombload of 2750 pounds.

The He111B-1's introduction to service was with I/KG154 (later KG27 'Boelcke'), and it was followed

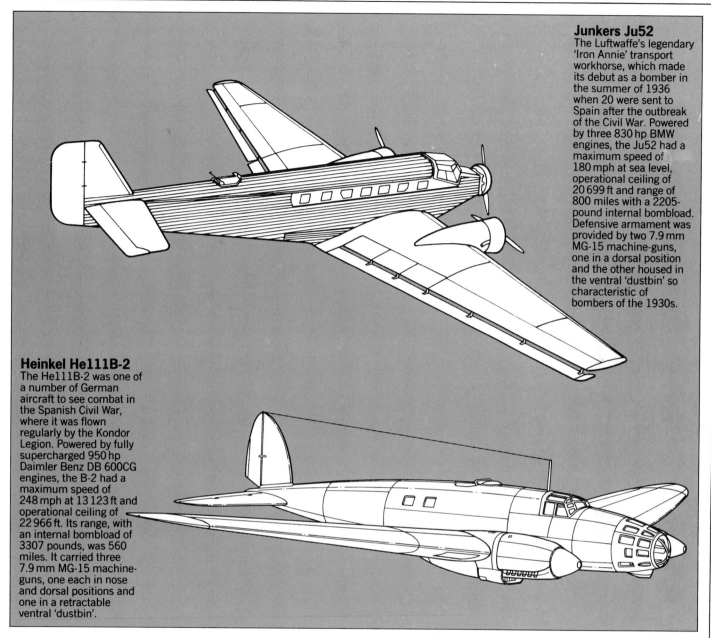

Junkers Ju52
The Luftwaffe's legendary 'Iron Annie' transport workhorse, which made its debut as a bomber in the summer of 1936 when 20 were sent to Spain after the outbreak of the Civil War. Powered by three 830 hp BMW engines, the Ju52 had a maximum speed of 180 mph at sea level, operational ceiling of 20 699 ft and range of 800 miles with a 2205-pound internal bombload. Defensive armament was provided by two 7.9 mm MG-15 machine-guns, one in a dorsal position and the other housed in the ventral 'dustbin' so characteristic of bombers of the 1930s.

Heinkel He111B-2
The He111B-2 was one of a number of German aircraft to see combat in the Spanish Civil War, where it was flown regularly by the Kondor Legion. Powered by fully supercharged 950 hp Daimler Benz DB 600CG engines, the B-2 had a maximum speed of 248 mph at 13 123 ft and operational ceiling of 22 966 ft. Its range, with an internal bombload of 3307 pounds, was 560 miles. It carried three 7.9 mm MG-15 machine-guns, one each in nose and dorsal positions and one in a retractable ventral 'dustbin'.

by the He111B-2, fitted with the more powerful DB600CG fully-supercharged engine developing 950 hp at critical altitude. Carrying a standard bombload of 1653 pounds, the B-2's range was 1000 miles, with a maximum speed of 217 mph at 19 600 ft. As it was to demonstrate in Spain, the He111's performance enabled it to outpace most of the fighters sent up to intercept it and to carry out unescorted raids with relative impunity.

Destined to join the He111 in Spain was the Dornier Do17, a slender twin-engined bomber whose origins lay in a Lufthansa order for a high-speed mailplane with additional accommodation for up to six passengers. The first of three prototypes built by Dornier was flown in the autumn of 1934, but the extreme slimness of the 'Flying Pencil's' fuselage – so narrow at the tail that a large man could encircle it with his arms – limited its possibilities as a civil

Banking over the Heinkel works airfield, this He111D displays its 'splinter' camouflage of jagged gray brown and green patches. The aircraft on the ground is one of the He118 dive bomber prototypes.

transport and Lufthansa lost interest in the aircraft. Shortly afterwards the RLM decided to investigate its potential as a medium bomber and a new prototype – Do17V4 – was produced with the twin-fin assembly which became standard in the subsequent production aircraft. By mid-1937 both the Do17E-1 bomber, powered by two 750hp BMWVI engines, and the Do17F-1 long-range reconnaissance bomber were in Luftwaffe squadron service; the E-1 had a maximum speed of 220mph and a 990-mile range with a bombload of 1750 pounds. In July 1937 a specially stripped prototype Do17, with uprated engines which gave it a top speed of 270mph, made a spectacular appearance at the International Military Aircraft Competition at Zurich, where it flew rings round the French Dewoitine D510, then thought to be the best single-seat fighter in Europe.

The Dive Bomber

In the spring of 1936 a new tactical bomber – the Junkers Ju87 dive bomber – appeared in Germany. Its gull-shaped wings were to cast a menacing shadow across the battlefields of Europe and, in the late 1930s, exercise an almost hypnotic grip on German air policy.

World War I reports contain many examples of pilots arriving over their objectives and then diving at full power to a height of only a few hundred feet before releasing their bombs when the axis of the aircraft was pointing straight at the target. Little was done to systematize this tactic before the end of the war, although the evolution in 1917–18 of sophisticated ground-attack techniques by both Allied and German units encouraged its employment in the search for greater accuracy. In the 1920s the dive bombing concept was kept alive in the United States Marine Corps, which used modified DH4s in a dive bombing role in a number of counter-insurgency operations in Central America and Haiti.

While modified fighters like the DH4 or Curtiss F6C proved relatively efficient in this new role, it was clear that priority should be given to the development of specialized dive bombing aircraft. This in turn accelerated the evolution of a body of tactics which addressed itself to the uses and advantages of a dive bombing force in a modern fleet. A blow was struck for the dive bomber in the US Navy's war games of 1929. The carrier *Saratoga's* fighter-escorted torpedo and dive bombers gained complete tactical surprise when they launched attacks on targets in the Panama Canal Zone which were heavily defended by both land- and carrier-based aircraft.

By the end of the 1920s the advantages of the dive bomber against naval targets had begun to crystallize: in those pre-radar days it was capable of achieving a considerable degree of surprise, appearing without warning and launching its attacks from heights to which only the most specialized guns could elevate and at speeds which cut the firing time down to a few seconds. The high degree of accuracy with which bombs could be placed posed an enormous threat to smaller warships, which could be sunk by this method alone, while capital ships could be 'swamped' by a combination of dive and torpedo bombing, the former suppressing anti-aircraft fire while the more vulnerable torpedo bombers delivered their attacks in straight and level flight.

The first purpose-built dive bomber to be ordered by the US Navy was the Martin BM-1, a two-seater biplane fitted with an under-fuselage bomb-release crutch which swung the projectile down and away from the body of the aircraft, clearing the propellers and undercarriage in one quick movement. Taking a keen interest in dive bomber development in the United States was a German journalist, Walther Kelffel. In 1930 Kelffel had attended a number of airshows in which the Curtiss XF8C-2 Helldiver had been put through its paces, filing glowing reports of the potential of the dive bomber. A year later the Curtiss Wright Company extended its hospitality to a distinguished visitor, the World War I fighter ace Ernst Udet, by then a civilian. After Udet had test-flown the Helldiver, Curtiss Wright offered to sell him a machine for $14000. The former ace had become a dive bomber convert, but at the time had little influence on German air policy. When the Nazis came to power he was better placed to press his claims. As an honorary Air Vice Commodore in the DLV, he returned to the United States in the summer of 1933. With money provided by Hermann Goering, Udet acquired two Curtiss F2C Hawks, which he whimsically named *Iris* and *Ilse* before they were crated up and despatched by sea to Bremerhaven.

Germany and the Dive Bomber

German interest in the dive bomber, however, pre-dated the arrival of the Curtiss Hawks in the autumn of 1933. In 1928 one of the aircraft to fly in tests at Litepsk was the K-47, designed by Flyingindustri of Malmo, a subsidiary of Junkers. A low-wing two-seater monoplane powered by a Bristol Jupiter radial, it was specifically braced to handle the stress of a pull-out from a high-speed dive in fighter combat. The K-47 was rejected as a fighter but showed up well in subsequent dive bombing tests.

Although the K-47 opened a new chapter in German aviation history, it was the Heinkel He50A biplane of the early 1930s which marked the first stage in the dive bomber program. A single-seat dive bomber capable of carrying a 1102-pound bombload, the He50A had a maximum speed of 143mph at sea level and a range of 370 miles. It was fitted with a three-bladed two-pitch airscrew, which enabled the pilot to select his airscrew pitch before entering the dive. In October 1933 the first production aircraft were delivered to JG132, which had been given prime responsibility for dive bomber training. Another 51 aircraft were ordered at the beginning of 1934, principally for service with flying training schools and also as part of the establishment of the first German dive bomber unit, Fliegergruppe Schwerin.

A rugged 'throwaway' replacement for the He50A was found in the Henschel Hs123, a sturdy biplane of clean aerodynamic design utilizing a single inter-plane strut with no external bracing. In 1937 the first Hs123A-1s began to enter service. Powered by an 880hp BMW 132Dc engine housed in a short cowl with 18 distinctive blisters enclosing the valve gear, the Hs123A could lift a single 550-pound bomb in an under-fuselage crutch and carry four 110-pound bombs under the wings; maximum speed was 248mph, with a diving speed of 350mph (no air brakes were fitted) and a range of 530 miles.

The stage was now set for the Ju87 to emerge as the key element in the Luftwaffe's third and final stage of dive bomber expansion before 1939. There have been few warplanes whose appearance so starkly conveyed its function, the cranked monoplane wings and heavy fixed undercarriage resembling in silhouette a monstrous bird of prey. Such was its mystique that it rapidly appropriated a contraction of the dive bomber class name, Sturkampfflugzeug, as its own - Stuka. The first Stuka prototype, powered by a Rolls Royce Kestrel V engine driving a two-blade fixed-pitch wooden airscrew, underwent tests at Dessau in the summer of 1935. The two-man crew sat back-to-back under a roomy 'greenhouse' canopy with an excellent all-round view, the rear gunner's field of fire being enhanced by a twin tail. The prototype had been designed to accommodate air brakes, but these were not fitted for the tests. As a result excessive vibration in sharp dives caused the tail section to break up and the aircraft to crash. The second prototype, Ju87V2, incorporated a redesigned single-fin unit and under-wing dive brakes, consisting of a hinged slot which could be turned to 90 degrees during a dive. It also had a new engine, the 610 hp Junkers Jumo 210A and a three-blade variable pitch airscrew. In trials held in June 1936 the Ju87 overcame its principal rivals, the Arado Ar81 biplane and the Heinkel He118, the latter a sleek all-metal monoplane with retractable undercarriage and powered by the 900 hp DB600 engine, which gave it a top speed of 250 mph. However, in the trials the He118 failed to achieve a diving angle of more than 50 degrees, possibly because of over-cautious handling by the test pilot.

The outcome of the trials was dramatically put beyond doubt on June 27 when the third He118 prototype crashed when being flown by Ernst Udet, the impulsive fighter ace having ignored a clear instruction to change the airscrew to a coarse pitch before going into the terminal drive. As a result the dive nearly proved to be terminal for Udet. The propeller flew off and the He118 hurtled to the ground, closely followed by the parachute-borne Udet, who had only just managed to struggle free in the nick of time.

The first production models of the Ju87A1 ('Anton') entered service with I/StG162 'Immelmann' in the spring of 1937. Two hundred 'Antons' were eventually delivered to the Luftwaffe. They were initially equipped with the 635 hp Jumo 210a, which late in 1937 was replaced by the Jumo 211, the standard power plant of the Ju87B1 ('Bertha'), the major wartime variant. The Ju87B1's standard bombload was a single 1,102-pound bomb slung under the fuselage, or one crutch-carried 550-pound bomb and four 110-pound bombs dropped from hard points under the wings. Defensive armament was provided by two fixed 7.9 mm MG-17s mounted in the leading edges of the wings just clear of the propeller arc, and a hand-trained MG-15 operated by the radio operator/gunner in the rear of the canopy. This gun had a very restricted field of fire, with blind spots under the rear fuselage and tail unit, making the Ju87 highly vulnerable to fighter attacks from underneath or the beam. Range was 370 miles with a moderate top speed of 211 mph and a cruising speed of 175 mph. These modest figures belie the dramatic impact which the Stuka made in 1939–40.

It was perhaps fitting that the Ju87 should have first entered service with I/StG162 'Immelmann', for it was in the hands of the great WW1 ace Max Immelmann that the Fokker Eindecker briefly held sway over the Western Front as the first true fighter aircraft. The Eindecker was another essentially modest performer, and within a year its supremacy had been challenged by improved Allied types. The Stuka's heyday was equally brief, but before it suffered a similar fate it had exercised a crucial influence in the opening campaigns of World War II.

Hindsight lends a certain inevitability to the Ju87's progress into service, as it also does to the subsequent exposure of its vulnerability. However, in the mid-1930s the German advocates of dive bombing did not have things all their own way. A particularly fierce opponent of this form of attack was General Wolfram von Richthofen, Head of the Luftwaffe's Technical Office, who on June 9, 1936 – shortly before the final dive bombing trails – issued a confidential memorandum recommending a moratorium on all development in this area. On the same day he was replaced by Udet, keenest advocate of the dive bomber, and the program forged ahead.

After the war General Marquadt, who had served in the Luftwaffe's Engineering Corps, referred to the Curtiss Hawks which Udet had brought back to Germany as 'Trojan horses within the walls of traditional aircraft design'. But it is debatable if the arrival of the two American dive bombers was a crucial factor in the formulation of German air policy. More important was the fact that they delivered the dashing Udet into the hands of the Luftwaffe, which he joined in January 1936 as Inspector of Fighters and Stukas. The former fighter ace was by temperament more drawn to to the dramatic concept of dive-bombing assault rather than the more pedestrian notion of medium and heavy bombers attacking from high altitude in straight and level flight. Moreover, in terms of Germany's limited material resources and developing war plans, the cost-effectiveness and the tactical advantages of the dive bomber were extremely persuasive. The acquisition of a fleet of heavy bombers would inevitably be an expensive and lengthy business. The Ju87 could be mass-produced quickly and relatively cheaply, and was ideally suited to the waging of short-range campaigns against Germany's neighbors, when the maximum precision in destroying significant military targets at the point of advance of the armored forces was one of the principal elements in the doctrine of *Blitzkrieg*. In the tactical requirements summary issued by the General Staff in the spring of 1938, the following appears: 'The emphasis in offensive bombardment has clearly shifted from area to pinpoint bombardment. For this reason the development of a bombsight suitable for use in dive bomber aircraft is more important than any other aiming device'. This argument was reinforced by the results of the bombing trials conducted by the Luftwaffe's Training Wing, the Lehrgeschwader, at Greifswald. The most experienced He111 and Do17 crews, bombing horizontally from 13 000 ft with no interference from fighters or AA fire, were able to place only two per cent of their bombs within a circle

The FW200 Kondor, a modified four-engined airliner thrust into the heavy bomber role at the beginning of the war. Armed with a 20 mm cannon in a dorsal turret, plus five machine-guns, the Kondor could carry a 2000-pound bombload over an effective operational radius of 860 miles. A Kondor squadron was formed in 1940 for reconnaissance and strike missions over the British naval approaches and was subsequently elevated to Geschwader (Group) status. In all, 263 Kondors were built.

330 ft in diameter. At 7500 ft the average hovered between 12 and 15 per cent. When the Ju87s took over, they were able to place 25 per cent of their bombs in a circle 165 ft in diameter. The disappointing performance in horizontal bombing of the Goerz-Visier 219 sight, and the slow development of the Lofte 7 and 7D sights, suggested that only the dive bomber could be relied upon as a weapon of immediate effectiveness in the event of war*. Henceforward all Luftwaffe bombers were to be built to deliver their bombs in a dive.

The Ju88 and the Heavy Bomber

The insistence on a dive bombing requirement had a crucial effect on a new aircraft designed by Junkers. In 1934 the Technical Office had issued a specification for a heavily armed Kampfzerstorer, a multi-purpose warplane capable of fulfilling the roles of bomber, bomber destroyer, reconnaissance and close-support aircraft. By the beginning of 1935 this approach had been abandoned in favour of a Schnellbomber, an unarmed high-speed bomber whose performance would not be compromised by concern as to its suitability for other roles. The basic requirement was for a three-seat bomber, with a maximum bombload of 1765 pounds, top speed of 310 mph and a cruising speed of 280 mph. The result was the Ju88VI prototype, which made its maiden

*Similar trials in the United States in the late 1930s prompted the conclusion that dive bombing reduced the radial error of horizontal bombing against stationary targets by at least half. Against moving targets, 'the dive bomber is at least four times as effective as the horizontal bomber carrying the same weight of bombs'.

flight on December 21, 1936. Weighing only six tons and powered by two 900 hp DB600 liquid-cooled engines, the Ju88VI attained a maximum speed of 340 mph. Speed notwithstanding, combat experience in the Spanish Civil War led Oberkommando der Luftwaffe (OKL) to request the addition of defensive armament. Work stopped while extensive alterations were made to the cabin enclosure to accommodate the necessary armament.

But at this point Junkers were overtaken by the new dive-bombing requirement. The Schnellbomber was taken apart and rebuilt with strengthened wings, fuselage and tail unit and dive brakes. At one point the Junkers managing director Dr Heinrich Koppenburg complained that he had been presented with no fewer than 2,500 demands for alterations by the Technical Office's engineers. Finally, all the requirements – dive bombing capability, increased defensive armament and a fourth crew member – were embodied in the Ju88V4, which introduced a 'beetle's eye' of optically flat panels in the nose, and a ventral gondola terminating in a position for a single aft-firing 7.99mm machine-gun on a flexible mounting. The aircraft's weight had more than doubled, to 13 tons, and maximum speed had fallen by 60 mph. Erhard Milch, the Secretary of State for Air, contemptuously referred to the Ju88 as 'a flying barn door which was capable of becoming a bird again only after it had dropped its bombs'.

This was a hasty judgement on an aircraft which, at the beginning of the war, was the best all-round bomber in service with any of Europe's air forces. The first production model, the Ju88A-1, was powered by two 1200 Jumo 211B engines, giving it a top speed of 258 mph at a height of 18 000 ft when carrying a 2000-pound bombload. With this load the effective attack radius was about 550 miles, cruising at 190 mph – falling to 250 miles with an offensive load of 4000 pounds. The four crew members sat in extremely cramped positions, which they could not exchange, closely grouped in the fuselage forward of the front wing spar. The pilot sat in a relatively comfortable seat, with the bombardier squeezed in beside him when not lying over his Lofte tachometric bombsight, which was uncomfortably close to the rudder pedals and bomb switches. Behind the pilot sat the upper gunner/wireless operator, while the lower gunner perched on a small rest seat above his station in the ventral gondola, which was virtually impossible to occupy in a prone position for more than an hour at a time. In addition to the hand-trained rear and ventral guns there was a single 7.9 mm MG-15 mounted in the starboard side of the cockpit windscreen and fired by the pilot. The close grouping of the crew made for excellent communications but also for increased vulnerability to an accurate burst of fire from a fighter.

The first Luftwaffe unit to receive the Ju88, in September 1939, was I/KG30. In design terms the Ju88 had come full circle to the original Kampf-zerstorer requirement of 1934. Having started life as a specialized high-speed bomber, it had evolved into the most adaptable general-purpose aircraft of World War II, serving not only as a horizontal, dive- and torpedo-bomber but also as a day and night fighter and reconnaissance aircraft. From the basic design was evolved the more advanced Ju188, which appeared in 1942 powered by two 1700 hp BMW 801 radials, with a maximum speed of 310 mph and operational radius of 800 miles with a 2000-pound bombload.

The Uralbomber
In the spring of 1935 Colonel Wilhelm Wimmer, of the Technical Office escorted Hermann Goering around the Junkers factory at Dessau. Passing through sliding doors into an immense hangar they were con-fronted with a full-scale wooden mock-up of a giant aircraft. Turning to Wimmer, Goering spluttered, 'What on earth is that?' Wimmer informed the astonished Goering that this was the Ju89 'Ural-bomber', a project which had been initiated in 1933 as part of the German rearmament program. The name 'Uralbomber' was an indication of the range required of the four-engined strategic bomber and an accurate anticipation of the inbuilt eastward thrust of Hitler's war plans. By 1936 two designs – the Ju89 and the Dornier Do19 – were ready for testing. According to General Deichmann, who was then Chief of Branch 1 (Operations) of the Luftwaffe General Staff, both aircraft displayed promise although their 620 hp Jumo engines left them somewhat underpowered. At this point Goering ordered a halt. Both aircraft appeared in the priority list issued by the Technical Office in April 1937, but by then they were effectively dead. After the war, Deichmann recalled a meeting in 1937, at which Erhard Milch poured scorn on the idea of a four-engined bomber, pointing out that the skies over Germany were so overcast that this would make high-altitude bomb aiming impossible – a serious problem which was indeed encountered by the B-17s of the US 8th Air Force in 1943–45. Moreover, Milch argued, German industrial capacity would permit a

fleet of 1000 heavy bombers only at the expense of the Ju88 medium bomber program. Deichmann claims to have voiced the opinion 'that 1000 four-engined bombers, whose longer range, greater speed and high degree of invulnerability to enemy attack would enable them to reach their targets safely, were of far greater value than 10000 twin-engined bombers which would probably be shot down by the enemy before reaching their destination'.

Germany did enter the war with a four-engined bomber, the Focke-Wulf Fw200 Kondor, derived from the design for a commercial transport and powered by four 1200 hp Bramo radials. However, the Kondor's inherently weak structure was easily overstressed in combat, and its principal wartime duties were as a highly effective long-range anti-shipping bomber operating against convoys in the North Atlantic. Ultimately the development of a German four-engined bomber was sidetracked into the dead end of the Heinkel He177. To provide this 32-ton strategic bomber with the mandatory dive bombing capability, its designers resorted to highly unreliable coupled twin-engine power plants, each driving a single propeller. These engines were extremely difficult to maintain and, in the hands of all but the most experienced pilots, liable to seize up if the throttles were not handled with the greatest care. To ensure added excitement for the aircrew, there were frequent fires caused by fuel leaking from the injectors. In all, nearly 50 of these hugely expensive aircraft broke up in the air or were destroyed by fire when put into dives by their hapless test pilots. In 1943, with the He177 still not in service, even Goering had to admit that the tandem-engine approach was sheer lunacy. But by then such was the pressing need for a four-engined bomber, and so great was the reluctance to write off so much effort and expense, that it was decided to continue with the doomed experiment rather than adopt a simple four-engine arrangement. Eventually 1466 He177s were produced, to no discernible effect.

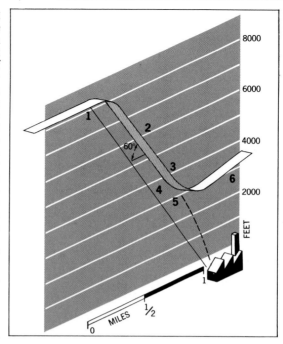

Ju88 dive bombing sequence
Before the attack, the bomb release altitude is set on the contact altimeter in the cockpit and the drift angle caused by the wind set on the BZ1A sight. As he prepares to dive, the pilot observes the target through a small window in the floor of the cockpit. A series of etched lines on the glass enables him to align the aircraft on the target and to judge distance.
1 At the moment the target passes beyond the last of the lines, the pilot pulls a knob to extend the aircraft's dive brakes, while trim tabs fitted to the elevators automatically bring the Ju88's tail up and the nose down to push the aircraft into a 60 degree dive.
2 Now the target comes into view through the pilot's windscreen just above his reflector sight. The pilot eases up the nose, bringing the target into alignment with the top of the sighting circle.
3 820 ft above the pull-out altitude set on the contact altimeter a pair of electrical contacts close to sound a horn in the cockpit. Easing back the stick, the pilot places the target under the base of the sighting reticule.
4 The horn stops at the bomb-release altitude and the pilot presses a button on his control column to initiate bomb releases and the automatic pull-out system.
5 Elevator trim tab brings the nose up and the Ju88 begins to pull out of the dive at a pre-determined rate, while the bombs are released at intervals set on the bomb release mechanism. To prevent them wrecking the propeller, they cannot be released until after the pull out has begun.
6 With the aircraft out of the dive, the pilot retracts the dive brakes and accelerates away. A dive through 4000 ft lasted approximately 12 seconds, with the pilot lightly holding the stick and allowing the elegant system to do the rest of the work.

The Spanish Civil War

In times of 'peace' the military establishments of the major powers are seldom reluctant to test their latest weaponry in combat conditions. This battle proving can be effectively managed by proxy, as has been demonstrated in the Middle East in recent years. In the mid-1930s the Spanish Civil War provided a similar, albeit limited, arena for such an exercise and marked a significant staging post on the way to world war.

On July 18, 1936 the garrisons in 12 cities in Spain and five in Spanish Morocco revolted against Manuel Azaña's Leftist coalition government. Command of the mutineers was assumed by General Francisco Franco who, within a week, had appealed to Germany for help in ferrying colonial troops from Tetuan in Morocco to Seville. Twenty Ju52s were flown via Italy to Spain, eventually airlifting some 15 000 armed troops, together with artillery and ammunition. Within a month nine of the Ju52s had been formed into an improvized bombing unit based at Tablada. On August 14 the Ju52s flew their first mission, attacking Government troops south of Madrid. Theirs were the first bombs to be dropped in action from German aircraft since 1918.

The makeshift bomber unit was followed into action by an experimental Staffel, commanded by Hauptmann Rudolf von Moreau and consisting of four Do17Es and the same number of He111B-0s and Ju86Ds, twin-engined contemporaries of the He111. The Staffel went into action for the first time in the Albacete sector, losing one of the He111s to ground fire. Its crew were taken prisoner.

Enthusiastic support for Franco's Nationalist forces also came from the Italian dictator Benito Mussolini. On the outbreak of the war the Regia Aeronautica had organized the Aviacion del Tercio (Air Force of the Spanish Foreign Legion), whose bombing element was equipped with the three-engined Savoia Marchetti S.81, which had played a large part in the Italian invasion of Ethiopia in 1935–36. In February 1937 three S.79s of the 12° Stormo were despatched to San Juan, Majorca, establishing a base from which they raided Government shipping and land targets such as the airfield at Reus and the arsenal at Cartagena. By the spring of 1937 the Italian bomber units on Majorca comprised 25° Gruppo Bombardamento Notturno 'Pipistrelli della Baleari', equipped with S.81s of the 251° and 252° Squadriglie and the S.79s of 8° Stormo BV 'Falci di Baleari', consisting of 17° Gruppo (18°, 52° Squadriglie) and 28° Gruppo (10°, 19° Squadriglie). On its arrival 25° Gruppo was disbanded and reformed on the mainland, where its new 215° and 216° Squadriglie joined 24° Gruppo to form 21° Stormo BP.

The principal components of the Republican bombing units were the French twin-engined Potez 540 M4 'multiplaces de combat', of which 49 had arrived in Spain by the end of 1936, and the Soviet-supplied SB-2 ('Katiuska'), which had initially formed a Gruppo manned entirely by Russian aircrew. Ordered under the French Air Ministry's Plan 1, the first series-built Potez 540s entered service with the Armée de L'Air in November 1934. The Potez 540 was a graceless aircraft in the French interwar style, with shoulder-mounted wings under which were slung two nacelles containing the 690 hp Hispano-Suiza engines and retractable undercarriage. Top speed was 193 mph at 13 000 ft and maximum bombload 2205 pounds. A marked contrast was presented by the sleek Tupolev SB-2, which began to enter service with the Soviet air force early in 1936. A twin-engined monoplane of exceptionally clean aerodynamic lines, the SB-2 had a maximum speed of 225 mph at 13 000 ft and a bomb capacity of up to 2205 pounds. By 1937 13 SB-2s a day were rolling off the Soviet production lines and by 1941 over 6500 had been delivered, just over 200 of them flying operationally in Spain in the years 1936–39.

By November 1936 the German aerial contingent in Spain had grown sufficiently large to adopt the title of Kondor Legion. Manned by 4500 Luftwaffe volunteers, its establishment initially comprised some 30 Ju52s, 27 He51 single-seater biplanes, 12 He70 reconnaissance/bombers, six He45 biplane reconnaissance/bombers, nine He59s and a single He60 for contact patrols. Its first commander was Generalmajor Hugo von Sperrle, with Oberstleutnant von Richthofen, a cousin of the WWI ace of aces, as his Chief of Staff. The Legion's bombing element was provided by three Ju52 Staffeln, Kampfgruppe 88, which began its operations on November 15 with an attack on Cartagena. On the following day Ju52s and S.81s launched a heavy raid on Madrid. Von Richthofen, who had carefully studied the photographs brought back by He70 reconnaissance aircraft, directed his crews to concentrate their bombing on public buildings to create the maximum psychological effect on the population of the Spanish capital. The first wave of 40 bombers went in by daylight dropping, in addition to their HE bombs, large quantities of thermite incendiaries, which caused widespread fires and lit the way for the bombers which followed them in by night.

In February 1937 the Kondor Legion re-equipped two Staffeln of Kampfgruppe 88 with 30 He111Bs. They were to be followed by 15 Do17F-1 reconnaissance/bombers and 20 Do17E-1 bombers. Until the arrival at the front of the stubby, rugged highly maneuverable Soviet-supplied I-16 monoplane fighter, these new arrivals had little to fear from Government interceptors.

Terror Bombing

The first major action in which the re-equipped Kondor Legion took part was the Vizcaya offensive launched at the end of March 1937 with the aim of breaching the so-called 'Iron Ring' around the city of Bilbao. On March 31 the Kondor Legion struck hard at the rail and road center of Durango. Ju52s armed with 550-pound bombs attacked first, followed by He51s, swooping low over the rubble-strewn streets to strafe and scatter fragmentation bombs. It was the first of a series of raids throughout April, most of them directed against Bilbao. On April 18 three Do17s and two He111s flew three sorties against the city, destroying a glue factory and a block of flats in the old quarter. On the third sortie two of the Do17s were shot down by a Soviet I-15 fighter.

As the Nationalist forces advanced towards Bilbao a number of fortified towns stood between them and the 'Iron Ring'. One of these was the Basque town of Guernica, a communications center about

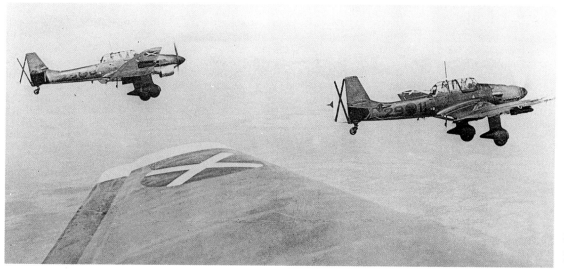

Ju87s over Spain, where they were introduced to combat during the Civil War.

ten miles from the front line with an important bridge crossing the River Oca. At the time Guernica's population of 7000 was swollen by an estimated 3000 refugees, many of them from Durango. It is clear that Generalmajor Sperrle ordered the destruction of the bridge at Guernica, but there is also little doubt that Oberstleutnant von Richthofen had a wider purpose in mind – the deliberate terror bombing of the town in an attempt to destroy the morale of the Government's troops and its supporters. The Kondor Legion's He111s and Ju52s attacked in poor visibility and with inadequate bombsights, but the large quantities of incendiary bombs carried on the operation would have been little use against a stone bridge. After a bombardment lasting three and a half hours, combined with strafing, the heart of the town lay in ruins.

Three Ju87A1s arrived in Spain in September 1937. The Stukas first saw action late in December, supporting Nationalist ground forces in the drive to the Mediterranean coast and in the fighting in Catalonia. They were flown by rotating crews in Kette 'Jolanthe', a reference to a pig which appeared in a popular German stage comedy of the time. In due course a pig made its appearance on the wheel spats of the Stukas, and it remained the Stuka mascot throughout World War II. Pilots found the dive bomber easy to handle, and steady as a rock in the dive, but technical problems dogged its introduction to combat. Better results were obtained in the autumn of 1938, when K/88 took delivery of five of the new Ju87Bs. Nevertheless its evaluation staff noted that, '*IT DID NOT PROVE POSSIBLE TO inflict lasting damage on, or to put out of action completely, any enemy air installations on the ground. It also proved impossible to knock out enemy air forces on the ground. The reason for this was the high degree of flexibility of the enemy formations and the effective use of dummy installations and dummy aircraft on the ground*'.

There were a number of lessons to be gained from combat experience in the Spanish Civil War, but not all of them were absorbed by the Germans and Italians. The experience had been bought relatively

cheaply. Of the 90 aircraft lost by the Kondor Legion during the conflict about 40 had been shot down, while the Legion claimed to have destroyed 277 Republican aircraft in combat. The speed of the He111s, Do17s and S.79s had given them a fair measure of immunity in daylight operations, and even the agile I-16s found it extremely difficult to intercept them. As a result a fatal lack of attention was paid to defensive armament. German designers persisted with single hand-trained 7.9mm MG-15 machine-guns, restricted by small magazines, at a time when the British were developing the eight-gun fighter. Seven months after the bombardment of Guernica the first Hawker Hurricanes were delivered to No. 111 Squadron RAF. It is all the more ironic when one considers that during the course of the Spanish Civil War the Legion's top-scoring ace Werner Molders, flying an Me109D, reshaped fighter tactics as radically as Oswald Boelcke had done in 1916, laying the foundation for the triumph of the Luftwaffe's fighter arm in the Battle of France.

One of the most important lessons the Luftwaffe learnt from its Spanish experience was the extreme vulnerability of light alloy fuel tanks to holing from enemy bullets and shell fragments. The loss of fuel could result in a forced landing in enemy territory. Worse, within minutes a fire might consume the wing or, in extreme cases, an explosion might tear the aircraft apart if a critical fuel-air mixture above the fuel was ignited. Armor protection conferred a heavy weight penalty, so designers turned to the possibilities offered by tanks which would seal themselves after being holed. Before World War II only German aircraft were fitted with self-sealing tanks as standard equipment. The tanks were usually constructed of compressed cellulose fiber with a 2mm wall thickness. The outer covering comprised a series of layers – 3mm thick chrome leather, 3mm thick unvulcanized rubber, two layers of lightly vulcanized rubber .5mm thick and an outer covering of highly vulcanized rubber 3mm thick. The chemical reaction set up when the wall of the tank was pierced and the fuel ran out caused the layer of unvulcanized rubber to swell and seal the hole. This important development was ignored by the RAF – with disastrous results in 1939.

Spain – a Proving Ground for New Ideas

Italian Savoia Marchetti S.79s of the Aviacion del Tercio (Spanish Foreign Legion). When the S.79 arrived in Spain it was one of the most advanced warplanes in Europe, with little to fear from Republican fighters, even the rugged little Soviet-supplied I-16 seen here pursuing them.

A total of 99 S.79s were sent to Spain. At the end of the war the 61 surviving Italian machines were handed over to General Franco's air force. By June 10, 1940, when Mussolini declared war on France and Britain a total of 612 S.79s equipped 14 of Italy's 23 bomber Stormi and one independent Gruppo in East Africa. They were severely mauled in daylight encounters with modern British monoplane fighters and suffered heavy losses in massed formation attacks on the British Fleet in the Mediterranean, the fortress island of Malta, and over the Western Desert. Modified as a torpedo bomber, the S.79 achieved some success against British shipping, notably in the fierce battles which raged over the convoys fighting their way to Malta in 1942.

Powered by three Alfa Romeo 126 radials, the S.79 had a cruising speed of 233 mph, range of 1181 miles and operational ceiling of 21 325 ft. Standard offensive loads were two 1320-pound bombs, five 550-pound bombs or 12 220-pound bombs. Defensive armament was provided by a fixed forward-firing machine-gun and a hand held rearward-firing gun housed in an open position behind the S.79's distinctive 'hump'. There was also provision for ventral and beam machine-guns, but these were frequently omitted in Spain as the S.79's speed was considered sufficient protection against Republican interceptors.

Spanish Civil War Speed Comparisons (maxima)

S.79	267 mph
Potez 540	193 mph
Amiot 143	183 mph
Tupolev SB-2	255 mph
He111 B-2	248 mph
Do 17F	222 mph

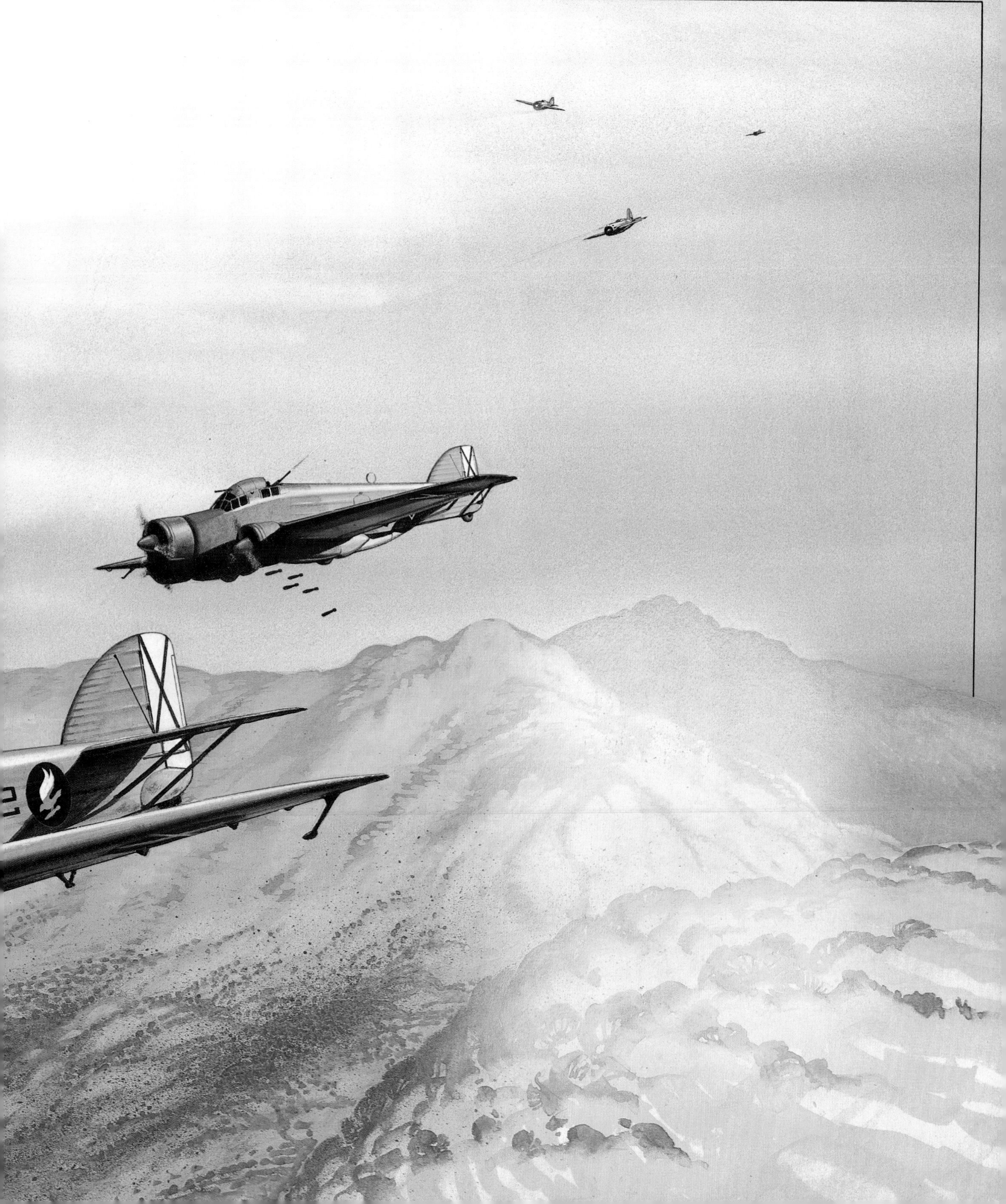

The British Response

In the early 1920s France, which after 1918 had maintained a relatively large air force, had been seen (briefly) to pose a military threat to Britain – a threat which existed more in the minds of British politicians than in reality. Ten years later the focus of concern had shifted eastwards to a rearming Germany. In 1934, according to the Air Staff's Scheme A, RAF strength in the United Kingdom was planned to expand by April 1939 from 316 to 476 bombers and from 156 to 336 fighters. Successive schemes leapfrogged each other until the submission, in December 1937, of Scheme J in which the Staff proposed an increased strength of 1442 bombers and 532 fighters by April 1941. Sir Thomas Inskip, for the government, regarded this plan as too costly, arguing that the expansion of the RAF should be based on the calculation that 'at the outset of war our first task is to repulse a knockout blow within the first two weeks'. Inskip, who was no air specialist, briefly flirted with the idea of increasing the medium bomber force at the expense of the planned heavy bombers. Finally, after a prolonged debate, a revised Scheme was approved in which the RAF would reach a strength of 1352 bombers and 608 first-line fighters. This marginal clawing back of the ratio in favour of the fighters is to secure Britain's survival in the summer of 1940.

Nevertheless, the continuing numerical preponderance of the bomber over the fighter reflected the Air Staff's belief that the former was the key element in its rearmament program and its offensive capability one of the principal pillars of national security. However, bombers were not only more costly to build than fighters but also presented planners and designers with the problem of the choosing from a wide range of competing options.

Ultimately most of these problems were resolved by the pressures of war rather than by peacetime theories. The instrument was RAF Bomber Command, which came into existence in July 1936 when the old regional structure of air defense was abolished and replaced by functional RAF Commands (Bomber, Fighter, Training) and a Maintenance Group (later Maintenance Command). At the same time Bomber Command's squadrons were moved from stations in southern England, facing France, to a line stretching southwards from Yorkshire to Norfolk, facing east towards Germany.

In 1935 the RAF had been a force of wooden biplanes. Its fastest fighter, the Hawker Fury II, was armed with two machine-guns and had a top speed of 223 mph at 15 000 ft. The principal component of the bombing force was the Handley Page Heyford III, with a defensive armament of three guns, bombload of 1500 pounds over a range of 750 miles and a maximum speed of 137 mph. By 1939, however the all-metal monoplane was coming definitely into its own. The Spitfire was armed with eight guns and capable of 335 mph at 19 000 ft. The Vickers Wellington MkI, the best bomber in service with the RAF on the outbreak of war, was armed with six guns (mounted in three hydraulically powered turrets), possessed a maximum speed of 245 mph and an operational radius of about 700 miles with 2000 pounds of bombs.

Wellesley and Wellington

The Wellington's fuselage was constructed using the geodetic method evolved in 1919 by Dr Barnes Wallis when he was devising a graduated wire mesh to contain the hydrogen gasbags of the Vickers airship *R100*. This metal 'basketwork' was assembled from large numbers of standard metal sections. Riveted together by small tabs and connecters, they could

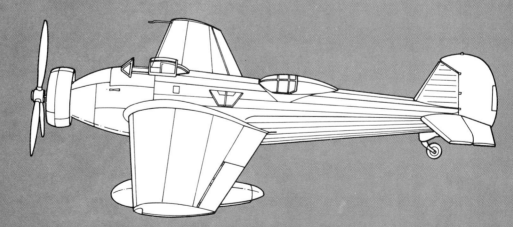

Vickers Wellesley
Originally developed as a monoplane alternative to the 1931 Air Ministry Specification G4/31 for a general-purpose biplane torpedo aircraft. An elegant two-seater monoplane with wings of exceptionally high aspect ratio, the Wellesley was powered by a 925 hp Pegasus XX engine, giving it a maximum speed of 228 mph at 19 680 ft and a service ceiling of 33 000 ft. Carrying a 2000-pound bombload housed in streamlined panniers mounted on pylons beneath the mainplanes, the Wellesley had a range of 1100 miles. This remarkable aircraft flew for the first time on June 19, 1935, and so impressed with its potential was the Air Ministry that it quickly drew up a retroactive specification, 22/35, and placed an order for 96

aircraft, the first delivery being made to No. 76 Squadron in April 1937. Eventually the Wellesley equipped Nos. 35, 77, 148 and 207 Squadrons in the United Kingdom and Nos. 14, 45 and 223 in the Middle East. The home-based Wellesley

units re-equipped with twin-engined types in 1939, while in Africa the aircraft continued to serve in the early part of the war. The Wellesley's high aspect ratio wings gave it an inherently long range. In November 1938 three modified three-

seater aircraft of the RAF's Long Range Development Flight – stripped of military equipment, powered by Pegasus XXII engines driving constant-speed propellers and fitted with extra fuel tanks – set out to break the world record for the greatest distance

flown in a straight line, navigating a 7162-mile route from Ismailia, in Egypt, to Darwin in Australia. Two of the aircraft – L2658 and L2680 – completed the trip without stopping to refuel, remaining airborne for just over 48 hours.

form a complete wing or fuselage. All the members had the shape of intersecting curves – a geodetic is the shortest distance between two given points on a curved surface – and each carried either tension or compression but no bending.

The first geodetic aircraft in service was the Vickers Wellesley of 1935. This two-seat monoplane had an inherently long range. In 1938 two RAF Wellesleys flew over 7,000 miles non-stop from Egypt to Australia.

One of the advantages offered by Barnes Wallis's design was that its reserves of strength gave bombing aircraft the potential to absorb heavy punishment and still remain airborne. Repair could be speedily effected by cutting out and replacing the small pieces of basketwork. Its drawbacks were a more complicated production process than with a stressed-skin aircraft, requiring more man-hours. Large holes had to be cut into the geodetic fuselage and wings to accommodate gun turrets, bury retractable wheels, and get men and bombs in and out of the aircraft. These holes had to be braced with heavy frames where they met the geodetics, and this added considerably to the weight of the aircraft.

These problems were encountered when Vickers turned their attention from the single-engined 6396-pound Wellesley to the design of the twin-engined 18 556-pound Wellington, developed to meet Air Ministry Specification B.9/32. The prototype, Vickers Type 271 (K4049), powered by two-air-cooled 850 hp Pegasus X engines, made its maiden flight on June 15, 1936. In contrast to the elegant Wellesley, the Wellington had a tubby appearance which belied its effective streamlining and tapered high-aspect ratio wings. Soon after its maiden flight the prototype, doped silver overall, appeared in the New Types Park at the Hendon Air Display. To conceal the geodetic structure from prying eyes, the glazed nose and tail cupolas were covered with fabric.

An order was placed for 180 production models of the Wellington MkI (as the new bomber was now called) and a revised specification, 29/36, was issued which provided for the installation of power-operated gun turrets. In April 1937 the prototype crashed during diving trials, and when the first production Wellington, L4212, was wheeled out it displayed a considerably redesigned tail unit and modified fuselage with space for five aircrew. The windows set in the side of the fuselage revealed the criss-cross geodetic structure, lending an engagingly rustic cottage-like air to the portly bomber.

Decidedly less rustic were the twin belt-fed .303 Brownings housed in the Vickers power-operated turrets. The RAF were particularly proud of their power-operated turrets, the first of which had been installed in the Boulton Paul Overstrand twin-engined medium bomber of 1935, 24 of which served with No. 101 squadron until 1938. The power-operated twin turret represented a considerable advance over the single hand-held machine-guns employed by the Luftwaffe. The Wellington's turrets were not mere windshields but precision aiming devices coupled with sighting system and operator controls to enable the gunner to train his weapons with accuracy and without effort even in a 200 mph slipstream or when being pulled in a tight turn. The provision of belted ammunition, fed from tanks in

the fuselage, eliminated the need to change magazines in combat.

The Hampden

A second twin-engined bomber was developed from Air Ministry Specification B.9/32. This was the Handley Page Hampden, the company's first monoplane bomber and a significant departure from the rugged biplanes which had characterized its style since the 0/100. The HP52 prototype K4240, which flew for the first time on June 22, 1936, was one of the most original of the mid-1930s generation of British bombers. In an attempt to minimize drag, the width of the fuselage was reduced to three feet, dwindling to a thin boom aft of the highly tapered, fully slotted and flapped wings. The first section of the slender fuselage was sufficiently deep to accommodate a 4000-pound bombload, while bringing the four-man crew together in a compact, if cramped, group. The abrupt reduction of its depth at the trailing edge of the wings was ideal for the installation of upper and lower gun positions.

In January 1937 Handley Page secured a production order for 180 aircraft, the manufacturing process being speeded up by the split-assembly method in which the fuselage was constructed in two halves, divided down the center-line, with most of the internal fitting completed before mating. The HP52 formally acquired the name Hampden in June 1938 and the first production aircraft, powered by 980 hp Pegasus XVIII engines driving three-bladed de Havilland constant-speed propellers, went into service with No. 49 Squadron in September 1938. Top speed was 265 mph at 15 000 ft, with a service

Above: The Vickers Wellington B.MkI; its geodetic structure can be glimpsed just below the cockpit.
Left: The Armstrong Whitworth Whitley MkI, 80 of which were ordered 'off the drawing board' in August 1935, seven months before the prototype flew for the first time. The MkI entered service with No. 10 Squadron in March 1937. Powered by two 795 hp Tiger IXs, the Whitley was the RAF's first heavy bomber equipped with both retractable undercarriage and turret armament, although this was initially restricted to manually operated installations in nose and tail, each housing a .303 gun. Bombload was 3365 pounds stowed internally with accommodation for small bombs available in 14 cells in the wing center section inboard of the engines. The wings were not flapped but given an 8.5-degree angle of incidence which ensured the appropriate ground angle when landing and reduced the ground run to 210 yds once the tail was on the runway, extremely important for an aircraft designed as a night bomber. The engines were upwardly canted to provide the correct thrust-line in flight and this gave the Whitley its characteristic nose-down flying attitude. A stream of modifications ensured its viability on the outbreak of war.

The Handley Page
Hampden, which entered
service with No. 49
Squadron in June 1938.
Top speed was 265 mph at
15 000 ft with a service
ceiling of 23 000 ft.
Carrying a standard
bombload of 4000
pounds, the Hampden had
a range of 2000 miles,
although the chances of
completing such a mission
in combat were limited by
the provision of
inadequate armament.
The pilot in a Hampden
B.MkI fired a fixed
Browning .303 installed in
the port foredecking and
each of the three gunners'
positions was provided
with a free-firing Vickers 'K'
gun. A sub-type, powered
by the temperamental
Napier Dagger XIII engine
and known as the
Hereford, was produced by
Short and Harland in
Belfast. A substantial
number of the 100
Herefords were eventually
modified as Hampdens.

ceiling of 23 000 ft. Carrying a standard bombload of 4000 pounds the Hampden's range was 1990 miles, but the chances of completing such a mission in combat were limited by the provision of inadequate armament. The pilot in a Hampden BMkI fired a fixed .303 Browning installed in the port foredecking and each of the three gunners' positions was provided with a free-firing .303 Vickers K gun. A sub-type, powered by the temperamental Napier Dagger XIII and known as the Hereford, was produced by Short and Harland in Belfast. A substantial number of the 100 Herefords manufactured were eventually modified as Hampdens.

The Whitley
Both the Wellington and the Hampden were conceived as day bombers. The Armstrong Whitworth Whitley was designed to operate at night. Unlike many of its contemporaries, the Whitley made few concessions to elegant contouring in the pursuit of aerodynamic excellence. Designed in response to a July 1934 Air Ministry Specification 3/34, the Whitley prototype, K4586, was a slab-sided two-engined mid-wing monoplane whose jutting nose gave the aircraft the slightly quizzical air of a middle-aged pipe smoker in a *Punch* cartoon of the period. Nevertheless, this was an exceptionally robust design, with an all-metal stressed-skin fuselage and immense box spars in each chunky, low aspect ratio wing conferring great strength.

A constant stream of modifications not only ensured that the Whitley played a significant role with the RAF in the early years of World War II but also underlined the rapid pace of change in the air environment of the late 1930s. Aircraft had to adapt to survive, and even those which in mid-decade seemed to be at the top of their class were reaching

obsolescence when put to the test. Two important examples were the Bristol Blenheim and the Fairey Battle.

The Blenheim and Battle
The origins of the Blenheim design lay in a proposal for a twin-engined monoplane fast passenger transport, the Type 135, designed in 1933 by F S Barnwell of the Bristol Aeroplane Company. The Type 135's fuselage, constructed of flush-riveted light alloy panels, was exhibited at the 1934 Paris Air Show, making a great impression on the newspaper magnate Lord Rothermere, a vigorous advocate of the potential of civil aviation who had declared his intention to possess 'the fastest commercial aeroplane in Europe, if not the world'. Rothermere placed an order for a complete aircraft, and the result was the Type 142, which made its maiden flight at Filton on April 12, 1935. Patriotically named 'Britain First' and powered by two 650 hp Mercury VI engines, the Type 142 attained a top speed of 307 mph at 14 000 ft, a staggering 100 mph faster than the RAF's best fighter aircraft of the day.

The Air Ministry immediately sat up and took notice, prompting Lord Rothermere to present the aircraft to the nation for evaluation as a potential bomber. On July 9 a conference was held at the Ministry to prepare the ground for the Bristol design team's conversion of K7557, as 'Britain First' was now prosaically designated, into a high-speed three-seater medium day bomber. A specification, B28/35, was drawn up around this development, which Bristol met with the Type 142M, raising the wings from a low to mid position and selecting a pair of Mercury engines as the power plants. Such was the Ministry's enthusiasm for the new bomber, and the pressures imposed by the expansion program, that

Above: Bristol Type 142 – 'Britain First' – flying at Martlesham Heath in 1936 after its presentation by Lord Rothermere to the Air Council.

Left: The ill-fated Fairey Battle. Battles were regarded as advanced aircraft when they went into service in 1937, but by the summer of 1940 they were too slow and lightly armed, and they suffered grievous casualties in the Battle for France.

150 aircraft were ordered 'off the drawing board' in September 1935. The first of these, K7033, flew on June 25, 1936 as the Blenheim MkI.

The Blenheim created a sensation, attaining 285 mph at 15 000 ft with a 1000-pound bombload and a range of 1125 miles. Its compact and robust design seated the pilot in a generously glazed cockpit flanked by a pair of 840 hp Mercury VIII engines, into whose nacelles sank the fully retractable main wheels. Defensive armament was provided by a fixed forward-firing machine-gun operated by the pilot and a semi-retractable dorsal turret fitted with a single Vickers 'K' gun.

In the spring of 1937, when the first Blenheims went into service with No. 114 Squadron, the Blenheim MkI was the fastest medium bomber in the world, a selling point which quickly secured export orders from the Finnish, Turkish, Greek, Romanian and Yugoslav air forces. By the autumn of 1938 the MkI equipped 16 UK-based RAF bomber squadrons. A year later nearly all of these units had been re-equipped with the extended-nose MkIV. On September 2, 1939 a Blenheim MkIV of No. 139 Squadron piloted by Flying Officer A McPherson was the first British service aircraft to cross the frontiers of Germany while conducting a reconnaissance of the port of Wilhelmshaven. The MkIV was to perform sterling service for the RAF throughout the war, but not in the day bomber role for which it had been designed in the mid-1930s. When the crunch came in the summer of 1940, the Blenheim was already obsolete for the task.

More tragic was the fate awaiting the Fairey Battle in the skies over France. In the mid-1930s the RAF still clung to the concept of the Single-Engine-Day-Bomber (SEDB), a tradition stretching back to the halcyon days of the DH4 and nourished by the success of the Hart and the Wapiti in interwar air control operations. In policing the colonies and mandated territories, the SEDB had proved itself an ideal workhorse, but its employment in a possible European war seemed more problematic. Nevertheless, in 1933 an Air Ministry specification, P27/32, was issued for a two-seat single-engined all-metal monoplane to carry a 1000-pound bombload at 200 mph for a distance of 1000 miles. The successful tender came from the Fairey Company whose prototype K4043, the work of M J O Lobelle, was an aircraft of immensely elegant lines and advanced design, which lends even greater poignancy to its brief combat career.

K4043 was a sleek low-wing monoplane whose engine merged cleanly into the nose of the gently tapering oval-section fuselage. Its two-man crew were seated under a long framed canopy stretching between the cockpits, which were placed at the leading and trailing edges of the wings. The 1000-pound bombload was stowed internally in four bays in the wings with provision for an additional 500 pounds of bombs on underwing racks. By the time K4043 made its maiden flight on March 10, 1936, the RAF had ordered 155 Battles 'off the drawing board'. The initial production Battle MkIs were delivered to No. 63 Squadron a year later and were the first Merlin-powered aircraft to enter service. Subsequent variants, from II to V, took their mark numbers from the Merlin engines which powered them. Modified to accommodate a third crew member – a wireless operator/air gunner – the MkI's maximum speed was 243 mph at 16 200 ft, 60 mph faster than the biplane Hart which it was to replace and with twice the Hart's bomb capacity and range.

The streamlined Battle, with its retractable under-carriage and variable pitch airscrew, was quint-essential mid-1930s high tech. One can imagine the type drawn up wing tip to wing tip on the stations of the totalitarian air force in Rex Warner's contemporary political fantasy, *The Aerodrome*. But an aircraft which seemed advanced in 1937 had become little more than a death trap in 1940. By the time the Battle was thrown into action on the Western Front it was both underpowered and grotesquely underarmed to meet the challenge of the Luftwaffe. In the cauldron of the Battle of France, the Battle was 'cold meat', its defensive armament consisting of a single .303 Browning installed in the starboard wing just beyond the landing wheel and a .303 Vickers 'K' gun on a Fairey high-speed mounting in the rear cockpit. Until the belated installation of a remotely controlled rearward-firing gun in the Battle's belly, the underside of the bomber was completely undefended, its lack of armor or self-sealing fuel tanks making it the most tempting of targets for German fighters.

The operational career of the Battle provides a grim example of the dangers of ordering military aircraft 'off the drawing board' at a time of rapid technological change and imminent war. The error was compounded as war approached by accelerated production of an aircraft already known to be dangerously vulnerable. At the time of the Munich Conference in August 1938, no fewer than 17 of the RAF's squadrons were equipped with the Battle, and before the end of 1940 over 3000 Battles would be produced. This demonstrated a misplaced faith in quantity rather than quality at a time of crisis, a weakness that can be a contagious disease. After he had cancelled the 'Uralbomber' project, Hermann Goering told Erhard Milch, 'The Fuhrer does not ask me what kind of bombers I have. He simply wants to know how many'.

The Luftwaffe had squandered its chances of developing an effective four-engine heavy bomber, but in 1936 the British Air Ministry issued specifications P/13/36 and B/12/36 for four-engined heavy bombers and twin-engined heavy-medium bombers which would produce, in 1941, the Stirling, the Halifax, the twin-engined Manchester and its ultimate modification, the Lancaster. Equally vital to Britain's wartime survival was the work under way on Radio Direction Finding (RDF) which, under the direction of Robert Watson Watt, would lead to a revolution in air defense. By 1937 the first of the Chain Home (CH) stations, intended to give warning of aircraft approaching the coast at a distance of 40 miles, had begun to operate.

The 'Great Fist' of Air Power

The bomber had cast a long shadow over the 1930s. At Munich, Adolf Hitler played on British Prime Minister Neville Chamberlain's fears, ominously observing that he too was a humanitarian and 'hated the thought of little babies being killed by gas bombs'. In a scenario plucked straight from the pages of Douhet, J B S Haldane wrote in his 1938 book ARP*: '*T*HEY (HITLER AND MUSSOLINI) would be prepared to lose half their air force to lay London in ruins. We may therefore expect an attack by successive waves of several hundred aeroplanes which would drop their bombs almost simultan-eously. A bombing aeroplane can carry a load which varies from half a ton upwards. But we may take one and a half tons as an average. Thus a squadron (sic) of 270 planes could drop 400 tons of bombs, or nearly double the weight dropped on Britain during the whole of the last war, in half a minute. This would probably kill about 8000 people and wound some 15 000. And this could be repeated several times a day, provided the enemy were willing to stand the heavy losses of aeroplanes involved. In fact the knockout blow might kill 50 000 to 100 000 Londoners'.*

Ironically in 1938 the very last thing on Hitler's mind was a strategic bombing offensive against London. The true disciples of Douhet wore the blue uniforms of the RAF. Having fought so hard to survive in the 1920s, the Air Staff of the 1930s sought to preserve its independence by advocating the war-winning potential of strategic bombing. But seldom has a force so fervently willed the ends it desired while at the same time failing to comprehend the means by which they could be achieved. While paying lip service to the concept of precision attacks on the enemy's vital industries, the RAF was firmly wedded to the terror bombing of civilian populations which was part and parcel of the Trenchard doctrine of 1928. In a memorandum of 1938 the Air Staff made a distinction between two forms of bombing:

(1) THE "PRECISE TARGET", EG A POWER station ... (2) "the target group", of considerable area in which are concentrated many targets of equal or nearly equal importance on which accurate bombing is not necessary to achieve valuable hits, eg parts of cities, industrial towns, distribution areas or storage areas'.

The second form of bombing was associated with the belief that civilian morale would be unable to withstand sustained bombardment from the air. In 1936 Group Captain (later Marshal of the Air Force Sir John) Slessor wrote: '*I*N AIR OPERATIONS against production, the weight of the attack will inevitably fall upon a vitally important, and not by nature very amenable, section of the community – the industrial workers, whose morale and sticking power cannot be expected to equal that of the disciplined soldier. And we should remember that if the morale effect of air bombardment was serious seventeen years ago, it will be immeasurably more so under modern conditions'.*

Trenchardian doctrine rested on the belief in a strategic air force's ability to 'penetrate the air defenses and attack direct the centers of production, transportation and communication from which the enemy effort is maintained'. However, Trenchard failed to foresee the absolute need first to defeat, rather than merely 'penetrate', the enemy's air defenses. As the Allies and the Axis powers were to learn the hard way in World War II, only when this had been achieved could the full weight of a strategic offensive be brought to bear.

In the 1930s there were two methods open to the

* ARP stands for Air Raid Precautions.

RAF to bypass the enemy's defenses: daylight raids flown by self-defending formations; and attacks launched under the cover of darkness. In the case of the former, the RAF entertained a false sense of security about the ease with which its bombers could find and destroy their targets while defending themselves against fighter attack. This stemmed partly from combat experience in World War I, when the Independent Force had faced relatively limited defenses, and partly from the success of air control operations which were unhindered by any opposition. It is significant that even in September 1941, after daylight bombing had been largely abandoned, the Directorate of Bomber Operations at the Air Ministry considered that attacking the morale of German civilians by bombing their cities was merely 'an adaptation, though on a greatly magnified scale, of Air Control'.

The Dangerous Illusions

The RAF was equally ill-prepared to wage a sustained night offensive. Right up to September 1939 a low priority was given to training in night flying. In 1936 the overall night hours logged were 2990 compared with 41 644 daylight hours; by 1938 the pattern remained the same with only 14 615 night hours logged compared with 148 458 by day. In 1937 only 84 Bomber Command pilots were qualified for night flying. Such training as there was invariably took place in good weather conditions. Bad weather was to be the dominant factor in the bombing campaigns of World War II. Even so, in the last two years of peace nearly 500 Bomber Command aircraft force landed on exercises in the United Kingdom. Given these figures, it is hardly surprising that training flights were not made over the sea. Lack of life-saving equipment was the official reason. Instead aircrews contented themselves with flying the short distances between Britain's brightly illuminated towns and cities.

The RAF had no access to the radio navigation aids which in the 1930s had revolutionized civil aviation in the United States and Europe. Navigation remained primarily a matter of Dead Reckoning, in which the navigator took the aircraft along a calculated heading which, allowing for wind, would bring him to the target after a certain flight time. There was little appreciation of the almost insuperable difficulties of applying this method to long flights over a blacked-out Europe in which incorrect predictions of the upper-air wind, and harassment by the enemy fighters, anti-aircraft guns and searchlights, could fatally compound the average Dead Reckoning error of seven miles to either side of the intended track for every hundred miles. If, like the Wellington, the bomber was fitted with a plexiglass astrodome, the navigator could attempt astro-navigation, 'shooting' the stars with a 'bubble sextant', an instrument specially designed for use in aircraft. But this required several minutes of straight and level flight and several more minutes for the navigator to complete his calculations. Nor could even the most experienced pilot prevent acceleration and turning forces from destabilizing the sextant's accuracy. A far from satisfactory solution was devised in which the navigator took a number of sights from a given star and then averaged them out. As Wing Commander F C Richardson, then an instructor at the RAF's School of Air Navigation, recalled, 'I would probably not be exaggerating to say that in war when astronomical navigation was resorted to over enemy territory and the aircraft was being flown in erratic courses in order to defeat the ack-ack being shot at you, the navigator trying to cope with an astro shot was really in trouble'. Anticipating the problems which lay ahead, the AOC of 3 Group told Bomber Command in May 1939 that 'Dead Reckoning navigation *by day* above cloud can only be expected to get aircraft to within 50 miles of the target'.

In 1938 nine squadrons of Whitleys represented Bomber Command's sole strategic night striking strength. Nevertheless, in the same year its planners confidently predicted that by concentrating on 45 power and manufacturing plants in the Ruhr, German war-making capacity could be brought to a halt – at an estimated cost of 174 aircraft. This recalls the forecasts of the Air Staff in 1918, painting pictures of the devastation to be visited on Germany by the fleet of V/1500s which never arrived. It was also in 1938 that the RAF arranged a fly-past of bombers for the benefit of a group of visiting senior officers from the Luftwaffe. The Wellingtons were kept discreetly in the distance, as they had no turrets; the Battles, sweeping overhead in immaculate formation, had neither radios nor guns.

It was this disparity between Bomber Command's stated aims and the weapons at its disposal which increasingly concerned its C-in-C, Air Chief Marshal Sir Edgar Ludlow Hewitt, as he considered the succession of Western Air Plans drawn up to convert bombing theory into reality in the event of war. His doubts grew. In May 1939 the thought of active operations caused Ludlow-Hewitt 'the most acute anxiety'. Even the RAF's power-operated turrets no longer seemed proof against enemy fighters: 'WE have all this valuable equipment and highly trained personnel depending for its safety upon one inadequately trained and inexperienced individual with a single relatively inadequate gun in a very exposed position in the tail of the aircraft. Here he has to face the full blast of the 8-gun battery of the modern fighter. The demands which will be made on the coolness, presence of mind, skill and efficiency of this single individual are, in exacting conditions, almost superhuman and in his present state of training and knowledge it is utterly fantastic to expect the efficient defense of our aircraft'.

Thus it was that shortly before the outbreak of war Ludlow Hewitt informed the Air Ministry that in an all-out offensive against Germany, his Blenheims would be destroyed in three and a half weeks and the Hampdens, Whitleys, and Wellingtons would go the same way in just under two months. It was perhaps with a degree of relief that the Air Staff bowed to the government's decision to avoid bomber operations which might cause civilian deaths for fear of provoking German retaliation. Far from providing 'an early termination of a European war', as Trenchard had informed the Salisbury Committee in 1923, the RAF's strategic bombing plans were, for the moment, quietly consigned to the shelf. In the air, as on land, the initiative in September 1939 lay with Germany.

SECTION THREE

WORLD WAR II

3.1 DAY OF THE DIVE BOMBER: FROM POLAND TO THE BLITZ

WORLD WAR II BEGAN, AS IT WOULD END, WITH AN AIR RAID. At 0430 hrs on September 1, 1939 three Ju87Bs of III/Stg1 took off from Elbing to attack the huge steel bridges spanning the River Vistula at Dirschau in Poland. The bridges had originally been targeted for seizure by paratroopers of General Kurt Student's 7th Division, to enable the armored mechanized infantry and support elements of 3rd Army to cross the river and link with 4th Army as it raced across the Polish corridor from its Pomeranian start line. But the dawn had broken to reveal a thick blanket of mist smothering the front. The planned air drop could not go ahead, and the three Stukas scrambled in an attempt to destroy the strongpoints from which detonation charges would be fired by Polish engineers. Forced low by the mist, the Stukas came in at 150 ft and, unhampered by any opposition, dropped three 550-pound and a dozen 110-pound bombs. An hour later a flight of Do17Zs of III/KG3 bombed the strongpoints through the cloud, returning to report that they had started fires in the town of Dirschau. As they flew away, Polish engineers fought to repair severed detonation wires and an hour later one of the bridges was blown, collapsing in a mangled heap of girders into the Vistula. The first Luftwaffe operation of the war had been a partial failure.

Failure lay ahead in the future, but for the next seven months the Luftwaffe gorged itself on an almost uninterrupted diet of triumph. The execution of 'Case White', the invasion of Poland, provided the first demonstration of the techniques of Blitzkrieg developed in the 1930s, a form of combined armored and aerial warfare which reasserted the supremacy of the offensive.

The Luftwaffe's Order of Battle comprised Luftlotte 1, commanded by General der Flieger Albert Kesselring, and Luftlotte 4, under General Alexander Löhre. The three principal bombing types at the disposal of Kesselring and Löhre were the He111P, the Do17Z and the Ju87B1. The P series He111 boasted a redesigned nose in which the original stepped-forward fuselage was replaced by a glazed continuous contour section. A total of 538 He111s were deployed in the Polish campaign, including some of the earlier stepped E- and D-series. The Do17 had also undergone modification after combat experience in Spain with the Condor legion. The Do17Z had appeared in the autumn of 1938 with a deeper fuselage and extensively glazed cockpit which afforded excellent visibility, particularly from the bomb aimer's position in the nose. In a qualified recognition of the increased threat posed by modern fighter aircraft, the Do17Z was more heavily armed than its predecessors, with two hand-held single 7.9 mm MG-15 machine-guns firing from port and starboard windows in the fuselage, two more MG-15s firing aft from dorsal and ventral positions and a single MG-15 mounted in the port windscreen and fired by the pilot. Powered by two 1000 hp BMW-Bramo radials, the Do17Z carried a standard bombload of 2205 pounds and, at operational weight, had a maximum speed of 225 mph at 13 200 ft. In Luftlotte 1, KG2 and KG3 were equipped with Do17Zs; in Luftlotte 4 they flew with KG76 and 77.

Completing the triumvirate of bombers was the Ju87B-1 powered by a single Junkers Jumo 211Da engine and with a normal bombload of a single 1100-pound bomb or, alternatively, a single 550-pound bomb supplemented by four 110-pound bombs carried on underwing racks. Swooping down on their targets, with the 'Jericho Trombones' attached to their undercarriages adding to the deafening cacophony, the Stukas provided the cutting edge of Blitzkrieg. Nevertheless, the Stuka's inherent vulnerability was already apparent to the Luftwaffe's senior commanders. The Ju87B1's top speed was only 238 mph: it cruised at 185 mph and dived at 150 mph. Defensive armament was little short of perfunctory: two fixed 7.9 mm machine-guns mounted on the leading edges of the wings, firing just clear of the propeller arc, and a single hand-held gun for the radio operator/rear gunner covering an extremely limited field of fire.

Twelve of the 16 Polish fighter squadrons facing

the Luftwaffe were equipped with the robust, maneuverable but obsolescent PZL P.11c, a single-engined interceptor with an open cockpit, braced wings and a top speed of 243 mph. The remainder flew even older and slower P7s. Five fighter squadrons were concentrated in a centrally controlled Pursuit Brigade for the defense of Warsaw against the anticipated major bombing attacks. During the last days of peace the Poles had prudently dispersed their aircraft to a number of concealed airfields. On the morning of September 1 not one Polish squadron remained on its pre-war base. In the first German blow only 28 obsolete or unserviceable machines were destroyed, at Rakowice.

The most modern bomber available to the Polish air force, although it equipped only four squadrons, was the PZL P.37B Los. This was a twin-engined medium bomber powered by the 918 hp PZL-built Bristol Pegasus XX radial and capable of carrying a 5688-pound bombload over a range of 1615 miles. Top speed was 276 mph with a service ceiling of 30 350 ft. The four P.37 squadrons were concentrated in a Bomber Brigade while the remainder, attached to individual army group units, flew the PZL P. 23B Karas, a single-engine low-wing monoplane with a fixed undercarriage. This obsolescent but rugged reconnaissance bomber was powered by a 680 hp PZL-built Bristol Pegasus VIII, which gave it a maximum speed of 198 mph, a service ceiling of 24 000 ft and a range of 782 miles with a 1500-pound bombload.

It had been Goering's original intention to launch Luftflotte 1 in a crushing bombardment of Warsaw – Operation Seebad (Seaside) – on the first day of the invasion. Luftflotte 4 had been tasked with the destruction of the airfields lying in the path of the German advance. But the lingering fog held up Luftflotte 1, allowing only six bomber Gruppen to get into the air that morning. Seebad was shelved and attention was switched to enemy airfields, naval installations on the Baltic coast, and operations in support of 3rd and 4th Armies.

It was while bombing airfields in the Krakow region that Stukas of I/StG2 were involved in the first aerial combat of World War II. As dawn broke on September 1, the P11cs of 121 Fighter Squadron

Dyon III/2, led by Captain Mieczyslaw Medwecki, scrambled to intercept He111s of I and III/KG4. Still climbing, the Polish fighters were pounced upon by the Stukas and Medwecki was shot down in flames. Rounding on the Ju87s, Lieutenant Wladislaw Gnys fought a brief and inconclusive combat with one of them before gaining height and accounting for two Do17Zs of KG77, which were flying at 3000 ft on their way back from bombing Krakow.

Later that day came a dramatic demonstration of the Stuka's ability to shatter formations of troops caught in the open. In an attempt to block the left wing of the German 10th Army, advancing in the south, the Polish C-in-C Field Marshal Smigley Rydz ordered a cavalry brigade some 3000 strong to drive westward from the town of Wielun, about 12 miles from the German frontier. The dust raised by the Polish cavalry – echo of an earlier age – was quickly

Above: The Do17Z, one of the medium bomber mainstays of the Kampfgruppen. Operating in Poland and France under a protective umbrella provided by the Luftwaffe's fighters, the Do17Z was initially effective. However it was soon revealed to be too lightly armed and armored and suffered heavily in the Battle of Britain.
Left: The PZL P.37B, the most modern bomber in service with the Polish air force on the outbreak of war. It compared well with similar types in other air forces but was unable to stem the tide of Blitzkrieg.

Junkers Ju87B2 'Stuka'

The spearhead of Blitzkrieg in Poland and France, the Ju87's fearsome reputation belied its relatively modest performance. Powered by the 1400 hp Junkers Jumo 211D, the Stuka could reach 238 mph at 13 500 ft and possessed an operational ceiling of 26 248 ft. With a bombload of 1540 pounds, its range was 380 miles. After its withdrawal from the Battle of Britain on August 16, 1940 the Ju87 proved highly successful against enemy shipping, particularly during the battle for Crete in May 1941.

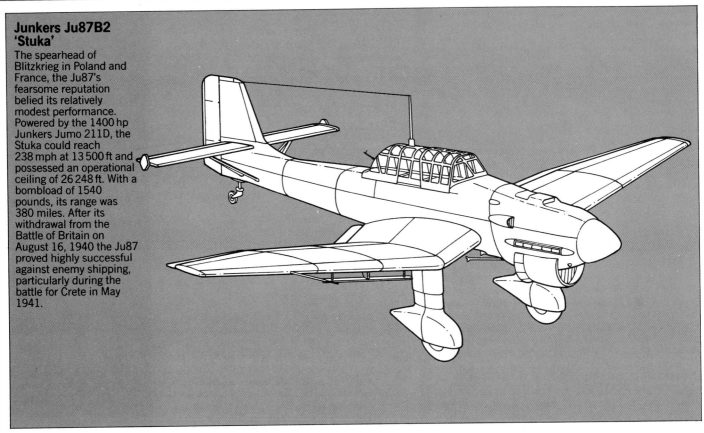

spotted by one of the many German reconnaissance aircraft flying at leisurely pace across the battlefields. Thirty minutes later the column came under heavy attack from Stukas of I/StG2 and I/StG77, howling down to release their bombs at 2500 ft. The destruction of the brigade was completed by 30 Do17Zs of I/KG77. After 90 air sorties, the cavalry brigade had ceased to exist as a fighting unit.

A similar fate overtook an infantry column at Radomsko on September 2, when it was caught by StG77. At Piotrkow, troops in the process of detraining were decimated by I/StG2 and I/StG76. A week later General von Richthofen, Fliegerfuehrer Zbv (Air Commander for Special Duties) threw in 135 Stukas of StG77 and LG2 to pound a concentration of Polish troops encircled in the forests around Ilza. After five days of virtually uninterrupted bombardment, supported by Luftwaffe flak batteries, the Poles surrendered.

With the inner pincer of the German envelopment closing around Warsaw, a final Polish counterblow was launched on the River Bzura, aimed at the exposed left flank of 8th Army. As the threat developed, General von Rundstedt, commander of Army Group South, called for a maximum air effort. Between September 9 and 12, massed dive-bomber attacks were launched from forward airstrips at Tschenstochau and Kruszyna. The impetus of the Polish attack was halted by the destruction of the bridges over the Bzura and then its principal elements broken up in two days of concentrated bombardment by Luftlotte 4's Stukas reinforced by Fliegerdivision 1 from Luflotte 1 and the Hs123

ground-attack aircraft of II/LG2. He111s of KG1, 4 and 26 bombed from higher altitudes, adding to the chaos and destruction racing in waves back and forth across the shrinking Kutno pocket in which the remnants of the Army of Poznan were now trapped. By September 19, nearly 200 000 Polish troops had surrendered.

At the end of the first week of the campaign the gallant Polish air force had shot its bolt. In the first six days of fighting Polish fighter pilots had claimed 105 victories, 63 by army units and 42 by the Pursuit Brigade. Their own losses were 79 fighters, 38 of them Brigade aircraft. The most successful unit was III/4 Dyon of the Army of Pomorze, whose 21 victories included six Ju87s and the same number of He126s for the loss of nine P.11s. But with fronts collapsing all round them, fuel supplies drying up, early warning systems breaking down and their bases engulfed by the German advance, Polish fighter activity dwindled to the heroic efforts of a few aircraft from the Army of Poznan flying over Warsaw. The last Polish bombing sorties were flown by the P.37s of the Bomber Brigade on September 16. On the following day the Poles' fate was sealed when the Red Army crossed the eastern border of Poland to occupy territory which had been lost in 1919. With that, the remainder of the Polish air force was evacuated to Romania.

As early as September 12 the Luftwaffe had begun hurriedly to transfer units to the West. At the same time Operation Seaside was revived. On September 13, 183 bombers attacked Warsaw, now defended by a unit calling itself the Deblin Group, composed of P7s, the remnants of the P11s and a single prototype

PZL P.24. Flying this aircraft, Lieutenant Hwyk Szczesny shot down two German bombers on September 14 and 15. Below the Polish fighters and circling German bombers Warsaw lay hidden under a pall of smoke as the aerial bombardment and constant shelling set the Polish capital ablaze from end to end. Von Richthofen complained of 'chaos over the target' and of 'aircraft nearly colliding in the act of bombing'.

With the arrival of the Russians, Hitler considered it imperative to bring hostilities to a swift conclusion. The survivors of the shattered Polish armies had fallen back on Warsaw, determined to make a last stand. For several days leaflets were dropped on the city calling for a surrender. No reply came, and at 0800 hrs on September 25 over 400 bombers, including eight Stukagruppen, attacked Warsaw in relays. To plug the gap left by the withdrawal of units to the West, 30 Ju52s were employed as makeshift bombers, their aircrews literally shovelling incendiaries from the loading doors. By the end of the day, 500 tons of HE and 72 tons of incendiaries had been dropped on Warsaw. The city surrendered on September 27, as did the garrison at Modlin, which had been subjected to non-stop air attacks during the preceding 36 hours. The last organized Polish resistance collapsed on October 5.

The Sinking of the Königsberg

The German invasion of Norway, launched on April 9, 1940, provided conclusive proof of the importance of air power on the battlefield. Within 24 hours the Luftwaffe controlled all seven of Norway's operational airfields. This gave them a virtually free hand against the ill-fated Allied counter-landings at Andalsnes, Namsos and Narvik. The last Allied troops were evacuated on June 8, and on the same day the British aircraft carrier *Glorious* – carrying Hurricanes and Gloster Gladiators which had been covering the withdrawal from Narvik – was sunk by the battlecruisers *Scharnhorst* and *Gneisenau*.

Amid this catalog of disaster the Fleet Air Arm had given the Germans a taste of their own medicine in an operation flown by 16 Blackburn Skua two-seat dive bombers from Nos. 800 and 803 Squadrons. By April 1940 the Skua could boast a number of firsts: it was the first monoplane to serve operationally with the Fleet Air Arm; the first British dive bomber (a type which the RAF had done its best to ignore during the 1930s); and the first British aircraft to shoot down an enemy plane in World War II – on September 25, 1939. It was about to become the first aircraft type to sink a major warship in battle.

On April 8 a powerful German naval force had landed troops in the Norwegian port of Bergen. British aerial reconnaissance showed that on the 9th two cruisers – *Köln* and *Königsberg* – still lay in the harbor. Bomber Command despatched 12 Wellingtons of Nos. 9 and 115 Squadrons against the cruisers. According to German reports the attack was 'vigorously pressed home', but the Wellingtons failed to score a single hit, and *Köln* sailed back to Germany unscathed. *Königsberg*, which had earlier sustained damage from a Norwegian shore battery and was having problems with one of its engines, was left behind. Unaware of the departure of *Köln*,

the 16 Skuas took off from the bleak airfield at Hatston in the Orkneys at 0515 hrs on April 10. They were fully laden with fuel for the 300-mile flight to Bergen and each was armed with a single 500-pound Semi-Armor-Piercing (SAP) bomb. Approaching Bergen harbor in two groups, they located *Königsberg* berthed alongside the Skoltegrund mole, her starboard side secured, facing east towards the shore. The 6600-ton cruiser was perfectly placed for dive-bomber attack: stationary and alongside a jetty whose resistance would magnify the water-hammer effects of any near misses falling into the harbor. *Königsberg's* armor protection at the waterline was only 2 inches thick and the deck armor at its thickest a mere ¾ of an inch; turrets and barbettes had 1¼-inch-thick protection.

At 0720 hrs the two Skua sections fell into line astern and began the first phase of the approach dive, clearing a thin layer of cloud at 8000 ft. The anti-aircraft defenses were caught cold as the dive bombers flew in out of the sun, and at angles of between 50 and 70 degrees, to deliver their bombs at altitudes between 3000 and 1500 ft. One pilot, Lieutenant W C A Church of No. 803 Squadron, chose not to release on his first dive, pulled up and came round in a second attack, flying over *Königsberg* from stern to bow in a shallow 40-degree dive, dropping his bomb from 200 ft, then climbing away to 3000 ft in a hail of anti-aircraft and tracer fire. *Königsberg* sustained at least three hits, one of them amidships between the two funnels. Five bombs struck the mole alongside her and two exploded in the space between the mole and the cruiser. Within minutes *Königsberg* was burning fiercely and sinking by the bows. An hour after the attack she rolled over and capsized.

The view through the nose glazing of a Heinkel He111 as it overflys a harbor in Norway. The observer enjoyed excellent visibility forward and downward, but behind him the pilot had a more restricted view. For landing, the pilot had to raise his seat so that his head projected through a sliding hatch in the roof of the cockpit.

The Battle for France

After the Munich crisis in September 1938 plans had been drawn up for the transfer to France, in the event of war with Germany, of a British Advanced Air Striking Force (AASF). The object was not to support the French Army, or even the British Expeditionary Force, but to place the RAF's shorter-ranged bombers within striking distance of targets in Germany. As war approached in the early summer of 1939, the Anglo-French plans were set in motion and the AASF's bombs laid down near Rheims under cover of a sale to the French Armée de L'Air. But times had changed since the days in 1917 when the dashing Colonel Barès had collaborated so enthusiastically with the RNAS. There was no discussion of a joint air offensive against Germany, for the simple reason that the French had no bombing force worth the name.

At the beginning of the war the French bombing squadrons were equipped with such obsolete types as the Amiot 143 and the Bloch 210, the latter flown by the Republican forces in the Spanish Civil War but by 1940 at least 100 mph slower than German bombers. A chaotic rearmament program was under way, but it was not due for completion until 1942. France did possess the fastest bomber in service at the beginning of the war, the LeO 451, which in prototype form had achieved 307 mph in level flight as early as 1937. Powered by two 1060 hp Gnome-Rhône 14N radials, the LeO 451 had a maximum speed of 307 mph carrying a 2000-pound bombload with an operational radius of about 450 miles. In the dorsal position it carried a Hispano 20 mm cannon fitted on an electro-hydraulically powered mounting and firing 4.4-ounce rounds at a rate of 700 a minute

with a muzzle velocity of 2820 ft a second – a firepower eight times that of the RAF .303s. Deployed in strength, the LeO 451 might have made a significant intervention in the fighting of May 1940. But only a handful had been delivered by the time Hitler decided to strike in the West.

On August 22, 1939 Hitler informed his commanders-in-chief, gathered at Obersalzberg, that as the result of the Russo-German Pact he could now fulfil his promise of May 23 and attack Poland when conditions were favorable. As the crisis deepened, the British War Cabinet authorized the mobilization of the RAF to war establishment. Two days after the meeting at Obersalzberg, members of the Auxiliary Air Force and the RAF Volunteer Reserve received a green envelope bearing the word 'MOBILIZATION' – a security lapse not entirely hidden by heavy overstamping. While the Reservists made their way to the mobilization centers and Hitler - thrown temporarily off balance by the Anglo-Polish Pact of August 25 - hesitated on the brink, aircraft of Coastal Command began to fly continuous patrols over the North Sea. The die was cast on September 1 and on the following day the ten Fairey Battle squadrons of the AASF flew to France. In a sense, they were 'all bombed with nowhere to go'. The Battles were already seen as the 'expendable' element in Bomber Command, and it was not long before there was an ominous indication of their frailty.

During the opening weeks of the war Battles had flown regular reconnaissance missions 10–20 miles over the Franco-German border. These were abruptly abandoned after an incident on September 30 when four of five Battles from No. 150 Squadron were shot down by Me109s. The fifth was damaged

The French Amiot 143, hopelessly outclassed in September 1939 with a top speed of 190 mph at 13 000 ft and range of 800 miles carrying a bombload of 1984 pounds. In the background is the equally ineffective Fairey Battle.

beyond repair. So much for the Battle's hopes of raiding industrial targets inside Germany.

The prospect of committing them, along with Blenheims, to a land battle raised even greater misgivings. The operational instructions issued by the British Air Forces in France (BAFF) and Bomber Command stated that 'Bomber aircraft have proved extremely useful in support of an advancing army, especially against weak anti-aircraft resistance, but it is not clear that a bomber force used against an advancing army, well-supported by all forms of anti-aircraft defense and a large force of fighter aircraft, will be economically effective'.

If nothing else, this was an economical summary of the debacle about to engulf the Advanced Air Striking Force. The Luftwaffe was ready to confirm the first half of the statement and the AASF the second. The campaign in Poland had sharpened the cutting edge of Blitzkrieg. When the so-called Phoney War came to an end and the assault in the West began on May 10, 1940, the doctrine of the offensive was set to roll up the French Army and bundle the British out of mainland Europe. Advance troops maintained constant wireless contact with Stuka control at the rear, calling in dive bombers by map grid reference to pulverize strongpoints of resistance. With the gap prised open in the Allied line and the armored units pouring through, the Stukas move on to paralyse further resistance, severing supply lines and breaking up formations of troops and armor deploying for a counter-attack.

The initial dive bomber assault was directed against airfields and fortress systems near Liége in Belgium. On May 12 they were moved south to support the armored breakthrough at Sedan. It is possible to pinpoint the precise moment at which the Battle of France was lost, at 1500 hrs on May 13, when the first German troops crossed the Meuse. Clearing the path for them had been 200 Ju87s of StG2 and StG77. In all there were over 700 aircraft of Fliegerkorps II and VIII over Sedan, but it was the Stuka which broke the raw reservists of the French 55th Division holding the key sector on the western bank of the Meuse.

Protected by a fighter umbrella of Me109s and Me110s, the Stukas operated in three large groups: the first attacked from 5000 ft with two or three aircraft at a time; the second group, circling at 12 000 ft, carefully noted the targets missed by the first before pulling over into their attack dives; the third group was allotted individual or moving targets. After the Stukas it was the turn of the Do17s, and then the Stukas moved in again, pounding the thin-skinned French pillboxes and shallow gunpits, destroying vital telephone wires, clogging the working parts of anti-aircraft machine-guns with soil and grit and blinding the observers with the swirling clouds of dust raised by their 550-pound bombs. Pinpoint accuracy was not achieved, as is indicated by the low number of casualties sustained by the French in the Stuka attacks. But the saturation bombing utterly demoralized the defenders. Before the smoke from the Stuka bombardment cleared, the first wave of German infantry was crossing the Meuse.

Air Marshal Barratt, in command of the RAF forces in France, received the news of the German breakthrough on the night of May 13. By then the AASF had already lost 25 per cent of its Battles and Blenheims. From the first the Battles had proved inadequate. Their vulnerability could not be reduced by close fighter escort as there were insufficient Hurricanes to provide more than short offensive patrols over target areas. On the afternoon of May 10, 32 Battles had been despatched to make low-level attacks – using delayed action bombs fused for 11 seconds – against the armored columns advancing through Luxembourg. Flying through a storm of light flak, and cut up by the ever-present Me109s, 13 of the Battles were shot down and every one of the remaining 19 damaged. The German column rolled on unchecked. On May 11 eight Battles of Nos. 88 and 218 Squadrons took off to strike at German columns moving up towards the Luxembourg border. Only one pilot returned. The tale was repeated on the 12th when five Battles of No. 12 Squadron attacked the bridges at Veldwezelt and Vroenhoven, on the Albert Canal near Maastricht. In a low-level operation pressed home with the greatest gallantry, the bridge at Veldwezelt was badly damaged, but at the cost of all five aircraft and four crews killed or captured.

Before the end of the day the AASF had lost a further six out of 15 Battles in attacks near Bouillon. Excluding aircraft badly damaged, the Battle loss rate had been 40 per cent of sorties flown on May 10, 100 per cent on May 11 and 62 per cent on May 12. In three days the number of operational bombers had been almost halved, from 135 to 72. On the 13th, the day on which the fate of France was sealed on the Meuse, the AASF flew only one operation.

On May 14 Barratt responded to urgent requests from the French High Command and threw in a maximum effort at Sedan, where the ground forces massing for a counter-attack had been broken up by German bombers. No longer flying at low level, concealed from the light flak by early morning mist and unhampered by Me109s, ten Battles from Nos. 103 and 150 Squadrons attacked pontoon bridges on the Meuse, suffering no losses. The Battles and Blenheims which flew in between 1500 and 1600 hrs to attack Rommel's bridges at Dinant were less fortunate. The Me109s, absent in the morning, were now back in force. Of the 71 bombers which took off, 40 failed to return, the highest loss ratio ever experienced by the RAF in an operation of this scale. No. 12 Squadron, which had flown so heroically against the bridges at Maastricht, lost four of its five remaining aircraft.

On May 16 the Battle was withdrawn from daylight operations and, for the brief remaining span of its fighting career, flew at night. Aircrews experienced considerable problems with the conversion. There was a brilliant glare from the exhaust, which dazzled the pilot, and the observer's field of vision was extremely limited. But there was a dramatic decline in the previously crippling casualty rate. Between May 10 and 14 one aircraft had been lost in every two sorties. Between May 20 and June 4 the loss rate hovered at just over one in every 200. However, safety was purchased at the cost of accuracy, and most pilots resorted to bombing on the ETA (Estimated Time of Arrival). The flickering influence which the Battle had exercised on the course of events had been blown out.

Extinguished with equally ruthless efficiency

were the increasingly desperate Allied attempts to mount counter-attacks. On May 17 150 tanks of the French 4th Armored Division, led by Colonel Charles de Gaulle, launched a northward thrust on the River Serre towards Moncornet with the aim of cutting General Guderian's Panzer corridor. After making initial gains, the attack ground to a halt under constant dive bombing attacks. Two days later de Gaulle made a second thrust, towards Laon, which was swiftly blunted by the Stukas. On May 21 the BEF attempted a limited counterblow at Arras, seeking to link up with French armies to the south. It ground to a halt after advancing ten miles, and the remnants withdrew under non-stop Stuka bombardment.

As Rommel's 7th Panzer Division drove into Arras the leading elements of Guderian's corps reached the Normandy coast at Abbeville. Boulogne fell on May 23 and the BEF was pushed back into the shrinking defensive perimeter around Dunkirk. The Wehrmacht was on the point of a stunning victory. But on May 26 von Rundstedt's request to rest the Panzer units was endorsed by Hitler, who was preoccupied with the imminent offensive against the remaining French armies south of the Somme and still fearful of an Allied counterstroke against his armor in an area protected by canals and inundations. The destruction of the trapped Allied troops waiting to be evacuated was entrusted to the Luftwaffe.

This was a task beyond its resources, a fact of which Goering's subordinates were well aware. Bad weather and dense smoke over the target area meant that during the nine days of the Dunkirk evacuations – May 26 to June 4 – the Luftwaffe was able to launch effective attacks over a period of only two and a half days. Stukas arrived over the beaches at 0740 hrs on May 27, claiming their first victim, the French troopship *Côte D'Azur*. In the following days they accounted for seven French destroyers and torpedo boats, six British destroyers, five large passenger ships, and dozens of the 'little ships' flung into Operation Dynamo by the British. But they failed to prevent the escape to England of 338 226 British and French troops. In the furious air battles over the beaches, the Luftwaffe lost 156 aircraft and the RAF lost 106. On May 27, the day the Luftwaffe launched its first heavy attacks, Fliegerkorps II lost 23 aircraft, more than the combined total of the last ten days. It had been the most punishing round fought by the Luftwaffe since the offensive had opened on May 10.

The Battle of Britain and the German Day Offensive

When it became clear to Hitler that the British government would reject his peace overtures, he began to consider plans for a cross-Channel invasion, Operation Seelowe (Sealion), set for September 15. Complete control of the air over the Channel and southeast England was vital to the success of Sealion – the same kind of air superiority which had first been contested over the trenches of the Western Front during the 'Fokker Scourge' in the winter of 1915-16.

Reichsmarschall Hermann Goering was confident that a mere four days would be sufficient to eliminate the RAF south of a line from Chelmsford to Gloucester, an early demonstration of the combination of over-optimism and faulty intelligence which were to characterize the German conduct of the battle. After the triumphs in Poland and France, Goering was convinced that Britain could be brought to its knees by air power alone. Here, surely, was the perfect opportunity to translate the theories of Douhet into action.

At Goering's disposal were three Luftflotten: the largest, Luflotte 2 commanded by General der Flieger Albert Kesselring, was based in Belgium and northern France, facing England from the east; Luftlotte 3, commanded by Generalmajor Hugo Sperrle, was stationed in Normandy and poised to strike at the south coast; the smaller Luftflotte 5 had been based in Denmark and Norway since the spring, and its targets were in Scotland and the north of England. Together these three air fleets could muster some 3500 aircraft. With 75 per cent serviceability, Goering could count on approximately 1000 Ju88s, Do17Zs and He111s, 250 Ju87s and 1000 Me109s and Me110s to throw against the 700 Spitfires and Hurricanes of Air Chief Marshal Sir Hugh Dowding's Fighter Command which were immediately available for operations.

Hindsight has given the various stages of the Battle of Britain a sharper definition than was apparent at the time. Seen as the prelude to a battle which was never fought – the invasion of England – it passed through a series of stages marked by the Luftwaffe switching targets as it went along. At the beginning both sides were feeling their way, neither able fully to control the forces available to them or to dictate the course of the battle. Even at this stage the RAF possessed two crucial advantages.

First, it had the 'Chain Home' system of 30 radar stations established on the coastline from Land's End to Newcastle and from which reports were fed to Fighter Command HQ at Bentley Priory. Along with the information from coastal and inland observation posts, these reports were cross-checked and the 'filtered' results transmitted simultaneously to the relevant Group and sector stations. Making allowance for the six-minute time lag between the radar observation and the plot of the enemy formation on the map, the Group Controller allocated interceptor squadrons which were then scrambled to meet the incoming aircraft. During the first ten months of the war regular Luftwaffe reconnaissance flights and attacks on coastal shipping had enabled the RAF to develop the system to a high degree of effectiveness. The radar itself was capable of extremely accurate bearings, although it was less reliable when it came to gauge the height and numbers of the attacking force. But its value can be judged from the postwar assessment of the fighter ace Adolf Galland, then commander of II/JG26: ' *I*N *the battle we had to rely on our own human eyes. The British fighter pilots could depend on the radar eye, which was far more reliable and had a longer range. When we made contact with the enemy our briefings were already three hours old, the British only as many as seconds old – the time it took to assess the latest position by means of radar to the transmission of attacking orders from Fighter Control to the already airborne force'.*

The second advantage enjoyed by the RAF lay in the realm of intelligence. Using a combination of 'Ultra', the top-secret device which had broken the German code, and the radio-listening 'Y' service, the RAF was able to build up a reasonably accurate picture of the numbers and dispositions of the Luftwaffe.

At the same time the Luftwaffe's apparent invincibility concealed a number of crucial weaknesses. By the end of the Battle of France, the Luftwaffe had suffered heavy overall casualties and needed time to rest and regroup. On the eve of the Battle of Britain, deliveries of aircraft were actually slowing down. The number of aircraft planned for production dropped from 227 in July 1940 to 177 in September. During the same period British fighter production plans were exceeded by 40 per cent, while the German forecast lagged by 40 per cent.

Conceived and equipped as a weapon of Blitzkrieg, the Luftwaffe was about to mount a strategic offensive for which it had never been designed and against an enemy it was facing on roughly equal terms. The Luftwaffe badly underestimated the vulnerability of its bombers and the absolute need for fighter escort in daylight operations. It was assumed that once the RAF's fighters had been swept from the sky, the bombers would fly to their targets as untroubled as they had been in Poland and France. The flaw in this line of reasoning lay in the extremely short range of the Me109. Although it was a superb air superiority

weapon when operating over advancing armor, the Me109E could remain over England for a maximum of 30 minutes. Even this time was eaten away at combat settings. Nor was it fitted with the suspension lugs to carry external drop tanks. While the twin-engined Me110 had the range to operate for longer periods over England, its effectiveness as an escort fighter was severely limited by the weight of guns, armor, engines and extra fuel, reducing its already indifferent man-euverability to a point where it fell an easy victim to the RAF Hurricanes and Spitfires.

In the first phase of the Battle of Britain the Luftwaffe launched a series of probing attacks on coastal targets and convoys, seeking to entice Fighter Command squadrons over the Channel and into a fight in which they would be cut up by superior numbers. They frequently flew fighter sweeps in the vicinity of the raiding force. These the RAF learned to ignore, provided they could be recognised in time. The convoy battles reached a climax on August 8, when CW9, comprising some 20 cargo vessels with naval escort, came under heavy attack from elements of Luftflotte 3. The initial sparring was now over and the attrition about to begin. On July 30 Hitler had ordered Goering to prepare 'immediately and with the greatest haste ... the great battle of the German air force against England'. On August 2 Goering issued the final orders for Adlertag ('Eagle Day') on which the destruction of Fighter Command was to be accomplished.

Adlertag was set for August 10 but bad weather

He111-Hs over England in the summer of 1940. The He111's successful performance against second-rate opposition in Spain encouraged the Luftwaffe to underestimate the threat posed by the RAF's eight-gun fighters. The He111's gimbal-mounted MG-15s were fed by 75-round saddle magazines, each of which contained ammunition for only about four seconds' firing. In a protracted engagement the gunner had either to change magazines after each burst, cluttering his station with half-empty magazines, or leave the magazine on his gun until it was empty – in which case it would take him a possibly fatal five seconds to fit a new one.

The Ju87, cutting edge of Blitzkrieg in Poland and France, but blunted over the south coast of England during the Battle of Britain. It was withdrawn from the battle on August 16.

caused its postponement for three days. However, the fighting was already moving into a higher gear. He111P-4s carried out extensive minelaying operations in the Thames and Humber estuaries and the dock entrances of Penzance, Plymouth, Liverpool, Southampton, Falmouth and Belfast. On August 12 a big raid was launched on the Portsmouth docks by Ju88s of KG51 escorted by 120 Me110s of ZG2 and 76 and by 25 Me109s of JG53. Fifteen of the Ju88s diverted to attack the radar station at Ventnor, whose tall latticed masts offered conspicuous targets for the dive bombers. The Ventnor station was put out of action until August 23 but those at Dover, Rye and Pevensey – which also came under attack – were quickly working again using their 'Buried Reserve'. Ventnor's disappearance from the chain was effectively camouflaged by the remaining stations, and to the listening German radio intelligence operators there appeared to be no appreciable reduction in the 'Chain Home' network's efficiency. Fatally, the Luftwaffe chose not to press home its attacks on the radar stations. On August 15 Goering, presiding over a meeting of his three air fleet commanders, had concluded, 'It is doubtful whether there is any point in continuing the attacks on the radar stations, in view of the fact that not one of those attacked has so far been out of operation'.

The effort was maintained against the RAF's bases and their installations, but its impact was dissipated by similar failures of intelligence. Repeatedly bombs fell on stations not used by Fighter Command. The pattern was established on August 13, the day which had been set for Adlerangriff ('Eagle Attack'). Once again bad weather halted operations, but the recall orders were not received by 74 Do17s of KG2, which had taken off to raid the airfield at Eastchurch. The Do17s completed their mission at a cost of five aircraft shot down and a further four heavily battle damaged and written off on return. The KG2 aircrew were confident that they had put the airfield out of action and reported to this effect, adding for good measure that they had destroyed ten Spitfires on the ground. German intelligence accepted the report at face value and Eastchurch was duly struck off the RAF's Order

of Battle. In fact, Eastchurch was a Coastal Command station, the aircraft destroyed were five Blenheims, and the field was fully operational the following day.

There were other ominous signs for the Luftwaffe. In the afternoon of August 13, 40 Ju87s of IV(St)/LG1 had made a damaging attack on the airfield at Detling (another station not used by Fighter Command). But Stukas of II/StG2 raiding the airfield at Middle Wallop were severely mauled by the Spitfires of the resident No. 609 Squadron. Nine Stukas were lost, six of them from one formation. RAF fighter pilots had quickly learnt that the Stuka was a sitting target as it pulled out of its dive and lost its forward speed. The day ended with an attack on Southampton flown by 120 Ju88s of KG54 and LG1. During the course of August 13 the Luftwaffe had lost 43 aircraft, the highest total thus far in the battle, while shooting down 14 of the defenders.

The weaknesses of the German bombers were now emerging. The He111's speed was no guarantee of safety from the attentions of Spitfires and Hurricanes, and a feature of the Battle of Britain was the high proportion of bombers which returned to their bases with dead and severely wounded crew. Of the five main crew positions in the Heinkel the ventral gondola was considered the most hazardous. A clear target for RAF fighters, it was dubbed 'das Sterbett' (The Death Bed) in at least one Gruppe. The bomber's gimbel-mounted MG-15 machine-guns compared unfavorably with the RAF's power-operated turrets and it was extremely difficult for the air gunner to fire a steady, continuous burst. The He111 was well protected from stern attacks, and the pilot's seat was fitted with an armored back and head piece. The upper gunner had a face shield and the whole of the upper half of the main cabin directly aft of his position was fitted with a semi-circular cross-section of armor. The lower half of the cabin was protected by a deflector plate fitted across the bottom of the fuselage behind the entrance hatch. The beam guns had curved shields bolted to the side of the fuselage behind the windows. The main part of the ventral gondola was protected by slabs of armor, with the exception of the window through which the gun was mounted. However, the He111 was less well-protected against quarter and head-on attacks. The close grouping of the crew in the extensively glazed cockpit, limited field of fire for the forward gun, and lack of protection for the engines, made the aircraft vulnerable to head-on attack.

Although it was extensively armored against stern and quarter attacks, the Ju88 was entirely unprotected against the head-on attack and, with its large circular radials, presented a good target. This type of attack was ideal, provided a fighter pilot could get into position unobserved. If he was spotted by the Ju88, the bomber's speed would come to its aid. Not surprisingly an evasive maneuver favoured by Ju88 pilots was the dive.

The Pressure Intensifies
On August 15 the Luftwaffe entered the most intensive phase of the daylight campaign. For the first and last time all three air fleets combined to throw five successive waves against targets as widely separated as Portland in the southwest and Tyneside in the northeast. Just over 2000 sorties

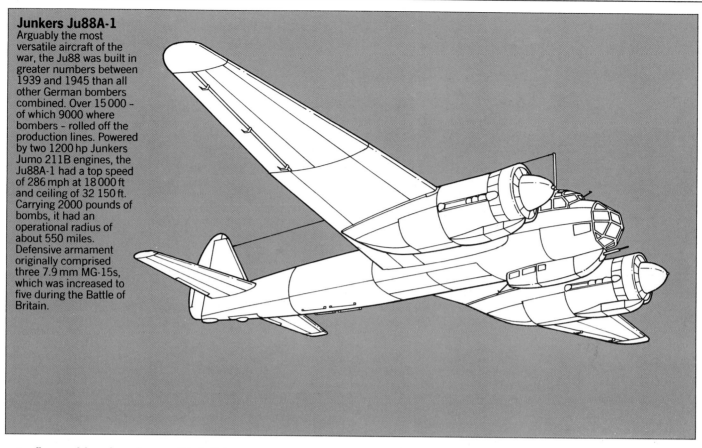

Junkers Ju88A-1
Arguably the most versatile aircraft of the war, the Ju88 was built in greater numbers between 1939 and 1945 than all other German bombers combined. Over 15 000 – of which 9000 where bombers – rolled off the production lines. Powered by two 1200 hp Junkers Jumo 211B engines, the Ju88A-1 had a top speed of 286 mph at 18 000 ft and ceiling of 32 150 ft. Carrying 2000 pounds of bombs, it had an operational radius of about 550 miles. Defensive armament originally comprised three 7.9 mm MG-15s, which was increased to five during the Battle of Britain.

were flown, although under one-third of these were by bombers. Confident that the attrition of the previous four days had forced Fighter Command to drain its northern region for the battle in the southeast, Luftflotte 5 was committed to the fighting. That morning 63 He111s of KG26, escorted by 21 Me110s of I/ZG76 took off to raid Newcastle. Just after noon they were picked up by radar (which badly underestimated their numbers) while still 100 miles out to sea. The formation was intercepted and split into two by No. 72 Squadron before it crossed the coast. Harassed by aircraft of No. 74 Squadron the Me110s, which in the words of the Official History were 'short of petrol and uneasy in the presence of Spitfires and Hurricanes', turned tail, leaving the He111s to the attentions of Nos. 41, 605 and 607 Squadrons. Seven of the Heinkels were shot down, and the only damage suffered on the British mainland was the destruction of a couple of dozen houses in a suburb of Sunderland.

Towards the end of the day Luftflotte 5 mounted a second attack in which 50 unescorted Ju88s from KG30, based at Aalborg in Denmark, attacked 4 Group's airfield at Driffield in Yorkshire. Four hangars were destroyed, along with ten Whitleys, at a cost of seven of the Ju88s. The day's losses were sufficient to force Luftflotte 5 out of the Battle of Britain. Before August was out, KG26 and 30 had been transferred to Luftflotte 2's area of operations.

With overall losses of 72 aircraft, August 15 went down in the annals of the Luftwaffe as 'Black Thursday'. However, there were some successes. Eighty-eight Do17s from KG3, heavily escorted by

JG51, 52 and 54, had bombed Eastchurch airfield and the Short Brothers factory at Rochester, Kent, disrupting production of the new Stirling four-engined bomber. But target identification had again proved faulty. Much effort had been expended in raids on relatively minor stations, such as Croydon and West Malling, rather than key bases like Biggin Hill, one of the nerve centers of the air defense system. On the same day Goering issued instructions that no aircrew operating over England should contain more than one officer.

The Luftwaffe maintained the pressure on the 16th, but suffered a significant reverse over the airfield at Tangmere when nine Ju87s of StG2 were shot down and three more badly damaged by pilots of No. 43 Squadron. After a lull on the following day battle was resumed on the 18th, with concerted attacks on the sector airfields at Biggin Hill and Kenley, the latter being severely damaged by Do17s and Ju88s of KG76. Once again the day was marked by heavy losses sustained by the Stuka units. In attacks on targets on the Hampshire coastline, StG77 lost 18 aircraft, either shot down or written off, among them the machine piloted by the I Gruppen-kommandeur, Hauptmann Maisel. After these heavy losses, the Stukageschwadern were pulled out of the battle.

With the prize still eluding its grasp, the Luftwaffe now narrowed its aim to the destruction of No. 11 Group's seven sector stations – Biggin Hill, Debden, Hornchurch, Kenley, Northolt, North Weald and Tangmere. Biggin Hill and Kenley had already been badly hit on August 18. Then poor weather caused a lull until the 26th, when North Weald was in the front line. The battle entered a critical phase on August 30, when Biggin Hill suffered the first of six major attacks which by September 1 had destroyed most of its buildings. Littered with wreckage, and with much of its vital equipment being worked in the open, the airfield nevertheless remained operational. On September 4 the sector stations were given a respite, but so many other raids were being plotted at Bentley Priory that the operations table was temporarily saturated. No air raid warnings were received at the Vickers aircraft factory at Weybridge – producing two-thirds of Bomber Command's Wellingtons – which was raided by 20 Me110s. Two days later it was the turn of the Hawker plant at Weybridge, which was responsible for more than half of the total supply of Hurricanes.

Both sides were now feeling the strain. The Luftwaffe continued to suffer heavy losses, and in the first six days of September 125 of its aircraft were destroyed. Of the 1000 aircraft crossing the Channel every day only about 25 per cent were bombers. But in the same period Fighter Command had lost 119 aircraft, and its reserves of experienced pilots were running dangerously low. By the opening week of September Dowding's squadrons had, on average, only 16 operational pilots out of their full complement of 26. By the end of the week there were no fresh squadrons to replace. No. 11 Group's

mauled units in the southeast. As Churchill wrote later, 'The scales had tipped against Fighter Command. There was much anxiety'.

The Luftwaffe, too, was finding it hard to make up the losses in men and matériel. Moreover, it had signally failed to solve the escort problem. From August 16 the fighters had been pulled in tightly on top, ahead and on the flanks of the bomber formations. This made further inroads into the combat efficiency of the Me109 and, as Adolf Galland recalled, '*THE SHORT RANGE OF THE Me109 became more and more of a disadvantage. During a single sortie my group lost 12 fighter planes, not by enemy action but simply because after two hours flying time the bombers had not yet reached the mainland on their return journey*'.

At this point the German strategy took a new turn. Late in the afternoon of September 7 the Luftwaffe began its first daylight raid on London. Ordered by Hitler in retaliation for the Bomber Command raid on Berlin on the night of August 25/26, it gave Fighter Command – reeling on the ropes – a crucial breathing space. A total of 348 bombers from KG1, 2, 3, 26 and 76, escorted by 617 fighters, bombed the Woolwich oil tanks at Thameshaven and the London docks. As darkness fell 318 Heinkels and Dorniers arrived in steady procession until dawn to add 300 tons of HE and 13 000 incendiaries to the inferno below. Between them London's anti-aircraft defenses and night fighters managed to account for only one of the raiders. As the last of the bombers flew off early in the morning of the 8th, some Londoners may have recalled that the day marked an anniversary; it was exactly 35 years since London had experienced the first raid by Kapitanleutnant Strasser's Zeppelins.

Once again Goering succumbed to the easy optimism with which the battle had begun. On the basis of German intelligence estimates that Fighter Command could now muster only 100 aircraft, a new pattern of bombing was adopted based on the apparent success of September 7/8. The Luftwaffe would continue to raid London by night, confident that it would sustain minimal losses, while smaller daylight raids – escorted in overwhelming strength – would clear the remaining British fighters from the sky. For Fighter Command this had the crucial effect of taking the pressure off its battered sector stations. In addition, the concentration on a target further inland gave the British fighter squadrons the opportunity to attack the incoming German raiders in larger formations. Where possible, Hurricane and Spitfire squadrons operated in pairs, the former attacking the bombers and the latter engaging the fighters.

Far from dealing the death blow to the RAF, the Luftwaffe now faced its deepest crisis of the battle. At 1130 hrs on September 15 100 Do17s of KG3, flying in stepped-up formations from 15 000 to 26 000 ft, crossed the English Channel at Dungeness. They were struggling into a strong headwind and their slow approach not only gave the fighters time to deploy but also forced the German escorts to turn back as their fuel began to run low. The Dorniers were harried all the way to the outskirts of London, where they were met by the five squadrons of the Duxford 'Big Wing' – 60 fighters attacking in close

St Paul's Cathedral rises majestic and unscathed above the fires raised at the height of an incendiary attack on London on December 29, 1940

formation – which accounted for six Do17s as the raiding force jettisoned its bombs and turned for home.

In the afternoon British radar operators began to pick up the slow assembly of another big formation, this time comprising 150 Heinkels and Dorniers of KG2, 53 and 76. To assemble the standard Gruppenkeil formation, the German bombers took off either in Vics of three from grass runways or singly from concrete runways, in the latter case forming into Vics shortly after becoming airborne. The procedure was then to fly straight and level away from the airfield for a short time before the leading Vic turned back, collecting the Vics behind it on the way. By the time they reached the airfield the bombers were in formation, ready to set course for the target and begin the climb to attack altitude.

The raiders flew in over Kent at 1400 hrs, escorted by two crack units, JG26 and 54. They were met by 170 fighters of No.11 Group. An intense battle with the escorts developed over the outskirts of London while the bombers flew on to encounter the Duxford 'Big Wing' and eight additional squadrons of Nos. 10 and 11 Groups. Nearly 300 fighters were operating over the British capital. By the end of the day German losses were 55 and at least a quarter of the remainder were put out of action by battle damage. Fighter Command lost 28 aircraft and, in one of the exultant bursts of overclaiming which were such a feature of the battle, claimed 185 enemy aircraft shot down. German losses had not been as heavy as those sustained on 'Black Thursday', but the proportion of bombers destroyed and the huge fighter effort required to escort them were particularly discouraging. Henceforth the He111s and Do17s were switched to night operations. Daytime raids were maintained by the Ju88s and the bomb-carrying Me110s and Me109s of the Zerstörergeschwadern and Erprobungs Gruppe (EGr) 210. As air superiority had been so decisively denied the Luftwaffe, Hitler ordered the indefinite postponement of Operation Sealion. The last major daylight raids occurred on September 30, the Luftwaffe losing 41 aircraft in attacks on London and the West Country town of Yeovil. During the autumn the Kampfflieger were to concentrate their attention on bombing by night.

The Blitz and KGr100

In June 1940 Winston Churchill received a painful shock. His scentific adviser, Professor Lindemann, reported to him that the Germans were preparing a device by means of which they would be able to bomb by day or night whatever the weather.

'*I*T APPEARED THAT THE GERMANS HAD developed a radio beam which, like an invisible searchlight, would guide bombers with considerable precision to their target. They might not hit a particular factory, but they could certainly hit a city or town. No longer therefore had we only to fear moonlight nights, in which our fighters could at any rate see as well as the enemy, but we must expect the heaviest attacks to be delivered in cloud and fog'.

Throughout the 1930s British and German scientists had been working hard on the idea of using radio beams as a guide to aerial navigation. Because of the two countries' differing strategic aims – defensive in the case of Britain, offensive in the case of Germany – developments had followed opposing courses. The British built up the radar system as the vital link in their air defense web, while the Germans concentrated on the development of radio aids to bombing, using the short-range blind-landing system devised by the Lorenz Company.

In simple terms the 'Lorenz beam' consisted of two slightly overlapping radio beams, one transmitting Morse dots and the other Morse dashes. When the signals interlocked, the aircraft flying along the beam received a steady note; any deviation from the predetermined course changed the signal. In the hands of Telefunken GmbH this system was adapted for long-range night bombing using a method dubbed 'Knickebein' (crooked leg). Two beams were employed. The first, a mile wide at a distance of 180 miles from the transmitter, kept the pilot on course with a steady monotone signal, any deviation being signalled either by dash or dot signals. The point where the second beam intersected the 'on-course' beam triggered the signal to release the bombs. Unlimited numbers of aircraft could use this simple system at the same time to achieve an accuracy of within one mile at a range of 180 miles. No special equipment was required as the Lorenz airfield approach receivers were standard in all Luftwaffe bombers. The transmitter, a huge oblong array 315 ft wide and 100 ft long, was pivoted at the center and mounted on bogies running along rails, enabling the beam to be aligned on the target with great accuracy. Somewhat naively, the Germans did not anticipate any problems with British counter-measures.

A second, more complicated system, aimed at precision bombing, was also devised before the outbreak of war. Using the X-Verfahren method*, four beams were employed, each on a different frequency. An approach beam held the bomber on course to the target while the other three crossed it at precise intervals. Before reaching the first intersecting beam, which was simply an approach warning, a special X-Uhr 'bombing clock', powered by a clockwork motor, was wound up. On crossing the second beam (indicated like the first either aurally or visually by means of a Zielfluginstrumente deviation display) the X-Uhr was activated by the observer/bomb aimer. This set in motion a hand much like the sweep seconds hand of a stop-watch. Over the center of the third cross beam a button was pressed to stop the first hand and start a second which moved at three times the speed. At the same time the bomb door opened and, as the second hand caught up with the first, an electrical contact released the bombs.

This was an extremely sophisticated system in which the clock and the beams combined to provide accurate data on the bomber's speed over the ground, the key element in precision bombing

---

*The airborne radio receivers and ancillary equipment associated with the system were collectively called X-Gerät (X-Equipment), a term often incorrectly used to describe the complete system, including the ground transmitters.

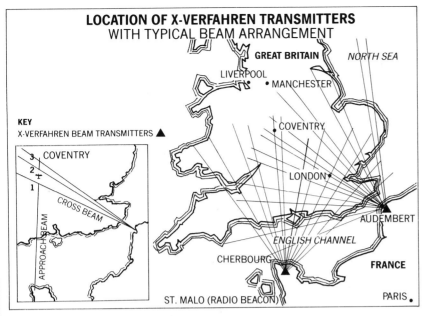

LOCATION OF X-VERFAHREN TRANSMITTERS
WITH TYPICAL BEAM ARRANGEMENT

GREAT BRITAIN   *NORTH SEA*

LIVERPOOL   • MANCHESTER

KEY
X-VERFAHREN BEAM TRANSMITTERS ▲

• COVENTRY

3   COVENTRY
2
1
CROSS BEAM

APPROACH BEAM

LONDON •

AUDEMBERT ▲

ENGLISH CHANNEL

CHERBOURG ▲

FRANCE

ST. MALO (RADIO BEACON)

PARIS •

The layout of the X-beams on November 14/15, 1940.
1 The first beam warns the pilot that he is nearing the target and that he must position the aircraft in the center of the approach beam.
2 As he hears the steady note signal from the second beam, 12 miles from the bomb release point, the observer presses a button to start the X-uhr bombing clock.
3 As he hears the steady note signal from the third beam, 4 miles from the Aiming Point, the observer presses the button on the X-uhr clock, stopping the moving hand and starting a second faster hand. When the two hands meet, a pair of electrical contacts close and the bombs are automatically released.

once the aircraft was routed correctly over the target. However, its complexity demanded special equipment and highly trained crews.

These were provided by Kampfgruppe 100, which became operational on November 18, 1939 with the status of an independent Bomber Wing. In December, its He111s, carrying no bombs, flew three experimental X-Verfahren sorties over London. On February 13, 1940 another trial sortie, flown by the unit's commanding officer, Oberstleutnant Joachim Stollbrock, ended in disaster when the specially equipped He111 was shot down off the north Kent coast by Spitfires of No. 54 Squadron.

Stollbrock's He111 had carried its secrets into the sea. It was the Knickebein system which was first revealed to the RAF. In March 1940 the routine examination of an He111 of KG26, which had been shot down by a night fighter, revealed a curious reference in the recovered radio operator's log to 'Radio Beam Knickebein on 315°'. Interrogation of the crew provided further clues and on the night of June 21/22 the beams were located by a specially equipped Avro Anson of the Blind Approach Training and Development Unit. The point of intersection was the Rolls Royce factory at Derby.

With what amounted to astonishing tactical naivety the Luftwaffe had chosen to test the system over Britain at a time when Germany was not contemplating large-scale night bombing operations. Scientists at the Air Ministry and the Telecommunications Research Establishment immediately set about devising countermeasures. When the beams were needed by the Luftwaffe, in September 1940, the jamming was sufficiently powerful to render the system unusable over much of Britain.

The X-Verfahren system then came into its own. Operating from a base at Vannes, on the northwest coast of France, 21 He111s of KGr100 took off on their first mission on the night of August 13. The targets were the Nuffield (Morris Motors) factory,

Castle Bromwich, and the nearby Dunlop Company factory on the outskirts of Birmingham. The aircraft took off in Kettes of three at 30-minute intervals, the individual aircraft in each Kette flying a different route to the target. The Nuffield plant, a center of Spitfire production, was hit by eleven HE bombs but in neither plant was production seriously disrupted.

On August 29/30 the Luftwaffe mounted its first big night raid when 340 bombers attacked the docks at Liverpool and Birkenhead. Although five Bristol Blenheim night fighter squadrons were flying that night, they failed to make a single interception. The only loss suffered by Luftflotte 3 during the operation was a single Ju88 of KGr806 which crashed in France after sustaining flak damage over England.

At this stage in the war the RAF's night fighter defenses were little more than a collection of hasty improvizations. A number of converted Blenheim IVs had been fitted with AI (Airborne Interception) radar sets and their first success had been achieved on July 22 when an AI-equipped Blenheim based at Tangmere intercepted a Dornier bomber and claimed it as probably destroyed. However, when the German night raids began in earnest, the Blenheim, Boulton Paul Defiant, Hurricane and Spitfire night fighters were still groping in the dark, much as their RFC predecessors had done in 1917–18. It was not until the introduction of the improved AI MkIV that a victory tally began to mount. Nor had the German night bombers much to fear from Britain's anti-aircraft guns. In September 1940 an expenditure of 20,000 AA shells was required to down each enemy aircraft. By the following February the figure had fallen to 3,000, but in the winter of 1940–41 German aircraft were able to operate almost at will by night over the British mainland.

Beginning on August 29, the Liverpool and Birkenhead area was bombed on four successive nights by Luftflotte 3. Only seven bombers were lost, a rate of one per cent, which could be sustained indefinitely. On 'Black Thursday' alone, the Luftwaffe had lost 72 aircraft in daylight operations. Between November 1940 and February 1941 the number destroyed by anti-aircraft defenses and night fighters was 75. To an air force which had been savagely mauled in a contest which it had anticipated to be a walkover, night bombing had a great deal to recommend it. Nevertheless there was already concern about the amount of damage being inflicted. Reconnaissance missions flown after the four-day offensive against Merseyside revealed a depressing lack of concentration, with the dock areas emerging virtually unscathed. Decoy fires had lured many aircraft away from the target, and there was now a growing suspicion that the British were interfering with the bombing beams.

Central London remained out of bounds, but on the night of August 24/25 several He111s, possibly confused by jamming of their Knickebein beams, missed their targets around the River Medway and dropped their bombs on the East End of London. On the following night the British retaliated: 14 Whitleys of No. 51 Squadron, 12 Hampdens of Nos. 61 and 144 Squadrons and 17 Wellingtons of Nos. 99 and 149 Squadrons bombed Berlin for the first time, returning on subsequent nights. Enraged by the 'nightly piracy of the British', Hitler withdrew his embargo on the bombing of London. The capital endured the first night of the Blitz on September 7/8.

It was not until mid-October that the Luftwaffe began to concentrate on night raids. On the face of it, no beams were needed to guide the bombers to London, the biggest target in the world and, when flying up the River Thames, the easiest to locate. Nevertheless on the first night of the Blitz, eight of KGr100's He111s flew to the British capital, using X-Verfahren in the opening stages of the attack and dropping a mixture of HE and 250 kg incendiaries.

It was during the opening stages of the Blitz that KGr100 first began to operate as a fire-lighting Beleuchte-Gruppe, attacking precision targets to provide aiming points for the Main Force. This 'pathfinding' technique was subsequently refined to a high degree of sophistication by RAF Bomber Command. In the hands of KGr100, it remained an effective but relatively crude weapon. Unlike the Pathfinders of Bomber Command, KGr 100 made no special effort to concentrate over the target at the beginning of a raid. Its He111s were usually among the early arrivals, but there was often a time gap of as many as five minutes between each of the Gruppe's aircraft, and it might take them up to an hour to bomb the target with a mixture of incendiaries and HE. [By the closing stages of the war Bomber Command was able to concentrate massive attacks within a time span of as little as 15 minutes.]

By the end of September the interrogation of captured aircrew and a growing pile of Enigma intercepts were enabling British intelligence to build up an accurate picture of the X-Verfahren system and its connection with KGr100. At the same time the pattern of German operations was changing. The greater part of the Luftwaffe was still engaged in the bombing of London, but the capital was not the center of British industrial production. Its dock area had taken a hammering, but in spite of its size and importance it was still only one among many. The influx of foodstuffs and war material had not slackened appreciably since the beginning of the German onslaught. The Luftwaffe turned its attention to the Midlands and the North, the home of Britain's heavy industries and war production over which German Zeppelins of the Naval Airship Division had blundered so ineffectually 25 years before. X-Verfahren would provide the means of locating the targets which had almost universally eluded the airships. During the month of October 1940 only five of KGr100's 19 operations were over London. Its principal targets were Liverpool, Birmingham and the city of Coventry, Luftwaffe target No. 53.

The Coventry Raid

Late in the afternoon of November 14 an aircraft of No. 80 Wing, the RAF's Radio Countermeasures unit, intercepted an X-beam laid across the Midlands, an area which had thus far escaped heavy night raids. This provided confirmation of an Air Intelligence forecast that the Germans were planning a major night offensive, 'Mondscheinserenade' (Moonlight Serenade) to take advantage of the full moon.

Less than two hours later the opening blow fell. At 1920 hrs the first of 13 He111s of KGr100 arrived over Coventry. In conditions of excellent visibility the X-beams were hardly needed, but the operation was used to make a visual check of their alignment. The aiming point was to the east of the city center, and by 2005 hrs, when the last of KGr100's aircraft flew away from the target, 48 SC50 HE bombs and 10 224 incendiaries had started numerous fires. These lit the way for aircraft of I/LG1, II/KG27, I/KG51, II/KG55 and KGr606. Each unit had a specific target: I/LG1 attacked the Standard Motor Company and the Coventry Radiator and Press Company; II/KG27 the Alvis Aero Engine Works; I/KG51 the British Piston Ring Company; II/KG55 the Daimler Works; and KGr606 the city gas holders. In the 11-hour attack 1500 HE bombs, 50 2000-pound parachute and land mines and approximately 30 000 incendiaries were dropped by 449 aircraft. Five hundred people were killed and over 1200 injured; 60 000 buildings, including three-quarters of the city center were destroyed; the medieval cathedral was gutted. In the immediate aftermath of the raid the feeling was that 'Coventry is finished'.

Coventry Survives

Twenty-one of Coventry's factories – 12 of them connected with the aircraft industry – had been severely damaged. In addition, the city's public utilities – its gas, water, electricity and transportation systems – had been thrown into chaos. This in turn brought to a standstill a number of factories which had escaped serious bomb damage. It had been the obliteration of the heart of the city, rather than the precision bombing of the factories, which had temporarily paralysed Coventry's war industries. If the Luftwaffe had returned on three successive nights (a task which would have been made easier by the fires still burning from previous attacks) a vital sector of Britain's war economy might have been dealt a crippling blow. But the Luftwaffe did not return, shifting its attention first back to London and then to Southampton and Birmingham.

Nor was Coventry 'finished'. Just over a month of production had been lost, but most of the factories were back in production within days. Civilian morale also survived the effects of the raid. After the initial shock there had been no mass panic, as the authorities in the 1930s had feared might happen. Several lessons can be drawn from the Coventry raid. First, it provided a clear indication of the results which could be achieved by 'area' bombing. This had not necessarily been the Luftwaffe's intent but it had assuredly been the result of the operation. The swamping of the civil defenses, the dislocation of the city's utilities and the creation of uncontrollable fires in a compact conurbation could prove far more effective than the precision bombing of specific industrial targets. Equally important was the maintenance of aim, the pressure of nightly attrition which the Luftwaffe was either unable or unwilling to maintain. However, the raid also demonstrated the remarkable resilience under aerial bombardment of both civilians and industrial plant. Shattered dwellings did not remove the work force; and under shattered factory roofs vital machine tools often survived intact. The bombers had got through. They had inflicted terrible damage. But they had won only a qualified victory.

The First Pathfinders

An He111H3 of Kgr100 over Coventry on the night of November 14/15, 1940. Thirteen He111s of KGr100 bombed the city between 1920 and 2005 hrs, starting eight large and numerous small fires. The incendiary bombs dropped by KGr100 were of two essentially similar types, the B1 E1 (Brandbomb, 1 kilogram, Elektron) and a derivative containing a small explosive charge, the B1 E1 ZA. During the Blitz, KGr100 dropped both types in cannisters, containing 36 incendiaries (BSK36), which fell apart a few seconds after release, scattering the bombs sufficiently to start large numbers of individual fires over a small area. KGr100 also used two large incendiary weapons, the Flam C250 (250 kg) and the Flam C500 (500 kg). Their thin pressed-steel cases contained a central 'burster' charge of three pounds of TNT and a main charge of a heavy highly inflammable oil mixture. These were phased out after December 1940.

When dropping a load composed entirely of incendiaries, it was customary to select a 50-meter spacing between each of the 32 BSK36s which an He111 could carry. This created an incendiary 'ribbon' approximately a mile in length, comprising 1152 magnesium bombs, each of which was capable of starting a fire. In the Coventry raid KGr100 dropped over 10 224 incendiaries. A total of 503 tons of HE also fell on the city – nearly twice the cumulative total on any one London borough during all the preceding month. Civilian morale was close to collapse immediately after the raid but had recovered within days, along with most of Coventry's essential services. Coventry was not hit hard again until April 8, 1941. Nor was the Luftwaffe ever again to throw so many bombers (449) against a similar middle-sized industrial town. Clydeside came nearest with an attack by 386 aircraft on May 5, when the Blitz had nearly run its course.

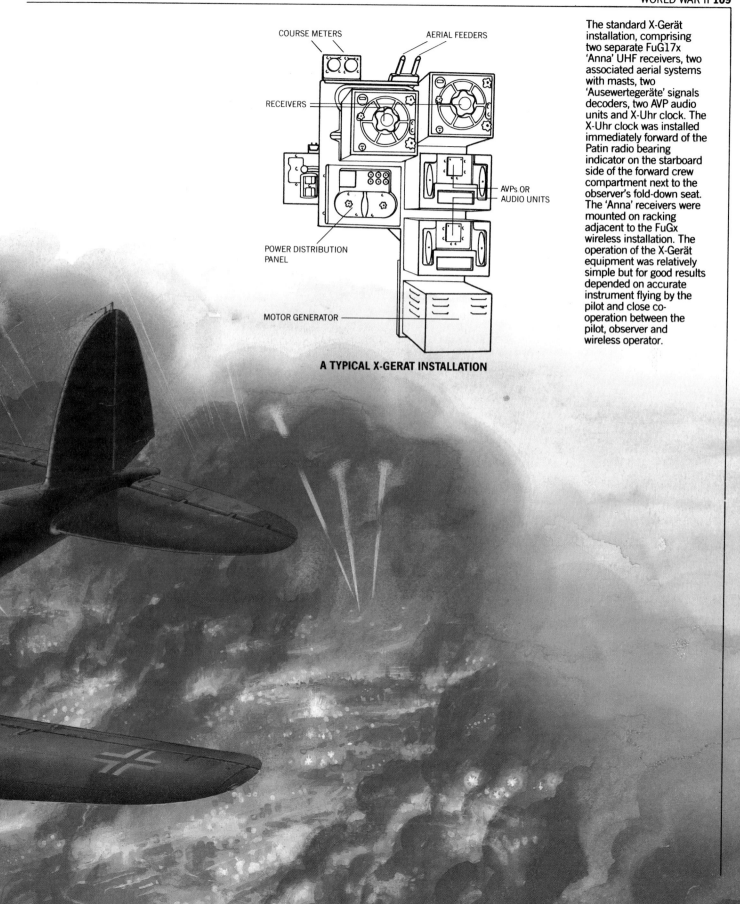

COURSE METERS

AERIAL FEEDERS

RECEIVERS

AVPs OR
AUDIO UNITS

POWER DISTRIBUTION
PANEL

MOTOR GENERATOR

A TYPICAL X-GERAT INSTALLATION

The standard X-Gerät installation, comprising two separate FuG17x 'Anna' UHF receivers, two associated aerial systems with masts, two 'Ausewertegeräte' signals decoders, two AVP audio units and X-Uhr clock. The X-Uhr clock was installed immediately forward of the Patin radio bearing indicator on the starboard side of the forward crew compartment next to the observer's fold-down seat. The 'Anna' receivers were mounted on racking adjacent to the FuGx wireless installation. The operation of the X-Gerät equipment was relatively simple but for good results depended on accurate instrument flying by the pilot and close co-operation between the pilot, observer and wireless operator.

The Technological See-Saw

There was only one occasion on which the Luftwaffe threatened to create conditions similar to those which, after Allied raids, were to lead to the firestorms in Hamburg (1943) and Dresden (1945). On December 29, 1940 a heavy incendiary raid on the City of London, led by KGr100, was compounded by a neap tide on the Thames which made it all but impossible for the hoses of the fire brigade to reach down to the surface of the river. Throughout January and February, in the face of increasingly severe winter weather, the Luftwaffe fought hard to maintain the pressure against London, the industrial centers in the Midlands and Britain's western ports, the last links in the Atlantic supply chain. Of 61 raids involving more than 50 aircraft, no fewer than 46 were directed at Portsmouth, Plymouth, Bristol and Avonmouth, Swansea, Merseyside, Belfast and Clydeside. Winter weather and improving air defenses were now making life more hazardous for the German bombers. By March, Fighter Command's AI squadrons were all equipped with the new AIMkIV. Within a month individual aircraft were beginning to operate a system of ground-controlled interception. Using a Plan Position Indicator (PPI), which presented a radar picture of the attacking bomber and the intercepting fighter in relation to the surrounding countryside, a ground operator could direct a fighter to within 1000 yds of the target, at which point the latter's AI would bring it into visual contact. In March, 22 bombers were claimed by the night fighters and another 17 fell to anti-aircraft fire. The figure rose to 48 and 39 respectively in April and reached a peak in May, with 96 fighter victories and 31.5 claimed by the guns, although this still represented only 3.5 per cent of German sorties. 'Starfish' decoy fires and increased interference with the X-beams, following the retrieval of an intact X-Gerat set from one of KGr100's crashed Heinkels, also played their part. So too did the 'meaconing' (masked beacon) system, in which signals from medium-frequency German direction-finding beacons were picked up and re-radiated in sufficient strength to confuse the bombers' aircrew.

Early in 1941 the Luftwaffe began using a third beam system, Y-Verfahren, in the aircraft flown by III/KG26, which had joined KGr100 in November 1940. The Y-system employed a single beam and a separate radio ranging signal which the bomber picked up and then re-radiated to the ground station, the time lapse enabling ground operators to calculate the position of the aircraft along the beam with great accuracy. Orders to release the bombs were radioed to the aircraft when it was directly over the target. The British threw this system out of joint by infiltrating their own false ranging signals, and the Y-Verfahren method quickly proved as fallible as its predecessors.

The final phase of the Blitz began in mid-April and ended with a savage raid on London on the night of May 10/11 in which 700 tons of HE and incendiaries were dropped, starting 2,200 fires and killing 1436 civilians. Sixteen aircraft were destroyed by the air defenses, the highest total in a single night during the campaign. These losses were not sufficient to bring a halt to the night offensive. Rather it was the transfer to the East of units earmarked for the invasion of the Soviet Union, which Hitler launched on June 22, 1941. By the end of June two-thirds of the Luftwaffe had been withdrawn from the Blitz attacks and the grinding routine of raids on Britain's cities was replaced by seaside 'tip and run' attacks which would have been familiar to the veterans of the World War I unit Kagohl 4.

By the late spring of 1941 the Blitz had reached a point almost of stalemate. Air defenses, initially powerless, had significantly improved: in December one bomber in every 326 had been brought down; in January one in every 110; in February one in every 95; and in the first twelve days of March one in every 63. But the Luftwaffe could sustain these losses indefinitely and at the same time inflict severe damage on Britain's cities and industries. Not until February 1941 did British aircraft production creep back up to the level which it had reached in August 1940. Over 600 000 personnel had been tied down in air defense; some 40 000 civilians killed and another 46 000 injured. All this had been achieved at the cost of 600 aircraft. Nevertheless, the British war economy had contrived to soak up this punishment, and the overall effect on production remained negligible. Douhet's predictions had been proved false. Between September and May 20 000 tons of bombs had been dropped on London but it remained the nation's administrative and economic capital; Portsmouth and Plymouth continued to serve the Royal Navy; the Liverpool docks stayed open; and Coventry absorbed the trauma of November 14/15 to increase its war production. Civilian morale, although severely tested, had not cracked.

Russian Nemesis

In the Battle of Britain and the Blitz the Luftwaffe had been checked for the first time. But it would be facile to say that after these reverses it was never the same again. In 1941 it swept through the Balkans in a month, dealt a series of near-crippling blows to the Royal Navy in the Mediterranean, and in the opening phase of the Eastern campaign destroyed more than 4000 Soviet aircraft for the loss of only 150 machines in a devastating demonstration of Blitzkrieg.

Close cooperation between Panzer units and the new Ju87D – faster, more heavily armed, better protected and with a 4000-pound bombload-reached a level at which officers riding in the tanks were able to call up the dive bombers to overwhelm strongpoints. In spite of these dazzling successes the whole concept of Blitzkrieg was undermined by the vast spaces of the Soviet Union. Envelopment succeeded envelopment in the summer of 1941, but the final victory eluded Hitler and the advance ground to a halt in the snows of winter. Then it was the turn of the Soviet air force to defeat the Luftwaffe at its own game. The tactical use of air power was the principal characteristic of the war on the Eastern front, and in the Ilyushin Il-2 Shturmovik ground-attack aircraft and the Petlyakov Pe-2 dive bomber the Soviet Union had two superb instruments of close-support operations. Developed from a design for a twin-engined fighter, the Pe2FT of 1943 was capable of operating as a level or dive bomber. Powered by two 1260 hp Klimov M-105Pf in-line engines, it had an impressive top speed of 361 mph at 16 400 ft, service ceiling of 29 530 ft and a range of

1100 miles. It could carry up to 12 1000 kg bombs, six of them internally, four under the wings and one in a bay at the rear of each engine. Defensive armament was provided by two fixed 12.7 mm B5 machine-guns in the nose, one flexible gun of similar caliber in a rear turret and one in a ventral position. Two 7.62 mm ShKAS machine-guns were sometimes fitted in the side panels of the cockpit.

Large numbers of these businesslike aircraft were deployed in the titanic struggle at Kursk in July 1943. Operation Zitadelle was not only the last great German offensive on the Eastern Front but also the swansong of the Ju87 in a pure dive bombing role. After Kursk it continued in production as a specialized tank buster while dive bombing operations were undertaken by high-performance 'Jabo' units equipped with FW109As. As the role of the dive bomber declined in the Luftwaffe, so it rose in importance in the Soviet Air Force, notably in the hands of Colonel I S Poblin, inventor of the 'Dipping Wheel' method of attack, first used in the Stalingrad offensive and subsequently employed against German armor at Kursk. The finishing touches to the technique were applied by Colonel A G Fedorov of the 9th Bomber Air Regiment; attacks were carried out by Pe2s in sections of three, each of which broke into a 60-degree dive at the target. Wave after wave, each coming in from a different angle, were calculated to overwhelm anti-aircraft defenses and expose German armor to heavy punishment. Experienced dive bomber pilots were also trained in 'sniper' techniques against pinpoint targets.

Immediately after the outbreak of war the Russians had begun to move their factories east, from the Ukraine to beyond the Urals. Entire plants were dismantled and sent trundling eastwards by train. In the period before the Ukraine fell some 500 factories were moved in this way. These strategic targets were now beyond the range of the Luftwaffe's Ju88s, Do17s and He111s, which were turned over to the more immediate support of the Wehrmacht. In low-altitude operations the He111 proved particularly vulnerable. The heavy losses it suffered were compounded by the size of its crew, the cost and time which had gone into their training and the amount of material and armament carried by the aircraft. By the end of September 1941 536 bombers had been lost on the Eastern front and a further 337 returned to Germany for repair. Having started the war against the Soviet Union with 510 bombers, the Luftwaffe had lost almost double that number in three months.

On July 8 Hitler had announced that Moscow and Leningrad were to be razed to the ground, but the demands made on the Luftwaffe by the Wehrmacht delayed the operations until July 21/22. Moscow was raided by nearly 200 aircraft of KG27, 53, 55 and 54, with KGr100 and III/KG26 acting as Pathfinders. There was intense anti-aircraft fire over the Russian capital, and when the attack was resumed the following night only 159 aircraft were operational. By the third attack the figure had fallen to 100. In all, 76 attacks were made on Moscow during 1941, but the remainder were harassing sorties seldom involving more than 10 bombers.

One of the Luftwaffe's few strategic efforts was mounted between 3 and 5 June 1943 by Luftflotte 4. The target was the T-34 factory at Novgorod, and in the first of four raids the He111s of I/KG100 lit the way for 168 aircraft of KG3, 27, 55 and III/KG4, reinforced by III/KG1, II/KG4 and II/KG51 of I Fliegerdivision. The tank complex was badly damaged, but as the Wehrmacht was remorselessly pushed back after its failure to break the Red Army at Kursk, the few remaining strategic targets disappeared out of range. There was no 'Uralbomber'

A Ju88A-4 on the Eastern Front is loaded with 550-pound bombs on external underwing racks. On the port side of the nose can be seen the window in the floor under the pilot's position, through which he observed the target before making a dive-bombing attack. The blister on the starboard side of the nose housed the Lofte tachometric bombsight used in level bombing missions.

to fill the yawning gap in the Luftwaffe's inventory. A measure of its strategic impotence can be gauged by comparing the night of June 20/21 1943, when 88 German bombers dropped 295 420 pounds of bombs on the rubber plant at Yaroslavl, with the night of June 16/17, when 179 British bombers dropped 1 446 220 pounds of bombs on Cologne. Twice the number of bombers had dropped four times the weight of bombs.

Hamstrung by the fatal decision to reject the heavy bomber program, the Luftwaffe's bombing arm withered away after 1943. Only on increasingly rare occasions was it able to show its claws. In June 1944 American bombers flew to Soviet airfields at Poltava and Mogilev to launch 'shuttle' bombing raids against Germany. They were shadowed to their destination by an He177 and then, on the night of June 22, attacked on their bases by 200 German bombers. A flight of 600 miles was involved with the aircraft 'streamed' in Bomber Command style. Total surprise was achieved: 43 B-17s and 15 Mustangs were destroyed on the ground, together with 300 000 gallons of fuel. It had been a daring raid but its effects were hardly noticed when on the following day the Red Army launched a massive summer offensive, rolling the Wehrmacht back to the Vistula. Bombs can destroy; but only troops can occupy ground.

Long-range bombing played little or no part in the Soviet strategy. The campaigns in the East were dominated by the use of aircraft in combined operations. Major offensives were invariably preceded on both sides by pre-emptive strikes and fierce air-to-air combat, tactics made simpler by the relatively shallow combat zones on the Eastern front, which allowed for greater ease of concentration. The Soviet Air Force devoted a mere five per cent of its effort to long-range bombing operations. Many of them, like those on Berlin, were purely propaganda exercises. The long-range air force (AAD) established in May 1942 was principally used in a battlefield role, on supply and transport work and in supporting the partisans operating behind German lines. Its workhorse was

the Ilyushin IL-4, which could carry only a light bombload over long distances. Later models were built largely of wood owing to severe metal shortages, although this had only a marginal effect on the aircraft's performance. The scarcity of resources also restricted production of the four-engined Petlyakov Pe-8, which had a range of 2038 miles with a 4400-pound bombload and, at altitudes above 14 000 ft, a speed which matched that of the Me109. It also carried the most powerful defensive armament of the mid-war period, with 20 mm ShVAK fast-firing cannon in dorsal and rear turrets and a single hand-held 12.7 UBS machine-gun installed in open positions at the rear of the inboard engine nacelles.

This combination of brute strength and primitive technology – the nacelle-mounted guns recall those in the R-Types of World War I – is characteristic of the Russian approach to waging war. In contrast, the Luftwaffe continued to break new technological ground, even in the closing stages of the war, but was no longer in a position to bring it to bear at a decisive point.

Rockets and Jets

The Fritz X (FX) armor-piercing bomb was a forerunner of the stand-off missile, controlled by radio from the launch aircraft. In similar fashion the rocket-boosted Hs293 was guided by the bomb aimer via a single control lever activating the FuG203 Kehl III transmitter which sent control impulses to the FuG 230 Strassburg receiver fitted in the missile's tail. Both the FX and Hs293 became operational in August 1943 with units of KGr100 equipped with special sub-types of the Do217. They proved highly effective against Allied shipping in the Mediterranean, although the British battleship *Warspite* survived three direct hits to limp into Malta.

Beyond the scope of this book, but crucial to postwar missile development, were Hitler's Vergeltungswaffen ('Revenge Weapons'), the V-1 flying bomb and the V-2 liquid-fueled rocket. The

The Petlyakov Pe-8, the sole modern Soviet bomber to see action during the war, although only 80 were built. It had the most powerful defensive armament of the mid-war period, with dorsal and rear turrets carrying a 20 mm ShVak fast-firing cannon. Two more gun positions, equipped with 12.77 mm UBS machine-guns, were located in open positions at the rear of the inboard engine nacelles.

RAF fighter pilots examine the wreckage of a downed V-1 in southern England. To combat the V-1s, London's anti-aircraft defenses were moved to the south coast and squadrons of fighters patrolled what became known as 'flying bomb alley' above the fields of Sussex and Kent. As backup, an immense balloon barrage was set up on the approach to London along the 20-mile ridge between Cobham and Limpsfield. Of the 9000 V-1 firings between June and September 1944, a quarter failed to cross the coast and only a quarter of the remainder got near the capital. Croydon was the favorite flight path – one observant dentist counted 37 V-1s droning over his surgery in one day. Just under 6200 people were killed by the V-1s and 18 000 seriously injured.

first V-1 was launched against England on June 13, 1944, to be followed on September 8 by the first V-2. The V-1s could be destroyed by fighters and anti-aircraft guns, but the V-2s reached a speed of 3600 mph and were impossible to intercept. The German V-weapon campaign against England continued until the end of March 1945, killing some 9000 people.

When the V-1 launching sites on the Channel coast were overrun, He111Hs were converted to air-launch the missiles. In the late summer of 1944 III/KG3 'Blitz Geschwader' flew launching missions from Gilze-Rijen in Holland. In September KG53 was reconstituted for training in northwest Germany. It commenced operations from Venlo, launching the V-1s by night on a westerly course over the North Sea. The missiles were released from an underwing carrier between the fuselage and the starboard engine, at an altitude of 1500 ft. More than 800 V-1s were launched in this way before the Allied advance closed the program at the end of 1944. Losses through accidents and RAF night fighters were appalling.

Equally risky was one of the more spectacular Allied methods of destroying the V-weapon sites in the Pas de Calais. War-weary B-17s and Liberators were crammed with high explosive, transforming them into huge flying bombs containing 27 000 pounds of Torpex triggered by an impact fuse system. The aircraft were flown by two pilots, who took off manually in an open cockpit and then baled out near the British coast after setting the fuses. The aircraft was then guided to the target by a control aircraft – usually an ex-RAF Ventura. An indication of the colossal explosive power of these 'Aphrodite' aircraft can be appreciated from the fact that when a converted US Navy Liberator piloted by Joseph P Kennedy (brother of the future President) exploded prematurely 15 000 ft over the Blyth estuary, with the crew still aboard, severe blast damage on the ground extended over a radius of six miles. The Luftwaffe's 'Mistel' program also exploited remotely controlled bombers, and explosives-crammed Ju88s

slung underneath a manned fighter and uncoupled to fly on to their targets steered by auto-pilot in a shallow dive.

No gas turbine engines were used by Allied bombers before the end of the war, but the Luftwaffe fitted the V-1 with a primitive Argus pulse jet welded from mild sheet steel. More sophisticated were the Jumo 004B turbojets which powered the Arado Ar234 jet reconnaissance bomber which entered service with KG76 in its B-2 bomber form in October 1944. In the previous July bombing missions against the Normandy bridgehead had been flown by the Me262 jet fighter. But the Ar234 was the first true jet bomber type to go into action when, in December 1944, it was flown from Rheine and Achmer to attack Allied targets during the Ardennes offensive.

Carrying two 1100-pound bombs, the Ar234 had a maximum speed of 420 mph and an effective operational radius of about 300 miles at high altitude. The B-2 had a tail parachute stored in the rear fuselage for braking to reduce landing distance, two rearward-firing 20 mm cannon and Patin PDS three-axis autopilot to enable the pilot (the only aircrew) to aim the Lofte 7K bombsight. The 004B engines, each generating 1984 pounds thrust, were augmented by two 1100-pound-thrust Walther 109-500 rocket pods.

During its brief operational career the Ar234 led a peripatetic existence dictated by the chaotic fuel situation and the inexorable Allied advance. On February 24, 1945 an Ar234 of III/KG76 was forced down by American fighters near Segelsdorf. The jet fell into the hands of Allied ground troops the following day, the first to be captured intact by the Allies. In March KG76 was thrown into the battle to hold up the Rhine crossings, flying a number of missions against the bridge at Remagen. This was the high point of its operational life, but the sorties had been flown in a cause which was clearly lost. Two hundred Ar234s had been flown by the end of the war, too few to exercise an influence in the last battles to stave off the collapse of the Third Reich.

3.2 BOMBER COMMAND LEARNING THE HARD WAY

In 1939 RAF Bomber Command was convinced that its fast modern bombers, bristling with power-operated turrets, would be able to fight their way to and from any target. The concept of the self-defending bomber force flying in tight formation – Douhet's theory in action – was about to be put to the test. However, the implementation of the second element in the Douhet equation – the bombardment of the enemy's industries and cities – was initially restrained by the stance which the RAF was obliged to adopt at the beginning of the war. The reluctance to trigger a bludgeoning response by the Luftwaffe was expressed by the French air attaché in Warsaw, who advised his government that it was in the Allies' best interests to accept the German claim that the bombing of the Polish capital had been justified by the fact that it was a fortified and defended city;

'ONLY MILITARY TARGETS HAVE BEEN *attacked. If civilians have been killed and wounded, it was only because they remained in proximity to such targets. It is important that this becomes known in France and England, lest reprisals be taken for which there is no cause, and so that we ourselves do not unleash total war in the air'.*

The British government adopted an equally cautious approach to the employment of air power. To a suggestion that the RAF might bomb the Ruhr, the Air Minister, Sir Kingsley Wood, made the now famous remark that factories were private property.

Thus in the opening months of the war the RAF confined its bombing operations to attacks on the German Navy. This was an indisputably military target but one for which Bomber Command had not prepared in the 1930s. On September 4, 14 Wellingtons of 3 Group and 15 Blenheims of 2 Group flew in the first of a series of raids on the German Navy in its bases. The Wellingtons, from Nos. 9 and 149 Squadrons, attacked two unidentified warships at Brunsbüttel, but bad weather and fierce anti-aircraft fire shielded the targets. Two of the Wellingtons were shot down by Me109s, a hint of disasters to come. The Blenheims, from Nos. 107, 110 and 139 Squadrons, were tasked to attack the pocket battleship *Admiral Scheer* in the Schillig Roads, off Wilhelmshaven. No. 139 Squadron failed to find the target, but Nos. 107 and 110, armed with 500-pound General Purpose (GP) bombs with 11-second delay fuses, pressed home the attack at 500 ft. The only damage suffered by the German Navy was caused by one of the missing Blenheims, which had crashed on to the forecastle of the cruiser *Emden*. The four bombs which had hit the *Admiral Scheer* had simply bounced overboard (proving as ineffective as many of the bombs dropped by Argentine fighter-bombers on British ships in San Carlos Water during the Falklands conflict in 1982). In both cases they had been dropped from too low a height for the delayed action fuses to detonate the bombs on the armored target.

Towards the end of September Bomber Command introduced the concept of 'reconnaissance in force', in which nine or more aircraft swept the Heligoland Bight with orders to attack any warships or U-boats they might find there. On September 29, 11 Hampdens from Nos. 61 and 144 Squadrons were intercepted by Me109Es of II/JG77, based on the North Frisian island of Wangerooge. As the Hampdens maneuvered to attack two German destroyers, the Me109s razored into them, shooting five into the sea, all of them from No. 144 squadron. Fortunately for Bomber Command bad weather intervened at the end of September, bringing a halt to any further large-scale operations. But it chose to ignore these sobering demonstrations of the vulnerability of bombers flying unescorted daylight missions. The lesson had still to be learnt.

On December 3 the weather improved and a force of 24 Wellingtons from Nos. 38, 115 and 149 Squadrons were despatched on a shipping strike off Heligoland, claiming one hit on a cruiser. They attacked from 7000 ft in cloudy conditions, which confused the German anti-aircraft gunners and also enabled the Wellingtons to escape unscathed from a brush with enemy fighters. Although 12 of the Wellingtons returned with their bombs still on board there were no losses. On December 14 a second operation was mounted against the Schillig Roads. The results were less encouraging. Five out of 12 Wellingtons from No. 99 Squadron were shot down and a sixth was blown up by its own bombs. Four days later another formation of 24 Wellingtons flew an 'armed reconnaissance' to the same target. Two turned back with engine trouble and the rest pressed on. As the Wellingtons turned in two groups to fly on a westerly course to the north of the Frisian islands, their progress was being plotted by German Freya early warning radar.

The Wellingtons flew over Wilhelmshaven but not a single bomb fell on warships, as the orders were to avoid bombing if there was the slightest risk of hitting the shore. Fierce flak over Wilhelmshaven obliged six Me109s of 10/JG26 (a night fighter unit) to stand off, but it also forced the Wellingtons' tight formation to open out. As they flew away from the target they were intercepted by Me110s of I/ZG76 and Me109s of II/JG77. In a running fight which lasted 80 miles out into the North Sea, ten Wellingtons were shot down and two more ditched in the sea. Three more were so badly shot up that they crash-landed in England. The Germans lost two Me109s in the 30-minute battle and one more which was written off after crash-landing. At first they claimed 36 Wellingtons shot down, a figure which was later revised down to 26. The figures were irrelevant. It had been a catastrophic day for Bomber Command.

The unescorted Wellingtons had been savaged. This time the bomber had not got through. Lacking self-sealing fuel tanks, the Wellingtons were fatally vulnerable to attacks from the cannon-armed fighters on the beam, a quarter not covered by the

Vickers Wellington MkIII

The 'Wimpey' formed the backbone of Bomber Command's strategic offensive against Germany until the arrival of the four-engined 'heavies'. Not the least of its virtues was the ability to sustain colossal amounts of damage and still return to base. The production MkIII was powered by 1509 hp Hercules XI engines, with a maximum speed of 255 mph at 12 500 ft and service ceiling of 19 500 ft. Typical ranges and associated bombloads were 2220 miles with 1500 pounds or 1540 miles with 4500 pounds. Defensive armament was provided by six .303 machine-guns in nose and tail turrets.

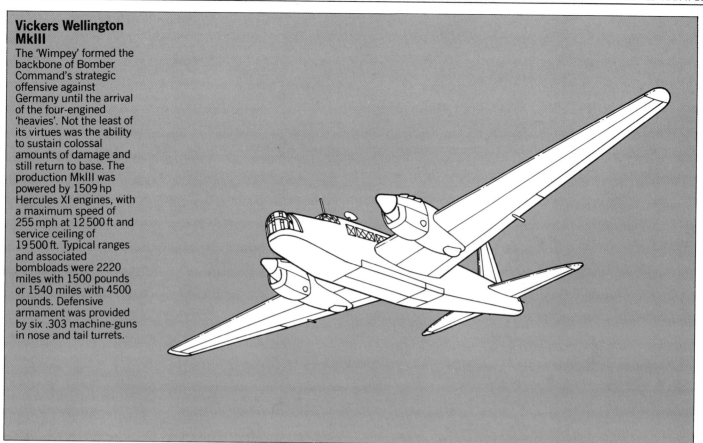

bombers' rear turrets which were unable to traverse to a full right angle with the aircraft.

But it was only with the greatest reluctance that Bomber Command began to question the tactical concepts underpinning the operation. Ludlow-Hewitt preferred to blame the heavy losses on 'poor leadership and consequent poor formation flying'. In 3 Group there was 'every reason to believe that a very close formation of six Wellington aircraft will emerge from a long and heavy attack by enemy fighters with very few, if any, casualties to its own aircraft'. Nevertheless, caution secured a priority program to fit self-sealing fuel tanks to Bomber Command's aircraft, and all further daylight operations by Hampdens, Whitleys and Wellingtons were suspended.

The belief that bomber formations would be able to repel enemy fighters had collided head-on with reality and had been revealed as an illusion. In contrast minelaying operations – known as 'Gardening' – and the dropping of propaganda leaflets – known as 'Nickelling' – had incurred more manageable losses. At the beginning of the war Bomber Command possessed 17 squadrons of aircraft which were suitable for use as night bombers. Of these the Whitleys of 4 Group shouldered the main burden of Nickelling operations, flying over Germany to bombard its population with paper rather than high explosive. These flights had begun on the first night of hostilities when ten aircraft of Nos. 51 and 58 Squadrons dropped 5.4 million leaflets on Hamburg, Bremen and the Ruhr. Many of the leaflets dropped in the

following six months were ingenious, although their effect of the German population was not discernible. The pamphlets dropped on Berlin on the night of October 1/2 provided the citizens of the German capital with detailed information about the personal fortunes salted away abroad by the Nazi leaders. These revelations failed to shame Hitler and his cronies into surrender.

On the Nickelling operations the savage winter weather was a greater hazard to the Whitleys than German air defenses. Inches of ice built up on the control surfaces, airspeed indicators froze up and oxygen supplies failed. Snow frequently caked the windows and clogged the front turret. Some crews reported battering their heads on the floor or navigation table to seek distraction from the cold.

Losses were running at six per cent when, on April 6, 1940, the Nickelling operations were suspended. These casualties were too high for any immediate effect achieved on the enemy. Nickelling had provided aircrews with vital operational experience and introduced them to the enormous difficulty of navigating over a blacked-out Germany. One navigator likened his task to '... sitting in a freezing cold stair cupboard with the door shut and the Hoover running and trying to do calculus'. Recognition of these limitations was to lead to systematic improvements in instrumentation, layout, navigation aids, emergency drills and the wellbeing of aircrews at high altitudes. However, dropping leaflets on Germany shed little light on target finding and bomb aiming, which led Ludlow-Hewitt to comfort himself with the assertion that, 'I see no reason why the major destructive part of our plans cannot take place in the form of precision bombing by night'.

Although Bomber Command had shifted the emphasis towards night operations, the German invasion of Scandinavia, Holland, Belgium and France forced the RAF back into daylight battles from which it emerged grievously mauled. On May 17, at the height of the crisis in France, 12 Blenheims of No. 82 Squadron were ordered to attack German armored columns near Gembloux. Although Hurricanes were operating over the area, the Blenheims were intercepted by 15 Me109s, which shot down 11 of them. On August 13 the same squadron mounted a 'maximum effort' in daylight on the Luftwaffe base at Aälborg, in northern Denmark, a target at the very limit of their range. Six Blenheims were shot down by anti-aircraft fire; the remainder fell to fighters. After this catastrophe No. 82 Squadron was switched to night operations against the growing German concentration of motorized barges being assembled along 'Blackpool Front', the invasion coast west of Dunkirk. The Battle of Britain is automatically associated with Fighter Command, but between July 1 and October 31 1940, Bomber Command lost 185 aircraft on night operations while a further 35 were lost by day. Perhaps its most significant contribution to the Battle was the Berlin raid of August 25/26, which prompted the German High Command to make the fateful switch of the main Luftwaffe effort to London.

The Strategic Air Offensive

It was not until March 19, 1940 that Bomber Command launched its first attack against a land target when 20 Hampdens from 5 Group and 30 Whitleys from 4 Group – including seven from No. 10 Squadron – raided the German seaplane base at Hornum, on the island of Sylt. Hindsight enables us to pinpoint this operation as the beginning of the long, grinding road which led to the terrible climax of 1944–45. At the time the Hornum raid was given maximum Press coverage. No. 10 Squadron's CO, Bill 'Crack 'Em' Staton, became a national hero, and the squadron's record book proudly noted that 'From Captains' reports it is very evident that considerable damage has been done to Hornum'.

However, the truth was more complicated. Nine of the aircraft despatched failed to reach the target area. The remaining 41 claimed to have attacked the base, at heights of around 2000 ft, with 20 tons of HE and 1200 incendiaries. Only one aircraft failed to return. The Official History records that at the debriefing, 'All the bomb-aimers reported that the target was easily recognizable and could be seen through the bombsight. They said they had experienced no difficulty in aiming the bombs'. But German propaganda broadcasts claimed that the base had suffered no damage, and this was confirmed a few days later when photo-reconnaissance aircraft returned with conclusive evidence that the buildings and hangars around the base were virtually undamaged.

Bomber Command anticipated more encouraging results when on May 15 the ban on attacks on

German territory was lifted following the Luftwaffe's attack on Rotterdam. That night 99 bombers were ordered to attack oil and rail targets in the Ruhr. At this stage in the war Bomber Command's methods differed little from those of the Independent Force in 1918. Within the general scope of a mission, commanders were allowed a considerable degree of freedom. German night fighters were not a major threat – Nachtjagsgeschwader 1 was not formed until July 1940 – and there was no attempt to fly in formation. Crews detailed for a night raid were able to take off at any time they chose within a period of two or three hours, flying on their own out and back. The staggered departures were intended to prolong air raid alarms over Germany, thus disrupting sleep-work schedules. Briefings were given as much as 24 hours in advance, leaving crews free to arrange a sequence of timed departures with their comrades. They worked out their own routes, and even had some say in the bombloads carried. Methods of attack were often a matter of individual initiative.

In the summer of 1940 there was a growing debate over the priority which should be given to different targets in Germany. Sir Charles Portal, then C-in-C RAF Bomber Command, supported an offensive against the enemy's synthetic oil plants, which were the subject of Western Air Plan 5(c). In the welter of shifting priorities listed by the Air Ministry in the summer and autumn of 1940, the oil plants retained a

leading place. In December 1940 the Lloyd Committee on German oil resources made a remarkably optimistic assessment of a 15 per cent reduction in the enemy's fuel availability, achieved by the dropping of 539 tons of bombs – representing 6.7 per cent of Bomber Command's effort in the preceding five months. Doubt was immediately cast on these figures by examination of daylight photo-reconnaissance pictures taken on December 24, which revealed that the two oil plants at Gelsenkirchen were still in full operation in spite of repeated night attacks. Air Vice-Marshal Coningham, commander of 4 Group, reflected, 'For my part I have little idea what the Whitleys do, and it causes me the greatest anxiety',

On July 13 the Air Ministry had ordered Portal to narrow the focus of Bomber Command's attacks 'with a view to complete destruction rather than harassing effect'. Priority was to be given to 15 key installations: five aircraft assembly plants, five aircraft depots and five oil refineries. Portal's reply contained the observation that of the ten aircraft industry targets only three 'could be found with any certainty by moonlight by average crews'. Portal went on to point out that as the majority of these new targets stood on their own in sparsely populated areas, 'the very high percentage of the bombers which inevitably miss the actual target will hit nothing else important and do no damage'.

These observations provide an early indication of the direction in which Bomber Command's policy would move – towards area bombing. For, as Portal noted, his aircraft would be more effectively deployed over targets which, while containing a high proportion of industrial installations, were also surrounded by the conurbations in which their workers lived. Oil remained Bomber Command's top priority until March 1941, but the seeds of area bombing were now taking root.

On December 16, 134 Bomber Command aircraft flew to Mannheim in Operation Abigail Rachel. The raid was mounted as a direct response to the bombing of Coventry on November 14/15 and, in the words of the War Cabinet, the aim was to cause 'the maximum possible destruction in a selected German town'. The attack was led by a number of experienced Wellington crews, who lit the target with incendiaries, raising fires to guide the Main Force. In clear moonlight skies 103 bombers claimed to have released their bombs over the Aiming Point – a factory producing diesel engines for U-boats – dropping 90 tons of HE and 14 000 incendiaries over a period of six hours. Ten aircraft were lost.

The oil offensive continued until March 1941, when the critical situation in the Battle of the Atlantic raised naval targets to the head of Bomber Command's list of priorities until the following July. Among the most important were the U-boat

A Wellington of No. 149 Squadron, based at Mildenhall, is bombed up with 250-pound GP bombs. No. 149 Squadron participated in the disastrous daylight raid on Wilhelmshaven on December 18, 1939.

construction yards and their bases at St Nazaire, Bordeaux and Lorient; the battle-cruisers *Scharnhorst* and *Gneisenau* at Brest; and the industrial complex at Bremen producing the FW200 maritime bomber.

At the end of Harry Watt's evocative wartime documentary film *Target for Tonight*, made in 1941, 'F-Freddy's' aircrew make their report in suitably laconic style while the audience is left with an impression of the unflustered infallibility of Bomber Command. It is a picture of a world in which the bomber always got through to hit the target right on the nose. But in July 1941, at the end of a series of 'maximum effort' raids, the Air Staff concluded that the bomb-aiming error at night might be as much as 1000 yds.

A month later Bomber Command received another body blow. In August 1941 the Prime Minister, Winston Churchill, received a report instigated by his scientific adviser Lord Cherwell and compiled by D M Butt, a member of the War Cabinet Secretariat. Butt's task had been to assess the performance of Bomber Command aircraft against targets in France and Germany. He had examined hundreds of flashlit photographs taken at the moment of bomb release and reached the depressing conclusion that in June and July 1941 only one-third of Bomber Command's aircrews had succeeded in placing their bombs within five miles of the Aiming Point. Against targets in the Ruhr the figure fell to one-tenth.

Any doubts Bomber Command had over the accuracy of its bomb aiming now paled into insignificance in comparison with the difficulties of navigation which Butt's findings implied. Equally disquieting was the revelation of the indispensability of moonlight to the success of its operations. On full-moon nights two crews in five flew to within five miles of their target. When there was no moon the figure slumped to one in 15. But the advantage conferred by moonlight was offset by the improvement in German night fighter defenses. During the summer of 1941 Bomber Command's losses began steadily to rise. In the period from August 1 to October 31 over 350 aircraft had been shot down or had crashed, more than Bomber Command's entire front-line strength in September 1939. On November 7, 37 out of 392 bombers despatched to raid Germany failed to return. The 'great fist' of air power still seemed more like a tentative jab flickering in the enemy's face, unable to deliver the 'knock-out' blow envisaged by Air Staffs of the 1930s. Had the Air Ministry and the Ministry of Economic Warfare also been fully aware of the as yet unrealised strength of the German war economy [which was still operating on a single-shift system] its potential for dispersal, and ready access to raw materials in the occupied territories, the picture would have appeared almost unrelievedly bleak. Most of the bombers had got through, but the damage they had inflicted had been negligible.

One answer was more bombers. In September 1941 Portal once again struck echoes of 1918 when he presented the outline of a new bombing plan which, had it been implemented, would have devoured the resources of the entire British war economy. If 4000 bombers could be produced, Portal argued, then in six months 43 cities could be flattened and Germany brought to its knees. Churchill was keenly aware that at this stage in the war the bomber was the only weapon on which he could call to strike blows at the heart of Germany. But he did not subscribe to the belief that bombing alone could win the war. Nor was he impressed with the Air Ministry's increasingly unrealistic statistical projections of the weight of explosives required to bring the enemy to the point of surrender. In October he dealt with the 4000 Plan, informing Portal that: '... *THE AIR staff would make a mistake to put their claims too high ... It may well be that German morale will crack, and that our bombing will play a very important part in bringing the result about.... One has to do the best one can, but he is an unwise man who thinks there is any certain method of winning the war, or indeed any other war between equals in strength. The only plan is to persevere...*'

But even perseverance had its limits. On November 13 Churchill concluded that it was pointless to attempt to defeat both the Germans and the winter weather. Bomber Command was instructed to scale down its operations in preparation for a new offensive in the spring. The tonnage of bombs dropped fell from the August level of 4242 to 1011 in February 1942.

By the winter of 1941 Bomber Command had passed through two crises. The first had revealed the inadequacy of unescorted daylight bomber formations when pitted against cannon-armed German fighters. The second had demonstrated that the Command remained too primitive an instrument to mount a decisive campaign by night. Bomber Command had reached a low point in its fortunes, but new aircraft and navigational aids were waiting in the wings.

New Arms for the Offensive

The first of the RAF's new four-engined bombers to enter service was the Short Stirling, which began its operational career with 3 Group on the night of February 10/11 1941 when three aircraft of No. 7 Squadron dropped 56 500-pound bombs on oil storage tanks at Rotterdam. By the end of the year 150 Stirlings had been delivered to the RAF and three squadrons – Nos. 7, 15 and 149 – were operational. Although by 1943 the Stirling had become increasingly vulnerable, it could nevertheless absorb terrific punishment and still keep flying. In the opening raid of the Battle of Hamburg in July 1943 a Stirling of No. 75 (New Zealand) Squadron survived a head-on collision with an Me109 which sheared away four feet of the starboard wing. When the pilot regained control of the aircraft he found that he could only keep the Stirling level by pushing the control column hard over to port. Aided by the co-pilot, he flew the plane homewards for about 30 minutes before they were both overtaken by exhaustion. The journey was completed by lashing the control column over with parachute elastic.

The Stirling was followed by the Handley Page Halifax, which entered service with 4 Group's No. 35 Squadron early in March 1941, only five months after the completion of the first production aircraft.

Handley Page Halifax MkII Series IA

The successor to the twin-engined Hampden, the Halifax was the second of the Bomber Command heavies to enter service. The performance of the MkII was improved by its four 1175 hp Merlin XX engines and the removal of the nose gun turret, which was replaced by a streamlined Perspex fairing. In the summer of 1943, MkII Series 1A Halifaxes were equipped with a low-drag four-gun dorsal turret. Powered by Merlin XXIs or XXIIs, this cleaned-up Halifax had a maximum speed of 260 mph at 19 000 ft and service ceiling of 21 000 ft. Range was 1860 miles with 13 000 pounds of bombs.

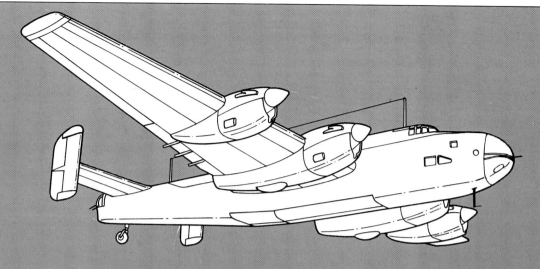

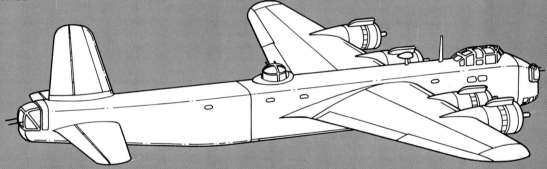

Short Stirling MkIII

Required to keep within Air Ministry Specification B12/36's limit of 100 ft wingspan – which had been dictated by the maximum width of pre-war hangar doors – the Stirling had expectionally low aspect ratio wings of 99 ft 1 in. This resulted in a service ceiling of 18 000 ft, and (frequently much lower when fully loaded) which made the Stirling extremely vulnerable to anti-aircraft fire. A further disadvantage lay in the division of the Stirling's 42 ft 3 in bomb bay into separate compartments, which prevented it from carrying any bombs heavier than 4000 pounds. The third and final mark of the Stirling, the B MkIII, appeared in 1942. Powered by 1635 hp Hercules XVI engines, its maximum speed was 270 mph at 14 500 ft. It could fly 2000 miles with 3500 pounds of bombs or 600 miles with 14 000 pounds.

The Halifax made its operational debut, in a raid on Le Havre, on the night of March 10/11. Two nights later Halifaxes became the first of the four-engined bombers to attack a target in Germany when they raided Hamburg.

A decidedly less successful contemporary of the Halifax was the ill-fated Avro Manchester, which in 1939 had been seen as one of the key elements in a re-equipped Bomber Command. But from the beginning the Manchester was dogged by technical problems, at the root of which were its unreliable 1845 hp Vulture engines. The first of the Manchesters were delivered to 5 Group's No. 207 Squadron at the end of 1940, making their operational debut on February 24/25 1941, in a raid on Brest. All six Manchesters completed the mission, but one of them crash-landed on return to base owing to a hydraulic fault, the first of many undercarriage failures. Aircrews quickly became acquainted with the aircraft's shortcomings. Carrying a maximum bombload of 10 350 pounds, the Manchester could not even reach the 20 000 ft ceiling of the Hampdens it was supposed to replace. A Y-shaped coolant pipe under each engine nacelle was alarmingly vulnerable to shrapnel bursts, and if one engine caught fire the aircraft quickly lost height. The temperamental behaviour of the engines kept the Manchesters grounded for weeks at a time. All in all, as one pilot of No. 50 Squadron commented, the aircraft was 'ideal for going out to lunch', but little more.

Above: The ungainly profile of the Short Stirling. When fully loaded with bombs, the Stirlings frequently had difficulty in climbing above 12 000 ft. On long-range trips to Italy, clearance of the Alps was marginal, the Stirling flying through rather than over the mountains. From late 1943 the increasing Stirling loss rate over Germany resulted in its relegation to less heavily defended targets, including the V-1 sites which the Germans were building in northern France. It was also assigned to minelaying duties and supply dropping to the French Resistance.
Right: Ground crew tend a Stirling's engines. Stirlings with Bomber Command flew a total of 18 440 operational sorties of all types, dropping 27 821 tons of bombs. Aircraft losses from all causes totalled 769.

However, this Ugly Duckling underwent a remarkable metamorphosis to emerge as the finest heavy night bomber of the war, the Lancaster. Using a modified Manchester airframe, the brilliant Avro designer Roy Chadwick produced a four-engined bomber powered by the 1280 hp Rolls Royce Merlin XX. The early production Lancasters made use of about 80 per cent of Manchester parts, and the first Lancaster MkI (L7527) followed the 159th and last Manchester (L7526) on the Avro production line. The Merlins gave the Mk1 a maximum speed, when fully loaded, of 275 mph at 15 000 ft, service ceiling of 24 500 ft and range of 1730 miles with a 12 000 pound bombload accommodated in its long, deep, unobstructed bay. Such was the adaptability of Roy Chadwick's airframe that by the end of the war modified Lancasters could carry Barnes Wallis' 22 000 pound 'Grand Slam' bomb. The first three Lancasters were delivered to No. 44 Squadron on December 24, 1941, and the aircraft made its operational debut on March 3, 1942.

The arrival of these new bombers in quantity was a necessarily protracted affair, and the robust, vice-free Wellington remained the mainstay of Bomber Command until well into 1942, its resilient geodetic structure shouldering successive increases in power, all-up weight and armament. The problems Bomber Command encountered when converting to the heavies are illustrated by the fact that at Armstrong Whitworth's Babington factory the changeover from Whitley to Lancaster production took 12 months. The Whitley was withdrawn from front-line service

in August 1942, but in 1943 277 Whitleys were built at Babington compared with 96 Lancasters. By the end of the war 56 home-based squadrons were equipped with Lancasters. The logistics of re-equipping and refurbishing airfields were even more formidable than the conversion of production lines. A typical Lancaster base had a main runway of 2000 yds, aligned to the direction of the prevailing winds and of sufficient strength to handle the stress of a fully loaded Lancaster, which by 1945 tipped the scales at 67 000 pounds. Two auxiliary 1400 yd runways were also provided for use when high winds made the cross-wind component of the main runway unacceptable. The impact of the new bombers was felt in every department. For example, it was quickly discovered that existing crew transport buses were not big enough to service a full Lancaster squadron with its seven-man crews. The

A bomb-aimer over a Lancaster's MkXIV sight. The MkXIV, which entered service late in 1942, was a stabilized vector bombsight mounted over a large, flat panel of glass. It was fitted with a gyro which could accommodate a 60-degree bank and 40-degree dive without spinning. Evasive action on the bombing run did not affect the sight's accuracy provided that at least ten seconds of the run were made in steady flight. If there was no sideslip, the aircraft could be banked at the moment of bomb release without appreciable loss of accuracy. The MkXIV consisted of two principal units, the sighting head and the computer. Mounted on the port side of the nose and level with the bomb aimer's elbow, was the computer, a complex analogue which correlated the various factors associated with aiming, automatically conveying adjustments to the bombsight.

The sighting head contained the gyro, collimeter, reflector and drift scale. The collimeter was a tube which projected a graticule on the reflector. Looking through the reflector, the bomb-aimer saw the graticule moving over the ground below him. If the aircraft was flying a correct course, the target appeared with agonizing slowness down the graticule's longer axis while the bomb-aimer provided the pilot with the necessary corrections over the intercom. When the graticule's shorter axis bisected the target, the bombs were released.

Lancaster's increased bomb capacity frequently led to station office staff, WAAFs and cooks being roped in to help harassed RAF armorers bomb up for a big raid.

The Coming of Area Bombing

On 14 February 1942 Bomber Command received a new directive. The main weight of operations was now to be thrown into 'area' attacks on German cities beginning with Essen, Duisberg, Dusselldorf and Cologne. On 15 February Sir Charles Portal, Chief of Air Staff, commented on the appendix listing the towns in a memorandum he directed to his deputy, Sir Norman Bottomley: 'Ref. the new bombing directive; I suppose it is clear that the aiming points are to be built-up areas, *not*, for instance, the dockyards or aircraft factories when these are mentioned. This must be made quite clear if it is not already understood'. Bottomley replied that, in a telephone conversation, he had specifically confirmed the point with Bomber Command.

Precision raids were to remain a frequently spectacular, albeit spasmodic feature of Bomber Command operations, but from this point until May 1945 75 per cent of the total tonnage of bombs dropped fell on area targets. This was the final rationalization of the view which had been expressed as early as the autumn of 1940 by Air Vice-Marshal Sir Robert Saundby. At Bomber Command HQ, High Wycombe, there was a map of Germany covered with small red and black squares, the former denoting existing German oil plants, the latter indicating those which had been 'flattened' by Bomber Command. The officer responsible for the map explained to the sceptical Saundby that as statistics had demonstrated that 100 tons of bombs would destroy half an oil plant, and each of the plants marked in black had received 200 tons, they must have been destroyed. To which Saundby replied, 'You have not dropped 200 tons of bombs on these oil plants; you have exported 200 tons of bombs, and you must hope that some of them went near the target'.

A more 'scientific' basis for the area bombing policy was provided by Lord Cherwell in a paper presented to Churchill on March 30, 1942. Analysing the effects of the German raids on Hull, Birmingham and elsewhere, Cherwell concluded that, on average, 'one ton of bombs dropped on a built-up area demolishes 20–40 dwellings and turns 100–200 people out of house and home'. Extrapolating from these figures, and assuming that bomber production forecasts would be met, Cherwell estimated that Bomber Command would be able to destroy the homes of one-third of the population of Germany:

'*I*NVESTIGATION SEEMS TO SHOW THAT having one's house demolished is most damaging to morale. People seem to mind it more than having their friends or even relatives killed. At Hull signs of strain were evident though only one-tenth of the

Avro Lancaster

A magnificent view of a Lancaster's Merlin engines as it warms up at the dispersal point on the airfield perimeter. Lancasters of Bomber Command flew 156 192 operational sorties in World War II, including 116 under Coastal Command control. They dropped 608 612 tons of bombs and laid a large number of sea mines–one of the least glamorous but most effective aspects of the war in the air; 3345 Lancasters were reported missing. The arrival in numbers of the heavies in the spring of 1942 prompted important changes in the composition of Bomber Command crews. Co-pilots were dropped, doubling the number of operational pilots; autopilots (known to the crews as 'George') were fitted to relieve the tedium experienced by a single pilot when flying his aircraft on instruments for several hours without respite. As a safety measure in the event of a pilot being killed or incapacitated, many captains gave their flight engineer sufficient informal training to enable him to fly the aircraft straight and level to friendly territory over which the crew could bale out. The post of flight engineer had been created when the four-engined bombers went into service. Another new crew member was the bomb aimer. This role had originally been undertaken by the observer/navigator, who now had his work cut out handling the Gee installation. The bomb aimer also manned the front turret, although this was rarely used at night, Luftwaffe pilots seldom choosing to attack from this quarter. The increase in the size of the crew was offset by the easing of the training program; it was far simpler to train a flight engineer than a pilot. The practice of training air gunners in the dual role of wireless operator/gunner was also abandoned, thus saving several weeks of instruction.

Above: Ill-fated predecessor of the Lancaster, this Manchester, L7380 of No.207 Squadron (the first unit to be equipped with the type) failed to return on September 8, 1941. Flight Lieutenant Lewis and his crew were made prisoners after crash-landing at Ameland.
Left: Bombing up Lancasters in the winter snows of February 1944, when the Battle of Berlin was making dangerous inroads on the morale of aircrews.

The business end of a Lancaster – the rear gunner in his 'Mighty Wurlitzer'. Many rear gunners dispensed entirely with the central Perspex panel in their turrets to improve visibility and reduce searchlight glare. This appreciably increased their discomfort during icing conditions. The turret and gun control column, equipped with a pair of handlebar grips, was fitted in the floor between the gunner's legs. On the grip were two triggers, for firing the .303 Brownings and two buttons for signalling evasive maneuvers to the pilot if the intercom was put out of action. The seat and ring sight were placed centrally between the guns. The ammunition was stored in four big tanks in the fuselage. Each of the tanks contained 2000 rounds of ammunition (mixed ball, armor-piercing, incendiary and trace) the proportion being laid down by the Group.

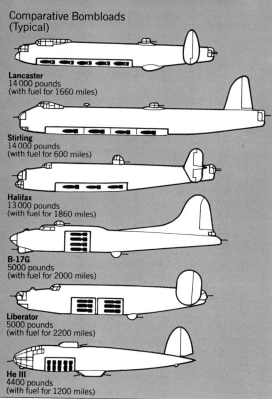

Comparative Bombloads
(Typical)

Lancaster
14 000 pounds
(with fuel for 1660 miles)

Stirling
14 000 pounds
(with fuel for 600 miles)

Halifax
13 000 pounds
(with fuel for 1860 miles)

B-17G
5000 pounds
(with fuel for 2000 miles)

Liberator
5000 pounds
(with fuel for 2200 miles)

He III
4400 pounds
(with fuel for 1200 miles)

houses were demolished. On the above figure we should be able to do ten times as much harm to each of the 58 principal German towns. There seems little doubt that this would break the spirit of the people.'

Morale, rather than oil plants or transportation and communications systems, was to be Bomber Command's principal target.

By the spring of 1942 Bomber Command was better placed to execute the new directive with the arrival of the four-engined heavy bombers and the phasing out of the Whitleys, Blenheims and Hampdens after stalwart service. The cargoes which its aircraft were now 'exporting' were also capable of inflicting greater damage on Germany than hitherto. Bomber Command had entered the war with 250-pound and 500-pound GP bombs which had a poor ratio of explosive charge to casing. In a grisly series of tests on live animals conducted by Professor S Zuckerman, it had been shown that German light case bombs were, weight for weight, twice as destructive as their British equivalents. The depressing results of these experiments were confirmed by Professor P M S Blackett, an Admiralty expert on Operational Research: 'Static detonation trials showed that the British General Purpose bombs then in use were about half as effective as the German light case bombs of the same weight. In the ten months from August 1940 to June 1941 the total weight of bombs dropped on the United Kingdom was about 50 000 tons; the number of persons killed was 40 000, giving 0.8 of a person killed per ton of bombs'. Adding Bomber Command's disappointing performances to the equation, Blackett concluded that the RAF's bombs were killing only 0.2 of a German per ton dropped.

Bomber Command thereafter introduced a range of bombs designed to do their work more efficiently. At the end of 1941 the first 500-pound medium-capacity bombs, with a 40 per cent explosive content, entered service. However, the brunt of the offensive was to be shouldered by high capacity bombs, with an 80 per cent explosive content. These were the result of Bomber Command's decision to abandon the concept of the bomb as an appropriately streamlined artillery shell and concentrate on the delivery of the maximum amount of chemical energy to the target. The metal part of the bomb was merely a necessary evil, to be reduced to the minimum. As the four-engined heavies carried their loads internally, there was no need for streamlining. The result was the Light Case (LC) high capacity bomb, with all the aesthetic appeal of a big boiler, which it closely resembled.

Bomber Command already had some experience with high-capacity bombs, having modified a 2000-pound parachute-delivered sea mine for use by Hampdens of 5 Group. The first LC bomb, the 4000-pound 'cookie', was a welded drum of thin mild steel, painted dark olive and fitted with three windmill armed fuses on its front face. The cases were filled by pouring in molten RDX, an explosive which was simple and safe to manufacture and possessed an extremely powerful blast effect. The cookies made their debut in March 1941 when they were dropped on Emden by specially modified Wellington IIs of Nos. 9 and 149 Squadrons.

A 12 000-pound 'Tallboy' bomb, riding alongside its 1000-pound and 500-pound predecessors. The Tallboy was a triple unit of 4000 'cookies' fitted with a stabilizing tail. Even this was dwarfed by Dr Barnes Wallis's 22 000-pound 'Grand Slam' bomb, a beautifully streamlined projectile designed to deal with hardened targets such as U-boat pens and railway viaducts. Dropped on the Bielefeld viaduct in 1945, the Grand Slam detonated deep underground, causing tremors so violent that the whole structure was undermined by the shock waves.

Finding the Target

The embarrassing revelations of the Butt Report were quickly followed by the development of British navigational systems, the first of which, Gee, appeared in late 1941. Gee employed three ground stations, about 100 miles apart and working in concert, which transmitted a complex train of pulses in a pre-determined order across the continent of Europe. Thus, unlike Knickebein or the X-system, which once intercepted led the air defense to the target, the Gee pulses led everywhere and nowhere. Using a special receiver, the aircraft navigator measured the time differences between the different pulses and with the aid of a special Gee grid chart determined the aircraft's position, to within six miles at an absolute maximum range of 400 miles. By February 1942, 200 bombers had been fitted with Gee, and the modification led to the introduction of specialist bomb-aimers. This job had formerly been done by the observer/navigator, who now had his hands full 'box bashing' his Gee equipment. Gee was not as accurate as Knickebein had been over England, but its arrival resulted in a marked improvement in accuracy until, inevitably, the Germans began to jam it in the autumn of 1942.

As Gee was going into service a new C-in-C arrived at Bomber Command's HQ in High Wycombe. Sir Richard Peirse, a remote leader with a faltering grasp of operational possibilities, was replaced by Air Marshal Sir Arthur Harris, perhaps the single most important factor in the systemization of the strategic bombing offensive. One of the outstanding operational commanders of the war, 'Bomber' Harris rapidly imposed on Bomber Command his formidable personality and unshakeable belief in the war-winning potential of strategic bombing. His caustic wit was legendary throughout the service, and it was often employed at the expense of the Army and the Royal Navy with whom, it can be said, Harris did not always see eye to eye. In a newspaper interview which he gave shortly before his arrival at High Wycombe, Harris declared, 'There are a lot of people who say that bombing cannot win the war. My reply is that it has never been tried yet. We shall see'.

The force which Harris had inherited in February 1942 was still far from being a war-winning weapon. Of its 38 nominally operational squadrons only 14 were equipped with the Stirling, Manchester and Halifax. The Manchester had already been discounted and the Halifax I was exhibiting an alarming tendency to fall into uncontrollable spins (a fault which was rectified in the MkII Series 1, whose enhanced performance was obtained by the deletion of the front gun turret and, in many of the Series 1, the mid-upper turret). To launch his spring offensive, Harris had at his disposal approximately 380 front-line bombers, 200 of them Wellingtons.

On the night of March 3/4, 235 aircraft attacked the Renault works at Billancourt. Gee was not used as the Seine provided a perfectly adequate navigation aid. Using tactics reminiscent of those employed by KGr100, the first wave – composed of Stirlings and Halifaxes – illuminated the target with a mixture of HE and flares. The second wave carried maximum incendiary loads to fire the center of the target, followed by the Main Force with high explosive. The concentration achieved was 121 aircraft to the hour, an early step towards the saturation raids to come. Production at the factory was not resumed for at least three months.

On March 28, 234 aircraft, led by ten Wellingtons equipped with Gee, carried out a devastating incendiary attack on the port of Lubeck. In clear moonlight conditions 191 aircraft reached the target to deliver over 400 tons of bombs (two-thirds of them incendiaries), starting a fire which razed 200 acres of the close-packed streets in Lubeck's medieval heart. In Harris' brutally candid words, the houses in this ancient city were like 'firelighters', and its operational vulnerability had been the principal reason for its choice as a target. At the end of April, four similar attacks were made on Rostock, another tinderbox of a city on whose southern outskirts lay the Heinkel works. After the fourth attack the Nazi Minister of Propaganda, Josef Goebbels, proclaimed that 'Community life in Rostock is almost at an end'. The British Ministry of Economic Affairs concurred: 'It seems little exaggeration to say that Rostock has for the time being ceased to exist as a going concern'. In fact, the cities of Lubeck and Rostock recovered as quickly as Coventry in the winter of 1940. Within days Lubeck's industrial output had returned to 80 per cent of normal. At Rostock the Heinkel works had been badly damaged but was back to full production in a matter of weeks. This provided further evidence of the resilience of war industry under aerial bombardment, but at the time the full extent of the recovery was not appreciated in Britain.

Harris faced two immediate tasks: the restoration of aircrew morale; and the preservation of Bomber Command strength in the face of demands for the diversion of large numbers of his aircraft to the Middle East and the Battle of the Atlantic. One of the weapons he used in this internal battle was his unerring flair for publicity. He exploited this to the full in the 1000-bomber raid flown against Cologne on May 30/31.

The 1000-Bomber Raid

The largest number of aircraft previously despatched against a single target had been the 272 which flew against Hamburg on the night of April 8/9, 1942. Now Harris and his deputy, Air Vice-Marshal Sir Robert Saundby, conceived 'The Thousand Plan', a single massive raid against a major German city into which they would throw the whole of their front-line strength and all the reserves. It was a tremendous gamble, but the prize to be won was the very survival of the one offensive weapon without which they believed the war could never be won – the strategic air offensive against Germany. 'At best', Harris wrote, 'the result may bring the war to a more or less abrupt conclusion owing to the enemy's unwillingness to accept the worse that must befall him increasingly as our bomber force and that of the United States of America build up. At worst it must have the most dire and material effect on the enemy's war effort as a whole and force him to withdraw vast forces from his exterior aggressions for his own protection'.

To mount Operation Millennium, Harris drew heavily on his Operational Training and Conversion units, courting a considerable risk for the long-term if large numbers of instructors and advanced pupils failed to return. Of the 1047 aircraft which took off that night, 367 were from the training units, among them venerable Hampdens and Whitleys, veterans of the Nickelling Operations of 1939–40. The first aircraft of the leading wave, Gee-equipped Wellingtons of 3 Group, arrived over the target at 0047 hrs. At 0225 hrs the last aircraft flew away from a blazing city on which approximately 870 bombers had dropped 1445 tons of bombs. Aircrews flying at 17 000 ft could see the framework of white-hot building joists glowing below them in the immense fire raging in central Cologne. The aircraft flying beneath them were silhouetted against the flames. Some of the tail gunners reported seeing the glow of the burning city at distances of up to 150 miles. Forty-one aircraft failed to return and, somewhat surprisingly, the loss rate suffered by the training units was lower than that of the operational crews. When the smoke cleared over Cologne, the recently introduced photo-reconnaissance Mosquitos of 2 Group returned with confirmation of the raid's success: 3300 houses had been destroyed, more than 2000 badly damaged and a further 7000 partially damaged. Thirty-six factories had been destroyed and 70 had suffered severe damage. The docks and railway system had been severely hit and the city's trams put out of action for a week. In the midst of shattered water and gas mains, severed power cables and a wrecked telephone system 12 000 fires burnt on for several days. About 475 people had been killed, 384 of them civilians, and 50 000 of the town's inhabitants had been 'dehoused'.

In the aftermath of Operation Millennium, Harris launched two more 1000-bomber raids, neither of which repeated the success of the original. On June 1 bad weather disrupted an attack on Essen by 965 aircraft. In this operation Bomber Command attempted to use Gee as a blind-bombing device, a development which was codenamed 'Shaker'. Its failure can be gauged from the fact that the German air defense did not even recognize Essen as the target. Thirty-one aircraft were lost. On June 25 904 aircraft flew to Bremen, inflicting some damage on the Focke Wulf plant but at the cost of 44 aircraft – a loss rate of 4.9 per cent – and a further 65 badly damaged.

The mounting losses were the result of the Luftwaffe's rapidly improving night fighter defenses. These were the responsibility of General Kammhuber, who had been appointed General of Night Fighters in October 1940. An immensely able technical expert and organizer, Kammhuber had built up a system of closely controlled fighter-defended areas covering every approach to Germany from Denmark to France. The searchlight batteries which had originally co-operated with the night fighters had now been moved back to the German cities and replaced by a series of 'boxes', each of which was controlled by a small radar station.

In its simplest form, each of the boxes relied upon three ground radar sets. The first was the long-range Freya, the rough equivalent of the British CH chain, which could pick out an approaching bomber stream at a range of up to 100 miles. This early warning system then brought into play two narrow-beam Würzburg radars, smaller versions of which were also used to direct master searchlights and flak batteries. The Würzburgs were sensitive enough to

A Bomber Command navigator 'box bashing' his Gee installation.

pick up an individual bomber at a range of 30 miles. While one Würzburg held the bomber, a second picked up and tracked a night fighter which was vectored on to the target. Under Kammhuber's direction, the "Himmelbett" ("bed in the sky") system reached a high degree of efficiency. The RAF acknowledged this by calling it the Kammhuber Line.

Nevertheless the system was at best the result of the long series of improvizations which had begun with the conversion of the Me110, Ju88 and Do217 to the night-fighter role. Pilots had to learn on the job as there were no operational training units in which a novice crew could be taught night-fighter tactics. And no matter how quickly they became expert, they were the slaves of a system in which only one fighter could operate in a box at any given time. 'Experten' usually flew in the busiest boxes, but if a big attack developed in a quiet sector, an ace might be flown in to take over from a less experienced pilot. While the night fighter was intercepting one bomber, another 40 might have flown through the same air space. When one considers that in June 1943 the Luftwaffe could field only 371 serviceable night fighters, it is clear that for all its virtues the Kammhuber Line was employing its scant resources in a singularly inflexible manner. By concentrating its aircraft into a 'stream', Bomber Command could pass through as few as four boxes on an inward flight, although there was a natural tendency for the stream to spread out on the way home, which brought more night fighters into action. The bomber stream itself bore no resemblance to a formation. Pilots did not rely on visual contact to hold position on their neighbors. Indeed, on the outward and return flights they might not see any other aircraft, as on a dark night visibility was limited to about 200 yds. Navigators were given a route and timing points, to which they did their best to conform. Inevitably the stream spread out across the sky. In 1942–43 a stream of 650 bombers might occupy a volume of sky 150 miles long, six miles wide and two miles deep. Some of the aircraft might be flying up to 30 miles off the route on the exposed fringes of the stream. By the end of the war far greater concentrations were obtained but even at this stage it was sufficient to pose considerable problems for the radar-directed flak and fighters.

3.3 THE US 8TH AIR FORCE ENTERS THE WAR

THE UNITED STATES ENTERED THE WAR on December 7, 1941, after the Japanese strike on Pearl Harbor. Four days later in Germany the Reichstag convened to hear Adolf Hitler declare war on the United States. In Britain, Winston Churchill concluded that 'we had won after all'.

Even before the United States entered the war Anglo-American strategic discussions had resulted in the decision that the main weight of the Allied effort would be directed against Germany. To defeat Germany the United States pledged complete land, sea and air participation in the joint Anglo-American effort, but the United States Army Air Force (USAAF) was confident that given a sufficient number of aircraft, it could conduct a strategic bombing offensive which would bring Germany to its knees. Heading the list of plans prepared by the Air War Plans Division before the United States entered the war was the use of air power to destroy the industrial and economic structure of Germany. 'If the air offensive is successful', it declared, 'a land offensive may not be necessary'.

At the core of the USAAF's philosophy were the conviction that high-level daylight precision bombing could be employed to break down the key elements in the German war economy, and the belief that, in the absence of a satisfactory long-range fighter, its bombers could fight their way to and from their targets without suffering unacceptable losses. Both the Luftwaffe and Bomber Command had tried this strategy and failed. In April 1942 Bomber Command received a sharp reminder of the vulnerablility of the unescorted daylight bomber when 12 Lancasters of Nos. 44 and 97 Squadrons carried out a low-level raid on the MAN diesel engine works at Augsburg. Seven of the Lancasters were lost in this gallant action, and although the Germans conceded that the raid had exhibited 'precision bombing of the highest quality', the factory was quickly back to full production.

Initially some pressure was put on the Americans to join Bomber Command's night offensive. However, they remained confident that their strategic bombers, more heavily armed than those of the RAF and flying in formation to provide mutual fire support, could penetrate to the important industrial targets lying deep in the heart of Germany. Ironically, the RAF had flown both of the principal components of the American strategic bombing force – the B-17 and the B-24 Liberator – before they saw action in Europe.

In the spring of 1940 the British acquired the first 20 B-17Cs to come off the production line. These Fortress Is, as they were known, were allocated to No. 90 Squadron. After numerous modifications, including the fitting of self-sealing fuel tanks, they began their operational career in the summer of 1941. From the start Bomber Command displayed a barely concealed mistrust of an aircraft which was so big and costly in terms of scarce manpower resources but could only carry a 4000-pound bombload to its targets. Tactically, the RAF used the Fortress in small groups, which did little to shake the Americans' confidence in their employment en masse. The British combat analysis, passed on to the Americans, stated that the B-17C was a mediocre bombing platform which was highly vulnerable to head-on fire and attacks from the rear and below. Some of these weaknesses had been anticipated by Boeing, and the B-17E, of which 512 were ordered before Pearl Harbor, incorporated significant technical improvements. The rear fuselage was considerably enlarged, allowing for increased empennage which was incorporated in a massive dorsal fin. This conferred greater stability at extreme altitude and bomb release. The strengthening and widening of the fuselage also facilitated the installation of a manually operated tail turret armed with 0.5 Browning machine-guns. Additional defensive armament was provided by a ventral Sperry ball turret [adopted on the 112th production aircraft after the failure of an experiment with a retractable turret], a twin set of machine-guns installed in a power-operated turret aft of the flight deck, and the provision of gun mountings in the radio compartment. These and other modifications made the aircraft a ton heavier but with no apparent decline in performance. B-17Es began to enter service in 1941, shortly before the United States was plunged into war.

The Liberator MKII, of which 139 had entered service with the RAF early in 1942, was the first version of the aircraft to fly as a bomber. The Liberator had progressed from drawing board to production in three years, a sprint by heavy bomber standards but leaving many teething problems in an aircraft which had not been engineered for mass production. Eventually it underwent 1820 engineering changes. The first bomber version of the Liberator to enter large-scale production for the USAAF was the B-24D. Although nearly 19 000 B-24s were built during the war, the Liberator has always lived in the shadow of the B-17. A slab-sided Ugly Sister with unusually high aspect ratio Davis wings, the B-24 had a range of 2100 miles with a 5000-pound bombload. The high aspect ratio wings gave the B-24 a cruising speed 20 mph faster than the B-17 with similar loadings at 20 000 ft. This made it a poor formation keeper, a problem exacerbated by very heavy controls, lack of stability and proneness to fall away violently in propeller wash. The aircraft's slow rate of roll, inherent because of the large wingspan, was aggravated by the addition of outer wing tanks. The B-24's extensive interior and hydraulic lines also caused it to blow up or burn quickly when damaged. B-17 pilots used to refer to the B-24 as 'our best escort. When they're along, Jerry leaves us alone'.

Other B-24 problems included a slow initial rate of climb, a tendency to take-off crashes when power was lost on an outboard engine soon after becoming airborne, and the difficulty a pilot faced when abandoning a badly damaged machine. On many occasions crew members would bale out, only for the

Consolidated B-24 Liberator

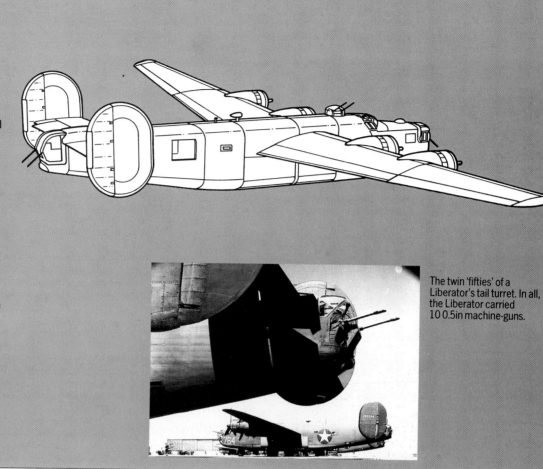

The second US heavy bomber, the B-24 was of later design than the B-17, but offered no significant improvement in performance. It was always heavily outnumbered by the Fortress in 8th Air Force. Powered by four Pratt and Whitney R-1830-65 radials, the Liberator had a top speed of 290 mph at 25 000 ft and service ceiling of 28 000 ft. Up to 5000 pounds of bombs could be carried over its excellent range of 2200 miles. Defensive armament comprised pairs of 0.5 Brownings in power-operated turrets in nose, tail, dorsal and ventral 'ball' positions, plus two more hand-held guns in waist openings. In combat the B-24 had a tendency to catch fire more easily than the B-17, and when damaged was inclined to break up if a wheels-up landing was attempted.

The twin 'fifties' of a Liberator's tail turret. In all, the Liberator carried 10 0.5in machine-guns.

pilot to be trapped in a viciously spinning aircraft as soon as he left the controls. The recommended way for a pilot to vacate a Liberator with damaged flight surfaces was to jump from the flight deck through the open bomb bay immediately after relinquishing controls – not a course of action for the fainthearted.

The first B-17s of 97th Bombardment Group (BG) flew into Polebrook airfield in Northamptonshire on July 6, 1942. On August 17, 12 of the Group's B-17Fs, under the command of Colonel Frank A Armstrong Jr, raided the rail yards at Rouen. RAF Spitfire IXs gave them close cover to the target while six more B-17s flew a diversionary sortie. The lead aircraft of the second flight, appropriately named Yankee Doodle, carried the commander of VIII Bomber Command, Brigadier-General Ira Eaker. In Colonel Armstrong's aircraft Butcher Shop, leading the first flight of six, the co-pilot was Major Paul W Tibbets (who was to fly on an even more historic mission in August 1945 at the controls of Enola Gay). From a height of 23 000 ft the B-17s dropped 39 000 pounds of 600- and 1100-pound bombs, returning to Polebrook without loss.

Eighth Air Force spent the rest of 1942 in a preparatory campaign in which the principal elements were training, deployment and initial limited operations. When they entered the war the Americans aimed to concentrate in England no fewer than 3500 aircraft, in 60 combat groups, by the spring of 1943. Of these, 33 were to be Bombardment Groups – 17 heavy, 10 medium and 6 light. This ambitious plan proved impossible to fulfil, and by August 1943 there were only six groups in England with a nominal strength of 288 aircraft. Demands in the Far East and North Africa diverted many of the aircraft originally intended for Britain. The landings in Sicily in July 1943 and the campaign in Italy, in which 15th Air Force played a crucial role in paralysing German communications and bombing targets in southern Germany and the Balkans, also limited the concentration of Bombardment Groups on British soil.

In addition to the loss of aircraft to other combat zones 8th Air Force faced fearsome logistical problems. The British war effort was already stretched up to and beyond the limit. Thus the American effort had to be self-sufficient, with every item of military equipment being shipped across the Atlantic at the height of the U-boat offensive. Simply to mount a 500-bomber raid, it was necessary to draw on a pool of at least 1250 aircraft to allow for maintenance and the repair of battle damage. To put these 500 bombers in the air over Occupied Europe and Germany required a total force of 75 000 officers and men, 300 tons of operational equipment, plus fuel and bombs, and a standing reserve of 8500 tons of spare parts. Each airfield from which they flew consumed concrete requirements the equivalent of a 60-mile road 18 ft wide. The first of these took ten months to complete, at a cost of 1.5 million man hours and five million dollars. Eighth Air Force eventually occupied 112 airfields in Britain, eight of which were pre-war RAF stations and the remainder wartime constructions.

Thus it was that, in the first five months of operations, 8th Air Force mounted only 30 raids flown against targets in Holland, Belgium and northern France. Most of these raids were provided with heavy fighter escort, and out of the 1369 sorties despatched only 46 aircraft were lost, an acceptable loss ratio of 3.4 per cent. These were useful acclimatization exercises, but they had little or no effect on the German war economy, and the relatively small scale of these operations was compounded by the B-17's light payload.

Formation Flying

The bedrock of American tactics was formation flying, the success of which depends on the concentration of defensive firepower and ease of flying. As the accompanying diagrams show in detail, 8th Air Force's basic formation at the beginning of the war was based on the six-bomber squadron. In September 1942 a greater concentration of firepower was achieved by the introduction of 18-aircraft groups, each comprising two squadrons of nine aircraft.

After two partially successful experiments, the first significant combat formation was introduced in December 1942, principally at the urging of Colonel Curtis LeMay, commander of 305th BG and the driving force behind the rolling program of tactical improvements in formation flying and bombing technique which was adopted by 8th Air Force. Now the 18 aircraft, broken down into three squadrons of 6, flew stacked towards the sun with the leading squadron in the center and the high and low squadrons flying a short distance behind. This effectively unmasked the B-17s' fields of fire, but the staggering and stacking of the bombers led to considerable problems when the formations were used in successive waves. In what was known as the 'Javelin', up to four Groups flew at 1½-mile intervals, each one flying slightly above the Group in front and echeloned towards the sun. As each Group incorporated a 900-ft height differential, this meant that the lowest aircraft in the lead formation were flying 4000 ft below the trailing aircraft in the formation bringing up the rear; the speed differential caused by the altitude variation made it extremely difficult for the higher aircraft to keep in touch. At the same time the 1½-mile gap between formations – intended to deny German fighters the optimum line in head-on attacks – had a natural tendency to widen and defeat the object of the exercise. A partial answer to these problems was the 'Vertical Wedge' experiment, introduced in February 1943, which retained the 18 aircraft Groups and the 1½ miles between formations while deploying the trailing formations in echelon above and below the leader. This went some way towards eliminating the speed differential between the leader and the highest Groups, although it failed to reduce the tendency for the latter's aircraft to straggle.

Formation Flying

The basis of USAAF tactics was formation flying, which was both gruelling and dangerous. Extreme physical effort was required from the pilot to keep station in the turbulence generated by hundreds of propellers. The pilots flying in wing positions depended completely on the skill of the various leaders from element to combat wing level. Poor flying by the leaders and the constant see-sawing of positions inevitably added to the pilots' fatigue and courted the risk of collisions or the shaking out of part of a formation to provide 'cold meat' for the Luftwaffe. Flying itself consisted principally of sliding the big bombers around. Banking or 'winging up' was too dangerous because of the close proximity of other aircraft. Frequent throttle changes were required which in turn could lead to excessive fuel consumption, particularly by those flying in the high groups. All these problems had been encountered by DH4 pilots on the Western Front in World War I, but on a miniature scale.

Right: B-17s of 303rd BG plough through flak on their way to Berlin in March 1944.
Above: 8th Air Force Liberators bomb Tours, in France. Note the formation leaders' smoke markers which triggered simultaneous release of their bombs by the following aircraft. The method produced a pattern of bombs around the Aiming Point – very different from the precision bombing on which American pre-war planning had been based.

The Evolution of 8th Air Force Formations

At the beginning of the war 8th Air Force's basic formation was the six-bomber squadron. Although the squadron had a nominal strength of 12 aircraft, it was customary for six to fly operationally. Within the squadron the six aircraft flew in two staggered inverted Vics. The two nearmost aircraft flew below and the two outermost aircraft flew above the two aircraft in the center of the formation. Height variation in the formation was 150 ft. Two flanking squadrons, 4 miles apart, kept station 1.5 miles behind and 1000 ft below the lead squadron while a fourth brought up the rear flying 1.5 miles behind and 2000 ft above the echeloned squadrons. This had the virtue of simplicity and ease of formation, allowing good maneuverability for bomb sighting. However it soon became clear that the 24 aircraft were spread out over too large an area of sky to provide adequate mutual support or to discourage German fighters.

SEPTEMBER 1942
THE 18-AIRCRAFT GROUP FORMATION

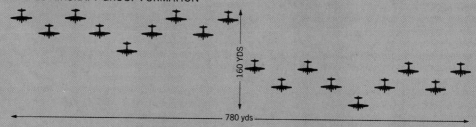

In September 1942 the units were brought closer together with the introduction of 18-aircraft groups, each comprising two squadrons of nine aircraft. The squadrons flew in three unstaggered Vics with the lead squadron 500 ft below the second squadron which was slightly behind and echeloned towards the sun. This widened the frontage and concentrated firepower but imposed an inflexible linear formation in which the outer aircraft not only found it difficult to respond to a turn by the leader but also tended to straggle and lose touch. The linear deployment also closed down fields of fire, reducing mutual support.

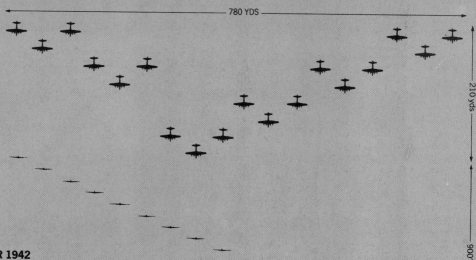

DECEMBER 1942
REVISED 18-AIRCRAFT GROUP

In December 1942 the 18-aircraft group was split into squadrons of six stacked towards the sun with the leading squadron in the center and the high and low squadrons trailing slightly behind. In the 'Javelin', up to four groups flew at 1.5-mile intervals, each one slightly above the group in front and echeloned towards the sun.

MARCH 1943
THE 54 AIRCRAFT COMBAT WING FORMATION

By March 1943 heavy losses to German fighters led to a greater concentration of defensive firepower in the 54-aircraft combat wing. The 18-aircraft group (below) was retained but three of these formations were brought together in a compact unit.

Left: A dramatic example of the Combat Wing. The high and low groups are maintaining compact boxes, but only at the expense of losing touch with the lead groups. This has shaken out sufficiently to allow German fighters to dive through the formation. A straggler from the lead formation has fallen back to find temporary shelter between the high and low groups.

Below The flashes indicate the most vulnerable positions in the 18-aircraft group.

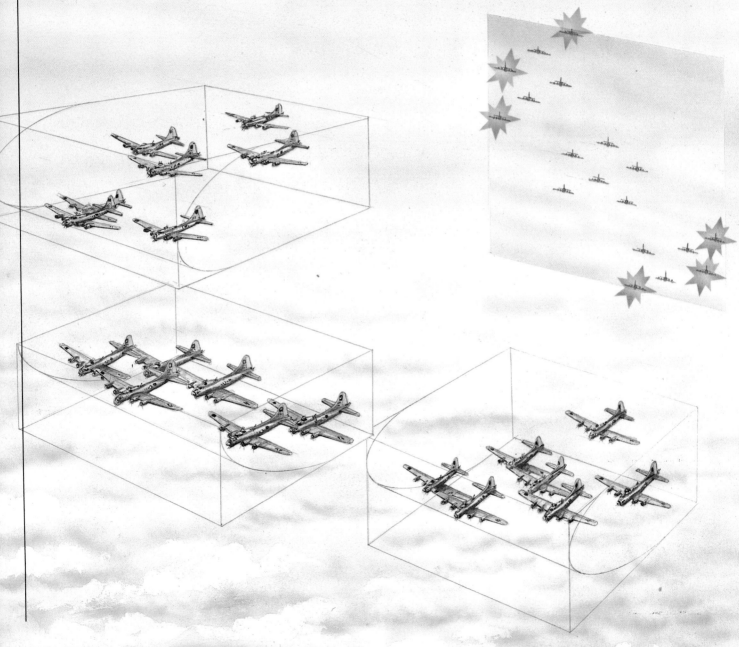

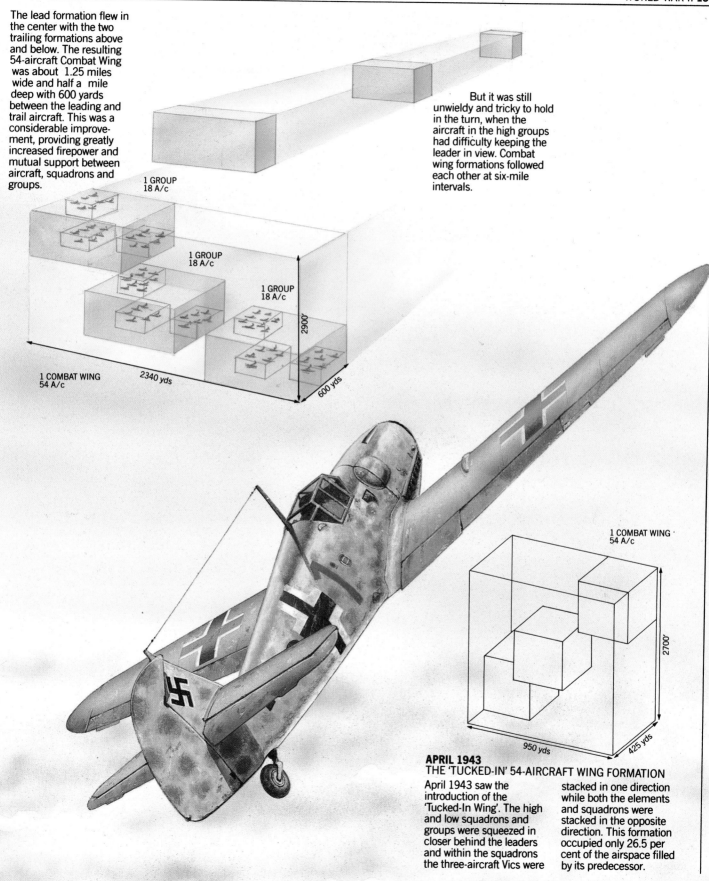

The lead formation flew in the center with the two trailing formations above and below. The resulting 54-aircraft Combat Wing was about 1.25 miles wide and half a mile deep with 600 yards between the leading and trail aircraft. This was a considerable improvement, providing greatly increased firepower and mutual support between aircraft, squadrons and groups.

But it was still unwieldy and tricky to hold in the turn, when the aircraft in the high groups had difficulty keeping the leader in view. Combat wing formations followed each other at six-mile intervals.

1 GROUP 18 A/c

1 GROUP 18 A/c

1 GROUP 18 A/c

2900'

1 COMBAT WING 54 A/c

2340 yds

600 yds

1 COMBAT WING 54 A/c

2700'

950 yds

425 yds

APRIL 1943
THE 'TUCKED-IN' 54-AIRCRAFT WING FORMATION

April 1943 saw the introduction of the 'Tucked-In Wing'. The high and low squadrons and groups were squeezed in closer behind the leaders and within the squadrons the three-aircraft Vics were stacked in one direction while both the elements and squadrons were stacked in the opposite direction. This formation occupied only 26.5 per cent of the airspace filled by its predecessor.

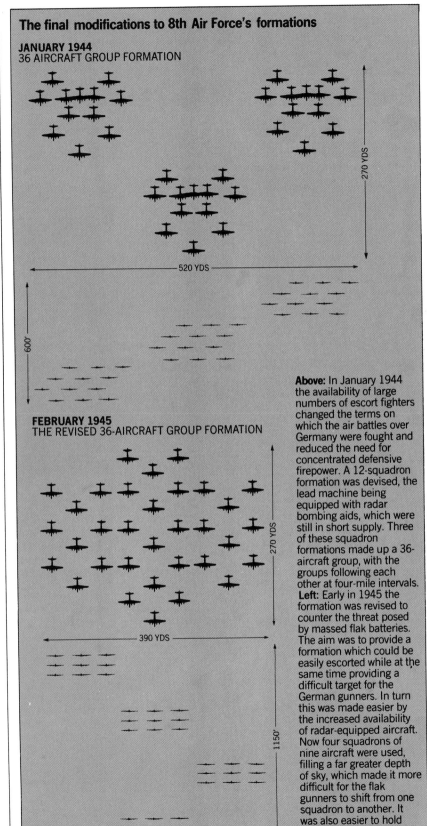

The final modifications to 8th Air Force's formations

JANUARY 1944
36 AIRCRAFT GROUP FORMATION

270 YDS

520 YDS

600'

FEBRUARY 1945
THE REVISED 36-AIRCRAFT GROUP FORMATION

270 YDS

390 YDS

1150'

Above: In January 1944 the availability of large numbers of escort fighters changed the terms on which the air battles over Germany were fought and reduced the need for concentrated defensive firepower. A 12-squadron formation was devised, the lead machine being equipped with radar bombing aids, which were still in short supply. Three of these squadron formations made up a 36-aircraft group, with the groups following each other at four-mile intervals.
Left: Early in 1945 the formation was revised to counter the threat posed by massed flak batteries. The aim was to provide a formation which could be easily escorted while at the same time providing a difficult target for the German gunners. In turn this was made easier by the increased availability of radar-equipped aircraft. Now four squadrons of nine aircraft were used, filling a far greater depth of sky, which made it more difficult for the flak gunners to shift from one squadron to another. It was also easier to hold formation and there were fewer stragglers.

The 'Vertical Wedge' and the 54-aircraft Combat Wing introduced in March 1943 proved inadequate to meet the challenge mounted by the Luftwaffe, which was now being transferred from other theaters to defend the cities of Germany. By October 1943 nearly 800 fighters (65 per cent of the Luftwaffe's front-line strength) were deployed on home defense duties. They developed a high degree of mobility by using expendable fuel tanks, and on occasion flew up to 250 miles from their bases to join battle with 8th Air Force, flying at low level to avoid detection.

In April 1943 the 'Combat Wing' underwent a modification which resulted in the introduction of the 'Tucked-In Wing', the most formidable concentration of defensive firepower yet devised by the Americans. During the remainder of 1943 the Tucked-In Wing was the principal element in 8th Air Force's philosophy of the self-defending formation. Heavy fighter escort could be provided on shallow penetrations into Occupied Europe, but on longer raids into Germany the bombers were on their own.

Another major innovation prompted by LeMay was the introduction of 'pattern' bombing, in which the bombers held their postions on the leading aircraft, releasing their bombs simultaneously when a smoke marker fell from the leader. At the beginning of the bombing run, the pilots in the lead aircraft switched on the AFCE (Automatic Flight Control Equipment) which was linked to the Norden bombsight. From that moment the bombardier, making constant small adjustments, flew the aircraft on to the target and the release point. The system had the obvious disadvantage that all the bombs could be wasted if a serious error was made by the lead bombardier. But there was a greater probability that more bombs would straddle and saturate the target if they were dropped on the orders of the most battle-experienced crew available. In this way the bombs of even the weakest crew could be made to count.

The introduction of the 'Wedge' coincided with 8th Air Force's first attacks on the Reich itself. In January 1943 Churchill and Roosevelt met at Casablanca to plan the future conduct of the war. Although a cross-Channel invasion was ruled out until 1944, it was considered of the utmost importance to commit American forces to operations in Europe as quickly as possible. The solution at hand was an Anglo-American bombing offensive which would clear the way for the invasion of northern Europe. This would also relieve pressure from Stalin for the opening of a 'second front' on land and stem the demand for the diversion of resources, including long-range aircraft, to the Pacific. On January 21, 1943 a directive was issued which was sufficiently broad to accommodate the different methods and aims of Bomber Command and 8th Air Force. The objective was to be 'the progressive destruction and dislocation of the German military, industrial and economic system, and the undermining of the morale of the German people to a point where their capacity for armed resistance is fatally weakened'.

The transformation of the directive into operational reality was embodied in a plan drawn up by General Eaker and - under the codename Pointblank - endorsed by Portal and Harris in April 1943. A number of Eaker's projections reflect the almost euphoric confidence of 8th Air Force as it prepared to mount the long-awaited offensive against Germany. Anticipating a strength of 2702 aircraft by April 1 1944, the plan predicted an 89 per cent reduction of German submarine construction, with figures of 43 per cent for fighters, 65 per cent for bombers, 76 per cent for ball bearings and 56 per cent for rubber production. They are reminiscent of the Sykes paper of April 1918, which had suggested that as much as 95 per cent of the German magneto industry could be destroyed in as few as three raids; and Bomber Command's unrealistic deletion of successive oil plants from the map in the winter of 1940. Now the unbounded confidence of 8th Air Force was to be tested, almost to the point of destruction, in the skies over Germany.

On January 27, 1943 64 B-17s, headed by 306th BG with Colonel Frank Armstrong in the leading aircraft, took off to raid Wilhemshaven. Fifty-eight aircraft bombed the target through gaps in the thin cloud and a smoke screen put up by the defenses. Three aircraft were lost on the operation, one B-17 and two B-24s, from a small force which made an unsuccessful attempt to bomb the same target. Eighth's gunners were credited with 22 victories. In fact the Luftwaffe lost seven fighters, which represented a considerable success for the American gunners, but wildly exaggerated claiming was to bedevil the bombing offensive throughout 1943.

After this initial modest success losses began to rise steadily. In February they amounted to 22 of the average effective combat strength of 84 aircraft and 74 crews. On April 17, 117 aircraft raided the Focke Wulf factory at Bremen, flying in two 'Wedge' combat wings. There was a height difference of nearly 3000 ft between the highest and lowest elements, and the formations were far from easy to control. Over the North Sea the Combat Wings were spotted by a Luftwaffe reconnaissance aircraft. As they began their bombing run they were attacked by two Gruppen of JG1, which shot down 15 B-17s from the leading wing, most of them over the target. A sixteenth was lost to anti-aircraft fire. Six of the downed bombers had made up the entire low squadron (401st) of 91st BG, leading the first Combat Wing. This was the most exposed and vulnerable element in the formation and had rapidly earned the nickname 'Purple Heart Corner'. It had already become necessary to rotate squadrons through the position. The remaining ten losses had been suffered by 306th BG, also in the leading wing. Another 48 B-17s incurred varying degrees of damage.

Weaknesses of the B-17

At the moment 8th Air Force was readying itself for deeper penetrations into Germany, the inherent weaknesses in the B-17 began to unravel. In comparison with the bombers of the late 1930s, the B-17 was bristling with firepower. A combat wing of 54 aircraft, each carrying about 9000 rounds of ammunition, could bring to bear 648 0.5 guns firing 14 rounds a second with an effective range of 600 yds. (Massed firing in formation accounts for much of the over-claiming as well as damage and loss as a result of 'friendly' bullets.) The two-ounce bullets remained lethal on a human body at ranges up to four miles. Fighter pilots attacking the combat wings in the classic curve of pursuit from astern flew straight into a wall of fire. Breaking away under the formation invited fire from the ball turret gunner hunched up beneath the B-17's fuselage as well as fire from left or right waist gunners. Pulling up and over meant running the gauntlet of fire from the waist gunners, upper turret gunners and the gun in the B-17's radio room. However, fire from the hand-held waist guns was fairly inaccurate – controlling a reverberating 0.5 gun weighing 64 pounds in a 200 mph slipstream was no easy task – and the waist gunners faced the added hazard of being thrown together and having the guns and ammunition belts entangled by the violent gyrations of the aircraft.

These were minor drawbacks compared with the B-17's deficiencies in protection. Although nearly 30 pieces of armor and flak curtains were incorporated in the aircraft, the lack of armor in the nose, and the absence of bullet-proof glass, were potentially lethal weaknesses. Here the B-17Es were particularly at risk. Numerous rear gunners were killed as fire from head-on attacks ripped through the nose and along the length of the fuselage before slamming into the rear turret and its gunner. And it was from head-on that German fighter pilots chose to mount the great majority of their attacks, a tactic first exploited in November 1942 by Major Egon Mayer, Commander of III/JG2. Initially the B-17's nose armament consisted of a flexible socket-mounted .300 machine-gun fired by the bombardier. The B-24 had two 0.5 'cheek' guns firing from ports in the nose and a 0.5 gun projecting through the lower part of the Perspex nose which could not be elevated beyond the horizontal plane, leaving a blind spot dead ahead. B-17s were modified to fire a nose-mounted 0.5 gun, fitted with a special support frame and mounted so as not to interfere with the bombsight. 'Cheek' guns were also added, and in combat some B-17 and B-24 pilots maneuvered in a slight diving turn to allow the 'cheek' guns and the upper turret to be brought to

B-17s plaster the Luftwaffe fighter base at Amiens-Glisy, in France, on August 31, 1943.

Boeing B-17, The Flying Fortress

Right: B-17s of 91st BG, 'The Ragged Irregulars', which led the famous Schweinfurt raid on August 17, 1943. On January 5, 1944 it became the first 8th Air Force group to complete 100 missions. It also suffered the highest loss total of all of 8th Air Force's bomb groups, with 197 aircraft missing in action. In January 1944 camouflaged paint was discarded on most USAAF aircraft, marginally improving performance through reduced weight and smoother skin, and also saving valuable man hours in the war factories. When the first natural metal deliveries began in February 1944, some units had misgivings that 'silver' bombers would become natural targets in a camouflaged formation. Initially the new aircraft flew together until sufficient numbers arrived to make them less of a curiosity.

Above: First of a mighty line, the Y1B-17, which entered service with 2nd BG in 1937.

Right: The B-17 played a crucial role in the Battle of the Atlantic, flying long-range patrols against U-boat 'wolf packs' and closing the mid-ocean gap. This RAF Coastal Command Flying Fortress is taking off from an airfield in the Azores.

Above: Sand-filled practice bombs are loaded on to a B-17 during training exercises. The Norden bombsight is discreetly covered.

The development of the Flying Fortress

The B-17E, the first of which flew in September 1941, marked a radical break with the original design, incorporating enlarged rear fuselage and rudder plus tail and ball turrets. The first B-17F left the production line in May 1942 and 3405 were produced in the following 15 months. Over 400 internal alterations were worked into the aircraft, including self-sealing fuel tanks, an improved oxygen system for the crew, more power sources, changes in the layout of the controls, and better radio communications. A one-piece moulded Plexiglass nosepiece was fitted into which was slotted the flat bomb-aiming panel. The B-17F was powered by the new R-1820-97 engines with an emergency 1320 hp rating. These and other modifications raised the loaded weight to 65 000 pounds and led to the strengthening of the undercarriage and the introduction of a dual braking system. In the later B-17Fs extra fuel could be carried in so-called 'Tokyo tanks' in the outer wing sections. The B-17G appeared in the autumn of 1943 with chin turret and glazed-over waist windows housing specially mounted guns. In the later B-17Gs the tail gunner's field of fire was improved, which resulted in the shortening of the fuselage by five inches.

YB-17

B-17B

B-17C

B-17E

B-17F

B-17G

Left: The chin turret of 'Pistol Packin' Mama'. The turret appeared on the later B-17Fs and was standard on the B-17G. No gun on a B-17 carried more than one minute's supply of ammunition. Experienced gunners fired short, sharp bursts rather than hosing their fire around the sky.

bear on fighters making frontal attacks. However, this tended to disrupt the formation, and also presented the incoming fighter with a slightly larger target.

Another problem was introduced by the composition of the crew. The gun positions covering the rear of the B-17 were all occupied by enlisted men who had graduated from aerial gunnery courses. The guns in the B-17's nose compartment were manned by two officers – the bombardier and the navigator – whose gunnery training had frequently been extremely sketchy. Thus the design emphasis of the B-17 had been turned inside out. With the exception of the top turret, the trained gunners were at the back of the bomber, powerless to assist in repelling the frontal attacks which represented the greatest threat.

The B-17's Strengths

A B-17 formation, dubbed a Pulk (Herd) by the Germans, was an unnerving sight for novice fighter pilots. With a combined closing speed of 500 mph both sides had only seconds to make their fire count. Barrelling in at 200 yds per second a fighter pilot might have time for only a half-second burst before taking avoiding action. On the face of it, the German aircraft seemed adequately armed for the task. In the summer of 1943 an FW190A4 carried two 7.9 mm machine-guns and four 20 mm cannon. With all guns functioning, a three-second burst loosed off about 130 rounds of ammunition. The Luftwaffe estimated that an average of 20 hits from the 20 mm cannon were sufficient to destroy a B-17. But analysis of air-to-air combat films by German armaments experts revealed that the average pilot scored hits with only 2 per cent of rounds fired. To obtain the necessary 20 hits, 1000 rounds of cannon ammunition would have to be expended, the equivalent of 23 seconds' firing.

From the autumn of 1943 fighter armament became progressively more heavy. The Mk108 30 mm heavy cannon fired over 600 11-ounce high-explosive rounds a minute; as few as three of these could prove fatal. Underwing mountings were devised for the 210 mm rocket mortar, firing tube-launched spin-stabilized projectiles weighing 248 pounds and time-fused to detonate at a pre-set range of between 600 and 1200 yds from the launch point. The Me109G carried one 30 mm cannon, two 13 mm machine-guns and either two 20 mm cannon or two 210 mm rocket launchers. The specially modified Me110G was armed with four 20 mm cannon, two 30 mm cannon and four 210 mm rocket launchers. The rockets were not particularly accurate, but they served the function of 'loosening up' the formation.

For the B-17's aircrew, operating conditions were gruelling. Of the personnel screened by the RAF in 1941 for the 20 B-17Cs, nearly 60 per cent were rejected on medical grounds alone, being unable to withstand the effects of decompression and altitude sickness. Malfunctioning oxygen sets were a constant problem in the early types, and the B-17's aircrew shared with their World War I predecessors the hazards of anoxia and frostbite. Tail and waist gunners – who wore electrically heated suits – ran the greatest risk. Until the introduction of glazed windows in the waist positions of the B-17G, which entered service in the autumn of 1943, hurricane-force winds often lashed the inside of the fuselage

A B-17 of 483rd BG, 15th Air Force, goes down over Nis in Yugoslavia. For heavy bombers the greatest single cause of loss was hits to the engines, followed by damage to the hydraulic, fuel and oil systems. Serious damage to the engines, combined with fuel or oil fire, frequently proved fatal. The pilot and the controls were also vulnerable, although presenting a smaller target.

and temperatures could fall to as low as 40 degrees below zero. Movement in the bomb bays and along the rear fuselage was by swaying, rope-handled catwalks, while the rear turret could only be entered in a crawl. The only station in the aircraft where a 6 ft man could stand upright was the radio room, but this could be as cold as the rear fuselage, and operators usually transmitted wearing gloves.

The B-17 may have been uncomfortable, but it was easy to fly and capable of surviving colossal structural damage. On October 2, 1942, while attacking the Meaulte aircraft factory in France, B-17 Phyllis of 301st BG was hit in the upper turret – where the gunner was badly wounded – and the inboard starboard engine, which was put out of action. Then the outboard starboard engine 'ran away', defying control. More hits aft badly damaged the control wires to the tail, whereupon Phyllis rose in a steep climb which required the efforts of both pilots to bring under control. The starboard wing was so badly damaged that it needed almost full left aileron to keep the aircraft level. Two of the crew in the radio room passed out after a partial failure of the oxygen system, and the pilot, Lieutenant Charles W Paine Jr, brought Phyllis down to a lower altitude. After struggling back over the Channel Phyllis made a wheels-up landing at Gatwick, narrowly missing a hangar. Subsequent examination showed that 16 canon shells had penetrated or exploded against the B-17, while the wings, tail and fuselage were peppered with 300 small-caliber bullet holes.

Lining up the Cavalry

At its most basic level, 8th Air Force's concept of strategic bombing reflected the unwavering American belief in the application of maximum firepower. Colonel Maurice A Preston, commander of 379th BG, put it this way: '*IT WAS LIKE LINING up the cavalry, shooting your way in and then shooting your way out again. This was definitely the concept of the early Air Corps leaders - also the*

concept of the design of the aircraft. The Flying Fortress was simply an aircraft with a lot of guns hanging on it. There was the idea of massing aircraft together to mass the firepower. If it didn't work, the answer was to get still more aircraft up and even more firepower. The fellows who had to do it weren't too keen on it, but we had to get on with it'.

The problem with this approach was that the 'Indians' were equally well-armed. In 1943 heavy losses became the norm. On June 13, 4th Bombardment Wing lost 22 bombers out of 60 in a raid on the submarine yards at Kiel, nine of them shot down off the Norfolk coast on the return journey by a dozen Ju88 night fighters. Nine days later 8th Air Force mounted its first large-scale penetration of the Ruhr, attacking the synthetic rubber plants at Hüls. Only 16 bombers were lost out of 235, but of those which returned no fewer than 170 had received some kind of damage.

Operations were also handicapped by poor weather conditions. Crews who had trained for high-altitude bombing with the excellent Norden bomb-sight could achieve pinpoint accuracy in the clear, sunny conditions of the Nevada desert. Bombing targets in Germany through 10/10ths cloud, smoke screens or industrial haze was another matter. Throughout the summer of 1943 cloud afforded German industry its best defense against attack, by both blanketing targets and dispersing closely knit formations. One of the worst examples occurred on September 6 when 388 B-17s took off to bomb an instrument bearings factory in Stuttgart. In heavy cloud only 4th Wing located the target. 388th Group, in the low position, lost one of its B-17s before the release point and ten more shortly afterwards; 563rd Squadron, occupying 'Purple Heart Corner,' was wiped out. The leading formations of 1st Wing vainly flew search patterns over the target area, making dangerous inroads into their fuel, while other Groups completely overshot the objective. Climbing out of the cloud, taking violent evasive action or flying two or three runs over the target all took their toll. On the return journey from Stuttgart rescue services were swamped with Mayday calls, and 12 Fortresses were forced to ditch in the Channel where RAF launches picked up all 118 aircrew. Forty-five aircraft were lost on the mission, almost half of them because of the fuel shortage, human error and equipment failure attributable to the bad weather conditions.

In the last week of July 1943 the predominantly cloudless skies over Europe enabled 8th Air Force to mount a series of raids in what became known as 'Blitz Week', during which 100 of its 330 operational aircraft were destroyed or written off and some 90 of its crews wounded or reported missing or killed. This was the equivalent of losing two complete Groups of the 15 which had now been brought up to battle-worthiness. In addition another 150 bombers had sustained some form of damage. The attrition reached a peak on August 17, the first anniversary of the Rouen raid, when 8th Air Force made its deepest penetration into the Reich, attacking the Me109 assembly plant at Regensburg and the ball-bearing factories at Schweinfurt. This famous double raid was one of the epics of the war over Germany.

Schweinfurt and Regensburg both lay far beyond

the deepest penetration made into Germany by the USAAF. Regensburg was over 500 miles from its East Anglian bases and a mere 40 miles from the Czech border. Schweinfurt was little nearer, but still almost 400 miles away. On July 27 B-17s of 94th BG had flown to the FW190 assembly plant at Oschersleben, but this was still 100 miles north of Schweinfurt. No Allied aircraft had been seen over this tranquil part of southern Germany since April 17, 1942, when a force of 12 RAF Lancasters from Nos. 44 and 97 Squadrons had carried out a near-suicidal low-level daylight attack on the MAN diesel works at Augsburg. A flight to and from such a distant target as Regensburg would inevitably give the Luftwaffe more than ample time to deploy its defensive units in strength. Thus after bombing its target the Regensburg force – 4th Bombardment Wing – would fly on over the Alps and the Mediterranean to airfields in North Africa. Fighter escort for 4th Wing and 1st Wing – attacking Schweinfurt – could be provided only as far as Eupen, a small Belgian town ten miles from the German border and 300 miles short of Regensburg.

Heavy early morning fog over both Wings' bases dislocated the original plan for the two forces to fly into Germany together and the complex escort and diversionary operations laid on to achieve that end. 4th Wing aircraft began to take off at 0621 hrs followed five hours later by 1st Wing. Criss-crossing huge tracks of airspace over central and eastern England, 4th Wing took three hours to complete its combat wing assembly. By now German listening devices and radar stations on the Dutch coast had picked up the huge formation. The listening devices were sophisticated enough to provide an accurate estimate of the number of individual bombers' radio sets being turned on and warming up as the B-17s climbed away from their bases. As 4th Wing crossed the English coast at Lowestoft – flying at heights between 17 000 and 20 000 ft – German radar was at work plotting its course. The first serious attacks on the stream were made at 1025 hrs by I/JG26, sweeping down in a head-on pass which carried it across the top of the leading combat wing and into 94th and 95 BGs. The first B-17 to go down was the 'tail end Charlie' in 94th Group's high squadron, Dear Mom, which was flying its 14th and last mission. It crashed into the ground at Lummen, a village seven miles from the east of the Belgian town of Diest.

Of the 376 aircraft despatched on the twin raids of August 17, 60 were lost and many more written off. The Luftwaffe lost 21 fighters. Of 4th Wing's 146 B-17s, 122 dropped 250 tons of bombs on Regensburg; of 1st Wing's 230 aircraft, 184 dropped 380 tons on Schweinfurt. Most of the machine tools in the Regensburg assembly plant survived the bombardment, and a limited production of fighters was under way in less than a month German estimates put overall loss of production at between 800–1000 fighters. Also destroyed in the bombing were the new jigs for the fuselage of the projected Me262 jet fighter, although it is not known how long a delay this caused in the introduction of the aircraft. These were successes (the damage to the Me262 jigs was not known at the time), but they had been achieved with a loss rate of 16.4 per cent. At Schweinfurt one of the three principal ball bearing factories suffered about a 50 per cent drop in ball

bearing output during the following 10 weeks, but in September German ball bearing production actually rose. 1st Bombardment Wing's loss rate had been 15.7 per cent. Both Wings' 500- and 1000-pound bombs had not been heavy enough to destroy the all-important machine tools. An attempt to renew the assault on Schweinfurt in October cost the Americans 77 aircraft lost and a further 133 damaged out of a total of 291 B-17s despatched.

Average losses per mission were now running at nearly 10 per cent, and by the late summer of 1943 morale was reaching a dangerously low ebb. After the second Schweinfurt raid bombing operations were temporarily suspended. Among the measures taken to enhance the formation's ability to defend itself was the conversion of a number of B-17s to a bomber escort role. These massively armored YB-40s carried a total of 14 0.5 machine-guns and 12 500 rounds of ammunition. The YB-40s made their operational debut on May 29 when seven flew in a raid on St Nazaire. However, it rapidly became clear that, laden with ammunition, they could not keep pace with the formation, particularly after it had released its bombs, and the experiment was abandoned. More practical measures were the addition of a powered twin-gun 'chin' turret in the nose of the B-17G and a modified Cheyenne reflector sight in its tail gun station. Nevertheless, in the autumn of 1943 German fighters, warned by radar and deployed in depth across the homeland, were destroying the USAAF's bombers and their crews more quickly than they could be replaced.

A basic USAAF heavy bomber tour consisted of 25 flights crossing the coast of enemy-occupied territory. The overall loss figures in 1943 were 967 aircraft lost from 22 779 sorties, a casualty rate of 4.24 per cent compared with the 3.6 per cent sustained by Bomber Command. Thirty-four per cent of USAAF aircrew could expect to complete their tour in Europe. As Colonel Maurice Preston, commander of 379th BG, told his men after their first mission: 'Is anyone scared? If not, there's something wrong with you. I'll give you a little clue how to fight this war – make believe you're dead already; the rest comes easy'.

The celebrated 'Memphis Belle'. As the bombs on her fuselage indicate, she was the first B-17 in 91st BG to complete 25 missions and the first in VIII Bomber Command to be returned to the United States with her crew. Piloted by Captain Robert Morgan, the 'Memphis Belle' was the subject of a remarkable documentary film shot by the distinguished Hollywood director William Wyler.

3.4 THE CLIMAX OF AREA BOMBING

BY THE SPRING OF 1943, BOMBER Command had the weapons and navigational aids in its hands to proceed with the implementation of the Pointblank directive. Gee now had only a limited usefulness but a new radar device was being introduced which was not tied to ground stations and had unlimited range. H2S was an airborne downward-tilted radar which scanned the ground beneath the aircraft. The echoes, displayed on a circular cathode-ray tube (Plan Position Indicator or PPI), presented a continuous representation of the terrain over which the aircraft was flying. Built-up areas, which gave the strongest returns, showed up brightly; open land and water-covered areas showed up in varying degrees of darkness, enabling the picture on the PPI to be compared with a map of the area. The usefulness of H2S depended on the interpretative skills of the operator and the nature of the terrain over which the aircraft was passing. The port of Hamburg, situated on a wide river estuary, provided a distinct H2S image, while inland targets like Stuttgart, which was surrounded by broken terrain, produced less distinct echoes and presented greater problems to the H2S operator trying to decipher the 'clutter' on his screen. When an H2S set fell into German hands, they added to the potential confusion by attempting to alter the H2S silhouette of some key targets. In Berlin huge strips of metal were laid across the city's lakes on rafts. H2S was initially installed only in heavy bombers, but it later found a home in many of No. 139 Squadron's Mosquitos. Its signals could be intercepted with some ease, and the Germans built up an efficient organization to track the movement of bombers by their H2S emissions. In 1944 night fighters were fitted with Naxos receivers which homed in on H2S radiations. As a result Bomber Command issued an instruction that sets should only be switched on at short intervals over enemy territory.

H2S could be used as a primitive blind bombing device but Bomber Command had now acquired a more sophisticated instrument in 'Oboe'. A brilliant short-wave variation on the X-system, Oboe employed two ground stations. The first station, codenamed 'Cat', tracked an aircraft as it flew along an arc of constant range running through the target. If the aircraft deviated from the arc, it could be corrected by the transmission of Morse dots when the aircraft was on the 'Cat' or western side of the arc and of dashes if it had strayed to the east. Once the beam had been intercepted the pilot maintained a predetermined height and airspeed until reaching the previously computed bomb release point when a Morse signal was transmitted from the second, 'Mouse', station.

Oboe's potential as a fail-safe blind bombing device was limited by several factors. First, its range was restricted by the curvature of the earth to about 280 miles, which just took in the Ruhr. Second, two transmitters could handle only one bomber at a time on its ten minute bomb-run.* Moreover, the airborne Oboe installation radiated a strong signal which could be used by the Germans to vector a night fighter on to the carrying aircraft. But in the twin-engined, all-wooden Mosquito Bomber Command possessed a fighter-bomber capable of out-running all of the Luftwaffe's pre-jet fighters. It was in six Mosquito MkVs of No. 109 Squadron that the first Oboe calibration raid was made on December 20/21, 1942 against a power station at Lutterade in Holland. Ultimately Oboe's operational error from 30 000 ft at speeds of over 300 mph was only 300 yds, and at lower levels even less.

8 Group: Pathfinding

No. 109 Squadron was the third Mosquito squadron to join 8 Group, the Pathfinder Force (PFF) commanded by Air Vice-Marshal D C T Bennett. The PFF had been formed in August 1942 specifically to exploit the new radar devices in locating and marking targets. Although Harris backed the principle of pathfinding, he was initially opposed to the formation of elite corps which, he felt, would lower morale in Bomber Command by depriving the individual Groups of their best crews. The rancorous argument over the formation of the PFF which rumbled on through the spring of 1942 was exacerbated by the fact that one of its leading advocates was Group Captain S O Bufton, the Director of Operations at the Air Ministry and a supporter of precision rather than area bombing.

In the end Harris suffered one of his rare defeats and the nucleus of what was to become 8 Group was formed by five squadrons: No. 156 Squadron from 1 Group; No. 7 Squadron from 3 Group; No. 35 Squadron from 4 Group; No. 83 Squadron from 5 Group; and No. 109 Squadron from the Wireless Intelligence Development. Aircrews were initially required to complete 50 operations. This was subsequently reduced to 45, and in June 1944 a points system was introduced – 5 for German targets and 3 points for non-German targets, 5 points equalling an operation.

In the autumn of 1942 the role of the PFF was principally that of finding and illuminating the target area. Its target markers were makeshift 250 pound and 4000 pound cases filled with an incendiary charge of benzole, rubber and phosphorus and known respectively as Red Blob Fires and Pink Pansies. In the New Year specially designed Target Indicators (TIs) were introduced to provide the Main Force with distinctive, eye-catching pyrotechnic displays which would be easy to recognize and difficult for the Germans to imitate. The first of these was a 250-pound bomb case filled with 60 12-inch pyrotechnic candles, each with its own igniter, which were ejected at a pre-determined height by a barometric fuse. From 1500 ft the TI made a ground pattern approximately 60 yds in diameter. Red, green or yellow candles

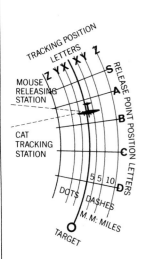

The Oboe blind bombing system, controlled by two ground stations, one of which (Cat) transmitted a beam along which the aircraft flew; the other signal (Mouse) told it when it was at the bomb release point. The Luftwaffe was sufficiently impressed with Oboe to copy it in their 'Egon' system, which was used in attacks against England in 1944.

*Later in the war the somewhat confusingly named G-H system enabled about 80 aircraft to be handled simultaneously.

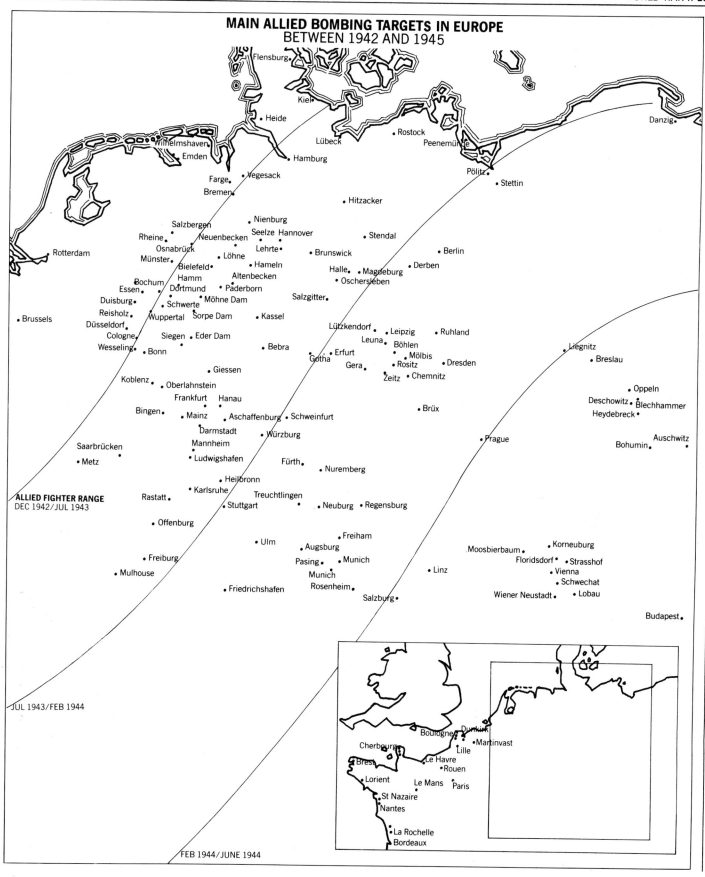

MAIN ALLIED BOMBING TARGETS IN EUROPE
BETWEEN 1942 AND 1945

Flensburg
Kiel
Heide
Rostock
Danzig
Lübeck
Peenemünde
Wilhelmshaven
Emden
Hamburg
Pölitz
Farge
Vegesack
Stettin
Bremen
Hitzacker
Nienburg
Salzbergen
Seelze Hannover
Stendal
Rheine
Neuenbecken
Osnabrück
Lehrte
Berlin
Rotterdam
Münster
Löhne
Brunswick
Derben
Bielefeld
Hameln
Bochum Hamm
Altenbecken
Halle Magdeburg
Essen
Dortmund
Paderborn
Oschersleben
Duisburg
Möhne Dam
Salzgitter
Brussels
Reisholz
Schwerte
Düsseldorf
Wuppertal
Sorpe Dam
Kassel
Lützkendorf
Leipzig
Ruhland
Cologne
Siegen
Eder Dam
Leuna
Böhlen
Liegnitz
Wesseling
Bonn
Bebra
Erfurt
Mölbis
Dresden
Breslau
Gotha
Gera Rositz
Giessen
Zeitz
Chemnitz
Oppeln
Koblenz
Oberlahnstein
Deschowitz
Blechhammer
Frankfurt
Hanau
Brüx
Heydebreck
Bingen
Mainz
Aschaffenburg
Schweinfurt
Auschwitz
Darmstadt
Würzburg
Prague
Bohumin
Saarbrücken
Mannheim
Metz
Ludwigshafen
Fürth
Nuremberg
Heilbronn
Karlsruhe
ALLIED FIGHTER RANGE
DEC 1942/JUL 1943
Rastatt
Treuchtlingen
Offenburg
Stuttgart
Neuburg
Regensburg
Freiham
Korneuburg
Ulm
Augsburg
Moosbierbaum
Freiburg
Pasing
Munich
Floridsdorf
Strasshof
Mulhouse
Munich
Linz
Vienna
Rosenheim
Schwechat
Friedrichshafen
Salzburg
Wiener Neustadt
Lobau
Budapest

JUL 1943/FEB 1944

Dunkirk
Boulogne
Martinvast
Cherbourg
Lille
Brest
Le Havre
Rouen
Lorient
Le Mans
Paris
St Nazaire
Nantes
La Rochelle
Bordeaux

FEB 1944/JUNE 1944

were used in the device, which was first employed operationally over Berlin on January 16/17, 1943.

H2S was now helping the PFF heavy squadrons to find the target with greater consistency; Oboe was proving its value as a blind bombing device; and the TIs were marking the Aiming Point distinctively. By the end of February 1943 the Main Force was being instructed to bomb the TIs instead of trying to locate the target itself. The PFF had progressed from being a target-finding force to a target marking force.

The PFF's marking techniques broke down into three categories: visual groundmarking (codenamed Newhaven), blind groundmarking (Parramatta) and skymarking (Wanganui)*; the addition of the prefix 'Musical' indicated that the initial markers had been dropped by Oboe-equipped Mosquitos. In Parramatta and Newhaven operations, the Aiming Point was marked continuously by a secondary force, known as Backers-Up, who dropped TIs of a contrasting color. Main Force's task was to drop its bombs as near as possible to the Pathfinder markers. This sounds ridiculously simple, but a great deal depended on the timing and accuracy of the PFF crews. High winds could play havoc with the marker flares dropped in Wanganui attacks, although the technique enabled Bomber Command to operate on nights when British bases were clear and cloud obscured the targets over Germany. If tail winds were stronger than forecast, Main Force might arrive over the target before or at the same time as the PFF, obliterating the TIs. The Germans developed their own decoy markers, which in turn prompted increasingly sophisticated variations on the basic TI theme.

Another complicating factor was the phenomenon known as 'creepback'. On the straight and level run to the target, with flak and searchlights making life distinctly disagreeable, a bomb aimer was under enormous strain. His orders were to bomb the center of any group of TIs he could see in his bombsight. But there was a natural tendency for some bomb aimers, referred to as 'fringe merchants' within Bomber Command, to drop their bombs short of the markers. Even though the time factor involved might be measured in fractions of a second, this process could set in motion a steady falling away from the Aiming Point. If the Backer-Up also dropped short, the bombing would inexorably 'creep back' along the line of the bombing run. To counter this effect, 'Re-Centerers' were employed to keep the attack on the aiming point by overshooting it with their markers, encouraging Main Force's bomb aimers to wait a second or two longer before releasing their load and thus bringing the weight of the attack back towards the original Aiming Point.

The search for greater concentration also led to the selection of Master Bombers to orchestrate important raids. The Master Bomber remained over the target throughout the raid, instructing Main Force where to aim their bombs to achieve maximum concentration. The first time the Master Bomber technique was used operationally was in No. 617 Squadron's attack on the Möhne and Eder dams in May 1943. Wing Commander J H Searby was the first to use it in conjunction with Main Force, over

Turin on August 7/8, 1943 and then ten days later in the attack on the V-weapons plant at Peenemünde. Over large well-defined targets, as opposed to small strategic ones like Peenemünde, the value of the Master Bomber was principally psychological. There were usually enough Markers, Backers-Up and Re-Centerers to keep the Aiming Point illuminated from start to finish. The chief assets of the Master Bomber were a cool head and a calm voice, maintained in conditions of considerable danger. As an Australian pilot remarked after a raid on Leipzig: 'It's not always so much the instructions that you notice, but the relief at hearing a good English voice getting things organized ahead of you after that long struggle through flak and dirty weather'.

All in a Day's Work: Before a Raid

How was a raid planned? the nerve center of Bomber Command was the operations room at the Naphill complex, High Wycombe. A concrete-lined, air-conditioned bunker sunk underneath a grassy, tree-covered knoll, it was known as 'The Hole'. Inside, the subdued lighting and rubber floors created an almost unreal air of calm. It was a world away from the flak-torn skies over Europe, and its remoteness from the battlefield – inevitable though it was – evoked comparisons with the elegant French chateaux, miles behind the trenches, from which Allied generals launched the doomed offensives of World War I. Three of its walls were covered with huge maps of Europe and target priority lists, which were updated daily and whose comprehensiveness allowed Harris enormous tactical latitude. On the fourth, main wall there were three giant blackboards deploying Bomber Command's Order of Battle.

At 0900 hrs every morning the C-in-C held a conference in the operations room. With heavy irony this was known as 'Morning Prayers'. The meeting was attended by the Deputy C-in-C (who was responsible for detailed planning), the Senior Air Staff Officer (SASO) (who set the operational machine in motion), a naval staff officer, the Chief Intelligence Officer, the Senior Meteorological Officer, the operations room staff and liasion officers, including those from the US forces. After a report on the previous night's operations, the Senior Meteorological Officer briefed the meeting on the weather for the coming night, both over Bomber Command's bases and all targets within range. The weather was the dominant factor in the air war; it established the framework within which operational decisions were made; and it also provided Harris with a ready excuse for ignoring the target lists handed down by the Combined Strategic Targets Committee and making his own unfettered decisions.

Having established the area to be attacked, the Intelligence Officer handed Harris the files on the most suitable objectives. At the end of the day it was Harris who made the final decision on the targets, numbers of aircraft to be despatched and H-Hour (time over the target). The detailed planning of the operation was undertaken by Harris' faithful deputy, Sir Robert Saundby. Working with key staff

Parramatta was the Australian Bennett's home town; his personal WAAF came from Newhaven; Squadron Leader Ashworth (of 156 Squadron) came from Wanganui.

Dealing with the V-2 Menace

The V-2 weapons research and development establishment on the Baltic island of Peenemünde was a critical target for Bomber Command. The target areas are shown on the map (right) and the photo-reconnaissance 'mosaic'. On August 17/18, 1943 596 aircraft (324 Lancasters, 218 Halifaxes and 54 Stirlings) attacked the plant. It was the only occasion in the war when the whole weight of Bomber Command was thrown into a precision raid on such a small target. At the end of a very long flight, Main Force attacked Peenemünde on timed runs from a small island off Mecklenburg. A Mosquito diversionary raid on Berlin drew off most of the German night fighters.

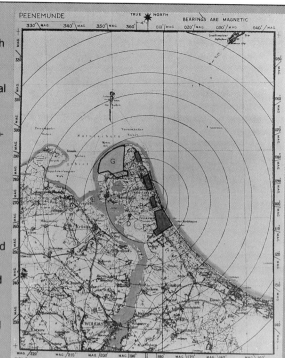

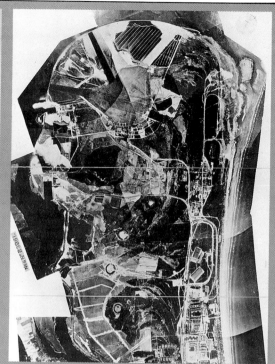

The main aiming areas – the assembly works, drawing offices, administrative block and scientists' housing settlement – were all hit, with PFF 'shifters' moving the bombing from one target to the next. Forty-one aircraft were lost, mostly in the last wave when German night fighters arrived in force and exploited the clear, moonlight conditions. Among the 735 German dead was Professor Thiel, a propulsion specialist, and the plant's chief engineer, Herr Walther. The V-2 program was set back by at least two months.

Above: As can be seen from these photo-reconnaissance pictures, the pressure was maintained on the Peenemünde plant. In this 'before and after' sequence from June and September 1944, 'A' indicates light flak positions, 'B' cradles for transporting the rockets and 'C' two V-2s.

Left: A Lancaster attacks a V-1 site in northern France in July 1944.

officers, and in telephone conversations with Group commanders, Saundby prepared precise breakdowns of routes, bombloads, take-off times and Aiming Points for Harris' approval. This was then committed to a Form 'A' (Operational Order) and passed to the operations room controller, who telephoned the 'order of batting' to the Group controllers. This was read simultaneously on a 'broadcast', enabling the Group controllers to interject or to ask for extra information. The order was confirmed by signal.

The 'Morning Prayers' routine was repeated at Group level, with each Group Commander addressing a similar meeting. The Group AOC, Air Vice-Marshal and SASO decided which squadrons were required for the night's operations, if necessary in consultation with the station commanders. Then each Group controller made another 'broadcast' telephone call to his opposite numbers at the stations, informing them of the target, time over the target and all other details necessary for smooth functioning of the operation.

It was now midday, and in the station operation rooms the controllers and squadron commanders were deciding which crews and aircraft would be flying that night. Having selected the crews, lists of pilots' names were posted in all the messes and flight rooms. Maintenance and armament officers were briefed on the night's operations and the intelligence officers were hard at work assembling all the relevant information for the briefing. Navigation officers were studying the routes allotted by Bomber Command headquarters. The controller was organizing the timed departure of each aircraft, and the bombing time over the target. By now the station was a hive of activity. Pilots conferred with the aero-engine mechanics. Flight engineers and wireless operators went about their inspections and checks. Gunners were harmonizing and cleaning their guns, and polishing the Perspex in their turrets. Another part of the routine was a brief air test for each aircraft to ensure that all was in order.

Now it was time for the crews to snatch some sleep. This had become second nature as they still did not know where they were flying or how long the mission would take. While they napped or played cards, huge fuel bowsers refuelled the aircraft and trucks hauling long caterpillar-like trolleys of fused bombs snaked out to the dispersal points.

Briefing took place in mid-afternoon, by which time the crews might already have eaten their operational meal of bacon and eggs. At the end of the briefing room there was a big operations map of Europe, covered by a curtain until the arrival of the station commander. At this point the curtain was drawn aside to reveal the target. The CO would then outline the overall plans and type of attack before handing over the briefing to a series of specialists. The Intelligence Officer, who supplied details on the nature of the target and its defenses; the Navigation and Bombing Leaders, and the Signals and Meteorological Officers. The Gunnery Leader provided information on the types of night fighters which might be encountered on the trip; and the Engineering Officer detailed the amount of fuel to be carried and the changeover over the bombers' tanks, vital in maintaining the trim of the aircraft. Flying Control gave intervals for take-off, together with a note of diversionary airfields.

The airmen then surrendered the contents of their pockets, collecting their personal medical packs and escape kits, which might prove useful if they came down in Europe. Soon it was time to don their flying clothes: sweaters, scarves, battledress, Mae Wests and parachute harness; over the silk socks, the woollen stockings, and over these flying boots lined with lamb's wool; then the flying helmet with its oxygen mask. For the rear gunner there was an electrically heated suit, an all-in-one garment with a heating element woven throughout. Carrying their parachutes and ration boxes, they boarded the crew tenders, which drove slowly around the airfield perimeter to the dispersal points where their aircraft stood waiting for them in the darkness.

The Battle of the Ruhr

On March 5, 1943 Harris delivered the first blow in what became known as the Battle of the Ruhr. A Main Force of 442 aircraft led by 35 PFF crews flew to raid Essen. The operation was planned as a Musical Parramatta and five Mosquitos marked the target with red TIs at 2058 hrs. Twenty-two PFF heavies backed up with greens, and yellow land marker TIs were also dropped 15 miles from the target so that all crews could bomb from a datum point to reduce the risk of collisions. (The dropping of route-marking flares at turning points was also to become standard PFF practice.) Main Force, carrying bombloads of one-third HE and two-thirds incendiaries, attacked in three waves concentrated within 40 minutes. For the loss of only 14 aircraft severe damage was done to the great Krupps armament complex and 160 acres of Essen laid waste.

Greater concentration was now being achieved by Bomber Command, but it was fighting the Battle of the Ruhr over the most heavily defended targets in the Reich. Between March and July 18 506 sorties were flown at a cost of 872 aircraft missing over Germany, a loss rate of 4.7 per cent. There were successes; on May 12/13 of 572 aircraft despatched to Duisberg, 410 bombed within three miles of the Aiming Point. There were failures: on April 16/17, in a raid on the Skoda works at Pilsen, many Main Force crews mistook a lunatic asylum for the factory. Night fighters were out in strength over the target and 36 bombers from this force were shot down, as well as 18 attacking Mannheim. The 11 per cent loss rate on this night was the highest of the Battle of the Ruhr. The most effective attack was that of May 29/30 when a force of 719 aircraft attacked Wuppertal-Bremen. Eighty per cent of a target area two miles long and a mile wide was devastated. The Battle of the Ruhr ended on July 13/14 with an attack on Aachen, by which time nearly 60 000 tons of bombs had been dropped on Germany, more than the total delivered by Bomber Command in 1942. Photo-reconnaissance pictures revealed devastation beyond the wildest hopes of Bomber Command in 1940. Intelligence estimated that in the Wuppertal raid of May 29/30, 118 000 people had been made homeless. In one sense, however, Bomber Command was waging a war in which decisive victory seemed always to be tantalisingly beyond its grasp. As the US Official History commented: 'The heavy bomber offensive was an impersonal sort of war, and monotonous in its own peculiar way ... Rarely was a single mission or series of missions decisive; whatever earlier they had taught of sudden paralysis of a nation by strategic bombing, in actual practice the forces available in 1942–43 were quite inadequate for such Douhet-like tactics'.

The high water mark of the area bombing campaign was reached at the end of July. The objective was Hamburg, Germany's second city and thus an important political target. Its situation on the coast reduced the opportunities for German night fighter interception; and its position on the Elbe, surrounded by a network of canals and waterways, was ideal for H2S location.

Hamburg had been Harris's original choice for the first 1000-bomber raid and, as he observed, 'I had always wanted to have a real dead set at Hamburg ... I wanted to make a tremendous show'. In the attack on Hamburg 8th Air Force was to complement the Bomber Command offensive with daylight raids.

On the night of July 24/25 791 bombers flew to Hamburg on the first of four raids. Not only had the 872 bombers lost in the Battle of the Ruhr been replaced but a further 300, all of them four-engined, had been added to the strength of Bomber Command. Of the 791 aircraft flying on July 24/25, 347 were Lancasters (118 of which were in the first of the six waves), 247 were Halifaxes, 125 were Stirlings and the remaining 73 were Wellingtons. Nearly 2460 tons of bombs were readied for the attack, of which 1006 tons were incendiaries (26 858 30-pound and 327 250 four-pound thermite or magnesium 'sticks'). The raiding force also carried a new weapon; more than 90 million metallized strips, known as 'Window'.

Window was a simple and ingenious counter to the radar on which the German night fighters and anti-aircraft defenses were absolutely dependent. The lightweight Window foil strips were 26.5 cm long, exactly half the wavelength of Würzburg radar pulses. Dropped in massive quantities, they would jam the radar by cluttering its tubes with false returns, swamping the echoes from genuine aircraft. Oboe and H2S, operating on 9 cm, were unaffected. The RAF had delayed using Window for a year, fearful that once its simple workings were revealed, it could be turned against British radar. The Germans, who had developed an equivalent device codenamed Düppel, held back for the same reason.

In the first attack on Hamburg, Window achieved complete tactical surprise, creating utter confusion in the Kammhuber Line and over the target. As a member of Hamburg's 608th Searchlight Battalion recalled, 'It was like going around with a torch in a dark room, trying to find a fly'. As they approached Hamburg, Bomber Command aircrews could clearly see the effect of Window. For Flight Lieutenant V Wood flying with No. 12 Squadron. '*T*HE SIGHT *approaching Hamburg was quite fantastic. It was as if a black swath had been cut through a sea of light and flashes. The few lights and flashes from guns within the black area, such as there still were, were completely out of control, the searchlight beams quickly traversing the area at random. The searchlights and guns at either side of the swath were under control but at too far a distance to cause any problems. My navigator told me I was slightly*

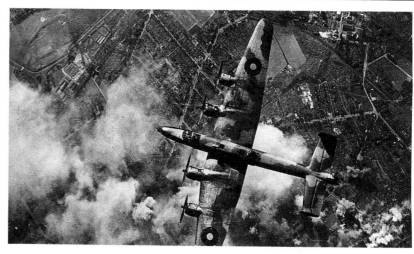

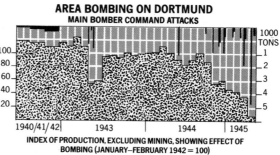

AREA BOMBING ON DORTMUND
MAIN BOMBER COMMAND ATTACKS

INDEX OF PRODUCTION, EXCLUDING MINING, SHOWING EFFECT OF BOMBING (JANUARY–FEBRUARY 1942 = 100)

off course, but I was happy to fly the aircraft down the center of this dark corridor. It was obviously safe to keep to the middle of the road'.

From a bomber the scene below resembled an immense fireworks display. The red and yellow primary TIs were steadily replaced by the brilliant greens of the Backers-Up. Bright, quick flashes marked the point of impact of the smaller HE bombs while the 4000-pound 'cookies' exploded more slowly, spreading white concussion circles around them as they detonated before relapsing into a dull red flame. The entire bombing area was carpeted with the bright pinpoints of igniting incendiaries.

It was different on the ground. The raid achieved the principal area bombing objective of saturating the city's civil defenses, dislocating communications, blocking the streets and overwhelming the fire-fighting forces. At one point in the western sector of Hamburg alone an estimated combined street frontage of 54 miles was ablaze. The city was still hidden under a dense pall of black smoke 15 000 ft high when, on the following day, 109 B-17s of 1st Bombardment Wing flew in to attack the Blohm and Voss U-boat yards and the Klöckner aero-engine factory. Only the leading formations were able to place their bombs with any degree of precision before cloud and smoke obscured the targets. Fifteen B-17s were lost and 78 returned with varying degrees of damage.

On the night of July 25/26 six Mosquitos of No. 139 Squadron flew a 'nuisance raid' over Hamburg, and on the 26th the city was revisited by four Groups of 1st Bombardment Wing. Bomber Command struck again in force on July 27/28, when a number of

Above: A Halifax overflies an oil plant at Wanne-Gickel, in the Ruhr, on October 12, 1944. One aircraft was lost out of 147 despatched on the raid. During October Sir Arthur Harris sent heavy bombers against oil targets on only four other occasions, preferring to devote his resources to area bombing.

Left: The effect of area bombing on production at Dortmund, where the principal factories were on the outskirts of the town. The immediate effect, clearly shown on the graph, was the result of the disruption of essential services (gas, electricity, water) and damage to the small industries scattered through the town. Production loss in the three main factories was relatively small until the autumn of 1944 when systematic attacks caused additional damage before repairs could be completed. The cumulative damage to the essential services, caused principally by the preponderance of HE in the bombloads, eventually brought a halt to production irrespective of the damage to the factories which was by then extensive.

factors combined to produce a terrifying firestorm in eastern Hamburg. To an hour of ferociously concentrated bombing by 729 aircraft were added exceptionally low humidity and a fire-fighting service on the verge of breakdown and deployed on the western side of the city still extinguishing the fires started on the night of 24/25th.

The firestorm engulfed an area approximately four miles square, encompassing about 130 miles of street frontage and reaching its height at 0315 hrs amid scenes of horror which were to be repeated in Dresden and Tokyo in 1945. Dead and dying lay stuck where they fell in the melting, glutinous asphalt of the Hamburg streets, their clothes burnt away, their bodies shrivelled like mummies. The corpses of children lay 'like fried eels' on the pavements. In some basement shelters all that remained after the raid was a thin layer of grey ash on the floor, the vestiges of corpses incinerated as fresh air had penetrated the firestorm at its end. The majority of the 40 000 deaths were caused by asphyxiation as the fire gobbled up the air, replacing it with smoke and colorless toxic gases. A million of Hamburg's citizens fled into the countryside. Nearly 600 individual plants had been wrecked and thousands of smaller workshops obliterated, along with 214 350 homes. Josef Goebbels declared the raid 'a catastrophe, the extent of which staggers the imagination'. Albert Speer, the Reich's Armaments Minister, informed Hitler that if another six major German cities were to receive similar treatment, armaments production would break down.

There was another heavy raid, by 777 aircraft on July 29/30. The fourth and last attack, by 740 aircraft, came on 2/3 August and was badly disrupted. The last bombs to fall on Hamburg were dropped at 0255 hrs by a Wellington of No. 466 Squadron. Bomber Command did not return in strength for another year. In the four raids 3091 bomber sorties had been despatched, and 2592 of these had dropped 8334 tons of bombs in the Hamburg area. Bomber Command had lost only 87 aircraft, a rate of 2.8 per cent, approximately 60 of them to night fighters. Thanks to Window, only 12 aircraft had been lost on July 24/25, although by 29/30 losses were beginning to rise as the defenses regained their balance and the weather took its toll. Thirty-three aircraft were lost in the last raid of the battle.

The Battle of Hamburg had resulted in a remarkable victory for Bomber Command. But even more remarkable than the scale of destruction was the speed of the stricken city's recovery. Within three weeks gas and electricity supplies had been restored. During September Hamburg's badly hit port handled 160 000 tons, only 40 000 less than the figure for July. The raids had resulted in two months' loss of industrial output, but Hamburg's aircraft plants – the destruction of which lay at the heart of the Pointblank directive – had been largely dispersed by the end of July. U-boat construction was not seriously disrupted because the USAAF's precision bombing had been hampered by smoke, and Bomber Command had not targeted the areas where the submarines were manufactured. Five months after the raid industrial production had risen to 80 per cent of normal.

In one night Window had sounded the death knell of the controlled night fighter in the boxes of the Kammhuber line. But even as Hamburg burned, the Luftwaffe was experimenting with new Wilde Sau (Wild Boar) tactics, developed by Major Hans-

The versatile Mosquito. Here a B.XVI of No. 128 Squadron, Fast Night Striking Force, bombs up with a 4000-pound 'cookie' before a raid on Berlin in March 1945. On February 23/24, 1944 three modified B.IVs of No.627 Squadron became the first Mosquitos to drop the 4000-pounder operationally during a raid on Düsseldorf. Between January 1945 and the fall of Berlin no fewer than 3900 Mosquito sorties were despatched to the German capital, dropping more than 4400 tons of bombs including 1479 'cookies'. Only 14 Mosquitos were lost in these operations.

Joachim Hermann, in which freelance night fighters operated directly over the city under attack.

Wild Boar tactics were soon replaced by the Zahme Sau (Tame Boar) method, in which twin-engined fighters were scrambled to orbit a radio beacon as soon as the approximate course of the bomber stream had been ascertained. The Tame Boars were directed into the stream by a running commentary from a ground controller. In the closing stages of the interception the tremendous turbulence caused by the propeller wash of hundreds of four-engined bombers alerted the pilots to the close presence of the stream. These flexible tactics, which gave the night fighters a great deal of freedom, achieved considerable success, particularly when in 1944 they were equipped with the SN-2 radar, which was not affected by Window. On the ground Window was partially countered by the Würzlaus (Delousing) and Nürnberg systems. In the former the operators learnt to distinguish between the bomber returns, which exhibited a pronounced 'Doppler' shift, and the Window, which did not. As the strips had practically no mass, they quickly lost momentum in the air and, in a light wind, drifted down without any forward speed, returning the radar pulses at precisely the same frequency as transmitted. In turn this led to Nürnberg, in which skilled operators could pick up the faint modulation introduced into the radar pulses by the bombers' propellers. Both these counter-measures were fully operational a month after the Battle of Hamburg.

The Radio War

Radio and radar countermeasures were now playing an increasingly important part in the battle over Germany. Boozer was a receiver which lit up a

warning light when the aircraft was 'illuminated' by gun and searchlight radar. Monica was a rearward-looking radar whose signals were translated into a series of pips over the intercom when reflected back from an aircraft approaching from astern. Monica was of limited usefulness, as in a concentrated stream it was almost constantly on the bleep. Nor could it distinguish between friend and foe or indicate the line of approach of the other aircraft. It was withdrawn after the Germans fitted their fighters with Flensburg radar, which homed in on its signals. It was succeeded by Fishpond, whose echoes were received on a cathode-ray tube linked to the H2S scanner. This was a more effective system, although the signals were received only when the aircraft was below the bomber. The bearing and distance of the approaching aircraft could be measured, and if several blips appeared on the screen it was odds on that the one approaching at the fastest rate was an enemy fighter. Fishpond also reduced the danger of collisions in the dark, and when it remained blank gave its operator the chilling indication that the aircraft had probably strayed out of the stream. When the German night fighters were fitted with Naxos receivers, they used H2S and Fishpond signals to home in on the bombers.

Tinsel was a microphone fitted in one of the engine nacelles and transmitting noises on the frequency of the nearest German fighter control net, jamming the instructions to the pilots. Tinsel was supplemented by special radio-countermeasures aircraft carrying jamming transmitters known as Cigar and Jostle. In addition there was Mandrel, a device for jamming the early warning Freya radar. A screen of eight Mandrel-equipped Halifaxes could swamp a 130-mile-wide sector in German early warning radar cover.

At the monitoring station at Kingsdown, in Kent, highly trained German-speaking personnel issued false instructions and weather reports to German night fighters in a deception tactic known as Corona, first used on the night of October 22/23, 1943 in a big raid on Kassel, the center of German tank production. A month later Bomber Command formed 100 Group whose sole purpose was to use radio and radar countermeasures against the enemy's night defenses. Eventually it expanded to a strength of 13 squadrons. Towards the end of the war 100 Group might put as many as 90 aircraft into the air for a big operation.

The capture of a Lichstenstein-equipped Ju88 in May 1943 led to the development of a Serrate receiver which enabled British intruder fighters to home in on their German opposite numbers. A month later No. 141 Squadron, equipped with twin-engined Beaufighters, began Serrate operations, flying individual patrols near the bomber stream, intercepting night fighters as they orbited their radio beacons or flew towards the target area. The Beaufighter's principal weakness was its lack of range, a problem only partially overcome by the fitting of 100-gallon drop tanks. Eventually Mosquitos also flew on these intruder missions, destroying an average of three enemy fighters a night with the aid of Serrate IV and Perfectos, one of the most elegant systems in the radio war, which tripped off the enemy aircraft's IFF (Identification Friend or Foe) device.

Target Amiens, February 18, 1944

Mosquitos of No. 487 Squadron sweep in to attack Amiens jail in one of the most famous examples of the aircraft's ability to bomb pinpoint targets. The operation was mounted to enable 700 members of the French Resistance to break out of the jail, a collecting point for those awaiting execution by the Gestapo. This was to be achieved by the precision bombing of the outer walls and the buildings inside the prison housing German guards. Success depended on split-second timing and accuracy during the low-level bombing run to the target. The attacking force comprised three formations of six aircraft from Nos. 487 (New Zealand), 464 (Australian) and 21 Squadrons of 140 Wing, 2 Group. They were to be accompanied by a Mosquito from the Film Production Unit which would photograph the raid. Commanding the operation in the air was Group Captain Percy Pickard in Mosquito HX922 'F-Freddie'. Fighter cover was provided by 12 Typhoons of No. 198 Squadron. Each Mosquito carried two 500-pound bombs fitted with 11-second delay detonators. No. 487 Squadron's task was to breach the outer wall of the prison in two places. No. 464 Squadron's aircraft were allotted the guards' annexe inside the prison. In the two hours before take-off, the crews made a detailed study of a model of the prison, calculating angles, heights, obstructions, gun-points and run-out routes.

Timetable

At 1100 hrs the 19 Mosquitos took off from Hunsdon airfield.

At 1203 hrs, having followed the snow-covered, poplar-lined road running from Albert to Amiens, No. 487 Squadron's first Vic of Mosquitos, led by Wing Commander I S 'Black' Smith, flew in as slowly as possible and at 15 ft, pitching their bombs towards the base of the corner of the east walls of the prison. Later Smith recalled: 'Navigation was perfect, and I'd never done a better flight. It was like a Hendon demonstration … I dropped my own bombs from a height of 10 ft, pulling hard on the stick, The Vic's bombs fell across the first wall and across a courtyard, exploding against the wall on the other side. The second Vic followed up with an attack on the north wall.

1204 hrs: No.487 Squadron was followed in by No.464 Squadron. Led by Wing Commander R W 'Bob' Iredale, they scraped over the outer walls, skidding their bombs on to the guards' annexe and flying out through the billowing smoke and debris thrown up by No. 487 Squadron's attack.

Circling overhead, Pickard observed the breaches in the outer walls through which prisoners were already pouring, tiny black figures in the white landscape. Satisfied that the mission had been accomplished, he gave the order to No.21 Squadron to return to base without bombing. The photo Mosquito started its first run over the target.

As the second Vic of No.464 Squadron reformed near Albert, Squadron Leader I R McRitchie's aircraft was hit by flak and his navigator, Flight Lieutenant R W Sampson, instantly killed. McRitchie crashed at 200 mph but survived to be taken prisoner. His fate attracted the attention of Pickard, who was seen to fly over the spot where McRitchie came down. Within seconds he was pounced upon by two FW190s, his Mosquito flipping over and ploughing straight into the ground. Pickard and his navigator, Flight Lieutenant J A 'Bill' Broadley, were killed. The remaining Mosquitos returned to Hunsdon, but three were seriously damaged. Fifty Germans were killed in the attack and 258 prisoners made good their escape, including 12 due to be shot the next day.

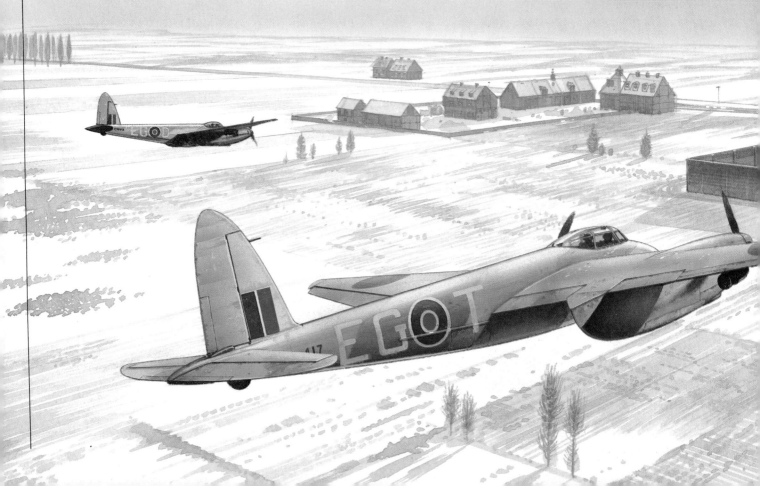

Another example of the Mosquito's precision capability. On October 31 1944, Mosquitos of 2nd Tactical Air Force attacked and destroyed the Gestapo HQ housed in the University of Aarhus, in Denmark.

The Battle of Berlin

While paying lipservice to the Pointblank directive Harris went his own way. In 1918 Trenchard had displayed a similar independence while conducting a basically tactical campaign when under orders to mount a strategic offensive. Late in 1943 Harris persisted with area bombing while under constant pressure to attack more specific targets linked with the German war effort. Reluctant to make the German aircraft industry his first priority, he believed that area bombing, by its cumulative effects on the economy and civilian population of the Third Reich, would reduce Germany to such an enfeebled state that the Allied invasion of northern Europe would be no more than a 'mopping up operation'. Furthermore, he argued that if an invasion was launched before this point was reached, the bloody deadlock of 1914–18 would be repeated.

Inevitably, for all his outstanding qualities, Harris himself recalls a World War I general, convinced that one more big push would secure victory. If the pressure was kept up, something had to give.

On November 3, 1943 Harris told Churchill: 'We can wreck Berlin from end to end if the US Army Air Force will come in on it. It will cost us between 400 and 500 aircraft. It will cost Germany the war'. The third of Harris's great battles of 1943 began on November 18 when 398 Lancasters out of 440 despatched bombed 'The Big City'. The Battle lasted until the Nuremberg raid of March 30/31, 1944; in that period Bomber Command mounted 16 major attacks (9 111 sorties) against Berlin and 19 attacks against other cities, notably Mannheim, Stuttgart, Frankfurt, Nuremberg, Leipzig, Brunswick and Schweinfurt. It was the last great drive to win the war by area bombing.

As Sir Ralph Cochrane, AOC 5 Group, remarked, 'Berlin won. It was just too tough a nut'. The four raids on Hamburg had been compressed within ten days, while the 16 attacks on Berlin – nearly 30 times larger in area – were spread over four months. The essence of strategic bombing lies in continuity and unrelenting attrition. But Berlin was too big, too well-defended and too far away for Bomber Command to deal with it as it had with Hamburg. Even those areas of the city which were badly hit served as effective firebreaks in subsequent raids.

Lying well beyond Oboe range, almost perpetually cloud-covered, and painting an ill-defined H2S picture, Berlin presented formidable problems for the PFF. It devised its own 'Berlin Method', keeping up a barrage of ground and sky markers throughout the attack. Their difficulties, and those of Main Force, can be gauged from the fact that in the first six big raids on Berlin only 400 of the 2650 attacking aircraft reported sighting the ground markers. Also waiting to lead them astray were numerous decoy fire sites, the most elaborate of which was at Nauen, 15 miles west of Berlin. A dummy city nine miles long, it boasted a panoply of searchlights, dummy TIs, simulated bomb flashes and fires.

Although the long winter nights enabled Bomber Command to make regular deep penetrations into Germany, it also exposed its aircrews to atrocious weather conditions in which long hours at sub-zero temperatures dulled performance and sapped morale. To gain height and speed in aircraft which took off loaded to the limit with bombs and fuel for the 1150-mile trip, some crews resorted to dropping their 'cookies' into the North Sea. The practice was curtailed by the rewiring of bomb release circuits so that the aircraft's photoflash exploded automatically when the 'cookies' were released. Nevertheless, the episode had chipped away at the confidence of many crews and their faith in the aircraft they were flying in such hazardous conditions.

The Luftwaffe's night fighter force was also operating with increasing effectiveness. Bomber Command's streaming was now turned against it as fighters were fed into the concentration. Over the target the cloud cover was illuminated by massed searchlights, a tactic codenamed Mattschiebe (Ground Glass), silhouetting the bombers above for Wild Boar fighters. In January 1944 Harris was losing 6.1 per cent of aircraft despatched to Berlin

A Handley Page Halifax III of No. 425 (RCAF) Squadron preparing to take off. The aircraft incorporates an interesting local modification, a ventral turret housing a single 0.5 machine-gun. Bomber Command's Halifaxes flew 82 773 operational sorties including 365 under Coastal Command control, dropping 224 207 tons of bombs; 1 837 Halifaxes were reported missing.

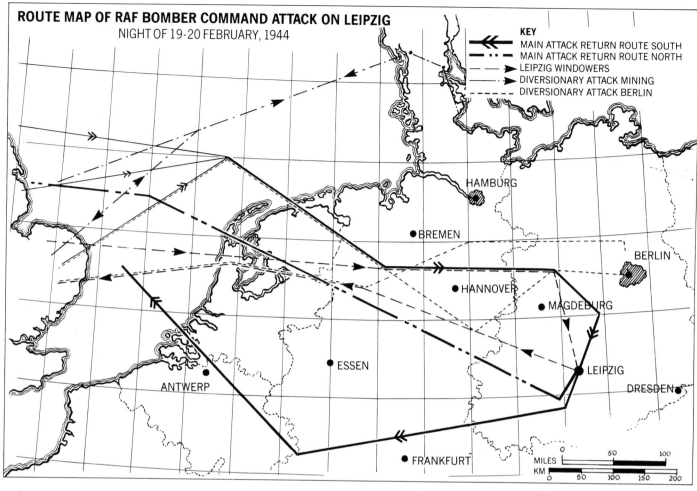

ROUTE MAP OF RAF BOMBER COMMAND ATTACK ON LEIPZIG
NIGHT OF 19-20 FEBRUARY, 1944

KEY
MAIN ATTACK RETURN ROUTE SOUTH
MAIN ATTACK RETURN ROUTE NORTH
LEIPZIG WINDOWERS
DIVERSIONARY ATTACK MINING
DIVERSIONARY ATTACK BERLIN

HAMBURG
BREMEN
BERLIN
HANNOVER
MAGDEBURG
ESSEN
LEIPZIG
ANTWERP
DRESDEN
FRANKFURT

MILES
KM

and 7.2 of those which flew to Stettin, Brunswick and Magdeburg.

Towards the end of February Harris committed his forces to the Pointblank 'shopping list' of targets, in support of 8th Air Force's Operation Avalanche, the series of daylight attacks which became known as 'Big Week'. On February 19 113 aircraft of the PFF and 741 Main Force heavies flew to attack the Junkers factory at Leipzig. The planning of the operation provides a good example of Bomber Command's methods at this stage in the war. An initial feint was to be made by 50 minelaying aircraft of 3 Group, despatched towards the Baltic with the aim of drawing German night fighters northwards. This was to be followed by a 'spoof' attack on Berlin by Mosquitos. The Main Force would also head towards Berlin, swinging half-south in the direction before turning again for the run-up to the target. Three more PFF Mosquitos were tasked with a nuisance raid on Aachen, while another 16 from 8 Group's Light Night Striking Force were to bomb Luftwaffe fighter bases. In support of these operations 100 Group despatched 12 intruder Mosquitos together with a handful of similar aircraft from Fighter Command stations to attack aircraft around German bases.

The carefully devised blend of feints, 'spoofs' and countermeasures failed to work in all its essentials. Partly by luck, partly by good judgement on the part of the ground controllers, night fighters infiltrated the stream in force, particularly at the turning points marked by PFF flares. Although the Junkers factory suffered considerable damage, Bomber Command lost 78 aircraft missing, 9.5 per cent of those despatched. A month later, on March 24, 72 aircraft (9.1 of those despatched) were lost in a raid on Berlin which ran into fierce unpredicted winds which blew the stream over the most heavily defended flak belts in Germany. As the battle drew to its close, Bomber Command suffered its worst losses in a single night when 96 of the 795 aircraft attacking Nuremberg failed to return.

Even Harris had to accept that these losses could not be sustained. At the beginning of April he came as close as he ever would to an admission of defeat when he suggested that ten squadrons of night fighters be made available to support the bombers. The 'Window' which had been opened over Hamburg was now fast being closed by the Luftwaffe. The tactics of evasion and deception by night were close to being exhausted. Even under cover of darkness Bomber Command was discovering what the USAAF had learned by day: an air force has first to defeat the opposing air force before it can attack the enemy nation. After the Battle of Berlin, Lieutenant-General Carl Spaatz, in overall command of the newly formed US Strategic Air Forces in Europe, privately concluded that Harris was 'all washed up'.

The Nuremberg Raid, March 30-31, 1944

Halifax B.III LK 795 of No.76 Squadron, piloted by
Lieutenant Henry Coverley, is shot down by the
upward-firing 'schrage musik' guns of an Me110
flown by Feldwebel Otto Kutzner of V/NJG3.
Two more of No.76 Squadron's aircraft fell in
similar fashion on Bomber Command's worst night
of the war. This would normally have been a stand-
down period for Bomber Command, because of the
moon, but the raid was mounted on the basis of an
early weather forecast that there would be
protective high cloud on the outward route, when
the moon was up, with the target area remaining
clear for ground-marked bombing. This was
contradicted by a Met Flight Mosquito which
reported that it was unlikely that there would be
cloud, but the warning was disregarded.

Bomber Command despatched 795 heavies on the
raid. The weather was clear, with a half-moon
silhouetting aircraft against an 8/10ths layer of alto-
stratus at 14 000 ft and a strong, unforecast
jetstream blowing from the northwest across
Germany. In the very cold conditions each bomber
left a telltale condensation trail in its wake, glowing
phosphorescent in the moonlight. The German
fighter controller ignored all the diversions and
concentrated his night fighters on two radio
beacons, Otto and Ida, astride the route to
Nuremberg. The first interceptions were made over
Belgium and 85 bombers were shot down on their
outward flight or over the target. The winds
dispersed the stream and Coverley strayed some 20
miles north of the track, flying straight over beacon
Ida where night fighters were circling to await
vectors. LK795 was attacked by a Ju88 which
caused some damage amidships and to the
starboard engine before breaking away. Then,
unseen, Feldwebel Kutzner delivered the *coup de
grâce* from below, opening up the Halifax's
starboard wing, rupturing the fuel lines and
shooting away the rudder and elevator controls.
With the wing ablaze, Coverley gave the order to
abandon the aircraft, which was normally used by
the station commander and dubbed the 'Royal
Barge'. Coverley remained fighting with the controls
while the crew baled out; the parachute of the flight
engineer, Flight Sergeant Motts, caught fire as he left
the burning Halifax and he fell to his death.
Coverley recalls: *'The flight engineer had passed
me my chest pack parachute just in case before
going back after the first attack to see what he
could do about the fire aft. Now something hit me
in the face knocking my oxygen mask off and
temporarily blinding me. I got out of my seat and
fell backwards down the steps leading to the nose
and found myself outside the aircraft. I cannot
recall clipping on my parachute, but it was there
when I reached for and pulled the handle'.*

His Halifax was the 22nd to fall. At least 120
aircraft bombed Schweinfurt, blown off course by
the winds and misled by mistakenly placed PFF
flares. Nuremberg itself was covered in thick
cloud, and a fierce crosswind on the final
approach caused many PFF aircraft to mark too
far to the east. A ten-mile creepback developed
into the country to the north of the city. Overall
losses were 95 aircraft with 71 more badly
damaged; 12 of these were subsequently written off.

Command of the Air and Overlord

There had also been problems in the American camp. The autumn of 1943 had witnessed a crisis in 8th Air Force's morale. The problem was brutally simple; 8th Air Force's P-38 Lightnings and P-47 Thunderbolts lacked the performance to meet enemy fighters on equal terms and the range to escort the bombers over Germany. The Luftwaffe could choose the time and the place to attack the bombers, even when the P-47's range was extended by 108-gallon drop tanks. German fighters would frequently draw the Thunderbolts on, encouraging them to drop the tanks for combat before turning away, having successfully reduced the American fighters' range.

The P-38F had a longer range than the Thunderbolt and was capable of providing cover over the target, having flown there directly, or escort on deeper penetrations. However, although the P-38 handled well below 20 000 ft, its performance fell away badly above this altitude, and the majority of combats over Germany took place well above this height. Without adequate escort the bombers were suffering a fate similar to that of the DH9 formations in 1918. Insult was added to injury in the winter of 1943 when 8th Air Force, and 15th Air Force in Italy, found the Norden bombsight practically useless in poor weather conditions. They were forced to spend much of their time flying limited penetration blind-bombing missions using H2X, the American version of H2S.*

*8th Air Force formed its own Pathfinder unit, 482nd BG, in September 1943. H2X-equipped aircraft of the Group flew at the head of the leading wings.

The situation underwent a dramatic change with the arrival in December 1943 of the P-51B Mustang, powered by the Rolls Royce Merlin. Fitted with a 75-gallon drop tank, the P-51B had a range of 1000 miles, enabling it to fly escort to such targets as Emden, Kiel and Bremen. The bubble-canopied P-51D, which arrived in May 1944, had a boosted performance, with reinforced wings allowing good fuel loads and, with drop tanks, a range of 1500 miles, sufficient for escort to any target and even the shuttle missions which flew on to the Soviet Union. The P-51D could match the Me109G in level maneuvering flight and had the edge in the climb and dive. Only in the rate of roll could the German fighters compete on equal terms.

In the P-51 the Americans possessed a superb escort fighter, which Spaatz and his fighter commander, General William E Kepner, used to provoke and win a series of air supremacy battles. In January 1944 the Americans introduced a modified bomber support relay system which remained standard for the remainder of the war. Rather than flying to a pre-determined rendezvous point and then accompanying part of the bomber stream until relieved by another unit, a group was allocated an area along the route, which it patrolled while the stream passed through. The most experienced P-47 Groups were assigned those sectors where enemy opposition was anticipated, while the target leg of the bomber route was flown by the P-38s and P-51s.

The arrival of the Mustang prompted another tactical adjustment of the American bombing formations. They were now reduced to three squadrons of 12 aircraft, with the lead squadron in the center and the trail squadrons formed up above and below. Although overall strength had been cut

Group Assembly

Rigid timing and precision flying were required to assemble the huge American bomber formations. Cloud cover increased the risk of collision and confusion as the aircraft climbed away from their airfields. A heavily-laden bomber had little room for maneuver in the crowded sky. A controlled penetration of the cloud was achieved with the introduction of the 'Buncher' radio beacon. The bombers took off at one-minute intervals, climbing at 300 ft per minute. They flew five-mile legs towards and away from the beacon until they were clear of the cloud. Circling the beacon, they formed into high, lead and low squadrons. Having completed its assembly, the group flew on to the Combat Wing Assembly Point.

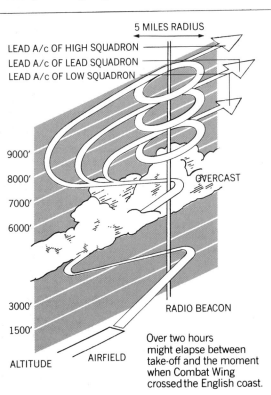

5 MILES RADIUS
LEAD A/c OF HIGH SQUADRON
LEAD A/c OF LEAD SQUADRON
LEAD A/c OF LOW SQUADRON

OVERCAST

9000'
8000'
7000'
6000'

3000'
1500'

RADIO BEACON

ALTITUDE   AIRFIELD

Over two hours might elapse between take-off and the moment when Combat Wing crossed the English coast.

by one-third, the new formation occupied 17 per cent more airspace than its predecessor, reducing the strain on pilots and making it easier for the Mustangs to provide escort.

Kepner employed his Mustangs not simply as close escorts, hugging the bomber formation as had the German Me109s in the Battle of Britain, but as fighting patrols whose role was to seek out and destroy the enemy. Although plagued with gun stoppages at high altitude, caused by the extreme cold, the P-51 quickly began to make its presence felt. On January 5, Fighter Group claimed 18 victories for no loss. Six days later the Group claimed 15 of an overall 28 victories, again with no loss, ten of the remainder falling to 56th Fighter Group, commanded by the legendary ace Hub Zemke.

The Effect on Fighter Production
On February 20, 1944 8th and 15th Air Forces launched Operation Argument, popularly known as 'Big Week', an all-out offensive against the Luftwaffe fighter force in which 3800 Fortress and Liberator sorties dropped 10 000 tons of bombs for the loss of 226 heavy aircraft – 6 per cent of sorties despatched – and 28 fighter escorts. Combined with Bomber Command raids, Operation Argument either destroyed or damaged 68 per cent of the factory buildings associated with the German aircraft industry. German fighter production fell sharply in the following month, but then began to rise again, thanks to effective dispersal and the reclaiming of plant surviving relatively undamaged beneath shattered roofs and piles of rubble.

Much has been made of the role in fighter production played by dispersal. It is perhaps ironic that by dictating the terms on which German war industry should be organized, the bombing offensive succeeded in making it more efficient. But dispersal proved problematic. Economy of scale was sacrificed and greater demands were placed on badly stretched skilled labor resources. Moreover, dispersal increased the chance of the interruption of the production flow by the bombing of communications. A few crucial missing parts could keep an aircraft grounded. The more elaborate the system of dispersal, the greater the problems of supply. Nevertheless, the fighter production figures for the period are revealing. In the last six months of 1943 Germany was producing approximately 851 single-engined fighters a month. In the first six months of 1944 output climbed to 1581 fighters a month. The real impact of the American daylight offensive is to be found in the air loss figures from all causes, running at over 2000 in February and March, and the attrition of experienced pilots, particularly those 'Experten' who were potential formation leaders. According to Adolf Galland, 'between January and April 1944 our daytime fighters lost over 1000 pilots'. On March 16 alone, 26 Me110s were shot down by 345th Fighter Group. The same month saw the death of Egon Mayer, inventor of the head-on attack.

However, the Luftwaffe was still capable of inflicting heavy losses on 8th Air Force. On March 6 the Americans mounted the first raid in strength on Berlin, flown by 730 bombers and 796 escorts. Sixty-nine of the bombers were lost, three more written off after landing, and 102 suffered major damage. To counter the massed formations flying into Germany, the Luftwaffe introduced Sturmgruppen, composed of massively armored FW190As attacking head-on in Gruppe strength of 30 aircraft. Their aim was to take maximum advantage of the initial surprise and

On the Bombing Run
As the bombers neared their target, the Combat Wings shook out into 'column of groups', in which the groups which made up each Wing formed a 'follow my leader' procession. Within each group the squadrons moved from their Vic formations into trail to ensure a concentrated bombing pattern. Each group maintained its original altitude so that it could return to the defensive formation as quickly as possible after bombing. The process was achieved with a dog leg at the Initial Point, the position from which the bombers would make their final run to the target. After releasing their bombs the aircraft descended 2000 ft, picking up speed to clear the target area as quickly as possible and making flak prediction more difficult for the gunners below. There was another dog leg at the Rally Point, where the aircraft reformed into Vics for the flight home.

Left: B-17s of 390th BG, 13th Bomb Wing, on a mission over Germany. Note the vapor trails of the escorting P-47s.

Above: A stricken B-17 of 94th BG over Berlin, its tailplane mangled by bombs falling from higher in the formation.

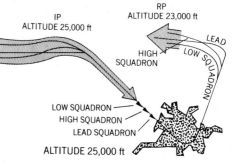

RP
ALTITUDE 23,000 ft

IP
ALTITUDE 25,000 ft

LEAD

HIGH SQUADRON

LOW SQUADRON

LOW SQUADRON
HIGH SQUADRON
LEAD SQUADRON

ALTITUDE 25,000 ft

saturate the defensive fire of the bomber formations. The Sturmgruppe was first used effectively on July 7, 1944 on a force of 756 B-17s and 373 B-24s raiding aircraft factories in the Leipzig area and oil plants at Luetzgendorf, Boehlen and Leuna-Merseburg. All eleven B-24s in the low squadron of 492nd BG were shot down in one pass. Had the Luftwaffe adopted these tactics in the summer of 1943, they would have wrought havoc with 8th Air Force. A year later the presence of Mustangs forced each Sturmgruppe to operate with, its own close and top-cover escorts, as the weight of its FW190s' armor and armament made them highly vulnerable, not least when forming up in their Gefechtsverbrand battle formation.

Anti-aircraft fire was still taking a heavy toll, thanks to improved gunlaying radar. In the summer of 1944 approximately 25 per cent of US bombers could expect to be hit by flak in their combat life, and one would be lost for every 13 damaged. By June 1944 the average life of a heavy bomber in the 8th Air Force Combat Groups was 145 days, inclusive of time spent on the ground. It is a measure of the attrition of the bombing offensive that, of the B-17Fs which made up the greater part of 8th Air Force in the autumn of 1943, approximately 75 per cent had been shot down or wrecked during the following six months. During 1944, 30 per cent of all artillery weapons manufactured in the Third Reich were of the flak type, most of them the supremely efficient 88 mm gun. A million men and women were engaged in the manufacture or maintenance of anti-aircraft guns. But none of these huge efforts could begin to match the size and power of the US war machine, which was now stepping up another gear. On May 7 8th Air Force despatched its first 1000-bomber raid, the Main Force droning over a sea of unbroken cloud to bomb Berlin and other targets in central Germany. The Americans had now overtaken Bomber Command in terms of numbers, if not in load-carrying capacity. As the war began to enter its final phase, the British were now the junior partners in the alliance against the Axis.

By March 1944 8th Air Force's loss rate had fallen to 3.5 per cent, encouraging Spaatz to believe that major land operations would be rendered unnecessary by the strategic air offensive. Now he fixed his attention on German oil production, over 75 per cent of which depended on the output of synthetic plants grouped around the German coalfields. The immediate implementation of this plan was overtaken by the demands of Overlord, the invasion of northern Europe. With the utmost reluctance, Harris and Spaatz agreed at the beginning of April to the placing of Bomber Command and the US Strategic Air Forces under the control of the Allied Supreme Commander, General Eisenhower. Their principal role would be the tactical support of the invasion. At the core of the invasion strategy was a scheme known as the Transportation Plan, in which the British and American heavy and tactical bombers were to undertake the destruction of rail communications in France to prevent the rapid reinforcement of the invasion area by the Germans. In January 1944 Harris had complained to Portal that, 'it is clear that the best and indeed the only effective support which Bomber Command can give to Overlord is the intensification of attacks on suitable industrial centers in Germany'. In Harris's opinion Bomber Command would be unable to hit specific targets by night. This marked a return to the arguments which had raged over precision bombing in 1940 although, ironically, in those days Harris had been a firm believer in Bomber Command's accuracy. Churchill joined in the argument, concerned that inaccurate attacks on targets in France might result in heavy civilian casualties.

Precision Targeting, Precision Bombing

In spite of Harris's reservations, Bomber Command possessed in 5 Group an expert precision bombing force. Its commander, Air Chief Marshal Sir Ralph Cochrane, was an advocate of low-level marking, and it had been 5 Group's 617 Squadron which had flown one of the great precision bombing missions of the war, attacking the Ruhr dams from a height of 60 ft with Barnes Wallis's 'bouncing bomb'. On December 16, 1943, No. 617 Squadron, using their Stabilized Automatic Bombsights, had achieved an error of only 94 yds in a raid on a V-weapon launching site at Abbeville. Perhaps the most brilliant of all 5 Group's pilots was Group Captain Leonard Cheshire, who pioneered low-level marking techniques in a Mosquito FBVI of No. 617 Squadron. Cheshire's method was to dive towards the Aiming Point at an angle of 30 degrees to release Red Spot TIs from a height of 1000 ft (or lower), using his gunsight to aim. The initial marking was then backed up by more Red Spot TIs dropped by Lancasters from higher altitudes, which in turn were bombed from still higher altitudes by Main Force. After delivering his TIs, Cheshire controlled the operation from his Mosquito, flying low enough to observe the Aiming Point clearly. No aircraft was to bomb until the Master Bomber was satisfied with the placing of the markers and transmitted the order to bomb by RT.

On February 8/9, flying a Lancaster, Cheshire marked the Gnome-Rhône factory at Limoges from a height of 200 ft. On April 24/25 he flew one of four 617 Squadron Mosquitos tasked with marking Munich for a Main Force of 250 heavies. Munich was defended by at least 200 anti-aircraft guns and lay at the extreme limit of the Mosquito's range. For this mission they could count of a maximum of only 15 minutes reserve of fuel. Six Lancasters flew a feint attack on Milan, while 11 Mosquitos of No. 627 Squadron flew ahead to drop Window over the target. Cheshire and his companions flew a direct route to Munich, attracting heavy fire from the moment they reached Augsburg. Over the target Cheshire was 'coned' by searchlights, whereupon he put his Mosquito into a steep dive, flattening out at 700 ft and releasing his Red Spot markers accurately over the Aiming Point at 0141 hrs. The remaining Mosquitos marked the target with equal precision, followed by Lancaster Backers-Up. While Main Force bombed on the markers, Cheshire circled the city at 1000 ft, flak exploding all around him and bombs raining down from above. Using every ounce of his immense skill, it took Cheshire 12 minutes to disengage himself from the flak zone. Over Manston, he evaded a Luftwaffe intruder by turning off his lights and landing in the dark. When he touched down his tanks were dry. For this operation Cheshire was decorated with the Victoria Cross.

On occasion these low-level methods could

achieve greater accuracy than 8th Air Force's daylight raids. At the end of April, the Lictard factory at Tours escaped unscathed from a high-altitude attack by American bombers. On May 1/2, Mosquitos of No. 627 Squadron (recently transferred from 8 to 5 Group) marked the target with ease, placing their first TIs through the factory's glass roof, where they almost disappeared from view. It was 5 Group's good fortune to have made this breakthrough precisely at a time when accuracy was required not only to destroy invasion targets in France but also to minimize what is nowadays coyly termed 'collateral damage'. Precision bombing was by now a necessary adjunct to Allied success.

In his single-minded pursuit of area bombing, Harris had underestimated the skill of his élite aircrews. On the night of March 6 rail yards at Trappes, near Paris, were attacked in a series of raids designed to test the practicability of the Transportation Plan. Other targets included the yards at Aulnoye, Le Mans, Courtrai and Laon all of which had suffered the similar attentions of RFC pilots in World War I. The results demonstrated a high degree of precision and minimal civilian casualties. On April 14 the US Strategic Air Forces and Bomber Command were directed to make the Transportation Plan and the continuing battle with the Luftwaffe their two top priorities. The attacks on railway targets, upon which 76 000 tons of bombs had been dropped by June 6, were an important factor in disrupting German attempts to mount a swift counter-attack on the Allied bridgehead. In March 1944 over 70 per cent of British bombs had fallen on Germany; in April the figure dropped to below 50 per cent; in May to 25 per cent; and in June it virtually fell off the scale at 8 per cent as Bomber Command provided support for the ground forces fighting in Normandy.

Statistics of Survival

On Bomber Command Main Force Squadrons the first tour was 30 operational flights. The first half dozen were considered the most hazardous. After this aircrews felt that they had some chances of surviving to the end of the tour, although the statistics were not encouraging. The historian Martin Middlebrook has shown that in 1943, when the average operational loss was 3.6 per cent, 33 per cent of Main Force crews would survive their first tour. Those who opted for a second tour of 25 operations had a 16 per cent chance of completing both tours. Crews who were badly shaken up in their first operations sometimes never recovered their equilibrium and were prey to the dreaded failure of nerve known as LMF, 'Lacking in Moral Fibre'. Having survived the first six operations, aircrews were at greatest risk in mid-tour, when over-confidence might betray them into carelessness, and during the last few trips, when concentration was eroded by fatigue. Survival depended on a combination of minute attention to detail and sheer good luck. The very best pilots went to remarkable lengths. When Flying Officer Leonard Cheshire joined his first operational unit, No. 102 Squadron, in June 1940, he got to know his Whitley by blindfolding himself and then feeling his way around it until he could identify every item he needed in the dark. No. 50 Squadron's renowned Mickey Martin personally polished every inch of Perspex in his cockpit canopy. These superb airmen made their own luck. Less brilliant but equally careful pilots observed a range of simple but vital procedures; gently banking the aircraft every few moments to enable the gunners to search the sky below them; cutting down unnecessary chatter on the intercom; making regular checks on each member of the crew. Gunners were forbidden to stare down into the flames of a burning city, a natural tendency during a raid but one which would rob them of their night vision.

Left: The crew of No. 9 Squadron's Lancaster W4964 pose in front of their aircraft on the completion of its 100th operation.

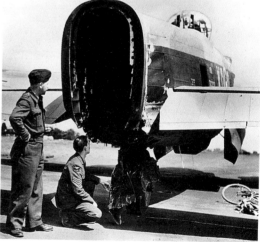

Above: A Lancaster of No. 115 Squadron photographed on the morning of June 29, 1943, after its rear turret (and gunner) had been sliced away over Germany during the previous night, probably by a bomb falling from a higher aircraft.

Above: A Lancaster takes off surrounded by the flames of a FIDO (Fog Investigation Dispersal Operations) installation. A continuous line of burners on each side of the main runway provided sufficient heat to disperse fog for take-off and landing.
Right: A Halifax overflies a less controlled blaze during a raid on oil storage facilities north of the French city of Bordeaux on August 4, 1944.

The Oil Plan

Even before the first troops had stepped ashore in Normandy, Spaatz had been able to launch a limited offensive against German oil production under the pretext of meeting the first priority of the Supreme Commander's direction to the Strategic Forces – the neutralization of the enemy's air force. Bad weather prevented operations until May 12 when 886 aircraft flew to attack the plants around Leipzig and the FW190 repair depot at Zwickau. Bombing was from 18 000 ft to achieve maximum accuracy, and in the clear conditions some Groups produced outstanding results: 385th BG placed 97 per cent of its bombs within 2000 ft of the Aiming Point at Zwickau. Forty-six aircraft were lost, but for the first time Spaatz had got his fingers around the jugular of Germany's war economy. In June tactical support of the Allied armies in Normandy, and the offensive against the V-weapon sites, restricted Spaatz's oil raids to only 11.6 per cent of his total effort. In July and August the figures hovered around 16 per cent, but the results were nonetheless significant. German petroleum availability fell from a March figure of 927 000 tons to 477 000 in June. During the same period the Luftwaffe's supplies of aviation fuel fell by two-thirds, from 180 000 tons to 50 000 tons. In August it slumped to 10 000 tons. The fruits of Albert Speer's organizational genius were now being cast to the winds. The Luftwaffe had the aircraft, but only a dwindling reserve of pilots and fuel to keep them in the air. By the autumn of 1944 the USAAF and Bomber Command had brought German oil production to a standstill. With the onset of winter weather, it crawled back up again, to 24 500 tons in December, just sufficient to launch the Ardennes

offensive but insufficient to sustain it. As Field Marshal von Rundstedt commented after the war,

'*TAKING ACCOUNT OF THE EXTRA DIF-ficulties likely to be met in a winter battle in such difficult country as the Ardennes, I told Hitler personally that five times the standard scale of petrol supply ought to be provided. Actually, when the offensive was launched, only one and a half times the standard scale had been provided. Worse still, much of it was kept too far back, in large truck columns on the east bank of the Rhine. Once the foggy weather cleared and the Allied air forces came into action, its forwarding was badly interrupted*'.

The Germans strove mightily to protect their fuel supplies. By the end of November there were over 1000 anti-aircraft guns in the Leipzig area. The 88s were usually sited in groups (Grossbatteries) of up to 24 guns, firing a concentrated pattern of bursts with a shotgun effect. The more powerful 108 mm and 128 mm guns were grouped in batteries of 12 or

synthetic and reclaimed rubber. The brake drums had a tendency to overheat and the 30 mm ammunition belts often broke during high g turns. On November 8 Nowotny was killed in a crash, shortly after downing three bombers, and the unit was withdrawn, having lost 26 of its 30 aircraft in just over a month.

Early in 1945 the veterans of Kommando Nowotny were reformed in JG7 and their aircraft equipped with the R4M air-to-air missile. Twelve of these were carried under each wing on wooden racks and were ripple-fired to form a dense pattern. Their two-pound impact-fused warheads were powerful enough to inflict terminal damage on a heavy bomber. However, it was not until March 1945 that the Me262s were used in large numbers against the daylight formations. On March 18 II/JG7 put up 37 aircraft against a big raid on Berlin, destroying eight heavies for the loss of four of their own number (two of them in a mid-air collision). At the end of March Jagdverband 44 was formed, under Adolf Galland. This was an ace-packed unit of 50 pilots; but it seldom had more than 15 serviceable Me262s operating at any one time. Their method of attack was to dive behind and below a formation, then pull up, level off and fire at a single aircraft at a range of about 650 yds, continuing to press home the attack with cannon before breaking away above the formation to avoid being hit by falling debris.

Crescendo

In March 1944, as the Battle of Berlin reached its climax, RAF Bomber Command was passing through one of its recurring periods of crisis. Six months later the situation had undergone a dramatic change. Not only was Germany slowly bleeding to death as it lost its oil supplies and pilots, but as the Allied armies advanced through Europe, it was also losing its early warning stations. In 12 major attacks on Germany in September 1944, Bomber Command lost only 2.4 per cent of the aircraft despatched.

At the same time Harris was released from his commitment to SHAEF. A decision now had to be made on the most effective method of prosecuting the combined bombing offensive. Spaatz, supported by Portal, argued for the priority to be given to oil targets. Sir Arthur Tedder, Deputy Supreme Commander at SHAEF, supported a concentrated attack on Germany's rail and water transportation links, an extension of the Overlord Transportation Plan to the German homeland.

Harris was impervious to these arguments. To the end he remained convinced that there were no key weaknesses in the German economy, or 'panaceas' as he scornfully called them. He had been told on many occasions that this or that target was crucial, but such expectations had always remained ill-founded. Harris had been dragged kicking and screaming into the oil offensive – between July and September only 11 per cent of Bomber Command's sorties had been sent to oil targets, compared with 20 per cent devoted to area bombing. Now, as the Oboe transmitting stations pushed eastwards across Europe, extending the range of accurate marking, Harris returned to his principal preoccupation, the progressive destruction

four. There were no fewer than 506 guns around the much-raided oil plant at Merseburg, which explains why in August 1944 8th Air Force lost 131 aircraft to flak compared with 39 to fighters. Lieutenant Gordon Courtenay, a bombardier in 398th BG, flew his first mission over this objective. Ahead of him he saw what he assumed to be a pall of black smoke hanging over the target. In fact his aircraft was flying into the smoke of several thousand shell bursts aimed at the preceding Groups. Window was used in huge quantities to jam the gunlaying radar, and 8th Air Force's monthly requirement rose to 2000 tons. However, aircraft in the leading formations, unable to take advantage of a Window screen, continued to suffer heavy losses. In November, 8th Air Force began to employ small formations of Mosquitos, equipped with an electric Window dispenser in the bomb bay, which flew ahead of Main Force. Blanket Windowing of these massive flak concentrations was crucial as the Grossbatteries were often linked by a 'Zug 44' Central Conversion Mechanism, which enabled a jammed battery to draw on data from a set functioning in an adjacent area.

Another consequence of these flak concentrations was an opening out of the American formations. Four nine-aircraft squadrons were deployed over 43 per cent more airspace, making it harder for the flak to assess altitude and shift fire with rapidity and accuracy. This formation saw out the war.

A final threat in the skies over Germany was the Me262 jet fighter which in October 1944 began to make its presence felt in the Kommando Nowotny, led by the ace Walther Nowotny. However, the Me262 was plagued by problems with its guns and undercarriage, its landing speed of 120 mph resulting in frequent bursting of the tyres, which were made of

The Corkscrew

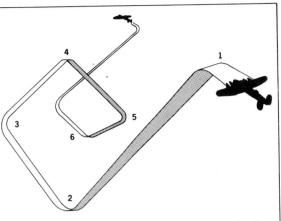

The RAF heavy bomber's standard evasive maneuver enabled it to continue on course while presenting an attacking fighter with an extremely difficult target. This diagram shows the maneuver following a port fighter attack.

1 The pilot opens his throttles and banks at 45 degrees to make a diving turn to port; descending through 1000ft in six seconds, the bomber reaches a speed of nearly 300mph.
2 After the 1000ft descent, the pilot pulls the aircraft into a climb, still turning to port.
3 He reverses the turn, halfway through the climb which has caused his speed to fall sharply, possibly forcing the attacking night fighter to overshoot.
4 Regaining his original altitude, with speed down to 185mph and still in the starboard turn, the pilot pushes the aircraft down into another dive.
5 Picking up speed in the dive, he descends through 500ft before reversing the direction of the turn.
6 If the fighter is still on his tail, he stands by to repeat the maneuver. The physical effort required by the pilot has been compared with that of an oarsman pulling hard in a boat race.

of Germany's cities. On November 1 he wrote to Portal. '*IN THE PAST 18 MONTHS Bomber Command has virtually destroyed 45 out of the leading 60 German cities. In spite of the invasion diversions we have so far managed to keep up and even extend our average of two and a half cities devastated a month ... There are not many industrial centers of population now left intact. Are we going to abandon this vast task, which the Germans themselves have long admitted to be their worst headache, just as it nears completion?*'

Harris was briefly checked by Portal in November, during which Bomber Command devoted 25 per cent of its effort to oil targets, delivering a higher tonnage than 8th Air Force. Thereafter, like Trenchard in 1918, he went his own way. Secure in the prestige and authority which had made him all but irreplaceable, Harris not only survived but, as Anthony Verrier has observed, ensured that he was 'one of the very few senior British officers who seemed able to ignore, let alone deny the American predominance in the conduct of grand strategy'.

Bomber Command in 1945

Bomber Command entered 1945 as a force both quantitatively and qualitatively light years removed from that of September 1939. Its daily availability of 1600 aircraft was dominated by the Lancaster, of which there were over 1000 on strength. A 'stretched' version, the Lincoln, was being prepared for operations with the RAF's Tiger Force in the Far East. All the heavy bombers were equipped with Gee and H2S. Rather late in the day some Lancaster rear turrets were being modified to accommodate 0.5 guns equipped with 'Village Inn' gunlaying radar. The scanner dish traversed and elevated with the guns, projecting a radar picture and ranging information on to the gunner's sight. This enabled a gunner to engage enemy fighters beyond visual range but left the problem of identification unresolved. Clearly a jumpy gunner blazing away at anything behind him could create havoc. Late in the war the problem was overcome with the installation of a special nose-mounted infra-red identification system, but this development came too late for Village Inn to be employed to its full effect.

The Browning .303, Bomber Command's standard armament throughout the war, was often accused of being too light to deal with cannon-armed enemy fighters. However, in the hands of an experienced gunner, it could prove a highly efficient weapon. On May 27/28, 1944 Sergeant P Engelbrecht, a mid-upper gunner in a Halifax III of No. 424 Squadron, shot down an FW190 and an Me110 with his four-gun dorsal armament while beating off no less than 14 attacks. The FW190 blew up in the air and the Me110 exploded on the ground. This was the first of three 'doubles' in which Engelbrecht was involved. However, ninety per cent of all sorties were made without contact with night fighters, and many crews completed a tour without encountering the enemy. Of the 10 per cent who were intercepted, about half were shot down, most of them taken completely by surprise.

Little had changed since World War I. The fighter the crew didn't see was the fighter that would administer the 'chop'. Intense concentration and attention to detail were the hallmarks of the good air gunner. The rear gunner occupied the most hazardous position, as this was the quarter from which the great majority of attacks were mounted. It was also the coldest, and the gunner frequently pulled six-inch long icicles from his oxygen mask while blinking his eyes to keep the lashes from freezing in the intense cold. Coned by searchlights over the target, he might keep one eye closed to retain at least part of his night vision. In an open-ended rear turret he could smell the explosive fumes of flak shells exploding nearby, just as his predecessors had done over the Western Front in World War I. A sliver of sky in which the stars were unaccountably blacked out might be the only warning of imminent attack, and fractions of a second the time in which he had to instruct the pilot to corkscrew to port or starboard. Few night fighters followed a bomber down into a corkscrew, and a burst from the guns was often sufficient to send the predator off in a search for less vigilant prey. A five-second burst from the six .303s in the rear and mid-upper turrets delivered about 1200 rounds of mixed ball, armor-piercing, tracer and incendiary bullets.

Bomber Command was now flying regularly in daylight, a far cry from the disasters of 1939. On August 27, 1944 216 Halifaxes of 4 Group, and 14 Mosquitos and 13 Lancasters of 8 Group raided the Meerbeck refinery in the first major daylight attack by Bomber Command since August 12, 1941, when 54 Blenheims had bombed power stations near Cologne. On the outward journey escort was provided by nine squadrons of Spitfires, and the withdrawal was covered by a further seven squadrons. The heavies did not fly in formation, like the B-17s, but in loose 'gaggles'. There was intense flak over the target, which had been marked by Oboe, but there were no losses. Production at Meerbeck was not resumed until October. In the following December, 19 out of 41 of Bomber Command's operations were by day.

By night 5 Group's target-marking techniques had reached a new level of sophistication. In the summer of 1944 the Group developed the system of 'offset' marking, in which each Main Force aircraft approached the Aiming Point on one of several different pre-instructed bearings. Although Main Force aimed for the same single marking point, the different approach angles and timed overshoots provided a number of Aiming Points for one successful marking attack. Over Königsberg on August 29, 1944 there were three approach lines. In the attack on Bremerhaven on September 18/19 there were five, a method ideally suited to an elongated port stretching eight miles along the eastern shores of the Weser estuary. Two hundred aircraft dropped 863 tons of bombs on the target, including 420 000 thermite incendiaries. Photo-reconnaissance revealed that of a total built-up area of 375 acres, 297 acres had been destroyed. The technique had been further refined in the Darmstadt raid of September 11. After the target had been marked by No. 627 Squadron's Mosquitos, 234 heavies approached the Aiming Point – an old army parade ground one mile west of the city center – along seven different lines of approach, at varying heights and with each aircraft timing its overshoot by between three and 12 seconds. In this fashion the destruction was spread in an unfolding V-shape across the city. The Germans called it der Todesfacher – the 'Death Fan'. Destruction in the center of Darmstadt was 78 per cent, and 70 000 of the city's population of 115 000 were made homeless. In the Old City only five buildings remained. About 8500 people had perished in the 45-minute raid, 90 per cent of them from asphyxiation or burning. A similar technique was employed in the attack on Brunswick on 14/15 October. A firestorm was started in the area of the city which contained six giant bunkers and two air raid shelters housing over 20 000 people. They were saved by a 'water alley' driven through the fire-torn streets by high-pressure fire hoses and screened on each side by overlapping jets of water. Nevertheless, the city had suffered such fearful damage that although the raid had been carried out by only one Group, the Brunswick authorities estimated that at least 1000 bombers must have taken part in the attack. In the space of 40 minutes over one-third of the population of 200 000 had been made homeless and 655 of 1400 built-up acres laid waste.

Operation Thunderclap

These crushing raids were the prelude to Operation Thunderclap, the triple blow to the city of Dresden delivered between February 13 and 15 1945 by Bomber Command and 8th Air Force. Above all others, the Dresden raid has provided a focus for the postwar debate on the morality of area bombing. At the time it was seen in a different perspective. It was just 'another operation', albeit conducted on a scale and with a precision inconceivable to Bomber Command at the beginning of the war. Its origins lay in the 1943 Thunderclap scheme to destroy German civilian morale in a series of cataclysmic raids. Its implementation in February 1944 also had much to do with Churchill's desire to strengthen his hand

when dealing with Stalin at Yalta, the last great Allied conference of the war. In the event diplomatic imperatives and the inbuilt dynamic of Harris's area bombing philosophy combined to destroy a city crammed with refugees, virtually undefended and of doubtful military importance. It was the last great convulsion in the process which had begun over Mannheim on December 12, 1940, and the culmination of the philosophy which Harris had preached so vigorously since 1942. For the C-in-C of Bomber Command, it was both a triumph and a disaster. After the war Harris was shunned by the British Establishment, and those who had fought with Bomber Command were denied the campaign medal they so richly deserved.

The ancient city of Dresden had survived the war virtually unscathed. It was a 'virgin' target and, like Lübeck in 1942, ready for the torch. Target marking on the night of February 13/14 was of a very high order. After the first wave of Blind Illuminators dropped by Lancasters, the low-level Mosquito Marker Leader placed the initial red TIs within 100 yds of the Aiming Point, the Dresden-Friedrichstadt Sportsplatz. Each of the first wave of 244 Main Force Lancasters flew on to the brilliantly marked Aiming Point on a different heading, fanning out across the city. This was an area attack par excellence. The 4000- and 8000-pound bombs smashed roofs and blew in windows; the incendiaries set individual buildings ablaze. Floors collapsed and huge tongues of flame burst through the shattered roofs, turning individual buildings into giant Roman candles. Then the fires coalesced, heating the air above and setting up a violent updraught, which in turn sucked in air from all sides into the center of the fire area. The colossal suction brought with it hurricane-force winds. During the worst night of the Blitz on London, the fires had spread as fast as a man could walk. In Dresden, they spread faster than a man could run.

The first attack ended at 2221 hrs. The second wave of 529 Lancasters – carrying 75 per cent incendiary bombloads – flew in at 0130 hrs. Two minutes before them the Master Bomber had arrived over the target to find a huge firestorm raging through the center of the city. The glow could be seen

A shower of incendiaries falls from the bomb bay of a Lancaster during a daylight raid on Duisburg on October 14, 1944. In the last three months of 1944, 14 254 Bomber Command sorties were despatched to Duisburg, Essen, Cologne, Düsseldorf and smaller industrial targets. Over 60 000 tons of bombs were dropped, 85 per cent of them HE, as there was little left that was combustible in the shattered cities below the bomber streams. Only 136 aircraft were lost in this phase of operations. As the German fighter defenses fell apart under the relentless battering, it was possible to despatch 1000 bombers on a nightly basis.

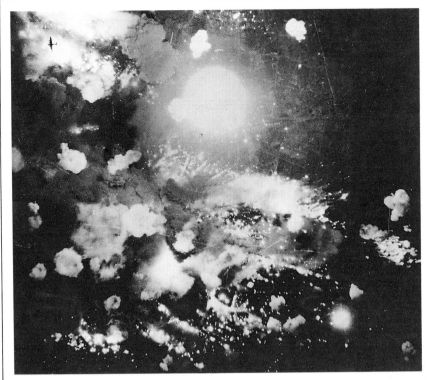

A vivid picture of the scene below Bomber Command aircraft on the night of February 23/24, 1945, during a raid on Pforzheim, deemed at the time to be a 'communications center' and industrial target. An idea of the size of the fire raging below can be gauged from the small silhouette of a Lancaster in the top left-hand corner of the picture.

by approaching Main Force aircrews at distances of up to 200 miles.

On the 14th 316 B-17s of 8th Air Force also bombed the stricken city. That night Bomber Command returned, this time to bomb Chemnitz, 30 miles west of Dresden. As part of a complex plan of feints and diversions, 244 Lancasters of 5 Group attacked the Deutsche Petroleum AG refineries at Rositz, near Leipzig. Their course took them 50 miles northwest of Dresden, and the aircrews could see the fires still blazing on the horizon as they flew in to their new target. On the ground, British POWs in Stalag IVB, 25 miles southeast of Dresden, also watched the distant pall of smoke hanging in the air for three days. Scraps of charred paper and clothing floated into the camp for days afterwards, sucked up in the artificial tornado of the firestorm and then carried by the wind across the surrounding countryside. It is impossible to give a completely accurate estimate of the casualties in Dresden, but some authorities have put the figure as high as 135 000.

Hindsight lends a certain irony to Churchill's subsequent moves to distance himself from the Dresden raid. His determination to have something to show Stalin at Yalta had been largely responsible for the resurrection of Thunderclap. On March 28 he wrote: '*IT SEEMS TO ME THAT THE MOMENT has come when the question of bombing of German cities simply for the sake of increasing the terror, though under other contexts, should be reviewed. Otherwise we shall come into control of an utterly ruined land.*'

Germany was already a ruined land. For every ton of bombs dropped by the Luftwaffe on Britain, Germany had received 315 tons. The devastation was the result of the cumulative effect of strategic bombing – steady attrition rather than the knock-out blow. Much of this had been accomplished after the point at which Germany's defeat had become inevitable. Seventy-five per cent of 8th Air Force's bombs fell on Germany after June 6, 1944, when the Luftwaffe – although still dangerous – was being bludgeoned into a corner from which there was no escape. As the German war economy disintegrated under the remorseless pressure to which it was subjected in the closing months of the war, it is difficult to isolate specific factors as decisive. In March 1945 strategic bombing had achieved the neutralization and isolation of the industrial region of the Ruhr, an achievement obscured at the time by the swift advance of the Allied armies, which had secured the area within days. It was the speed and totality of the German collapse which denied the proponents of strategic bombing the proof that theirs had been the decisive contribution.

As the war neared its end Bomber Command was able to deploy all the professionalism and technique which it had acquired since 1939. On March 14, 1945 the great Bielefeld railway viaduct linking Hamm and Hannover was destroyed by 14 specially modified Lancasters of No. 617 Squadron carrying the 22 000-pound 'Grand Slam' bomb designed by Barnes Wallis. On March 23/24, immediately prior to Montgomery's crossing of the Rhine, 200 heavies dropped 1092 tons of HE and 7.5 tons of incendiaries on German troop concentrations. On April 9 the pocket battleship *Admiral Scheer* was capsized in Kiel harbor. On March 21/22, in the climax of 8 Group's Light Night Striking Force's campaign against Berlin, 139 Mosquito sorties were flown against the German capital. In the closing months of the war, Mosquito losses had fallen to one for every 2000 sorties – a Bomber Command record. In the last four months of the war Bomber Command flew 67 487 sorties for the loss of 608 aircraft. It is an indication of the scale of strategic operations that although this figure represents nearly twice the 1939 front-line strength, it was considered a small price to pay for the defeat of Nazi Germany.

In one final spasm the Luftwaffe caught Bomber Command unawares. On the night of March 1, Bomber Command's main targets were the synthetic oil plant at Kamen and the Dortmund-Ems canal at Ladbergen. As the Main Force streamed homewards, over 100 German night fighters launched Operation Gisella, their first big intruder operation against Bomber Command's British bases since the summer of 1941. Two waves of Ju88s and He219s attacked 27 airfields in Suffolk, Norfolk, Lincolnshire and Yorkshire, and the aircraft returning to them from Germany. There were a number of OTU units in the air that night, and they were caught cold by the night fighters. Twenty-seven aircraft were shot down and eight badly damaged. John Albers, whose Lancaster was returning from a raid on Ladbergen, flew straight into the thick of it, and recalled 45 minutes of sickening corkscrewing before the shaken crew put down. With Gisella the Luftwaffe had all but shot its bolt. Two weeks later, on March 17, a similar operation was flown by 18 Ju88s. But there were no heavy bomber raids planned for that night and the intruders succeeded only in shooting down a single training aircraft. It was the Luftwaffe's last offensive action over Britain.

3.5 THE WAR IN THE PACIFIC

AS A J P TAYLOR HAS OBSERVED, WORLD War II might well be said to have begun in April 1932 when Mao Tse Tung and Chou Teh declared war on Japan in the name of the Kiangsi Soviet. In the 1930s Japanese expansion was signposted by a series of so-called 'Incidents' – the first of which was the 'Manchurian Incident' of 1931 – which provided Japan with convenient pretexts to resort to force against China and the Soviet Union. In 1937 there was an armed clash between Chinese and Japanese troops near Peking. The Japanese struck back and within seven weeks they had taken Shanghai. By the end of 1938 they controlled the entire Chinese coast, a victory won at the price of 500 000 Chinese dead and 50 million driven from their homes. In 1938 and 1939 there were fierce border clashes between the Soviet Union and Japan as the latter sought to strengthen its position in Manchuria by destroying the Russian forces across the frontier.

By the late 1930s the United States and the Western colonial powers viewed Japanese expansion with increasing alarm. Unfortunately this went hand in hand with an almost wilful ignorance of the high state of preparedness and efficiency of Japan's armed air forces, not least its air element.

Serious Japanese interest in military aviation dates from the years following World War I. First the Japanese acquired considerable quantities of Allied surplus aircraft, including Sopwith 1½ Strutters, Nieuport Bébés and Spads. Then they obtained licences to build a variety of aircraft in Japan, among them the French Salmson bomber, which was manufactured by the Kawasaki Company. Kawasaki retained a European connection when it engaged a German, Dr Richard Vogt, as its chief designer. In 1928 Vogt supervised the production of Japan's first original bomber, the Type 88, which was powered by a licence-built BMW engine.

By the early 1930s the efficient Japanese had made the breakthrough to technological self-sufficiency. Japan was well-placed to assimilate new aviation technology into the increasingly large and sophisticated inventories of its Army and Navy Air Forces. War with China, and large-scale clashes with the Soviet Union on the Manchurian frontier provided the opportunity to test men and equipment in combat conditions.

The Japanese Bomber Force

Several of the military aircraft developed by the Japanese in the mid-1930s were well-matched with the leading European equivalents. In the development of their Pacific grand strategy, the crucial element of distance had an overriding influence on Japanese aircraft design. In the Mitsubishi GM3 Type 96 bomber (Allied codename Nell), which entered service in 1937, the Navy had an aircraft well-equipped to undertake operations at extreme range. In order to obtain the maximum endurance from a twin-engined bomber which, in the G3M2 version, was powered by 1075 hp radials, Mitsubishi's designers achieved a drastic reduction in weight. Unladen, the G3M2 tipped the scales at less than 11 000 pounds, approximately 65 per cent of the weight of the Wellington and the Ju88, neither of which carried armor at this stage in their development. Capable of lifting impressive quantities of fuel, the G3M2 had a range of 2000 miles with an externally carried 1760-pound bombload. However, range was purchased at the expense of armor protection for engines and crew. The G3M's vulnerability when unescorted by fighters was exposed as soon as it was committed to the fighting in China. On August 14, 1937, 18 G3M1 and G3M2 bombers of the Konoya Naval Air Corps raided Hangchow and the surrounding area to support the drive on Shanghai. Six of them were shot down by Curtiss Hawk biplanes of the Chinese Air Force. On the following day 24 G3Ms of the Zizaniza Naval Air Corps made a dramatic 1200-mile round trip over the waters of the East China Sea, flying southwest from the island of Kyushu to strike at Shanghai and Nanking. What the Japanese did not tell the world was that in three subsequent raids they lost 54 bombers over Nanking alone, as the G3M demonstrated a tendency to explode in a ball of flame when the unprotected fuel tanks were hit.

The G3M's successor, the G4M (Allied codename Betty), entered service in 1941. Built in larger numbers than any other Japanese bomber, the G4M was bigger, faster and more heavily armed than its predecessor, with an impressive range of 3000 miles. But like the G3M, its heavy fuel load – carried in unprotected tanks – made it extremely vulnerable. During the Pacific War the Betty was dubbed the 'one shot lighter' by American pilots, a soubriquet with which few of its crew would have disagreed. To remedy this major defect, Mitsubishi redesigned the aircraft in the winter of 1942, installing self-sealing tanks of reduced capacity and providing armor plating in the crew areas. The additional protection reduced performance, a problem which afflicted many Japanese types after 1941, when they came face to face with increasingly stiff opposition.

The standard Army medium bomber at the outbreak of the World War II was the Mitsubishi Ki-21 Type 97 (Sally). Powered by two 1450 hp engines, the Mitsubishi Ki-21 IIB had a maximum speed of 297 mph at 13 000 ft, ceiling of 32 180 ft and range of 1350 miles with a 2205-pound bombload. Facing obsolete Allied aircraft in the opening phase of the war, the Ki-21 was relatively successful, but when pitted against RAF Hurricanes and P-40s of the American Volunteer Group over Burma and China, losses increased sharply. The Ki-21's defensive armament was improved by the removal of its distinctive long dorsal 'greenhouse', which was replaced by a large conical turret housing a 12.7 mm machine-gun operated by bicycle pedals and chain drive for gun reverse. Although the Ki-21 had outlived its operational lifespan, it was forced to soldier on since its replacement, the Nakajima Ki-49 (Helen) suffered from poor range and inadequate bombload in trying to achieve higher speed with heavier armament.

If the G3M was the technical equivalent of the Bristol Blenheim, the Aichi D3A (Val) Type 99 Navy dive bomber stands comparison with the Ju87. Japanese interest in the potential of the dive bomber was bound up with their development of a strong aircraft carrier component in their Fleet Replenishment Program. The Navy's first dive bomber was the Nakajima D1A1 Type 94 biplane, an export version of the Heinkel He50. This was quickly followed by the Type 96, a two-seat biplane with a 550-pound bombload, powered by a 600 hp Hikari engine and capable of around 140 mph. Both types saw service in China, but were overshadowed by the Aichi Val single-engined monoplane, which had been designed from the outset to operate from fleet carriers. Powered by an 810 hp Kinsei radial, the prototype flew for the first time in January 1938 and made its combat debut with 12th Air Corps on September 3, 1940 in raids on Chungking. With the sky swept clear of fighter opposition by the Mitsubishi A6M Zero, the Vals were able to carry out pinpoint attacks undisturbed by largely primitive anti-aircraft defenses. After extensive deck trials on *Akagi* and *Kaga*, the D3As joined their squadrons aboard the carriers, and in September 1941 the Val was withdrawn from the Chinese campaign.

In December 1941 the Val, with its fixed, spatted undercarriage, was already approaching obsolescence. In contrast the Nakajima B5NA Type 97 (Kate) single-engined Navy bomber incorporated a number of advanced design features, including Fowler-type flaps, mechanically folding wings, retractable landing gear, variable pitch propeller and integral fuel tanks. A contemporary of the G3M, the Kate carried either one 1764-pound torpedo or three 550-pound bombs. The Val, the Kate and the Zero formed a trio of outstanding Japanese carrier aircraft on the eve of war. In 1941 the Air Groups (Koku Sentai) embarked aboard the six big fleet carriers comprised a mixture of fighters, dive bombers, and level bomber/torpedo aircraft. For example, Akagi, flagship of the fleet carriers, embarked 18 Zero fighters, 18 Val dive bombers and 27 Kate bomber/torpedo planes. The three smaller carriers generally carried only two types of aircraft – fighters and bomber/torpedo.

Japan in the Ascendant

At 0630 hrs on December 7, 1941 the first of 120 Kates, 51 Vals and 43 Zeros took off from the six carriers of Admiral Nagumo's striking force which lay 275 miles north of the great American naval base at Pearl Harbor on the Hawaian island of Oahu. Fifty of the Kates were armed with a single 1760-pound armor-piercing bomb and 70 more carried a torpedo; the Vals in the first wave carried 250-pound fragmentation bombs to destroy parked aircraft. The Japanese targets were the US air bases, the Kaneohe seaplane base, the battleships of the Navy's Pacific Fleet and also, it was anticipated, the aircraft carriers moored beside Ford Island in Pearl Harbor. From endless hours of practice and meticulous studies of maps and models of Oahu, every member of the aircrews knew his target and task. Nothing had been left to chance. An hour later they were followed by a second wave of 54 Kates, 80 Vals and 36 Zeros. Within four hours, the Japanese had disabled the entire battleship component of the US Pacific Fleet and destroyed over 300 aircraft on the ground.

The victory might have been even greater had Nagumo heeded the pleas of his squadron commanders to launch a second attack. This would have caught the carrier *Enterprise* on its approach to Pearl Harbor from Wake Island. It would also have wrecked Pearl Harbor's repair facilities and destroyed the huge American oil stocks – almost equal to the entire Japanese supply – which although intact were now defenseless. In turn this would have forced the US Navy out of Pearl Harbor and back to the American west coast, out of range of the imminent theater of war in the southeast Pacific.

Japanese aircrews wait on the tarmac in 1945 beside a Mitsubishi G4M 'Betty', under whose belly is slung an Okha piloted suicide bomb. The 'Betty' entered service in 1941 and took part in the sinking of *Prince of Wales* and *Repulse* on December 10, 1941. It had an impressive range of more than 3000 miles, but its large fuel load – carried in unprotected tanks – made it one of the most vulnerable of all Japanese military aircraft. Heavy losses were suffered, particularly in the battle for the Solomon Islands in 1942, but it was not until 1943 that any attempt was made to provide smaller, fully-protected tanks.

This Japanese omission allowed the Americans not only to keep the naval base but also to survive this appalling setback with their carrier force intact. Three of the Navy carriers had been at sea during the attack and the fourth was under repair in California. And it was the aircraft carrier, not the big guns of the battleships, which was to be the arbiter of sea power in the Pacific war.

In the six months following Pearl Harbor, the Japanese cut a swathe through the Pacific, gaining vast territories for their Greater East Asia Co-Prosperity Sphere. In the air the Western powers faced them with obsolescent, scattered forces outnumbered by at least 2:1 and functioning with no overall co-ordination. Japanese victories had been secured by superb intelligence, central planning and tactical superiority, and the smooth linkage of naval, air, and ground forces. The air forces provided the preliminary strikes, protection for fleet and transport movements, and air cover over the battlefield. The last was of particular importance as Japan's bomber force was designed to destroy air installations and aircraft on the ground and needed fighter escort to carry out its primary function. To make this possible, the Japanese 11th Air Fleet, based in Formosa, had conducted experiments to extend the range of the Zero fighter, enabling it to provide fighter cover direct from Formosa to the Philippines and back.

At 1235 hrs on December 7, 53 Japanese bombers, escorted by 36 fighters, appeared over the US base at Clark Field, 80 miles from Manila. They achieved complete tactical surprise, catching B-17s and P-40 fighters on the ground with their tanks full. With anti-aircraft shells exploding harmlessly 3000 ft below them the bombers set about the systematic destruction of the base, while the Zeros flew strafing attacks for over an hour. To the west, the Iba field had suffered a similar fate as 54 bombers, escorted by 53 fighters, attacked barracks, warehouses, and the radar station. Zero pilots pounced on a flight of P-40s of the US 3rd Pursuit Squadron circling to land, and all but two were shot down. These were the first in a series of raids which by December 11 had reduced the number of serviceable American aircraft from 235 to 70. The next day the Japanese put almost 200 aircraft over the Philippines, and on December 19 Admiral Hart despatched the surviving B-17s to Darwin in northern Australia.

The elimination of the American air forces in the northern Philippines, and the scattered disposition of Allied air strength, gave the Japanese an overwhelming tactical advantage which they used to concentrate their air forces to maximum effect at each stage of their advance. On December 8, 1941 the British battleships *Prince of Wales* and *Repulse* sailed from Singapore to strike at Japanese transports supporting the landings in northern Malaya. Before the unit commander, Admiral Phillips, had left London, Air Chief Marshal Harris had told him, 'Tom, don't get out from under your air cover. If you do, you've had it'. Phillips had no air cover; the carrier which had been intended to support his 'Force Z' had scraped its bottom in Jamaica and was unable to move. Moreover, the Japanese capture of Kota Bharu deprived the British ships of a base from which air cover could have been flown from the Malayan mainland. Phillips failed to

A formation of Mitsubishi Ki-21 'Sally', the standard Japanese Army medium bomber at the beginning of the war.

find the Japanese transports, and the fate which Harris had predicted overtook his command at 1107 hrs on December 10 when the two capital ships – racing at 25 knots back to Singapore – were intercepted by G3Ms and G4Ms of 22nd Air Flotilla. At precisely 1113 hrs the high-angle guns of Force Z began firing at the attackers. Under a barrage of bombs and torpedoes *Repulse* sank at 1233 hrs. At 1320 hrs the 11 Buffalo fighters from the mainland, charged with the protection of Force Z in response to a belated distress call from Captain W G Tennant, commander of *Repulse*, arrived to see *Prince of Wales* roll over ponderously to port and sink with Admiral Phillips still on the bridge. The loss of the two ships sealed the fate of Malaya and confirmed Japan's command of the Pacific and Indian Oceans – for the loss of three aircraft. Churchill wrote, 'over all this vast expanse of water Japan was supreme, and we everywhere weak and naked'. On the day after the action a Japanese aircraft dropped a wreath of flowers over the spot where the ships had gone down, to honor the British dead.

The Naval War Intensifies

On February 19, 1942 the carriers *Akagi*, *Kaga*, *Hiryu* and *Soryu* flew off a strike force of 188 aircraft, reinforced by 54 land-based planes, to attack Darwin, the only major port in Australia capable of reinforcing the Allied forces resisting the southern Japanese advance. Opposition over Darwin was negligible. The eight defending fighters which managed to get airborne were summarily despatched, and another 15 destroyed on the ground. Val dive bombers then created havoc in the shipping massed in the harbor, sinking the American destroyer *Peary* and seven transports, one of them an ammunition ship whose cargo of 200 depth charges went up in a colossal explosion.

Nagumo's force then turned on the British navy in the Indian Ocean – sinking the heavy cruisers *Cornwall* and *Dorsetshire* and the light carrier *Hermes*. Then the Japanese focused their attention on the isolation of Australia and the eastward extension of their defensive perimeter in the central Pacific. Early in April they planned to occupy Port Moresby in New Guinea. The Americans were able to lay their plans on the basis of the broken Japanese ciphers, and were ready to stand and fight.

The Coral Sea was the gateway to Port Moresby,

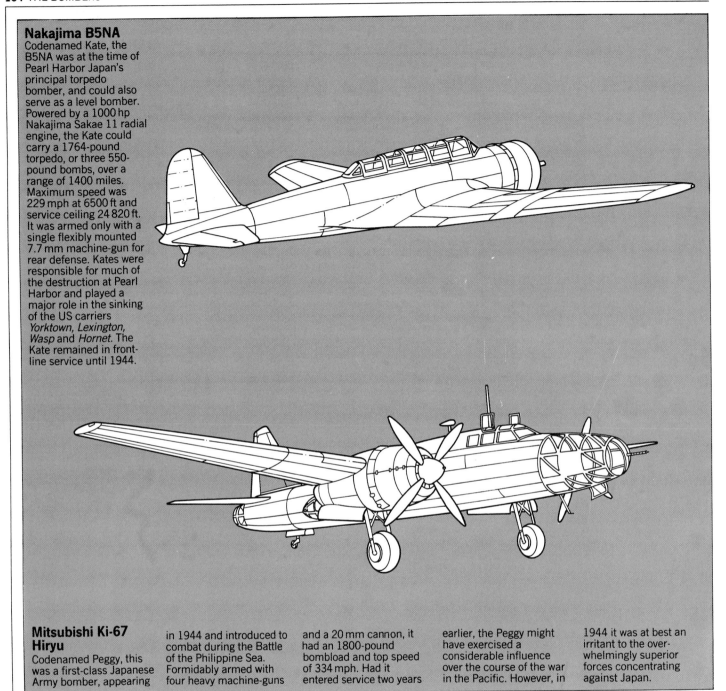

Nakajima B5NA

Codenamed Kate, the B5NA was at the time of Pearl Harbor Japan's principal torpedo bomber, and could also serve as a level bomber. Powered by a 1000 hp Nakajima Sakae 11 radial engine, the Kate could carry a 1764-pound torpedo, or three 550-pound bombs, over a range of 1400 miles. Maximum speed was 229 mph at 6500 ft and service ceiling 24 820 ft. It was armed only with a single flexibly mounted 7.7 mm machine-gun for rear defense. Kates were responsible for much of the destruction at Pearl Harbor and played a major role in the sinking of the US carriers *Yorktown, Lexington, Wasp* and *Hornet*. The Kate remained in front-line service until 1944.

Mitsubishi Ki-67 Hiryu

Codenamed Peggy, this was a first-class Japanese Army bomber, appearing in 1944 and introduced to combat during the Battle of the Philippine Sea. Formidably armed with four heavy machine-guns and a 20 mm cannon, it had an 1800-pound bombload and top speed of 334 mph. Had it entered service two years earlier, the Peggy might have exercised a considerable influence over the course of the war in the Pacific. However, in 1944 it was at best an irritant to the overwhelmingly superior forces concentrating against Japan.

in New Guinea, control of which would isolate Australia. While the Japanese Invasion Group took the transports to Port Moresby, covered by the light carrier *Shoho*, the Carrier Striking Force – commanded by Admiral Takagi and comprising *Shokaku* and *Zuikaku* – was to cruise into the Coral Sea and past the Solomon Islands to block any American attempt to interfere with the invasion.

Admiral Chester Nimitz, C-in-C US Pacific Fleet, ordered a concentration in the Coral Sea of the forces at his disposal: Admiral Fletcher's Task force 17, with the carrier *Yorktown*; Admiral Fitch's Task Force 11, with the carrier *Lexington*; and Admiral

Crace's Task Force 44, with US and Australian cruisers and destroyers.

The standard US naval dive bomber was the Douglas SBD-3 Dauntless. Like the Val, it was an obsolescent but extremely rugged aircraft whose ability to absorb punishment meant that it had the lowest loss rate of any US carrier type. Between 1939 and 1944 nearly 6000 Dauntlesses rolled off the production line. Powered by a 1000 hp engine, the Dauntless had a maximum speed of 250 mph at 16 000 ft, service ceiling of 27 000 ft and combat range of 1345 miles with a single 1000-pound crutch-carried bomb. The offensive load was augmented by the provision of underwing racks for 100-pound bombs. Defensive armament comprised two 0.5 guns in the engine cowlings and two 3 in guns for the observer. Armor protection was provided for the crew, and the Dauntless was fitted with self-sealing rubber-lined fuel tanks. The outer wing panels were designed to accommodate two additional 65-gallon fuel tanks to increase the aircraft's range. The first carrier air group to re-equip with the Dauntless was VB-2 aboard *Lexington*. In May 1941 it had participated in a mock attack on the island of Oahu.

The Dauntless formation adopted by the US Navy was the 18-aircraft squadron, stacked up towards the sun and split into three divisions, each of which flew in two Vics. Cruising altitude was 18 000 ft and the attack sequence was initiated down-sun and up-wind from 15 000 ft. The squadron leader kicked his rudders and peeled off from the top of the stack, followed by the rest of the formation in sequence. To dive, each pilot throttled back, lifting the Dauntless's nose slightly above the horizon into the stall position. Operating a lever to his right, he opened the dive and landing flaps and then pulled the aircraft over on its side to follow his squadron leader down at an angle of 70 degrees and at a braked speed of 275 mph. The crutch gear was released, swinging the bomb down clear of the propeller arc. The dive to a release height of about 1500 to 2500 ft took some 30 seconds, during which the pilot lined up the target in the crosshairs of his sight, and calculated wind direction and drift, maintaining alignment with touches on the ailerons. The bombs were released manually; electrical release equipment was installed later in the war, but most pilots preferred to operate the manual release, just to make certain. As soon as the bombs fell away, the pilot opened the throttle and pulled the stick back. The dive brakes retracted and the Dauntless shot clear of the target, like a pip squeezed from an orange, to reform outside the immediate combat zone. At this stage the crew were experiencing forces up to 6 g.

At Coral Sea Nimitz's aim was to concentrate his forces by May 4. But the Japanese attack began on May 3 with the occupation of Tulagi. On the following day Fletcher launched air strikes on the landings before turning south to join *Lexington*. For the next two days the Japanese and American carrier groups hunted each other without success. On May 7, the Japanese found and attacked Crace's Task Force 44, which had been moved up to harass the Port Moresby Invasion Group, sinking the destroyer *Sims* and the tanker *Neosho*. Then, at 1100 hrs, 53 SBDs from *Lexington* and *Yorktown*, accompanied by torpedo bombers and fighters, found and sank the light carrier *Shoho*. This was the first Japanese carrier to be lost, and her destruction was immortalized by the jubilant signal to *Lexington* from Lieutenant-Commander Bob Dixon: 'Scratch one flattop. Dixon to carrier. Scratch one flattop!'

Takagi's striking force launched an unsuccessful attack which was overtaken by nightfall. The next morning, shortly after 0800 hrs, both sides located each other. *Lexington* and *Yorktown* were dive-bombed by 33 Vals, the latter suffering a direct hit which sliced through four decks and killed 66 of her crew. *Yorktown* remained operational but at 1200 hrs *Lexington* was hit by two torpedoes. Ninety minutes later she was racked by a huge internal explosion and was abandoned at 1710 hrs. At 1950 hrs she was sunk by the destroyer *Phelps*.

The American strike on *Zuikaku* and *Shokaku* included 46 SBDs from VB5, VS5, VB2 and VS2. *Zuikaku* steamed to safety through a tropical squall. The majority of the dive bombers attacked *Shokaku*, hitting her three times. The heavy carrier was badly damaged but stayed afloat; like the *Yorktown*, she lived to fight another day.

The Battle of the Coral Sea had been a confused but crucial engagement. For the first time in history two fleets had fought at a range of over 100 miles without once seeing each other. The Americans had lost a heavy carrier and 81 aircraft; the Japanese had lost a light carrier and 105 aircraft. Tactically the Japanese had gained a victory, but they abandoned the attack on Port Moresby, ceding for the first time the strategic initiative to the Americans.

At Coral Sea the Japanese had been checked. At Midway they were defeated. Convinced that both *Yorktown* and *Lexington* had been sunk at Coral Sea, the Japanese C-in-C Admiral Yamamoto pushed ahead with his plans to capture the island of Midway, which offered a base within striking distance of Hawaii.

The Battle of Midway
The Japanese possessed a potentially decisive advantage in a battle at sea: seven battleships, six heavy and light carriers, 13 cruisers and 50 destroyers were ranged against an American force of three carriers, eight cruisers and 14 destroyers. Air strength, however, was more equal: Nagumo had brought with him only 325 aircraft while Nimitz could assemble an assortment of 350 land-based and carrier-borne machines. The Americans were not in a position to offer battle at sea, but their chances of success had been increased by the faulty dispositions of the principal Japanese units. The victors of Pearl Harbor had not yet been forced to integrate the carrier squadrons with the rest of the fleet.

At 0430 hrs on June 4 Nagumo launched half of his aircraft in a strike on Midway to soften up the island for the Occupation Force landings. He was still unaware of the approach of the US Task Forces 16 (commanded by Admiral Spruance) and 17 (led by Admiral Fletcher). Once again code-breakers had alerted Admiral Nimitz to Japanese intentions. While Nagumo was preparing for a second strike, his carriers came under attack from US bombers based on Midway. They inflicted little damage and were severely mauled by Nagumo's Zeros. At 0820 hrs Nagumo received news of the US carrier forces to the northeast. He immediately changed course and as a result the first American carrier strike failed to find its target. A second attack by Douglas Devastator torpedo bombers was pushed home without fighter escort and at great cost; 35 out of 41 aircraft were lost. However, this apparently suicidal attack had pulled the Japanese fighter cover down to deck level in pursuit of their lumbering prey. At 1030, with Nagumo's decks still cluttered with aircraft refuelling for the second strike, 37 dive bombers from *Enterprise* and *Yorktown* arrived over the Japanese carriers. Thirty-four of the dive bombers concentrated on the *Kaga*; four bombs scored direct hits and started a fatal chain of fires and explosions.

The Dauntless at Midway, June 4, 1942

Lieutenant Paul Holmberg of VB-3 from the US carrier *Yorktown* evades Japanese naval gunfire as he hurtles away from the stricken Japanese carrier *Kaga*. At the moment of pull-out from the dive a Dauntless pilot often had to grasp his neck with his left hand, pressing the arteries to prevent black-out on the recovery while holding the stick back with his right hand. A US carrier air group usually comprised two squadrons of fighters (Grumman F4F Wildcats or later F6F Hellcats), one of torpedo bombers (Douglas TBD Devastators, later Grumman TBF Avengers) and two Dauntless squadrons – one for scouting and one for bombing, respectively designated VS and VB. The scouting role had been envisaged before the US carriers were fitted with radar, which was operational at the beginning of the war. In practice there was little distinction made between the VB and VS squadrons, and scouting pilots underwent the same training and preparation for

dive-bombing missions as their colleagues in the VB squadrons.

Armed with two nose-mounted 0.5 in Brownings for the pilot and a pair of flexible 0.3 in guns for the rear gunner, the Dauntless could carry a 1000-pound bomb or a 500-pound bomb and two 250-pound weapons. It had a top speed of 250 mph at 16000 ft, service ceiling of 27000 ft and range of 1345 miles as a bomber, extended to 1580 miles in its scouting role. Early in the war it frequently doubled as a fighter in defense of US carriers.

Timetable

0616 hrs: Japanese carrier aircraft bomb Midway Island.

0918 hrs, after recovering the Midway strike force, the Japanese fleet alters course towards the reported position of the approaching US carrier force

0930 hrs, the Japanese change of direction caused the first US strike to miss the Japanese. Dive bombers from *Hornet* turn south and torpedo bombers from *Yorktown* and *Enterprise* turn north – both search for the Japanese – while the fighters, running out of fuel, are forced to ditch. Deprived of their escort, the bombers suffer heavy losses from Zeros.

1015 hrs, the torpedo bombers from *Yorktown* and *Enterprise* also find the Japanese, but lacking fighter support, they are massacred without damaging the enemy.

1030 hrs: Dive bombers, from *Enterprise* and *Yorktown* arrive overhead undetected and within five minutes the carriers *Kaga*, *Akagi* and *Soryu* are crippled.

1400 hrs, a force of dive bombers from *Hiryu* locate and damage *Yorktown*. A second strike by torpedo bombers cripple her and she is abandoned.

2123 hrs, *Hiryu* is located and crippled.

The Douglas SBD Dauntless dive bomber, 5936 of which were produced before the end of World War II. Underpowered, lacking range and exhausting to fly for any length of time, the Dauntless nevertheless managed to sink a greater tonnage of Japanese shipping than any other Allied aircraft.

DAUNTLESS 18-AIRCRAFT FORMATION

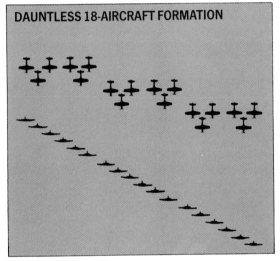

Yorktown's SBDs also made short work of *Soryu*. Their commander on *Yorktown*, Lieutenant-Commander Leslie, was one of the most battle-experienced aviators in the US Navy. His SBD aircraft attacked in three closely concentrated waves from the starboard bow, the starboard quarter and the port quarter, climbing away without a single casualty. Three 1000-pound bombs struck home, the first penetrating the hangar deck, blasting the elevator platform and folding it back against the bridge. The others ploughed into the massed aircraft on *Soryu's* flight deck, engulfing the carrier in flames. In five minutes half of the Japanese carrier fleet had been destroyed. *Akagi* was abandoned and sunk by a Japanese destroyer the following morning. *Kaga* was abandoned at 1640 hrs and three hours later sank after two internal explosions had ripped her apart. *Soryu*, had gone to the bottom 10 minutes earlier, taking with her 718 of her crew.

While Nagumo's carriers were entering their death throes, *Yorktown* came under attack from 18 dive bombers and six fighters from *Hiryu*. Six of the Vals survived Wildcat interceptions and ferocious anti-aircraft fire to scream down on *Yorktown*. One Val disintegrated over the carrier, its bomb exploding on the flight deck, starting a huge fire below. A second bomb tore into the smokestack and exploded inside, igniting more fires. With three boiler uptakes smashed and the furnaces of six boilers extinguished, *Yorktown* was stopped in the water. A third bomb had sliced through three of her decks, causing fires which threatened the carrier's fuel tanks and magazines. Admiral Fletcher transferred his flag to the cruiser *Astoria* and ordered *Portland* to take the carrier in tow. Before the towline had been passed, frantic damage control work had got *Yorktown* under way again. But almost immediately her radar picked up incoming enemy aircraft. This was the second wave from *Hiryu*, ten Kate torpedo bombers and six Zero escorts. They flew into an inferno of bursting shells while the cruisers around *Yorktown* raised a barrage of splashes with their main armament through which it seemed impossible that the sea-skimming Kates could fly. Five were shot down but the survivors, approaching from four different angles, dropped their torpedoes at the pointblank range of 500 yds. Two struck *Yorktown* on her port side, ripping open the double-bottom fuel tanks. Water poured in, and the carrier was soon listing at 26 degrees. At 1500 hrs Captain Buckmaster gave the orders to abandon ship. On June 7, while under tow, she sank after being torpedoed by a Japanese submarine.

Hiryu's moment of triumph was shortlived. She was located by 24 dive bombers from *Enterprise*, among them 10 transferred from *Yorktown*, and 16 from *Hornet*. They scored four hits for the loss of three aircraft. Like her sister ships, *Hiryu* underwent a prolonged death agony as uncontrollable fires took hold. At 0230 hrs on the following morning she was abandoned and sunk by her attendant destroyers. This brought the main actions of Midway to an end, and Spruance prudently withdrew. The initiative, both at sea and in the air, had passed from the Japanese to the Americans.

At the beginning of the war Admiral Yamamoto, the architect of the triumph at Pearl Harbor, warned that he could only guarantee six months of victory. After Midway the tide of war began to flow back against Japan. Even before the battle the balance of carrier forces had begun to swing towards the Americans. In 1942 the number of aircraft planned for production for the US Navy exceeded total Japanese production for all purposes in the same year. Japan had won its first, stunning victories against a nation still at peace. But as the British Foreign Secretary Sir Edward Grey had observed in the days before World War I, the US economy was like 'a gigantic boiler. Once the fire is lighted under it, there is no limit to the power it can generate'. Only 15 per cent of the total US war effort was devoted to the Pacific, but once it had hit its stride the Japanese were always going to be outgunned and outpunched in the critical encounters. From mid-1942 the Japanese air forces fought an increasingly uphill battle against an implacable juggernaut equipped with more powerful, and more heavily armed aircraft – among them the Curtiss SB2C Helldiver, the Chance-Vought FU Corsair (a fighter which was adapted to carry twice the offensive load of a Dauntless in the dive bombing role), and the B-29 Superfortress.

Like the Luftwaffe, the Japanese air forces were ground up in the mincing machine of attrition. By January 1943 American front-line air strength in the Pacific had overtaken that of Japan. A year later it had reached a total of 11 442 aircraft against a Japanese figure of 4050. The campaigns of 1943 relentlessly chewed up the Japanese bomber arm. In the final attempt to relieve New Guinea in June 1943 a force of 120 medium bombers and fighter escorts

were met by an equal force of American fighters. Over 100 of the Japanese aircraft were destroyed at the cost of six of the American force. In November 1943 Admiral Koga lost 75 per cent of the Vals he despatched against the American landings on Bougainville in the Solomons. Significantly in August, during the New Georgia campaign, heavy close-support attacks by Marine Air Corps SBDs played an important part in breaking Japanese resistance.

The War of Attrition

The loss of aircraft was compounded by the wholesale destruction of Japan's élite aircrew cadres. Thus even when potent new types were brought into service there were insufficient experienced crews to make their presence felt. After 1942 every advance in Japanese warplane design was accompanied by a corresponding decline in the ability of Japanese air power to influence the course of events. By mid-1944 the paradox had become acute. All 15 aircraft carriers brought into service since 1941 had been sunk or irreparably damaged, while of 27 fleet carriers added to the US Navy only one had been sunk. Japanese air plans, intended to cover the period January 1944-August 1945, set out a requirement of 97 000 aircraft, of which 40 000 were produced. By 1945 the overall proportion of fighters was 49 per cent, compared with 17 per cent for bombers, an indication of Japan's defensive posture. The task of regaining the initiative with increased bomber production was beyond the Japanese war economy. A measure of Japan's desperate straits is the fact that the ratio of engines to airframes fell from the 1941 level of 2.3:1 to 1:1 in 1945, condemning all its aircraft to a severely reduced service life. By a tremendous effort Japan produced 28 000 aircraft in 1944. This

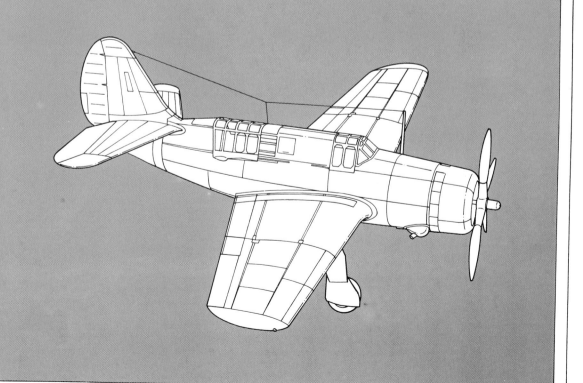

Curtiss SB2C Helldiver

A powerful two-seat dive bomber which carried a 1000-pound bomb internally and was armed with four wing-mounted 0.5 in Brownings and two 0.3 in Brownings on flexible mountings in the rear cockpit. Powered by a 1700 hp Wright radial, the Helldiver had a top speed of 281 mph at 12 400 ft, service ceiling of 24 700 ft and range of 1110 miles. The most numerous Allied dive bomber of World War II, the Helldiver made its debut with VB-17 over Rabaul on November 11, 1943. However, it was never popular with aircrews (who dubbed it 'Son of a Bitch, 2nd Class') principally because of its poor handling and instability.

represented about eight per cent of total US production. Thus the original Japanese strategy was turned inside out. Declining intelligence, the impossibility of concentrating scattered forces, and a policy of defending every outer area to the last man, accelerated the process of collapse.

In mid-1944 the Japanese Army and Navy air forces took delivery of an impressive new bomber, the twin-engined Mitsubishi Ki-67 Type 4 Hiryu (Peggy), which compared well with Allied medium bomber types like the B-26 Marauder. But it could be thrown into operations only in the hands of inexperienced crews fresh out of training school and flying in almost suicidal conditions. In similar fashion, the elegant Yokosuka D4Y Type 2 Suisei (Judy) dive bomber arrived too late to turn the tide, but just in time to be shot down in great numbers during the battle of the Philippine Sea in June 1944. Developed as a replacement for the Val, the D4Y was an exceptionally fast and clean midwing monoplane powered by a 1011 hp engine which gave it a top speed of 343 mph at 15 585 ft, nearly matching that of contemporary fighters. Its two-man crew were defended by two 7.7 mm fixed forward-firing guns and a single flexible 7.92 mm gun operated by the observer. The D4Y carried two 550 pound or one 1102-pound bomb over a range of 978 miles. Range, however, was a less crucial requirement in 1944 as the perimeters of the Greater East Asia Co-Prosperity Sphere began to shrink towards the home islands.

In the Battles of the Philippine Sea and Leyte Gulf, the reformed Japanese carrier fleets were utterly broken on the anvil of American air power. In the fighting between June and August 1944 the Japanese lost over 750 aircraft, one third of them shot down on June 19 in what became known as the 'Great Marianas Turkey Shoot'. Japan emerged from the Battle of the Philippine Sea with most of its carrier fleet intact but with its air arm irretrievably mauled. At Leyte Gulf, in October 1944, four carriers were sent to the bottom. One small incident provides an illustration of Japanese impotence. On October 15, 13 Judys, led by Rear-Admiral Masafumi Arima, took off from Nicholls Field in the Philippines to attack the huge US Task Force approaching Leyte. They were intercepted and massacred by Hellcat Combat Air Patrols before they reached the ships. Arima penetrated the defensive screen, diving on the carrier *Franklin* in a suicide attack. Fierce anti-aircraft fire from the carrier and her escorts caught Arima in a cone of fire which deflected the Judy off course. The dive bomber crashed into the sea alongside the carrier, one of its wings landing on the flight deck.

New types were still trickling into service, notably the Aichi B7A Ryusei (Grace) dive bomber, powered by a 1670 hp engine which gave it a maximum speed of 352 mph. But there were no carriers left to accommodate them. From October 1944 the recurring theme of the Japanese air effort was the *Kamikaze* suicide attack. One of the grimmest developments in this rush to self-immolation was the Yokosuka MXY-7 Ohka (Cherry Blossom) piloted suicide bomb. Carried to within 50 miles of its target by a conventional bomber motherplane – usually a G4M2 Betty – the Ohka was then released and flown by its pilot seated in a cramped cockpit between the stubby 16.5 ft wing and the twin-finned tail. Covering most of the distance to the target in a fast glide, the device was extremely difficult to intercept, even though it was incapable of evasive maneuver. Three miles from the target the pilot ignited three solid-fuel rockets in the tail, arriving in a steep dive at speeds approaching 650 mph. The front of the fuselage was a massive warhead containing 2645 pounds of tri-nitrol aminol. Once it had begun the attack dive, the Ohka was virtually unstoppable. US fighters preferred to concentrate on destroying the motherplanes before the missiles were launched. As the war drew to an end, *Kamikaze* missions were usually flown by conventional aircraft packed with explosive.

The largest single *Kamikaze* was the 78 000-ton battleship *Yamato*, which on April 6, 1945 sailed from the Inland Sea to attack the US landings on Okinawa. She carried only sufficient fuel for a one-way trip, and the plan was to run her aground on Okinawa to bombard US positions. On April 7 *Yamato* and her screening destroyer were located and attacked by waves of aircraft from the US carrier fleet. Nearly 400 sorties were flown and the *Yamato* was repeatedly hit by bombs and torpedoes. At the cost of only ten US aircraft the largest battleship ever built was sent to the bottom. The Japanese fleet never ventured from its bases again.

The US Strategic Bomber in the Pacific

In December 1941 the USAAF had only 150 B-17s on its strength, of which one-third were the combat-worthy B-17Es. Based in Hawaii were 12 B-17Cs and Ds of 5th Bombardment Group. In the Philippines 7th and 19th BGs mustered between them a total of 35 Fortresses, none of them B-17Es.

This token force was rapidly dissipated in the opening phase of the war. Five B-17s were lost at Pearl Harbor and 14 destroyed on the ground in the first Japanese strike on the Philippines. On December 10, 1941 six B-17s of 14th Squadron, 19th BG, flew the first American bombing raid of the war, attacking the Japanese invasion fleet supporting the landings at Aparri on the north coast of Luzon. Their intervention had no effect, although the B-17C piloted by Lieutenant Colin Kelly Jr was incorrectly credited with the sinking of the battleship *Haruna*. Kelly's B-17 was intercepted by Zeros which had been patrolling near Vigan, and as he approached Clark Field it was burning fiercely. While Kelly held the aircraft steady the crew baled out. Then it blew up before he could follow them. The gallant Kelly was awarded a posthumous DSO. A second B-17 raid on the Aparri landings was engaged by Japanese Army Ki-27s of the 50th Sentai, which inflicted severe damage on one of the Fortresses.

The air fighting over the Aparri landings marked the first Japanese combats with the Fortress. They presented their fighter pilots with problems which were to become familiar during the B-17's combat life in the Pacific. Although it was obsolescent, the B-17C was still a tough proposition for a Zero pilot. It flew at over 20 000 ft, an altitude at which the Zero's performance fell away sharply, and at a speed which forced Japanese pilots to use full throttle to catch it. Its size also proved troublesome. Like the RFC night-

Martin B-26B Marauder

A medium bomber of exceptionally clean lines, the B-26B saw extensive service in the Southwest Pacific with the rear bomb bay used as a fuel tank. Because of its high accident rate, Martin extended the wing and vertical tail from the 641st B model. On May 4, 1943 the Marauder began a distinguished career as the principal medium bomber of the 9th Air Force in Europe. By May 1945 the B-26 could claim the lowest loss rate of any US bomber in European operations. Powered by two 2000 hp Pratt and Whitney R-2800-39 engines, the B-26B had a maximum speed of 282 mph; carrying 3000 pounds of bombs it had a range of 1150 miles. Defensive armament was provided by one manually aimed 0.5 machine-gun in the nose, a twin 0.5 dorsal turret, two manually aimed 0.5 waist guns, one 'tunnel gun' (usually 0.5), four 0.5 'package guns' on both sides of the forward fuselage, and a twin 0.5 tail turret.

fighter aircrew encountering the R-types in 1918, the Zero pilots found it hard to judge their firing distance, while the B-17's speed caused their range finders to misread. Their small-caliber guns made it extremely difficult to down shoot a B-17, while the Zero's lack of armor and self-sealing fuel tanks made it vulnerable to the Fortress's 0.5 gunfire. However, the early B-17s were themselves vulnerable to a close-range tail attack, where the absence of a turret enabled a pilot to stay right behind the bomber, shielded by the B-17's huge tail fin. New tactics had to be developed to deal with the B-17E, whose tail turret presented a more formidable defense. Zero pilots turned to head-on attacks, aiming for the pilots or engines. These in turn, were negated by evasive maneuvers which brought the B-17s heavy machine-guns to bear. The most effective tactic proved to be a rolling dive from above, repeated until the bomber went down.

The B-17 Leaves the Fray

On December 19, 1941 the surviving B-17s were withdrawn to Australia, where only ten were judged fit to resume combat duties. They were immediately assigned to Java, being the only Allied aircraft capable of offering resistance to the Japanese invasion of the Dutch East Indies. At the same time reinforcements in the form of 43rd BG began to arrive in the Pacific, flying via the Caribbean, Africa, and India. By March 1942, when the Dutch East Indies capitulated, 49 B-17s had seen action in Java. Thirty of them had been lost; of this figure 19 had been destroyed on the ground and six shot down by Japanese fighters. Overall loss figures in the Pacific were 52 out of 80 aircraft, with a further six written in accidents in Australia. There was little to show for it. Postwar analysis established that, in the 350 missions flown in the opening months of the war, only two Japanese ships had been sunk by the Fortresses.

The B-17, designed as an offensive strategic weapon, had been pressed into service as a defensive tactical bomber. Reinforcements arrived piecemeal from the United States, often flown straight from the factory and requiring a degree of servicing which it was impossible to sustain at this stage in the war. Crews lacked combat experience, and several months passed before 43rd BG became an effective fighting unit. By then the B-17s had been further dispersed, with 7th BG redeployed to India and 19th BG reconcentrated in Australia. This reorganization coincided with the highwater mark of the Japanese advance in the Pacific, which was followed by the check at Coral Sea and the decisive encounter at Midway. B-17s flew at Midway but exercised no influence over the battle. They played a more significant part in the battle for Guadalcanal, by which time the USAAF deployed four B-17 Groups in the Pacific as part of 13th Air Force. In September 1942 B-17 strength in the Pacific reached a peak of 155 aircraft, a relatively small number which nevertheless imposed a tremendous strain on shipping resources. Many B-17s were forced into a transport role in order to keep their sisters in service.

This build-up was almost immediately followed by the decision to phase out the B-17 from the Pacific war. The B-24, with its longer range, was considered more effective over the vast area of the Pacific, and in October 1942 a major re-equipment began. The last B-17 missions in the Pacific were flown by 5th and 11th BGs in September 1943. Two months later, with the exception of the transport commands, only one B-17 remained in service in the entire theater. The aircraft had achieved only a limited degree of success, arriving at a time of defeat and disorganization and living a hand-to-mouth existence on rudimentary groundstrips where effective ground maintenance was next to impossible. As ever, weather was a crucial factor, and the alternating heat and rain, bringing choking dust and glutinous mud in turn, made servicing a nightmare. Once airborne, the B-17s often ran into cloud and violent tropical storms stretching across the horizon and over which they were unable to climb. In seven months of operations, 11th BG lost six Fortresses to enemy action and 12 to the weather. These factors forced the B-17 groups to fly into action in penny packets. An entire Group attack might consist of only five aircraft. Against shipping these small numbers could achieve little. Even when attacking in formation – an Inverted Vee – in order to pattern the bombs in a straddle, the chances of hitting a ship were extremely slim. Frequently operating at the extreme limit of their range, with correspondingly reduced bombloads, the B-17s were perhaps fortunate not to suffer heavier losses. Had the Japanese possessed early-warning radar, this would almost certainly have been the case.

The role played by the B-24 in the Pacific from 1943 was also primarily tactical. The overwhelming majority of its missions were directed against enemy airfields, ports, supply depots and communications as part of combined land-sea-air operations. Other targets for the Liberator were provided by Japanese bases bypassed in the island-hopping campaigns. Operating conditions were very different from those in Europe. Attacks went in at 6000 ft for precision bombing of targets, with the exception of those heavily defended by flak. The Liberator also operated by night and at low level against shipping, locating its targets by radar. At peak unit strength there were 11½ B-24 Bombardment Groups in the Pacific, divided among the seven theater air forces whose combined area of operations totalled 16 million square miles.

Four Groups were assigned to 5th Air Force, flying in the campaigns in New Guinea, the Philippines and the Ryukyus. There were two Groups with 13th Air Force, which began operations in the New Hebrides island group – 1000 miles east of Australia – and leapfrogged through the Solomons to join 5th Air Force in New Guinea and the Philippines. The 7th Air Force operated three Groups in the central Pacific, moving eastward through the island chains towards Japan. Both 10th Air Force (in India) and 14th Air Force (in China) were assigned a single Group, and two squadrons flew with 11th Air Force in the Aleutians. The 10th Air Force was particularly active on the Burma front, and in the winter of 1942 7th BG raided Bangkok in a mission which involved a round trip of 1850 miles.

Strategic operations were on a small scale compared with those in Europe. In August 1943 380th BG, 5th Air Force, flew three missions from Darwin to attack oil refineries at Balikpapan, Borneo, by night. The B-24s made this round trip of

A B-24 of US Army 14th Air Force in action over the railroad repair works at Vinh in French Indo-China.

2000 miles with only a 2500-pound bombload and were in the air for nearly 17 hours. Twelve months passed before Balikpapan was attacked again, when September 30 saw the first of five strikes launched by stripped down B-24Js of 5th and 13th Air Forces, once again carrying 2500-pound bombloads. P-38 support was provided on the last three missions, the fighters flying from Morotai, 850 miles from the target. In the five raids 321 B-24s dropped 433 tons of bombs at a cost of 22 aircraft.

The B-29

On April 18, 1942 16 B-25B Mitchell bombers, led by Lieutenant-Colonel James Doolittle, took off from the aircraft carrier *Hornet* to attack targets 800 miles away in Tokyo. To save weight, broomhandles replaced the guns normally fitted in the Mitchell's rear turrets. The raid caused little damage, and all the aircraft were lost while attempting to find safety in China. Most of the crews survived, although the Chinese suffered terribly when the Japanese launched an offensive to capture all territory within flying range of their home islands.

A month later the Battle of the Coral Sea provided a complete vindication of Billy Mitchell's efforts, almost 20 years earlier, to demonstrate the influence which air power could have on the conduct of operations at sea. However, the extent of the Japanese conquests in the first six months of the war had pushed the Allied forces back beyond the range at which it was possible for bombers to carry out strategic raids on the Japanese home islands. Two years were to pass before a full-scale air offensive could be launched against Japan.

On September 21, 1942 the prototype of a new American heavy bomber flew for the first time when XB-29 Number One took off on a 75-minute flight at Seattle. The origins of the B-29 can be found in a request, made in 1939 by Major-General Henry Arnold, for authority to contract major aircraft companies to produce studies of a Very Long Range (VLR) bomber capable of waging war well beyond the shores of the United States. Approval was granted at the end of the year and the AAC engineering officers began to draw up the official specification, XC-218. It called for an aircraft with a range of 5333 miles and a bigger bombload and speed than the B-17.

The Boeing Company had already developed a full-scale mock-up of their Model 341 which, with its projected wingloading of 64 pounds per sq ft, 12-man crew and range in excess of 5000 miles with a 2000-pound bombload, anticipated the requirements of XC-218. Using Model 341 as a basis, Boeing submitted a proposal for a four-engined aircraft of advanced design, incorporating pressurized accommodation for the crew, tricycle undercarriage, and cruising speed of 290 mph with one ton of bombs over the stipulated 5333 miles. Defensive armament was to be provided by four retractable turrets, each mounting 0.5 machine-guns, and a tail turret fitted with twin 0.5 machine-guns and a 20 mm cannon. The wingspan was to be 114 ft 2in, length 98 ft and weight 97 700 pounds.

Designated XB-29, the new bomber appeared in full-scale mock-up form in November 1940, by which time Boeing had already secured a contract for two

B-25Bs on the flight deck of the carrier *Hornet* prepare to take off for the 'Doolittle' raid on Tokyo on April 18, 1942.

prototypes. The aircraft's subsequent progress was marked by the struggle to overcome the considerable technical problems posed by its bold design. The B-29's colossal wingloading required a wing area of 1736 sq ft. In turn this threatened an impossibly high landing speed. The problem was overcome by the installation of immense flaps, covering 322 sq ft or approximately one-sixth of the wing area. The long thin wings were reinforced by specially developed trusses, constructed in a web-like pattern out of flat pieces of sheet metal. The clean, cigar-like contours of the fuselage were enhanced by countersunk rivet heads which lay flush with the aluminum alloy skin surfaces.

Pressurization – to enable the crew to operate at great heights – presented further difficulties. The B-29 was not the first operational bomber with a pressurized cabin. This honor went to the German Ju86R, a few of which carried out attacks on southern England from altitudes of over 40 000 ft during the summer of 1942. The Ju86R's two-man crew were housed in a cramped cabin which, at altitudes of over 40 000 ft, had a pressure differential of about 8 pounds per square inch (psi) above the outside air. This enabled them to breathe normally without oxygen masks. If the Ju86R came under attack at lower altitudes, the cabin had to be depressurized to avoid a fatal explosion if it was holed by enemy fire. Two years later the Mosquito MkXVI entered service with a more rudimentary pressurized cabin, providing a pressure differential of 2 psi. This obliged the crew to retain their oxygen masks but, combined with a Maxwell blower which permitted full exploitation of the aircraft's Merlin 72 engines, gave the Mosquito an operational ceiling of 35 000 ft.

Pressurization of the much larger crew areas in the B-29 was complicated by the basic need to open the bomb bay doors during high-altitude flight. The Boeing designers' solution was the provision of three pressurized areas – in the nose, center fuselage and the tail. The nose and mid-fuselage areas (the latter housing the gunners amidships) were connected by a tunnel 34 in in diameter, through which a man could crawl. The third compartment, housing the tail gunner, was unconnected with the forward pressurized areas. At 30 000 ft the 6.5 psi pressure held the cabin to the equivalent of 8000 ft, relieving the crew of the necessity of wearing oxygen masks by day and reducing the fatigue which inevitably accompanied long flights. At night masks had to be worn when the cabin altitude exceeded 4000 ft, in order to retain night vision.

The B-29's armament also broke new ground. Towards the end of 1941 the General Electric Company produced a small computer capable of automatically correcting range, altitude, air speed and temperature. This was the basis of a central control mechanism enabling any gunner (with the exception of the tail gunner) to fire more than one of the B-29's 0.5 guns at a time. The German Me210 fighter bomber of mid-1942 was armed with an FDL 131 barbette on either side of its fuselage, each firing a single 13 mm MG131 machine-gun; the same system was also fitted to the more successful Me410. However, the B-29 unquestionably represented the most sophisticated application of the barbette concept during World War II. There were five gun mountings: four 0.5 in guns above the forward fuselage; two 0.5 guns above the rear fuselage; two 0.5 guns below the forward fuselage; two 0.5 guns beneath the rear fuselage; and two 0.5 guns and a 20 mm cannon on a common power-driven mounting in the tail. The five sighting stations were located in the extreme nose, above the rear fuselage, on either side of the rear fuselage and in the tail. The installation of the system to the prototype increased the weight of the B-29 to 105 000 pounds and led to the removal of such crew comforts as auxiliary bunks and sound proofing.

In May 1941, four months before it's maiden flight, an order was placed for 250 B-29s. Immediately after the attack on Pearl Harbor this was increased to 500. Thereafter the aircraft's progress into service was dogged by persistent problems with the new Wright R-3350 engines. On February 18, 1943 a double engine failure in the second prototype resulted in a crash which killed the entire test crew. In the next 18 months at least 19 B-29s suffered a similar fate. The complicated business of training the 11-man crew also slowed the pace at which the B-29 moved towards combat readiness. Training was placed in the hands of XX Bomber Command, established in November 1943, which would also be responsible for the B-29's initial strategic deployment. The Command comprised two Bombardment Wings, 58th and 73rd, each made up of four groups. At the outset XX Command was based at four airfields in Kansas, with headquarters conveniently close to the B-29 plant at Wichita. It took up to 27 weeks to produce a pilot, 15 to complete the navigator's training and 12 to turn out a gunner. These preliminaries had to be completed before they were brought together as a complete crew to train on the B-29 itself. To accelerate the process, volunteer B-24 crews, recently returned from Europe and North Africa, were added to the program. Understandably they experienced considerable difficulty in converting to the bigger, more sophisticated aircraft. Further delay was caused by the decision to train two crews for each B-29, a measure adopted to offset the very long ranges over which it was expected the bomber would fly when its combat life began. By December 1943 only 67 pilots had flown a B-29 and a handful of crews been assembled as complete teams.

B-29 Operations

The first specific reference to the B-29 in US wartime strategic planning is to be found in General Arnold's 'Air Plan for the Defeat of Japan', which was discussed at the Quadrant Conference held at Quebec in August 1943. Up to that point various possibilities for its deployment had been canvassed, including the stationing of 12 groups in Northern Ireland and 12 more in Egypt. Arnold's Air Plan proposed the deployment of 58th Bombardment Wing to the China-Burma-India theater (CBI) by the end of 1943. The B-29s were to operate from Chengtu, in south-central China, supplied by airlifts from India flown over the 'Hump' of the Himalayas. The forward base at Chengtu still necessitated long flights over Japanese-occupied territory to attack the enemy's home islands, and even then only brought

the southern island of Kyushu within range of the B-29. Nevertheless, this coincided with Roosevelt's desire to provide air support for Chiang Kai Shek, which had previously been frustrated by the shorter ranges of the B-17 and the Liberator and the calls made on aircraft supply by the strategic precedence taken by the plans for the invasion of northern Europe.

Arnold aimed to concentrate 150 B-29s in the CBI theater by mid-April 1944, rising to 800 by the autumn when full-scale operations could begin. Once they were under way he forecast that Japan would be brought to the point of surrender by mid-1945, without the need for a seaborne invasion. Arnold's optimism belied the continuing teething troubles of the B-29, not least with the engines but also affecting the GEC remotely controlled fire system and the AN/APQ-13 bombing-navigation aid, derived from Bomber Command's H2S and installed in a retractable radome between the B-29's two bomb bays. Arnold's personal intervention galvanized the flagging modification program, and by April 15, 1944 150 B-29s had been handed over to XX Bomber Command.

At this stage in the war the B-29 stood in a class of its own. Its uniqueness lay in its size rather than any revolutionary approach to design. Its wingspan exceeded that of the B-17 by almost 40 ft, and its maximum take-off weight of 135 000 pounds was three times greater than that of the B-17A of 1939. The B-29 was twice as heavy as the Lancaster or the He177. Over shorter ranges and at low altitude, it would prove capable of carrying an offensive load of 22 000 pound, the equivalent of a fully loaded Ju88A-1. Cruising at 200–250 mph at 30 000 ft, the B-29 could carry a 5000 pound bombload over a 1600-mile radius.

By the end of the first week in May 1944 130 B-29s had reached their airfields in India, staging through Marrakesh, Cairo, Karachi and Calcutta. In India XX Bomber Command headquarters were established at Kharagpur airfield west of Calcutta. This field also provided a base for 468th BG, while 40th, 444th and 462nd BGs were respectively assigned to the fields at Chakulia, Charra (later Dudhkundi), and Piardoba. The airfields had been prepared in 1942–43 as bases for B-24s, and their runways had not yet been extended to the 7200 ft which would enable the B-29s to take off fully loaded. Progress had also been slow at the five forward bases around Chengtu, where tens of thousands of Chinese peasants made up the work force. The fuel, bombs and spares required to

Boeing B-29 Superfortress

The B-29 represented the supreme application of 'state of the art' aviation technology of the mid-1940s.

Below: The defensive options available with the B-29's GEC barbettes and sighting positions. All the guns were fitted with interrupter gear to prevent them blasting away great chunks of the aircraft.

3 The rear upper gunner co-ordinated the fire of all the other gunners and exercised sole control of the rear upper barbette (C) and secondary control of the forward upper barbette (E).

The tail gunner **1** controlled only his own guns (A).

2 The waist gunners had primary control over the aft lower barbette (B) and secondary control over the lower forward barbette (D) and the tail guns (A).

4 The bombardier in the nose had primary control of the two forward barbettes (D and E). A gunner in control of more than one barbette could use them simultaneously to engage an attacking fighter.

Far Left: Bombing up a B-29.
Left: Maintenance on a B-29's lower barbette.

keep XX Bomber Command flying had to be ferried into Chengtu from eastern India by B-24 transports and stripped B-29s fitted with extra fuel tanks. The transportation of fuel posed special problems. In good weather conditions the B-29s burned two gallons of fuel for every gallon they delivered to Chengtu. When faced with headwinds or if diverted to avoid bad weather over the Himalayas, the ratio would leap to 12 gallons burned for every one delivered. The 1000-mile leg over the Hump was considered so hazardous that each time it was flown, it counted as a combat mission and a camel was painted on the B-29's nose.

By May 1 only 1400 tons of supplies had been delivered to Chengtu. The commencement of operations was further postponed by the Japanese 'Ichi Go' offensive launched in central China on April 19. Among its objectives were the 14th USAAF bases in the Kweilun and Liuchow areas, which they feared would be used for B-29 operations. Although these eastern bases had originally been earmarked for use by the heavy bombers, they had finally been ruled out precisely because of the vulnerability underlined by the 'Ichi Go' offensive. As the Japanese advance continued, General Joseph W 'Vinegar Joe' Stilwell, Chiang Kai Shek's Chief of Staff, withdrew the Transport Command contingent from Chengtu supply operations.

The Assault Begins
General Wolfe, C-in-C XX Command, was now under increasing pressure to begin operations. This was heightened by the autonomy which Arnold had secured for the Command, which was now the spearhead of the newly formed special strategic force, 20th Air Force. Commanded by Arnold at Joint Chiefs of Staff level, it had been given a wide-ranging brief to undertake 'the earliest possible progressive destruction and dislocation of the Japanese military, industrial and economic systems and to undermine the morale of the Japanese people to the point where their capacity for war is decisively defeated'. Complete control of the B-29s was to be retained by Arnold, even when assigning the aircraft to local commanders for tactical use in an emergency. However, like RAF Bomber Command, 20th Air Force needed to demonstrate its strategic capability in order to secure its continued survival as an independent force.

On June 5, 1944, 98 B-29s took off from their airfields in eastern India to attack the Makasan rail yards in Bangkok, in Thailand, a 2000-mile round trip. Engine failure caused 14 aborts and added to the problems of maintaining the four-aircraft diamond formations. Bombing through heavy overcast at heights varying between 17 000 and 27 000 ft, the B-29s placed only 18 bombs in the target area. Five aircraft crashed on landing and 42 more put down on a variety of airfields as their fuel ran out.

Nine days later, on the night of June 14, Wolfe launched the first raid on Japan when 68 B-29s took off to attack the Imperial Iron and Steel Works at Yawata, on the island of Kyushu. Forty-seven aircraft arrived over the target but could deliver only one bomb within three-quarters of a mile of the Aiming Point. Six B-29s were lost in accidents and one fell to enemy fire. After the Yawata raid fuel stocks at Chengtu stood at less than 5000 gallons. It took nearly 9000 gallons to despatch a single B-29 against Japan.

On July 4 Wolfe was recalled to Washington and reassigned. During the next two months the campaign lurched forward in desultory fashion, by day and night, against industrial targets in Kyushu, the steel complex at Anshan in Manchuria and, staging through bases on Ceylon, oil storage facilities at Palembang in Borneo. The situation changed dramatically with the arrival of Wolfe's replacement, the hard-driving, uncompromising Curtis LeMay, who had contributed so much to the bombing tactics and formation features evolved in Europe by 8th Air Force. LeMay's sure grasp of operational techniques was soon at work, and the diamond formation was replaced by a 12-aircraft box modeled on the formations employed by the B-17s in Europe. Night operations were abandoned and the emphasis placed firmly on daylight precision bombing led by experienced crews with the responsibility for finding and marking the target area. LeMay also decided that in future both the bombardier and the radar operator should control the bombing run, so that whoever had sight of the target at the critical moment could release the bombs. This was principally intended to avoid confusion in the hazy or cloudy conditions which were frequently encountered in the Far East. At the same time 58th Bombardment Wing was reorganized, the four groups emerging with three squadrons of ten B-29s each, a measure which it was hoped would simplify administration and control.

By early autumn results were improving. On October 25 considerable damage was inflicted on the Omura aircraft factory at Kyushu with a 2:1 mixture of HE and incendiaries. However, when the B-29s returned on November 21 they met stiffening resistance from fighters and light bombers, which dropped phosphorus bombs on the American formations. Six of the B-29s failed to return, a loss figure repeated on December 7 in a raid on the Manchurian Aircraft Company plant at Mukden. Continuing problems of supply and a high accident rate stood in the way of the concentration which strategic bombing requires. Additional losses were caused by Japanese air raids on the Chengtu base. When these were added to aircraft destroyed in landing accidents and combat by the end of 1944, the figure was 147. Thus, in the space of seven months 20th Air Force had lost the equivalent of its entire front-line strength in May.

At the end of the year the decision was taken to wind up operations at Chengtu. The last raid mounted from the forward bases – a tactical mission against targets in Formosa to divert attention from the landings at Luzon – was flown on January 15. Before re-deployment to the new bases in the Marianas, 58th Bombardment Wing flew a number of missions from India, the last of which was a raid on March 29 against oil storage facilities in Singapore. At enormous cost, 20th Air Force had flown 49 missions, involving 3058 aircraft sorties, dropping 11 477 tons of bombs. In the four raids on Hamburg between July 24 and August 2 1943, RAF Bomber Command had flown 3091 sorties and dropped 8344 tons of bombs. There was some way to go before the B-29 assumed a strategic bombing role in the Pacific.

The Destruction of Japan

The date of the first B-29 raid on Japan – June 15, 1944 – has a double significance. This was also the day which marked the beginning of operations to take the island of Saipan in the Marianas chain. Its capture, together with Guam and Tinian, gave the B-29 a springboard 1500 miles southeast of Tokyo, lying just within the aircraft's range. Virtually immune from large-scale Japanese counter-attack and on a direct supply route from the United States, these islands provided the bases for the resumption of the campaign against the Japanese home islands. On Saipan, construction work on a former Japanese fighter airstrip began while the fighting was still raging. Saipan was cleared by July 9 and a month later US control was established over Guam and Tinian. On October 12 the first B-29 of 73rd Bombardment Wing touched down on Isley Field, Saipan. It was piloted by Major-General Haywood S Hansell Jr, commander of XXI Bomber Command, established specifically for operations from the Marianas.

Much remained to be done. Two 9000 ft paved runways had been planned for Isley Field, but when Hansell arrived only one had been paved to 6000 ft, and there were no hardstandings or buildings. Nevertheless, by November 22 over 100 aircraft had flown to Saipan directly from their training bases. Target priority had been switched from steel to one offering more immediate results, the Japanese aircraft industry. This was to be accomplished by high-level daylight precision bombing, the goal still fervently sought by the United States' senior air commanders. However, the problems encountered on a series of 'shakedown' raids at the end of October forced Hansell to the conclusion that 73rd BW's crews were too inexperienced for this method of attack. The bulk of the Wing's training had focussed on blind bombing with the use of radar, which allowed crews a certain latitude in choosing attack altitudes and bombing runs. Through no fault of their own, the crews lacked the expertise for high-level formation flying. Poor results obtained in raids on targets in Truk were aggravated by the recurrence of engine problems and Japanese air strikes on the Saipan field launched from Iwo Jima. The Chengtu pattern was unfolding in the Marianas and as it did the autonomous future of Arnold's B-29s was placed in jeopardy.

On November 24 111 B-29s flew from Saipan to attack the Nakajima Aircraft Company's Musashi plant, on the outskirts of Tokyo, which produced approximately 30 per cent of the Japanese air forces' engines. Engine failures forced 17 B-29s to turn back, and as the remainder approached the home islands at altitudes of 27000–32000 ft they encountered the jetstream. During the winter months this powerful wind blew out of the west at precisely the altitudes flown by the B-29s. Plucked up like leaves in a gale, the aircraft attained speeds of up to 450 mph as formations disintegrated and bombing became a matter of guesswork. Cloud obscured the target and the majority of the B-29s dropped their bombs at random over the Tokyo area. One of the B-29s was rammed and destroyed by a Japanese fighter.

In ten subsequent raids on the Musashi plant, a mere two per cent of the bombs dropped hit any of the complex's buildings; only ten per cent of the overall damage caused fell within the 130 acres occupied by the plant. In 11 raids on this resilient target, 40 bombers had been lost, while Japanese casualties in the plant were about half the figure of 440 airmen who had failed to return.

The Musashi plant was a tough nut to crack, but the B-29's failure to punch its weight was graphically illustrated early in February 1945 when US Navy fighters and bombers from Vice-Admiral Marc A Mitscher's Task Force 58 caused more damage to the Mushashi plant than the combined B-29 raids. 73rd Bombardment Wing's second principal target had been the Mitsubishi engine plant at Nagoya, 17 per cent of which was destroyed in raids during the course of December, although at disquieting cost. The average loss of five aircraft – or 55 crew – a mission was placing a heavy strain on the Wing's ability to sustain the offensive. By mid-January the mission abort rate was running at 23 per cent, another cause for concern. The principal reason was overloading of the B-29s. Removal of one of the fuel tanks in the bomb bay and a reduction in the amount of ammunition carried saved over 6000 pounds in each aircraft. Performance rose dramatically. With an improved maintenance system, individual engine life was stretched from 220 to 750 hours.

Once again LeMay was brought in as the 'fireman', assuming command of XXI BC at the end of January 1945. His appointment coincided with a considerable expansion of the Command, marked by the arrival of 313th BW under Brigadier-General John H Davies. His wing was based at the North Field, Tinian, the largest bomber field ever built, which boasted four parallel 8500 ft runways.

In November 1944, General Arnold had received a report on the structure of the Japanese war economy. It indicated that production in Japan tended to be dispersed in numerous small businesses, and suggested that as there was a high proportion of wooden buildings in Japanese cities, area incendiary attacks might be up to five times more effective than precision bombing. The acceptance of these conclusions marked a crucial turning point in American bombing policy. From November 1944, the B-29s had been striking at precise economic targets, which nevertheless involved a degree of indiscriminate destruction. They were now about to launch a general urban bombing offensive aimed at demoralizing the population and taking advantage of the particular vulnerability of the Japanese cities to incendiary raids. The fate which had overtaken Lübeck, Hamburg, Darmstadt and Dresden was about to overwhelm the cities of Japan.

On January 3 4900-pound incendiary clusters were used in a raid on Nagoya, and on February 3 160 tons of incendiaries were dropped by 313th and 73rd Wings on Kobe, hitting fabric and synthetic rubber plants and halving the capacity of the shipyard. LeMay issued a directive embodying these new tactics on February 19. On February 25 and March 4 they were tested in two raids on Tokyo. In the first, 30000 buildings were gutted by 172 B-29s, which dropped 450 tons of incendiaries. The pattern was established and by May 1945 75 per cent of the B-29s' bombloads comprised incendiaries; among the most effective was the 500-pound M76 'pyrotechnic gel' bomb which had a special mixture of jellied oil,

Fire Raids on Japan

B-29 Dina Might of 421st Bomb Squadron, 504th BG, over Yokohama. The raging firestorms started by the B-29s' concentrated incendiary attacks created tremendous turbulence at low-altitude over the target. One pilot from 29th BG described it as, 'Worse than any Texas thunderstorm I'd experienced. The smoke was filled with the litter and smells of a burning and dying city'. On one occasion his B-29 was tossed upside down, surviving a 90-degree split-S recovery as a mountain loomed dead ahead through the pall of smoke.

The oft-quoted maximum speeds of aircraft are a useful rule of thumb but can be misleading when it comes to considering the practicalities of operational flying. The diagram (right) compares the upper limits of a B-29's performance – maximum speed 342 mph, economical cruising speed 220 mph, maximum bombload of 20 000 pounds and practical bombload of 5000 pounds over 3250 miles – with the realities of a typical mission. Crucial to planning is a calculation which has not changed since 1914. The fuel-bomb ratio is determined by the difference between the maximum take-off weight and minimum landing weight and the distance to be flown on the raid. Here we chart a B-29's progress from its base to a target 1730 miles away and its return journey. The target is to be attacked from 20 000 ft, an altitude flow for 60 miles either side of the objective. On this mission the B-29's bombload is 12 1000-pound bombs and fuel load 34 557 pounds (excluding a reserve of 5610 pounds). No allowance had been made for wind in this hypothetical mission.

1. Taxiing
500 pounds of fuel burnt before take off.

2. Take-off
240 pounds of fuel burnt.

3. Climb to 5000 feet at 450 feet per minute burning
30 pounds of fuel per minute;
levels off after 34 miles.

4. 5000 ft
Seven hours at 205 mph
burning 11 pounds of fuel per mile;
1530 miles covered
burning 16240 pounds of fuel.

Total time 15 hours 28 minutes
Round trip 3460 miles
Average speed of 224 mph

Max. take-off weight 135 000 pounds
Min. landing weight   88 000 pounds
Including reserve fuel
                      47 000 pounds
Fuel for mission.   34 557 pounds
(excluding reserve)
Bomb capacity.   12 443 pounds

6. Level off at 20 000 feet/
260 mph burning 11 pounds of fuel per mile.

5. 166 miles from target
climb to 20 000 feet at 550 feet per minute;
106 miles in 27 minutes 23 pounds of fuel per mile.

000's feet

— 15
— 10
— 5
— 0

Target

9. Level out 15 000 ft
1330 miles in 5½ hours;
burning 7.8 pounds per mile.

8. 60 miles from target
descent at 200 feet per minute next 100 miles;
240 mph at 8 pounds per mile.

10. 240 miles from base
descent at 200 feet per minute for 1 hour 10 mins;
burning 6.6 pounds of fuel per mile.

7. Over target
12 000 pounds of bombs shed;
fuel consumption down to 10 pounds per mile.

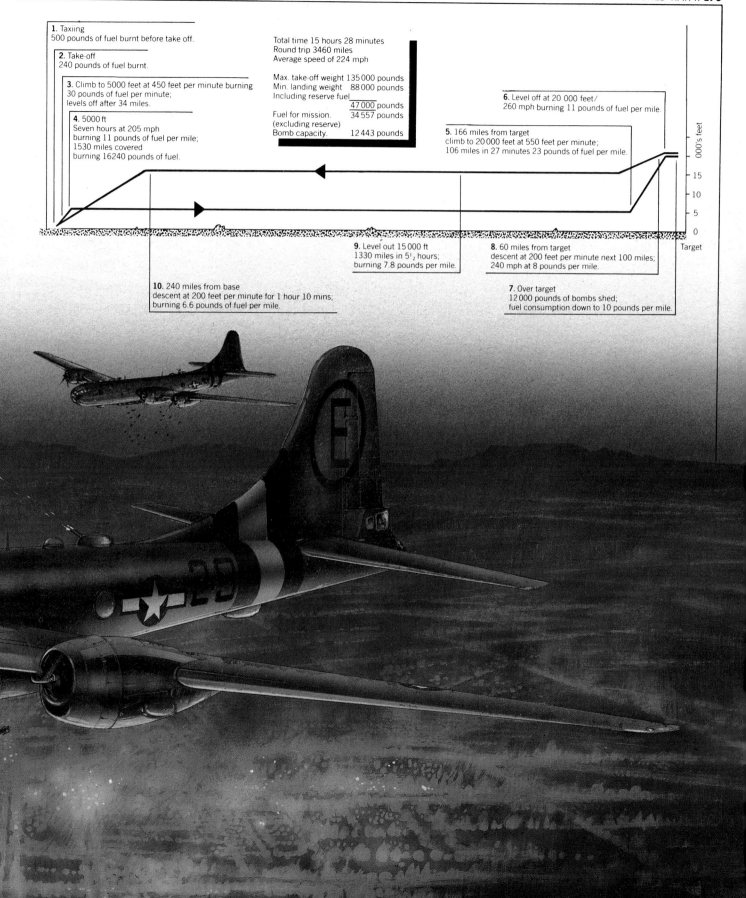

heavy oil, petrol, magnesium powder and sodium nitrate. These bombs were all but impossible to extinguish.

LeMay now introduced additional tactical refinements. To counter the jetstream, high-level daylight raids were replaced by low-level high-intensity incendiary attacks, preferably by night. The B-29s were stripped of their GEC gun systems, leaving only the tail gun for defense, packed with incendiaries and pulled down to an operating height of 6000 ft. The first raid of this kind was flown against Tokyo on the night of March 9/10 by 325 B-29s led by special pathfinder crews. Of these 279 arrived over the target and in two hours of bombing razed the central area of Tokyo. Sixteen square miles of the city were destroyed and 84 000 people killed for the loss of 14 B-29s.

On March 11/12 285 B-29s unloaded 1700 tons of incendiaries on Nagoya, leveling two square miles of the city for the loss of only one aircraft. There were now only 500 aircraft of low serviceability defending Japan, including two night fighter groups equipped with rudimentary radar. Because of the system of Army command over the home defense units, each fighter group was assigned to a specific territory and could not be used for operations in support of neighboring areas. Ground-to-air communications were too poor for concentrated control of fighters, even in the relatively small defense areas.

On March 13/14 eight square miles of Osaka were swept by a firestorm; on March 16/17 three square miles of Kobe were razed, and three nights later a similar blow was delivered to Nagoya. In two weeks over 120 000 Japanese civilians were killed or injured, for the loss of 22 B-29s. By March 20 XXI BG had exhausted its stock of incendiaries. It was the final triumph of area bombing.

By April 1945 LeMay had over 700 B-29s at his disposal, enabling him to divide his force between the tactical support of the Okinawa landings and the continuing incendiary offensive against the major Japanese cities – Tokyo, Nagoya, Osaka, Kawasaki, Kobe and Yokohama. On April 13 327 B-29s destroyed another 11 square miles of Tokyo with over 2000 tons of incendiaries. The Japanese night defenses had rallied and five aircraft were lost on this raid and 13 more on April 15 in attacks on Tokyo, Kawasaki and Yokohama. These were negligible losses, and the arrival of 58th Wing from the CBI now enabled LeMay to contemplate the use of 500 B-29s in a single raid and the ending of the war with the bludgeon of air power.

On May 14 a new series of crippling fire raids began with an attack by 472 B-29s on the area surrounding the Mitsubishi engine plant at Nagoya. In this and another attack on May 16/17 a total of nine square miles were engulfed by firestorms, stampeding the terrified population into the surrounding countryside. On May 23 LeMay mounted the largest single B-29 raid of the war when 562 aircraft took off to raid Tokyo and 510 bombed the target. Two days later 464 B-29s returned to drop incendiaries in the areas which had not been hit. Although 43 aircraft were lost in these two raids, the Japanese capital had been reduced to a charred wasteland. By the end of May over 50 per cent of the city area of Tokyo, about 56 square miles, had been destroyed.

Troubled by the losses on these raids, LeMay changed his tactics, with the twin aim of catching the defenses off balance and drawing the Japanese fighters into an air battle which would drain their remaining strength. On May 29, in a high-altitude raid, 454 B-29s appeared over Yokohama heavily escorted by P-51 Mustangs from Iwo Jima. In the ensuing dogfights 26 Japanese fighters were shot down for the loss of four B-29s and three Mustangs. Japanese interference with the raiders now fell away as they husbanded their dwindling strength for a final spasm of *Kamikaze* attacks against the anticipated Allied invasion force. By June 1945 the B-29s flew unmolested over the shattered cities of Japan. At the end of the month no less than 105.6 of the combined 257.2 square miles of Tokyo, Nagoya, Osaka, Kawasaki, Kobe and Yokohama had been flattened.

Operating with almost complete freedom, LeMay adopted a variety of tactics. On April 7 he initiated a program of high-level precision strikes with an attack by 153 B-29s on the aircraft engine plant at Nagoya. Six hundred tons of HE wrecked 90 per cent of the remaining facilities. Five days later 93 B-29s completed the destruction of the Nakajima factory at Musashi. The task of neutralizing Japan's remaining oil-producing and storage facilities was given to 315th BW, stationed on Northwest Field, Guam, and equipped with the stripped-down B-29B capable of carrying a standard load of 18 000 pounds. Navigation and bombing accuracy were improved by the AN/ADQ-7 'Eagle' radar, housed in a wing-shaped radome underneath the fuselage. The aircrew in 315th BW had received a rigorous training in low-level nighttime bombing. The task was completed by August 10. The last nails were hammered into the Japanese coffin by 313th BW, which between March 27 and August 10 sowed nearly 13 000 acoustic and magnetic mines in the western approaches to the

B-29s over Yokohama on May 29, 1945. This was a daylight high-altitude attack flown by 459 aircraft heavily escorted by P-51 Mustangs. In a series of ferocious dog-fights, 26 Japanese fighters were shot down at a cost of four B-29s and three P-51s.

Shimonoseki strait and the Inland Sea, and around the harbors of Hiroshima, Kure, Tokyo, Nagoya, Tokuyama, Aki and Noda. By the end of April Japanese coastal shipping movements had been brought to a standstill. In May, 85 ships totalling 213 000 tons were sunk in attempts to break out.

With Japan's major cities lying in ruins, LeMay focused his attention on smaller conurbations of between 100 000 and 200 000 people. The program began on June 17 with low-level incendiary raids on Kagashima, Omuta, Hamamatsu and Yokkaichi. Fifty-seven cities were hit in these secondary attacks. One of them, Toyama, was 99.5 per cent destroyed. In July a refinement was introduced – reminiscent of the plans to 'proscribe' German cities which had been discussed by the British Air Staff in 1918 and 1941. Leaflets warning of forthcoming attacks were dropped over selected Japanese cities and every third night thereafter the B-29s returned with their cargoes of incendiaries.

After four months of relentless bombardment LeMay was running out of targets to attack. Japan had been brought to the brink of surrender.

The Problem: And the Solution

The American Joint Chiefs of Staff were divided. The naval chiefs were convinced that their blockade would end the war. The air chiefs urged the continuation of the bombing. Over these arguments hung the fear of the million Allied casualties which, it was believed, would be sustained in an invasion of the Japanese home islands. Roosevelt's successor, Harry S Truman also viewed the prospect of Soviet intervention in the East with something less than enthusiasm. There were already sufficient problems in Europe to sort out with Stalin. However, the Americans had a trump card up their sleeve.

For three years the Manhattan project had been pushing ahead with the development of a controlled nuclear explosion. As early as the summer of 1943 General Arnold had been asked to provide specially modified B-29s for flight and dropping tests for a new bomb. Modification of one of the early production B-29s began in December 1943 and the first test, using dummy bombs, began on February 28, 1944. By August 46 B-29s had been fitted with a new H-frame hoist, carrier assembly and release units. At a remote air base near Wendover, Utah, Colonel Paul W Tibbets Jr – a veteran B-17 pilot – began to put the newly formed 509th Composite Group through its paces. Self-sufficient, wrapped in secrecy and with only one Bombardment Group – 393rd under Major Charles W Sweeney – 509th was the unit chosen to drop 'the bomb'.

There was little doubt that it would be dropped. True, General Marshall believed that Soviet intervention would lever the Japanese into capitulation. And when, during the Potsdam Conference, General Eisenhower was told of its intended use, he judged that it was 'completely unnecessary'. But Truman had already made up his mind. Once the bomb had been produced, it was inevitable that it was going to be used. Too much money had been spent on its development for it to be quietly placed on the shelf.

Two types of bomb had been developed by the scientists working on the Manhattan Project. The first, relying for its chain reaction on uranium and

nicknamed 'Little Boy', weighed about 900 pounds and was 28in in diameter. The second, using plutonium and called 'Fat Man', had a diameter of 60 in. In July, 509th was transferred to North Field, Tinian. On the 16th of that month the Manhattan scientists exploded the first atomic device at Alamogordo, in the New Mexico desert.

On July 24 a mission directive was issued by General Spaatz, commander of the newly formed US Strategic Air Forces in the Pacific. He ordered 509th Group to 'deliver its first special bomb as soon as weather will permit visual bombing after August 3 1945 on one of the targets; Hiroshima, Kokura, Niigata and Nagasaki'. By August 2 'Little Boy' had been assembled on Tinian, and during the course of the afternoon LeMay's staff prepared a field order specifying Hiroshima as the primary target, with Kokura and Nagasaki as alternative targets if bad weather prevented a visual drop. B-29 Enola Gay was commanded by Colonel Paul W Tibbets. Enola Gay was his mother's name; the bomber had been blessed by a Catholic priest; and on 'Little Boy' was a pin-up of Rita Hayworth. The B-29 approached Hiroshima in good visibility, the crew pulling on arc-welder's goggles to protect their eyes from the flash. At 0811hrs Tibbets handed over to his bomb aimer, Major Thomas Ferebee, who quickly found the aiming point, a bridge over the widest branch of the River Ota. Enola Gay was now flying over the target at 285 mph, and at 17 seconds past 0815 hrs the B-29's bomb bay doors opened and 'Little Boy' began its six-mile descent. Tibbets pulled Enola Gay away sharply in a 150-degree turn, to put as great a distance as possible between the aircraft and the explosion. The crew started counting. Fifty-one seconds later 'Little Boy' exploded 1850 ft over Hiroshima, only 200 yds from the aiming point.

As Enola Gay pulled away, the crew saw a vivid flash, then felt the double shock wave as it struck the aircraft. Below them, 15 miles away, a ball of fire seethed skyward. They witnessed the instant obliteration of the heart of Hiroshima and the deaths of 75,000 human beings. A new age in warfare had arrived. When Truman was told, he said 'This is the greatest thing in history'.

Still the Japanese insisted that continued resistance might secure 'honourable conditions'. On August 9 a second, 'Fat Man', bomb was dropped on the city of Nagasaki by B-29 Bock's Car, named after its commander Captain Frederick C Bock but flown on the mission by Major Sweeney. The city of Kokura, the primary target, had been covered by cloud, and after three abortive bombing runs Major Sweeney diverted to Nagasaki. At 1058 hrs Sweeney's bomb aimer released from 28 900 ft through a break in 8/10 cloud cover. Because of Nagasaki's bowl-shaped terrain, the damage extended in an oval shape 2.3 by 1.9 miles, within which every building was destroyed or rendered uninhabitable. Approximately 35 000 people died.

This was not the last air raid of the Pacific War. On August 14 804 B-29s flew to bomb Japan. On the same day Japan's leaders agreed to an unconditional surrender. On September 2 General McArthur received the formal surrender on board the battleship USS *Missouri* in Tokyo Bay. With his customary flair for the theatrical gesture he declared, 'These proceedings are closed'.

The mushroom cloud rising over Nagasaki after the second atom bomb raid on August 9, 1945. It has often been pointed out that the casualties in the Tokyo fire raid of March 9/10, 1945 were greater than those resulting from the dropping of the first atomic bomb on Hiroshima. However, in relation to density of population per square mile destroyed, casualties at Hiroshima were four times higher. A new era in warfare had arrived. When President Truman was told of the first raid he said, 'This is the greatest thing in history'.

SECTION FOUR

THE BOMBER IN THE MODERN WORLD

4.1 COLD WAR POLITICS AND SAC

WORLD WAR II ENDED WITH THE EMERGENCE OF TWO superpowers: the Soviet Union, grievously mauled but master of Eastern Europe; and the United States, riding a war-generated boom, the economic powerhouse of the Western World, and the sole possessor of the atomic bomb. The atomic bombs dropped on Hiroshima and Nagasaki were the harbingers of a revolution in the nature of war more sweeping than anything anticipated by Douhet and Mitchell in the 1920s. When President Truman almost casually told Stalin about the bomb at Potsdam on July 24, 1945, the Soviet leader betrayed no emotion. Churchill was convinced that he had not understood what he had been told.

The United States' initial lead in the nuclear race might seem to have secured it an overwhelming strategic advantage as East-West tensions began to shape the contours of the postwar world. Indeed, the first war plans approved by the Joint Chiefs of Staff in 1948 focused and relied on a strategic offensive employing atomic bombs. It was anticipated that, in a European war, the enormous destructive power of the West's nuclear weaponry would counterbalance the Soviet superiority on the ground. Once again the vision arose of the strategic bomber as the single decisive factor in any future conflict. In words which recall those of Trenchard and Mitchell, Arnold's successor as Chief of Staff, General Carl Spaatz, declared, 'the attackers do not have to plod laboriously and bloodily along the Minsk-Smolensk-Moscow road in order to strike at Russia's vitals. Hence the war may be concluded within weeks and perhaps days'.

This optimism that victory could be swift and total ignored immediate postwar realities and recalls the RAF's Western Air Plans of the 1930s. There was an appreciable gap between real and potential capability, which was not closed until the early 1950s. Peace brought with it demobilization and cutbacks which, although not on the swingeing scale of 1918, nevertheless bit deeply into the USAAF's combat capability. In the five months following Japan's surrender, the Army Air Forces alone returned nearly 750 000 men to civilian status. Personnel shortages and an imbalance of available skills prevented the USAAF from reaching its original peacetime goal of 70 air groups.

Experience in World War II had shown how long it took to build up a strategic bombing force. With the advent of the atomic bomb, the element of time had been removed. General Arnold was not alone in considering that the new weapons made air power 'all important' and that 'offensive and defensive power in a state of immediate readiness is the primary requisite of national survival'. Arnold anticipated that the United States would not long retain a nuclear monopoly. As early as the summer of 1943 he had written to General Marshall a memorandum on future warfare which both revived the air theories of the 1920s and anticipated the link between national security, technological development, and deterrence from attack which remains the bedrock of US strategic doctrine: '*IT IS CLEAR THAT THE ONLY defense against such warfare is the ability to attack. We must, therefore, secure our nation by developing and maintaining those weapons, forces, and techniques required to pose a warning to aggressors in order to deter them from launching a modern, devastating war*'.

A crucial moment in the development of postwar US air power was the decision to create a force with global capabilities, Strategic Air Command (SAC), which came into being in March 1946. The brainchild of 'Tooey' Spaatz, it reorganized AAF combat power into three Commands – Strategic, Tactical and Air Defense. The next step stemmed from the great strategic offensives of World War II. Before the war had ended, a committee had recommended the establishment of a US Air Force, on an equal footing with the Army and the Navy, under the umbrella of a single Department of Defense. Predictably, this revived the battles which had been fought in the 1920s and '30s over air force independence, but on July 26, 1947 President Truman signed the National Security Act, which brought into being the US Air Force, and Executive Order 9877 which defined the roles of the three services and appointed the disgruntled Navy Secretary James Forrestal as the

first Secretary of Defense. At the end of September General Spaatz, wearing the service's new sky-blue uniform, was sworn in as the USAAF's first commander-in-chief.

The Soviet Union had not yet developed an atomic bomb of its own. However, its ground forces seemed to present a formidable threat. In the autumn of 1945 the Soviet Union maintained an absolute minimum of nine million men under arms, while Eastern European nations under its sway fielded 84 divisions and played host to 213 Soviet divisions. There was little argument about the Soviets' ability to overrun most of Continental Europe – if they chose to do so – and the American inability to stem the tide. By 1947 US forces in Europe amounted to no more than two divisions and 12 air groups. The best hope of halting a Soviet drive into Western Europe seemed to be in strategic bombing with nuclear weapons. One USAF general estimated that 200 successful atomic sorties could inflict on the Soviet Union damage comparable to that suffered by Germany during the last nine months of World War II.

But the integration of the atomic weapon into the USAF was painfully slow. In January 1946 the Army Air Force designated 58th Bomb Wing and its three Groups, including 509th BG, as its strategic atomic force. These units were to form the nucleus for the anticipated conversion of the entire strategic bombing component to an atomic striking role. A year later SAC possessed only 27 B-29s modified to deliver atomic bombs, and for several years 509th remained the only unit capable of flying atomic strike missions. There was also a limited supply of bombs. In the immediate postwar period only the Hanford Plant in Washington produced plutonium, and this in very small amounts. The scarce supply of fissionable material limited the number of atomic weapons manufactured. When Major-General Curtis

LeMay, then Chief of Staff for Research and Development, was instructed to prepare a contingency war plan, he estimated an availability not of 200 but of 25 atomic bombs. Even at this level, by mid-1948 the Armed Forces Special Weapons Project – which supplied and controlled the technical teams assembling atomic weapons – could assemble only two bombs per day for combat operations.

Delivering the Bomb
Delivering the bombs against Soviet targets presented formidable problems. In World War II the USAAF had concentrated on visual bombing by daylight, generally avoiding night-time operations. The only hope of penetrating Soviet fighter defenses lay in night attacks with radar bombing, a method in which most airmen lacked experience. The night bombing of Japanese cities in 1945 had, it is true, been devastatingly effective, but had been accomplished against an enfeebled enemy and targets on which there was no lack of intelligence and which lay within the B-29's range. Flying over blacked-out Soviet territory through intense jamming, and against heavily defended targets on which there was often little or no intelligence, left little margin for error. Flying from European bases, crews would have little difficulty in finding major cities, like Moscow and Gorki, but these areas contained only a fraction of the Soviet Union's warmaking industry. The important industrial centers would be defended in depth, which was not a problem which had been encountered by Enola Gay. It was not enough merely to possess atomic weapons; if they were to be used, overseas bases, intelligence and aircrews with the ability to fly their bombers through air defenses were needed.

SAC's first commander, General George Kenney, flinched in the face of these unpalatable facts. Just as

The B-47E Stratojet, which throughout the 1950s equipped 28 Strategic Air Command Bomb Wings, each with 45-combat ready aircraft.

RAF Bomber Command had avoided the rigors of night flying in the 1930s, so SAC neglected high-altitude bombing practice and night flights while concentrating on low-level visual bombing. This produced misleadingly encouraging bombing results and a good maintenance record, as aborts occurred less frequently at low altitude. But it bore little relation to the operational conditions which aircrews would face in a war against the Soviet Union.

SAC's difficulties were compounded by the Atomic Energy Act of 1946, establishing the Atomic Energy Commission and placing very strict limitations on the dissemination of information on the atomic bomb and all related equipment. Under the new 'Restricted Data' category of classification, equipment associated with the handling, loading, and dropping of the bomb was classified, and crews who were to fly these missions were, somewhat farcically, not cleared to see or use the equipment. Because of the 'Restricted Data' equipment in their B-29s, 509th BG was not allowed out of the United States for training missions on the foreign bases it would have to use if war came.

In February 1948 SAC took delivery of its first B-50, an improved version of the B-29 with more powerful 3500 hp Pratt and Whitney Wasp Major radials, taller fin and hydraulically boosted rudder, and provision for probe/drogue flight refueling by modified B-29s designated KB-29M. The B-50 was a strategic bomber firmly rooted in the past, as was the remarkable Convair B-36 Peacemaker, the first of which was delivered to SAC in June 1948. The origins of the B-36 lay in US wartime contingency plans in the event of the possible collapse of Britain. The B-36 was developed to continue the war at extreme range by operating against occupied Europe from bases in the United States and Canada. The challenging specification called for a bombload of 10 000 pounds delivered to a target 5000 miles away. The B-36 fell foul of wartime shortages and more pressing priorities, and it was only after hostilities ceased that work on the giant bomber began. The result was a majestic aircraft and the world's largest bomber, 160 ft long with a wingspan of 230 ft. The early models were powered by six 3500 hp Wasp Majors driving 19 ft pusher-type propellers. The B-

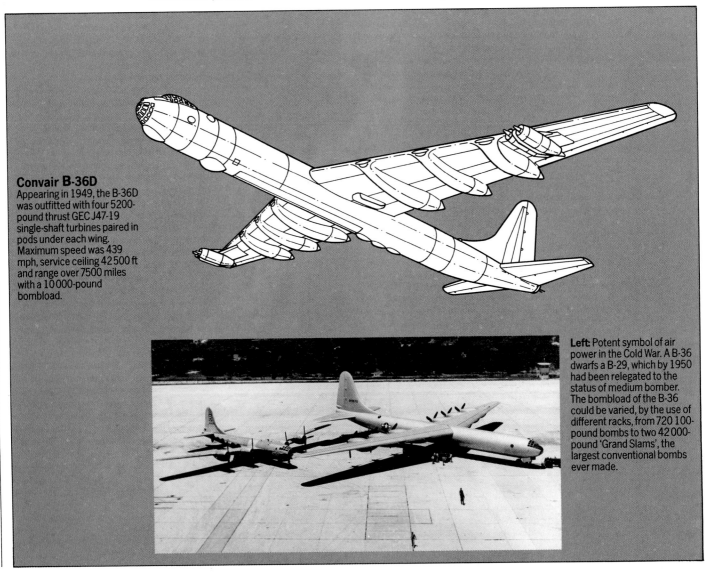

Convair B-36D
Appearing in 1949, the B-36D was outfitted with four 5200-pound thrust GEC J47-19 single-shaft turbines paired in pods under each wing. Maximum speed was 439 mph, service ceiling 42 500 ft and range over 7500 miles with a 10 000-pound bombload.

Left: Potent symbol of air power in the Cold War. A B-36 dwarfs a B-29, which by 1950 had been relegated to the status of medium bomber. The bombload of the B-36 could be varied, by the use of different racks, from 720 100-pound bombs to two 42 000-pound 'Grand Slams', the largest conventional bombs ever made.

36D, which appeared in 1949, was outfitted with four 5200-pound thrust GEC J47-19 single-shaft turbojets paired in pods under each wing. The B-36D had a crew of 15, a maximum speed of 439 mph, a service ceiling of 42 500 ft and a range of over 7500 miles with a 10 000-pound bombload. Maximum bombload was a staggering 86 000 pounds, far more than the take-off weight of a wartime Lancaster carrying a 22 000-pound bomb. Defensive armament was provided by 16 20 mm cannon housed in six remotely controlled fuselage, nose and tail turrets. The tiny XF-85 fighter escort was developed to be launched from a B-36 with an articulated trapeze, an idea which had first been tried in the 1920s when the US airships *Macon* and *Akron* had acted as motherships for four Curtiss F9C-2 Sparrowhawk biplane fighters. The XF-85 had a wingspan of 21.1 ft and length of 14.9 ft, to allow it to be carried in the B-36's bomb bay. Only one XF-85 was built.

Snarling through the skies of an uncertain postwar world, the mighty B-36 provided a potent image of the Cold War which had begun almost immediately after the defeat of the Axis powers. The year in which it appeared, 1948, saw the Communist take-over in Czechoslovakia and the Berlin Airlift, the latter dramatically underlining the vital importance of strategic air planning. In October 1948 a familiar figure once again strode center stage when Curtis LeMay succeeded General Kenney as commander of SAC with orders to upgrade its combat capability. In the first exercise conducted under LeMay's command, SAC B-29 crews simulated an attack on specific targets in Dayton, Ohio. Bombing by night and by radar from high altitude, not one of the 150 participating aircrews successfully flew the mission as directed. The aircraft which penetrated to the target recorded bombing errors of over two miles. With pardonable exaggeration, LeMay described the exercise as the darkest night in the history of US aviation. With characteristic determination he set about revitalizing SAC.

The Growing Might of SAC
In December 1949, SAC had 72 000 men, 14 Bomb Groups and 610 strategic aircraft, two strategic Fighter Groups and six air refueling squadrons. Four years later LeMay commanded 171 000 men, 37 Bomb Wings comprising over 1000 aircraft (mostly B-36s and the all-jet B-47s) six Fighter Wings, and 28 air-refueling squadrons. The most significant aircraft in this inventory was the Boeing B-47, which was committed to production in 1949 and entered service with 306th Bomb Wing in October 1951.

The USAF's first four-engined jet bomber had been the North American B-45 Tornado, which entered service with 47th BG late in 1948. In all but its engines it was of straight-wing conventional design, with the two pilots seated in tandem under a large fixed canopy, the bombardier in the nose and a gunner in the tail firing two 0.5 guns. Maximum speed at low level was 580 mph, service ceiling 42 500 ft and range 1910 miles with a 22 000-pound (including nuclear) bombload. The B-45 had been designed before American aero-engineers had gained access to the swept-wing technology developed in Germany during World War II. Immediately after the war Boeing engineers had visited Germany and sub-

sequently designed a swept wing into their Model 450 bomber, whose thin shoulder-mounted wings were given a 35-degree angle of sweepback. The Model 450 prototype of the B-47 was acquired by the USAAF in 1945, and it immediately impressed with its advanced design. Its podded engine installations held six all-American axial turbojets and, in early versions, rocket boost was provided for maximum-weight take-off boost. A large braking parachute was another innovation, as were the remotely controlled tail turret (initially firing twin 0.5 guns), and the bicycle landing gear. The two pilots were seated in tandem under a large fighter-type canopy and the bombardier/navigator was housed in the nose. The first major service version of the 'Stratojet', was the B-47B, incorporating 1500-gallon drop tanks and Flying Boom flight refueling.

American involvement in the Korean War led to an immediate expansion of the Stratojet program and in 1951 production was switched to the more powerful B-47E, equipped with a new radar bombing system, 20 mm guns, jettisonable rocket pack, water-injected engines, and ejection seats. The B-47E had a range of 3600 miles with a bombload of 22 000 pounds, combat speed of 557 mph and service ceiling of 32 000 ft early in the mission, rising to 38 000 ft with fuel burn-off. During the 1950s the B-47 equipped 28 Strategic Air Command Bomb Wings, each comprising 45 combat-ready aircraft. In addition there were over 300 RB-47E and RB-47K reconnaissance and ERB-47H Elint 'Ferret' aircraft and a variety of test, weather, and drone versions. Production for SAC ceased in 1957 and the last B-47s were retired from the USAF in 1969. As late as 1976 two US Navy EB-47Es remained in support of Aegis system testing.

Mention should also be made of the remarkable Northrop YB-49 Flying Wing project. Developed as the XB-35, powered by four R-4360 engines driving pusher propellers, the aircraft's radical configuration dates back to research conducted before the United States' entry into World War II. When it was unveiled in 1946, the XB-35 seemed to have flown straight out of the pages of Buck Rogers. The aircraft was a 172 ft wing constructed in one piece from aluminum alloy. The chord at the centerline was a staggering 37 ft 6 in and the wing area was some 4000 sq ft. Defensive armament was provided by two four-gun turrets and four two-gun turrets located above and below the wing and controlled by the gunner from his cockpit in the sharply pointed tail nacelle. XB-35 made its maiden flight on June 25, 1946, and this led to an order for 13 YB-35 development and service test aircraft. Two of the YB-35s were modified to take eight J35-A-19 turbojets, and in 1949 one of them flew 2258 miles between Muroc Air Force Base, California, and Washington DC, averaging a speed during the flight of 511 mph. During another flight the Flying Wing achieved a ceiling of over 40 000 ft. These impressive performances failed to secure its acceptance by the USAF, although a single six-jet version appeared as the experimental YRB-49A reconnaissance bomber. An order for 30 B-49s was placed in 1948 and was then canceled a year later. Appropriately, in 1953 the Flying Wing made a 'posthumous' appearance in George Pal's updated screen version of HG Wells' science fiction classic, *The War of the Worlds*.

4.2 THE KOREAN WAR AND THE SWANSONG OF THE B-29

BY 1950 THE B-29 WAS MOVING QUICKLY towards obsolescence as potent new bombers like the B-47 prepared to enter service. Production of the Superfortress had ceased in 1946, by which time a total of 3960 had been built. Four years later most of them were in storage and the B-29 had suffered the indignity of being redesignated a 'medium bomber'. Its role as the Very Heavy Component of US air power had been assumed by the B-50 and the B-36. But there was one more campaign to fight.

On August 15, 1945 an Allied agreement laid down that Japanese forces north of the 38th Parallel in Korea would surrender to the Russians, and those in the south to US forces. This decision established the 38th Parallel as a political frontier. Following an abortive attempt to achieve a unification of Korea, the Republic of Korea was formed in the South on August 15, 1947. In the North, the Soviet Union set up the Democratic People's Republic of Korea, and in an 'advisory' capacity created the North Korean Army (NKA). On June 25, 1950 NKA units comprising seven infantry divisions and one tank brigade crossed the 38th Parallel and invaded South Korea, rapidly advancing to take the capital, Seoul. On the day the invasion began the UN Security Council invited its members to assist in obtaining the withdrawal of the NKA forces. The Soviet Union, boycotting the Council, had no representative present to veto the decision. On June 27 President Truman sent orders to General MacArthur, the US commander in the Far East, to provide air and naval assistance to South Korea. Three days later the order was extended to ground troops.

When the war broke out, the only US bombers in the region capable of operating effectively with conventional ordnance over the Korean peninsula were the 22 B-29s of 19th BG stationed at Andersen Field, Guam, as part of the Far Eastern Air Forces (FEAF). They were almost immediately thrown into action in a tactical role with orders to strike at NKA troop concentrations, supply depots, communications and targets of opportunity between the front line and the 38th Parallel. On June 28 four of the 19th BG's Superfortresses flew the unit's first mission, attacking targets of opportunity along the railway network north of Seoul. During the next chaotic ten days targets were switched from North Korean airfields to NKA formations massing on the Han River in preparation for a major southward thrust. The results were poor, emphasising a fundamental conflict over the B-29's employment in the Korean War which was never satisfactorily resolved. While USAF planners cast around for a proper strategic function for the aging bomber, land commanders insisted on its use as a close tactical support weapon, a role for which it had never been designed.

On July 8 a FEAF Bomber Command was established under the command of Major-General Emmett O'Donnell, with its headquarters at Yokata in Japan. Reinforcements arrived in the shape of 22nd and 92nd Bomb Wings, transferred from SAC on July 3. Including six RB-29 long-range reconnais-

sance aircraft of 31st Strategic Reconnaissance Squadron, based on Okinawa, 24 weather reconnaissance WB-29s and four SB-29 'Superdumbo' rescue aircraft, O'Donnell's command had a nominal strength of 100 machines. O'Donnell was eager to use the B-29s in incendiary attacks on North Korea's cities, just as they had been used against Japan five years before, but this was ruled out by Washington, fearful that there might be a political backlash if large numbers of civilians were killed in fire raids. This was an early indication of the political constraints at play in Korea, a factor which was to be repeated on a bigger scale 15 years later in the Vietnam conflict.

There were no incendiary raids. Once again the B-29s were thrown into tactical operations north of the Han River, with predictably indifferent results. At this point a personal intervention by SAC's Chief of Staff, General Hoyt S Vandenburg, secured the diversion of the B-29s to interdiction raids near the 38th Parallel. These were still tactical missions, but they allowed FEAF to adopt a more formalized approach to operations, which had previously been conducted on an ad hoc basis. During Interdiction Campaign No. 1 the principal targets were the strategic road and rail bridges north of the 38th Parallel. Crews trained for atomic strikes at high altitude and, in the case of 22nd and 92nd Bomb Wings, equipped with aircraft capable of carrying only 500-pound bombs, found the bridges extremely difficult targets to destroy. One railway bridge near Seoul resisted three weeks of concentrated bombardment before it finally went down. By the end of August 37 of the 44 targeted bridges had been destroyed and the remainder so badly wrecked that they were unusable.

B29s in the Strategic Role
By now the B-29s had finally acquired a strategic role. Intelligence gathering by the RB-29s of 31st SRS led to the targeting of five industrial centers in North Korea: the North Korean capital of Pyongyang, a rail center and source of aircraft and armaments, Wonsan, a port with oil refining facilities; Hungnam, with its chemical and metallurgical plants; Chongjin, with its iron foundries and railyards; and the naval base and port at Rashin, 17 miles from the Soviet border. Secondary targets included five hydroelectric plants on North Korea's eastern coastline.

The campaign against Hungnam opened at the end of July. In Mission Nannie Able, 47 B-29s bombed the Chosen nitrogen explosives factory, using radar bombing techniques for the first time in the conflict. They dropped all their bombs in the target area, destroying 30 per cent of the factory. Two days later the Superfortresses knocked out the Chosen nitrogen fertilizer factory, bombing visually from 16000 ft. Next to be hit, after another two-day gap, was the Bogun chemical plant. In three missions the largest explosives and chemical complex in North Korea had been put out of action. This contrasts with an operation launched on August 15 when, in the biggest ground-support mission since the fighting in Normandy, 98 B-29s plastered an area 25 miles square near Wangwan, ostensibly attacking heavy troop formations which were massing against the US Ist Cavalry Division near Pusan. The B-29s dropped several thousand tons of bombs, only to discover after the raid that there was no evidence that the area had contained large numbers of enemy troops.

At the end of August, General O'Donnell reported the destruction of the entire industrial infrastructure of North Korea, with the exception of the facilities at Rashin. Its proximity to the Soviet border had led President Truman to strike it from the target list to avoid the risk of bombing error widening the conflict.

The B-29's strategic triumph was shortlived. As O'Donnell began to move on to the secondary targets, the war underwent a dramatic upheaval. On September 15 the US 10th Corps under General Edward M Almond, began the amphibious landings at Inchon, 20 miles west of Seoul and 150 miles north of the Pusan Perimeter, into which the US and South Korean forces had been penned by the NKA. These forces now broke out from the Perimeter, linking with the Inchon landing force on September 26. Seoul was liberated on the same day, and the territory occupied by the NKA cut in half. UN troops drove northward, crossing the 38th Parallel on October 10 and taking Pyongyang on the 19th. By November 24 they had occupied two-thirds of North Korea and were almost at the Yalu River, which marks the border with China. So complete seemed the victory that as early as October 27, FEAF Bomber Command was disbanded and 22nd and 92nd BWs returned to SAC duties in the United States. The remaining B-29s continued to fly tactical operations.

This confidence was premature. As the UN forces advanced through North Korea, the Chinese began massing troops on the frontier, and on November 1 Chinese MiG-15 jet fighters made their first appearance in combat. FEAF was hastily reformed, but its operations in the second half of the war were to be circumscribed by the decision not to use it strategically against the Chinese homeland. Not only was there an extreme reluctance to widen the conflict with the Chinese, but also a fear of intervention by the Soviet Union. Political considerations propelled the war down a 'limited' path which in turn confined the B-29s to operations against targets in the North Korean peninsula. The war industries in the heart of China, which were sustaining the Communist effort, remained out of bounds.

Early in November FEAF Bomber Command was thrust back into the tactical straitjacket when it was ordered to attack the bridges on the Yalu, across which supplies of all kinds were pouring into North Korea. Bombing was limited to the southern approaches to the bridges, as the destruction of their northern spans would have been construed as an attack on Chinese territory. One B-29 was shot down and ten more badly damaged in a series of raids which did little to check the flow of supplies. Those spans which were broken were replaced by pontoons, which the Chinese then used at night.

On November 25 the Chinese launched a full-scale counter-offensive, rolling back the UN forces to the 38th Parallel by the end of the year. In December, the front congealed over the lines it had occupied before the Inchon landings. In January, a renewed Communist offensive forced the evacuation of Seoul and tied the B-29s to close-support missions. At the end of January, the new UN commander, General Matthew B Ridgway, initiated a series of counterblows while USAF planners once more attempted to formulate a targeting policy which would unlock the strike potential of the B-29. Much of the Chinese matériel was routed through northwest Korea, but this area was thickly populated with anti-aircraft defenses and MiG fighter bases. When Interdiction Campaign No. 4 began in February 1951 the B-29s were provided with F-80C Shooting Star and F-84E Thunderjet escorts, neither of which were able to hold their own against the MiG-15. Their lack of performance, and a lack of co-ordination between bomber and fighter commanders, meant that the B-29s often flew on to their targets unescorted. On March 1, 1951, 18 B-29s from 98th BG arrived late at a rendezvous, forcing their escort to return to base before the bombing-run began. The bombers were jumped by nine MiGs and ten were damaged, three of them so badly that they force-landed on the fighter strip at Taegu. On April 12 48 B-29s of 19th BG and 98th and 307th BWs from Okinawa, close escorted by 36 F-84Es and with 18 F-86A Sabres providing top cover, attacked the rail bridge over the Yalu at Antung. Over the target they were intercepted by the entire regiment of Antung-based MiGs. As the Superfortress formations shook out to start their bombing run, the MiGs swooped on the stragglers. Three bombers were shot down and seven badly damaged. The Sabres accounted for four enemy fighters and the bombers' gunners claimed another nine shot down.

New Weapons, New Tactics

A new range of weapons had also been tried and found wanting. Towards the end of 1950, 19th BG took delivery of the Razon radio-controlled bomb, which was guided on to its target by the bombardier, who could alter RAnge and AZimuth ONly once it had left the aircraft. The Razons were used by 19th BG to destroy a number of bridges, but at 1000 pounds they were too light to be effective. The Razons were succeeded by the 2000-pound Tarzon, which proved even less successful. The B-29 had great difficulty in accommodating the unwieldy Tarzon, most of which protruded from its bomb bay. Filled with unstable wartime RDX explosive, the Tarzons blew up at least two B-29s which had tried to ditch them in the sea, exploding as soon as they hit the water. The Tarzon experiment was abandoned after 30 had been dropped in Korea, wrecking six bridges.

B-29s next found employment in a ploy reminiscent of the 'Circus' missions mounted by the RAF during 1940–42, flying as heavily escorted bait over the Communist air bases in the North in an attempt to lure the MiGs into battle with their F-86 guardians. The Communist countered these tactics with a widespread dispersal of their MiG units, which always seemed to be one jump ahead of USAF intelligence. The raids failed to achieve their objective and between October 13 and 27 five B-29s were shot down and 20 badly damaged.

These losses prompted another change of tactics,

in which small numbers of B-29s equipped with Shoran (SHOrt RANge) navigation radar flew precision night raids against well-defined targets. Night raids were also flown against enemy troop concentrations, following directions from ground radar stations. This technique used pre-surveyed ground stations to locate, track and direct bombers on their run-in. Using 500-pound fragmentation bombs with proximity fuses set to air burst, the bombers were able to saturate ground areas about 150 yds in diameter with each burst. This anti-personnel bombing was employed in support of ground troops, often within 400 yds of the UN front lines.

Once again losses began to mount as the Communists brought effective countermeasures to bear. Against some of the strikes they flew night fighters directed into the bomber stream by an airborne controller aircraft orbiting above the B-29s and co-ordinating the attack. On June 10, 1952 four Shoran B-29s were picked up over Sinuiju by radar-controlled searchlights. Night fighters shot down two of the B-29s and damaged a third so badly that it crashed just inside the UN lines. By now the Superfortresses sported black bellies, coated with gloss lacquer to cut down visibility in sectors defended by radar-controlled searchlights.

More successful had been the continued use of the B-29s in an interdiction role. Rashin was now back on the target list, and on August 25, 1951 35 B-29s of 19th BG and 98th and 307th BWs mounted the first in a series of heavy raids on its rail yards. A sustained campaign against the rail network in North Korea culminated in the 44-day bombardment – beginning in January 1952 – of the small town of Wadong, a 'choke point' where North Korea's lateral rail route entered a narrow defile.

Still searching for the cloak of strategic respectability, the FEAF planners revived the plan to destroy North Korea's hydroelectric facilities. Four targets were chosen – Sui-Ho, Fusen, Chosen and Kyosen – with the B-29s committed to night-time Shoran-guided strikes following fighter-bomber raids during the day. The raids began on June 24 with an attack on Chosen. Within a week 90 per cent of North Korea's power supplies had been destroyed. From this success a policy was evolved which, in its essentials, foreshadowed the bombing strategy in Vietnam. Selected targets were subjected to crushing bombardment in the expectation that the Communists would be forced to sign the armistice over which they had been haggling for months. On July 11 targets in Pyongyang were attacked, and in the following weeks Sungho-Ri, Chosen, Sindok and Sinuiju were hit. On the night of July 30/31, 63 B-29s flew the biggest raid of the war against the Oriental Light Metals Company at Sinuiju. Ninety per cent of the plant was destroyed, denying major quantities of aluminum and magnesium alloys to North Korea. On September 12/13 six B-29s flew in to attack the Sui-Ho power plant. Electronic countermeasures were employed to confuse North Korean radar while 5th Air Force Douglas B-26s worked over the searchlights at low level with bombs and machine-guns. The B-29s, dropping 2000-pound SAP bombs, scored five direct hits, four probables and three near misses on the plant, also hitting the adjacent railway yards and transformers. On September 30 similar tactics

were used when 45 Superfortresses flattened the Namsan-Ri chemical plant on the Yalu, the last strategic target in the North.

In October the tactical pattern underwent further modification. The bomber stream was compressed, with the aircraft attacking at one-minute intervals. Countermeasures were strengthened, with 91st SRS flying 'ferret' missions to monitor and measure the operating frequencies, strengths and locations of enemy radars. Marine Corps Douglas F-3D Skynight jet fighters provided a protective screen, flying overhead cover between the stream's arrival at the Initial Point and breakaway after the bomb drop. Subsequently the arrival of the Lockheed F-94 night fighter enabled the F-3Ds to concentrate on top cover missions while F-94s made up the barrier screen. Attacks were delivered at irregular intervals and flown at varying altitudes carefully chosen to avoid tell-tale con-trails. Taking a leaf out of the RAF Bomber Command's book, heavily defended targets were attacked on nights when there was no moon. A mission analysis program established that between December 1952 and May 1953 the force virtually doubled its combat effectiveness in terms of target destruction accomplished for weight of bombs

dropped and damage or loss sustained.

The last Korean mission, a leaflet drop by B-29s of 91st SRS, was flown on July 17, 1953 – ten days before the war came to an end. The fighting in Korea had lasted just over three years, but only a single month of that time had been devoted to strategic bombing – an indication of the paucity of truly strategic targets as well as the growing vulnerability of the B-29. More than 21 000 B-29 sorties had been flown and 167 000 tons of bombs dropped. Combat losses were 34 machines: 16 shot down by enemy fighters, four by anti-aircraft fire and 14 lost as a result of various operational causes. The B-29 had given doughty service, but had now been left behind by postwar developments in aviation technology. The Superfortress was a product of the 1940s, an age before the jet fighter and superpower confrontation. Over Japan in 1945 it had ultimately proved an instrument of terrible destruction. Seven years later it was but one component in an air offensive which employed the fighter-bomber to equal effect. The Superfortress was soon to be succeeded by the Stratofortress – the very name evoking the relentless technological strides made since the B-29 first took to the skies.

Above: B-29s of SAC's 22nd BW en route to targets in North Korea.

Left: Approaching retirement: B-29s at the end of the Korean War.

The Soviet Union

In 1946 Josef Stalin dismissed the atomic bomb as a 'device to terrify the weaknerved'. Even when the Soviet Union exploded its first atomic bomb in 1949, the role of strategic air bombardment was played down in favour of the ground offensive, the traditional Russian 'steamroller'. One can only speculate on whether, in the immediate postwar years, the Russians were overly impressed by the United States' nuclear monopoly or chose to belittle it because of national pride. In the Soviet Union Douhet was dismissed as a 'bourgeois military adventurist', but the destruction of Hiroshima and Nagasaki had nevertheless forced the USSR to revise its approach to the use of air power in war.

When the Russians entered Berlin, their victorious armies were supported by over 20 000 aircraft and production was running at over 40 000 machines a year. But with the exception of the Pe-8 and a few Mitchell B-25s acquired in 1943, they did not possess an effective long-range bomber force. They had no jet interceptor aircraft and no radar early warning or controlled interception systems. After the German surrender, the top Soviet military and political leaders were able to inspect the results of the British and American combined strategic bombing offensive. The shells of Germany's shattered cities made a great impression on them. Nor had they neglected to remove from their zones of occupation huge quantities of German high-technology equipment and information, along with scientists, engineers and technicians.

Among the establishments taken over by the Russians were the secret research plants at Peenemünde and Rechlin. The capture of the Argus and Walter works provided invaluable material on liquid-fueled ramjet engines and liquid-fueled rockets respectively. Among the advanced aircraft which disappeared behind the Iron Curtain were the two prototypes of the Junkers Ju287 heavy jet bomber, which had been designed with swept-forward wings. A number of the Junkers staff went to Podberezhye in the USSR to work on the Ju287 which flew – with swept-back wings – in 1947.

The Ju287 did not exercise a crucial influence over Soviet jet bomber development. One of the most significant boosts to the Soviet program came in 1947 when the British government exported 25 Rolls Royce Nene and Derwent 5 turbojets to the Soviet Union. These were more sophisticated than the Junkers Jumo 004 and BMW 003 engines and enabled the Russians to bypass the lengthy development of low-thrust turbojets. The Nenes and the Derwents were immediately fitted into both fighter and bomber prototypes and went into mass production in the Soviet Union as the RD-45 (Nene) and RD-500 (Derwent).

Assistance, albeit unintended, also came from the United States. Towards the end of World War II three B-29s force landed in Soviet territory. They were not returned and, under the direction of the Tupolev design bureau, were copied and produced as the Tu-4 (NATO codename Bull). The Tu-4 remained the principal component of the Soviet Union's Long Range Aviation (Dal' naya Aviatsiya, or DA) arm until the early 1950s, by which time more than 1400 had been produced. It was also the Soviet Union's first strategic weapons delivery system. The first Soviet atomic device was tested in 1949, very much sooner than had been predicted by Western intelligence.

Much of the technology derived from the impounded B-29s found its way into the Tupolev Tu-16 (Badger), which represented a robust, straightforward approach to the strategic jet bomber requirements of the early 1950s. Entering service in 1953, the Tu-16 was powered by two Mikulin AM-3M singleshaft turbojets, each rated at 20 590 pounds thrust. Its maximum speed was 616 mph, with a range of 4000 miles carrying a 8360-pound bombload (maximum bombload was 19 842 pounds). In the tradition of the Pe-8, the Tu-16 incorporated extremely heavy defensive armament, with six 23 mm NR-23 cannon in radar-directed manned tail turret and remotely controlled upper dorsal and rear ventral barbettes and a seventh NR-23 in the nose.

The All-Purpose Badger

Production of this durable bomber continued into the early 1960s, with 2000 eventually being built. Since its appearance the Tu-16 has flown in a wide variety of roles. The Badger B carried two 'Kennel' anti-shipping cruise missiles on underwing pylons. The Badger C anti-shipping aircraft carried two 'Kipper' and later 'Kingfish' nuclear or conventional missiles. Badger D maritime and electronic reconnaissance aircraft are equipped with comprehensive radars housed in a large under-nose radome and electronic countermeasures (ECM) in other fairings. The Badger E was a photo- and multi-sensor type, superseded by the F with significantly improved photo-reconnaissance and electronic intelligence equipment. The Badger G is an updated version of the B armed with 'Kelt' stand-off missiles or 'Kingfish' nuclear missiles. Conventional or nuclear bombs can also be carried. The 'Kelt', with a range of up to 140 miles at high altitude, was the first Soviet air-to-surface missile to enter service. In the Arab-Israeli Yom Kippur war of 1973, 35 Tu-16s armed with 'Kelts' were supplied to the Egyptian Air Force. Out of 25 missiles launched, 20 were destroyed by Israeli air defenses; of the five which reached their targets, one hit a supply store and at least two homed automatically on to Israeli radar emissions. Finally, the Badger H and J versions are ECM jamming aircraft whose task is to escort and protect armed aircraft. The Badger K is another reconnaissance model. Approximately 800 Badgers remain in service with the DA and Naval Aviation. These include Badger Bs carrying nuclear or conventional bombs, various strategic and strike versions, and about 125 air force and 110 naval ECM, reconnaissance and flight refueling aircraft. They are in service with the Egyptian and Iraqi air forces, and China – which manufactures them as the Xian H-6s – deploys about 100.

In the early 1950s the only bomber with true intercontinental strategic capability was the B-36. The B-47 could reach the Soviet homeland only when flying from forward bases in Western Europe or North Africa. As a result the United States never abandoned its 'forward military position' in Europe and, when NATO was formed in 1949, the pattern of confrontation in Europe was set. The Soviet Union moved towards closing the intercontinental gap with the introduction into service of the Myasishchev M-4 and the Tupolev Tu-20, whose NATO codenames were, respectively, Bison and Bear. The M-4 proved something of a disappointment. The first Soviet production four-turbojet bomber, it was powered by Mikulin AM-3D engines carried as podded pairs in the wing roots and each rated at 19 180 pounds thrust. Although its maximum speed of 560 mph was satisfactory for a big jet aircraft of the mid-1950s, its range of approximately 5000 miles with a 12 000 pound load fell far short of the 10 000 miles achieved by the B-36. Its moderate service ceiling of 42 000 ft necessitated a heavy defensive armament of ten 23 mm cannon. A handful of obsolescent Bisons remain with the DA as bombers and a small number soldier on as tankers and in the long-range ECM role.

While the Tu-20 made use of identical systems, techniques and even similar airframe structures as the Tu-16, it achieved double the range of its immediate predecessor. Powered by four huge Kutsnetsov NK-12M turboprop engines driving contra-rotating propellers, the Bear emerged as an authentic strategic bomber with a maximum speed of 575 mph and range of 7800 miles with 25 000-pound bombload. Defensive armament was provided by six 23 mm cannon. Entering service in 1956, the Bear's B and C versions were first seen in 1961, carrying as their primary armament either a (400-mile-range) 'Kangaroo' or (185-mile-range) 'Kitchen' supersonic missile for strategic and stand-off attacks on surface targets. The Tu-20D flown by Soviet Naval Aviation is a major reconnaissance ECM reconnaissance type with chin radar, very large belly radar and up to 21 avionic features visible from stem to stern. The Bear E is a naval maritime reconnaissance aircraft with up to seven camera windows, while the Bear F is a naval anti-submarine strike aircraft.

Bombers v. Missiles

The Tu-20 had flown as a prototype in mid-1954, the high water mark of the strategic bomber's career. In 1952–53 the successful testing of thermonuclear (hydrogen) bombs promised another revolution in warfare. The hydrogen bomb multiplied the strategic bomber's striking power by a factor of 200. The bomb which had been dropped on Hiroshima had yielded less than the equivalent of 20 000 tons of TNT (20 kilotons). The device exploded by the United States in the 1948 Operation Sandstone yielded a 49 000-ton equivalent (49 kilotons). On October 31, 1952, in Operation Ivy, a thermonuclear device was exploded with a yield of 10 400 000 tons equivalent (10 400 kilotons or 10.4 megatons). The thermonuclear breakthrough provided production-line weapons with yields of 1–2 million tons weighing under 3000 pounds and small enough to be carried in tactical aircraft or in the warheads of ballistic missiles.

On January 12, 1954 the American Secretary of State, John Foster Dulles, declared that, 'Local defenses must be reinforced by the further deterrent of massive retaliatory power', and that the defense of the West depended 'primarily upon a capacity to retaliate instantly, by means and at places of our own choosing'. The thrust of the policy of 'massive retaliation' was that any act of aggression by a member of the Communist bloc might be countered by American strategic nuclear strikes on targets

Left: The Myasishchev M-4 Bison, which entered service with the Soviet air force in 1955. Bisons are still encountered over the Arctic, Atlantic and Pacific in high- and low-level probing missions.
Below: A Tu-20 Bear F naval strike aircraft photographed under the watchful eyes of USAF Phantom II fighters in September 1980.

deep within the Soviet or Chinese homelands. The strategic bomber had now assumed Douhet's mantle of the ultimate weapon, assigned the task of deterring all forms of armed conflict or, if necessary, of winning them.

The embodiment of this philosophy was the Boeing B-52 Stratofortress which became operational with 93rd Bomb Wing in the summer of 1955. Originally conceived in the late 1940s as a turbine-engined replacement for the B-36, the YB-52 prototype flew for the first time on April 15, 1952 powered by eight 8700-pound thrust Pratt and Whitney J57-P-1W turbojets, carried in twin pods under the 35-degree-swept wings. The colossal new silver aircraft incorporated many novel features. Fuel capacity, at 38 865 US gallons, was greater than in any previous production aircraft, giving a maximum take-off weight of 405 000 pounds. On the ground the bomber rested on four twin-wheel trucks, all of which were steerable and which could be slewed in unison to allow cross-wind landings to be made with the

Boeing B-52F

Supreme example of the durability and adaptability of the strategic bomber's airframe, the B-52 was planned in 1948 as turboprop and emerged in 1952 as a jet because of the availability of the advanced J57 engine. By 1962 the last of 744 had been delivered in eight main versions. The B-52F – of which 89 were built – was powered by eight J57-43Ws, fitted like earlier versions with water injection to boost take-off power. Painted black underneath, the B-52F was rebuilt in the early 1960s to accommodate Hound Dog pylons on which were hung long triple ejector racks for 24 750-pound bombs; internal bombload was 38 000 pounds and defensive armament was provided by four 0.5 M-3 guns in a pressurized, manned rear turret. Typical cruising speed was 565 mph at 36 000 ft.

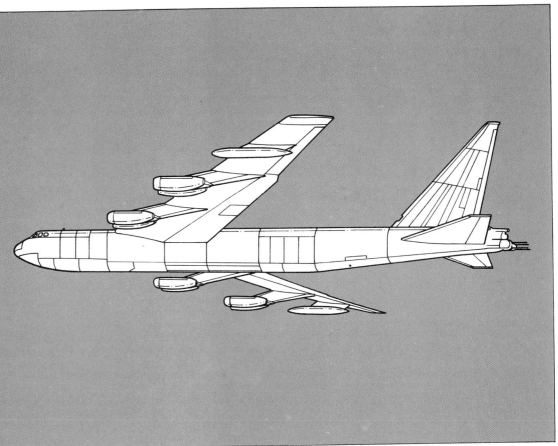

wings level and the aircraft crabbed diagonally on to the runway. The huge fin, only the very trailing edge of which was hinged to form a rudder, could be power-folded to the right to allow the aircraft to enter standard USAF hangars. All accessory power for the on-board systems was taken from the engines in the form of high pressure bleed air, ducted through stainless steel pipes to small high-speed turbines, which set up a tremendous noise driving everything from the hydraulic pumps to the air conditioning.

The initial production variant was the B-52A, powered by J57-P-9W engines, with side-by-side pilot seating in a stepped cockpit, of which only three of an order for 13 were built. The remaining ten were absorbed into the total of 50 B-52Bs, which began to enter service in 1955. Like its predecessor, the B-52B had many teething problems. Turbos exploded to cause fire or wreck sections of the fuselage; main-gear trucks had a nasty habit of trying to swivel in two directions simultaneously, or jamming at the maximum 20-degree slewed position; and the huge Fowler-type flaps cracked and broke under the strenuous sonic buffeting caused by repeated take-offs with the engines at full power with water injection. In February 1956 the 78 B-52s then in service were grounded while the problem of exploding air turbos was tackled (the system was finally replaced on the B-52F by conventional shaft drive). The B-52C, of which 35 were built, first flew on March 9, 1956. It was quickly followed in June of the same year by the B-57D, 170 of which eventually equipped SAC.

Cruising at altitudes above 50 000 ft and with an unlimited range provided by in-flight refueling, the B-52 was the awesome instrument of 'massive retaliation', but even as the C variants entered service the bomber's primacy came under threat from developments in the field of missile technology. In this crucial area the Russians possessed a lead which can be traced back to the military situation which confronted Stalin at the end of World War II. After 1945 the Soviet Union was faced with the need to prepare for a possible conflict with an adversary who was not accessible by land, as were Russia's traditional enemies, and which possessed the capability to project military power at great distances from his own homeland – most dramatically in the form of nuclear weapons. The Soviet Union could no longer rely on geography and physical size – both of which had proved too much for Napoleon and Hitler – to ensure victory in the event of a major conflict with the West. Its Tu-4s could have reached the United States on a one-way mission, or with air-refueling, but the Soviets did not develop a capability for the latter until the late 1950s. Rocketry provided the means to redress the balance.

At the end of World War II the Soviets acquired large stocks of German V-2 rockets and set captured German scientists to work on more advanced systems. As early as 1947 a small number of 'Scunner' SRBMS (Short Range Ballistic Missiles) had been deployed. In 1948 Stalin initiated an ICBM (Intercontinental Ballistic Missile) program to advance the work which had been conducted on the

V-2 types. Only one significant rocket was developed before Stalin died in 1953, the SS-2 'Sibling' SRBM.

Stalin's death led to a fierce struggle over strategic priorities. His successor, Georgii Malenkov, believed that when the Soviet Union and the United States both possessed adequate strategic nuclear forces, a mutual state of deterrence would make conventional conflict more likely than nuclear war. His opponents, among them, Molotov, Bulganin, Marshal Zhukov and, finally, Nikita Khrushchev, placed the emphasis on preparation for nuclear war and the overriding importance of achieving strategic surprise. Malenkov lost the argument, and the power struggle, and was deposed in February 1955. Under Khrushchev the development of long-range missile delivery systems continued apace, a program encouraged by the destructive power of the hydrogen bomb, which meant that the relative inaccuracy of the missiles was of little significance.

The first full-range test of a Soviet ICBM, involving an early version of the SS-6 'Sapwood', was made on August 26, 1957. In 1959 the Strategic Rocket Forces were formed as a new element in the Soviet armed forces and were referred to as the 'primary service'. Today, the C-in-C of the Strategic Rocket Forces automatically takes precedence over the other service chiefs, regardless of actual rank, a measure of the force's central importance in Soviet strategy.

If the United States unleashed its strategic bombers against the Soviet Union, the Russians would respond by destroying the major cities of America with ICBMs carrying compact hydrogen warheads. If either side crossed the nuclear threshold with strategic attacks on the enemy's homeland, it courted the risk of committing national suicide. Each side's strategic forces were now in place to deter their use by the enemy. The prospect of 'mutually assured destruction' had carried air warfare beyond the territory staked out by Douhet and fought over from 1917 to 1950. The hydrogen bomb was simply too destructive to be accommodated into a system based on the proposition that all future wars would be decided by the exercise of strategic air power.

By 1957 the development by the Soviets of the ICBM led to the adoption by SAC of the 'ground alert concept'. In order to ensure an effective and immediate retaliatory force in the face of missile threat, SAC initiated a program to bring one-third of its aircraft to a state of constant ground alert, with weapons loaded and crews standing by for immediate take-off. This state of preparedness, combined with a wide-scale dispersal of the B-52s from their previously crowded bases, was achieved by the summer of 1960. At the same time the United States strove to close the 'missile gap' with an ICBM development program for Atlas and Titan missiles. These were liquid-fueled, took several hours to prepare for firing, and so remained extremely vulnerable to surprise attack. Second-generation ICBMs like Minuteman were solid-fueled and could be fired almost instantly from 'hardened' underground silos. The submarine-launched missile, Polaris, was invulnerable to an enemy first strike.

The solid-fueled ICBM, tipped with a thermonuclear warhead of immense destructive power, was a weapon which, in the early 1960s, threatened always to get through. Not so the strategic bomber. Both offensive and defensive missiles were growing increasingly effective and accurate. The development of the big surface-to-air missile threatened the bomber's ability to deliver sure and certain destruction to any designated target. On May 1, 1960 a USAAF U-2 reconnaissance aircraft was shot down while flying over Sverdlosk at a height of 65 000 ft by a Soviet SA-1 'Guild' SAM (Surface to Air Missile). Between 1956 and 1960 U-2s roamed at will over the entire Soviet Union from bases in Norway, Turkey, Germany and Japan. The destruction of the aircraft flown by Lieutenant Gary Powers, and his subsequently highly publicised trial, suggested that in future the bomber might never get through. No longer could it be considered the United States' primary means of delivering nuclear weapons. In 1964 the US Secretary of Defense, Robert McNamara, stated that although long-range bombers would be employed in follow-up attacks, 'most of the aiming points in the Soviet target system can be best attacked by missiles'.

Seven years earlier Nikita Khrushchev had predicted that 'fighter and bomber planes can all now be put in museums'. This was a point of view echoed in the same year by the British Defence White Paper, which also forecast the imminent demise of the manned aircraft. The days of the big bomber, cruising majestically and unstoppably at high altitude, seemed numbered.

Suspect, but the Bomber Survives

In this climate governments considered it prudent to cancel or curtail a number of costly supersonic bomber projects, thereby releasing funds for the equally costly development of missiles. An early casualty, in March 1957, was the British Avro 730, a proposal for a supersonic bomber, powered by eight Armstrong Siddeley P.176 turbojets, which never progressed beyond the drawing board. Another supersonic bomber which never went into production was the Soviet Myasishchev M-52 'Bounder'. The USAF's delta-winged Convair B-58 Hustler was the first supersonic bomber to enter service, in the summer of 1960, but only 116 were built, 30 for development and 86 for combat duty. Nevertheless, it remains a significant aircraft. It was the first bomber to reach a speed of Mach 2; the first aircraft constructed mainly from stainless-steel honeycomb sandwich; the first bomber to carry its payload in a jettisonable pod, which also contained the fuel for the outward journey; the first to incorporate a stellar-inertial navigation system; and the first to use the escape capsule concept, in which the crew of three sat in individual capsules which could be ejected in an emergency even at supersonic speed. The Soviet equivalent was the Tupolev Tu-22 'Blinder', which entered service in 1963.

A spectacular casualty of doubts about the strategic bomber was the North American XB-70 Valkyrie, an immense delta-winged aircraft powered by six General Electric YJ93-GE-3 turbojet engines and capable of cruising to and from its targets at a constant Mach 3 and operational height of 75 000 ft. The prototype was rolled out at the North American (Rockwell) plant at Palmdale in May 1964. It flew for the first time in the following September and was canceled shortly thereafter.

The North American Valkyrie. First flown in September 1964, the bomber was canceled before it went into production.

out chinks in one's clothing ... the shattering noise; the constant teeth-jarring vibration; the turbulence causing the whole airframe to flex and creak; having to wear an oxygen mask which made every breath reek of wet rubber; the cramp which the tight harness made it impossible to relieve...'

Nearly 30 years later a B-52D crew member, flying over North Vietnam in the 'Linebacker II' campaign, recorded his impressions: '*OUR B-52D HAD almost no creature comforts. They don't nowadays, either. Room in which to move around is minimal. Finding a comfortable place at some crew positions merely to prop your foot for a change of posture can be an adventure. The air conditioning is usually either too hot or too cold [a problem shared with World War II aircrew] and its whine plus the noise of eight jet engines combines with the rushing of the slipstream and the sounds made by the actuators and motors to create a din which drowns out a shouted message in just a couple of feet. It can only be overcome without loss of voice by use of the interphone; however, the fatiguing background roar is ever-present'.*

Clearly some things had not changed. Nevertheless, change has been the feature of the B-52's long career. During the Vietnam conflict the B-52D was structurally rebuilt for high-density bombing with conventional bombs - a role not anticipated in the original design. Modifications were required in all models to permit sustained and punishing operations a low level, flying under hostile radar - a method of attack not envisaged when the B-52 was designed. In continuous improvement programs, the B-52Gs and Hs have received considerable updating of both offensive and defensive electronic systems. These include the installation of the Electro-Optical Viewing System (EVS), Phase VI ECM, satellite communications facilities, and 'smart noise' jammers to swamp enemy radars. In 1980 a $126.3 million program was initiated to equip the aging B-52Ds with a new digital navigation/bombing system. The installation of an Offensive Avionics System (OAS) in the B-52Gs and Hs, under way in the mid-1980s, will cost at least $1,662 million.

SAC's B-52 bomber force now numbers approximately 300, supported by small numbers of training and back-up aircraft. Sixteen squadrons (including two training) are equipped with 151 B52Gs and 90 B-52Hs, of which 30 fulfil conventional roles - maritime reconnaissance, minelaying and acting as a 'Strategic Projection Force' within the Rapid Deployment Joint Task Force. In 1981, during the 'Bright Star' exercise in Egypt, B-52s flew direct from the east coast of the United States, made strikes in the desert and then flew back, refueling in-flight on the journey.

In the early 1970s the B-52 ceased to be a high-level strategic bomber. From 1972 the B-52Gs and Hs were armed with the nuclear-tipped AGN-69A SRAM (Short Range Attack Missile), of which there are estimated to be approximately 1200 with the SAC Bomb Wings. The SRAM was designed to enable the B-52 to blast its way through to the target at low altitude, obliterating the radar and missile sites in its path. The B-52s can carry up to 24 SRAMs

The Valkyrie had been developed as a replacement for the B-52. But while the XB-70 has slipped into the gallery of aviation curiosities, along with the Beardmore Inflexible and the Barling bomber, the B-52 - conceived in 1948 and ordered in 1951 - is still with us and will remain operational until well into the 1990s. In spite of exaggerated reports of its death, the strategic bomber has survived.

One of the principal reasons for the B-52's longevity is its sheer size. Large strategic bombers have the slowest rate of change of any type of combat aircraft. Each one represents a huge financial investment, but their big airframes are capable of absorbing successive engineering changes, new weapons systems, and electronic warfare equipment, preserving a modern combat capability in an aging airframe.

The major production version of the Stratofortress was the B-52G, 193 of which were built between 1958 and 1961. The first was delivered to SAC's 5th BW on February 13, 1959. Its extended unrefueled range of 10 000 miles was the result of redesigned wings with integral tanks, while other new features included a shorter tail fin and rudder and a pressure cabin for the rear gunner, firing the four 0.5 guns in the tail by remote control. Significant changes in the aircraft's offensive load underlined the rapidly changing air environment and were designed to provide the B-52 with a stand-off capability. Previous versions of the Stratofortress could carry up to 60 000 pounds of conventional or nuclear weapons in the fuselage bomb bay. The B-52G introduced the Hound Dog strategic air-to-surface missile, two of which were usually carried. Powered by a single J52 turbojet engine, the nuclear-tipped Hound Dog could be launched over 500 miles from its target. The B-52G also carried in its bomb bay four Quail unarmed air decoy missiles. Launched en route to the target and powered by a single turbojet, the Quail flew at approximately the same speed and altitude as the B-52 and creating a similar 'blip' on the enemy's radar screens.

Recalling flying in a Wellington over Hamburg on July 24, 1943 Air Commodore H I Cozens wrote: '*ANYONE WHOSE SOLE EXPERIENCE OF flying is confined to holiday jets has simply no idea of what it was like to fly in a wartime piston-engined bomber: the numbing cold, with icy winds seeking*

internally on three rotary launchers. The missile has a range of between 35 and 105 miles, depending on launch height, following a ballistic trajectory on inertial guidance or using pre-programmed terrain-following maneuvers. The B-52 can also carry eight Mk28 free-fall nuclear weapons, each with a yield of 25 megatons, over a thousand times more powerful than the bombs which fell on Hiroshima.

By the mid-1970s it was clear that the B-52's SRAMS, its successive electronic overhauls, and its ability to fly low, would still not be proof against the increasingly sophisticated Soviet air defense network. An answer, and yet another modification, to the B-52Gs and Hs, was provided by the parallel development of the cruise missile – the direct descendant of the German V-1 of World War II. With its future as a penetration bomber virtually at an end, the B-52 was converted to use as a launch platform for long-range missiles. The first production models of an order for 3,418 AGM-86B ALCMs (Air Launched Cruise Missiles) were delivered to 416th BW, SAC, at Griffiss Air Force Base in January 1981. In December 1982 the first squadron of 14 AGM-86B-equipped aircraft became operational. Over 100 B-52Gs have been subsequently modified to carry 12 externally-mounted ALCMs and a progam is in hand to convert 96 B-52Hs, each of which will carry 20 ALCMs. Powered by a Williams F-107-101 turbofan engine, the missile has a range of between 1000 and 1550 miles, cruising at 500 mph. The ALCM is a force multiplyer, giving the B-52 a multi-target capability, with its missile able to approach from any direction on a variety of flight profiles. Another cruise missile available to the B-52 is the GD AGM-109H MRAS (Medium Range Air to Surface Missile), a shorter range version of the Tomahawk with a conventional warhead dispensing sub-munitions, the usual design being for cratering enemy runways. Maritime B-52s are equipped with the GBU-15 (V) stand-off precision-guided conventional weapon for use against shipping and other clearly defined targets.

Long life in ageing airframes:
Above: Aircrew scramble to a B-52.
Left: A Soviet Bear H cruise missile carrier intercepted by 21st Tactical Fighter Wing off the north coast of Alaska on April 5, 1985.

4.3 VIETNAM AND ROLLING THUNDER

THE VIETNAM WAR, THE LONGEST conflict in which US armed forces have ever been engaged and the only one since 1945 in which strategic bombing took place on a major scale. However, the strategic aims of the United States were pursued not by its B-52s but by USAF, Navy and Marine fighter-bombers. It was only towards the end of the war, in 1972, that the B-52s were involved in a fierce quasi-strategic 11-day campaign waged against targets in North Vietnam.

The bombing of North Vietnam began in August 1964, after incidents in the Gulf of Tonkin in which North Vietnamese torpedo boats attacked the US Navy destroyers *Maddox* and *C Turner Joy*. The precise truth behind these engagements has been the subject of fierce debate, but at the time it enabled the US President Lyndon Baines Johnson to secure the passage through Congress of the Gulf of Tonkin resolution empowering him to use all measures – including the commitment of armed forces – to assist South Vietnam in the defense of its independence against North Vietnamese aggression.

The bombing campaign began before the massive commitment of ground troops which gathered pace from the summer of 1965. On August 18, 1964 the US ambassador in South Vietnam, General Maxwell D Taylor, recommended to Washington, as one of the steps to shore up the regime in South Vietnam, a 'carefully orchestrated bombing attack against North Vietnam, aimed primarily at infiltration and other military targets'. This advice was given greater urgency on November 1 when Viet Cong units shelled the Bien Hoa airfield near Saigon, destroying five USAAF B-57 Canberra tactical bombers, damaging another 15 and killing four American personnel. On December 2 President Johnson approved a limited Air Force and Navy program against Communist lines of communication used to supply the insurgents in South Vietnam. The second series of air strikes against North Vietnam, code-named Flaming Dart, was launched at the beginning of February 1965 following an incident in which Viet Cong mortar and demolition teams attacked US and South Vietnamese military facilities near Pleiku. This was quickly followed by Flaming Dart II, provoked by an attack on Qui Nhon on February 10. These purely retaliatory strikes were the preliminaries to the Rolling Thunder bombing offensive, which lasted from March 1965 to October 1968.

Rolling Thunder differed materially from the strategic bombing campaigns of World War II, in its essentials resembling the geographically limited air war fought in Korea 15 years before. In formulating a policy for bombing North Vietnam, President Johnson faced three distinct options: first the launching of retaliatory strikes, as in the Flaming Dart operations; second, a swift no-holds-barred offensive against targets of military significance; and third, a 'slow squeeze' in the form of a gradually escalating campaign in which the punishment inflicted on the enemy was geared directly to his own aggression. It was anticipated that the bombing would reduce the North's ability to supply the Viet Cong in the South by destroying its war economy, weaken the North's will to continue the struggle while simultaneously raising morale in the South, and exploiting the United States' clear technological superiority.

The third option was adopted. This failed to take account of the relatively under-developed state of the North Vietnamese economy and communications systems, which meant that there were few elements in either which could not be repaired or dispensed with if irretrievably damaged by bombing. Moreover, the bulk of North Vietnam's military equipment was supplied by China and the Soviet Union. President Johnson considered that there was too great a risk attached to any attempt directly to interrupt these supplies. He was also concerned about the wider effect of any bombing campaign on world opinion and the immediate reaction of the electorate at home to a widening of the conflict. This led to frequent pauses in the campaign in response to North Vietnamese hints that they were willing to negotiate. General Westmoreland, the American commander in Vietnam from June 20, 1964 to June 24, 1968, later wrote, 'To North Vietnam it must have been clear that the bombing demonstrated not strength and determination but political weakness and uncertainty'.

The assumptions underlying Rolling Thunder were flawed in their application to both North and South Vietnam. As the Presidential adviser John P Roche observed in May 1967, '*WHAT HAS me is the notion (expressed time and again by the Air Force boys) that air power could provide a strategic route to victory; and the parallel assumption that by bombing the North we could get a cut-rate solution in the South and escape the problems of building a South Vietnamese army*'.

In the North the gradual build-up of the campaign – and the failure to interdict the inward flow of matériel – allowed the North Vietnamese a vital breathing space in which to place their country on a war footing and upgrade their initially primitive anti-aircraft defenses into a formidably integrated system capable of inflicting heavy casualties on the Americans. There is a parallel to be drawn here with World War II: the US bombing offensive made the conflict a 'total war' for the North Vietnamese, which in turn strengthened rather than weakened their morale. Paradoxically it had precisely the opposite effect in the United States, providing the anti-war movement with some of its heaviest ammunition.

Tight control of all Rolling Thunder operations was exercised from Washington. There was none of the freedom which had been enjoyed by Trenchard or craftily engineered by Harris. No important target or target area in North Vietnam could be hit without prior approval of the President. His decisions were handed down by Secretary of Defense Robert S

McNamara to the Joint Chiefs, who then issued strike directives to the Commander-in-Chief Pacific (CINCPAC). It was the latter's task to assign targets and armed reconnaissance routes between the USAF, US Navy and the Vietnamese Air Force (VNAF), with USAF crews usually providing air cover for the VNAF, which was subsequently withdrawn from operations against the North to concentrate on supporting their own ground forces in South Vietnam.

Operational constraints flowed directly from the political underpinning of the campaign. The day, time, strength, and direction of attacks was determined by Washington. They were limited to primary targets or one of two secondaries. If the mission was aborted because of bad weather, it could only be rescheduled by repeating the laborious process of gaining approval from Washington. Enemy aircraft had to be positively identified before being engaged, not always simple when flying at speeds of Mach 1. Only military trucks could be attacked, but they had to be moving along the roads. If they were parked in villages, they were out of bounds. The overriding concern to minimize civilian casualties, and the removal of the element of surprise (a problem exacerbated by the relatively small geographical area overflown by Rolling Thunder crews), led to a certain stereotyping of American tactics, which enabled the North Vietnamese to deploy their air defenses to considerable effect.

There was one factor over which the Americans had no control – the weather, as crucial over North Vietnam in 1968 as it had been over the Western Front in 1918. The northeast monsoon, which lasted from October to March, often ruled out full-scale attacks on fixed targets and played havoc with armed reconnaissance operations. Torrential rain, low cloud and wretched visibility hid the enemy's anti-aircraft defenses, masking the launching and in-flight targeting of his SAM missiles. When US aircraft dropped below the cloud cover, they came within range of radar-controlled guns and small arms. At night in these conditions, the only aircraft able to locate a pinpoint target without flares – flying low enough to hit it and maneuver to avoid mountain tops, missiles and anti-aircraft fire – was the US Navy's carrier-based all-weather attack aircraft, the A-6 Intruder. The frequently unpredictable weather conditions over Vietnam were never fully appreciated in Washington. With centralized control being exercised from afar, it was impossible to keep in touch with the ever-changing weather, which often demanded on-the-spot changes in targets and weapons assignments.

The principal Air Force tactical strike aircraft during Rolling Thunder was the Republic F-105D Thunderchief, which from early 1965 began flying combat missions north of the 17th Parallel. A key target during these initial operations was the strategically important Than Hoah bridge carrying a highway and rail line across the Ma River which flows into the Gulf of Tonkin. On April 4 Thunderchiefs, escorted by USAF North American F-100 Super Sabres, were intercepted during their bombing run on the bridge by four North Vietnamese MiG-17s. Two of the Thunderchiefs were shot down.

MiG-17s, and later MiG-19s and MiG-21s, formed but one element in North Vietnam's air defenses. The

second was the Soviet-supplied SA-2 'Guideline' radar-guided SAM missile, particularly dangerous when launched through a layer of cloud. The SAM missiles were first detected by a SAC U-2 aircraft on April 5, 1965. By the end of the year USAF and Navy reconnaissance had pinpointed nearly 60 SAM sites. Tied to the policy of gradual escalation, the United States refrained from attacking the missile launchers until it could be demonstrated that they were operational. Confirmation was provided by a USAF Douglas EB-66C Destroyer electronic warfare aircraft when it intercepted radar signals from one of the sites. Then, on July 24, 1965, a SAM launched west of Hanoi claimed its first victim, a USAF F-4C Phantom.

The North Vietnamese skilfully concealed the SAM sites, readily abandoning them to build new ones, many equipped with dummy missiles. Their 'launch and move' tactics were also applied to the anti-aircraft gun sites. There were approximately 400 sites by the end of 1965, the guns controlled by radar and varying in caliber from 37 mm to 100 mm. At this stage in the war a typical North Vietnamese ruse was to erect a dummy SAM battery and then surround it with camouflaged anti-aircraft guns. Also effective against low-flying aircraft was small arms and machine-gun fire, which by mid-1965 was credited with shooting down the majority of the 50 Air Force and Navy aircraft lost over North Vietnam.

Among the countermeasures employed against the MiGs was the airborne radar carried by the USAF EC-121Ds, a military version of the Lockheed Super Constellation. Patrolling over the Gulf of Tonkin, the EC-121D alerted US fighter and support aircraft to approaching MiGs and also served as air-borne radar and communications platforms. Later in the war the radar web was expanded to include the Navy's sea-based radars, increasing the information available on their own and the enemy's operations over the North.

The drive to suppress the radar-controlled SAMs, anti-aircraft guns and other defense radars resulted

An aerial reconnaissance photograph of a North Vietnamese SAM site near Haiphong, taken by a North American RA5C Vigilante from the carrier *Constellation*. The arrows indicate launch pads with the SAMs in position. At both high and low altitudes the Vigilante was kept precisely on course by a radar inertial guidance system and automatic flight controls. The aircraft was particularly effective in photographing missile sites or other pinpoint targets as each photo carried a marginal notation showing the plan's longitude and latitude when the picture was taken. All the information brought back by the Vigilante was fed into the computerized databank on board the carrier, providing a vital intelligence base for mission planners.

Republic F-105D Thunderchiefs bombing near Khe Sanh on Combat Skyspot guidance from radar-equipped ground operators. The Thunderchief made more strikes against North Vietnam than any other US aircraft, and also suffered more losses. Between 1965 and 1971 the F-105Ds were fitted with armor plate, a secondary flight control system, an improved pilot ejection seat and underwing ECM pods. Modified F-105Fs formed the backbone of the 'Wild Weasel' countermeasures program designed to improve the US Air Force's electronic warfare capability.

in a complex electronic battle reminiscent of that fought over Germany in World War II. The technology used was infinitely more sophisticated but the aims were the same. The first counter-measures were provided by USAF EB-66C Destroyers and the Navy's almost identical EA-3 Skywarriors. The EB-66C featured a pressurized capsule in its bomb bay which housed four technicians operating electronic reconnaissance equipment. This provided warning that SAM guidance radar was transmitting. On October 17, 1965 radar detection played its part in the first successful attack on a SAM site. In this operation an 'Iron Hand' flight of four McDonnell Douglas A-4C Skyhawk carrier bombers, led by an A-6 Intruder flown by Lieutenant-Commander E 'Pete' Garber, knocked out the SAM site at Kep airfield, 50 miles northeast of Hanoi, with Shrike missiles which identified and homed on a SAM battery's guidance radar.

The 'Iron Hand' missions were paralleled by the USAF's employment of 'Wild Weasel' F-105Fs carrying radar warning and homing gear. When the 'Wild Weasel' picked up radar emissions from the enemy's 'Fan Song' radar, it turned towards the transmitter and launched a Shrike missile which followed the radar beam to its source. In the early stages of the war USAF EB-66Bs packed with powerful jamming equipment also flew radar support missions, although their lack of speed prevented them from accompanying the bombers over the target and they were forced to operate at a distance. Of approximately 180 SAMs launched in 1965, only 11 succeeded in downing American aircraft.

From late 1966 individual fighter-bombers were equipped with a 'countermeasures pod' in a stream-lined underwing housing which broadcast a signal capable of jamming enemy radar. The pod could be adjusted to jam radars controlling either anti-aircraft guns or SAMs. American pilots tended to concentrate on the SAM sites, flying out of range of the light flak and at altitudes at which the missiles would normally have been effective.

Effect of the Bombing Pauses
The first two years of Rolling Thunder were marked by periodic bombing pauses ordered by President Johnson in the hope that these would encourage Hanoi's leaders to enter negotiations for a political settlement of the war. The first, approximately a week long, was ordered in May 1965. The second began on December 24, 1965 and continued until the end of January. Bomber stand-downs were also ordered to permit celebration of the Vietnamese New Year ('Tet'), Buddha's birthday, Christmas and New Year's Day. The principal effect of these pauses was to enable the North Vietnamese to undertake a massive and well-organized resupply of their ground forces. The dramatic effect of the stand-downs can be gauged by some figures for 1967. During the 24-hour Christmas and 36-hour New Year stand-downs US pilots and photo-interpreters identified over 3000 supply trucks in North Vietnam. Pilots from the carrier *Kittyhawk* counted 560 trucks jammed on one seven-mile stretch of road. This compares with a daily average of 170 trucks for the other days between December 22, 1967 and January 4, 1968.

The North Vietnamese showed no inclination to come to the peace table and early in 1966 Rolling Thunder strikes were resumed against military targets in North Vietnam. Road and rail bridges were hit, along with industrial targets such as cement factories and power plants. In the summer the focus was shifted to oil storage facilities, most of which were situated near Hanoi and Haiphong. It was an echo of Spaatz's Oil Plan of 1944, but the results were not similarly decisive. The first major oil strike was made on June 29, 1966, when USAF F-105s raided a 32-tank complex less than four miles from Hanoi, destroying 95 per cent of the target. Navy aircraft also joined the offensive. On the same day 28 aircraft from the carrier *Ranger* attacked the Haiphong complex, which blew up in three huge fireballs leaving thick columns of greasy black smoke hanging over the city at 20 000 ft. The leader of the strike, Commander Frederick F Palmer of Air Wing 14, recalled: '*I* PUT THE A-4Cs, SLOWEST OF *the jets in the attack group, in the van. Commander Al "Shoes" Shaufelberger, Commanding Officer of VA-146 (Blue Diamonds), did a perfect job of navigating to the target area and the fireball from his bombs provided an interesting obstacle for subsequent attackers during their pull-out. Commander Bob Holt, leading the War Horses of VA-55, peppered and ignited several tanks with his load of 2.74 Mighty Mouse rockets. The flak was heavy, initially, in the target area, but flak suppressors – F-4s of VF-142 led by Commander Jim Brown – were so accurate in placing their bombs that it seemed as if a switch had suddenly "turned off" the heavy caliber anti-aircraft fire. Finally Fighting 143, led by Commander Walt Spangenberg, positioned their Phantoms between the MiG bases and the attack group. There were no takers*'.

Oil storage facilities in Vinh were hit on July 23, resulting in another spectacular fire. In this attack Commander Wynne F Foster, leading VA-163 in an A-4E, was hit on the starboard side of the cockpit by gunfire and his right arm severed below the shoulder. Holding the stump of his shattered right arm to staunch the flow of blood, Foster steered the crippled Skyhawk out over the sea with his knees, finally making a left-handed ejection over water near USS *Reeves*, which rescued him.

At the end of July, Soviet tankers had ceased sailing to Haiphong. They reappeared in August but were now loaded with drums rather than bulk fuel. The North Vietnamese sought to protect their own diesel-powered oil barges by anchoring them next to tankers of other nations in the roadsteads off Haiphong and Hon Gai. Under cover of darkness or foul weather the barges would sprint for the ports, which were out of bounds to US aircraft. The task of intercepting them on this last leg of the journey was entrusted to the A-6s, with their all-weather attack systems, and A-4s working under flares.

By the end of 1966 all of Hanoi and Haiphong's above-ground oil storage facilities had been destroyed. Work at the Haiphong receiving terminal had been brought to a virtual standstill, with less than one-third of a shipload being handled a month. But the North Vietnamese retained a four-month military reserve dispersed in drums and buried or hidden in caves. The oil campaign – launched 15 months into the conflict – had come too late to cripple the North Vietnamese war effort. The long delay, and the 37-day bombing pause over Christmas in 1965–66, gave the North Vietnamese a breathing space in which to disperse their oil stocks, moving

them by truck rather than by the more vulnerable rail system, and beginning the construction of an underground pipeline system. Nevertheless, the effort required was considerable. It is estimated that up to 300 000 Vietnamese workers had to be diverted to keep road and rail networks working and man anti-aircraft defenses. By the end of the year, US tactical aircraft had flown 107 000 sorties over North Vietnam, dropping at least 165 000 tons of bombs for the loss of 455 machines. The number of SAM sites had risen to about 150, but improved tactics and the installation of countermeasures pods had reduced the effectiveness of their missiles.

Early in 1967 the targets moved closer to Hanoi, prompting Operation Bolo, the most spectacular air battle of the war, planned and led by Colonel Robin Olds of 8th Tactical Fighter Wing. The increasingly troublesome North Vietnamese MiG-21s could not be attacked on the ground, so on January 2 Olds lured them into the air with what appeared to be a standard Rolling Thunder strike by F-105s. When the enemy intercepted the strike force, they found themselves tangling with F-4C Phantoms which shot down seven MiGs in 12 minutes for no loss. Four days later another two MiGs were shot down, and the NVAF stood down to regroup and retrain.

Rolling Thunder had moved some way from its original aim of persuading the North Vietnamese to suspend their operations in the South. It had now assumed the shape of a massive interdiction campaign directed against southward movement of matériel. In March 1967 the Canal des Rapides, the rail and highway bridge four miles north of Hanoi, was hit for the first time. In July an extended target list was issued permitting attacks on 16 additional fixed targets and 23 road, rail and waterway segments inside the previously restricted Hanoi-Haiphong areas. From the end of August a concerted effort was made to isolate Haiphong by destroying its major bridges, mining trans-shipment points near the city and cutting its rail links with Hanoi. One of the first targets to be hit, on August 30, was the

Most missions flown by the Grumman A-6A involved attacks from the minimum safe altitude, but these aircraft from the carrier *Constellation* are on a level bombing sortie. The A-6A could carry a maximum of 15 000 pounds of ordnance, with a typical load comprising 30 500-pound bombs.

Haiphong highway bridge southeast of the city. Twenty-four A-4Cs from *Oriskany*, led by Commander Burton H Shepheard, flew through a barrage of SAMs and intense 37 mm, 57 mm and 85 mm fire, maintaining their group integrity to drop all of their bombs within 12 seconds and destroying three of the bridge's four spans. Within a few weeks all the principal bridges around Hanoi and Haiphong had been made unserviceable. It was estimated that some 200 000 tons of goods imported by sea had been piled up in colossal dumps near the Haiphong docks. Permission was never obtained to attack these dumps or the Haiphong docks and warehouses.

In the same month Haiphong's ship and barge-building yards came under heavy attack from carrier strikes launched from Task Force 77, forcing the North Vietnamese to remove construction to the sanctuaries of Haiphong's inner city, where strikes were not permitted. There is little doubt that the cumulative effect of the interdiction campaign placed the North Vietnamese war economy under great strain. The successive day and night attacks severely disrupted work in the Haiphong docks, and ship unloading times more than trebled. It required no more than the regular presence of US aircraft in the area to prevent the effective dredging of the approaches to Haiphong.

Rail and Bridge Busting

A key target was the rail line running south from Hanoi and Haiphong to Thanh Hoa. It was frequently cut by air strikes, which in turn provided opportunities to wreck the trains stranded between the wrecked sections of the line, tactics which would have been familiar to British pilots who had flown during the Battle of the Somme in 1916. The destruction of rail bridges seriously disrupted North Vietnamese supply lines, forcing them to offload at each crossing – usually by night – to ferry the cars and supplies across before reloading on the other side. Bridges – those targets which in 1918 Major-General Sykes had considered so difficult to destroy – absorbed much of the Rolling Thunder effort. On August 11 the Paul Doumer bridge, which carried road and rail traffic across the Red River at Hanoi, was hit by 26 F-105Ds, each armed with a single 3000-pound bomb and attacking in three waves. Each wave was provided with four F-4s flying top cover, four more attacking anti-aircraft batteries, and four 'Wild Weasels' for SAM suppression. As anti-personnel bombs burst among the enemy gun positions, the strike force climbed from tree-top height to 13 000 ft, dived on the bridge at an angle of 45 degrees, released their bombs, lowered their air brakes and then pulled out. The second Thunder-chief to attack released at 7000 ft, scoring a direct hit which dropped the center span into the river. Two more spans were destroyed in the attack, and the bridge was out of action until late October. No sooner had traffic been resumed than the Thunderchiefs brought it down again. Frantic repair work restored service by the end of November, whereupon the fighter-bombers delivered the coup de grâce in two December raids. The North Vietnamese abandoned the bridge and replaced it with a pontoon carrying rail traffic.

Equally important were the railroad ferries which the North Vietnamese were now using to cross the Red River. On the night of October 30, 1967 a single A-6A Intruder, flown by Lieutenant-Commander Charles B Hunter with Lieutenant Lyle F Bull as bombardier/navigator, took off from the carrier *Constellation* to attack a ferry slip near Hanoi. The Hanoi area was now bristling with the greatest concentration of anti-aircraft defenses in the history of aerial warfare. It was defended by 15 SAM sites, at least 560 anti-aircraft guns, and by MiG-17s and 21s flying from nearby bases. To attack the landing slip, Hunter had to make a low-level night approach across the rugged, mountainous terrain surrounding the Red River, dropping his 18 500-pound bombs along an impact line of 2800 ft. With Lieutenant Bull interpreting radar echoes to identify landmarks and avoid dangerous ridges, Hunter had flown to within 18 miles of the target when his instruments and earphones told him that the A-6A had been picked up by the North Vietnamese search radar. Hunter brought the Intruder down to a level at which he hoped to slip below the radar horizon, but as he reached the Initial Point he detected a SAM battery locking on to him. Descending again and turning on to the bombing heading, Hunter saw a SAM rising towards him. He recalled, 'WHEN I FIRST SAW IT, IT WAS *dead ahead and above me, and it appeared that it would pass overhead. However, just as it got overhead, I could see it turn directly downward and head for us. To me the rocket exhaust looked like a doughnut'.

Declining to jettison his bombs and head for home, Hunter executed a high-g low-altitude barrel roll, a near-suicidal maneuver. The SAM exploded within 200 ft of the A-6A, shaking it violently as Hunter rolled out at 2000 ft and commenced the bombing run within a few degrees of the inbound heading. As Hunter and Bull closed on the target they came under intense AA fire. At least five SAMs were also airborne and heading for them. For the last seven miles Hunter flew the Intruder at deck level on the radar altimeter, hoping that he was too low for the missile batteries to track and shoot him down. One by one the SAMs detonated 400 ft above him, filling the cockpit with a blinding flash and buffeting the aircraft as it bored in on the target. The flak barrage lit up the sky and searchlights illuminated Hunter's aircraft, enabling small arms and automatic weapon sites to add to the volume of fire directed at the lone A-6A. Flying through this inferno at tree-top height, Hunter located the ferry and released his bombs directly on the target, executing a seven-g turn as they fell away and four SAMs exploded aft and above him. Rolling out, Hunter streaked southeast-ward, varying his altitude and at one point jinking heavily to counter a MiG-17 which had briefly got on his tail. Flak followed him all the way until his A-6A cleared the coast.

The most intractable target in North Vietnam was the horizontal steel birdcage Thanh Hoa bridge on the Ma River, 80 miles south of Hanoi. During the 43 months of Rolling Thunder Navy, Air Force and Marine aircraft flew 700 sorties against the bridge, losing eight aircraft in the process. Over 1250 tons of bombs were dropped on this stubborn target, but the Thanh Hoa bridge defied destruction. In March 1967 Navy aircraft attacked the bridge with the recently

introduced 'Walleye' glide bomb. A television camera in the missile's nose was locked on to the target before its release – the picture appearing on a small monitor screen in the cockpit – and then guided the 'Walleye' to the target. Three hits were scored but only minor damage was inflicted on the bridge, which was beginning to acquire a legendary reputation. It was to survive until 1972, when it was finally wrecked by a laser-guided 'Smart' bomb.

By the end of 1967 the US air forces had gained virtual air supremacy over North Vietnam. From April the MiG bases at Kep, Hoa Lac, Hien An and Phuc Yen had come under heavy bombardment, obliging the NVAF to withdraw to Chinese bases. Seventy-five MiGs had been downed in air-to-air combat against American losses of 25. The bombing had inflicted heavy damage on North Vietnam and, in the pattern established during the two World Wars, diverted several hundred thousand personnel to home defense duties. But the North's determination to continue fighting had been underestimated while its vulnerability had been overestimated. As in Korea the number of big strategic targets was limited. These were duly flattened, but the North Vietnamese were able to withstand these losses – even that of their one and only steel mill. Nor had Rolling Thunder interrupted the flow of matériel from China, the Soviet Union and the Eastern bloc nations. The crucial move which might have terminated the war – the mining or blockading of Haiphong harbor – was ruled out because of the risk to third-country shipping. For several months the interdiction campaign had bottled up huge quantities of matériel in the port and disrupted its dispersal, but the stranglehold could not be maintained. Secretary of State McNamara reached the conclusion that the cost of Rolling Thunder could no longer be justified. On March 31, 1968 President Johnson suspended bombing north of the 20th Parallel (250 miles north of the Demilitarized Zone), announcing at the same time that he would not seek a second term as President of the United States. On October 31, on the eve of the Presidential election, he halted all bombing of North Vietnam.

An F4B Phantom of VF-154 from the attack carrier *Ranger* strikes at an artillery site north of the Demilitarized Zone in February 1968, in support of the US 3rd Marine Division. In spite of its comprehensive navigational systems, the F-4 was not equipped for accurate level bombing from medium altitudes. A technique was devised in which the Phantoms bombed on a signal from a fully-equipped lead ship, frequently an RB-66C. Typical loads included 18 750-pound bombs, 11 150-US gallon napalm bombs, four Bullpup air-to-surface missiles or 15 air-to-surface missiles or rockets.

B-52s in a Tactical Role

It is one of the ironies of the air war in Southeast Asia that while tactical fighter bombers conducted an essentially strategic campaign against North Vietnam in Rolling Thunder, the B-52s of Strategic Air Command dropped millions of 'iron bombs' in a tactical role. For more than seven years the Strato-fortresses were used to support friendly ground forces, bomb hostile base areas, blunt enemy offensives, and interdict infiltration routes in South Vietnam, Laos and Cambodia. It was not until the 11-day 'Linebacker II' operation launched in December 1972 that the B-52s swung into a quasi-strategic role, bringing the air war against North Vietnam to a close.

In the early 1960s President Kennedy's administration backed away from the policy of 'massive retaliation', adopting a strategy of 'flexible response' in which local challenges would initially be met with conventional forces. This change of direction prompted SAC to examine the tactical potential of its strategic bombers. The B-52 emerged as the most suitable contender for conversion, and at the beginning of 1964 Secretary of Defense McNamara directed SAC to improve the Strato-fortresses's capability to wage limited war. As a result the B-52F underwent an extensive series of modifications, enabling it to carry 27 750-pound general purpose bombs in its internal bomb bay and 24 more on external underwing pylon racks. After modification the nominal maximum weight of bombs which could be carried by a B-52F was 38 200 pounds.

In February 1965, as the situation in South Vietnam deteriorated, Strategic Air Command deployed two B-52F squadrons to Andersen Air Force Base on the island of Guam. There they stood by to fly against targets in North Vietnam, in response to Viet Cong attacks on US personnel in the South. However, General Westmoreland was already urging their employment in support of his ground forces in the South, arguing that the B-52s' heavy offensive load would provide a concentrated bombing pattern over the wide areas in which the Viet Cong dispersed their camps. Additionally, saturation bombing of the Viet Cong base areas would release tactical aircraft for operation against 'time urgent' battlefield targets. The B-52s, with their all-weather capability, would be of particular value during the northeast monsoon, when atrocious weather conditions frequently grounded tactical aircraft. These were persuasive arguments and at the end of April 1965, following a meeting with West-moreland in Honolulu, Secretary of Defense McNamara agreed to the tactical use of the B-52s over South Vietnam. In effect he was providing West-moreland with a reserve of flying heavy artillery. For the moment the strategic bomber had traveled full circle, and the B-52s were now being readied for a task which would have been warmly applauded by a brigade commander on the Western Front in 1917.

The first of these 'Arc Light' missions was flown on June 18, 1965. Thirty B-52Fs took off from Guam on a 5500-mile round trip to bomb Viet Cong strong-points in the Ben Cat Special Zone in Binh Duong province, northwest of Saigon. In-flight refueling was provided by KC-135 tankers from Kadena Air Base, Okinawa, and the B-52s flew in the three-aircraft cells which became the standard Arc Light formation. Two of the bombers were lost on the way to the target in a mid-air collision over the South China Sea while refueling, and eight of the 12 aircrew died. Post-strike reconnaissance revealed large tracts of mangled jungle but little evidence of any damage or losses suffered by the Viet Cong. It had been an inauspicious start.

B-52s flew more than 100 missions during the summer and autumn of 1965, with formations of up to 30 B-52s striking at reported enemy bases and troop concentrations. In November they were used for the first time in direct support of US ground forces, when 1st Cavalry Division clashed with units of the North Vietnamese Army (NVA) in the Ia Drang valley near the Cambodian border. Ninety-six sorties were flown in this operation, beginning on November 15, and 1603 tons of bombs dropped.

The Build-up of B-52 Strength

As the year drew to a close the B-52s began to fly in smaller numbers, averaging 300 sorties a month. At the same time the USAF launched a second major modification progam, to increase the bombload of its B-52Ds. Known as 'Big Belly', it raised the internal capacity to 42 750-pound bombs, with an alternate loading of 84 500-pounders, while retaining the external loading of 24 bombs of either weight on underwing 'stub' pylons. This raised the B-52's maximum offensive load to 108 iron bombs with a 'book' value of 60 000 pounds (in practice loads of over 80 000 pounds were often carried). The program also led to the development of 'C-racks', holding 28 500-pound bombs, which could be clipped into the bomb bays. Between December 1965 and September 1967 the entire B-52D fleet passed through the 'Big Belly' modification centers. The aircraft also under-went structural strengthening and were fitted with new radar transponders for ground-directed bombing. A camouflage scheme of mottled tan and green was adopted as a measure against visual detection of low-flying B-52s by enemy fighters. Following the Korean War example, the B-52D's undersides and tail were painted black to counter North Vietnamese searchlights and optically-guided anti-aircraft guns. The first modified B-52Ds arrived at Andersen in April 1966.

The first 12 months of SAC operations in the Southeast Asian theater saw a significant build-up in B-52 strength. By June 1966 Stratofortresses were dropping about 8000 tons of bombs a month against reported Viet Cong bases and in support of friendly ground troops. In August Secretary of Defense McNamara approved a monthly sortie level of 800 per month, but munitions shortages and construc-tion work at Guam prevented achievement of this target. It was not until November that the sortie level reached 600. At this stage in the war, 24 hours notice was required for an attack on a planned target box 1100 by 2200 yds in area. Nevertheless, during the same period the B-52F's performance and flexibility were considerably enhanced by the introduction of the Combat Skyspot bombing system, in which SAC ground radar units directed the bombers over enemy targets and indicated the exact moment of bomb release. The first of seven radar sites was established at Bien Hoa airfield in March. After a number of

modifications, Combat Skyspot operators could achieve a high degree of accuracy against targets 250 miles away. One minute before drop, the bombardier in the lead aircraft in the element opened the bomb bay doors and armed the bombs for release. The ground radar was locked on the B-52, and its data was displayed on a plotting board which also marked the target areas. The other crews in the element monitored the conversation between the lead aircraft and the ground controller, listening for the start of the controller's countdown. Calling off the approach to the release point, he began a ten-second countdown. On the release signal, the lead bombardier pressed the bomb release, which was displayed on annunciators in the cockpit. At the release signal the crews in the other aircraft started their stopwatches and made their drops at timed intervals after the lead aircraft. A DH4 pilot of 1918 would have quickly recognized the procedure. The arrival of Combat Skyspot also enabled Third Air Division to form a six-aircraft quick reaction force, standing by on a ten hour-alert at Guam to respond to battlefield emergencies, and allowed a controller to divert aircraft to new targets while they were in flight.

In 1967 the number of B-52 combat sorties nearly doubled. Arc Light rotations brought in crews and aircraft from 306th, 91st, 22nd, 454th, 461st, and 99th

Bomb Wings to Andersen AFB. Guam had now reached saturation point. To maintain the sortie rate and to relieve the pressure on Andersen's facilities, part of the bomber force was transferred to the U-Tapao base at Sattalip, in Thailand, from which the B-52s could fly to their targets without refueling. On May 6, 1967 an SAC B-52D took off on the 10 000th combat sortie flown since June 1965, during which time nearly 200 000 tons of bombs had been dropped.

B52s in Close Support

In the second half of 1967 the majority of Arc Light operations were flown around the Demilitarized Zone, where NVA artillery batteries were bombarding US Marine Corps fire support bases at Con Thien, Camp Carroll, and Dong Ha. Under the direction of Lieutenant-General William Momyer, commander of 7th Air Force and Westmoreland's deputy for air operations, an air plan was devised to deal with the troublesome NVA positions. Designated Operation Neutralize, and beginning on September 12, it employed artillery, naval gunfire, Air Force, Navy and Marine tactical aircraft and the B-52s in a 49-day round-the-clock SLAM (Seek, Locate, Annihilate, Monitor) operation against NVA positions north of the DMZ. Two Arc Light missions were flown every day, with 910 sorties hitting targets in the DMZ alone. It is estimated that

Loading the internal bomb bay of a Stratofortress. Note the four 0.5in guns in the occupied, pressurized tail turret of this B-52D.

Operation Neutralize succeeded in destroying 146 North Vietnamese gun, mortar and rocket positions. In November the shelling of the US bases fell away as the NVA turned its attention southward, to areas adjacent to its Cambodian sanctuaries, where it could more easily harass Allied positions in South Vietnam. However, one B-52 sortie over Con Thien in November was to have significant consequences. At this stage in the war the B-52s were limited to striking targets which were at least 3300 yds from friendly forces. But an Arc Light B-52 strayed to within 1500 yds of the Marines' positions at Con Thien, setting off a series of secondary explosions which revealed that the enemy was using the safety zone to hug the perimeter of the Marine base. This prompted a re-examination of the limits applied to B-52s when flying close-support missions.

Throughout 1967, Communist pressure had been mounting on the Marine combat base at Khe Sanh, which lay six miles from the Laotian border and 14 miles south of the DMZ. The base functioned as a support facility for surveillance units observing the DMZ and probing the outer edges of the Ho Chi Minh Trail in Laos. For General Giap, the North Vietnamese commander-in-chief, Khe Sanh was a key objective whose seizure would have posed a serious threat to US forces in the northern area and cleared the way for a North Vietnamese drive on Quang Tri and its heavily populated hinterland. As General Westmoreland commented, '*T*HERE is ... little doubt that the enemy hoped at Khe Sanh to obtain a climacteric victory such as he had done in 1954 at Dien Bien Phu in the expectation that this would produce a psychological shock and erode American morale'.

To counter this threat 'Operation Niagara' was devised, with the aim of disrupting the North Vietnamese preparations and supporting the Marines holding Khe Sanh. The operation had already entered its preliminary phase when the North Vietnamese launched their offensive on January 21, 1968.

During the course of the 77-day siege of Khe Sanh the area around the base became the most heavily bombed target in the history of aerial warfare. A daily average of 45 B-52 sorties and 300 tactical sorties by Air Force and Marine aircraft were flown against targets in the vicinity of the base. Every 90 minutes a three-aircraft B-52 cell arrived over Khe Sanh, plastering North Vietnamese bunkers and supply dumps, blowing up ammunition stores and collapsing the tunnels being driven towards the combat base's perimeter. Poor weather resulted in 62 per cent of all sorties being directed to their targets by Combat Skyspot. Over 550 close support sorties were flown in which strikes were made on enemy positions barely 1000 yds from the Khe Sanh perimeter. One B-52 strike is said to have killed 75 per cent of an 1800-strong NVA regiment.

By the time the siege was relieved at the beginning of April, 96 000 tons of bombs had been dropped in Operation Niagara, nearly twice as much as that delivered by the USAAF in the Pacific theater in 1942–43. The B-52s had flown 2548 sorties and dropped approximately 54 000 tons of bombs. Their effect had been as much psychological as physical.

On June 13 General Westmoreland told Third Air Division personnel at Andersen that 'the thing that broke their backs was basically the B-52s'.

Following the halting of Rolling Thunder at the end of October 1968 the focus shifted to the Ho Chi Minh Trail networks in Laos and its points of entry into South Vietnam. In an attempt to reduce infiltration through the Trail, the Air Force, Navy and Marines launched the 'Commando Hunt' campaign to destroy supplies and fuel moving down the trail in the Laotian dry season, tie down enemy manpower and test the effectiveness of the 'Igloo White' electronic anti-infiltration sensor system sown by aircraft in designated jungle areas. B-52s were heavily engaged in November–December, flying over 1200 'Commando Hunt' sorties principally against trans-shipment points and motor parks. By the spring of 1972 the B-52s were flying in 'Commando Hunt VII'.

On March 18, 1969, in 'Operation Breakfast', B-52s began the clandestine bombing of Communist sanctuaries in Cambodia. Over the next 14 months 3630 B-52 sorties were flown against suspected bases strung along the Cambodian border. 'Breakfast' was followed by 'Lunch', and so on until 'Supper' as the program was widened to embrace one reported sanctuary after another. The entire campaign was codenamed 'Menu'. Its naming was unintentionally apt. The bombing was a major ingredient in the recipe for disaster which was to overtake Cambodia in 1976, when it fell into the murderous hands of the Khmer Rouge. B-52s also flew in support of the ARVN and US incursions into Cambodia in May 1970 and in 'Lam Son 719', the shambolic ARVN attempt, in February 1971, to block the Communist trails in Laos by seizing Tchepone, a supply hub at the upper end of the Ho Chi Minh Trail. By February 23 nearly 400 B-52 sorties had cleared a path for the advancing ARVN, but two days later the NVA threw in a determined counter-offensive. By mid-March the South Vietnamese were in full retreat, abandoning huge quantities of armor, tanks, trucks and other hardware. They were extricated under massive tactical and B-52 cover, and by the end of the operation the B-52s had flown 1358 sorties in support of the ARVN.

In November 1968 Richard Milhouse Nixon had been elected as President of the United States, pledged to a gradual withdrawal from Vietnam. On June 8, 1969, while conferring at Midway with South Vietnam's President Nguyen Van Thieu, Nixon announced the planned withdrawal of 25 000 American combat troops. This was the beginning of the process by which the winning of the war would, by degrees, be turned over to South Vietnamese forces, which up to this point had been junior partners in all aspects of the fighting. However, few senior US commanders had any illusions about the ARVN's ability to cope with highly trained and motivated North Vietnamese regulars. The shift in American policy represented by 'Vietnamization' exerted conflicting influences over the air war. Secretary of Defense Melvin R Laird cut the monthly Arc Light sortie rate from 1800 to 1400 in October 1969 and 1000 by June 1971. However, when one considers that in the course of a year a single B-52 squadron was capable of dropping half the total tonnage delivered by US aircraft in the Pacific theater during World War II, it is clear that reductions in strength contained a strong element of window-dressing. Nixon's stated aim of withdrawal required a visible scaling down of operations, but the policy of Vietnamization – and the slow improvement in the capability of the ARVN as the US ground troops were withdrawn – also required the intensive use of air power. In the words of the Air Force history, this '*BRIDGED THE GAP ... BY applying air strikes for political purposes and by extending the geographic area of interdiction into Cambodia and back into North Vietnam. Thus the role of air power, though slated for reduction, continued to be emphasised*'.

Nevertheless, by the end of 1971 B-52 strength had fallen to 45, all of them flying from U-Tapao. There is a faint echo of the Korean War to be found here, for at the beginning of 1972 it was becoming increasingly clear that the North Vietnamese were concentrating forces for a large-scale offensive across the DMZ. In February 29 B-52s were despatched to Guam and the monthly Arc Light sortie rate climbed back to 1500. The anticipated North Vietnamese offensive began on March 30 with heavy artillery bombardment and infantry attacks across the DMZ in north Quang Tri province and an eastward thrust against Hue. To the south, Kontum-Pleiku and An Loc, northwest of Saigon, came under threat.

The offensive was in large part blunted by the B-52s. By the end of April, the Arc Light force had risen to 133 aircraft, capable of mounting 75 sorties a day and 2250 a month. In June Eighth Air Force* strength had increased to 200 bombers and the monthly sortie

*Third Air Force was redesignated Eighth Air Force in April 1970.

rate was running at 3150. Between April and the end of June the B-52s flew 6000 sorties in support of the ARVN in Quang Tri province, and at Kontum and An Loc. The invasion was smashed by air power. Its targets were not the elusive Viet Cong, hidden by the jungle canopy, but concentrations of troops and armor in the battle zone and the huge convoys of trucks supplying them from North Vietnam. Tanks were particularly vulnerable. In April an NVA armored division was spotted moving by road towards Dong Ha and passing through a designated B-52 target box. The Arc Light cells were called in by the Forward Air Controller, and within an hour the hulks of 35 tanks littered each side of Highway I. Time and again single Stratofortress strikes blanketed NVA troop concentrations, wiping out hundreds of men and entire units. In mid-May the NVA made a final effort to break through. At An Loc 56 B-52 sorties hit 91 targets, some of them as close as 650 yds to friendly forces. A month earlier the Stratofortresses had also flown over North Vietnam, venturing for the first time into the heavily defended Hanoi-Haiphong area to strike at airfields, oil storage facilities and trans-shipment points.

By the middle of June the invasion had ground to a halt. Now B-52s began to range across the southern part of North Vietnam as part of the 'Linebacker' operations which renewed strikes above the 20th Parallel. The Nixon administration also took the long-deferred decision to impose a naval blockade and lay mines in the waters of Haiphong and other North Vietnamese ports; the mines were dropped by modified B-52Ds. Peace talks resumed in Paris on July 13 and a month later the last American ground combat troops left South Vietnam, leaving 43 500 airmen and support personnel still in place in the Southeast Asian theater. On October 23, when it

A three-aircraft Arc Light cell of B-52s attacking a target 25 miles from Bien Hoa airbase in South Vietnam. Accurate assessment of many of the Arc Light strikes against more remote targets was problematic. Too great an emphasis was placed on tonnage dropped in designated boxes and sorties completed rather than any concrete evidence of enemy casualties. This was reminiscent of Bomber Command's optimistic assessment of the destruction of German oil plants in 1940-41. There were times in the air campaign in Southeast Asia when this approach caused severe morale problems in SAC crews flying Arc Light missions.

Enter the 'Smart' Bomb

A USAF F-4 Phantom, armed with two 2000-pound Paveway I laser-guided 'smart' bombs, maneuvers to attack the Than Hoa bridge on April 27, 1972. This road and railway bridge, 70 miles south of Hanoi, was one of the most stubborn targets in North Vietnam, acquiring an almost legendary reputation because of its apparent indestructibility. During Operation Rolling Thunder (March 1965 – October 31, 1968) nearly 700 sorties were flown against this vital link in North Vietnam's transportation system, delivering 1250 tons of all types of ordnance. Eight aircraft were lost in these missions, but the durable heavily trussed steel bridge, built into an outcrop of solid rock, defied all attempts to bring it down. Although the North Vietnamese soon established bypasses around the bridge – diminishing its value as a target – it assumed a psychological importance to US aircrews which outweighed purely tactical considerations. It was not until the spring of 1972, and the introduction of the 'smart bomb', that the bridge was badly damaged. It was put out of action on May 13, 1972 in another raid by Phantoms equipped with 2000-pound and 3000-pound laser-guided bombs.

The 'smart bomb' is fitted with a sensor which enables it to home on to a target acquired by the aircraft's Weapons Systems Officer and 'illuminated' by a laser carried in an underwing pod. The bomb rides down the laser 'basket' to the target. Guidance is provided by the four computer-driven variable fins. The system can also be operated in conjunction with a similarly equipped companion aircraft or forward ground troops. The target must be continuously illuminated and accuracy is affected by cloud and rain. In the 1970s Paveway production ran at some 20000 a year.

USAF LINEBACKER OFFENSIVE AGAINST NORTH VIETNAM

PEOPLE'S REPUBLIC OF CHINA

NANNING

CAO BANG

LAO CAI

NORTH VIETNAM

YEN BAI

PINGSIANG

LANG SON

VIET TRI · HANOI

HON GAI

DIEN BIEN PHU

HAIPHONG

PHA

PATHET LAO CONTROL

LAOS

THANH HOA

LUANGPRABANG

SEVENTH FLEET

PLAIN OF JARS

NA PE PASS · VINH

VIENTIANE

MU GIA PASS

HO CHI MINH TRAIL

THAILAND

DMZ

SOUTH VIETNAM

HUE

US Strike Group

The diagram on the right shows the composition of a typical US strike group and its supporting elements during the Linebacker I campaign against targets in North Vietnam (May-October 1972). One of its most interesting features is the number of support aircraft required at a time when air superiority had not yet been decisively gained by the United States.

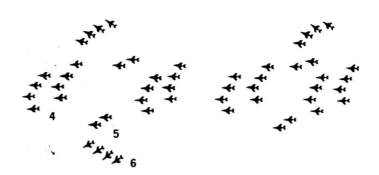

1

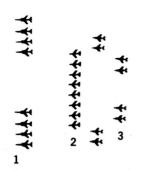

2   3

4

5

6

7

1 The raiding force is led by two 'Iron Hand' flights, each comprising F-4E Phantoms armed with AIM-7 Sparrow air-to-air missiles and cluster bombs and two Republic F-105G Thunderchief 'Wild Weasel' aircraft equipped with anti-radiation missiles for SAM suppression.

2 Approximately three minutes behind the 'Iron Hand' flight are eight A-7 Corsair IIs. Their task is to lay a 'chaff' screen to mask the strike force from enemy radars and SAM attacks. Accurate laying of their heavy 'chaff' loads required straight and level flight, which made the A-7s extremely vulnerable. In addition to their own ECM equipment they were provided with a close escort of two flights of F-4E Phantoms, **3**, flying two miles behind on either flank and keeping a sharp look-out for MG interceptors.

4 The Strike Group itself is made up of 32 McDonnell Douglas F-4E Phantoms armed with a combination of 'iron' and laser-guided bombs.

5 Close escort is provided by more F-4E Phantoms.
6 Outer defense against North Vietnamese interceptors is maintained by roving F-4E Combat Air Patrols.

7 Bringing up the rear, and some distance behind, are two McDonnell Douglas RF-4C reconnaissance aircraft tasked with photographing the target after the raid for subsequent analysis and damage assessment.

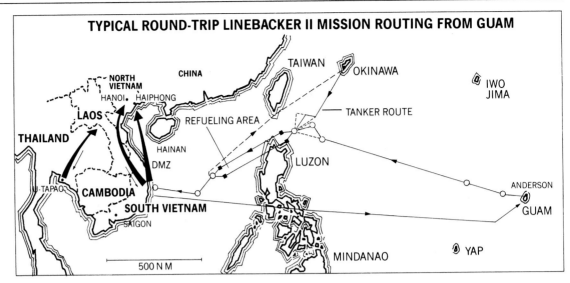

TYPICAL ROUND-TRIP LINEBACKER II MISSION ROUTING FROM GUAM

appeared that the Paris talks were leading to an agreement to end the war, President Nixon halted air operations above the 20th Parallel. However, it soon became clear that the talks were drifting up yet another blind alley, with Hanoi offering hints that it might renew its offensive in South Vietnam.

President Nixon determined to break the impasse with the resumption of bombing above the 20th Parallel. The North Vietnamese walked out of the talks on December 13 and there followed an 11-day bombing campaign, 'Linebacker II', the heaviest aerial offensive of the war launched against previously restricted targets around Hanoi-Haiphong.

The principal instrument of 'Linebacker II' were SAC's B-52Ds and B-52Gs. The B-52 had first flown over North Vietnam in April 1966, bombing the Mu Gia pass, through which men and supplies moved through Laos and thence into South Vietnam. But until March 1972 the Stratofortresses had been withheld from attacks on the fiercely defended Hanoi-Haiphong corridor. The first phase of 'Linebacker II' called for a three-day maximum effort against rail yards, power plants, communications facilities, air defense radars, Haiphong's docks, oil storage complexes, and ammunition supply areas. Of the 34 strategic targets attacked in 'Linebacker II', over 60 per cent were clustered within a 25-mile radius of Hanoi.

'Linebacker II' aimed to apply round-the-clock pressure to the North Vietnamese defensive network. The initial plan was for the B-52s to attack by night, in three waves, with F-111s and A-6s following up by day. The B-52 streams were to be preceded by F-111s tasked with attacking MiG fighter bases, and F-4s laying 'Chaff' corridors ('Chaff', millions of metallized strips cut to the right length to interfere with enemy radar frequencies, is the modern equivalent of 'Window'). The F-4s, sowing 'Chaff' from underwing dispensers, had to fly in formation straight and level and at reduced speed, which made them extremely vulnerable to SAM and MiG attack. To combat the MiGs they were provided with their own escort.

Only a limited amount of 'Chaff' screening was available at the beginning of 'Linebacker II', and this combined with other factors to limit the approach and exit routes available to the B-52s. Target approach was from the northwest, to take advantage of the strong winds blowing from that direction. After bomb release the B-52s were to swing in wide turns which, it was hoped, would take them out of SAM range as quickly as possible. The stream of three-aircraft cells was compressed to enhance electronic countermeasures protection and keep the B-52s within the 'Chaff' screens. The crews, who were unfamiliar with flying in large formations at night, were under orders to maneuver as little as possible to avoid collisions.

The Climax of Linebacker II

On the night of December 18/19, 129 B-52s took off from Guam and Thailand. Half an hour before the first Stratofortresses arrived over the target F-111s hit the MiG airfields and F-4s sowed two 'Chaff' corridors to screen strikes on the Kinh No and Yen Vien target areas north of Hanoi. The strong northwest wind dispersed the 'Chaff' before the B-52s arrived.

Over Hanoi Staff Sergeant Samuel O Turner, a tail gunner in a B-52D, claimed the first Stratofortress victory of the war. Picking up an enemy fighter on his radar screen, he squeezed off a short burst from his four 0.5 guns, shooting down what was later confirmed as a MiG-21. The night also saw the first B-52 casualties sustained in 'Linebacker II'. Among the aircraft in the first wave was Charcoal I (the leading aircraft in 'Charcoal' cell), a Guam-based B-52G. The B-52G had not been as extensively modified with ECM equipment as the B-52D. Charcoal 1's Initial Point-to-Target axis of attack took it over the most closely grouped SAM sites defending Hanoi. As it ran in on the Yen Vien rail-yards Charcoal 1 received a near-direct SAM hit at the very moment its bomb doors were opening. With the Stratofortress hopelessly damaged, and the pilot, co-pilot and gunner either dead or incapacitated, the radar navigator, navigator and electronic warfare officer (EWO) ejected and were taken prisoner.

The second wave flew in four hours later. 'Peach' cell was one of six renewing the attack on the Yen Vien railyards. Peach 2 had just released its bombs when it was crippled by a SAM, in all probability fired from the same site which had downed Charcoal 1. The B-52 limped back into friendly territory, with wing and engine fires taking hold, before the crew abandoned the aircraft.

The third wave arrived after a gap of five hours. Eighteen aircraft attacking the Hanoi railroad repair shops encountered fierce opposition, with more than 60 SAMs fired at their cells alone. Another seven cells, flying in from almost due west, came within range of 11 SAM sites. The lead aircraft in the last cell to bomb, Rose 1, fell to a SAM site which B-52 crews subsequently dubbed 'Killer Site 549'. On the first night of 'Linebacker II' Hanoi's defenses had fired more than 200 SAMs and thousands of rounds of anti-aircraft ammunition, shooting down three B-52s and damaging three others.

Analysis of the raid revealed serious short-comings in its planning and execution. The strength of the North Vietnamese air defenses had been underestimated. Tactics which had proved satisfactory on Arc Light missions were ill-suited to the crowded, dangerous skies over Hanoi and Haiphong. More 'Chaff' corridors were needed to enable each wave to gain maximum benefit from the high tailwinds. The wide spacing of the waves created considerable problems for the SAM-suppression and 'Chaff'-sowing aircraft, at the same time allowing the North Vietnamese air defenses time to recover before the attack was renewed. Greater concentration was required – the cardinal lesson of World War II. The long bomber streams, and the use of a single point for post-target turns, enabled the air defenses to direct their fire at the turning point after the first cell had passed. German night fighters in World War II used similar tactics to infiltrate the RAF's bomber streams where PFF flares marked turning points on the approach to the target. Finally, the steeply banked turns made by the B-52s after releasing their bombs brought them into a fierce headwind, which hampered their withdrawal and countermeasures patterns, enabling the probing SAM radars to penetrate chinks in their jamming barrage.

On the night of December 19 the B-52s' tactics remained essentially unchanged. There were no casualties as 120 aircraft hit targets around Hanoi, including the Bac Giang trans-shipment point, the city's radio station, and the Thai Nguyen thermal power plant. On the third night of operations, December 20, SAMs struck two B-52Gs in the first wave as they were making their post-target turns and both of them crashed in Hanoi. A badly damaged B-52D struggled back to Thailand before crashing. The last wave came under heavy fire; two more B-52Gs were claimed by SAMs and a crippled B-52D crashed in Laos. In the course of nine hours, 220 SAMs had been fired and six B-52s lost, four of them the B-52Gs with their less than adequate jamming transmitters. In three days over 300 sorties had been flown and nine aircraft lost. The overall loss rate of 3 per cent was acceptable, but if the casualties of December 20 were an indication of things to come, the offensive could not be sustained.

A thorough-going revision was now made of planning and tactics, particularly the B-52's vulnerability to SAMs during post-target turns, and a number of modifications were introduced for the raid of December 21. Among them were more freedom for pilots to employ evasive maneuvers; greater compression of the bomber stream, within which random spacing and altitudes would serve to confuse the air defenses; and authorization for pilots to make shallow post-target turns to withdraw with maximum speed, flying 'feet wet' over the Gulf of Tonkin. All sorties on the fourth day were flown from U-Tapao, releasing the Guam-based B-52s for Arc Light missions. By December 22, the fifth day of bombing, the new tactics had been absorbed and the B-52s flew away from Hanoi with no losses. The first week of 'Linebacker II' ended on Christmas Eve.

After a 36-hour Christmas stand-down, operations were resumed on the 26th with a brilliantly planned attack by 120 B-52s. Preceded and escorted by 113 aircraft, the B-52s flew through a massive 'Chaff' screen in seven highly compressed waves to batter ten targets in Hanoi and Haiphong. The plan called for the release of all weapons within a 15-minute time period. Two streams attacked Hanoi from the northwest, flying in from Laos and out over the Gulf of Tonkin; two more approached on a reverse course, from the northeast and southeast over the Gulf, flying away through Laos. Aircraft attacking Haiphong approached from the northeast and southeast. The more vulnerable B-52Gs were assigned to Thai Nguyen and Haiphong.

The raid of December 26 was the climax of 'Linebacker II' and the most concentrated bomber attack in history. The SAMs downed only one aircraft, and a second – heavily battle damaged – crashed short of U-Tapao's runway while trying to land. Sixty B-52s were despatched on each of the three remaining raids. By the eleventh day of 'Linebacker II' SAM firings had declined dramatically, as the combination of bombing and blockade had prevented fresh supplies reaching the North Vietnamese. The SAMs had been Hanoi's first line of defense; deprived of their air bases, the North Vietnamese were able to deploy only about 30 MiGs in the defense of Hanoi-Haiphong, eight of which were shot down.

Operations north of the 20th Parallel ceased at midnight on December 29, 1972. In all, 729 B-52 sorties had been flown during 'Linebacker II' – 340 from U-Tapao and 389 from Guam – at a cost of 15 aircraft lost (all to SAMs) and nine damaged. Over 13 000 tons of bombs had hit 34 targets, killing approximately 1500 civilians. Twenty-nine US airmen had been killed in action; 33 had become prisoners of war and were later returned; and 26 were rescued in post-strike operations.

There can be little doubt that the 'Linebacker' campaign had been instrumental in bringing the North Vietnamese back to the peace table, and talks were resumed on January 8. Bombing operations in the South continued until January 27, when the cease fire was signed. It continued in Laos until mid-April and in Cambodia until mid-August, when Congress cut off funds for the air war. Between June 1965 and August 1973, 126 615 B-52 sorties had been flown, 9800 of them against North Vietnam. Of these 124 499 reached their targets, delivering 2 633 035 tons of bombs. Eighteen aircraft were lost to enemy action and 13 more in mid-air collisions and accidents. The B-52s had won their battles, but not the war.

4.4 THE RAF AND THE STRATEGIC NUCLEAR DETERRENT

IN MAY 1944 THE BRITISH PRODUCED A paper entitled *Future Bomber Requirements*. Looking into the future, the paper emphasised height and speed as the primary qualities of the next generation of bomber aircraft. Considerations of defense became secondary. The higher a bomber flew, the harder it would be to catch; and the faster it traveled the less time there would be for air defenses to detect and attack it. The B-29 raids on Hiroshima and Nagasaki raised the prospect of a single bomber, able to outdistance and outpace anything else in the sky, penetrating hostile airspace to deliver nuclear weapons to the enemy heartland. The days of the bomber stream were numbered. *Future Bomber Requirements* observed, '*THERE IS NO EVIdence to support the theory that using larger numbers of night bombers causes saturation of the enemy's defenses. Mosquito losses have been low despite the small numbers in which they have operated, and there is no significant decrease in Lancaster wastage rate when the size of the raid increases. So, in night bombing, as numbers do not seem to offer any striking advantage, the decision of optimum size depends mainly on the relative vulnerability of large and small bombers*'.

In 1945 *Flight Magazine* declared that the RAF's 'stretched' Lancaster, the Lincoln, was 'the mightiest bomber in the world'. In truth it was already an anachronism. Between 1950 and 1955, when it was retired, the Lincoln performed valuable service in anti-terrorist operations in Malaya and Kenya. But with its maximum speed of 305 mph at 19 000 ft and range of 2250 miles carrying a bombload of 14 000 pounds, the Lincoln MkIII was a relic of the past in the age of the jet. It was the success of the Mosquito, highlighted in *Future Bomber Requirements*, which pointed the way to immediate postwar developments. Before the end of the war the British Air Ministry issued Specification B.3/45 for a light twin-jet tactical day bomber, incorporating bomb-aiming radar, to replace the Mosquito. This produced the English Electric Canberra, whose A.1 prototype took off on its maiden flight on May 13, 1949. Two years later No. 101 Squadron RAF took delivery of the first operational Canberra B.Mk2s, which replaced its Lincolns.

The Canberra bridged the gap between RAF Bomber Command's piston-engined heavy bombers and a new strategic striking force capable of delivering nuclear weapons. Denied access to the United States' nuclear secrets, by the McMahon Act of 1947, Britain's Labour government set about developing its own atom bomb, at great expense and in conditions of utmost secrecy. Britain's first atomic bomb was tested in October 1952, but two more years passed before the first of the new strategic 'V-bombers', the Vickers Valiant, entered service.

The Valiant was designed to meet the requirements of Air Ministry Specification B.35/46, drawn up in January 1947 to embrace the development of a long-range bomber incoporating advanced design features such as swept-back wings – data on which had become available from captured German material and original research. The first Valiant prototype, powered by four 6500-pound s.t. Avon RA3 engines, made its maiden flight on May 18, 1951 and No. 138 Squadron introduced the bomber to operational service in February 1955. The crew of five was accommodated in pressurized compartments, and a prone position for the bomber-aimer was provided in a teardrop fairing under the cabin. No defensive armament was considered necessary because of the Valiant's high speed – 554 mph at 36 000 ft – and service ceiling of 54 000 ft. In company with Canberras of Nos. 10 and 12 Squadrons, Valiants of Nos. 148 Squadron saw action in the Suez crisis during the autumn of 1956, flying from bases in Malta to drop a conventional payload of 21 1000-pound bombs on 12 Egyptian airfields along the length of the Canal Zone.

The Vulcan and Victor

1The Valiant was followed into service by the Avro Vulcan and the Handley Page Victor. Preliminary work on the delta-wing Vulcan had begun after the war, by Avro's chief aerodynamicist, Roy Chadwick (designer of the Lancaster). Chadwick's imagination had been fired by German wind tunnel experiments with delta aerofoils. In 1945 most designers were pre-occupied with jet fighter development, but Chadwick was already working on a 100ft-span delta sufficiently thick to contain all the engines and tanks, with only a slight swelling in the mid section for cockpit and bombs.

Chadwick died in an air accident on August 23, 1947, but his original work led to the development of the Avro Type 698 Vulcan. Its delta-wing configuration promised a number of significant advantages: huge storage capacity in the inboard portions of the wings, which was afforded by the great chord at the roots; a strong, inflexible structure provided by the delta's inherently low aspect ratio; and good handling characteristics at both ends of the speed range. Nevertheless, Avro was venturing into uncharted aerodynamic waters, and a number of experiments were made with one-third-scale deltas on single-engine research aircraft, the Avro Type 707s. The first prototype Vulcan, powered by four Avon RA3s and featuring delta wings with straight leading edges, took off on its maiden flight on August 30, 1952. On July 11, 1957 No. 83 Squadron took delivery of its first Vulcan B.Mk1s. The wings of the early B.Mk1s sported straight leading edges, but on October 5, 1955 the second prototype flew with modified 'kinked' wings, incorporating a reduced leading edge sweep with compound sweep on the outer half of the wing. This reduced previously encountered buffeting during high-altitude maneuvers and became standard on all later Vulcans.

The third of the strategic bombers prompted by Specification B.35/46 was the Handley Page Victor, which featured a unique 'crescent wing'. Initial

production Victor B.Mk1s were ordered six months before the first prototype flew on December 24, 1952, and B.Mk1s went into service with No. 10 Squadron at the beginning of 1958.

In 1958 A V Roe died. Roe, the founder of the Avro company and designer of the Avro 504s which had attacked the Zeppelin sheds at Friedrichshafen on November 20, 1914, had lived long enough to see his improvized bombers mature into a weapon with the power to obliterate cities with a single bomb. The British V-bomber force reached its greatest numerical strength in June 1964, with 50 Valiants, 39 Victors and 70 Vulcans in service. To counter the threat posed by the Soviet Union's Long Range Air Force and the low-trajectory missiles sited in Eastern Europe, special Quick Reaction Alert crews were at permanent readiness in caravans parked next to the bombers' Operational Readiness platforms at the end of the runways on Bomber Command's dispersal airfields. From February 1962 at least one Vulcan and crew from each squadron was on Quick Reaction Alert, never more than 15 and as few as four minutes away from getting airborne in permanently fueled, armed and checked aircraft.

The 'Skyshield' exercise of October 14, 1961, mounted to test the North American Air Defense Command to its peacetime limits, gave the RAF's Vulcans a chance to demonstrate their effectiveness. By the early 1960s the North American approaches were covered by an early warning system which meshed integrated and fully automated communications with fighters and surface-to-air missiles. In 'Skyshield', RAF Bomber Command contributed four Vulcan B.2s from No. 27 Squadron flying from Kindley AFB, Bermuda, and four from No. 83 Squadron, taking off from Lossiemouth (Scotland) to

launch an attack from the north. In the north the attack was led by USAF B-47s flying at low level and jamming ground radars, followed by B-52s and B-57s at heights between 42000 and 56000ft, and finally No. 83 Squadron's Vulcans at 56000 ft. Electronic countermeasures proved effective, and only one Vulcan heard an F-101 Voodoo fighter lock on. The fighters scrambled to intercept had focused their attention on the B-52s and, when the Vulcans flew in, they lacked sufficient fuel to climb to engage them. In the south No. 27 Squadron's Vulcans attacked on a broad front. Fifty miles from the coast they were met by F-102 Delta Dagger interceptors. As the F-102s concentrated on the lead Vulcans, the southernmost bomber turned to fly north behind the jamming screen provided by its companions, penetrating US airspace to land at Plattsburgh AFB, New York.

Top: The Handley Page Victor, which was designed and built with a unique crescent-shaped wing.
Above: In-flight refueling from one Vickers Valiant to another. A Valiant of No. 49 Squadron dropped the first British atomic bomb on October 11, 1956 over Maralinga, Australia. On May 15, 1957 an aircraft of the same squadron released the first British hydrogen bomb over the Christmas Island area in the Pacific.

The TSR2, tantalizing might-have-been of British military aviation. Only one of the four constructed took to the air, making its last flight on March 31, 1965.

However, the V-bomber force was already living under the shadow of obsolescence. Even before the Victor entered service, planners had looked forward to a time when manned aircraft would be replaced by missiles. Britain had been developing its own liquid-fueled ICBM, Blue Streak, but in May 1960 this was abandoned on the grounds of cost and vulnerability. As the high-altitude bombers were looking increasingly vulnerable to air defense missiles, it became necessary to find an alternative means of delivering Britain's independent nuclear deterrent.

One method of prolonging the V-bombers' useful lives was to equip them with an air-launched 'stand-off' missile. In the late 1950s Britain developed the Blue Steel missile, with a range of about 100 miles, which became fully operational with No. 617 Squadron in February 1963. At the outset Blue Steel was seen as the initial phase in a stand-off missile program intended to complement the development of the supersonic Avro 730 bomber. But the Avro 730 was canceled in 1957 and two years later work on Blue Steel 2 (with a 700-mile range and Mach 3 speed) was brought to a halt. The British government had decided to buy the Douglas AGM-87A Skybolt, an air-launched ballistic missile under development in the United States. While scientists at Aldermaston worked on a British thermonuclear warhead to fit Skybolt's small nose cone, Avro submitted a proposal for a 'Phase 6' Vulcan armed with six Skybolts and capable of maintaining a state of Continuous Airborne Alert, along the lines employed by SAC. Employing the Vulcan B.2s already in service and 48 'Phase 6' aircraft in a system of staggered take-offs, 84 Skybolts would have been deployed round the clock to deter a Soviet pre-emptive strike.

In December 1962 the US government canceled the Skybolt program and with it died the plans for the

'Phase 6' Vulcan and the Continuous Airborne Alert. At a meeting in the Bahamas between President John F Kennedy and Prime Minister Harold Macmillan it was agreed that Britain should be supplied with American Polaris missiles for four Royal Navy nuclear-powered submarines. As a stopgap measure, the V-bombers were converted to operate at low level, enabling them to penetrate below hostile radar defenses. The RAF now waited for the introduction into service of the British Aircraft Corporation TSR2, which could carry out either strategic or tactical missions at tree-top level.

The Ill-Fated TSR2

The TSR2 was one of the great 'might-have-beens' of British military aviation. The original concept behind the TSR2 was that of a complete weapons system integrated in one airframe and enabling the aircraft to operate in all weathers at very high speed at high or low level on tactical, strike and reconnaissance duties. However, impressive payload and range also qualified the TSR2 for a strategic role. At the time of its maiden flight in September 1964, it was arguably the most formidable aircraft of its type in the world. Seating pilot and observer in tandem in the lengthy nose, it could fly at Mach 2.05 to 2.5 and its range with underwing tanks approached 1700 miles. Its avionics would have allowed completely automatic high and low level attacks without visual reference. XR219 – the only one of four TSR2s constructed to fly – made its last flight on March 31, 1965. Shortly afterwards the entire program was canceled. The purchase of 50 American F-111s as a possible replacement was canceled in 1968.

Thus the RAF no longer had a new long-range bomber in prospect to maintain its strategic role. The Valiant was withdrawn from front-line service in

Avro Vulcan B.Mk2
Spearhead of Britain's V-bomber force and the last in the line of the heavies which had begun with the Handley Page O/100. The first Vulcan B.2 deliveries were made to No. 83 Squadron in July 1960. Powered by four Rolls Royce Olympus 301 engines, the B.2 had a maximum cruising speed of more than 625 mph at 50 000 ft, maximum cruising altitude of 55 000 ft and an unrefueled combat radius at altitude of 2300 miles. Its offensive load was 21 1000 - pound bombs or free-fall nuclear weapons, with additional provision for a single Blue Steel nuclear-tipped stand-off missile (which entered service early in 1963) carried semi-recessed below the fuselage.

1964, followed by the Victor in 1968. In the same year Bomber Command ceased to exist when it was merged with Fighter Command to form RAF Strike Command. The remaining Vulcan bombers were assigned to the North Atlantic Treaty Organization (NATO) in a tactical role. When the Navy's Polaris missile became operational in July 1969 the RAF lost its responsibility for Britain's strategic nuclear capability. In this there lay a certain irony, for in 1914 Britain's first attempts at long-range bombing had been undertaken by the RNAS. Fifty-five years later the Navy assumed control of Britain's strategic nuclear deterrent.

The Vulcan soldiered on in the role of low-level attack, a task to which it was adapted with considerable success. The introduction in 1966 of Terrain-Following Radar and the Vulcan's immensely robust airframe enabled it to absorb the punishment of low-level flight well into the 1970s. From 1977 selected Vulcan crews participated in the USAF's 'Red Flag' exercises initiated to sustain the combat capability acquired in the Vietnam conflict. Each Vulcan crew flew five sorties, over a range in Nevada approximately the size of Switzerland, against targets as diverse as truck convoys and industrial complexes defended by simulated SAM sites and fighter pilots flying F-5s to Warsaw Pact rules. Frequently attacking at only 300 ft above ground level, the Vulcans used terrain masking and three-axis jinking to evade the defenses, often completing their sorties without a single claim being made against them – a remarkable achievement in the crystal-clear skies of Nevada.

In the early 1980s the Vulcans' tactical strike role was assumed by the swing-wing Panavia Tornado Mach 2+ multipurpose combat aircraft. Capable of a wide variety of tasks, including close air support,

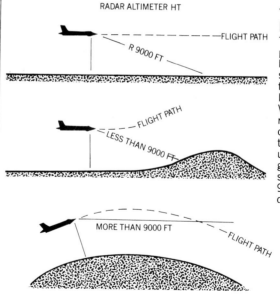

RADAR ALTIMETER HT

FLIGHT PATH

R 9000 FT

FLIGHT PATH

LESS THAN 9000 FT

MORE THAN 9000 FT

FLIGHT PATH

The Vulcan's Terrain-Following Radar.
The radar throws out a pencil beam ahead of and below the aircraft using a slanting range of 9000 ft as the measuring parameter. If the ground ahead of the Vulcan rises, the radar return gives a slant range of less than 9000 ft and the TFR computes a pull-up signal to the pilot. If the ground falls away, the slant range exceeds 9000 ft producing a dive demand from the TFR.

interdiction and naval strike, the Tornado can carry up to 20 000 pounds of weapons. Disbandment of the Vulcan squadrons began in the summer of 1981. By early March 1982 the B.2 fleet had been reduced to three squadrons, all based at Waddington. But the venerable bomber was given a temporary reprieve when, on April 2, Argentine forces invaded and occupied the Falkland Islands, in the South Atlantic. After 25 years of service, and on the brink of retirement, the Vulcan was to be used in anger for the first time.

The Falklands War

In the Falklands conflict of 1982 Argentine navy and air force pilots faced many of the problems encountered by their Bomber Command predecessors in the autumn and winter of 1939. Flying at the limit of their range, they were tasked with low-altitude attacks on ships of the British Task Force, operations for which they had little previous training. They suffered heavy losses but nevertheless inflicted severe damage on the warships screening the British landings at San Carlos, which began on May 20. On May 21 the frigate *Ardent* was sunk, followed on the 24th by her sister ship, the crippled *Antelope*. However, because of the low altitude at which the Argentine pilots were flying, many of the bombs they dropped were not fully armed on their descent. They found their targets but failed to explode. Later the Argentines used bombs whose descent was retarded by a small parachute, but by then the crisis had passed and the British had gained the upper hand.

May 25, Argentina's national day, saw particularly heavy air attacks. Here, Primer Teniente Velasco in an Argentine air force A4B Skyhawk C-207 of Grupo 5 pulls away from the stricken British Type 42 destroyer *Coventry*. *Coventry* and her 'goalkeeper', the Seawolf-armed frigate *Broadsword*, had been singled out for attack by Grupo 5, which was based at Rio Gallegos on the Argentine mainland. Both ships were providing British land forces on the Falklands with excellent radar intelligence from their picket position some 15 miles north of Pebble Island. Grupo 5 launched two flights of two Skyhawks against the warships, each of which was armed with three 1000-pound bombs.

The Attack

Captain Carballo and Teniente Rinke's Skyhawks of 'Vulcan' flight took off from Rio Gallegos, followed by Teniente Velasco and Alferez Barrioneuvo's 'Zeus' flight. Flying the last 150 miles to the attack zone at low altitude, Carballo experienced heavy windscreen salting as he flew a northerly track, passing over the Passage Islands en route to Pebble Island. The Skyhawks were untroubled by British Sea Harrier combat air patrols (CAPs), which had been directed out of the immediate area the moment *Broadsword*'s Seawolf missile system locked on to the approaching Argentine aircraft.

Carballo and Rinke ran in on *Broadsword* through only light gunfire, the frigate's missile control having 'tripped out' and broken the Seawolf lock on the Skyhawks. Five of their bombs missed the frigate but a sixth bounced off the sea, struck her aft on the starboard side and burst through the flight deck, damaging a Lynx helicopter before falling harmlessly into the sea, having failed to explode. As Carballo and Rinke pulled away, Velasco and Barrionuevo began their 10-mile run into *Coventry*. Simultaneously *Coventry* turned towards *Broadsword*, which declined CAP assistance. *Coventry* launched a Sea Dart missile, which in the clear conditions the Argentine pilots evaded with a co-ordinated course change as they skimmed in at wave-top height. *Coventry* attempted to confuse the Skyhawks with evasive maneuvers and fire from her 4.5in gun.

Passing across *Broadsword*'s bows, *Coventry* fatally broke the Seawolf missile lock. Barrioneuvo's bombs hung up, but Velasco placed all three in the destroyer's port side, where they exploded, causing fire and flooding. The ship took a heavy list to port within five minutes and capsized within 20 minutes; 19 men die. All four Skyhawks return safely.

ARGENTINE BASES IN USE DURING THE FALKLANDS CONFLICT, 1982

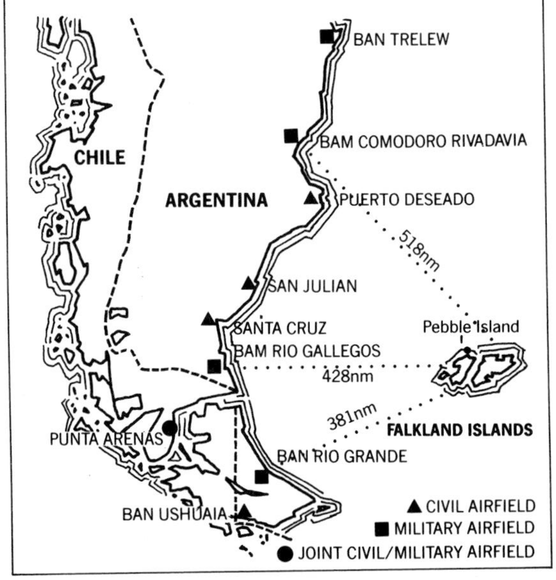

BAN TRELEW
BAM COMODORO RIVADAVIA
PUERTO DESEADO
CHILE
ARGENTINA
518nm
SAN JULIAN
SANTA CRUZ
Pebble Island
BAM RIO GALLEGOS
428nm
381nm
FALKLAND ISLANDS
PUNTA ARENAS
BAN RIO GRANDE
BAN USHUAIA
▲ CIVIL AIRFIELD
■ MILITARY AIRFIELD
● JOINT CIVIL/MILITARY AIRFIELD

A B.2 Vulcan of No. 44 Squadron. Note the 'squared-off' fin tip housing the passive warning radar receiver aerial which entered service in 1975. On low-level missions the camouflaged top surface minimised detection by downward-looking fighter pilots. From the autumn of 1979 the white underside – designed to minimise detectability at height from an upward-climbing fighter – was also camouflaged. This followed experience in 'Red Flag' exercises which showed that the white underside exposed the Vulcan to fighters when in a tight turn. The 'Black Buck' Vulcans XM607 and XM597 came from No. 44 Squadron, which was disbanded on December 31, 1982.

Vulcan route, with in-flight refueling points (R) for Black Buck 1

The 'Black Buck' Missions

Five of the six remaining Vulcans fitted with forward and aft Skybolt missile attachment points were selected for use in 'Operation Corporate', the re-occupation of the Falklands by British forces. The Vulcans were fitted with the Carousel inertial navigation system and extra ECM equipment in the shape of Westinghouse AN/ALQ-101 'Dash Ten' jamming pods carried on locally devised underwing pylons, the wiring running through the Skybolt refrigeration ducting. Training in conventional bombing and in-flight refueling began in mid-April. For greater accuracy in the delivery of its payload of 21 1000-pound bombs, each Vulcan was fitted with triple 'offset' radar equipment which had been rescued from a dump at Scampton.

On April 29 two aircraft, XM598 and XM607, flew to Wideawake airfield on Ascension Island, in mid-Atlantic, refueled twice in flight by Victor K.2 tankers. This was the first stage in the series of 'Black Buck' missions directed against the runway of the Falklands' airfield at Port Stanley with the aim of denying it to high-performance Argentine fighter aircraft. 'Black Buck 1' was launched on the night of April 30 when 11 Victor tankers, followed by the two Vulcans, took off at one-minute intervals from Wide-awake airfield. Almost immediately the primary aircraft, XM598, was forced to turn back with pressurization failure in the cabin. XM607 flew on to Port Stanley, nearly 4000 miles distant. Just under 300 miles from the target the Vulcan began a descent to 300 ft. With 60 miles to go, the H2S radar was switched on and the Vulcan eased up to 500 ft to widen the radar horizon. XM607 was exactly on track, and with 46 miles to go it began a rapid climb to 10 000 ft. This was designed to enable the bomber to overfly the Argentine air defenses – Tigercat anti-aircraft missiles and Oerlikon 35 mm fast-firing twin-barrelled anti-aircraft guns linked to Skyguard and Super Fledermaus fire-control radars. The attack altitude would also give the Vulcan's navigator/radar as much time as possible to identify his aiming offsets and ensure maximum penetration of the runway by the 1000-pound bombs. The bomb doors were opened ten miles from the target and with the range at two miles the Vulcan's bombing computer set the release mechanism in motion. Just before release, the Vulcan's radar warning receiver picked up transmissions from an Argentine fire-control radar, and this was promptly jammed by the Air Electronics Officer, using the ALQ-101. While XM607's pilot, Flight Lieutenant WFM Withers, flew the Vulcan straight and level for an agonising five seconds, the bombs fell away, dropping in a line which ran diagonally across the runway to ensure that at least one of them found its target. Twenty seconds later, as the first of the bombs impacted, Withers hauled the Vulcan into a full power climb, at the top of which the codeword 'Superforce' was transmitted to indicate a successful attack. After 16 hours in the air, XM607 landed at Wideawake.

Only one bomb hit the runway, another struck its edge and the remainder caused some damage to the airfield's facilities and blocked the road to Port Stanley. Although the airfield was not denied to Hercules transports, which continued to fly in and out until the end of the conflict, it could no longer be used by the Skyhawks, Mirages and Super Etendards which, while operating at short range, might have dealt crippling blows to the subsequent British landings at San Carlos.

On May 3 XM607 flew 'Black Buck 2', but failed to hit the runway. A third raid, planned for May 16, was canceled because of fierce headwinds. This was not the end of the Vulcan's contribution to 'Operation Corporate'. Armed with AGM-45 Shrike missiles, XM597 flew three missions (the first of which was aborted) against Argentine radars sited on the Falkland Islands. On June 12 XM607 flew the seventh and last 'Black Buck' raid, attacking Port Stanley airfield with iron bombs fused to air-burst over 'soft' targets. With the Argentine surrender, the Vulcan's withdrawal from service recommenced. The last six Vulcans of No. 50 Squadron were retired on March 31, 1984.

4.5: INTO THE FUTURE

THE CONFLICT IN SOUTHEAST ASIA underlined the crucial importance of electronic warfare in the battle for air supremacy. It is a battle which began in the mid-1930s, with the parallel development of the British Chain Home radar system and the German X-Verfahren program. In World War II radar, electronic navigation aids and jamming equipment played a decisive part in the major air campaigns in the West. They had little impact on the great tactical battles on the Eastern Front, but today the Soviet Union's investment in the technology of electronic warfare (EW) is as heavy as that in the West. EW is a primary military consideration, touching on every aspect of the exercise of air power. In the 1980s expenditure on electronics makes up at least one-third of the USAF's equipment costs, and the proportion of research funding it eats up exceeds that for weapons airframes or propulsion. USAF Systems Command tends over 40 000 computers and 250 000 'black boxes' within its fleets of aircraft. With each new generation of combat aircraft, the cost of developing and maintaining these elaborate systems leapfrogs far ahead of general inflation. The price of air supremacy has always been high. During World War II Bomber Command took the cream of Britain's high technology. The historian A J P Taylor has estimated that the strategic offensive absorbed up to one-third of the total war effort.

As its most basic, the prize at stake is simple survival over the real and potential battlefields of the last quarter of the 20th century. On June 5, 1967 – the first day of the Six Day War between Israel and her Arab neighbors – Israeli pre-emptive strikes destroyed on the ground 300 out of 340 serviceable Egyptian aircraft within the space of three hours. Six years later, in the Yom Kippur War of 1973, the Egyptians were better prepared, with an integrated modern air defense missile system shielding their bases. All the major Egyptian airfields lay within an hour's return flight from Israel, and as they sat in their cockpits before take-off, Israeli pilots could feel the effects of communications jamming. In the first six days of the 1973 war, nearly 100 Israeli aircraft were shot down by SA-6 surface-to-air missiles guided by continuous wave radars, while ZSU-23 radar-guided multiple cannon and man-portable heat-seeking SA-7s made low-level attack a hazardous proposition.

The Israelis were quick to react. In the June 1982 invasion of Lebanon – Operation Peace in Galilee – they lost no aircraft, having neutralized the Syrian SAM defenses with a brilliantly conducted electronic countermeasures offensive. Unmanned IAI Scout drones flew over the SA-6 batteries in the Bekkaa Valley, drawing their fire, while the electronic signatures were registered by Grumman E2-C Hawkeye EW aircraft. The recorded electronic intelligence (Elint) was programmed into aircraft jammers which completely swamped the air defense's frequencies in a devastating demonstration of the 'Mandrel' techniques developed by Bomber Command in 1943. Large numbers of decoy gliders were also launched by Israeli F-4s to saturate SAM sites. Ultra-sophisticated versions such as the Brunswick Maxi decoy system in service with the

Israeli air force can dispense Chaff, drop flares, carry jammers or radar signature augmentation which gives them the appearance of manned aircraft.

The importance of defense suppression was amply demonstrated in the Vietnam War. Among the types developed for this role was the US Navy's Grumman EA-6B Prowler, a redesigned A-6 Intruder accommodating a crew of four (pilot and three EW specialists) and equipped with the AN/ALQ-99 tactical jamming system used against microwave radars associated with Soviet-built anti-aircraft weapons such as the SA-5. The AN/ALQ-99 generates jamming signals aimed against early-warning, ground-control intercept, SAMs, air intercept, and naval radars. Its central computer analyses potential threats and coordinates the jamming operations.

Prowlers flew during Linebacker II, but the USAF rejected the aircraft – whose limited range and endurance would have been serious disadvantages in a European war – choosing instead the General Dynamics EF-111A, which accommodates the ALQ-99E tactical jamming system (developed for the Prowler) in the airframe of the F-111A swing-wing attack aircraft. Unlike the 'Wild Weasels' employed in Vietnam, the EF-111A uses massive electronic power, rather than missiles, to blind hostile radars. General Dynamics claim that five EF-111As can radiate jamming power sufficient to disrupt the greater part of the Warsaw Pact's air defense radars from the Baltic to southern Europe. The EF-111A can be employed in a defensive role, jamming the radars of intruding aircraft; or close to the line of conflict with the enemy, jamming hostile ground radars; or as an escort to a strike group penetrating hostile airspace. In this third mode the EF-111As – with wings swept and flying at supersonic speed – create a 'jamming corridor', thrusting back hostile radar coverage and neutralizing ground-control intercept stations and tactical communications between ground controllers and aircraft.

Putting Tactics to the Test

These tactics were among those employed on April 15, 1986, when USAF and US Navy aircraft attacked suspected terrorist training and bivouac sites in Libya – the first demonstration of many of the technologies developed after the experience of the Vietnam War. Planning for the strikes began a week earlier, but was hampered because Spain and France would not permit USAF F-111Fs based in Britain to overfly their territory en route to their designated targets in Libya. As a result, these aircraft were forced to fly a circuitous 2800-mile route to their objectives, refueling four times on the outward flight and twice on the way home. Targets in the Tripoli area assigned to the USAF F-111Fs were: the Al Azziziyah barracks, the principal headquarters for Libyan planning and direction of overseas terrorist attacks and the home and HQ of the Libyan leader, Colonel Muammar al-Qadaffi; the Sidi Bilal port facility, which reportedly provided a training establishment for a terrorist frogman unit; and Tripoli airport, used by Soviet-supplied Il-76 transports to provide worldwide military support.

The US Raid on Libya

Just before 1900 hrs on April 14, 28 McDonnell Douglas KC-10 and Boeing KC-135 tanker aircraft took off from the RAF stations at Mildenhall and Fairford in England. Twenty-three minutes later, 24 F-111Fs of the 48th Tactical Fighter Wing took off from RAF Lakenheath and were joined by five EF-111As launched from RAF Upper Heyford. After the first in-flight refueling, six F-111s and two EF-111s, flying as airborne spares, returned to base. The remaining 18 F-111s flew on, the majority of them armed with 2000-pound Paveway 2 laser-guided bombs. As the F-111s approached Libya in the first minutes of the new day, the carriers of the US Sixth Fleet, on station in the Gulf of Sidra, turned into the wind. The USS *America* launched six Grumman A-6Es and USS *Coral Sea* launched eight A-6Es to hit targets in Benghazi. Six McDonnell Douglas F/A-18 Hornet strike-support aircraft flew off from *Coral Sea* and six LTV Aerospace A-7Es from *America* provided surface-to-air weapon suppression over the Benghazi targets (the Al Jumahiriyah barracks and Benina military airfield) and Tripoli. Combat air patrols over the Gulf of Sidra were flown by carrier-borne Grumman F-14s and McDonnell Douglas F/A-18s controlled by Grumman Aerospace E-2Cs. Before attacks began, US Navy EA-6B Prowler and USAF EF-111As were employed in a defense suppression role.

Five minutes before the attacks hit Tripoli, EF-111As began to jam Libyan radar communications. They were followed in by the F-111Fs, using radar and infra-red systems to acquire targets and fly a low-level approach. The F-111F is equipped with an AN/AVQ-26 Pave Track laser designator/ranger which enables its Weapons System Officer (WSO) to acquire, track and designate ground targets at night for laser, infra-red and optically guided weapons. The WSO selects his target using an infra-red television camera. The Pave Track pods, housing the laser which the bombs will follow to the target, are then lowered from the aircraft's belly. The WSO selects the target and locks the beam on to it. No matter how the F-111 maneuvers, Pave Track holds the laser on the target while the bombs ride the beam, their on-board computers making constant adjustments to their fins during their descent.

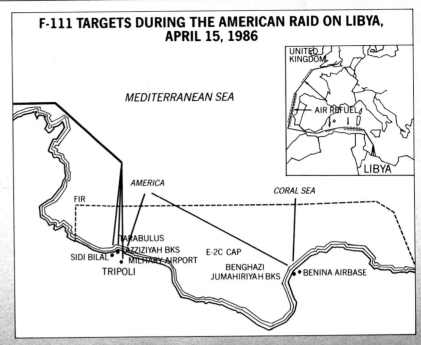

F-111 TARGETS DURING THE AMERICAN RAID ON LIBYA, APRIL 15, 1986

However, even with such sophisticated technology at work, there can be no guarantee of 100 per cent effectiveness. Over Tripoli the first wave of F-111Fs roared in at 500 ft, flashing over the villa occupied by the British consul to release their Paveway 2 bombs at the Al Azziziyah barracks. The main buildings were not damaged and four bombs demolished a tennis court. Two bombs aimed at the main office complex failed to find their target, and Qadaffi's celebrated tent escaped unscathed. One bomb exploded in front of the house where Qadaffi's family were sleeping – killing his 15-month-old adopted daughter and injuring two of his small sons. Damage was sustained by the French, Austrian, Finnish, Iranian and Swiss embassies. It was here, in the prosperous Bin Ashur district, that most of the approximately 100 civilian casualties occurred. At Tripoli airport a number of Il-76s were destroyed on the ground, and the 'frogman training center' received a direct hit.

At Benghazi US Navy A-6Es used similar tactics. The Intruders were armed with Mk82 Mod 1 retarded-delivery Snakeye bombs and Mk20 Rockeye cluster bombs. Approaching at low-level, the A-6Es used AN/APQ-148 multi-mode search radars to acquire the targets before passing the target location information to the aircraft's AN/AAS-33 target recognition attack multisensors (TRAM). Snakeye and Rockeye are conventionally released, with no guidance system, but the TRAM system's laser provides accurate ranging information for automatic release. At Benghazi airfield four Soviet-built MiG-23 'Floggers' were destroyed, along with two Mi-8 helicopters and four Fokker F-27 transports. The Navy and Air Force pilots attacking Benghazi and Tripoli were under strict orders to release their ordnance only when they had a positive identification of and perfect

approach to their targets. Some aircrews were unable to meet these requirements and returned with their weapons; five F-111Fs and two A-6Es did not complete their bombing missions. One F-111F was lost in the operation and another diverted to the US naval base at Rota, near Cadiz in Spain, with an overheating engine. The remainder touched down at their UK bases after 12 hours in the air.

EF IIIA JAMMING CORRIDOR

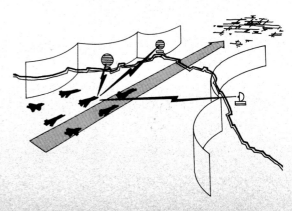

In spite of the apparently dominating role assumed in the early 1960s by the ICBM, neither the Soviet Long-Range Aviation nor US Strategic Air Command abandoned their interest in supersonic strategic bombers. One of the most significant military aircraft of the 1970s was the Tupolev Tu-26 'Backfire', first flown in 1971 and currently serving with the 46th Air Force, based at Smolensk, in a European theater strike role. The latest Soviet bomber is the Tupolev-designed 'Blackjack', a swing-wing penetration bomber with a maximum speed of Mach 2.3, an unrefueled range of 8400 miles, and maximum offensive load of 36 000 pounds.

In the mid-1960s SAC drew up a requirement for a bomber to replace the B-52, which would combine the latter's range and bombload with the performance of the FB-111A, the medium-range high-altitude strategic bomber variant of the F-111 tactical fighter-bomber. After a number of costly false starts, the Advanced Manned Strategic Aircraft (AMSA) program produced the Rockwell International Mach 2+ B-1 low-altitude penetration bomber. The swing-wing prototype flew for the first time on December 23, 1974, at Palmdale, California. The USAF originally wanted 244 B-1s, and six billion dollars were spent on building four prototypes. But in 1977 President Carter canceled the B-1 program, stating as the reasons cost, the effectiveness of ALCMs in fulfilling the same role and the forecast inability of the B-1 to penetrate Soviet air defenses.

The project was revived in October 1981 by Carter's successor, President Reagan, who announced plans to build 100 multi-role B-1Bs to be used as cruise missile carriers, deep penetration or conventional bombers. On October 1, 1986 the first B-1B squadron became operational with 96th BW at Dyess AFB, Texas. The B-1B remains a controversial aircraft but is nevertheless a potentially formidable weapon of war. Its variable-geometry wings are set forward for take-off from runways much shorter than those required for B-52 operations, and swept back to 67.5 degrees for low-level flight at high subsonic speed. The B-1B's shorter take-off opens the door to wide dispersal with a corresponding increase in the aircraft's ability to survive the opening phases of a major conflict. Employing the latest version of terrain-following radar, the B-1B can maneuver between hills and hug the contours of valleys to attack its targets at low level. The terrain-following computer is engaged at high altitude as the aircraft's wings are swept back. The computer, receiving a stream of inputs from the offensive radar system, directs the aircraft to descend quickly and then level off just above tree-top level. The B-1B can be flown on the deck at all times and in all weathers, the computer maintaining precise airspeed control and pinpoint navigation to the target. In front of the pilot is a visual display which gives altitude to the nearest foot, a vertical image of the terrain ahead, attitude, ground speed to the nearest knot, and distance to the next destination or target to the nearest tenth of a mile.

The B-1B has been aptly described as a huge computer system surrounded by fuel and engines. All the aircraft's systems are computer-based or computer-aided. Overseeing them all is the Central Integrated Test System (CITS), which continuously diagnoses the ground and in-flight operations of all

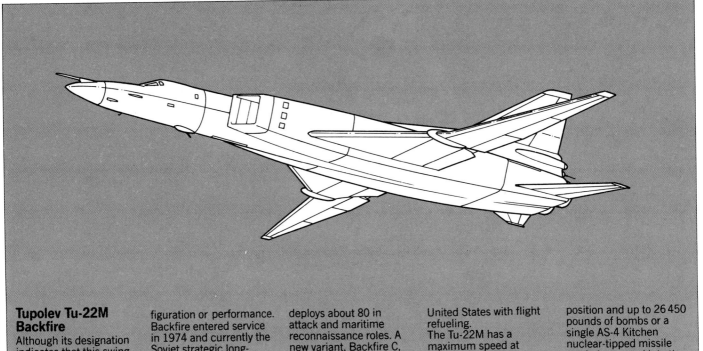

Tupolev Tu-22M Backfire

Although its designation indicates that this swing-wing strategic bomber was intended as a Blinder replacement, there are no similarities between the two types in terms of configuration or performance. Backfire entered service in 1974 and currently the Soviet strategic long-range airforce operates approximately 100 Backfire As and improved Backfire Bs. In addition, Soviet Naval Aviation deploys about 80 in attack and maritime reconnaissance roles. A new variant, Backfire C, began to enter service in 1983. These bombers operate in the European theater and North Atlantic but can also reach the United States with flight refueling.

The Tu-22M has a maximum speed at altitude of Mach 2 (1320 mph). Its armament consists of twin radar-directed 23 mm cannon in a tail position and up to 26 450 pounds of bombs or a single AS-4 Kitchen nuclear-tipped missile carried recessed into the weapons bay. With in-flight refueling, Backfire can fly to a target about 3400 miles from its base.

The Rockwell International B-1B, which has to reconcile a design originated in the 1960s with the demands of the 1990s and beyond. The Soviet equivalent, code-named Blackjack and designed by Tupolev, is nearly twice as big again as the TU-22M Backfire (see opposite page) and larger than the B-1B. Powered by four new turbofans aftermounted in pairs under the fixed section of the wing, Blackjack has a maximum speed of Mach 2.3 (1550 mph) and armament may include cruise missiles or other nuclear or conventional weapons to a weight of approximately 36 000 pounds.

the aircraft's systems by monitoring 10 000 electrical performances from the sub-systems every second. Even while the B-1B is turning off the runway after landing, the CITS is providing information on the exact temperature of each brake and printing a record of all malfunctions which might have occurred during the flight.

At the heart of the B-1B's defensive avionics is the AN/ALQ-161 electronic countermeasures system, controlling an array of jamming transmitters and antennae which generate 'jamming chains' around the bombers' periphery. A separate network of antennae receivers and processors pick up and identify new signals, directing the AN/ALQ-161's jamming operations. In an all-out jamming mode the system consumes as much as 120 kw of power. The B-1B also carries an ALQ-153 tail radar warning receiver, and the ALQ-161 can launch 'Chaff' and flares to blind hostile radar and draw off attacks from heat-seeking missiles.

First, or Last, of its Line?

Nevertheless, at the time of writing, serious doubts have been cast on the B-1B's ability to fulfil its potential. The aircraft is immensely costly to fly – $21,000 per flying hour or three times as much as the elderly B-52 – and burdened with an all-up weight which has risen by over 80 000 pounds since the B-1B was conceived nearly 20 years ago. Its wing-loading may inhibit maneuverability at the low altitudes at which it must fly to penetrate hostile air space. It has also been suggested that the bomber remains underpowered and at present would have considerable difficulty in carrying out long-range missions.

Built mostly of aluminum alloys and titanium,

hardened to withstand nuclear blast, the B-1B incorporates aspects of Stealth technology which reduce its radar cross-section (RCS, the measure of a target's apparent size on radar) to 0.1 per cent of that of the B-52. Originating in work begun in the 1950s on specialized covert reconnaissance aircraft, Stealth is not a single technology but rather a quality and design goal affecting all the major components of an aircraft's configuration. Computers enable designers to model an aircraft's characteristics to ensure that a low RCS is achieved at all significant aspects and at the differing wavelengths of the many hostile defensive systems it might encounter. The development of radar-absorbent materials has played a crucial part in the development of Stealth, while sophisticated signature control techniques can be employed to distort or refract an aircraft's reflection to make it appear like something else. Among a number of Stealth projects is the Northrop Advanced Technology Bomber (ATB), which closely resembles the company's legendary 'Flying Wing', the YB-49. The prototype is reputed to weigh approximately 180 tons with a wingspan of about 164 ft and range and payload roughly equivalent to that of the B-1B. Production of the ATB has yet to be approved and analysts estimate that each of the 132 aircraft planned may cost as much as $500 million, twice the price of the problematic B-1B. Supporters of the ATB argue that its value lies in its ability to penetrate air defenses at medium altitude to seek out and destroy imprecisely located mobile targets. If developments in Soviet air defenses seriously threaten the survivability of the B-1B, then it may prove no more than a bridge to the bomber of the future.

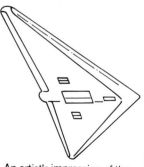

An artist's impression of the Advance Technology Bomber designed by Northrop.

INDEX